Software and Intelligent Sciences:

New Transdisciplinary Findings

Yingxu Wang
University of Calgary, Canada

Information Science
REFERENCE

Managing Director:	Lindsay Johnston
Senior Editorial Director:	Heather A. Probst
Book Production Manager:	Sean Woznicki
Development Manager:	Joel Gamon
Development Editor:	Myla Harty
Acquisitions Editor:	Erika Gallagher
Cover Design:	Nick Newcomer, Lisandro Gonzalez

Published in the United States of America by
Information Science Reference (an imprint of IGI Global)
701 E. Chocolate Avenue
Hershey PA 17033
Tel: 717-533-8845
Fax: 717-533-8661
E-mail: cust@igi-global.com
Web site: http://www.igi-global.com

Library of Congress Cataloging-in-Publication Data

Software and intelligent sciences: new transdisciplinary findings / Yingxu Wang, editor.
    p. cm.
  Summary: "This book discusses the transdisciplinary field known as software and intelligence sciences covering an array of developments in computer science, theoretical software engineering, cognitive science, cognitive informatics, and intelligence science"-- Provided by publisher.
  Includes bibliographical references and index.
  ISBN 978-1-4666-0261-8 (hardcover) -- ISBN 978-1-4666-0262-5 (ebook) -- ISBN 978-1-4666-0263-2 (print & perpetual access) 1. Computational intelligence. 2. Computer software. I. Wang, Yingxu, 1956-
  Q342.S54 2012
  003'.3--dc23
                            2011051852

British Cataloguing in Publication Data
A Cataloguing in Publication record for this book is available from the British Library.

All work contributed to this book is new, previously-unpublished material. The views expressed in this book are those of the authors, but not necessarily of the publisher.

Table of Contents

Section 1
Computational Intelligence

Section 2
Cognitive Computing

Section 4
Applications of Computational Intelligence and Cognitive Computing

Detailed Table of Contents

Section 1
Computational Intelligence

Yingxu Wang, University of Calgary, Canada

Software Science is a discipline that studies the theoretical framework of software as instructive and behavioral information, which can be embodied and executed by generic computers in order to create expected system behaviors and machine intelligence. Intelligence science is a discipline that studies the mechanisms and theories of abstract intelligence and its paradigms such as natural, artificial, machinable, and computational intelligence. The convergence of software and intelligent sciences forms the transdisciplinary field of computational intelligence, which provides a coherent set of fundamental theories, contemporary denotational mathematics, and engineering applications. This editorial addresses the objectives of the International Journal of Software Science and Computational Intelligence (IJSSCI), and explores the domain of the emerging discipline. The historical evolvement of software and intelligence sciences and their theoretical foundations are elucidated. The coverage of this inaugural issue and recent advances in software and intelligence sciences are reviewed. This editorial demonstrates that the investigation into software and intelligence sciences will result in fundamental findings toward the development of future generation computing theories, methodologies, and technologies, as well as novel mathematical structures.

Yingxu Wang, University of Calgary, Canada

Abstract intelligence is a human enquiry of both natural and artificial intelligence at the reductive embodying levels of neural, cognitive, functional, and logical from the bottom up. This paper describes the taxonomy and nature of intelligence. It analyzes roles of information in the evolution of human intelligence, and the needs for logical abstraction in modeling the brain and natural intelligence. A formal model of intelligence is developed known as the Generic Abstract Intelligence Mode (GAIM), which provides a foundation to explain the mechanisms of advanced natural intelligence such as thinking, learning, and inferences. A measurement framework of intelligent capability of humans and systems is comparatively studied in the forms of intelligent quotient, intelligent equivalence, and intelligent metrics. On the basis of the GAIM model and the abstract intelligence theories, the compatibility of natural and machine intelligence is revealed in order to investigate into a wide range of paradigms of abstract intelligence such as natural, artificial, machinable intelligence, and their engineering applications.

Chapter 3

Computational Intelligence (CI) supports a wealth of methodologies and a plethora of algorithmic developments essential to the construction of intelligent systems. Being faced with inherently distributed data which become evident, the paradigm of CI calls for further enhancements along the line of designing systems that are hierarchical and collaborative in nature. This emerging direction could be referred to as collaborative Computational Intelligence (or C2I for brief). The pervasive phenomenon encountered in architectures of C2I is that collaboration is synonym of knowledge sharing, knowledge reuse and knowledge reconciliation. Knowledge itself comes in different ways: as some structural findings in data and usually formalized in the framework of information granules, locally available models, some action plans, classification schemes, and alike. In such distributed systems sharing data is not feasible given existing technical constraints which are quite often exacerbated by non-technical requirements of privacy or security. In this study, we elaborate on the design of information granules which comes hand in hand with various clustering techniques and fuzzy clustering, in particular.

Chapter 4

Numerous attempts are being made to develop machines that could act not only autonomously, but also in an increasingly intelligent and cognitive manner. Such cognitive machines ought to be aware of their environments which include not only other machines, but also human beings. Such machines ought to understand the meaning of information in more human-like ways by grounding knowledge in the physical world and in the machines' own goals. The motivation for developing such machines range from self-evidenced practical reasons such as the expense of computer maintenance, to wearable computing in health care, and gaining a better understanding of the cognitive capabilities of the human brain. To achieve such an ambitious goal requires solutions to many problems, ranging from human perception, attention, concept creation, cognition, consciousness, executive processes guided by emotions and value, and symbiotic conversational human-machine interactions. This paper discusses some of the challenges emerging from this new design paradigm, including systemic problems, design issues, teaching the subjects to undergraduate students in electrical and computer engineering programs, research related to design.

Chapter 5

A new form of denotational mathematics known as Visual Semantic Algebra (VSA) is presented for abstract visual object and architecture manipulations. A set of cognitive theories for pattern recognition is explored such as cognitive principles of visual perception and basic mechanisms of object and pattern recognition. The cognitive process of pattern recognition is rigorously modeled using VSA and Real-Time Process Algebra (RTPA), which reveals the fundamental mechanisms of natural pattern recognition by the brain. Case studies on VSA in pattern recognition are presented to demonstrate VAS' expressive power for algebraic manipulations of visual objects. VSA can be applied not only in machinable visual and spatial reasoning, but also in computational intelligence as a powerful man-machine language for representing and manipulating visual objects and patterns. On the basis of VSA, computational intelligent systems such as robots and cognitive computers may process and inference visual and image objects rigorously and efficiently.

Section 2
Cognitive Computing

Inspired by the latest development in cognitive informatics and contemporary denotational mathematics, cognitive computing is an emerging paradigm of intelligent computing methodologies and systems, which implements computational intelligence by autonomous inferences and perceptions mimicking the mechanisms of the brain. This article presents a survey on the theoretical framework and architectural techniques of cognitive computing beyond conventional imperative and autonomic computing technologies. Theoretical foundations of cognitive computing are elaborated from the aspects of cognitive informatics, neural informatics, and denotational mathematics. Conceptual models of cognitive computing are explored on the basis of the latest advances in abstract intelligence and computational intelligence. Applications of cognitive computing are described from the aspects of autonomous agent systems and cognitive search engines, which demonstrate how machine and computational intelligence may be generated and implemented by cognitive computing theories and technologies toward autonomous knowledge processing.

Granular computing studies a novel approach to computing system modeling and information processing. Although a rich set of work has advanced the understanding of granular computing in dealing with the "to be" and "to have" problems of systems, the "to do" aspect of system modeling and behavioral implementation has been relatively overlooked. On the basis of a recent development in denotational mathematics known as system algebra, this paper presents a system metaphor of granules and explores the theoretical and mathematical foundations of granular computing. An abstract system model of granules is proposed in this paper. Rigorous manipulations of granular systems in computing are modeled by system algebra. The properties of granular systems are analyzed, which helps to explain the magnitudes and complexities of granular systems. Formal representation of granular systems for computing is demonstrated by real-world case studies, where concrete granules and their algebraic operations are explained.

Composition of software applications from component parts in response to high-level goals is a long-standing and highly challenging goal. We target the problem of composition in flow-based information processing systems and demonstrate how application composition and component development can be facilitated by the use of semantically described application metadata. The semantic metadata describe both the data flowing through each application and the processing performed in the associated application code. In this paper, we explore some of the key features of the semantic model, including the matching of outputs to input requirements, and the transformation and the propagation of semantic properties by components.

Chapter 9

The constant demand for complex applications, the ever increasing complexity and size of software systems, and the inherently complicated nature of the information drive the needs for developing radically new approaches for information representation. This drive is leading to creation of new and exciting interdisciplinary fields that investigate convergence of software science and intelligence science, as well as computational sciences and their applications. This survey article discusses the new paradigm of the algorithmic models of intelligence, based on the adaptive hierarchical model of computation, and presents the algorithms and applications utilizing this paradigm in data-intensive, collaborative environment. Examples from the various areas include references to adaptive paradigm in biometric technologies, evolutionary computing, swarm intelligence, robotics, networks, e-learning, knowledge representation and information system design. Special topics related to adaptive models design and geometric computing are also included in the survey.

We consider linguistic database summaries in the sense of Yager (1982), in an implementable form proposed by Kacprzyk & Yager (2001) and Kacprzyk, Yager & Zadrożny (2000), exemplified by, for a personnel database, "most employees are young and well paid" (with some degree of truth) and their extensions as a very general tool for a human consistent summarization of large data sets. We advocate the use of the concept of a protoform (prototypical form), vividly advocated by Zadeh and shown by Kacprzyk & Zadrożny (2005) as a general form of a linguistic data summary. Then, we present an extension of our interactive approach to fuzzy linguistic summaries, based on fuzzy logic and fuzzy database queries with linguistic quantifiers. We show how fuzzy queries are related to linguistic summaries, and that one can introduce a hierarchy of protoforms, or abstract summaries in the sense of latest Zadeh's (2002) ideas meant mainly for increasing deduction capabilities of search engines. We show an implementation for the summarization of Web server logs.

Based on the principle of cognitive economy, the complexity and the information of textual context are proposed to measure subjective cognitive degree of textual context. Based on minimization of Boolean complexity in human concept learning, the complexity and the difficulty of textual context are defined in order to mimic human's reading experience. Based on maximal relevance principle, the information and cognitive degree of textual context are defined in order to mimic human's cognitive sense. Experiments verify that more contexts are added, more easily the text is understood by a machine, which is consistent with the linguistic viewpoint that context can help to understand a text; furthermore, experiments verify that the author-given sentence sequence includes the less complexity and the more information than other sentence combinations, that is to say, author-given sentence sequence is more easily understood by a machine. So the principles of simplicity and maximal relevance actually exist in text writing process, which is consistent with the cognitive science viewpoint. Therefore, this chapter's measuring methods are validated from the linguistic and cognitive perspectives, and it could provide a theoretical foundation for machine-based text understanding.

Knowledge representation is essential for semantics modeling and intelligent information processing. For decades researchers have proposed many knowledge representation techniques. However, it is a daunting problem how to capture deep semantic information effectively and support the construction of a large-scale knowledge base efficiently. This paper describes a new knowledge representation model, SenseNet, which provides semantic support for commonsense reasoning and natural language processing. SenseNet is formalized with a Hidden Markov Model. An inference algorithm is proposed to simulate human-like natural language understanding procedure. A new measurement, confidence, is introduced to facilitate the natural language understanding. The authors present a detailed case study of applying SenseNet to retrieving compensation information from company proxy filings.

Firstly this article presents a thorough discussion of semantics formalization related issues in model driven engineering (MDE). Then motivated for the purpose of software implementation, and attempts to overcome the shortcomings of incompleteness and context-sensitivity in the existing models, we propose to study formalization of semantics from a cognitive background. Issues under study cover the broad scope of overlap vs. incomplete vs. complete, closed world assumption (CWA) vs. open world assumption (OWA), Y(Yes)/N(No) vs. T(True)/F(False), subjective (SUBJ) vs. objective (OBJ), static vs. dynamic, unconsciousness vs. conscious, human vs. machine aspects, and so forth. A semantics formalization approach called EID-SCE (Existence Identification Dualism-Semantics Cosmos Explosion) is designed to meet both the theoretical investigation and implementation of the proposed formalization goals. EID-SCE supports the measure/evaluation in a {complete, no overlap} manner whether a given concept or feature is an improvement. Some elementary cases are also shown to demonstrate the feasibility of EID-SCE.

Section 3
Software Science

Chapter 14

Yingxu Wang, University of Calgary, Canada
Shushma Patel, London South Bank University, UK

It is recognized that software is a unique abstract artifact that does not obey any known physical laws. For software engineering to become a matured engineering discipline like others, it must establish its own theoretical framework and laws, which are perceived to be mainly relied on cognitive informatics and denotational mathematics, supplementing to computing science, information science, and formal linguistics. This paper analyzes the basic properties of software and seeks the cognitive informatics foundations of software engineering. The nature of software is characterized by its informatics, behavioral, mathematical, and cognitive properties. The cognitive informatics foundations of software engineering are explored on the basis of the informatics laws of software and software engineering psychology. A set of fundamental cognitive constraints of software engineering, such as intangibility, complexity, indeterminacy, diversity, polymorphism, inexpressiveness, inexplicit embodiment, and unquantifiable quality measures, is identified. The conservative productivity of software is revealed based on the constraints of human cognitive capacity.

Chapter 15

Capers Jones, Software Productivity Research LLC, USA

The software engineering field has been a fountain of innovation. Ideas and inventions from the software domain have literally changed the world as we know it. For software development, we have a few proven innovations. The way software is built remains surprisingly primitive. Even in 2008 major software applications are cancelled, overrun their budgets and schedules, and often have hazardously bad quality levels when released. There have been many attempts to improve software development, but progress has resembled a drunkard's walk. Some attempts have been beneficial, but others have been either ineffective or harmful. This article puts forth the hypothesis that the main reason for the shortage of positive innovation in software development methods is due to a lack of understanding of the underlying problems of the software development domain. A corollary hypothesis is that lack of understanding of the problems is due to inadequate measurement of quality, productivity, costs, and the factors that affect project outcomes.

Chapter 16

Yingxu Wang, University of Calgary, Canada

The quantification and measurement of functional complexity of software are a persistent problem in software engineering. Measurement models of software complexities have been studied in two facets in computing and software engineering, where the former is machine-oriented in the small; while the latter is human-oriented in the large. The cognitive complexity of software presented in this paper is a new measurement for cross-platform analysis of complexities, functional sizes, and cognition efforts of software code and specifications in the phases of design, implementation, and maintenance in software engineering. This paper reveals that the cognitive complexity of software is a product of its architectural and operational complexities on the basis of deductive semantics. A set of ten Basic Control Structures (BCS's) are elicited from software architectural and behavioral modeling and specifications. The cognitive weights of the BCS's are derived and calibrated via a series of psychological experiments. Based on this work, the cognitive complexity of software systems can be rigorously and accurately measured and analyzed. Comparative case studies demonstrate that the cognitive complexity is highly distinguishable for software functional complexity and size measurement in software engineering.

Chapter 17

Du Zhang, California State University, USA

Software engineering research and practice thus far are primarily conducted in a value-neutral setting where each artifact in software development such as requirement, use case, test case, and defect, is treated as equally important during a software system development process. There are a number of shortcomings of such value-neutral software engineering. Value-based software engineering is to integrate value considerations into the full range of existing and emerging software engineering principles and practices. Machine learning has been playing an increasingly important role in helping develop and maintain large and complex software systems. However, machine learning applications to software engineering have been largely confined to the value-neutral software engineering setting. In this paper, the general message to be conveyed is to apply machine learning methods and algorithms to value-based software engineering. The training data or the background knowledge or domain theory or heuristics or bias used by machine learning methods in generating target models or functions should be aligned with stakeholders' value propositions. An initial research agenda is proposed for machine learning in value-based software engineering.

Chapter 18

Yingxu Wang, University of Calgary, Canada

A typical real-time system, the Telephone Switching System (TSS), is a highly complicated system in design and implementation. This paper presents the formal design, specification, and modeling of the TSS system using a denotational mathematics known as Real-Time Process Algebra (RTPA). The conceptual model of the TSS system is introduced as the initial requirements for the system. Then, the architectural model of the TSS system is created using the RTPA architectural modeling methodologies and refined by a set of Unified Data Models (UDMs). The static behaviors of the TSS system are specified and refined by a set of Unified Process Models (UPMs) such as call processing and support processes. The dynamic behaviors of the TSS system are specified and refined by process priority allocation, process deployment, and process dispatching models. Based on the formal design models of the TSS system, code can be automatically generated using the RTPA Code Generator (RTPA-CG), or be seamlessly transformed into programs by programmers. The formal model of TSS may not only serve as a formal design paradigm of real-time software systems, but also a test bench of the expressive power and modeling capability of exiting formal methods in software engineering.

Chapter 19

A Lift Dispatching System (LDS) is a typical real-time system that is highly complicated in design and implementation. This article presents the formal design, specification, and modeling of the LDS system using a denotational mathematics known as Real-Time Process Algebra (RTPA). The conceptual model of the LDS system is introduced as the initial requirements for the system. The architectural model of the LDS system is created using RTPA architectural modeling methodologies and refined by a set of Unified Data Models (UDMs). The static behaviors of the LDS system are specified and refined by a set of Unified Process Models (UPMs) for the lift dispatching and serving processes. The dynamic behaviors of the LDS system are specified and refined by process priority allocation and process deployment models. Based on the formal design models of the LDS system, code can be automatically generated using the RTPA Code Generator (RTPA-CG), or be seamlessly transferred into programs by programmers. The formal models of LDS may not only serve as a formal design paradigm of real-time software systems, but also a test bench of the expressive power and modeling capability of exiting formal methods in software engineering.

There exists an extensive literature on vision science, on the one hand, and on program comprehension, on the other hand. However, these two domains of research have been so far rather disjoint. Indeed, several cognitive theories have been proposed to explain program comprehension. These theories explain the processes taking place in the software engineers' minds when they understand programs. They explain how software engineers process available information to perform their tasks but not how software engineers acquire this information. Vision science provides explanations on the processes used by people to acquire visual information from their environment. Joining vision science and program comprehension provides a more comprehensive theoretical framework to explain facts on program comprehension, to predict new facts, and to frame experiments. We join theories in vision science and in program comprehension; the resulting theory is consistent with facts on program comprehension and helps in predicting new facts, in devising experiments, and in putting certain program comprehension concepts in perspective.

This paper aims to develop an Indian-logic based approach for automatic generation of software requirements from a domain-specific ontology. The structure of domain ontology is adapted from Indian logic. The interactive approach proposed in this paper parses the problem statement, and the section of domain ontology, which matches the problem statement, is identified. The software generates questions to stakeholders based on the identified concepts. The answer is analysed for presence of flaws or inconsistencies. Subsequent questions are recursively generated to repair the flaw in the previous answer. These answers are populated into requirements ontology, which contains problem specific information coupled with the interests of the stakeholder. The information gathered is stored in a database, which is later segregated into functional and non-functional requirements. These requirements are classified, validated and prioritized based on combined approach of AHP and stakeholders' defined priority. Conflict between requirements is resolved by the application of cosine correlation measure.

Chapter 22

One of the major issues in software engineering is the measurement. Since traditional measurement theory has problem in defining empirical observations on software entities in terms of their measured quantities, Morasca tried to solve this problem by proposing Weak Measurement theory. Further, in calculating complexity of software, the emphasis is mostly given to the computational complexity, algorithm complexity, functional complexity, which basically estimates the time, efforts, computability and efficiency. On the other hand, understandability and compressibility of the software which involves the human interaction are neglected in existing complexity measures. Recently, cognitive complexity (CC) to calculate the architectural and operational complexity of software was proposed to fill this gap. In this paper, we evaluated CC against the principle of weak measurement theory. We find that, the approach for measuring CC is more realistic and practical in comparison to existing approaches and satisfies most of the parameters required from measurement theory.

Chapter 23

Researchers in the field of information system (IS) endorse the view that there is always a discrepancy between the expressions of client's automation requirements and IS designers understanding of such requirement because of difference in the field of expertise. In this article an attempt is taken to develop a motivational gratification model (MGM) from the cognitive informatics perspective for the automation of employee motivation measurement, instead of developing a motivation theory from a management perspective and expecting the IS designers to develop a system based on the understanding of the theory that is alien to his/her field of expertise. Motivational Gratification is an integrated work motivation model which theoretically explains how employees self-regulate their effort intensity for 'production' or 'reduction' of motivational force towards future high performance, and it is developed using taxonomies of system approach from psychology and management. The practical implications of MGM in management and IS analysis and design are discussed.

This article presents an intelligent social grouping service for identifying right participants to support CSCW and CSCL. We construct a three-layer hierarchical social network, in which we identify two important relationship ties – a knowledge relationship tie and a social relationship tie. We use these relationship ties as metric to measure the collaboration strength between pairs of participants in a social network. The stronger the knowledge relationship tie, the more knowledgeable the participants; the stronger the social relationship tie, the more likely the participants are willing to share their knowledge. By analyzing and calculating these relationship ties among peers using our computational models, we present a systematic way to discover collaboration peers according to configurable and customizable requirements. Experiences of social grouping services for identifying communities of practice through peer-to-peer search are also reported.

Chapter 25

As the Neural-Symbolic Hybrid Systems (NSHS) gain acceptance, it increases the necessity to guarantee the automatic validation and verification of the knowledge contained in them. In the past, such processes were made manually. In this article, an enhanced Petri net model is presented to the detection and elimination of structural anomalies in the knowledge base of the NSHS. In addition, a reachability model is proposed to evaluate the obtained results of the system versus the expected results by the user. The validation and verification method is divided in two stages: 1) it consists of three phases: rule normalization, rule modeling and rule verification. 2) It consists of three phases: rule modeling, dynamic modeling and evaluation of results. Such method is useful to ensure that the results of a NSHS are correct. Examples are presented to demonstrate the effectiveness of the results obtained with the method.

Chapter 26

In the three-layered framework for knowledge discovery, it is necessary for technique layer to develop some data-driven algorithms, whose knowledge acquiring process is characterized by and hence advantageous for the unnecessity of prior domain knowledge or external information. System uncertainty is able to conduct data-driven knowledge acquiring process. It is crucial for such a knowledge acquiring framework to measure system uncertainty reasonably and precisely. Herein, in order to find a suitable measuring method, various uncertainty measures based on rough set theory are comprehensively studied: their algebraic characteristics and quantitative relations are disclosed; their performances are compared through a series of experimental tests; consequently, the optimal measure is determined. Then, a new data-driven knowledge acquiring algorithm is developed based on the optimal uncertainty measure and the Skowron's algorithm for mining propositional default decision rules. Results of simulation experiments illustrate that the proposed algorithm obviously outperforms some other congeneric algorithms.

Chapter 27

This article presents a neural network model that permits to build a conceptual hierarchy to approximate functions over a given interval. Bio-inspired axo-axonic connections are used. In these connections the signal weight between two neurons is computed by the output of other neuron. Such arquitecture can generate polynomial expressions with lineal activation functions. This network can approximate any pattern set with a polynomial equation. This neural system classifies an input pattern as an element belonging to a category that the system has, until an exhaustive classification is obtained. The proposed model is not a hierarchy of neural networks, it establishes relationships among all the different neural networks in order to propagate the activation. Each neural network is in charge of the input pattern recognition to any prototyped category, and also in charge of transmitting the activation to other neural networks to be able to continue with the approximation.

Using the TOPEX radar altimeter for land cover studies has been of great interest due to the TOPEX near global coverage and its consistent availability of waveform data for about one and a half decades from 1992 to 2005. However, the complexity of the TOPEX Sensor Data Records (SDRs) makes the recognition of the radar echoes particularly difficult. In this article, artificial neural computation as one of the most powerful algorithms in pattern recognition is investigated for water ratio assessment over Lake of the Woods area using TOPEX reflected radar signals. Results demonstrate that neural networks have the capability in identifying water proportion from the TOPEX radar information, controlling the predicted errors in a reasonable range.

The computerized modeling of cognitive visual information has been a research field of great interest in the past several decades. The research field is interesting not only from a biological perspective, but also from an engineering point of view when systems are developed that aim to achieve similar goals as biological cognitive systems. This paper introduces a general framework for the extraction and systematic storage of low-level visual features. The applicability of the framework is investigated in both unstructured and highly structured environments. In a first experiment, a linear categorization algorithm originally developed for the classification of text documents is used to classify natural images taken from the Caltech 101 database. In a second experiment, the framework is used to provide an automatically guided vehicle with obstacle detection and auto-positioning functionalities in highly structured environments. Results demonstrate that the model is highly applicable in structured environments, and also shows promising results in certain cases when used in unstructured environments.

Preface

Software Science is a discipline that studies the theoretical framework of software as instructive and behavioral information, which can be embodied and executed by generic computers in order to create expected system behaviors and machine intelligence. *Intelligence science* is a discipline that studies the mechanisms and theories of abstract intelligence and its paradigms such as natural, artificial, machinable, and computational intelligence. The convergence of software and intelligent sciences forms the transdisciplinary field of computational intelligence, which provides a coherent set of fundamental theories, contemporary denotational mathematics, and engineering applications.

This book, entitled *Software and Intelligent Sciences: New Transdisciplinary Findings,* is the first volume in the IGI Series of Advances in Software Science and Computational Intelligence. The book encompasses 29 chapters of expert contributions selected from the *International Journal of Software Science and Computational Intelligence* during 2009. The book is organized in five sections on: (i) Computational intelligence; (ii) Cognitive computing; (iii) Denotational mathematics; (iv) Computational intelligence; and (v) Applications in computational intelligence and cognitive computing.

Section 1. Computational Intelligence

Intelligence science studies theories and models of the brain at all levels, and the relationship between the concrete physiological brain and the abstract soft mind. Intelligence science is a new frontier with the fertilization of biology, psychology, neuroscience, cognitive science, cognitive informatics, philosophy, information science, computer science, anthropology, and linguistics. A fundamental view developed in software and intelligence sciences is known as abstract intelligence, which provides a unified foundation for the studies of all forms and paradigms of intelligence such as natural, artificial, machinable, and computational intelligence. *Abstract intelligence* (αI) is an enquiry of both natural and artificial intelligence at the neural, cognitive, functional, and logical levels from the bottom up. In the narrow sense, αI is a human or a system ability that transforms information into behaviors. However, in the broad sense, αI is any human or system ability that autonomously transfers the forms of abstract information between *data, information, knowledge,* and *behaviors* in the brain or intelligent systems.

Computational intelligence (CoI) is an embodying form of abstract intelligence (αI) that implements intelligent mechanisms and behaviors by computational methodologies and software systems, such as expert systems, fuzzy systems, cognitive computers, cognitive robots, software agent systems, genetic/ evolutionary systems, and autonomous learning systems. The theoretical foundations of computational intelligence root in cognitive informatics, software science, and denotational mathematics.

Chapter 1, **Convergence of Software Science and Computational Intelligence: A New Transdisciplinary Research Field**, by Yingxu Wang, presents two emerging fields of software science and computational intelligence as well as their relationship. Software Science is a discipline that studies the theoretical framework of software as instructive and behavioral information, which can be embodied and executed by generic computers in order to create expected system behaviors and machine intelligence. Intelligence science is a discipline that studies the mechanisms and theories of abstract intelligence and its paradigms such as natural, artificial, machinable, and computational intelligence. The convergence of software and intelligent sciences forms the transdisciplinary field of computational intelligence, which provides a coherent set of fundamental theories, contemporary denotational mathematics, and engineering applications. This editorial addresses the objectives of the *International Journal of Software Science and Computational Intelligence* (IJSSCI), and explores the domain of the emerging discipline. The historical evolvement of software and intelligence sciences and their theoretical foundations are elucidated. The coverage of this inaugural issue and orecent advances in software and intelligence sciences are reviewed. This chapter demonstrates that the investigation into software and intelligence sciences will result in fundamental findings toward the development of future generation computing theories, methodologies, and technologies, as well as novel mathematical structures.

Chapter 2, **On Abstract Intelligence: Toward a Unifying Theory of Natural, Artificial, Machinable, and Computational Intelligence**, by Yingxu Wang, presents a novel theory known as *abstract intelligence* that is an enquiry of both natural and artificial intelligence at the reductive embodying levels of neural, cognitive, functional, and logical from the bottom up. This chapter describes the taxonomy and nature of intelligence. It analyzes roles of information in the evolution of human intelligence, and the needs for logical abstraction in modeling the brain and natural intelligence. A formal model of intelligence is developed known as the *Generic Abstract Intelligence Mode* (GAIM), which provides a foundation to explain the mechanisms of advanced natural intelligence such as thinking, learning, and inferences. A measurement framework of intelligent capability of humans and systems is comparatively studied in the forms of intelligent quotient, intelligent equivalence, and intelligent metrics. On the basis of the GAIM model and the abstract intelligence theories, the compatibility of natural and machine intelligence is revealed in order to investigate into a wide range of paradigms of abstract intelligence such as natural, artificial, machinable intelligence, and their engineering applications.

Chapter 3, **Hierarchies of Architectures of Collaborative Computational Intelligence**, by Witold Pedrycz presents computational intelligence as a wealth of methodologies and a plethora of algorithmic developments essential to the construction of intelligent systems. Being faced with inherently distributed data, which becomes evident, the paradigm of CI calls for further enhancements along the line of designing systems that are hierarchical and collaborative in nature. This emerging direction could be referred to as collaborative Computational Intelligence (or C^2I, for short). The pervasive phenomenon encountered in architectures of C^2I is that collaboration is synonymous with knowledge sharing, knowledge reuse, and knowledge reconciliation. Knowledge itself comes in different ways: as some structural findings in data and usually formalized in the framework of information granules, locally available models, some action plans, classification schemes, and the like. In such distributed systems sharing data is not feasible given existing technical constraints, which are quite often exacerbated by non-technical requirements of privacy or security. In this study, the author elaborates on the design of information granules, which comes hand in hand with various clustering techniques and fuzzy clustering, in particular. Having stressed the role of information granules and Granular Computing, in general, the chapter demonstrates that such processing leads to the representatives of information granules and granular models in the form of metastructures and metamodels. The author elaborates on pertinent optimization strategies and emphasizes a combinatorial character of the problems, which underlines a need for advanced techniques of evolutionary optimization. Collaboration leads to consensus and the quality of consensus achieved in this manner is quantified in terms of information granules of higher order (say type-2 fuzzy sets). The concept of information granulation emerging as a result of forming constructs of justifiable granularity becomes instrumental in the quantification of the achieved quality of collaboration.

Chapter 4, **Challenges in the Design of Adoptive, Intelligent and Cognitive Systems**, by Witold Kinsner presents cognitive machines that could act not only autonomously, but also in an increasingly intelligent and cognitive manner. Such cognitive machines ought to be aware of their environments which include not only other machines, but also human beings. Such machines ought to understand the meaning of information in more human-like ways by grounding knowledge in the physical world and in the machines' own goals. The motivation for developing such machines range from self-evidenced practical reasons such as the expense of computer maintenance, to wearable computing (e.g., Mann, 2001) in healthcare, and gaining a better understanding of the cognitive capabilities of the human brain. To achieve such an ambitious goal requires solutions to many problems, ranging from human perception, attention, concept creation, cognition, consciousness, executive processes guided by emotions and value, and symbiotic conversational human-machine interactions. This chapter discusses some of the challenges emerging from this new design paradigm, including systemic problems, design issues, teaching the subjects to undergraduate students in electrical and computer engineering programs, research related to design.

Chapter 5, **On Visual Semantic Algebra (VSA): A Denotational Mathematical Structure for Modeling and Manipulating Visual Objects and Patterns**, by Yingxu Wang presents a new form of denotational mathematics known as Visual Semantic Algebra (VSA) for abstract visual object and architecture manipulations. A set of cognitive theories for pattern recognition is explored such as cognitive principles of visual perception and basic mechanisms of object and pattern recognition. The cognitive process of pattern recognition is rigorously modeled using VSA and Real-Time Process Algebra (RTPA), which reveals the fundamental mechanisms of natural pattern recognition by the brain. Case studies on VSA in pattern recognition are presented to demonstrate VAS' expressive power for algebraic manipulations of visual objects. VSA can be applied not only in machinable visual and spatial reasoning, but also in computational intelligence as a powerful man-machine language for representing and manipulating visual objects and patterns. On the basis of VSA, computational intelligent systems such as robots and cognitive computers may process and inference visual and image objects rigorously and efficiently.

Section 2. Cognitive Computing

Computing systems and technologies can be classified into the categories of *imperative, autonomic,* and *cognitive* computing from the bottom up. The imperative computers are a passive system based on stored-program controlled mechanisms for data processing. The autonomic computers are goal-driven and self-decision-driven machines that do not rely on instructive and procedural information. Cognitive computers are more intelligent computers beyond the imperative and autonomic computers, which embody major natural intelligence behaviors of the brain such as thinking, inference, and learning. The increasing demand for non von Neumann computers for knowledge and intelligence processing in the high-tech industry and everyday lives require novel cognitive computers for providing autonomous computing power for various cognitive systems mimicking the natural intelligence of the brain.

Cognitive Computing (CC) is a novel paradigm of intelligent computing methodologies and systems based on *Cognitive Informatics* (CI), which implements computational intelligence by autonomous inferences and perceptions mimicking the mechanisms of the brain. CC is emerged and developed based on the transdisciplinary research in cognitive informatics, abstract intelligence, and *Denotational Mathematics* (DM). The latest advances in CI, CC, and DM enable a systematic solution for the future generation of intelligent computers known as *Cognitive Computers* (CogCs) that think, perceive, learn, and reason. A CogC is an intelligent computer for knowledge processing as that of a conventional von Neumann computer for data processing. CogCs are designed to embody *machinable intelligence* such as computational inferences, causal analyses, knowledge manipulations, machine learning, and autonomous problem solving.

Chapter 6, **On Cognitive Computing**, by Yingxu Wang presents cognitive computing as an emerging paradigm of intelligent computing methodologies and systems, which implements computational intelligence by autonomous inferences and perceptions mimicking the mechanisms of the brain. This chapter presents a survey on the theoretical framework and architectural techniques of cognitive computing beyond conventional imperative and autonomic computing technologies. Theoretical foundations of cognitive computing are elaborated from the aspects of cognitive informatics, neural informatics, and denotational mathematics. Conceptual models of cognitive computing are explored on the basis of the latest advances in abstract intelligence and computational intelligence. Applications of cognitive computing are described from the aspects of autonomous agent systems and cognitive search engines, which demonstrate how machine and computational intelligence may be generated and implemented by cognitive computing theories and technologies toward autonomous knowledge processing.

Chapter 7, **On the System Algebra Foundations for Granular Computing**, by Yingxu Wang, Lotfi A. Zadeh, and Yiyu Yao, presents a new mathematical means, granular algebra, for granular computing to computing system modeling and information processing. Although a rich set of work has advanced the understanding of granular computing in dealing with the "*to be*" and "*to have*" problems of systems, the "*to do*" aspect of system modeling and behavioral implementation has been relatively overlooked. On the basis of a recent development in denotational mathematics known as *system algebra*, this chapter presents a system metaphor of granules and explores the theoretical and mathematical foundations of granular computing. An abstract system model of granules is proposed in this chapter. Rigorous manipulations of granular systems in computing are modeled by system algebra. The properties of granular systems are analyzed, which helps to explain the magnitudes and complexities of granular systems. Formal representation of granular systems for computing is demonstrated by real-world case studies, where concrete granules and their algebraic operations are explained. A wide range of applications of the system algebra theory for granular computing may be found in cognitive informatics, computing, software engineering, system engineering, and computational intelligence.

Chapter 8, **Semantic Matching, Propagation and Transformation for Composition in Component-Based Systems**, by Eric Bouillet, Mark Feblowitz, Zhen Liu, Anand Ranganathan, and Anton Riabov, presents the composition of software applications from component parts in response to high-level goals. The authors target the problem of composition in flow-based information processing systems and demonstrate how application composition and component development can be facilitated by the use of semantically described application metadata. The semantic metadata describe both the data flowing through each application and the processing performed in the associated application code. In this chapter, the authors explore some of the key features of the semantic model, including the matching of outputs to input requirements, and the transformation and the propagation of semantic properties by components.

Chapter 9, **Adaptive Computation Paradigm in Knowledge Representation: Traditional and Emerging Applications**, by Marina L. Gavrilova, presents the constant demand for complex applications, the ever increasing complexity and size of software systems, and the inherently complicated nature of the information, which drive the needs for developing radically new approaches for information representation and processing. This drive is leading to creation of new and exciting interdisciplinary fields that investigate convergence of software science and intelligence science, as well as computational sciences and their applications. This survey article presents the new paradigm of the algorithmic models of intelligence, based on the adaptive hierarchical model of computation, and presents the algorithms and applications utilizing this paradigm in data-intensive, collaborative environment. Examples from the various areas include references to adaptive paradigm in biometric technologies, evolutionary computing, swarm intelligence, robotics, networks, e-learning, knowledge representation, and Information System design. Special topics related to adaptive models design and geometric computing are also included in the survey.

Chapter 10, **Protoforms of Linguistic Database Summaries as a Human Consistent Tool for Using Natural Language in Data Mining**, by Janusz Kacprzyk and Slawomir Zadrozny, presents a linguistic database that summarizes a personnel database in which most employees are young and well paid and their extensions as a very general tool for a human consistent summarization of large data sets. The authors advocate the use of the concept of a protoform as a general form of a linguistic data summary. Then, they present an extension of our interactive approach to fuzzy linguistic summaries, based on fuzzy logic and fuzzy database queries with linguistic quantifiers. The authors show how fuzzy queries are related to linguistic summaries, and that one can introduce a hierarchy of protoforms, or abstract summaries in the sense of latest ideas meant mainly for increasing deduction capabilities of search engines. The chapter shows an implementation for the summarization of Web server logs.

Chapter 11, **Measuring Textual Context Based on Cognitive Principles**, by Ning Fang, Xiangfeng Luo, and Weimin Xu, presents a measurement of the complexity of textual context with subjective cognitive degree of information. Based on minimization of Boolean complexity in human concept learning, the complexity and the difficulty of textual context are defined in order to mimic human's reading experience. Based on maximal relevance principle, the information and cognitive degree of textual context are defined in order to mimic human's cognitive sense. Experiments verify that more contexts are added, more easily the text is understood by a machine, which is consistent with the linguistic viewpoint that context can help to understand a text; furthermore, experiments verify that the author-given sentence sequence includes the less complexity and the more information than other sentence combinations, that is to say, author-given sentence sequence is more easily understood by a machine. So the principles of simplicity and maximal relevance actually exist in text writing process, which is consistent with the cognitive science viewpoint. Therefore, the measuring methods are validated from the linguistic and cognitive perspectives, and it could provide a theoretical foundation for machine-based text understanding.

Chapter 12, **A Lexical Knowledge Representation Model for Natural Language Understanding**, by Ping Chen, Wei Ding and Chengmin Ding, presents knowledge representation as an essential technology for semantics modeling and intelligent information processing. For decades, researchers have proposed many knowledge representation techniques. However, it is a daunting problem how to capture deep semantic information effectively and support the construction of a large-scale knowledge base efficiently. This chapter describes a new knowledge representation model, SenseNet, which provides semantic support for commonsense reasoning and natural language processing. SenseNet is formalized with a Hidden Markov Model. An inference algorithm is proposed to simulate human-like natural language understanding procedure. A new measurement, confidence, is introduced to facilitate the natural language understanding. The authors present a detailed case study of applying SenseNet to retrieving compensation information from company proxy filings.

Chapter 13, **A Dualism Based Semantics Formalization Mechanism for Model Driven Engineering**, by Yucong Duan, presents a thorough discussion of semantics formalization related issues in model driven engineering (MDE). Motivated for the purpose of software implementation, and attempts to overcome the shortcomings of incompleteness and context-sensitivity in the existing models, the chapter proposes to study formalization of semantics from a cognitive background. Issues under study cover the broad scope of overlap vs. incomplete vs. complete, closed world assumption (CWA) vs. open world assumption (OWA), Y(Yes)/N(No) vs. T(True)/F(False), subjective (SUBJ) vs. objective (OBJ), static vs. dynamic, unconsciousness vs. conscious, human vs. machine aspects, et cetera. A semantics formalization approach called EID-SCE (Existence Identification Dualism-Semantics Cosmos Explosion) is designed to meet both the theoretical investigation and implementation of the proposed formalization goals. EID-SCE supports the measure/evaluation in a {complete, no overlap} manner whether a given concept or feature is an improvement. Some elementary cases are also shown to demonstrate the feasibility of EID-SCE.

Section 3. Software Science

Software as instructive behavioral information has been recognized as an entire range of widely and frequently used objects and phenomena in human knowledge. Software science is a theoretical inquiry of software and its constraints on the basis of empirical studies on engineering methodologies and techniques for software development and software engineering organization. In the history of science and engineering, a matured discipline always gave birth to new disciplines. For instance, theoretical physics was emerged from general and applied physics, and theoretical computing was emerged from computer engineering. So does software science that emerges from and grows in the fields of software, computer, information, knowledge, and system engineering.

Software Science (SS) is a discipline of enquiries that studies the theoretical framework of software as instructive and behavioral information, which can be embodied and executed by generic computers in order to create expected system behaviors and machine intelligence. The discipline of software science studies the common objects in the abstract world such as software, information, data, concepts, knowledge, instructions, executable behaviors, and their processing by natural and artificial intelligence. From this view, software science is theoretical software engineering; while software engineering is applied software science in order to efficiently, economically, and reliably develop large-scale software systems. The phenomena that almost all the fundamental problems, which could not be solved in the last four decades in software engineering, simply stemmed from the lack of coherent theories in the form of software science. The vast cumulated empirical knowledge and industrial practice in software engineering have made this possible to enable the emergence of software science.

Chapter 14, **Exploring the Cognitive Foundations of Software Engineering**, by Yingxu Wang and Shushma Patel, presents that software is a unique abstract artifact that does not obey any known physical laws. For software engineering to become a matured engineering discipline like others, it must establish its own theoretical framework and laws, which are perceived to be mainly relied on cognitive informatics and denotational mathematics, supplementing to computing science, information science, and formal linguistics. This chapter analyzes the basic properties of software and seeks the cognitive informatics foundations of software engineering. The nature of software is characterized by its informatics, behavioral, mathematical, and cognitive properties. The cognitive informatics foundations of software engineering are explored on the basis of the informatics laws of software and software engineering psychology. A set of fundamental cognitive constraints of software engineering, such as intangibility, complexity, indeterminacy, diversity, polymorphism, inexpressiveness, inexplicit embodiment, and unquantifiable quality measures, is identified. The conservative productivity of software is revealed based on the constraints of human cognitive capacity.

Chapter 15, **Positive and Negative Innovations in Software Engineering**, by Capers Jones, presents the software engineering field as a fountain of innovation. Ideas and inventions from the software domain have literally changed the world as we know it. For software development, we have a few proven innovations. The way software is built remains surprisingly primitive. Even in 2008, major software applications are cancelled, overrun their budgets and schedules, and often have hazardously bad quality levels when released. There have been many attempts to improve software development, but progress has resembled a drunkard's walk. Some attempts have been beneficial, but others have been either ineffective or harmful. This article puts forth the hypothesis that the main reason for the shortage of positive innovation in software development methods is due to a lack of understanding of the underlying problems of the software development domain. A corollary hypothesis is that lack of understanding of the problems is due to inadequate measurement of quality, productivity, costs, and the factors that affect project outcomes.

Chapter 16, **On the Cognitive Complexity of Software and its Quantification and Formal Measurement**, by Yingxu Wang, presents the quantification and measurement of functional complexity of software that were recognized as a persistent problem in software engineering. Measurement models of software complexities have been studied in two facets in computing and software engineering, where the former is machine-oriented in the small; while the latter is human-oriented in the large. The cognitive complexity of software presented in this chapter is a new measurement for cross-platform analysis of complexities, functional sizes, and cognition efforts of software code and specifications in the phases of design, implementation, and maintenance in software engineering. This chapter reveals that the cognitive complexity of software is a product of its architectural and operational complexities on the basis of deductive semantics. A set of ten Basic Control Structures (BCS's) are elicited from software architectural and behavioral modeling and specifications. The cognitive weights of the BCS's are derived and calibrated via a series of psychological experiments. Based on this work, the cognitive complexity of software systems can be rigorously and accurately measured and analyzed. Comparative case studies demonstrate that the cognitive complexity is highly distinguishable for software functional complexity and size measurement in software engineering.

Chapter 17, **Machine Learning and Value-Based Software Engineering**, by Du Zhang, presents a view of software engineering research and practice that are primarily conducted in a value-neutral setting where each artifact in software development such as requirement, use case, test case, and defect, is treated as equally important during a software system development process. There are a number of shortcomings of such value-neutral software engineering. Value-based software engineering is to integrate value considerations into the full range of existing and emerging software engineering principles and practices. Machine learning has been playing an increasingly important role in helping develop and maintain large and complex software systems. However, machine learning applications to software engineering have been largely confined to the value-neutral software engineering setting. In this chapter, the general message to be conveyed is to apply machine learning methods and algorithms to value-based software engineering. The training data or the background knowledge or domain theory or heuristics or bias used by machine learning methods in generating target models or functions should be aligned with stakeholders' value propositions. An initial research agenda is proposed for machine learning in value-based software engineering.

Chapter 18, **The Formal Design Model of a Telephone Switching System (TSS)**, by Yingxu Wang presents a typical real-time system, the Telephone Switching System (TSS), as a highly complicated system in design and implementation. This chapter presents the formal design, specification, and modeling of the TSS system using a denotational mathematics known as Real-Time Process Algebra (RTPA). The conceptual model of the TSS system is introduced as the initial requirements for the system. Then, the architectural model of the TSS system is created using the RTPA architectural modeling methodologies and refined by a set of Unified Data Models (UDMs). The static behaviors of the TSS system are specified and refined by a set of Unified Process Models (UPMs) such as call processing and support processes. The dynamic behaviors of the TSS system are specified and refined by process priority allocation, process deployment, and process dispatching models. Based on the formal design models of the TSS system, code can be automatically generated using the RTPA Code Generator (RTPA-CG), or be seamlessly transformed into programs by programmers. The formal model of TSS may not only serve as a formal design paradigm of real-time software systems, but also a test bench of the expressive power and modeling capability of exiting formal methods in software engineering.

Chapter 19, **The Formal Design Model of a Lift Dispatching System (LDS)**, by Yingxu Wang, Cyprian F. Ngolah, Hadi Ahmadi, Philip Sheu, and Shi Ying, presents a Lift Dispatching System (LDS) that is highly complicated in design and implementation. This chapter presents the formal design, specification, and modeling of the LDS system using a denotational mathematics known as Real-Time Process Algebra (RTPA). The conceptual model of the LDS system is introduced as the initial requirements for the system. The architectural model of the LDS system is created using RTPA architectural modeling methodologies and refined by a set of Unified Data Models (UDMs). The static behaviors of the LDS system are specified and refined by a set of Unified Process Models (UPMs) for the lift dispatching and serving processes. The dynamic behaviors of the LDS system are specified and refined by process priority allocation and process deployment models. Based on the formal design models of the LDS system, code can be automatically generated using the RTPA Code Generator (RTPA-CG), or be seamlessly transferred into programs by programmers. The formal models of LDS may not only serve as a formal design paradigm of real-time software systems, but also a test bench of the expressive power and modeling capability of exiting formal methods in software engineering.

Chapter 20, **A Theory of Program Comprehension: Joining Vision Science and Program Comprehension**, by Yann-Gaël Guéhéneuc, presents a program comprehension technology in vision science and software engineering. It is identified that these two domains of research have been so far rather disjoint. Indeed, several cognitive theories have been proposed to explain program comprehension. These theories explain the processes taking place in the software engineers' minds when they understand programs. They explain how software engineers *process* available information to perform their tasks but not how software engineers *acquire* this information. Vision science provides explanations on the processes used by people to acquire visual information from their environment. Joining vision science and program comprehension provides a more comprehensive theoretical framework to explain facts on program comprehension, to predict new facts, and to frame experiments. The author joins theories in vision science and in program comprehension; the resulting theory is consistent with facts on program comprehension and helps in predicting new facts, in devising experiments, and in putting certain program comprehension concepts in perspective.

Chapter 21, **Requirements Elicitation by Defect Elimination: An Indian Logic Perspective**, by G.S. Mahalakshmi and T.V. Geetha, presents an Indian-logic based approach for automatic generation of software requirements from a domain-specific ontology. The structure of domain ontology is adapted from Indian logic. Domain concepts and its member qualities, relations between concepts, relation-qualities etc. contribute to the Indian logic ontology. This is different from the western-logic based ontology, where only concepts and relations between concepts are classified into an ontological framework. The interactive approach proposed in this chapter parses the problem statement, and section or sub-section of the domain ontology, which matches the problem statement, is identified. The software generates questions to the stakeholders based on the concepts of the identified sections of the domain ontology. The answer to every question is collected and analysed for presence of flaws or inconsistencies. Subsequent questions are recursively generated to repair the flaw in the previous answer. The flaws or missing (or inconsistent) information are actually identified by mapping the answers (or values) with that of the concepts of the domain ontology. These answers are populated into requirements ontology, which contains problem specific information coupled with the interests of the stakeholder. The information gathered in this fashion is stored in a database, which is later segregated into functional and non-functional requirements. These requirements are classified, validated, and prioritized based on combined approach of AHP and stakeholders' defined priority. Conflict between requirements is resolved by the application of cosine correlation measure.

Chapter 22, **Measurement of Cognitive Functional Sizes of Software**, by Sanjay Misra, presents cognitive functional size measure based on Wang`s theory. Since traditional measurement theory has problem in defining empirical observations on software entities in terms of their measured quantities, Morasca has tried to solve this problem by proposing Weak Measurement theory. Further, in calculating complexity of software, the emphasis is mostly given to the computational complexity, algorithm complexity, functional complexity, which basically estimates the time, efforts, computability and efficiency. On the other hand, understandability and compressibility of the software, which involves the human interaction, are neglected in existing complexity measurement approaches. Recently, Wang has tried to fill this gap and developed the cognitive complexity to calculate the architectural and operational complexity of software. In this chapter, an attempt has been made to evaluate cognitive complexity against the principle of measurement theory/weak measurement theory. The author finds that the approach for measuring cognitive complexity is more realistic and practical in comparison to the existing approaches. Cognitive complexity satisfies most of the parameters required from measurement theory perspective. The chapter also investigates the applicability of Extensive Structure for deciding on the type of scale for cognitive complexity. It is found that the cognitive complexity is on weak ratio scale.

Chapter 23, **Motivational Gratification: An Integrated Work Motivation Model with Information System Design Perspective**, by Sugumar Mariappanadar, presents a view that researchers in the field of Information System (IS) endorse the view that there is always a discrepancy between the expressions of client's automation requirements and IS designers understanding of such requirement because of difference in the field of expertise. In this chapter, an attempt is taken to develop a motivational gratification model (MGM) from the cognitive informatics perspective for the automation of employee motivation measurement, instead of developing a motivation theory from a management perspective and expecting the IS designers to develop a system based on the understanding of the theory that is alien to his/her field of expertise. Motivational gratification is an integrated work motivation model that theoretically explains how employees self-regulate their effort intensity for "production" or "reduction" of motivational force towards future high performance, and it is developed using taxonomies of system approach from psychology and management. The practical implications of MGM in management and IS analysis and design are discussed.

Section 4. Applications of Computational Intelligence and Cognitive Computing

A series of fundamental breakthroughs have been recognized and a wide range of applications has been developed in software science, abstract intelligence, cognitive computing, and computational intelligence in the last decade. Because software science and computational intelligence provide a common and general platform for the next generation of cognitive computing, some expected innovations in these fields will emerge such as cognitive computers, cognitive knowledge representation technologies, semantic searching engines, cognitive learning engines, cognitive Internet, cognitive robots, and autonomous inference machines for complex and long-series of inferences, problem solving, and decision making beyond traditional logic- and rule-based technologies.

Chapter 24, **Supporting CSCW and CSCL with Intelligent Social Grouping Services**, by Jeffrey J.P. Tsai, Jia Zhang, Jeff J.S. Huang, and Stephen J.H. Yang, presents an intelligent social grouping service for identifying right participants to support CSCW and CSCL. The authors construct a three-layer hierarchical social network, in which they identify two important relationship ties – a knowledge relationship tie and a social relationship tie. They use these relationship ties as metric to measure the collaboration strength between pairs of participants in a social network. The stronger the knowledge relationship tie, the more knowledgeable the participants; the stronger the social relationship tie, the more likely the participants are willing to share their knowledge. By analyzing and calculating these relationship ties among peers using our computational models, the authors present a systematic way to discover collaboration peers according to configurable and customizable requirements. Experiences of social grouping services for identifying communities of practice through peer-to-peer search are also reported.

Chapter 25, **An Enhanced Petri Net Model to Verify and Validate a Neural-Symbolic Hybrid System**, by Ricardo R. Jorge, Gerardo R. Salgado, and Vianey G.C. Sánchez, presents that as the Neural-Symbolic Hybrid Systems (NSHS) gain acceptance, it increases the necessity to guarantee the automatic validation and verification of the knowledge contained in them. In the past, such processes were made manually. In this chapter, an enhanced Petri net model is presented to the detection and elimination of structural anomalies in the knowledge base of the NSHS. In addition, a reachability model is proposed to evaluate the obtained results of the system versus the expected results by the user. The validation and verification method is divided in two stages: 1) it consists of three phases: rule normalization, rule modeling and rule verification. 2) It consists of three phases: rule modeling, dynamic modeling and evaluation of results. Such method is useful to ensure that the results of a NSHS are correct. Examples are presented to demonstrate the effectiveness of the results obtained with the method.

Chapter 26, **System Uncertainty Based Data-Driven Knowledge Acquisition**, by Jun Zhao and Guoyin Wang, presents that in the three-layered framework for knowledge discovery, it is necessary for technique layer to develop some data-driven algorithms, whose knowledge acquiring process is characterized by and hence advantageous for the unnecessity of prior domain knowledge or external information. System uncertainty is able to conduct data-driven knowledge acquiring process. It is crucial for such a knowledge acquiring framework to measure system uncertainty reasonably and precisely. Herein, in order to find a suitable measuring method, various uncertainty measures based on rough set theory are comprehensively studied: their algebraic characteristics and quantitative relations are disclosed; their performances are compared through a series of experimental tests; consequently, the optimal measure is determined. Then, a new data-driven knowledge acquiring algorithm is developed based on the optimal uncertainty measure and the Skowron's algorithm for mining propositional default decision rules. Results of simulation experiments illustrate that the proposed algorithm obviously outperforms some other congeneric algorithms.

Chapter 27, **Hierarchical Function Approximation with a Neural Network Model**, by Luis F. de Mingo, Nuria Gómez, Fernando Arroyo, and Juan Castellanos, presents a model based on neural networks that permits to build a conceptual hierarchy in order to approximate functions over a given interval. A new kind of artificial neural networks using bio-inspired axo-axonic connections. These connections are based on the idea that the signal weight between two neurons is computed by the output of other neuron. Such model can generate polynomial expressions with lineal activation functions and the degree n of the output depends on the number $n - 2$ of hidden layers. This network can approximate any pattern set with a polynomial equation, similar to Taylor series approximation. Results concerning function approximation using artificial neural networks based on multi-layer perceptrons with axo-axonic connections are shown. This neural system classifies an input pattern as an element belonging to a category or subcategory that the system has, until an exhaustive classification is obtained, that is, a hierarchical neural model. The proposed neural system is not a hierarchy of neural networks; this model establishes relationships among all the different neural networks in order to propagate the neural activation when an external stimulus is presented to the system. Each neural network is in charge of the input pattern recognition to any prototyped class or category, and also in charge of transmitting the activation to other neural networks to be able to continue with the approximation. Therefore, the communication of the neural activation in the system depends on the output of each one of the neural networks, so as the functional links established among the different networks to represent the underlying conceptual hierarchy.

Chapter 28, **Application of Artificial Neural Computation in Topex Waveform Data: A Case Study on Water Ratio Regression**, by Bo Zhang, Franklin W. Schwartz, and Daoqin Tong, presents that using the TOPEX radar altimeter for land cover studies has been of great interest due to the TOPEX near global coverage and its consistent availability of waveform data for about one and a half decades from 1992 to 2005. However, the complexity of the TOPEX Sensor Data Records (SDRs) makes the recognition of the radar echoes particularly difficult. In this chapter, artificial neural computation as one of the most powerful algorithms in pattern recognition is investigated for water ratio assessment over Lake of the Woods area using TOPEX reflected radar signals. Results demonstrate that neural networks have the capability in identifying water proportion from the TOPEX radar information, controlling the predicted errors in a reasonable range.

Chapter 29, **A Generic Framework for Feature Representations in Image Categorization Tasks**, by Adam Csapo, Barna Resko, Morten Lind, and Peter Baranyi, presents computerized modeling of cognitive visual information. The research field is interesting not only from a biological perspective, but also from an engineering point of view when systems are developed that aim to achieve similar goals as biological cognitive systems. This chapter introduces a general framework for the extraction and systematic storage of low-level visual features. The applicability of the framework is investigated in both unstructured and highly structured environments. In a first experiment, a linear categorization algorithm originally developed for the classification of text documents is used to classify natural images taken from the Caltech 101 database. In a second experiment, the framework is used to provide an automatically guided vehicle with obstacle detection and auto-positioning functionalities in highly structured environments. Results demonstrate that the model is highly applicable in structured environments, and also shows promising results in certain cases when used in unstructured environments.

This book is intended to the readership of researchers, engineers, graduate students, senior-level undergraduate students, and instructors as an informative reference book in the emerging fields of software science, cognitive intelligence, and computational intelligence. The editor expects that readers of *Software and Intelligent Sciences: New Transdisciplinary Findings* will benefit from the 29 selected chapters of this book, which represents the latest advances in research in software science and computational intelligence and their engineering applications.

Yingxu Wang
University of Calgary, Canada

Acknowledgment

Many persons have contributed their dedicated work to this book and related research. The editor would like to thank all authors, the associate editors of IJSSCI, the editorial board members, and invited reviewers for their great contributions to this book. I would also like to thank the IEEE Steering Committee and organizers of the series of IEEE International Conference on Cognitive Informatics and Cognitive Computing (ICCI*CC) in the last ten years, particularly Lotfi A. Zadeh, Witold Kinsner, Witold Pedrycz, Bo Zhang, Du Zhang, George Baciu, Phillip Sheu, Jean-Claude Latombe, James Anderson, Robert C. Berwick, and Dilip Patel. I would like to acknowledge the publisher of this book, IGI Global, USA. I would like to thank Dr. Mehdi Khosrow-Pour, Jan Travers, Kristin M. Klinger, Erika L. Carter, and Myla Harty, for their professional editorship.

Yingxu Wang
University of Calgary, Canada

Section 1
Computational Intelligence

Chapter 1
Convergence of Software Science and Computational Intelligence:
A New Transdisciplinary Research Field

Yingxu Wang
University of Calgary, Canada

ABSTRACT

Software Science is a discipline that studies the theoretical framework of software as instructive and behavioral information, which can be embodied and executed by generic computers in order to create expected system behaviors and machine intelligence. Intelligence science is a discipline that studies the mechanisms and theories of abstract intelligence and its paradigms such as natural, artificial, machinable, and computational intelligence. The convergence of software and intelligent sciences forms the transdisciplinary field of computational intelligence, which provides a coherent set of fundamental theories, contemporary denotational mathematics, and engineering applications. This editorial addresses the objectives of the International Journal of Software Science and Computational Intelligence (IJSSCI), and explores the domain of the emerging discipline. The historical evolvement of software and intelligence sciences and their theoretical foundations are elucidated. The coverage of this inaugural issue and recent advances in software and intelligence sciences are reviewed. This editorial demonstrates that the investigation into software and intelligence sciences will result in fundamental findings toward the development of future generation computing theories, methodologies, and technologies, as well as novel mathematical structures.

DOI: 10.4018/978-1-4666-0261-8.ch001

INTRODUCTION

The latest developments in computer science, theoretical software engineering, cognitive science, cognitive informatics, and intelligence science, and the crystallization of accumulated knowledge by the fertilization of these areas, have led to the emergence of a transdisciplinary and convergence field known as software and intelligence sciences. The coverage of the International Journal of Software Science and Computational Intelligence (IJSSCI) includes theories, methodologies, technologies of software science and engineering, denotational mathematics, and their applications in engineering and industries.

Software Science is a discipline that studies the theoretical framework of software as instructive and behavioral information, which can be embodied and executed by generic computers in order to create expected system behaviors and machine intelligence (Wang, 2007a). Intelligence science is a discipline that studies the mechanisms and theories of abstract intelligence and its paradigms such as natural, artificial, machinable, and computational intelligence (Wilson and Frank, 1999; Wang, 2008a, 2009a). The convergence of software science and intelligent science forms the transdisciplinary field of computational intelligence, which provides a coherent set of fundamental theories, contemporary denotational mathematics, and engineering applications.

This editorial addresses the objectives of the International Journal of Software Science and Computational Intelligence (IJSSCI), and explores the domain of the emerging discipline. The historical evolvement of software and intelligence sciences and their theoretical foundations are elucidated. The coverage of this inaugural issue and recent advances in software and intelligence sciences are highlighted. This editorial demonstrates that the investigation into software and intelligence sciences will result in fundamental findings toward the development of future generation computing theories, methodologies, and technologies, as well as novel mathematical structures.

THE EMERGENCE OF SOFTWARE SCIENCE

Software as instructive behavioral information has been recognized as an entire range of widely and frequently used objects and phenomena in human knowledge. Software science is a theoretical inquiry of software and the laws constrain it on the basis of empirical studies on engineering methodologies and techniques for software development and software engineering organization. In the history of science and engineering, a matured discipline always gave birth to new disciplines. For instance, theoretical physics was emerged from general and applied physics, and theoretical computing was emerged from computer engineering. So will software science emerge and grow in the field of software, computer, information, knowledge, and system engineering (Wang, 2007a).

This section provides perspectives on the emerging discipline of software science along with the maturity of software engineering theories and methodologies in fundamental research. The architecture and roadmap of software science are presented. The theoretical framework, mathematical foundations, and basic methodologies of software science will be briefly introduced.

What is Software Science?

Definition 1. Software Science is a discipline of enquiries that studies the theoretical framework of software as instructive and behavioral information, which can be embodied and executed by generic computers in order to create expected system behaviors and machine intelligence.

The discipline of software science studies the common objects in the abstract world such as software, information, data, concepts, knowledge, instructions, executable behaviors, and their processing by natural and artificial intelligence. From this view, software science is theoretical software engineering; while software engineering is the engineering discipline that applies software science theories and methodologies to efficiently, economically, and reliably organize and develop large-scale software systems.

The relationship between software science and software engineering can be analogized to those of theoretical physics and applied physics, or dynamics and mechanical engineering. Without theoretical physics there would be no matured applied physics; without dynamics there would be no matured mechanical engineering. So is software science with software engineering. The phenomena that almost all the fundamental problems, which could not be solved in the last four decades in software engineering, simply stemmed from the lack of coherent theories in the form of software science. The vast cumulated empirical knowledge and industrial practice in software engineering have made this possible to enable the emergence of software science.

The disciplines of mathematics and physics are successful paradigms that adopt the formal framework of theoretical knowledge, which have the advantages of *stability* and *efficiency*. The former is a property of formal knowledge that once it is established and proven, users who refer to it will no longer need to reexamine or reprove it. The latter is a property of formal knowledge that is exclusively true or false that saves everybody's time to argue a proven theory. In contrasting the nature of theoretical and empirical knowledge, the following principle can be derived.

Theorem 1. *The rigorous levels of empirical and theoretical knowledge states that an empirical truth is a truth based on or verifiable by observations, experiments, or experiences. In contrary,* *a theoretical proposition is an assertion based on formal theories, logical, or mathematical inferences.*

Based on Theorem 1, a corollary on application domains of theoretical and empirical knowledge is stated as follows.

Corollary 1. *The validation scope of theoretical knowledge is universal in its domain such as* $\forall x \in S \Rightarrow p(x)$; *while the validation scope of empirical knowledge is based on limited observations such as* $\exists x \in S \Rightarrow p(x)$, *where S is the discourse of a problem x under study, and p a proven proposition or derived theory on x.*

The differences of the validated domains between theoretical and empirical knowledge indicates the levels of refinements of a given form of knowledge and its reliability. Huge empirical knowledge were reported and then disappeared over time. For example, there are tons of empirical knowledge on software engineering published each year in the last decades. However, those that would be included in a textbook on software engineering theories as proven and general truth, rather than specific cases partially working on certain given or nonspecified constraints, would be no more than a few handful pages. According to Corollary 1, the major risk of empirical knowledge is its uncertainty when applying in a different environment, even the same environment but at different time, because empirical knowledge and common sense are often error-prone. The differences of the validated domains between theoretical and empirical knowledge indicate the levels of refinements of different forms of knowledge and their reliability.

Empirical knowledge answers *how*; while theoretical knowledge reveals *why*. Theoretical knowledge is a formalization of generic truth and proven empirical knowledge. Although the discovery and development of a theory or a law may take decades even centuries, its acquisition and dissemination are much easier and faster with ordinary effort. However, empirical knowledge is very difficult to be indirectly gained. One may acquire knowledge in multiple scientific disciplines such as those offered at a university, but may not be an expert in multiple engineering disciplines such as in all areas of electrical, mechanical, chemical, and computer engineering. The reasons behind this are that each engineering area requires specific empirical knowledge, skills, and tools. All of them need a long period of training and practice to be an expert.

Architecture of Software Science

The architecture of software science can be classified into four categories namely theories and methodologies, denotational mathematics, cognitive informatics, and organizational theories as shown in Figure 1.

In the framework of software science, *theories and methodologies* encompass system modeling and refinement methodologies, computing theories, formal linguistic theories, and software code generation theories. All forms of imperative, autonomic, and cognitive computing theories as well as their engineering applications are explored in this category.

Denotational mathematics (Wang, 2002a, 2008b) for software science is the enquiry for its mathematical foundations in the forms of formal inference methodologies, concept algebra, system algebra, and Real-Time Process Algebra (RTPA). In the contemporary mathematics for software science and software engineering, *concept algebra* is designed to deal with the *to be* problems and knowledge manipulation (Wang, 2008c). *System algebra* is developed to formally treat the *to have* problems in terms of dynamic relations and possessions beyond set theory (Wang, 2008d). *RTPA* is adopted to formalize the *to do* problems such as system architectures, static and dynamic behaviors (Wang, 2002b, 2007a, 2008e). Further discussion

Figure 1. The architecture of software science

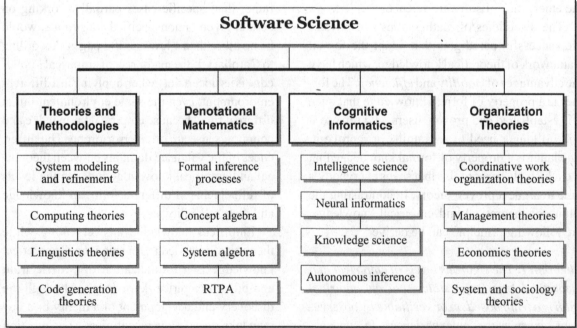

on denotational mathematics for software science may be referred to (Wang, 2008b).

Cognitive informatics for software science encompasses intelligence science, neural informatics, knowledge science, and computational intelligence (Wang, 2002a, 2006, 2007b; Wang et al., 2006). Cognitive informatics explains the fundamental mechanisms of natural intelligence and its products in terms of information and knowledge. It also studies the software implementation of intelligent behaviors by computational intelligence. Advances in cognitive informatics will help to overcome the cognitive barriers and inherited complicities in software engineering, which is called the *intellectually manageability* by Dijkstra (1976) and the *essential difficulties* by Brooks (1975) in software engineering.

Organizational theories of software science encompass coordinative work organization theories, management theories, economics theories, and system/sociology theories. The organizational facet of software science studies how large-scale software engineering projects may be optimally organized and what the underpinning laws are at different levels of coordinative complexities (Wang, 2007a).

Software Science: Theoretical Foundations for Software Engineering and Computational Intelligence

It is recognized that *theoretical software engineering* focuses on foundations and basic theories of software engineering; whilst *empirical software engineering* concentrates on heuristic principles, tools/environments, and best practices by *case studies*, *experiments*, *trials*, and *benchmarking*. It is noteworthy that, because software is the most abstract instructive information, software engineering is one of the most complicated branches of engineering, which requires intensive theoretical investigations rather than only empirical studies. Due to the widely impacted and applicable

objects and the complicated theories in software engineering, a scientific discipline known as software science is emerged.

The discipline of software science enquiries the common objects in the abstract world such as software, information, data, knowledge, instruction, executable behavior, and their processing by natural and machine intelligence. In other words, software science studies instructive and behavioral information and the mechanism of its translation into system behaviors. It is noteworthy that cognitive informatics perceives information as anything that can be inputted into and processed by the brain; while software science perceives software as any instructive information that can be executed and transformed into computational behaviors by computers. This forges a relationship between cognitive informatics and software science, which indicates that the former is the foundation for natural intelligence science, and the latter is the foundation for artificial intelligence science and software engineering. With the perception as applied software science, *software engineering* is an engineering discipline that applies software science theories and methodologies to efficiently, economically, and reliably organize and develop large-scale software systems.

FROM ARTIFICIAL INTELLIGENCE TO COMPUTATIONAL INTELLIGENCE

Intelligence science is naturally interdisciplinary in vertical based on reductionism and is transdisciplinary in horizontal based on holism. Intelligence science studies theories and models of the brain at all levels, and the relationship between the concrete physiological brain and the abstract soft mind. Intelligence science is a new frontier with the fertilization of biology, psychology, neuroscience, cognitive science, cognitive informatics, philosophy, information science, computer science, anthropology, and linguistics.

Approaches to Embody Abstract Intelligence

A fundamental view developed in software and intelligence sciences is known as abstract intelligence (Wang, 2008a), which provides a unified foundation for the studies of all forms and paradigms of intelligence such as natural, artificial, machinable, and computational intelligence.

Definition 2. Abstract intelligence, αI, is a human enquiry of both natural and artificial intelligence at the embody levels of neural, cognitive, functional, and logical from the bottom up.

In the *narrow sense*, αI is a human or a system ability that transforms information into behaviors. While, in the *broad sense*, αI is any human or system ability that autonomously transfers the forms of abstract information between *data, information, knowledge,* and *behaviors* in the brain or systems.

With the clarification of the intension and extension of the concept of the generic abstract intelligence, its paradigms or concrete forms in the real-world can be derived as summarized in Table 1. As shown in Table 1, computational intelligence can be defined below.

Definition 3. Computational intelligence (CoI) is an embodying form of abstract intelligence (αI) that implements intelligent mechanisms and behaviors by computational methodologies and software systems, such as expert systems, fuzzy systems, autonomous computing, intelligent agent systems, genetic/evolutionary systems, and autonomous learning systems.

Cognitive Informatics Foundations of Computational Intelligence

It is recognized that the theoretical foundations of computational intelligence root in cognitive informatics, software science, and denotational mathematics (Wang, 2002a, 2008b). Cognitive informatics is a cutting-edge and multidisciplinary research field that tackles the fundamental problems shared by modern informatics, computation, software engineering, AI, computational intelligence, cybernetics, cognitive science, neuropsychology, medical science, systems science, philosophy, linguistics, economics, management science, and life sciences. The development and the cross fertilization between the aforementioned science and engineering disciplines have led to a whole range of extremely interesting new research area known as cognitive informatics.

Definition 4. Cognitive informatics is the transdisciplinary enquiry of cognitive and information sciences that investigates into the internal information processing mechanisms and processes of the brain and natural intelligence, and their engineering applications via an interdisciplinary approach (Wang, 2002a, 2006, 2007b; Wang et al, 2006).

The architecture of the theoretical framework of cognitive informatics (Wang, 2007b) covers the Information-Matter-Energy (IME) model (Wang, 2003), the Layered Reference Model of the Brain (LRMB) (Wang et al., 2006), the Object-Attribute-Relation (OAR) model of information representation in the brain (Wang, 2007c), the cognitive informatics model of the brain (Wang and Wang, 2006), Natural Intelligence (NI) (Wang, 2002a), Neural Informatics (NeI) (Wang, 2007b), the mechanisms of human perception processes (Wang, 2007g), and cognitive computers (Wang, 2006; Wang and Sheu, 2008).

The key application areas of cognitive informatics can be divided into two categories. The first category of applications uses informatics and computing techniques to investigate cognitive science problems, such as memory, learning, and reasoning. The second category including the remainder areas uses cognitive theories to investigate problems in informatics, computing, soft-

Table 1. Taxonomy of abstract intelligence and its embodying forms

No.	Form of intelligence	Embodying Means	Paradigms
1	Natural intelligence (NI)	Naturally grown biological and physiological organisms	Human brains and brains of other well developed species
2	Artificial intelligence (AI)	Cognitively-inspired artificial models and man-made systems	Intelligent systems, knowledge systems, decision-making systems, and distributed agent systems
3	Machinable intelligence (MI)	Complex machine and wired systems	Computers, robots, autonomic circuits, neural networks, and autonomic mechanical machines
4	Computational intelligence (CoI)	Computational methodologies and software systems	Expert systems, fuzzy systems, autonomous computing, intelligent agent systems, genetic/evolutionary systems, and autonomous learning systems

ware/knowledge engineering and computational intelligence. cognitive informatics focuses on the nature of information processing in the brain, such as information acquisition, representation, memory, retrieve, generation, and communication. Through the interdisciplinary approach and with the support of modern information and neuroscience technologies, mechanisms of the brain and the mind may be systematically explored within the framework of cognitive informatics.

Recent advances in cognitive informatics reveal an entire set of cognitive functions of the brain (Wang, 2007b; Wang and Wang, 2006) and their cognitive process models (Wang et al., 2006). LRMB (Wang, et al., 2006) provides a reference model for the design and implementation of computational intelligence, which provides a systematical view toward the formal description and modeling of architectures and behaviors of computational intelligence. The LRMB model explains the functional mechanisms and cognitive processes of the natural intelligence with 39 cognitive processes at seven layers known as the *sensation, memory, perception, action, meta-cognitive, meta-inference,* and *higher cognitive layers* from the bottom up. LRMB elicits the core and highly repetitive recurrent cognitive processes from a huge variety of life functions, which may shed light on the study of the fundamental mechanisms and interactions of complicated mental processes and computational intelligence, particularly the relationships and interactions between the in-

herited and the acquired life functions as well as those of the subconscious and conscious cognitive processes. The cognitive model of the brain can be used as a reference model for goal- and inference-driven technologies in computational intelligence and autonomous agent systems (Wang, 2009b).

Denotational Mathematics Foundations of Computational Intelligence

Applied mathematics can be classified into two categories known as *analytic* and *denotational* mathematics (Wang, 2007a, 2008b). The former are mathematical structures that deal with functions of variables as well as their operations and behaviors; while the latter are mathematical structures that formalize rigorous expressions and inferences of system architectures and behaviors with abstract concepts, complex relations, and dynamic processes.

Definition 5. *Denotational mathematics is a category of expressive mathematical structures that deals with high-level mathematical entities beyond numbers and simple sets, such as abstract objects, complex relations, behavioral information, concepts, knowledge, processes, intelligence, and systems.*

Typical paradigms of denotational mathematics are comparatively presented in Table 2, where

Table 2. Paradigms of denotational mathematics

No.	Paradigm	Structure	Mathematical entities	Algebraic operations	Usage
1	Concept algebra	$CA \triangleq (C, OP, \Theta) = (\{O, A, R^c, R^i, R^o\},$ $\{\bullet_r, \bullet_c\}, \Theta_C)$	$c \triangleq (O, A, R^c, R^i, R^o)$	$\bullet_r \triangleq \{\leftrightarrow, \leftrightarrow\!\!\!\!/, \prec, \succ, =, \cong, \sim, \triangleq\}$ $\bullet_c \triangleq \{\overset{-}{\Rightarrow}, \overset{+}{\Rightarrow}, \overset{\sim}{\Rightarrow}, \uplus, \Cap, \Leftarrow, \vdash, \mapsto\}$	Algebraic manipulations on abstract concepts
2	System algebra	$SA \triangleq (S, OP, \Theta) = (\{C, R^c, R^i, R^o, B, \Omega\},$ $\{\bullet_r, \bullet_c\}, \Theta)$	$S \triangleq (C, R^c, R^i, R^o, B, \Omega, \Theta)$	$\bullet_r \triangleq \{\leftrightarrow, \leftrightarrow\!\!\!\!/, \prod, =, \sqsubseteq, \sqsupseteq\}$ $\bullet_c \triangleq \{\overset{-}{\Rightarrow}, \overset{+}{\Rightarrow}, \overset{\sim}{\Rightarrow}, \boxminus, \uplus, \Cap, \Leftarrow, \vdash\}$	Algebraic manipulations on abstract systems
3	Real-time process algebra (RTPA)	$RTPA \triangleq (\mathfrak{T}, \mathfrak{P}, \mathfrak{N})$	$\mathfrak{P} \triangleq \{:=, \blacklozenge\Rightarrow, \Leftarrow, \not\lessgtr, \gg, \lessdot, \rhd,$ $\lhd, @, \triangleq, \uparrow, \downarrow, !, \otimes, \boxtimes, \S\}$ $\mathfrak{T} \triangleq \{\mathbf{N, Z, R, S, BL, B, H, P, TI, D, DT,}$ $\mathbf{RT, ST,} @eS, @t\mathbf{TM}, @int\odot, \textcircled{S} s\mathbf{BL}\}$	$\mathfrak{R} \triangleq \{\to, \curvearrowright, \|\cdot\|\cdots\|\cdots, R^*, R^+, R^i,$ $\circlearrowleft, \hookleftarrow, \|, \oiint, \|\|, \gg, \swarrow, \hookleftarrow, \hookleftarrow\}$	Algebraic manipulations on abstract processes

their structures, mathematical entities, algebraic operations, and usages are contrasted. The paradigms of denotational mathematics as shown in Table 2 are *concept algebra* (Wang, 2008c), *system algebra* (Wang, 2008d), and *Real-Time Process Algebra* (RTPA) (Wang, 2002b, 2008e).

The emergence of denotational mathematics is driven by the practical needs in cognitive informatics, computational intelligence, computing science, software science, and knowledge engineering, because all these modern disciplines study complex human and machine behaviors and their rigorous treatments. Among the new forms of denotational mathematics, *concept algebra* is designed to deal with the abstract mathematical structure of concepts and their representation and manipulation in knowledge engineering. *System algebra* is created to the rigorous treatment of abstract systems and their algebraic relations and operations. RTPA is developed to deal with series of behavioral processes and architectures of human and systems.

Denotational mathematics provides a powerful mathematical means for modeling and formalizing computational intelligent systems. Not only the architectures of computational intelligent systems, but also their dynamic behaviors can be rigorously and systematically manipulated by denotational mathematics. A wide range of applications of de-

notational mathematics have been demonstrated in software science and computational intelligence, which demonstrate that denotational mathematics is an ideal mathematical means for dealing with concepts, knowledge, behavioral processes, and human/machine intelligence with real-world problems.

A NEW TRANSDISCIPLINARY RESEARCH FIELD OF SOFTWARE AND INTELLIGENCE SCIENCES

The transdisciplinary field between software science and computational intelligence brings two logically and interactively related disciplines together. This new field of enquiry will be helpful to explain how natural intelligence is generated on the basis of fundamental biological and physiological structures; How intelligence functions logically and physiologically; How natural and machine intelligence are converged on the basis of software and intelligence sciences.

The architectural framework of software and intelligence science is described in Table 3, which illustrates the structure and scope of the International Journal of Software Science and Computational Intelligence (IJSSCI). Because the implementation media and embody means

Table 3. The structure and scopes of IJSSCI

Theories and Methodologies	Denotational Mathematics	Applications in Engineering and Industries
• Transdisciplinary theories shared by software and intelligence science	• Denotational vs. analytic mathematics	• Future generation computers
• Functional models of the brain	• Mathematical structures for software modeling	• Cognitive computers
• Logical models of the brain	• Formal description of the brain	• Soft computing
• Software simulations of the brain	• Formal description of cognitive processes	• Intelligent software engineering
• Theories for computational intelligence	• Formal inference processes	• Autonomic/autonomous systems
• Software vs. brain processes	• Concept algebra for knowledge modeling	• Autonomous machine learning systems
• Formal language theories	• Process algebra for behavioral modeling	• Autonomous agent systems
• Cognitive informatics foundations of the brain	• System algebra for complex system modeling	• Software code generation technologies
• Intelligent behavioral foundations of software	• Real-Time Process Algebra (RTPA)	• Hyper programming
• Instructive information foundations of software	• Visual semantic algebra	• Hybrid man-machine systems
• Non-language centered programming	• Fuzzy/rough sets	• Novel computing methods
• Cognitive informatics	• Mathematical foundations of software	• Novel intelligence simulation systems
• Cognitive mechanisms of the brain and mind	• Universal mathematic models of software	• Novel memory devices
• Neural informatics	• Mathematical models of the brain and mind	• Cognitive complexity of software
• Knowledge representation methodologies	• Mathematical models of machine intelligence	• Cognitive machines that think and feel
• Autonomous computing	• Mathematical models of natural intelligence	• Granular computing
• Brain behavioral simulation	• Mathematical models of learning	• Bioinformatics
• Distributed intelligence	• Mathematical models of problem solving	• Machine inferences
• Machine perception and cognition	• Mathematical models of agent systems	• Novel memory forms and implementations

of computational intelligence are software or its instructive behaviors, to a certain extent, computational intelligence may be perceived as software intelligence, or shortly *intelware* in parallel to hardware and software. Typical paradigms of computational intelligence are expert systems, fuzzy systems, autonomous computing, intelligent agent systems, genetic/evolutionary systems, and autonomous learning systems.

As that of computing hardware is based on the mathematical foundation of Boolean algebra, the more intelligent capability of computational intelligence must be processed by more powerful mathematical structures known as denotational mathematics in the forms of concept algebra, system algebra, and RTPA as described in the preceding sections. The three new structures of contemporary mathematics extend the abstract objects under study in mathematics from basic entities such as numbers, Boolean variables, and sets to complex ones such as concepts, systems, and behavioral processes.

Computing systems and technologies can be classified into the categories of *imperative, autonomic,* and *cognitive* computers from the bottom up. The imperative computers are a traditional and passive system based on stored-program controlled behaviors for data processing (von Neumann, 1946, 1958). The autonomic computers are goal-driven and self-decision-driven machines that do not rely on instructive and procedural information (Kephart and Chess, 2003; IBM, 2006; Wang, 2004, 2007a). Cognitive computers are more intelligent computers beyond the imperative and autonomic computers, which embodies major natural intelligence behaviors of the brain such as thinking, inference, and learning (Wang, 2006, 2007a; Wang and Sheu, 2008).

Definition 6. A cognitive computer is an intelligent knowledge processor with the capabilities of autonomic inference and perception that mimics the mechanisms of the brain and abstract intelligence.

Cognitive computers are an expected paradigm of computational intelligence. The theories and methodologies of cognitive computers are inspired by the latest advances in cognitive informatics (Wang, 2002a, 2006, 2007b) and contemporary denotational mathematics (Wang, 2002b, 2008b). The theoretical foundations of cognitive computers encompass cognitive informatics, neural informatics, and abstract intelligence. As that of formal logic and Boolean algebra are the mathematical foundations of conventional computers. The mathematical foundations of cognitive computers are based on denotational mathematics. Cognitive computers will provide a powerful platform to implement all facets of computational intelligence such as the *perceptive, cognitive, instructive,* and *reflective* intelligence (Wang, 2008a, 2009a).

HIGHLIGHTS OF THE INAUGURAL ISSUE

IJSSCI will not only establish an important forum for the emerging field of software and intelligence sciences, but also facilitate the dissemination of engineering and industrial applications of the latest discoveries in the fields covered by the journal. The objective of this inaugural issue of IJSSCI is to provide an informative overview on the entire structure of software science and computational intelligence, and an in-depth survey of the latest advances in these fields from multidisciplinary researchers and practitioners.

This inaugural issue includes eight regular research articles from prestigious scholars as highlighted below:

a. Yingxu Wang introduces the concept of abstract intelligence in the work *On Abstract Intelligence: Toward a Unifying Theory of Natural, Artificial, Machinable, and Computational Intelligence*, which presents the *Generic Abstract Intelligence Mode* (GAIM) in order to explain the mechanisms of advanced intelligence and their denotational mathematical foundations.

b. Witold Pedrycz elaborates *Hierarchies of Architectures of Collaborative Computational Intelligence*, Which investigates into the hierarchical and collaborative properties of computational intelligence known as Collaborative Computational Intelligence (C^2I). A paradigm of information granules in granular computing are modeled and explained in the form of metastructures and metamodels of C^2I.

c. Eric Bouillet, Mark Feblowitz, Zhen Liu, Anand Ranganathan, and Anton Riabov from IBM T.J. Watson Research Center address a long-standing and highly challenging problem on *Semantic Matching, Propagation and Transformation for Composition in Component-Based Systems*. The work demonstrates how application architects craft components for dynamic assembly, and how they craft semantic descriptions using ontology that captures the essence of components' functionality to support composition in software engineering.

d. Jeffrey J.P. Tsai, Jia Zhang, Jeff J.S. Huang and Stephen J.H. Yang reported their finding in *Supporting CSCW and CSCL with Intelligent Social Grouping Sensors*. A hierarchical social network is constructed to model both knowledge and social relationships, where the former is the extent of knowledge of a participant; while the latter is the capability of a participant to share knowledge with peers. The model is adopted to measure the collaboration strength between pairs of participants in social sensor networks in the contexts of Computer Supported Cooperative Work (CSCW) and Computer-Supported Collaborative Learning (CSCL).

e. Yingxu Wang, Lotfi A. Zadeh, and Yiyu Yao develop a new approach to formally model the entities and methodologies of granular computing using system algebra in the work *On the System Algebra Foundation for Granular Computing*. It focuses not only on the architectural and relational modeling of system granules in granular computing, but also their computing behavioral modeling, which enables implementation of computable and distributed granules and granular computing systems.

f. *Marina Gavrilova* presents an intensive survey on *Adaptive Computation Paradigm in Knowledge Representation: Traditional and Emerging Applications*. The author finds that many fundamental needs in computing drive the investigation into convergence of software science and intelligence science, as well as computational sciences and their applications. A number of emerging paradigms of adaptive computation, such as the algorithmic models of intelligence, biometric technologies, evolutionary computing, swarm intelligence, knowledge representation, and geometric computing, are comparatively elaborated.

g. Janusz Kacprzyk and Sławomir Zadrożny investigate into *Protoforms of Linguistic Database Summaries as a Human Consistent Tool for Using Natural Language in Data Mining*. The authors advocate the use of Zadeh's concept of the prototypical form, shortly protoform, in linguistic database and their extensions as a general tool for consistent summarization of large data sets. They present an extended interactive approach to fuzzy linguistic summaries based on fuzzy logic and fuzzy database queries with linguistic quantifiers. This work shows how fuzzy queries are related to linguistic summaries by a hierarchy of protoforms. An implementation of the proposed technology for the summarization of Web server logs is demonstrated.

h. Du Zhang's work on *Machine Learning and Value-Based Software Engineering* synergizes a new link between computational intelligence and software intelligence. The author perceives that machine learning plays an increasingly important role in helping develop and maintain large and complex software systems. A set of machine learning methods and algorithms to enable value-based software engineering are proposed, which integrates value considerations into the full range of existing and emerging software engineering practices.

As an introductory orientation, the editorial of this inaugural issue highlights the architecture and a coherent framework of the convergence of software science and computational intelligence, which form a new transdisciplinary field that investigates into a unifying theory for abstract intelligence and its paradigms in forms of natural, artificial, machinable, computational, and web-based distributed intelligence.

CONCLUSION

The emerging field of software and intelligence sciences investigates into the theoretical foundations and denotational mathematical structures of computational intelligence and software engineering. This editorial has provided insightful perspectives on the convergent field of software science and computational intelligence. The coverage of the inaugural issue has been reviewed and highlighted. The Editor-in-Chief expects that readers of *the International Journal of Software Science and Computational Intelligence* (IJSSCI) will benefit from the set of articles presented in this inaugural issue in order to aware the recent advances and groundbreaking studies in the transdisciplinary filed of software and intelligence sciences.

ACKNOWLEDGMENT

Many people have contributed their dedicated work to the establishment of IJSSCI and the publication of its inaugural issue. The Editor-in-Chief would like to thank all authors, the associate editors, and the editorial board members, particularly *Lotfi A. Zadeh, Witold Pedrycz, James Anderson, Janusz Kacprzyk, Witold Kinsner, Philip Sheu, Jeffrey Tsai, Du Zhang, Yiyu Yao, Dilip Patel, Christine Chan, Keith Chan, Ling Guan,* and *Zhen Liu,* for their great contributions to IJSSCI. I would like to acknowledge the publisher of IJSSCI, IGI Publishing, USA, and to thank *Mehdi Khosrow-Pour* (President of IGI), *Jan Travers* (Managing Director), *Kristin M. Klinger* (Managing Acquisitions Editor), and the editorial staff of IGI, *Heather Probst* and *Elizabeth C. Duke,* for their excellent professional support.

REFERENCES

Brooks, F. P. Jr. (1975). *The Mythical Man-Month: Essays on Software Engineering.* Boston: Addison Wesley Longman, Inc.

Dijkstra, E. W. (1976). *A Discipline of Programming.* Englewood Cliffs, NJ: Prentice Hall.

IBM. (2006), Autonomic Computing White Paper: *An Architectural Blueprint for Autonomic Computing,* 4th ed., June, 1-37.

Kephart, J., & Chess, D. (2003). The Vision of Autonomic Computing. *Computer, 26*(1), 41–50. doi:10.1109/MC.2003.1160055

von Neumann, J. (1946), The Principles of Large-Scale Computing Machines, reprinted in *Annals of History of Computers*, 3(3), 263-273.

von Neumann, J. (1958). *The Computer and the Brain.* New Haven: Yale Univ. Press.

Wang, Y. (2002a), Keynote: On Cognitive Informatics, *Proc. 1st IEEE International Conference on Cognitive Informatics* (ICCI'02), Calgary, Canada, IEEE CS Press, August, 34-42.

Wang, Y. (2002b), The Real-Time Process Algebra (RTPA), *Annals of Software Engineering,* (14), USA, 235-274.

Wang, Y. (2003), On Cognitive Informatics, *Brain and Mind: A Transdisciplinary Journal of Neuroscience and Neurophilosophy*, 4(2), 151-167.

Wang, Y. (2004), Keynote: On Autonomic Computing and Cognitive Processes, *Proc. 3rd IEEE International Conference on Cognitive Informatics (ICCI'04),* Victoria, Canada, IEEE CS Press, August, 3-4.

Wang, Y. (2006), Keynote: Cognitive Informatics - Towards the Future Generation Computers that Think and Feel, *Proc. 5th IEEE International Conference on Cognitive Informatics* (ICCI'06), Beijing, China, IEEE CS Press, July, 3-7.

Wang, Y. (2007a), *Software Engineering Foundations: A Software Science Perspective*, CRC Series in Software Engineering, Vol. II, Auerbach Publications, NY, USA, July.

Wang, Y. (2007b), Wang, Y. (2007b), The Theoretical Framework of Cognitive Informatics, *International Journal of Cognitive Informatics and Natural Intelligence,* IGI, Hershey, PA, USA, Jan., 10-22

Wang, Y. (2007c). The OAR Model of Neural Informatics for Internal Knowledge Representation in the Brain, *International Journal of Cognitive Informatics and Natural Intelligence, 1*(3), 64–75.

Wang, Y. (2007d). On The Cognitive Processes of Human Perception with Emotions, Motivations, and Attitudes, *International Journal of Cognitive Informatics and Natural Intelligence, 1*(4), 1–13.

Wang, Y. (2008a), Keynote: Abstract Intelligence and Its Denotational Mathematics Foundations, *Proc. 7th IEEE International Conference on Cognitive Informatics* (ICCI'08), Stanford University, CA, USA, IEEE CS Press, August, 3-12.

Wang, Y. (2008b), *On Contemporary Denotational Mathematics for Computational Intelligence, Transactions of Computational Science,* (2), Springer, June, 6-29.

Wang, Y. (2008c). On Concept Algebra: A Denotational Mathematical Structure for Knowledge and Software Modeling. *International Journal of Cognitive Informatics and Natural Intelligence, 2*(2), 1–19. doi:10.4018/jcini.2008040101

Wang, Y. (2008d). On System Algebra: A Denotational Mathematical Structure for Abstract Systems, Modeling. *International Journal of Cognitive Informatics and Natural Intelligence, 2*(2), 20–43. doi:10.4018/jcini.2008040102

Wang, Y. (2008e). RTPA: A Denotational Mathematics for Manipulating Intelligent and Computational Behaviors. *International Journal of Cognitive Informatics and Natural Intelligence, 2*(2), 44–62. doi:10.4018/jcini.2008040103

Wang, Y. (2009a), On Abstract Intelligence: Toward a Unifying Theory of Natural, Artificial, Machinable, and Computational Intelligence, *International Journal of Software Science and Computational Intelligence,* IGI, USA, Jan., 1(1), 1-17.

Wang, Y. (2009b), A Cognitive Informatics Reference Model of Autonomous Agent Systems, *International Journal of Cognitive Informatics and Natural Intelligence,* Jan., 3(1), 1-16.

Wang, Y., & Sheu, P. (2008). (to appear). Toward Cognitive Computers that Learn and Think. *ACM Transactions on Autonomous and Adaptive Systems, 2*(4).

Wang, Y., & Wang, Y. (2006). On Cognitive Informatics Models of the Brain. *IEEE Transactions on Systems, Man, and Cybernetics, 36*(2), 16–20.

Wang, Y., Wang, Y., Patel, S., & Patel, D. (2006). A Layered Reference Model of the Brain (LRMB) [Part C]. *IEEE Transactions on Systems, Man, and Cybernetics, 36*(2), 124–133. doi:10.1109/TSMCC.2006.871126

This work was previously published in International Journal of Software Science and Computational Intelligence, Volume 1, Issue 1, edited by Yingxu Wang, pp. i-xii, copyright 2009 by IGI Publishing (an imprint of IGI Global).

Chapter 2
On Abstract Intelligence:
Toward a Unifying Theory of Natural, Artificial, Machinable, and Computational Intelligence

Yingxu Wang
University of Calgary, Canada

ABSTRACT

Abstract intelligence is a human enquiry of both natural and artificial intelligence at the reductive embodying levels of neural, cognitive, functional, and logical from the bottom up. This paper describes the taxonomy and nature of intelligence. It analyzes roles of information in the evolution of human intelligence, and the needs for logical abstraction in modeling the brain and natural intelligence. A formal model of intelligence is developed known as the Generic Abstract Intelligence Mode (GAIM), which provides a foundation to explain the mechanisms of advanced natural intelligence such as thinking, learning, and inferences. A measurement framework of intelligent capability of humans and systems is comparatively studied in the forms of intelligent quotient, intelligent equivalence, and intelligent metrics. On the basis of the GAIM model and the abstract intelligence theories, the compatibility of natural and machine intelligence is revealed in order to investigate into a wide range of paradigms of abstract intelligence such as natural, artificial, machinable intelligence, and their engineering applications.

INTRODUCTION

Intelligence is a driving force or an ability to acquire and use knowledge and skills, or to inference in problem solving. It is a profound human wonder on how conscious intelligence is generated as a highly complex cognitive state in human mind on the basis of biological and physiological structures. How natural intelligence functions logically and phisiologically? How natural and artificial intelligence are converged on the basis of brain, software, and intelligence science? It was conventionally deemed that only mankind and advanced species possess intelligence. However, the development of computers, robots, software agents, and autonomous systems indicates that intelligence may also be created or embodied by machines and man-made systems. Therefore, it is

DOI: 10.4018/978-1-4666-0261-8.ch002

one of the key objectives in cognitive informatics and intelligence science to seek a coherent theory for explaining the nature and mechanisms of both natural and artificial intelligence.

The history of investigation into the brain and natural intelligence is as long as the history of mankind, which can be traced back to the Aristotle's era and earlier. Early studies on intelligence are represented by works of Vygotsky, Spearman, and Thurstone (Bender, 1996; Matlin, 1998; Payne and Wenger, 1998; Parker and McKinney, 1999; Wilson and Keil, 2001; Lefton et al., 2005). Lev Vygotsky's (1896 - 1934) presents a communication view that perceives intelligence as inter- and intra-personal communication in a social context. Charles E. Spearman (1863 - 1945) and Lois L. Thurstone (1887 - 1955) proposed the *factor theory* (Lefton et al., 2005), in which seven factors of intelligence are identified such as the *verbal comprehension, word fluency, number facility, spatial visualization, associative memory, perceptual speed,* and *reasoning.*

David Wechsler's *intelligent measurement theory* (Lefton et al., 2005) models intelligence from the aspects of *verbal, quantitative, abstract visual,* and *short-term working memory reasoning.* He proposed the Wechsler Adult Intelligence Scale (WAIS) in 1932. Arthur Jensen's *two-level theory* (Jensen, 1969, 1970, 1987) classifies intelligence into two levels known as the *associative* ability level and the *cognitive* ability level. The former is the ability to process external stimuli and events; while the latter is the ability to carry out reasoning and problem solving.

Howard Gardner's *multiple intelligences theory* (Gardner, 1983, 1995) identifies eight forms of intelligence, which are those of *linguistic, logical-mathematical, musical, spatial, bodily-kinesthetic, naturalist, interpersonal,* and *intrapersonal.* He perceives that intelligence is an ability to solve a problem or create a product within a specific cultural setting. Robert J. Sternberg's *triarchic theory* (Sternberg, 1997, 2000, 2003)

models intelligence in three dimensions known as the *analytic, practical,* and *creative* intelligence. He perceives intelligence as the ability to adapt to, shape, and select environments to accomplish one's goals and those of society. Lester A. Lefton and his colleagues (Lefton et al., 2005) defined intelligence as the overall capacity of the individual to act purposefully, to think rationally, and to deal effectively with the social and cultural environment. They perceive that intelligence is not a thing but a process that is affected by a person's experiences in the environment.

J. *McCarthy, M.L. Minsky, N. Rochester, and C.E. Shannon* proposed the term *Artificial Intelligence* (AI) in 1955 (*McCarthy* et al., 1955; McCulloch, 1965). S.C. Kleene analyzed the relations of automata and nerve nets (Kleene, 1956), and Bernard Widrow initiated the technology of *Artificial Neural Networks* (ANNs) in the 1950s (Widrow and Lehr, 1990) based on multilevel, distributed, dynamic, interactive, and self-organizing nonlinear networks (Albus, 1991; Ellis and Fred, 1962; Haykin, 1998). The concepts of robotics (Brooks, 1970) and expert systems (Giarrantans and Riley, 1989) were developed in the 1970s and 1980s, respectively. Then, intelligent systems (Meystel and Albus, 2002) and software agents (Hewitt, 1977; Jennings, 2000) emerged in the 1990s.

Yingxu Wang's *real-time intelligent theory* (Wang, 2007a, 2007b; Wang and Wang, 2006; Wang et al., 2006) reveals that natural intelligence is the driving force that transforms cognitive information in the forms of data, knowledge, skill, and behavior. Intelligence can be modeled into two categories known as the *subconscious* (inherent) intelligence and *conscious* (acquired) intelligence. A *Layered Reference Model of the Brain* (LRMB) has been developed (Wang et al., 2006), which encompasses 39 cognitive processes at seven layers known as the *sensation, memory, perception, action, meta-cognitive, meta-inference,* and *higher-cognitive layers* from the bottom up.

Cognitive informatics (Wang, 2002a, 2003a, 2006b, 2007b) adopts a compatible perspective on natural and artificial intelligence (Wang, 2007d, 2008d). It is logical to perceive that natural intelligence should be fully understood before artificial intelligence can be scientifically studied. In this view, conventional machines are invented to extend human physical capability, while modern information processing machines such as computers, communication networks, and robots are developed for extending human intelligence, memory, and the capacity of information processing (Wang, 2006a, 2007b). Any machine that may implement a part of human behaviors and actions in information processing has possessed some extent of intelligence. This holistic view has led to the theory of *abstract intelligence* (Wang, 2008c) in order to unify all paradigms of intelligence such as natural, artificial, machinable, and computational intelligence.

This article reveals that abstract intelligence is a form of driving force which transfers information into behaviors or actions. The taxonomy and nature of intelligence is described and roles of information in the evolution of human intelligence and the need for logical abstraction in modeling the brain and natural intelligence are analyzed. A Generic Abstract Intelligence Mode (GAIM) is formally developed, which provides a foundation to explain the mechanisms of advanced natural intelligence such as thinking, learning, and inference. A measurement framework of intelligent capability of humans and systems is presented covering intelligent quotient, intelligent equivalence, and intelligent metrics. Then, the compatibility of nature and machine intelligence is formally established, which forms a theoretical foundation for more rigorous study in natural, artificial, machinable, and computational intelligence as well as their engineering applications.

THE COGNITIVE INFORMATICS FOUNDATIONS OF ABSTRACT INTELLIGENCE

Intelligence plays a central role in cognitive informatics, computing, software science, brain science, and knowledge science. However, it was perceived diversely from different facets. A key in the study of natural and artificial intelligence is the relationships between *information, knowledge, and behavior*. Therefore, the nature of intelligence is an ability *to know* and *to do* possessed by both human brains and man-made systems.

In this view, the major objectives of cognitive, software, and intelligence sciences are to answer:

- How the three forms of cognitive entities, i.e., information, knowledge, and behavior, are transformed in the brain or a system?
- What is the driving force to enable these transmissions?

A set of fundamental theories toward modeling and explaining the abstract intelligence has been developed in cognitive informatics, such as the Layered Reference Model of the Brain (LRMB) (Wang et al., 2006) and the OAR model (Wang, 2007c), which play important roles in exploring the abstract intelligence and its real-world paradigms.

Taxonomy of Cognitive Information in the Brain

Almost all modern disciplines of sciences and engineering deal with information and knowledge. However, data, information, and knowledge are conventionally considered as different entities in the literature (Debenham, 1989; Wilson and Keil, 2001). It is perceived that *data* are directly acquired raw information, usually a quantitative abstraction of external objects and/or their relations. *Information*, in a narrow sense, is meaningful data or a subjective interpretation of data. Then, *knowledge* is the consumed information or data related to existing knowledge in the brain.

Based on the investigations in cognitive informatics, particularly the research on the OAR model (Wang, 2007c) and the mechanisms of internal information representation, the empirical classification of the cognitive hierarchy of data, information, and knowledge may be revised. A cognitive informatics theory on the relationship among data (sensational inputs), actions (behavioral outputs), and their internal representations such as knowledge, experience, behavior, and skill, are that all of them are different forms of cognitive information, which may be classified on the basis of how the internal information relates to the inputs and outputs of the brain as shown in Table 1.

According to Table 1, the taxonomy of cognitive information is determined by types of inputs and outputs of information to and from the brain, where both inputs and outputs can be either information or action. For a given cognitive process, if both I/O are abstract information, the internal information acquired is *knowledge*; if both I/O are empirical actions, the type of internal information is *skill*; and the remainder combinations between action/information and information/action produce *experience* and *behaviors*, respectively. It is noteworthy in Table 1 that behavior is a new type of cognitive information modeled inside the brain, which embodies an abstract input to an observable behavioral output (Wang, 2007b).

Definition 1. *The Cognitive Information Model (CIM) classifies internal information in the brain* into four categories, according to their types of I/O information, known as knowledge (K), behavior (B), experience (E), and skill (S), i.e.:

a) Knowledge $K: I \rightarrow I$ (1)
b) Behavior $B: I \rightarrow A$ (2)
c) Experience $E: A \rightarrow I$ (3)
d) Skill $S: A \rightarrow A$ (4)

where I and A represent information and action, respectively.

The approaches to acquire knowledge/behavior and experience/skills are fundamentally different. Although knowledge or behaviors may be acquired directly and indirectly, skills and experiences can only be obtained directly by hands-on activities. Further, the associated memories of the abstract information are different, where knowledge and experience are retained as abstract relations in Long-Term Memory (LTM), while behaviors and skills are retained as wired neural connections in Action Buffer Memory (ABM) (Wang, 2007b, 2008h).

Roles of Information in the Evolution of Natural Intelligence

The profound uniqueness of the discipline of cognitive informatics, software science, and intelligence science lies on the fact that its objects under study are located in a dual world as described below.

Definition 2. *The general worldview, as shown in Figure 1, reveals that the natural world (NW)*

Table 1. The cognitive information model (CIM)

		Type of output		Ways of acquisition
		Information	**Action**	
Type of input	**Information**	Knowledge (K)	Behavior (B)	*Direct or indirect*
	Action	Experience (E)	Skill (S)	*Direct only*

is a dual world encompassing both the physical (concrete) world (PW) and the abstract (perceived) world (AW).

Theorem 1. *The Information-Matter-Energy-Intelligence (IME-I) model states that the natural world (NW) which forms the context of human and machine intelligence is a dual: one facet of it is the physical world (PW), and the other is the abstract world (AW), where intelligence (ℑ) plays a central role in the transformation between information (I), matter (M), and energy (E).*

According to the IME-I model, information is the general model for representing the abstract world. It is recognized that the basic evolutional need of mankind is to preserve both the species' biological traits and the cumulated information/knowledge bases (Wang, 2007a). For the former, the gene pools are adopted to pass human trait information via DNA from generation to generation. However, for the latter, because acquired knowledge cannot be inherited between generations and individuals, various information means and systems are adopted to pass information and knowledge of collectively cumulated by mankind.

Corollary 1. *Intelligence plays an irreplaceable role in the transformation between information, matter, and energy according to the IME-I model.*

It is observed that almost all cells in human body have a certain lifecycle in which they reproduce themselves via divisions. This mechanism allows human trait information to be transferred to offspring through gene (DNA) replications during cell reproduction. However, it is observed that the most special mechanism of neurons in the brain is that they are the only type of cells in human body that does not go through reproduction but remains alive throughout the entire human life (Thomas, 1974; Fried and Hademenos, 1999; Kandel et al., 2000). The advantage of this mechanism is that it enables the physiological representation and retention of acquired information and knowledge to be memorized permanently in long-term memory. But the vital disadvantage of this mechanism is that it does not allow acquired information to be physiologically passed on to the next generation, because there is no DNA replication among memory neurons.

This physiological mechanism of neurons in the brain explains not only the foundations of memory and memorization, but also the wonder why acquired information and knowledge cannot be passed and inherited physiologically through generation to generation. Therefore, to a certain extent, mankind relies very much on information for evolution than that of genes, because the basic characteristic of the human brain is intelligent information processing. In other words, the intelligent ability to cumulate and transfer information from generation to generation plays the vital role in mankind's evolution for both individuals and the species. This distinguishes human beings from other species in natural evolution, where the latter cannot systematically pass acquired information from generation to generation in order to grow their information/knowledge-bases cumulatively and exponentially (Wang, 2008g).

The Need for Logical Abstraction in Modeling the Brain and Abstract Intelligence

According to the functional model of the brain (Wang and Wang, 2006), genomes may only explain things at the level of *inherited* life functions, rather than that of *acquired* life functions, because the latter cannot be directly represented in genomes in order to be inherited. Therefore, high-level cognitive functional models of the brain are yet to be sought to explain the fundamental mechanisms of the abstract intelligence.

In recent genome research people expect that the decoding and probing of human genomes will solve almost all problems and answer almost all questions about the myths of the natural intelligence. Although the aim is important and encouraging, computer and software scientists would doubt this promising prediction. This is based on the basic reductionism of science and the following observations: Although the details of computer circuitry are fully observable at the bottom level, i.e., at the gate or even the molecular level, seeing computers only as the low-level structures would not help explaining the mechanisms of computing rather than get lost in an extremely large number of interconnected similar elements, if the high-level functional architectures and logical mechanisms of computers were unknown.

Corollary 2. *The principle of functional reductionism states that a logical model of the natural intelligence is needed in order to formally explain the high-level mechanisms of the brain on the basis of observations at the biological and physiological levels.*

The logical model of the brain is the highest level of abstraction for explaining its cognitive mechanisms. Based on it, a systematical investigation from the levels of logical, functional, physiological, and biological may be established in both the top-down and bottom-up approaches, which will enable the establishment of a coherent theory of abstract intelligence and brain science.

A FORMAL MODEL OF ABSTRACT INTELLIGENCE

Based on the principle of *functional reductionism*, a logical model of the general form of intelligence is needed, known as the abstract intelligence, in order to formally explain the high-level mechanisms of the brain on the basis of observations at the biological, physiological, functional, and logical levels. On the basis of the logical model of abstract intelligence, the studies on the paradigms of abstract intelligence, such as natural, artificial, machinable, and computational intelligence, may

be unified into a common framework as developed in cognitive informatics (Wang, 2002a, 2003a, 2007a, 2007b).

Abstract Intelligence and Its Paradigms

Definition 3. *Abstract intelligence, αI, is a human enquiry of both natural and artificial intelligence at the embody levels of neural, cognitive, functional, and logical from the bottom up.*

In the *narrow sense*, αI is a human or a system ability that transforms information into behaviors. While, in the *broad sense*, αI is any human or system ability that autonomously transfers the forms of abstract information between *data, information, knowledge,* and *behaviors* in the brain or systems.

With the clarification of the intension and extension of the concept of αI, its paradigms or concrete forms in the real-world can be derived as summarized in Table 2.

Definition 4. *Natural intelligence (NI) is an embodying form of αI that implements intelligent mechanisms and behaviors by naturally grown biological and physiological organisms such as human brains and those of other well developed species.*

Definition 5. *Artificial intelligence (AI) is an embodying form of αI that implements intelligent mechanisms and behaviors by cognitively-inspired artificial models and man-made systems such as intelligent systems, knowledge systems, decision-making systems, and distributed agent systems.*

Definition 6. *Machinable intelligence (MI) is an embodying form of αI that implements intelligent mechanisms and behaviors by complex machine and circuit systems such as computers, robots, circuits, neural networks, and autonomic mechanical machines.*

Table 2. Taxonomy of abstract intelligence and its embodying forms

No.	Form of intelligence	Embodying Means	Paradigms
1	Natural intelligence (NI)	Naturally grown biological and physiological organisms	Human brains and brains of other well developed species
2	Artificial intelligence (AI)	Cognitively-inspired artificial models and man-made systems	Intelligent systems, knowledge systems, decision-making systems, and distributed agent systems
3	Machinable intelligence (MI)	Complex machine and wired systems	Computers, robots, autonomic circuits, neural networks, and autonomic mechanical machines
4	Computational intelligence (CoI)	Computational methodologies and software systems	Expert systems, fuzzy systems, autonomous computing, intelligent agent systems, genetic/evolutionary systems, and autonomous learning systems

Definition 7. *Computational intelligence (CoI) is an embodying form of αI that implements intelligent mechanisms and behaviors by computational methodologies and software systems.*

Typical paradigms of CoI are expert systems, fuzzy systems, autonomous computing, intelligent agent systems, genetic/evolutionary systems, and autonomous learning systems (Jordan, 1999).

Definition 8. *The behavioral model of consciousness, §CS-BST, is an abstract logical model denoted by a set of parallel processes that encompasses the imperative intelligence I_P, autonomic intelligence I_A, and cognitive intelligence I_C from the bottom-up, i.e. Box 1.*

According to Definition 8, the relationship among the three-form intelligence is as follows:

$$\mathfrak{I}_I \subseteq \mathfrak{I}_A \subseteq \mathfrak{I}_C \qquad (6)$$

Both Eqs. 5 and 6 indicate that any lower layer intelligence and behavior is a subset of those of a higher layer. In other words, any higher layer intelligence and behavior is a natural extension of those of lower layers.

The Generic Abstract Intelligence Model (GAIM)

On the basis of the conceptual models developed in previous subsections, the mechanisms of αI can be described by a Generic Abstract Intelligence Model (GAIM) as shown in Figure 2.

In the GAIM model as shown in Figure 2, different forms of intelligence are described as a driving force that transfers between a pair of abstract objects in the brain such as *data* (*D*), *information* (*I*), *knowledge* (*K*), and *behavior* (*B*). It is noteworthy that each abstract object is physically retained in a particular type of memories. This is the neural informatics foundation of

---

Box 1.

$$\S CS\text{-}A^{ST} \triangleq (\mathfrak{I}_I, \mathfrak{I}_A, \mathfrak{I}_C)$$
$$= \{ \ (B_e, B_t, B_{int}) \qquad\qquad // \ \mathfrak{I}_I \text{ - Imperative intelligence}$$
$$\| (B_e, B_t, B_{int}, B_g, B_d) \qquad // \ \mathfrak{I}_A \text{ - Autonomic intelligence} \qquad (5)$$
$$\| (B_e, B_t, B_{int}, B_g^g, B_d^d, B_p, B_{inf}) \ // \ \mathfrak{I}_C \text{ - Cognitive intelligence}$$
$$\}$$

Figure 2. The generic abstract intelligence model (GAIM)

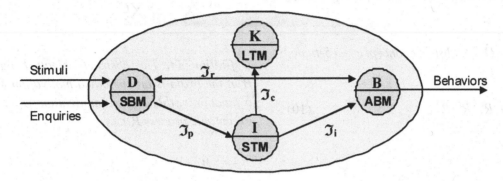

$\mathfrak{I}_p$– *Perceptive* intelligence $\mathfrak{I}_i$– *Instructive* intelligence

$\mathfrak{I}_c$– *Cognitive* intelligence $\mathfrak{I}_r$– *Reflective* intelligence

natural intelligence, and the physiological evidences of why natural intelligence can be classified into four forms as given in the following theorem.

Theorem 2. *The nature of intelligence states that abstract intelligence αI can be classified into four forms called the perceptive intelligence I_p, cognitive intelligence I_c, instructive intelligence I_i, and reflective intelligence I_r as modeled below:*

$$
\begin{aligned}
\alpha I \triangleq\ & \mathfrak{I}_p : D \rightarrow I \quad \text{(Perceptive)} \\
& \|\ \mathfrak{I}_c : I \rightarrow K \quad \text{(Cognitive)} \\
& \|\ \mathfrak{I}_i : I \rightarrow B \quad \text{(Instructive)} \\
& \|\ \mathfrak{I}_r : D \rightarrow B \quad \text{(Reflective)}
\end{aligned}
\tag{7}
$$

According to Definition 8 and Theorem 2 in the context of the GAIM model, the narrow sense of αI is corresponding to the instructive and reflective intelligence; while the broad sense of αI includes all four forms of intelligence, that is, the perceptive, cognitive, instructive and reflective intelligence.

The four abstract objects in Theorem 2 can be rigorously described in the following definitions.

Definition 9. *The abstract object data D in GAIM is a quantitative representation of external entities by a function r_d that maps external message or signal M into a specific measurement scale S_k, i.e.:*

$$
\begin{aligned}
D \triangleq\ & r_d : M \rightarrow S_k \\
& = \log_k M, \ k_{\min} = 2
\end{aligned}
\tag{8}
$$

where k is the base of the measurement scale, and the minimum of k, $k_{\min}$, is 2.

Definition 10. *The abstract object information I in GAIM in the narrow sense is a perceptive interpretation of data by a function r_i that maps the data into a concept C, i.e.:*

$$
I \triangleq r_i : D \rightarrow C, \ r_i \in \mathfrak{R}_{CA}
\tag{9}
$$

where $P\,\mathfrak{R}_{CA}$ is the nine compositional operations of concepts as defined in concept algebra, P

$\mathfrak{R}_{CA} = \{\Rightarrow, \overset{+}{\Rightarrow}, \overset{-}{\Rightarrow}, \overset{\sim}{\Rightarrow}, \uplus, \sqcap, \Leftarrow, \vdash, \rightarrow\}$, with C as a concept in the form given below (Wang, 2008a, 2008b).

Definition 11. *An abstract concept c is a 5-tuple, i.e.:*

$$c \triangleq (O, A, R^c, R^i, R^o) \tag{10}$$

where

- O is a finite nonempty set of object of the concept, $O = \{o_1, o_2, ..., o_m\} \subseteq \text{Þ}E$, where $\text{Þ}E$ denotes a power set of the universal entities in the discourse of concept environment Θ.
- A is a finite nonempty set of attributes, $A = \{a_1, a_2, ..., a_n\} \subseteq \text{Þ}M$, where M is the universal set of attributes of Θ.
- $R^c \subseteq O \times A$ is a finite nonempty set of internal relations.
- $R^i \subseteq A' \times A$, $A' \sqsubseteq C' \wedge A \sqsubseteq c$, is a finite nonempty set of input relations, where C' is a set of external concepts, $C' \sqsubseteq \Theta$, and $\sqsubseteq$ denotes that a set or structure (tuple) is a substructure or derivation of another structure. For convenience, $R^i = A' \times A$ may be simply denoted as $R^i = C' \times c$.
- $R^o \subseteq c \times C'$ is a finite nonempty set of output relations.

Definition 12. *The abstract object knowledge K in the brain is a perceptive representation of information by a function r_k that maps a given concept C_0 into all related concepts, i.e.:*

$$K \triangleq r_k : C_0 \rightarrow (\underset{i=1}{\overset{n}{\text{X}}} C_i), \ r_k \in \mathfrak{R}_{CA} \tag{11}$$

Definition 13. *The entire knowledge K is represented by a concept network, which is a hierarchical network of concepts interlinked by the set of nine associations P_{CA} defined in concept algebra, i.e.:*

$$\mathfrak{K} = \mathfrak{R} : \underset{i=1}{\overset{n}{\text{X}}} C_i \rightarrow \underset{j=1}{\overset{n}{\text{X}}} C_j \tag{12}$$

Definition 14. *The abstract objects behavior B in the brain is an embodied motivation M by a function r_b that maps a motivation M into an executable process P, i.e.:*

$$
\begin{aligned}
B &\triangleq r_b : M \rightarrow P \\
&= \underset{k=1}{\overset{m}{R}}(@e_k \hookrightarrow P_k) \\
&= \underset{k=1}{\overset{m}{R}}[@e_k \hookrightarrow \underset{i=1}{\overset{n-1}{R}}(p_i(k) \ r_{ij}(k) \ p_j(k))], j = i+1, r_{ij} \in \mathfrak{R}_{RTPA}
\end{aligned} \tag{13}
$$

where M is generated by external stimuli or events and/or internal emotions or willingness, which are collectively represented by a set of events E $= \{e_1, e_2, ..., e_m\}$.

In Definition 14, P_k is represented by a set of cumulative relational subprocesses $p_i(k)$. Mathematical model of the cumulative relational processes may be referred to (Wang, 2008d).

Consciousness of Abstract Intelligence: The Platform of Mind and Thought

The theory of αI may be used to explain how consciousness is generated as a highly complex cognitive state in human mind on the basis of biological and physiological structures. From a point of view of cognitive informatics, consciousness is the entire state of a human being and his/her environment encompassing the internal sates of the brain, internal states of the body, senses about the external environment, interactions (behaviors) between the brain and the body (Wang and Wang, 2006). Therefore, the brain is logically equivalent to a real-time system, and consciousness is logically equivalent to a real-time multi-thread operating system.

On the basis of the cognitive informatics model of the brain, the following analogies show interesting relations between the brain and computing in computational intelligence and software science:

$$\text{Brain: Mind} = \text{Hardware: Software} \qquad (14)$$

$$\begin{aligned} &Consciousness : Behaviors \\ &= Operating\, system\,(NI - OS) : Applications\,(NI - App) \end{aligned}$$

(15)

where NI-OS and NI-App denote natural intelligence operating system and applications, respectively.

A process model of consciousness as an NI-OS system can be described in Real-Time Process Algebra (RTPA) (Wang, 2002b, 2003b, 2006a, 2008d, 2008e) as shown in Figure 3. The consciousness process §CS**ST** is divided into two parts known as the architectural model and the behavioral model of consciousness.

Definition 15. *The architectural model of consciousness, §CS-A**ST**, is a logical model of the brain in term of the NI-OS**ST**, which is denoted by a set of parallel intelligent engines, such as the Sensory Engine (SE), Memory Engine (ME), Perception Engine (PE), Action Engine (AE), Meta-Cognition Engine (CE), Meta-Inference Engine (IE), and Higher Cognition Engine (HCE), from the bottom up according to LRMB, i.e.:*

$$\begin{array}{lll} \S CS\text{-}A\textbf{ST} \triangleq & SE & //\ \text{Sensory engine} \\ & \|\ ME & //\ \text{Memory engine} \\ & \|\ PE & //\ \text{Perception engine} \\ & \|\ AE & //\ \text{Action engine} \\ & \|\ CE & //\ \text{Cognitive engine} \\ & \|\ IE & //\ \text{Inference engine} \\ & \|\ HCE & //\ \text{Higher cognitive engine} \end{array}$$

(16)

where $\|$ denotes the parallel relation between given components of the system.

In Definition 15, each intelligent engine of §CS-A**ST** is further refined by detailed structures

and functions as given in Figure 3. In addition, a relative system clock §t**TM** is provided in §CS-A**ST** for synchronizing dispatching activities and behaviors in the natural intelligence system. The behavioral model of consciousness has been given in Definition 8. Detailed models of each behavior in the categories of imperative, autonomic, and cognitive intelligence are presented in the last section of the CSP**ST** model in Figure 3.

MEASUREMENT OF INTELLIGENCE

On the basis of the formal models of abstract intelligence as developed in previous sections, measurement of intelligence studies how intelligence may be quantified and rigorously evaluated and benchmarked. The measurement of intelligent ability of humans and systems can be classified into three categories known as *intelligent quotient*, *intelligent equivalence*, and *intelligent metrics*.

Intelligent Quotient

The first measurement for mental intelligence is proposed in psychology known as the intelligent quotient based on the *Stanford-Binet intelligence test* (Binet, 1905; Terman and Merrill, 1961). Intelligent quotient is determined by six subtests where the pass of each subtest is count for two equivalent months of mental intelligence.

Definition 16. *The mental age A_m in an intelligent quotient test is the sum of a base age A_b and an extra equivalent age ΔA, i.e.:*

$$\begin{aligned} A_m &= A_b + \Delta A \\ &= A_{\max} + \frac{2n_{sub}}{12} \\ &= A_{\max} + \frac{n_{sub}}{6} \quad [yr] \end{aligned}$$

(17)

Figure 3. The cognitive process of consciousness in RTPA

The Consciousness Process

$\S$ConsciousnessProcess**ST** $\triangleq$ CSP**ST** ::

$\quad\quad\S$CS-A**ST** $\quad\quad\quad\quad\quad$ // Architectures

$\quad\quad\|$ $\S$CS-B**ST** $\quad\quad\quad\quad\quad$ // Behaviors

$\quad = \{$ $\quad$// Consciousness Architectures

$\quad\quad\quad <$SE**ST**: $\overset{5}{\underset{ptr\mathbf{P}=0}{R}}$ SENSORS[ptr**P**]**ST**$>$ $\quad$ // Layer 1: Sensation

$\quad\quad\quad = <$S$_{Vision}$**ST** $\|$ S$_{Audition}$**ST** $\|$ S$_{Smell}$**ST** $\|$ S$_{Tactility}$**ST** $\|$ S$_{Taste}$**ST**$>$

$\quad\quad\quad \| <$ME**ST**: $\overset{5}{\underset{addr\mathbf{P}=0}{R}}$ MEM[addr**P**]**ST**$>$ $\quad$ // Layer 2: Memory

$\quad\quad\quad = <$SBM**ST** $\|$ STM**ST** $\|$ CSM**ST** $\|$ LTM**ST** $\|$ ABM**ST**$>$

$\quad\quad\quad \| <$PE**ST**: $\overset{7}{\underset{i\mathbf{P}=0}{R}}$ PROC[i**N**]**ST**$>$ $\quad$ // Layer 3: Perception

$\quad\quad\quad = <$Attention**ST** $\|$ Motivation**ST** $\|$ Emotion**ST** $\|$ Attitude**ST**
$\quad\quad\quad\quad \|$ SensOfSpatiality**ST** $\|$ SensOfTime**ST** $\|$ SensOfMotion**ST**$>$

$\quad\quad\quad \| <$AE**ST**: $\overset{n_{SERVO}\mathbf{N}-1}{\underset{ptr\mathbf{P}=0}{R}}$ SERVOS[ptr**P**]**ST**$>$ $\quad$ // Layer 4: Action

$\quad\quad\quad \| <$CE**ST**: $\overset{10}{\underset{i\mathbf{P}=0}{R}}$ PROC[i**N**]**ST** $>$ $\quad$ // Layer 5: Meta-cognition

$\quad\quad\quad = <$ObjectIdentification**ST** $\|$ Abstraction**ST** $\|$ ConceptEstablishment**ST**
$\quad\quad\quad\quad \|$ Search**ST** $\|$ Categorization**ST** $\|$ Comparison**ST** $\|$ Memorization**ST**
$\quad\quad\quad\quad \|$ Qualification**ST** $\|$ Quantification**ST** $\|$ Selection**ST**$>$

$\quad\quad\quad \| <$IE**ST**: $\overset{6}{\underset{i\mathbf{P}=0}{R}}$ PROC[i**N**]**ST** $>$ $\quad$ // Layer 6: Meta-inference

$\quad\quad\quad = <$Deduction**ST** $\|$ Induction**ST** $\|$ Abduction**ST** $\|$ Analogy**ST**
$\quad\quad\quad\quad \|$ Analysis**ST** $\|$ Synthesis**ST**$>$

$\quad\quad\quad \| <$HCE**ST**: $\overset{7}{\underset{i\mathbf{P}=0}{R}}$ PROC[i**N**]**ST** $>$ $\quad$ // Layer 7: Higher cognition

$\quad\quad\quad = <$Comprehension**ST** $\|$ Learning**ST** $\|$ Planning**ST** $\|$ ProblemSolving**ST**
$\quad\quad\quad\quad \|$ DecisionMaking**ST** $\|$ Creation**ST** $\|$ PattenRecognition**ST**$>$

$\quad\quad\quad \| <\S t$**TM**$>$ $\quad\quad\quad\quad\quad$ // Relative clock

$\quad\}$

$\quad\| \{$ $\quad$// Consciousness Behaviors

$\quad\quad\quad \| < \overset{n_e\mathbf{N}-1}{\underset{k\mathbf{N}=0}{R}}$ @e$_k$**S** $\hookrightarrow$ P$_k$**ST**$>$ $\quad$ // *Event*-driven behaviors (B_e)

$\quad\quad\quad \| < \overset{n_t\mathbf{N}-1}{\underset{k\mathbf{N}=0}{R}}$ @t$_k$**TM** $\hookrightarrow$ P$_k$**ST**$>$ $\quad$ // *Time*-driven behaviors (B_t)

$\quad\quad\quad \| < \overset{n_{int}\mathbf{N}-1}{\underset{k\mathbf{N}=0}{R}}$ @int$_k$$\odot$ $\hookrightarrow$ P$_k$**ST**$>$ $\quad$ // *Interrupt*-driven behaviors (B_{int})

$\quad\quad\quad \| < \overset{n_t\mathbf{N}-1}{\underset{k\mathbf{N}=0}{R}}$ @g$_k$**ST** $\hookrightarrow$ P$_k$**ST**$>$ $\quad$ // *Goal*-driven behaviors (B_g)

$\quad\quad\quad \| < \overset{n_t\mathbf{N}-1}{\underset{k\mathbf{N}=0}{R}}$ @d$_k$**ST** $\hookrightarrow$ P$_k$**ST**$>$ $\quad$ // *Decision*-driven behaviors (B_d)

$\quad\quad\quad \| < \overset{n_t\mathbf{N}-1}{\underset{k\mathbf{N}=0}{R}}$ @p$_k$**ST** $\hookrightarrow$ P$_k$**ST**$>$ $\quad$ // *Perception*-driven behaviors (B_p)

$\quad\quad\quad \| < \overset{n_{int}\mathbf{N}-1}{\underset{k\mathbf{N}=0}{R}}$ @inf$_k$**ST** $\hookrightarrow$ P$_k$**ST**$>$ $\quad$ // *Inference*-driven behaviors (B_{inf})

$\quad\}$

where A_b is the maximum age A_{max} gained by a testee who passes all six subtests required for an certain age, and $\varDelta A$ is determined by the number of passed subtests beyond A_{max}, i.e., n_{sub}.

Definition 17. *Intelligent quotient (IQ) is a ratio between the mental age A_m and the chronological (actual) age A_c, multiplied by 100, i.e.:*

$$
\begin{aligned}
IQ &= \frac{A_m}{A_c} \bullet 100 \\
&= \frac{A_{max} + \frac{1}{6}n_{sub}}{A_c} \bullet 100
\end{aligned}
\tag{18}
$$

According to Definition 17, an IQ score above 100 indicates a certain extent of a gifted intelligence. However, the measure is sensitive only to children rather than adults, because the differences between the mental ages of adults cannot be formally defined and measured. Further, the basic assumption that the intelligent capability is linearly proportional along the growth of testee's age is inaccurate. Third, the norms or benchmarks of the mental ages for determining IQ are not easy to objectively obtain, especially for adults, and were considered highly subjective. More fundamentally, the IQ tests do not cover all forms of abstract intelligence as defined in GAIM, particularly the instructive and reflective intelligent capabilities.

The Turing Test

The second type of measurement for comparative intelligence is proposed by Alan Turing based on the Turing test (Turing, 1950) known as Turing intelligent equivalence.

Definition 18. *Turing intelligent equivalence E_T is a ratio of conformance or equivalence evaluated in a comparative test between of a system under test and an equivalent human-based system, where both systems are treated as a black box and the tester do not know which is the tested system, i.e.:*

$$
E_T = \frac{T_c}{T_c + T_u} \bullet 100\%
\tag{19}
$$

where T_c is the number of conformable results between the two systems a tester evaluated, and T_u the number of unconformable results.

Turing tests with the layout above are informally defined based on empirical experiments and subjective judgement of conformance of testers, because the standard reference system of real human intelligent in the test is difficult to be defined and stabilized. Also, not all forms of intelligence as identified in GAIM may be tested by the black box setting such as the cognitive and reflective intelligent capabilities.

The Intelligent Metrics

Based on the understanding of the nature of abstract intelligence and the GAIM model (Wang, 2007d), a comprehensive measurement on human and system intelligence is proposed by the author known as the intelligent metrics as defined below.

Definition 19. *The Intelligent Capability $\mathfrak{C}_I$ is an average capability of the perceptive intelligence (C_p), cognitive intelligence (C_c), instructive intelligence (C_i), and reflective intelligence (C_r), i.e.:*

$$
\mathfrak{C}_I = \frac{C_p + C_c + C_i + C_r}{4}
\tag{20}
$$

where $\mathfrak{C}_I \geq 0$ and $\mathfrak{C}_I = 0$ represents no intelligence.

In Definition 19, the four forms of intelligent capabilities can be measured individually according to the following methods given in Definitions 20 through 23.

Definition 20. *The perceptive intelligent capability C_p is the ability to transfer a given number of data objects or events N_d into a number of information objects in term of derived or related concepts, N_i, i.e.:*

$$C_p = \frac{N_i}{N_d} \tag{21}$$

The perceptive intelligent capability is directly related to the association capability of a testee. The higher the ratio of C_p, the higher the capability of perceptive intelligence. If there is no concept that may be linked or derived for a given set of data or event, there is no perceptive intelligent capability.

Definition 21. *The cognitive intelligent capability C_c is the ability to transfer a given number of information objects N_i in terms of associated concepts into a number of knowledge objects N_k in terms of relations between concepts, i.e.:*

$$C_c = \frac{N_k}{N_i} \tag{22}$$

Definition 22. *The instructive intelligent capability C_i is the ability to transfer a given number of information objects N_i in terms of associated concepts into a number of behavioral actions N_b in terms of number of processes at LRMB Layers 5 through 7, i.e.:*

$$C_i = \frac{N_b}{N_i} \tag{23}$$

Definition 23. *The reflective intelligent capability C_r is the ability to transfer a given number of data objects or events N_d into a number of behavioral*

actions N_b *in terms of number of processes at LRMB Layers 5 through 7, i.e.:*

$$C_r = \frac{N_b}{N_d} \tag{24}$$

On the basis of Definitions 19 through 23, a benchmark of average intelligent capabilities can be established with a large set of test samples. Then, a particular testee's relative intelligent capability or intelligent merit may be derived based on the benchmark.

Definition 24. *The relative intelligent capability ΔX_I is the difference between a testee's absolute intelligent capability X_I and a given intelligent capability benchmark, $\overline{\mathfrak{C}}_I$ i.e.:*

$$\Delta \mathfrak{C}_I = \mathfrak{C}_I - \overline{\mathfrak{C}}_I$$
$$= \frac{1}{4}(\frac{N_i}{N_d} + \frac{N_k}{N_i} + \frac{N_b}{N_i} + \frac{N_b}{N_d}) - \overline{\mathfrak{C}}_I \tag{25}$$

The intelligent metrics provide a new approach to formally model and test abstract intelligence and their paradigms on the basis of GAIM. Adopting the intelligent metrics theory, natural and artificial intelligence may be quantitatively evaluated on the same foundation.

A UNIFIED FRAMEWORK OF ABSTRACT INTELLIGENCE AND ITS PARADIGMS

The preceding sections reveal the equivalence and compatibility between natural and artificial intelligence on the basis of abstract intelligence. Therefore, it is logical to state that natural intelligence should be fully understood before artificial intelligence can be rigorously studied on a scientific basis. It is also indicates that any machine which may implement a part of human behaviors and actions in information processing may be treated as the possession of some extent of intelligence.

The Architectural Framework of Abstract Intelligence

The architectural framework of abstract intelligence encompasses a wide range of coherent fields, as shown in Figure 4, from the computational, machinable, and artificial intelligence to natural intelligence in the horizontal scopes, and from the logical, functional, cognitive models to neural (biological) models in the vertical reductive hierarchy. Therefore, abstract intelligence forms the foundation of a multidisciplinary and transdisciplinary enquiry of intelligence science.

Compatibility of the Intelligence Paradigms

According to the GAIM model, all paradigms of abstract intelligence share the same cognitive informatics foundation as described in the following theorems, because they are an artificial or machine implementation of the abstract intelligence.

Theorem 3. *The compatible intelligent capability state that natural intelligence (NI), artificial intelligence (AI), machinable intelligence (MI), and computational intelligence (CoI), are compatible by sharing the same mechanisms of αI, i.e.:*

$$CoI \cong MI \cong AI \cong NI \cong \alpha I \qquad (26)$$

On the basis of Theorem 3, the differences between NI, AI, MI, and CoI are only distinguishable by: (a) The means of their implementation; and (b) The extent of their intelligent capability.

Figure 4. The architectural framework of abstract intelligence and intelligence science

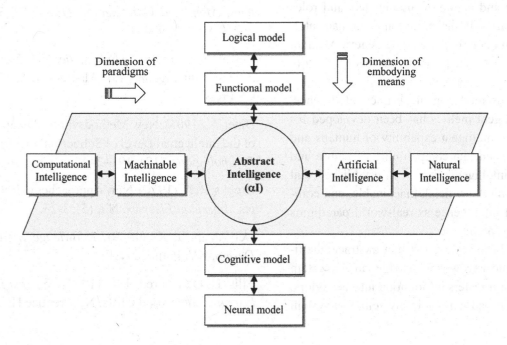

Corollary 3. *The inclusive intelligent capability states that all real-world paradigms of intelligence are a subset of αI, i.e.:*

$$CoI \subseteq MI \subseteq AI \subseteq NI \subseteq \alpha I \qquad (27)$$

Corollary 3 indicates that AI, CoI, and MI are dominated by NI and αI. Therefore, one should not expect a computer or a software system to solve a problem where human cannot. In other words, no AI or computer systems may be designed and/or implemented for a given problem where there is no solution being known collectively by human beings as a whole. Further, Theorem 3 and Corollary 3 explain that the development and implementation of AI rely on the understanding of the mechanisms and laws of NI.

CONCLUSION

This article has presented a coherent theory for explaining the mechanisms of abstract intelligence and its paradigms such as natural, artificial, machinable, and computational intelligence. The taxonomy and nature of intelligence, and roles of information in the evolution of human intelligence have been explored. The Generic Abstract Intelligence Mode (GAIM) has been formally developed that provides a foundation toward the rigorous modeling of abstract intelligence. The intelligent metrics has been developed for measuring intelligent capability of humans and systems. Then, the compatibility of nature and machine intelligence has been established that unifies natural, artificial, machinable, and computational intelligence as real-world paradigms of abstract intelligence.

It has been recognized that abstract intelligence, in the narrow sense, is a human or a system ability that transfers information into behaviors; and in the broad sense, it is any human or system ability that autonomously transfers the forms of abstract information between data, information, knowledge, and behaviors in the brain. The abstract intelligence has been classified into four forms known as the perceptive, cognitive, instructive, and reflective intelligence. The logical model of the brain has been developed as the highest level of abstraction for explaining its cognitive mechanisms. Based on it, a systematical reduction from the levels of logical, functional, physiological, and biological has been enabled in order to form a coherent theory for abstract intelligence, brain science, and intelligence science.

ACKNOWLEDGMENT

The author would like to acknowledge the Natural Science and Engineering Council of Canada (NSERC) for its partial support to this work.

REFERENCES

Albus, J. (1991). Outline for a Theory of Intelligence. *IEEE Transactions on Systems, Man, and Cybernetics*, *21*(3), 473–509. doi:10.1109/21.97471

Bender, E. A. (1996). *Mathematical Methods in Artificial Intelligence*. Los Alamitos, CA: IEEE CS Press.

Binet, A. (1905). New Methods for the Diagnosis of the Intellectual Level of Subnormals. *L'Année Psychologique*, (12): 191–244.

Brooks, R. A. (1970), New Approaches to Robotics, *American Elsevier*, NY, (5), 3-23.

Debenham, J. K. (1989). *Knowledge Systems Design*. NY: Prentice Hall.

Ellis, D. O., & Fred, J. L. (1962). *Systems Philosophy*. Englewood Cliffs, NJ: Prentice Hall.

Fried, G. H., & Hademenos, G. J. (1999). *Schaum's Outline of Theory and Problems of Biology* (2nd ed.). NY: McGraw-Hill.

Gardner, H. (1983). *Frames of Mind: The Theory of Multiple Intelligences*. New York, NY: Basic Books.

Giarrantans, J., & Riley, G. (1989). *Expert Systems: Principles and Programming*. Boston: PWS-KENT Pub. Co.

Haykin, S. (1998). *Neural Networks: A Comprehensive Foundation* (2nd ed.). Upper Saddle River, NJ: Prentice Hall.

Hewitt, C. (1977). Viewing Control Structures as Patterns of Passing Messages. *Artificial Intelligence*, *8*(3), 323–364. doi:10.1016/0004-3702(77)90033-9

Jeasen, A. R. (1969). How Much can We Boost IQ and Scholastic Achievement? *Harvard Educational Review*, (39): 1–123.

Jeasen, A. R. (1987). Psychometric g as a Focus on Concerted Research Effort. *Intelligence*, (11): 193–198. doi:10.1016/0160-2896(87)90005-5

Jennings, N. R. (2000). On Agent-Based Software Engineering. *Artificial Intelligence*, *17*(2), 277–296. doi:10.1016/S0004-3702(99)00107-1

Jordan, M. I. (1999), Computational Intelligence, in Wilson, R.A. and C.K. Frank eds., *The MIT Encyclopedia of the Cognitive Sciences*, MIT Press, pp. i73-i80.

Kandel, E. R., Schwartz, J. H., & Jessell, T. M. (Eds.). (2000). *Principles of Neural Science* (4th ed.). New York: McGraw-Hill.

Kleene, S. C. (1956), Representation of Events by Nerve Nets, in C.E. Shannon and J. McCarthy eds., *Automata Studies*, Princeton Univ. Press, 3-42.

Lefton, L. A., Brannon, L., Boyes, M. C., & Ogden, N. A. (2005). *Psychology* (2nd ed.). Toronto: Pearson Education Canada Inc.

Matlin, M. W. (1998). *Cognition* (4th ed.). Orlando, FL: Harcourt Brace College Publishers.

McCarthy, J., & Minsky, M. L. M. L., N. Rochester, and C.E. Shannon *(1955)*, Proposal for the 1956 Dartmouth Summer Research Project on Artificial Intelligence, *Dartmouth College, Hanover, NH, USA*, http://www.formal.stanford.edu/jmc/history/dartmouth/dartmouth.html.

McCulloch, W. S. (1965). *Embodiments of Mind*. Cambridge, MA: MIT Press.

Meystel, A. M., & Albus, J. S. (2002). *Intelligent Systems, Architecture, Design, and Control*. John Wiley & Sons, Inc.

Parker, S. T., & McKinney, M. L. (1999). *Origins of the Intelligence, The Evaluation of Cognitive Development in Monkeys, Apes and Humans*. The John Hopkins University Press.

Payne, D. G., & Wenger, M. J. (1998). *Cognitive Psychology*. Boston: Houghton Mifflin Co.

Sternberg, R. J. (1997). The Concept of Intelligence and the its Role in Lifelong Learning and Success. *The American Psychologist*, *52*(10), 1030–1037. doi:10.1037/0003-066X.52.10.1030

Sternberg, R.J. (2000), Implicit Theory of Intelligence as Exemplar Stories of Success: Why Intelligence Test Validity is in the Eye of the Beholder, *Journal of Psychology, Public Policy, and Law*, (6), 159-167.

Sternberg, R. J. (2003). *Cognitive Psychology* (3rd ed.). Thomson Wadsworth.

Terman, L. M., & Merrill, M. (1961). *Stanford-Binet Intelligence Scale, Manual for the Third Revision*. Houghton Mifflin.

Thomas, L. (1974). *The Lives of a Cell: Notes of a Biology Watcher*. NY: Viking Press.

Turing, A. M. (1950). Computing Machinery and Intelligence. *Mind*, (59): 433–460. doi:10.1093/mind/LIX.236.433

von Neumann, J., & Burks, A. W. (1966). *Theory of Self-Reproducing Automata*. Urbana, IL: Univ. of Illinois Press.

Wang, Y. (2002a), Keynote: On Cognitive Informatics, *Proc. 1st IEEE International Conference on Cognitive Informatics* (ICCI'02), Calgary, Canada, IEEE CS Press, August, 34-42.

Wang, Y. (2002b), The Real-Time Process Algebra (RTPA), *Annals of Software Engineering: A International Journal*, (14), USA, 235-274.

Wang, Y. (2003a), On Cognitive Informatics, *Brain and Mind: A Transdisciplinary Journal of Neuroscience and Neurophilosophy*, USA, August, 4(3), 151-167.

Wang, Y. (2003b). Using Process Algebra to Describe Human and Software System Behaviors. *Brain and Mind*, *4*(2), 199–213. doi:10.1023/A:1025457612549

Wang, Y. (2006a). On the Informatics Laws and Deductive Semantics of Software. *IEEE Transactions on Systems, Man and Cybernetics. Part C, Applications and Reviews*, *36*(2), 161–171. doi:10.1109/TSMCC.2006.871138

Wang, Y. (2006b), Cognitive Informatics and Contemporary Mathematics for Knowledge Representation and Manipulation, *Proc. 1st International Conference on Rough Set and Knowledge Technology* (RSKT'06), LNCS, Vol. 4062, Springer, Chongqing, China, July, 69-78.

Wang, Y. (2006c), Keynote: Cognitive Informatics - Towards the Future Generation Computers that Think and Feel, *Proc. 5th IEEE International Conference on Cognitive Informatics* (ICCI'06), Beijing, China, IEEE CS Press, July, 3-7.

Wang, Y. (2007a), *Software Engineering Foundations: A Software Science Perspective*, CRC Series in Software Engineering, Vol. II, Auerbach Publications, NY, USA, July.

Wang, Y. (2007b). The Theoretical Framework of Cognitive Informatics, *International Journal of Cognitive Informatics and Natural Intelligence*, *1*(1), 1–27.

Wang, Y. (2007c). The OAR Model of Neural Informatics for Internal Knowledge Representation in the Brain, *International Journal of Cognitive Informatics and Natural Intelligence*, *1*(3), 64–75.

Wang, Y. (2007d), Keynote: On Theoretical Foundations of Software Engineering and Denotational Mathematics, *Proc. 5th Asian Workshop on Foundations of Software*, Xiamen, China, 99-102.

Wang, Y. (2008a). On Contemporary Denotational Mathematics for Computational Intelligence, Transactions of Computational Science, 2. *Springer, LNCS, 5150*(June), 6–29.

Wang, Y. (2008b). On Concept Algebra: A Denotational Mathematical Structure for Knowledge and Software Modeling, *International Journal of Cognitive Informatics and Natural Intelligence*, *2*(2), 1–19.

Wang, Y. (2008c), Keynote: Abstract Intelligence and Its Denotational Mathematics Foundations, *Proc. 7th IEEE International Conference on Cognitive Informatics* (ICCI'08), Stanford University, CA, USA, IEEE CS Press, August.

Wang, Y. (2008d). RTPA: A Denotational Mathematics for Manipulating Intelligent and Computational Behaviors, *International Journal of Cognitive Informatics and Natural Intelligence*, *2*(2), 44–62.

Wang, Y. (2008e). Deductive Semantics of RTPA, *International Journal of Cognitive Informatics and Natural Intelligence*, *2*(2), 95–121.

Wang, Y. (2008f). On the Big-R Notation for Describing Iterative and Recursive Behaviors, *International Journal of Cognitive Informatics and Natural Intelligence*, *2*(1), 17–28.

Wang, Y. (2008g). On Cognitive Properties of Human Factors and Error Models in Engineering and Socialization. *International Journal of Cognitive Informatics and Natural Intelligence, 2*(4), 70–84. doi:10.4018/jcini.2008100106

Wang, Y. (2008h), Formal Description of the Cognitive Process of Memorization, *Transactions of Computational Science*, Springer, 2(4), Nov.

Wang, Y., & Wang, Y. (2006). Cognitive Informatics Models of the Brain. *IEEE Transactions on Systems, Man and Cybernetics. Part C, Applications and Reviews, 36*(2), 203–207. doi:10.1109/TSMCC.2006.871151

Wang, Y., Wang, Y., Patel, S., & Patel, D. (2006). A Layered Reference Model of the Brain (LRMB). *IEEE Transactions on Systems, Man, and Cybernetics, 36*(2), 124–133. doi:10.1109/TSMCC.2006.871126

Wilson, R. A., & Keil, F. C. (2001). *The MIT Encyclopedia of the Cognitive Sciences*. MIT Press.

This work was previously published in International Journal of Software Science and Computational Intelligence, Volume 1, Issue 1, edited by Yingxu Wang, pp. 1-17, copyright 2009 by IGI Publishing (an imprint of IGI Global).

Chapter 3
Hierarchies of Architectures of Collaborative Computational Intelligence

Witold Pedrycz
University of Alberta, Canada & Polish Academy of Sciences, Poland

ABSTRACT

Computational Intelligence (CI) supports a wealth of methodologies and a plethora of algorithmic developments essential to the construction of intelligent systems. Being faced with inherently distributed data which become evident, the paradigm of CI calls for further enhancements along the line of designing systems that are hierarchical and collaborative in nature. This emerging direction could be referred to as collaborative Computational Intelligence (or C^2I for brief). The pervasive phenomenon encountered in architectures of C^2I is that collaboration is synonym of knowledge sharing, knowledge reuse and knowledge reconciliation. Knowledge itself comes in different ways: as some structural findings in data and usually formalized in the framework of information granules, locally available models, some action plans, classification schemes, and alike. In such distributed systems sharing data is not feasible given existing technical constraints which are quite often exacerbated by non-technical requirements of privacy or security. In this study, we elaborate on the design of information granules which comes hand in hand with various clustering techniques and fuzzy clustering, in particular.

DOI: 10.4018/978-1-4666-0261-8.ch003

INTRODUCTION AND MOTIVATING INSIGHTS

Computational Intelligence (Zurada, Yen, and Wang, 2008) dwells on the synergy between its three pillars of Granular Computing (including fuzzy sets, interval calculations, and rough sets), biologically inspired optimization (exemplified through evolutionary algorithms, genetic algorithms, ant colonies, particle swarm optimization) and neurocomputing. Cognitive Informatics (Wang, 2003, 2006) stresses the cognitive facets of intelligent pursuits. The commonly encountered constructs of Granular Computing are concerned with processing individual data sets conveying experimental evidence. Numeric data are available locally by being collected at some single data site, as portrayed in Figure 1. The resulting information granules come as a result of processing of the data. The research agenda of Granular Computing has been predominantly focused on this general framework of data exploitation. For instance, in fuzzy modeling we can commonly witness design scenarios of using a single data set to construct fuzzy sets and afterwards treating them as building blocks (modules) in the realization of the fuzzy model. In particular, fuzzy rule-based models are representative examples of these modeling developments; we construct information granules which afterwards constitute a backbone of any fuzzy model.

There is, however, a growing interest in the design and analysis of distributed systems, multi-agent systems, and distributed modeling, cf. (Acampora and Loia, 2008; Bouchon-Meunier, 1998; Ferrero and Salicone; 2007; Genesereth and Ketchpel, 1994; Pedrycz and Vukovich, 2002). This interest is supported by a wealth of pertinent methodologies and algorithmic developments, cf. (Ayad and Kamel, 2003; Bickel and Scheffer, 2004; Campobello et al., 2006; Silva and Klusch, 2006; Gersho and Gray, 1992; Merugu and Ghosh, 2005; Pedrycz and Vukovich, 2002; Pedrycz, 2002; Pedrycz and Rai, 2008; Skillicorn and Mc-

Figure 1. From data to structure: a case of a single data

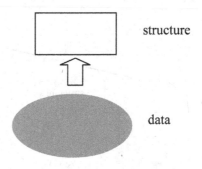

Connell, 2007; Stubberud and Kramer, 2006; Tsoumakas, Angelis, and Vlahavas, 2004; Wang, 2003).

Referring to Figure 2, let us now envision a number of individual data sets, denoted here by $D_1, D_2, ..., D_p$. There are situations in which we encounter a collection of data for which granulation is realized individually and therefore leads to the resulting structures as illustrated in this figure.

We would like to determine a global structure-*metastructure* which is regarded as the most representative topology of the individual structures and reconciles the locally formed information granules to the highest possible extent. Note the use of different graphic symbols in Figure 2 which emphasize the existence of different levels of the hierarchy emerging in this fashion. A task of forming metastructures could be of interest from several points of view. First, one could be interested in the determination of the most profound commonalities one could come across when dealing with the individual structures of some specific characteristics. The discovered commonalities are critical to the better understanding of the phenomenon at the global level. Second, we may identify differences across various perspectives (data sets) which in this way become properly exposed and could be further investigated. Interestingly enough, we are faced with a diversity of topologies with a few further examples included in Figure 3. Instead of the commonly distinguished

Figure 2. A conceptual hierarchy: from data to structures and metastructures

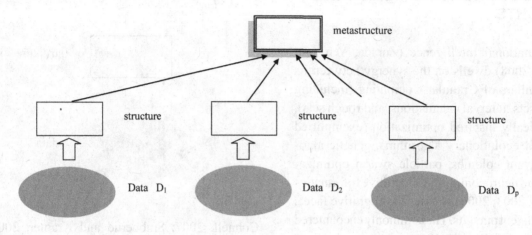

Figure 3. Example of development of metastructures in a diversified setup of data and information granules: (a) dedicated, high-level data site contributing directly to the realization of the metastructure, and (b) metastructure realization on a basis of several structures formed at the lower level.

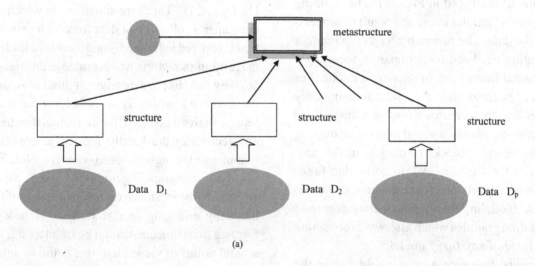

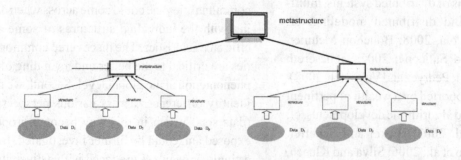

layers of data, the metastructure is built on a basis of structures as well as data themselves, Figure 3(a). They illustrate the effect of dealing with information granules of higher diversity (embracing both data and information granules).

The architecture shown in Figure 3(b) comes with several layers and metastructures are built in a consecutive manner, viz. starting with the collections of data which give rise to metastructures and those in turn are aggregated even further.

The main objective of this study is to extend a concept of structures (information granules) realized through information granulation by moving to the reconciliation of structures built for individual data sites and in this way supporting an idea of handling multiset data architectures being commonly encountered in multiagent architectures, distributed data processing, distributed data mining and alike. We demonstrate how granular constructs are formed. Two main types of constructs are investigated; in the first one we encounter metastructures while the second one is concerned with metamodels. While initially the underlying concept is presented for a regular topology of data sites in which we encounter a well delineated layer of hierarchy, we also elaborate on higher diversity by demonstrating how the same concept becomes refined and augmented. In the detailed investigations carried out in the consecutive sections, we consider that the structures formed at the level of individual data are represented in the form of a finite family of prototypes (centroids) constructed e.g., by running a certain clustering algorithm (producing Boolean or fuzzy set-based results). To invoke the formation of metastructures, we assume that the individual data are defined in the same feature space $\mathbf{F}$. If this assumption does not hold (which might be the case in practice), the ensuing analysis can be completed by considering an intersection of the features present at the level of the individual data sets. In other words, the common feature space for which metastructures are formed is taken in the form $\mathbf{F} = \mathbf{F}_1 \mathbf{I} \mathbf{F}_2 \mathbf{I} \mathbf{I} \mathbf{F}_p$. Throughout the study, we adhere to the standard

notation. Vectors are indicated in boldface. The underlying granulation process giving rise to some information granules is exemplified here within the setting of fuzzy sets. In particular, Fuzzy C-Means (FCM) (Bezdek, 1981; Pedrycz, 2005; Pedrycz and Gomide, 2007) can be sought as a certain vehicle to form information granules represented as fuzzy sets whose sound descriptors come in the form of prototypes (centroids). Those will be denoted by $\mathbf{v}_1$, $\mathbf{v}_2$, .. etc. Note that we are not confined ourselves to this particular scheme of fuzzy clustering and any other grouping technique giving rise to a family of prototypes could be anticipated here.

Before proceeding with the development of metastructures, it is instructive to elaborate on the concept of granulation –degranulation (or encoding-decoding) as it is realized in the setting of fuzzy clustering. Along the same line we discuss a principle of legitimate granularity which brings to existence some ideas of capturing a collection of entities through some granular constructs. These results will be of direct use in the assessment of the quality of the resulting metastructures.

GRANULATION AND DEGRANULATION: A CONCEPT AND A QUANTIFICATION OF THE PROCESS

The general scheme portrayed in Figure 4 is now made more detailed as we elaborate on the specific realization of the tasks of granulation and degranulation. These processes are closely related to encoding and decoding schemes which are their particular instances given the set-theoretic mechanism or fuzzy set-based scheme of information granulation. We show that the tandem granulation-degranulation is inherently associated with the functional components generated by the FCM. One can also refer here to some discussion on vector quantization and pertinent analysis of its quality (Gersho and Gray, 1992; Krogh and Vedelsby, 1995).

Let us assume that we are provided with a collection of prototypes $\mathbf{v}_1$, $\mathbf{v}_2$, ..., $\mathbf{v}_c$ that are generated by running the FCM clustering on some numeric data. Consider that we are provided with a certain input datum $\mathbf{x}$.

Encoding

The encoding is concerned with a representation of $\mathbf{x}$ in terms of the information granules associated with the given prototypes $\mathbf{v}_1, \mathbf{v}_2, ..., \mathbf{v}_c$. Denote the results of this representation by u_1, u_2, ..., $u_c \in [0,1]$. More formally, u_is are a direct outcome of following minimization task

$$\sum_{i=1}^{c} u_i^f \|\mathbf{v}_i - \mathbf{x}\|^2 \rightarrow \text{Min } u_1, u_2, ..., u_c$$

subject to the following constraint

$$\sum_{i=1}^{c} u_i = 1 \qquad (1)$$

Where $\|.\|$ is a certain distance function. Interestingly, we can recognize that this minimization is similar to the one we have encountered when dealing with the original FCM problem when optimizing its underlying objective function. The fuzzification coefficient "f" (f>1) offers an extra level of parametric flexibility. By solving (1), making use of the standard use of Lagrange multipliers, we arrive at the expression of the granular representation of the numeric datum to be in the form

$$u_i = \frac{1}{\sum_{j=1}^{c} \left(\frac{\|\mathbf{x} - \mathbf{v}_i\|}{\|\mathbf{x} - \mathbf{v}_j\|} \right)^{\frac{2}{f-1}}} \qquad (2)$$

The vector of the membership grades $\mathbf{u}(\mathbf{x}) = (u_1 \ u_2 \ ... \ u_c]$ is thus a result of encoding – hence a numeric datum becomes represented in the language of the information granules. We have used the notation $\mathbf{u}(\mathbf{x})$ to underline that $\mathbf{u}$ depends directly upon the numeric input $\mathbf{x}$ it encodes. As a side effect, note that this representation usually

Figure 4. A detailed insight into the encoding and decoding involving the resulting constructs of the FCM (prototypes)

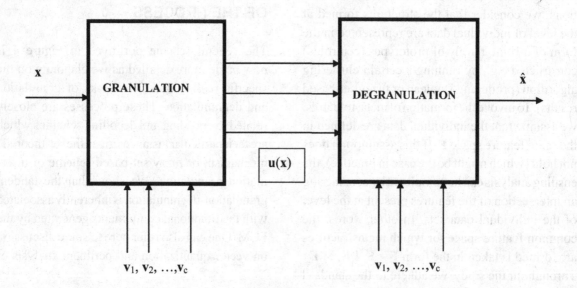

leads to a useful compression effect: instead of transmitting (storing) the original pattern **x**, we need to store and transmit "c-1" numeric values taking the values in the (0,1] interval (the last coordinate of **u** could be easily computed given the normalization condition).

Decoding

The decoding process relies on the two components. As before, we use the prototypes and involve the vector of membership grades, **u(x)**. The form of the decoding formula results from the minimization of the following expression (which quantifies the resulting decoding error)

$$F(x) = \sum_{i=1}^{c} u_i^f(\mathbf{x}) \| \mathbf{v}_i - \hat{\mathbf{x}} \|^2 \qquad (3)$$

The minimization of (3) is completed with respect to the result of decoding, that is $\hat{\mathbf{x}}$. In essence, we require that $\hat{\mathbf{x}}$ is positioned in such a way so that minimizes the distances from the prototypes; noticeable is an impact of the membership grades in the overall computing of F. Assuming the use of the Euclidean distance in (3) and zeroing the gradient of F(**x**) that has been computed with respect to the encoded vector, we obtain the following expression for the encoded numeric result of **u(x)**

$$\hat{\mathbf{x}} = \frac{\sum_{i=1}^{c} u_i^f \mathbf{v}_i}{\sum_{i=1}^{c} u_i^f} \qquad (4)$$

In this expression we note that each prototype is weighted by the corresponding coordinates of **u**. The fuzzification coefficient becomes also an integral part of this aggregation of the prototypes. A certain simplified variation of (4) comes as the expression of the form

$$\hat{\mathbf{x}} = \sum_{i=1}^{c} u_i^f \mathbf{v}_i \qquad (5)$$

The decoding error usually assumes nonzero values which are quite intuitive since we must have introduced some error by using the granular representation of the numeric data. The non ideal decoding and nonzero decoding error are typical for multivariable cases. While this error could be minimized, it cannot be completely eliminated. Note however that this is not the case in a one-dimensional case where $x \in \mathbf{R}$. It could be easily demonstrated, cf. (Pedrycz and Gomide, 2007] that fuzzy sets with triangular membership functions where each two successive fuzzy sets overlap at the level of 0.5 lead to the zero values of the decoding error. This somewhat explains the popularity of the use of triangular fuzzy sets (even though the concept of the encoding-decoding mechanisms is not widely known and embraced in the fuzzy set community).

Performance Evaluation of the Encoding-Decoding Scheme

So far we have demonstrated how for some input **x** the reconstruction error can be computed. In general, an overall performance of the reconstruction is more representative for the design of the encoding and decoding schemes. To assess this performance, we consider the dataset for which the clustering has been completed. This gives rise to the following index

$$V = \sum_{k=1}^{N} \| \mathbf{x}_k - \hat{\mathbf{x}}_k \|^2 \qquad (6)$$

(obviously, one could have consider some other sets of data for which the testing of the scheme could be realized). The optimization of V with respect to the number of clusters and the values of the fuzzification coefficient forms the essence of the design activities of the encoding-decoding tandem, $V = V(c, m)$.

There is an interesting alternative to the fuzzy decoding that is a Boolean (two-valued) option. Here instead of considering all the prototypes, we choose the one for which $\mathbf{x}$ is the closest and use this prototype in the decoding process. In other words, we choose the index of the prototype i_0 where the following relationship holds

$$i_0 = \arg\min_i \|\mathbf{x} - \mathbf{v}_i\| \tag{7}$$

Then the decoded result becomes the i_0-th prototype, $\hat{\mathbf{x}} = \mathbf{v}_{i0}$ for all x for which (7) holds. The evaluation of the Boolean decoding is quantified by the same performance index as given by (6).

THE PRINCIPLE OF JUSTIFIABLE GRANULARITY

The principle of justifiable granularity is in the center of aggregation of some experimental entities and capturing them in the form of some information granule. Let us consider a finite number of those denoted here by $z_1, z_2, .., z_n (=\mathbf{Z})$. A numeric representative of $\mathbf{Z}$ can be some statistical descriptor, say mean or median. Denote this representative by u. Consider now the values of z_i that are lower than u, $z_i < u$ We use them in the formation of the left-hand side of the linear portion of the membership function, refer to Figure 5.

There are two requirements guiding the design of the fuzzy set, namely

(a) maximize the experimental evidence of the fuzzy set; this implies that we tend to "cover" as many numeric data as possible, viz. the coverage has to be made as high as possible. Graphically, in the optimization of this requirement, we rotate the linear segment up (clockwise) as illustrated in Figure 5. Normally, the sum of the membership grades

$A(z_i), \sum_i A(z_i)$ where A is the linear membership function to be optimized with respect to its slope and z_i is located to the left to the modal value (u) has to be maximized

(b) Simultaneously, we would like to make the fuzzy set as specific as possible so that is comes with some well defined semantics.

Figure 5. Computation of a membership function of fuzzy set for some numeric data z_i

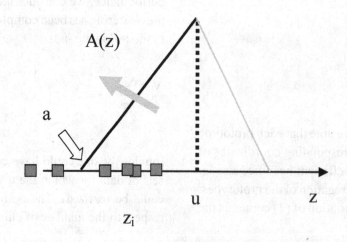

This requirement is met by making the support of A as small as possible, that is $\min_a |u - a|$

To accommodate the two conflicting requirements, we have to combine (a) and (b) into a form of a single scalar index which in turn becomes maximized. Two alternatives could be sought, say

$$\max_{a \neq u} \frac{\sum_i A(z_i)}{|u - a|} \tag{8}$$

or

$$\sum_i (1 - A(z_i))(u - a) \tag{9}$$

The linearly decreasing portion of the membership function positioned at the right-hand side of the modal value (u) is optimized in the same manner. The investigations presented here were carried out in a general setting not being confined to any particular nature of the objects to be aggregated. Two scenarios are worth presenting here:

- **Z** is a collection of numeric readings (provided by sensors) then the aggregate is a fuzzy set
- **Z** is a collection of membership grades of some object as being perceived by different observers then the result is a fuzzy set defined over a collection of numeric membership grades. So in fact we arrive at type-2 fuzzy sets. The principle of justifiable granularity is of particular interest in this setting given that there has been a long debate on the estimation of type-2 fuzzy sets.

Likewise we can consider here higher type fuzzy sets which emerge through the aggregation of lower type fuzzy sets. Say, a collection of type *n-1* fuzzy sets gives rise to a single type *n* fuzzy set

In this way there are emerging interesting and intuitively appealing hierarchies of granular concepts: The two examples discussed above underline this effect.

THE DESIGN OF METASTRUCTURE AND ITS COMBINATORIAL OPTIMIZATION

To elaborate on the essence of the formation of the metastructures, let us consider a generic scenario shown in Figure 6.

A number of data sets have been analyzed in the sequel resulting in some structures represented by a collection of the prototypes (those are shown as open circles in Figure 6). The number of prototypes at each data site could vary as we might envision several views (perspectives) realized at different levels of granularity. Considering all prototypes together we end up with their set of dimensionality n, that is $v_1, v_2, \ldots, v_n$. Denote by I the set of indexes of these prototypes, $I = \{1, 2, \ldots, n\}$. While several alternatives could be sought with a diversified category of averaging (aggregation) existing prototypes, all of these come with a quite visible drawback such that the results of aggregation are different than the originally available prototypes meaning that an interpretation of such constructs could be quite limited. Having this possible limitation in mind we consider a different development path where the metastructure is sought as a subset of the prototypes. Denote by J the set of "p" indexes from I where p is the number of prototypes selected from I. These prototypes v_j, $j \in J$ will be regarded as the resulting metastructure (again illustrated as black dots in Figure 6). While the formulation of the problem is straightforward, there is the underlying design procedure to be established which comes hand in hand with a way of assessing the quality of the metastructure.

Figure 6. Realization of the metastructure regarded as a certain selection process applied to the prototypes

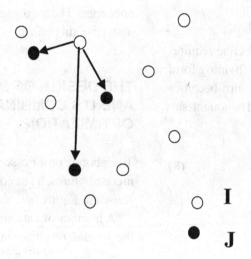

PERFORMANCE EVALUATION OF THE METASTRUCTURE

Let us assume that the prototypes of the metastructure v_j, $j \in J$ have been selected. Given this, we express each prototype v_i $i \in \mathbf{I}\text{-}\mathbf{J}$ in terms of the metastructure. The degranulation scheme presented in Section 2 offers a way of computing the values of u_{ij} as follows

$$u_{ij} = \frac{1}{\sum_{j \in J} \left(\frac{\|\mathbf{v}_i - \mathbf{v}_k\|}{|\mathbf{v}_i - \mathbf{v}_j|} \right)^{2/(f-1)}} \qquad (10)$$

In other words u_{ij} is a degree of matching achieved between the i-th prototype and the j-th element of the metastructure. The higher the value of the u_{ij}, the better match is reported between the two elements under discussion. The values of u_{ij} close to 1 are reflective of the close match between $\mathbf{v}_i$ and $\mathbf{v}_j$. The degranulation scheme allows us to represent each $\mathbf{v}_i$ in terms of the metastructure and u_{ij} by computing the following convex combination of the form

$$\hat{\mathbf{v}}_i = \sum_{j \in J} u_{ij}^f \mathbf{v}_j \qquad (11)$$

which could be treated as an expansion formula using which we describe all prototypes in **I-J** in terms of the elements of the metastructure. The quality of the metastructure could be expressed in a straightforward manner by calculating the distance $\| . \|$ between $\mathbf{v}_i$ $i \in \mathbf{I}\text{-}\mathbf{J}$ and the representation provided by (11), that is

$$Q = \sum_{i \in I-J} \|\hat{\mathbf{v}}_i - \mathbf{v}_i\|^2 \qquad (12)$$

The optimal metastructure **J** arises as a result of the minimization of the above performance index, $\min_J Q$.

One can also take another look at the expansion (11) by concentrating on the distribution of the values of u_{ij} which tell about the use of the components of the metastructure. If we consider a collection of values u_{ij} for some fixed index "j", this characterizes how different prototypes in **I-J** are expressed by the j-th component of the expansion. In this case the entropy function

$$H = \sum_{i \in I-J} u_{ij} \log_2 u_{ij} \qquad (13)$$

can serve as a suitable measure of uncertainty associated with the utilization of this component in the description of the structure.

An alternative approach used to the assessment of the nature of the activation levels of the elements of the metastructure can be envisioned as follows. Note that the values u_{ij} that are either close to 0.0 or close to 1.0, become indicative of a sound representation of the prototypes in terms of the metastructure. On the other hand, if the values of u_{ij} tend to be close to 1/c, we may talk about a high level of uncertainty when expressing the prototypes in the language of the available structure. More formally, we may quantify the structural diversity by introducing some functional φ defined on the set of membership degrees such that $\varphi(0) = \varphi(1) = 0$ which is increasing over [0, 1/c) attains the maximal value at 1/c and then monotonically decreases to zero. Here the sum of the following form

$$T_j = \sum_{i \in I-J} \varphi(u_{ij}) \qquad (14)$$

serves as a concise descriptor of the uncertainty of structural differences associated with the metastructure.

The minimization of Q is of combinatorial nature viz. we are concerned with the formation of the subset of the prototypes which realize the metastructure. The mechanisms of evolutionary optimization come here as an effective design alternative. Genetic algorithms (GAs), particle swarm optimization (PSO), evolutionary strategies (ES) and alike are sound algorithmic tools worth exploiting here. The representation of the combinatorial problem in the form suitable for further evolutionary optimization is central to this problem solving strategy. One of the approaches to

the representation is realized through the ranking mechanism. Its underlying essence is illustrated in Figure 7.

The original n-element set of the prototypes is processed through genetic optimization (say genetic algorithm or particle swarm optimization). Assuming that "p" components are sought as the contributor to the metastructure, the entries of the n-dimensional vector are ranked and the first "p" entries (here p=3) are selected.

There are two design parameters used in the development of the metastructure, that is (a) the number of its elements (p) and the fuzzification coefficient (f) used in the determination of the membership grades. The role of the first parameter is self-evident: it implies the level of generalization offered by the metastructure. A few prototypes induce the metastructure of high generality. More details are captured with the increasing values of "p" The general tendency of Q is that its values decrease when the values of "p" go up. Hence for the formation of the metastructure in terms of its abilities to capture details could be controlled. The choice of the fuzzification coefficient is not so obvious. While an impact of the fuzzification coefficient on the form of the membership function is known (low values of "f" give rise to Boolean-like relationships), it is not clear how the values of "f" affect the values of the performance index. Given this, the design strategy involves two phases. For fixed value of "f" the genetic optimization is carried out so that Q attains minimum (inner optimization loop) while the outer optimization loop is completed by adjusting the values of "f".

The strategy presented here is quite passive as we built upon the existing structures which are kept fixed while the metastructure is actively formed by being guided by the performance index. In what follows, we anticipate a different strategy where the buildup of the metastructure engages the existing structures and affects them so that the metastructure could achieve a higher level of consistency.

Figure 7. Representation of the set of prototypes and their ranking leading to the formation of the meta-structure (here n=5 and p=3). The coding scheme could be suitable for various vehicles of evolutionary optimization (GA, PSO, etc.)

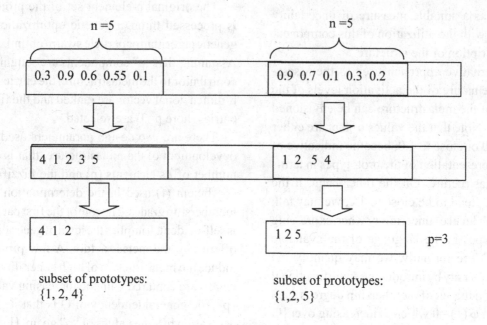

METASTRUCTURE CONSTRUCTION THROUGH A HIERARCHY OF CLUSTERS OF CLUSTERS

One can envision a different architecture and the underlying strategy of reconciling findings at the local level. This brings the concept of *clusters of clusters*. The essence of the method is that the structural findings formed at the lowest level are reconciled in the form of structure that is common to all local data sites. The prototypes at each lower level of data scheme are considered together and clustered into "cc" clusters formed at the higher level. In the sequel, the resulting partition matrix is used to convey information about the behavior of the original prototypes when being confronted with structural findings (prototypes) at other data sites. The essence of the scheme is visualized in Figure 8.

More specifically, using the partition matrix U formed at the higher level of this hierarchy, we form some relevancy index $\gamma(U)$ to quantify the impact on any of the prototypes coming from the data site. The index which applies to each column of U associates the ith prototype at data site D_{ii} with $\gamma_i(U)_{ii}$ which articulates how much identity this prototypes retains when confronted with the data structure obtained at other data sites. The index is included in the modified objective function used to cluster data at the ii-th data site

$$Q = \sum_{i=1}^{c_{ii}} \sum_{\mathbf{x}_k \in \mathbf{X}_{ii}} {}^3_i(U)_{ii} \| \mathbf{x}_k - \mathbf{v}_{i,ii} \|^2 \qquad (15)$$

The formation of the clusters of clusters is an interactive process: we start with the development of structure individually at D[ii], cluster the obtained prototypes and use the relevancy index to

Figure 8. The design of clusters of clusters – conceptual developments

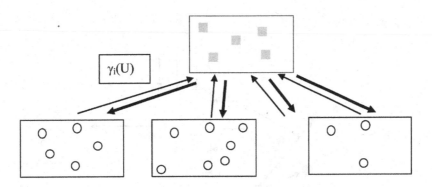

minimize the modified objective function as shown above. The clusters formed in this way are again clustered at the higher level of the hierarchy. This leads to the new values of the relevance index and the process iterates until it stabilizes. The number of clusters "cc" assumed at the higher level plays an important role as a measure to express the intensity of reconciliation of the individual findings. Strong interaction becomes realized when we consider only a few clusters. In case when cc = c[1] + c[2]+… + c[P] there is no interaction at all (each prototypes retains its identity) and the values of $\gamma_i(U)_{ii}$ are all equal to 1 not affecting the form of the objective function and thus not changing the prototypes. The strength of the structural interaction controlled by the values of the number of clusters "cc" may affect the dynamics of collaboration with the likelihood that its lower values associated with stronger collaboration may imply eventual instability.

THE DESIGN OF METASTRUCTURES FOR RULE-BASED GRANULAR MODELS

So far the metastructure design has been presented for information granules. The underlying concept can be directly applied to problems of forming metamodels (see Figure 9). To concentrate our discussion, we consider granular rule-based mod-

els where at each data site there are a collection of rules where the i-th rule reads as

- if A_i then y is $g_i(\mathbf{x}, a_i)$ (16)

The conclusion part $g_i(\mathbf{x}, a_i)$ is a local model whose region of "activity" is determined by the information granule Ai occurring in the condition part of this rule. The metastructure in this case could be referred to as a *metamodel*. Its realization follows the general scheme we discussed before however there are some refinement of the performance index using which we can assess the performance of the resulting construct.

Considering that a collection of rules – the metamodel has been selected from all rules, we express a condition of any rule in **I-J** by means of A_j's which are located in **J**. More specifically, a degree of matching A_i expressed in terms of A_j is denoted by $u_{ij}(\mathbf{x})$ The calculations of u_{ij} are realized with the use of (10). The i-th rule then arises as a combination of the rules which form the metamodel, namely

$$\hat{y}_i(\mathbf{x}) = \sum_{j \in \mathbf{J}} u_{ij}(\mathbf{x}) g_j(\mathbf{x})$$ (17)

where g_j is the conclusion of the j-th rule in **J**. The performance of the metamodel requires some attention as $u_{ij}(\mathbf{x})$ is a function of **x** and one has to exercise caution when considering the quality

Figure 9. The development of the metamodel (metastructure). Shown are main processing phases

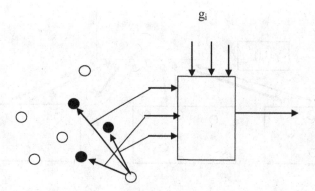

of the i-th rule. In general we could have written down the following performance index

$$Q = \sum_{i \in I-J} ||y_i(\mathbf{x}) - \hat{y}_i(\mathbf{x})||^2 \qquad (18)$$

However its practical feasibility is still limited as Q becomes an explicit function of **x** and hence it requires further interpretation and refinement. Intuitively, one could integrate (18) over the entire input space, that is

$$Q' = \int_{\mathbf{X}} \sum_{i \in I-J} ||y_i(\mathbf{x}) - \hat{y}_i(\mathbf{x})||^2 \, d\mathbf{x} \qquad (19)$$

However which this sounds like a viable solution, its practicality could be questionable particularly in case of highly dimensional input space. To come up with a practical version of (19) we confine ourselves to some selected values of **x** that is $\mathbf{v}_i$ $i \in \mathbf{I\text{-}J}$ so in essence the following criterion

$$Q = \sum_{i \in I-J} ||y_i(\mathbf{v}_i) - \hat{y}_i(\mathbf{v}_i)||^2 \qquad (20)$$

which concentrates on assuring that the i-th rule and its representation by expansion via the elements of the metamodel at some points (as shown above) are getting close as possible to each other. In this sense, the criterion considered here is a special case of the far more general (yet practically not viable) performance index (20).

CONCLUDING COMMENTS

C^2I opens a new avenue in the pursuits of intelligent systems by emphasizing the effect of collaborative activities involving a number of systems dealing with their local data and effectively exchanging available knowledge acquired at the local level. We stressed the role of information granules and information granulation, in general, as a sound vehicle to convey accumulated knowledge and complete its reconciliation and calibration.

In the study, we have introduced a concept of metastructures which arise through distributed processing carried out for a variety of local data where such metastructures can be regarded as a direct outcome of reconciliation of locally established information granules. We have presented two main categories of scenarios of practical relevance embracing situations of (i) establishing information granules at the global level, and (ii) forming rule-based metamodels. In this case, both a passive and active schemes of metamodeling have been introduced. The design of metastructures is guided by a well-articulated performance index whose minimization becomes feasible via combinatorial optimization (in which we stressed a role of biologically-inspired optimization).

This study has focused on the underlying concepts and while we elaborated on some development aspects and optimization tools, it should be stressed that further refinement and a thorough exploitation of optimization techniques in application to the inherently combinatorial facet of the problem are to be pursued in detail.

ACKNOWLEDGMENT

Support from the Natural Sciences and Engineering Research Council (NSERC) and the Canada Research Chair (CRC) is gratefully acknowledged.

REFERENCES

G. Acampora, V. Loia, A proposal of ubiquitous fuzzy computing for Ambient Intelligence, *Information Sciences*, 178, 3, 2008, 631-646.

Ayad, H., & Kamel, M. Finding natural clusters using multi-cluster combiner based on shared nearest neighbors, *Proc. 4th Int. Workshop on Multiple Classifier Systems*, 2003, 166-175.

Bezdek, J. C. *Pattern Recognition with Fuzzy Objective Function Algorithms*, Plenum Press, N. York, 1981.

Bickel, S., & Scheffer, T. Multi-view clustering, Proc. of the 4th IEEE Int. Conf. on Data Mining, ICDM'04, 2004, 19-26.

Bouchon-Meunier, B. (1998). *Aggregation and Fusion of Imperfect Information*. Heidelberg: Physica-Verlag.

G. Campobello, M. Mantineo, G. Patanè, M. Russo, LBGS: a smart approach for very large data sets vector quantization, *Signal Processing: Image Communication*, 20, 1, 2005, 91-114.

Costa da Silva, J., & Klusch, M. (2006). Inference in distributed data clustering. *Engineering Applications of Artificial Intelligence*, 19, 363–369. doi:10.1016/j.engappai.2006.01.013

A. Ferrero, S. Salicone, Fully comprehensive mathematical approach to the expression of uncertainty in measurement, *IEEE Transactions on Instrumentation and Measurement*, 56, 3, 2007, 706-712.

M. R. Genesereth, S. P. Ketchpel, Software agents, *Communications of the ACM*, 37, 7, 1994, 48-53.

A. Gersho, R.M. Gray, *Vector Quantization and Signal Compression*, Kluwer Academic Publishers, Norwell, 1992.

Krogh, A., & Vedelsby, J. (1995). Neural Networks Ensembles, Cross validation, and Active Learning. In *Advances in Neural Information Processing Systems* (pp. 231–238). MIT Press Cambridge.

Merugu, S., & Ghosh, J. (2005). A privacy-sensitive approach to distributed clustering. *Pattern Recognition Letters*, 26, 399–410. doi:10.1016/j.patrec.2004.08.003

Pedrycz, W. (2002). Collaborative fuzzy clustering. *Pattern Recognition Letters*, 23, 675–686. doi:10.1016/S0167-8655(02)00130-7

Pedrycz, W. *Knowledge-Based Fuzzy Clustering*, J. Wiley, N. York, 2005.

Pedrycz, W., & Gomide, F. (2007). *Fuzzy Systems Engineering*, J. Hoboken, NJ: Wiley. doi:10.1002/9780470168967

Pedrycz, W., & Rai, P. (to appear). Collaborative clustering with the use of Fuzzy C-Means and Its Quantification. *Fuzzy Sets and Systems*.

Pedrycz, W., & Valente de Oliveira, J. (1996). Optimization of fuzzy models. *IEEE Transaction on Systems, Man, and Cybernetics - Part B*, *26*(4), 627–636. doi:10.1109/3477.517038

Pedrycz, W., & Vukovich, G. Clustering in the framework of collaborative agents, *Proc. 2002 IEEE Int. Conference on Fuzzy Systems*, 1, 2002, 134-138.

D. B. Skillicorn, S. M. McConnell, Distributed prediction from vertically partitioned data, *Journal of Parallel and Distributed computing*, 2007.

S.C. Stubberud, K.A. Kramer, Data association for multiple sensor types using fuzzy logic, *IEEE Transactions on Instrumentation and Measurement*, 55, 6, 2006, 2292-2303.

Tsoumakas, G., Angelis, L., & Vlahavas, I. (2004). Clustering classifiers for knowledge discovery from physically distributed databases. *Data & Knowledge Engineering*, *49*(3), 223–242. doi:10.1016/j.datak.2003.09.002

Y. Wang, On Cognitive Informatics, *Brain and Mind*, 4, 2, 2003, 151-167.

Y. Wang, W. Kinsner, Recent advances in Cognitive Informatics, *IEEE Transactions on Systems, Man, and Cybernetics, Part C*, 36, 2, 2006, 121-123.

Wiswedel, B., & Berthold, M. R. (2007). Fuzzy clustering in parallel universes. *J. of Approximate Reasoning*, *45*, 439–454. doi:10.1016/j.ijar.2006.06.020

Zadeh, L. A. (1999). From computing with numbers to computing with words-from manipulation of measurements to manipulation of perceptions. *IEEE Transactions on Circuits and Systems*, *45*, 105–119.

Zadeh, L. A. (2005). Toward a generalized theory of uncertainty (GTU)—an outline. *Information Sciences*, *172*, 1–40. doi:10.1016/j.ins.2005.01.017

Zurada, J. M., Yen, G. G., & Wang, J. (Eds.). (2008). *Computational Intelligence: Research Frontiers, LNCS 5050*. Heidelberg: Springer Verlag. doi:10.1007/978-3-540-68860-0

This work was previously published in International Journal of Software Science and Computational Intelligence, Volume 1, Issue 1, edited by Yingxu Wang, pp. 18-31, copyright 2009 by IGI Publishing (an imprint of IGI Global).

Chapter 4
Challenges in the Design of Adoptive, Intelligent and Cognitive Systems

W. Kinsner
University of Manitoba, Canada

ABSTRACT

Numerous attempts are being made to develop machines that could act not only autonomously, but also in an increasingly intelligent and cognitive manner. Such cognitive machines ought to be aware of their environments which include not only other machines, but also human beings. Such machines ought to understand the meaning of information in more human-like ways by grounding knowledge in the physical world and in the machines' own goals. The motivation for developing such machines range from self-evidenced practical reasons such as the expense of computer maintenance, to wearable computing in health care, and gaining a better understanding of the cognitive capabilities of the human brain. To achieve such an ambitious goal requires solutions to many problems, ranging from human perception, attention, concept creation, cognition, consciousness, executive processes guided by emotions and value, and symbiotic conversational human-machine interactions. This paper discusses some of the challenges emerging from this new design paradigm, including systemic problems, design issues, teaching the subjects to undergraduate students in electrical and computer engineering programs, research related to design.

DOI: 10.4018/978-1-4666-0261-8.ch004

INTRODUCTION

Engineers cause change through their knowledge, skills and professional activities (Koen, 2003; p.11; Eder & Hosnedl, 2008). One of the major roles of engineers is to design, build and test new physical or logical systems that have not existed before. A system is a deliberate arrangement of parts (such as hardware and software components, functional units, subsystems, procedures, or people and facilities) required to achieve a desired goal and specific objectives (e.g., Hollnager & Woods, 2005). Following the scientific method, with its physical and mathematical principles augmented by ergonomics and aesthetics, a system is first specified, then simulated and emulated if necessary, and its different parts (subsystems) are built and put together, tested and installed in an environment for which it was intended. Finally, field testing and operational observations provide feedback for improvements and modifications of the system.

If the system is simple (i.e., linear, with few static non-interacting components), many well-established design techniques can be used. If the system is complex (nonlinear, with interacting components), the design techniques must be much more involved including many heuristics. When the system must involve human operators (not users), even more complex design techniques must be considered. This article describes some of the design challenges brought about by the emerging dynamical systems, as well as intelligent and cognitive machines and systems (Kinsner, 2007a; Kinsner, 2007b). These developments require profound changes to the design process as dictated by the new scientific and engineering principles involved.

ENGINEERING DESIGN

An Engineer

The American College Dictionary and other dictionaries define an engineer as a person who is not only versed in the design, construction and use of machines, but also is capable of employing the innovative and methodological application of scientific knowledge and technology to produce a device, or a system, or a process, all intended to satisfy human needs, subject to technological, economic and environmental constraints.

Similar definitions are provided by the engineering accreditation bodies such as the Canadian Engineering Accreditation Board (CEAB) of Engineers Canada (formerly the Canadian Council of Professional Engineers, CCEP) (CEAB, 2006), and the ABET Engineering Accreditation Commission (formerly the Accreditation Board of Engineering and Technology) in the USA (ABET, 2006).

The definitions stress design and implementation through innovative and methodological application of knowledge (not just of information, or even worse, data). As we shall see, innovation and creativity are of particular importance to the design of intelligent systems. We shall also see that the design process of such systems requires a well synchronized team of engineers and other professional from non-engineering disciplines, rather than an ensemble of isolated individuals. In fact, a concept of the world-class engineer has been developed at academics and industry (Leonhard, 1995, December).

The Engineering Design Process (EDP)

What is an engineering design process (EDP)? The process of developing a product is based on a design philosophy (Koen, 2003) and involves a number of steps that guide the designer from the concept to the implementation and testing in the field. All the engineering accreditation bodies define engineering design clearly. For example, according to the Canadian CEAB (CEAB, 2006; p. 12), engineering design integrates mathematics, basic sciences, engineering sciences and complementary studies in developing elements, systems and processes to meet specific needs. It is a creative, interactive and often open-ended process subject to constraints which may be governed by standards or legislation to varying degrees, depending upon the discipline. These constraints may relate to economic, health, safety, environmental, social, or other pertinent interdisciplinary factors.

According the American ABET (ABET, 2006), engineering design is the process of devising a system, component or process to meet desired needs. It is a decision-making process (often interactive), in which the basic sciences, mathematics, and engineering sciences are applied to convert resources optimally to meet a stated objective. Among the fundamental elements of the design process are the establishment of objectives and criteria, synthesis, analysis, construction, testing and evaluation.

The International Technology Education Association (ITEA) defines (ITEA, 2007) engineering design ad the systematic and creative application of scientific and mathematical principles to practical ends such as the design, manufacture and operation of efficient and economic structure, machines, processes, and systems.

Although the definitions differ in several marked aspects, they point to some common elements of the design process, including specifications, analysis, synthesis, implementation and testing, regardless of the discipline. The actual design methodologies may also differ considerably, depending on the discipline (e.g., computer engineering) and area such as integrated circuit design, embedded systems, and software systems, as described in the next section.

Two Types of the Engineering Design Process

Is there a single approach to the engineering design process? Cross (2000) distinguishes two types of processes: *prescriptive* (algorithmic) and *descriptive* (open-ended, holistic, gestalt). The prescriptive (procedural) approach involves the basic phases identified in the previous section. It can be applied to very simple, well established designs in which several conditions are satisfied: (i) the problem and needs are well understood, (ii) the requirements are known and can be improved from previous similar cases, and (iii) the implementation and product introduction have low risk. Although feedback (i.e., revisiting previous phases) occurs in the process to correct or improve product performance, the process is sequential.

More complex machines and systems require the descriptive approach in which various phases of the design process do not follow sequentially, but are interconnected in the sense that their future impact must be considered at each other phase at all times, as shown in Figure 1.

The process usually starts from the ***problem identification*** phase in which the need for the product (i.e., a device, or a module, or a system) is established clearly. Mistakes are frequent in this phase due to either misjudgment of the current needs or unexpected changes in the future economic or environmental conditions. Such mistakes may be very costly. To minimize this risk related to known factors, various procedures have been developed. The dashed lines emanating from this phase to all the other nine phases indicate an *awareness* of the limitations and constraints of the other stages in the design process. Although they do not imply any actual visitations of the other phases at this stage of the process, they indicate the parallel nature of this model. The simultaneous awareness increases with the experience of thee design team, and could improve the accuracy of the problem formulation. If similar lines were drawn from each phase, a

Figure 1. A descriptive approach to the engineering design process (after Ford & Coulston, 2000; p. 4)

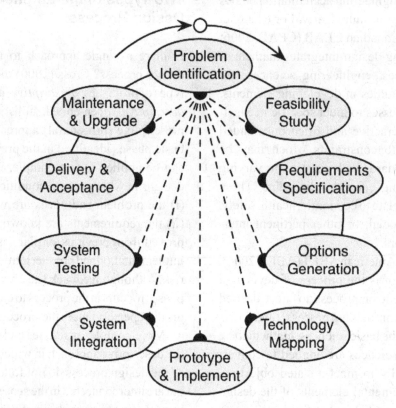

fully connected graph would result (see Ford & Coulston, 2000; p. 4). This is not done in Figure 1 to avoid overcrowding.

A preliminary design team is often established at this stage to conduct a *feasibility study* in order to identify the scientific and engineering principles involved, as well as the available technologies and prior art (available solutions). This establishes if the product is feasible within the available resources. Notice again that although not shown by the dashed lines in Figure 1, this stage is also connected to all the other nine phases, with the strongest link going to the previous phase.

During the *requirements specification* phase, the team describes what the product is, and what it must do in order to satisfy the needs. The specifications must be formulated in writing as both text and graphics in the form of a functional (architectural) block diagram. The block diagram represents a partitioning of the system into subsys-

tems (modules), and identifies all the interfaces between the various functional units, together with their levels of difficulty. This requirements stage is often assisted by computer-based tools and languages in order to improve and maintain product documentation. Although this phase does not provide an optimal solution, it is a guide for the entire remaining design process.

The distinguishing feature of the descriptive (open-ended) design approach is demonstrated in the next *option generation* phase. By developing the necessary solution to the problem, a cost function must also be established to performed a constrained optimization and grade the solutions. This phase is often marked by extreme innovation and creativity.

The *technology mapping* phase converts the selected optimal functional (architectural) solution into a detailed technological solution. This transformed product organization involves all the specific available parts, their specific interconnections (buses), and specific protocols to communicate between the components. Based on the technology mapping, the system partitioning may also be revisited to search for a better solution. To minimize logical mistakes, this stage often uses computer-based simulators (software), or emulators (software augmented with some actual hardware). Logical verification and testing are integral part of this phase. *Verification* is intended to prove that each module does what it should, while *testing* establishes its performance limits. Testing may be very time consuming at this stage due to the complexity of test vectors.

The *prototyping and implementation* phase provides the proof-of-concept because specific components are acquired, assembled and tested as physical prototypes in order to gain understanding of the physical limitations of the actual implementation. Prior experience with similar components may not be sufficient because of the technological changes in their manufacture. The subsystems are often implemented using rapid prototyping such as the *field-programmable gate arrays* (FPGAs) from Xilinx (e.g., Coffman, 2000), or other *programmable logic devices* (PLDs) such as the *complex PLDs* (CPLDs) from Altera (e.g., Dueck, 2001), or 3D printing and stereolithography (Castle Island, 2007). The prototypes further remove either logical or physical mistakes such as speed limitation. This phase also includes verification and testing.

The *system integration* phase is responsible for bringing all the subsystems together. This phase is often very difficult because the functional subsystems may not work together due to interface problems such as timing in the protocols, or improper utilization of resources such as memory conflicts. Real-time systems are particularly difficult to integrate.

The *system verification and testing* phase is an extension of similar activities in the technology mapping and prototyping phases. The system is verified against standards, and the overall performance is tested so that it is consistent with the system specifications.

The last two stages are *delivery and acceptance* and *maintenance and upgrading*. They follow procedures agreed upon in the preliminary phases of the product design process. The last stage may be very costly if the usable product lifetime is long. Since, for some systems such as computer installations, the cost of maintenance may be up to ten times the cost of the equipment, the systems must be designed in new ways. For example, autonomic computing (Kinsner, 2005; Kinsner, 2007a) and intelligent systems may alleviate some of the problems.

Notice that although the ten phases apply to any engineering design process, their description has been slanted towards computer engineering to reflect the experience of this author.

AREA-SPECIFIC EDP

Electronic Circuit Engineering Design Process

In computer engineering, the general descriptive engineering design process of Figure 1 has been used for years in several specialized forms to suit various application domains, such as circuit design in the form of chips, or FPLDs, or CPLDs, or printed circuit boards (PCBs), as well as embedded systems, and software development. For example, the design process of electronic circuits in the form of PCBs or FPGAs is illustrated in Figure 2 (e.g., Kinsner, (1985, July); Wolf, (2002)).

The need to develop a new electronic circuit intended to function in a larger system leads to the *specification stage* in which the detailed specifications are formulated in writing. The *feasibility study* stage is intended to establish if the concept is feasible within the available resources, and to establish a system partitioning to minimize cost, space and risk.

If the project is feasible, this stage is followed by *circuit architecture* stage in which a functional (architectural) block diagrams is developed, and the *circuit design* stage, including the actual partitioning into analog and digital subcircuits, translation of the functional block diagram into a circuit schematic (organization) by logical mapping (selection) of optimal components to be used. This stage also includes schematic capture (i.e., component selection from a library, new symbol creation, and netlist generation). The schematic capture can be either graphical, or through high-level hardware description languages such as Verilog (e.g., Arnold, 1999; Ciletti, 1999; Ciletti, 2003; Ciletti, 2004; Coffman, 2000; Navabi, 1999; Palnitkar, 1996; Smith, 1996; Thomas & Moorby, 1998) or VHDL (e.g., Ashenden, 1998; Smith, 1996). In either case, it is intended to facilitate circuit verification. This complicated stage is followed by the *analysis stage*, which includes logic simulation, timing analysis, analog analysis, and implementing the circuit on a breadboard, or in an FPGA or in a CPLD. If the analysis reveals that the circuit is either too slow, or consumes too much power, or takes too much real estate on the chip or board, it is sent for redesign.

However, if all appears to be according to the specifications, the *physical layout stage* can commence with respect to the specific target implementation such as a PCB, FPGA, CPLD, or a thin-film hybrid (TFH) for mixed analog-digital circuits. This layout stage may be followed by a *post-layout analysis stage* which includes simulation of the physical layout to calculate the characteristic impedances of the traces which, in turn, affect the electrical characteristics of the entire circuit, cross-talk between the traces to estimate the internal noise of the circuit and its survivability, transient analysis, and thermal analysis of the physical circuit with the physical currents. In some cases, a three-dimensional (3-D) modelling may be required if the product is intended for tight spaces. If the circuit is not up to par, it must be redesigned. Otherwise, the

Figure 2. The design process of electronic circuits

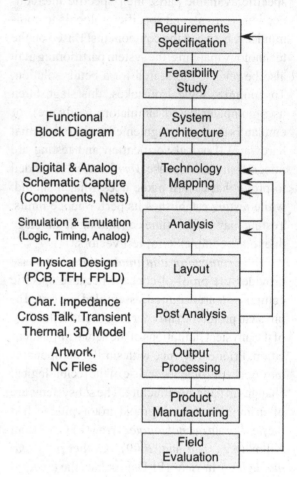

output stage produces all the artwork, the files required for the numerically-controlled (NC) drilling machines to make holes for all the feed-through components, or files designated for the FPGA or CPLD.

The manufacturing stage can be done either in-house for low-volume production, or it may be transferred to foundries for larger volumes or more complex designs. Finally, the product must be *evaluated for performance* in the field. If improvements or modifications are required, the cycle must be repeated, and the product may be either replaced or upgraded in the field, without returning it. The latter mode of upgrading is dominant today due to three major factors: (i) the availability of in-circuit reprogrammable devices

Figure 3. The almost-sashimi waterfall design process of software (after Royce, 1970)

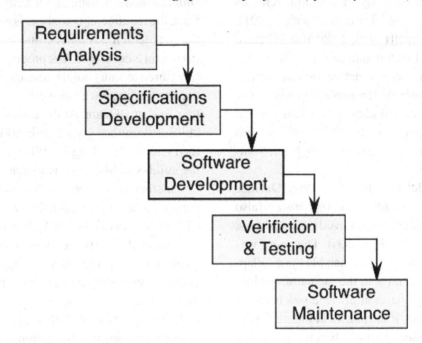

(software replacement) and reconFigureurable devices (hardware modifications), (ii) high-speed wired (Internet) or wireless networking, and (iii) the fast turn around, lower cost, and convenience to the customer.

Software Engineering Design Process

Development of software appears to be a complex undertaking, except for very simple applications (e.g., Brooks (1975); Ghezzi, Jazayeri, & Mandrioli, 1991; Schach, 1999; Sommerville, 2006; McConnell, 2006). This is particularly true in the design of real-time software that must respond to events within strictly predefined periods of time (e.g., Sommerville, 2006; Ch. 2; Ghezzi, Jazayeri, & Mandrioli, 1991; Sec. 2.3.2). The discipline of software engineering has been developing various approaches and metrics to improve the five basic phases, as illustrated in Figure 3.

The software engineering design process is depicted as strictly sequential (prescriptive) suc-

cession of phases, like in a waterfall. Although this *waterfall model* is attributed to Royce (1970), his article presented this model as one of the least realistic, and introduced iterations not only between adjacent phases, but also between other phases. Based on his experience with the development of military software, Royce also elaborated on many details required to reach a high level of reliability of the software developed. This expanded waterfall model is also discussed by Schach (1999; p. 66).

Many other authors have introduced models with *backtracking* (feedback) because essential details become available only when one progresses through the various phases in the design process. This eliminates the possibility of developing perfect specifications, regardless of how much time one would spend in that phase (in other words, the principle "measure twice, cut once" could not apply to software development). For example, David Parnas (Parnas & Clements, 2001) advocated the rational software design process.

He also introduced many major improvements to the design process (Hoffman & Weiss, 2001).

Steve McConnell (1996; 2006) also criticized the wide-spread of the simple waterfall model, and described many alternative models such as the *spiral software design process* in which one traverses the waterfall phases to obtain a rough idea of the system, and revisits the phases with more details (see also Schach, 1999; p. 80; Sommerville, 2006).

Anther model introduced by Peter DeGace (1998) is the *sashimi software design process* (also known as the waterfall with overlapping phases, and waterfall with subprojects). The name was coined because the phases resemble the overlapping slices of fish meat in the Japanese sashimi. The overlapping phases imply feedback between the phases. In fact, if the phases in Figure 3 were drawn a bit closer, it would become a sashimi waterfall.

Another model is the *evolutionary prototyping process* in which the initial concept is designed and implemented as a rough prototype. This prototype is then improved iteratively, until acceptable for release.

A modified version of the previous model is the *staged delivery model* in which the conceptual formulation is also followed be the analysis of requirements and architectural design, but the customer is now involved in each stage, rather in the final prototype only, and phases are revisited when needed. A mixture of the two previous models is called the *evolutionary delivery model*.

One of the largest software companies, Microsoft, uses a version of the *incremental model* just described (also see Schach, 1999; p. 72) in which software is built (not written) incrementally day by day, with input from the customer. This approach uses a unit called a build. A *build* includes the code developed for various modules, interacting together to form the expected function. Since it is very difficult to integrate the software if there are too many builds, Microsoft modified the incremental model into their *synchronize and stabilize model* (Cusumano & Selby, 1997, June). First, the requirements analysis is conducted with many potential customers, and a specifications document is developed. The product is divided into few (three to four) builds, arranged according to their criticality. Each build is developed by more than one small team. At the end of each day, the build is discussed (synchronized) by the teams, then tested and debugged. When all is well (i.e., the build is stabilized) it is frozen.

Another new recent software development paradigms has emerged as *eXtreme Programming* (XP) (Beck & Andres, 2004). It is intended to reduce the cost of software changes. It is marked by the development and analysis of test cases before coding, then coding using pairs of programmers, and placing most of the documentation into the code. The central tenet of this approach is the *participatory design*, with the customer involved in as many phases as possible. Fred Brooks promoted this idea of user-centered design in his classical book on software management [Brook75].

A number of important software design ideas have emerged around the time of object-oriented languages. One of the examples is the object-oriented engineering design paradigm as described in (Schach, 1999; p.82) and (Douglass, 1999). Objects are small scalable modules of the fundamental problem-domain concepts. Objects are intended to increase the performance of the systems, and their robustness to change. The third-generation modelling languages such as the Unified Modelling Language (UML) provides a rigorous development environment (Douglass, 1999). Schach also compares and contrasts the models to assist in the selection of an appropriate one for a specific application.

One of the object-oriented models is the *fountain software engineering design process* (Henderson-Sellers & Edwards, 1990, September), as shown in Figure 4.

The circles represent the different phases in the process. Many of the phases are overlapping (like in the sashimi model). The arrows indicate

Figure 4. The fountain software engineering design process (after Henderson-Sellers & Edwards, 1990, September)

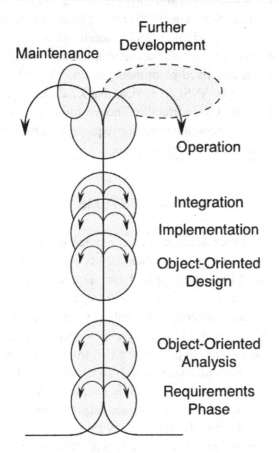

backtracking within the phases and between different phases. Notice that the maintenance phase is smaller than the other circles to signify the advantage of the object-oriented methodology.

The review of the software design methodologies was also intended to show that a professional software or computer engineer is required to assure to quality of the process. A software engineer must be not only a good programmer, fluent in more than one programming language, but also fully familiar with theory and practice of data structures, algorithms, artificial intelligence, real-time operating systems, various applications areas, requirements engineering, as well as various abstraction levels through specific modelling languages, with verification and testing. Furthermore, since teams develop software projects, a software engineer must have good communication and interpersonal skills.

Based on the previous electronic circuit and software EDPs, we are ready to discuss one of the more challenging design methodologies related to embedded systems.

Embedded Systems Engineering Design Process

One of the important activities in computer engineering is the design of embedded systems (e.g., Gajski, Vahid, Narayan, & Gong, 1994; Valvano, 2000, Vahid & Givargis, 2002; Kamal, 2008). Embedded systems are hardware-software computing and controlling systems encapsulated into larger electromechanical systems to perform dedicated operations in a way that is often inconspicuous to the outside observer. Unlike the stand-alone computer systems (e.g., personal computers, laptops, workstations, mainframes, and servers), embedded systems are integral parts of larger systems such as those found in consumer electronics (cell phones, pagers, global positioning systems, digital cameras, camcorders, MP3 sound players, DVD players, video games, calculators, and personal digital assistants), home appliances (microwave ovens, washing and drying machines, answering machines, thermostats, security systems), office automation (Copiers, printers, scanners, fax machines, office telephones), business equipment (cash registers, card readers, product scanners, alarm systems), automobiles (fuel injection, transmission control, emission control, cruise control, antilock brakes, active suspension). Other applications such as avionics and industrial machinery have even a wider range of embedded systems. In 2004, a typical household had more than 300 embedded systems (Vahid & Givargis, 2002). Around 1995, approximately 3 billion embedded processors were sold each year (Cole, 1995, March 20).

Embedded systems have several common characteristics: (i) repeated single-function operation, (ii) very stringent constraints (low cost, low power, single chip), (iii) real-time operation (i.e., the system must acquire data, compute, and respond in time that is no slower than the natural time), (iv) very high reliability, (v) long life time, (vi) adaptability to its environment, and (vii) a very tight time-to-market. The latter feature appears to be so stringent that it has led to major changes in the design of embedded systems. In order to meet this challenge, hardware (HW), software (SW) and the interface (IF) had to be developed concurrently. This codesign of HW and SW and IF (HSI for shot) has displaced the traditional sequential design process, and has led to starting the HIS design before the architecture or even specifications are finalized. The HIS codesign has also resulted in the concept of practical reuse of components from previous internal designs or from outside designs. This engineering design process of embedded systems (Ernst, 1998, April-June) is illustrated in Figure 5.

Notice that although the design process in Figure 5 looks quite prescriptive (sequential), it is an extreme example of a very descriptive (concurrent) process in that the HIS codesign starts even before the specifications and system architecture are completed. The codesign has led to many new tools for computer-assisted design space exploration, cosynthesis, cosimulation, coverification and testing, automatic code generation, and reusability.

The reusability of HIS modules has become an essential part not only of the rapid design of embedded systems, but also in many other electronic designs. An example of such reusable software modules for embedded systems has been provided by Labrosse (2000), with some of the most common building blocks, including real-time software (dedicated to the μC/OS II real-time operating system, RTOS), keyboard scanners, multiplexed light-emitting diodes (LEDs), character liquid-crystal displays (LCDs), timers, discrete input (e.g., limit and status switches) drivers, discrete output (e.g., stepping motors, fans, lamps) drivers, analog input and output (I/O) (e.g., for sensor signals (Soloman, 1999) related to temperature, pressure, position, velocity, acceleration, as well as analog motors and actuators), data communications, and fixed-point mathematics. The code is written in ANSI (American National Standards Institute) C for portability. These software modules reflect the common function required in embedded systems, as shown in Figure 6.

EVOLUTION OF SYSTEMS

Computer science and computer engineering have contributed to many shifts in technological and computing paradigms. For example, we have seen shifts (i) from large batch computers to personal and embedded real-time computers, (ii) from control-driven microprocessors to data- and demand-driven processors, (iii) from uniprocessors to multiple-processors (loosely coupled) and multiprocessors (tightly coupled), (iv) from data-path processors to structural processors (e.g., neural networks, (Bishop, 1995; Austin, 1998)), quantum processors (Nielsen & Chuang, 2000) and biomolecular processors (Sienko, Adamatzky, Rambidi, & Conrad, 2003), (v) from silicon-based processors to biochips (Ruaro, Bonifazi., & Torre, 2005, March), (vi) from vacuum tubes to transistors to microelectronics to nanotechnology, (vii) from large passive sensors to very small smart active sensors (Soloman, 1999), (viii) from local computing to distributed computing and network-wide computing, (vii) from traditional videoconferencing to telepresence (e.g., WearTel and EyeTap (Mann, 2002)), (viii) from machines that require attention (like a palmtop or a wristwatch computer) to those that have a constant online connectivity that drops below the conscious level of awareness of users (like autonomic computers (Ganek & Corbi, 2003; IBM, 2006), and eyeglass-based systems (Mann,

Figure 5. The design process of embedded systems, involving hardware (HD), software (SW) and interface (IF) (after Ernst, 1998, April-June)

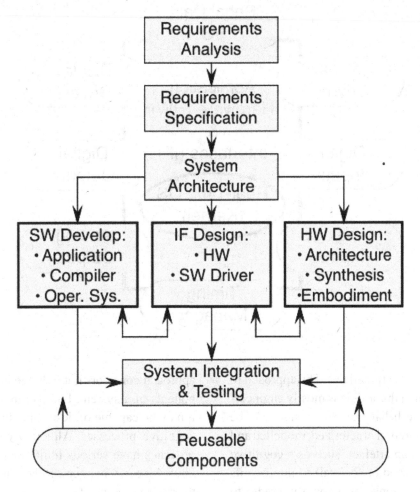

2002; Haykin & Kosko, 2001), (ix) from crisp-logic-based computers to fuzzy or neurofuzzy computers (Pedrycz & Gomide, 1998), as well as (x) from control-driven (imperative) systems to cognitive systems such as cognitive radio (Haykin, 2005, February), cognitive radar (Haykin, 2006, January), active audition (Haykin & Chen, 2005), and cognitive robots. These remarkable shifts have been necessitated by the system complexity, which now exceeds our ability to maintain them (Ganek & Corbi, 2003), while being facilitated by new developments in technology, intelligent signal processing, and machine learning (Haykin, Principe, Sejnowski, & McWhirter, 2006).

Since the 1950s, philosophers, mathematicians, physicists, cognitive scientists, neuroscientists, computer scientists, and computer engineers have debated the question of what could constitute *digital sentience* (*i.e.*, the ability to feel or perceive in the absence of thought and inner speech), as well as machine consciousness or artificial consciousness (*e.g.*, von Neumann, 1958; Searle, 1980; Minsky, 1986; Rumelhart & McClelland, 1986; Cotterill, 1988; Posner, 1989; Klivington, 1989; Penrose, 1989; Kurzweil, 1990; Dennett, 1991; Searle, 1992; Penrose, 1994). Consequently, many approaches have been developed to modelling consciousness, including biological, neurologi-

Figure 6. Candidates for reusable software modules in embedded systems (after Labrosse, 2000, p. xix)

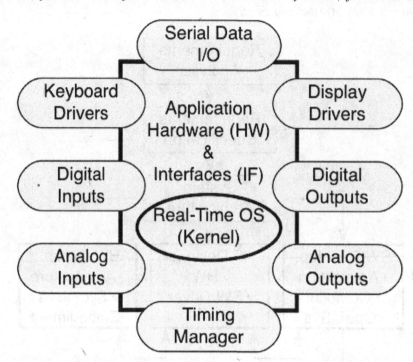

cal, and engineering (practical). The approach to cognition taken in this article is mostly engineering in which the behaviour of a system can be observed, measured, characterized, modelled and implemented as an artefact, such as a cognitive robot (either isolated or societal) to improve its interaction with people, or a cognitive radio to improve the utilization of a precious resource, *i.e.*, the frequency spectrum.

In general, the intent of such cognitive systems is to improve their performance in changing environments, to reduce waste in resource utilization, to help human operators interact with the controlled process, to guard against catastrophic failure, to age gracefully, and to provide a test-bed for learning about cognition and cognitive processes.

If an approach to understanding cognition is purely reductionist (i.e., reducing the system to its constituent elements, without their interactions, and then reconstructing the whole from the individual contributions), it may not be capable of describing its complexities. Since our engineering

approach considers not only the individual components of a system, but also their interactions, it may be capable of describing the dynamics of cognitive processes. Although engineering approaches have serious limitations (e.g., Parsell, 2005, March; Chalmers, 1997), they are intended to produce a range of specific practical outcomes.

Kinsner (2007a) described several models of cognitive machines, including those proposed by Haikonen (2003); Franklin (1995), Aleksander (1998), Taylor (2003), with specific examples such as cognitive radio (Haykin, 2005, February), cognitive radar (Haykin, 2006, January), active audition (Haykin & Chen, 2005), affective computing, and autonomic computing. His paper also discusses several critical aspects related to cognitive machines, including intelligent signal processing (Haykin & Kosko, 2001), real-time learning, adaptive control (Zak, 2003), and metrics. Without this framework, the challenges of designing intelligent and cognitive systems might not be appreciated fully.

CHALLENGES IN THE DESIGN OF COMPLEX SYSTEMS

The previous sections provided a review of the commonalities and differences in the engineering design process (EDP) of electronic hardware, software and embedded systems. These models are well understood, and are used in practice in industry, as well as in research and development (R&D) organizations. When a limitation of a specific model is identified, the model is improved. This has been practised for decades. So, is there a problem? Yes, there may be a fundamental problem with all the existing EDP models if the complexity of a system increases beyond what is known (i.e., the system becomes unmanageable), or when limited resources prevent the use of the system, or when the system includes human operators as an integral part of the system. In such cases, intelligent and cognitive systems ought to be considered. However, there is no EDP model developed for such systems. This discussion may be helpful in the development of such a model. The discussion is grouped into several topics related to outsourcing of manufacturing, the new role of design teams, complex systems, the EDP, teaching, and research.

Outsourcing of Manufacturing

One of the major challenges in EDP is the outsourcing of manufacturing in our global economy. How can we sustain design without knowing how to manufacture the designs? For example, in chip manufacturing, since the physical parameters of the wafer may change from day to day, they are measured and fed back into the parameters used in simulation of the circuit to estimate its speed and other performance criteria. Without knowing the details of manufacturing, our designs cannot be optimal, or even may fail prematurely.

The problem is compounded by the number of engineers graduated in those countries that are handed over the manufacturing. For example in 2006, the number of graduating engineers was around 600,000 in China and around half of that in India, while North America graduated just around one tenth of that number. One of the outcomes of not meeting this challenge is the declining enrollment in some areas of engineering, as the perception is that there will be no engineering jobs here.

The Role of Engineers and Engineering Teams

The engineer must be not only a good designer, but also a user's advocate (user-centred designs). The engineer must also be a design diplomat, capable of guiding the design in a team, enhancing the environment of all the team members by balancing their interests, and keeping the client fully involved and aware of the status of the project.

The complexity of intelligent systems requires teams of professionals whose individual detailed knowledge of the entire system may be next to impossible. Many teams may also be distributed physically in a city, country, or even the world. In the later case, the teams may not be working at the same time due to the opposite time zones. Encapsulation of expertise and reusable software may be necessary in such cases.

System Challenges

Autonomic Computing: Designing intelligent and cognitive systems is a long-term goal. Autonomic computing (AC) is a scaled-down form of cognitive machines (Ganek & Corbi, 2003; IBM, 2006; Kinsner, 2005; Kinsner, 2007; Wang, 2003; Wang, 2004; Wang, 2006). The systems are evolving earnestly because the cost-performance of hardware improvements (speed and capacity) have lead to escalating complexity of software (features and interfaces). However, this increased complexity requires elaborate managing systems that are now six to ten times the cost of the equipment itself. Autonomic computing is intended to simplify this problem by making the systems self-conFigureuring, self-optimizing, self-organizing, self-healing, self-protecting, and self-telecommunicating, thus leading to increased reliability, robustness, and dynamic flexibility. This involves not only the traditional fault tolerant computing (i.e., tolerating hardware and software faults), but also tolerating various faults made by human operators and users, thus shifting attention from the *mean-time-between failures* (MTBF) to the *mean-time-to-recover* (MTTR) in order to make the systems more available. AC applies to both desktop computing, portable computing, pervasive computing, and embedded systems.

A number of new concepts must also be developed, such as the real-time process algebra (RTPA) (Wang, 2002, October). RTPA can provide a multidimensional (space, time and action) representation of the behaviour of autonomous systems.

Mechatronics: Many of the developments of intelligent machines involve mechatronics (e.g., Bolton, 2003; Cetinkunt, 2007) which is a system-level approach to designing electromechanical systems. It combines several engineering disciplines, including mechanical, electrical, electronic, control, wireless, and computer, with an extended embedded systems design methodology. Machines that perform one task are no longer in great demand. Flexible machines require control, human-machine interfaces (HMI), networking, remote machine monitoring and reporting over the Internet. However, such complexities increase cost, risk, and design time. Mechatronics-based approach mitigates some of the problems.

Networking: How can we provide resilient networking for intelligent and cognitive machines? Should the networking be wired or wireless? How can the Internet be used for telerobotics and telepresence in view of the unpredictable delays on the network? Boosting the Internet routers will not solve the problem. ReconFigureureable hardware and network-embedded computational resources

will not solve the problem either. Can the network be redesigned to make the attached computing resources not only a distributed computing system, but also a cognitive global computer?

Direct Challenges Within the EDP

The EDP itself has many challenges, particularly when applied to complex systems, including rapid EDP cycle, requirements, specifications, design and evaluation, hardware and sensors, and software, as discussed next.

Short EDP Cycle: The turn-around time for product specification, design and delivery has been decreasing not only in embedded systems and mechatronics, but also in automotive and aerospace industries with very complex environments spanning many departments and partners. Rapid evaluation and alternative designs require massive computing resources. Can grid computing be helpful to resolve this problem? Grid computing is a service-oriented architecture approach that uses open standards and resource virtualization to make distributed computing possible over the Internet. An example may be IBM's Grid-Aided Engineering (GAE) (IBM, 2007).

Requirements: Identifying the current needs for a product, its characteristics, functionality, reliability and life span is a difficult process. How can future users and operators, their needs, and characteristics of their work be analyzed and understood? Although adaptive systems may solve some of such issues, there is a strong need for intelligent and cognitive systems to help alleviate some of the problems.

Specifications: How can the scope and specifications of intelligent systems be defined and described adequately? A large portion (84%) of today's designs of simple systems fails due to incomplete or unclear specifications. On the other hand, how many people read and understand complete specifications in a 1000-page or so document? What methodologies and tools must be developed to help in this mater?

Design and Evaluations: How do we design an interactive, intelligent, or cognitive system optimally for current and future users? It is relatively easy to design complex systems that are complicated and hard-to-use. It is very hard to design complex systems that are neither complicated nor hard-to-operate. The very nature of cognitive systems is to help in this matter.

What new tools should we develop? The tools to design small subsystems are formidable. Assembling such subsystems into larger systems requires many solutions to the management of interfaces between the subsystems and coordination of parallel operations between the subsystems. What method and strategies must be introduced to predict and prevent errors in product development? Are the current solutions (Chao & Ishii, 2004, August) satisfactory for such systems? Would tools such as LabVIEW from National Instruments be helpful in teaching students how to model and evaluate designs in embedded systems and mechatronics?

Hardware and Sensors: Should parallel hardware be used? How should parallel software match the parallel hardware and parallel network? Should the hardware be event or time driven? Should it be synchronous or anachronous? Should it be control or data driven? What granularity should be employed? Should it use crisp or fuzzy logic? Should it be structural (e.g., neural network based)? Should it be purely digital or hybrid (digital and analog)?

Sensing of the environment is central to intelligent and cognitive machines. How can we provide new reliable sensors with self-calibration, self-correcting, and resilient to aging? How can we improve computer vision, as well as real-time natural speech recognition and understanding? Since single sensors are not sufficient to provide input to cognitive systems, reliable and robust mesh networking is required, both wired and wireless.

Software: Software requires many advances to be suitable for intelligent and cognitive systems. An example of how far we are from this level of sophistication is the low usability of help files in most application software. However, within the EDP itself, the Unified Modelling Language (UML) and similar approaches have been found very useful to build blueprints, with a common vocabulary for software modelling and reduced differences in software methodologies. The UML uses the best practices of the object-oriented software design (OOD) process. The OOD is fundamentally different from the functional design process. It emphasizes objects rather than functions. Objects identify both data (attributes) and methods (functions) that can act on the data. Objects are instances of a class (with the same attributes and methods). An object encapsulates this information, and cannot change it by itself. This encapsulation improves the reliability and maintainability of software, as changes appear to be local.

Teaching Challenges

Methodological and Innovative Design: Our engineering students have an extensive exposure to mathematics (algebra, calculus, analysis, and discrete mathematics), basic sciences (physics, chemistry, and some geological and environmental sciences), and basic engineering sciences (electronics, computing, signal and image processing, information theory, coding, electromagnetics, telecommunications, and computer networking). This exposure in itself does not convert a student into and engineer; it just provides the required scientific and engineering knowledge. This model is well established in many countries (CEAB, 2006; ABET, 2006; De Bon, Wolfe, Chagnon, & Paterson, 2002).

Any good engineering program must also incorporate the *methodological* application of the knowledge in order to design and produce a new device, system, or process, each satisfying human needs and safety. In addition, for a program to be excellent, it should develop the concept of *innovative* design (which is in some contradiction with the concept of methodological design). This is of particular importance to the design of intelligent systems that must be autonomous, autonomic, survivable, immune to external and internal attacks, and recognize the changing human needs and safety. How do we teach and develop such design skills?

Extended Coverage: The design of intelligent and cognitive systems requires a major extension of the topics taught to our students, including intelligent signal processing (Haykin, Principe, Sejnowski, & McWhirter, 2006), biology, cognitive informatics (Wang, 2003), and new computing paradigms such as structural computing (i.e., neural networks, particularly with recurrence and full connectivity in which emergence can occur), as well as quantum and biomolecular computing. In signal processing, we already teach autocorrelation, convolution, and Fourier transforms, but must extend it to time-scale (wavelet) transforms (Mallat, 1998; Weeks, 2007). Control theory should be extended to include nonlinear dynamical systems with the fourth stable state, chaos. This necessitates extensions to discrete mathematics to include self-affinity, multiscale analysis, fuzzy logic, and higher-order statistics. Electronics must also emphasize the physics of computing and discuss challenges in high-speed circuit design.

New Emerging Areas vs Specialization: How do we respond to the emerging areas of engineering such as Genetic Engineering, Cognitive Engineering? Will biology, neuroscience, bioinformatics, cognitive informatics be all required as Basic Sciences? Will Computer Science be ever considered as one of the Basic Sciences?

How do we distinguish between a new emerging area (discipline) and a highly-specialized sub-area? Many off-shore engineers graduate from very narrow specialties. Does this approach (narrow, but deep) help or hinder the design process? Will teams be helped by such narrow specialties? Do broadly-based engineers defined by their discipline adapt to change faster?

Experiential Learning: How do we deal with experiential learning (i.e., co-op terms, 16-month internship, stage projects)? Companies no longer tolerate extended years of on-the-job training for new engineering graduates because of the short product life cycles, fast turn-around of graduates (the old model of seven years with a company no longer applies). The recent shift from a *graduating thesis* to a *capstone project* based on teams who practise the engineering design process is a reflection on how engineering schools cope with the problem.

Research Challenges

The engineering design process (EDP) is used in industry, research and development (R&D) institutions, research laboratories, educational institutions, and many other places where new concepts must be developed and made operational. We have seen that the process itself is multi-facet and requires much knowledge and experience. How are the EDP tools and methodologies developed? Is there a room for research related to EDP?

The Cambridge Engineering Design Centre (2007) has been conducting research in several areas. For example, their *knowledge management* includes acquisition, storage, and retrieval of engineering knowledge related to design. *Process management* addresses the modelling aspects of the design process. *Change management* studies how to model change in products. *Computational design* focuses on integrated optimization methods and tools. *Design practice* has been developing understanding of the practices used in the design process.

CONCLUDING REMARKS

Intelligent signal processing, real-time machine learning, and cognitive informatics are essential in solving some design and implementation issues of adaptive, intelligent and cognitive machines. The engineering design process will be critical to the development and introduction of such machines. Since the classical EDP models have not been involved with the design of such complex machines, a new improved paradigm must be developed. This article addresses some of the challenges of developing the new paradigm.

ACKNOWLEDGMENT

Partial financial support of this work from the Natural Sciences and Engineering Research Council (NSERC) of Canada is gratefully acknowledged.

REFERENCES

ABET. (2006). ABET Engineering Accreditation Commission: Criteria for accreditation engineering programs. *Report*, 29 pp. Retrieved June 2007, from http://www.abet.org/forms.shtml

Aleksander, I. (1998). From WISARD to MAGNUS: A family of weightless neural machines. In Austin, J. (Ed.), *RAM-Based Neural Networks* (pp. 18–30). Singapore: World Scientific. doi:10.1142/9789812816849_0002

Arnold, M. G. (1999). *Verilog Digital Computer Design: Algorithms into Hardware* (p. 602). Upper Saddle River, NJ: Prentice Hall.

Ashenden, P. J. (1998). *The Student's Guide To VHDLs* (p. 312). San Francisco, CA: Morgan Kaufmann.

Austin, J. (Ed.). (1998). *RAM-Based Neural Networks* (p. 240). Singapore: World Scientific.

Beck, K., & Andres, C. (2004). *Extreme Programming Explained: Embrace Change* (2nd ed., p. 224). Upper Saddle River, NJ: Addison-Wesley Professional.

Bishop, C. M. (1995). *Neural Networks for Pattern Recognition* (p. 482). Oxford, UK: Oxford Univ. Press.

Bolton, W. (2003). *Mechatronics: Electronic Control Systems in Mechanical and Electrical Engineering* (3rd ed., p. 574). Edinburgh Gate, UK: Pearson Education.

Brooks, F. P. (1975). *The Mythical Man Month*. Reading, MA: Addison-Wesley, (p. 195). {ISBN 0-201-00650-2 pbk}

Cambridge Engineering Design Centre. (2007), Research (Report). Cambridge, UK: Cambridge Engineering Design Centre, 2007. (Retrieved June 2007 from http://www-edc.eng.cam.ac.uk/research/)

Castle Island. (2007). The worldwide guide to rapid prototyping. *Tutorials and Directories*. Retrieved June 2007 from http://home.att.net/~castleisland/home.html

CEAB. (2006). Canadian Engineering Accreditation Board: Accreditation criteria and procedures, (*Report*),(p. 40). Retrieved June 2007 from http://www.engineerscanda.ca/e/prog_publications_3.cfm

Cetinkunt, S. (2007). *Mechatronics*. New York, NY: Wiley.

Chalmers, D. (1997). The Conscious Mind. In *Search of a Fundamental Theory* (p. 432). Oxford, UK: Oxford Univ. Press.

Chao, L. P., & Ishii, K. (2004, August). Design process error-proofing: Challenges and methods in quantifying design elements. In *Proc. Tenth ISSAT Intern. Conf. on Reliability and Quality in Design* (Las Vegas, NV; August 2004) 5 pp. Retrieved June 2007 from http://www-mml.standford.edu/publications/2004/ISSATquality-C04-24.pdf

Ciletti, M. D. (1999). *Modelling, Synthesis and Rapid Prototyping with Verilog HDL* (p. 724). Upper Saddle River, NJ: Prentice Hall/Pearson Education.

Ciletti, M. D. (2003). *Advanced Digital Design with the Verilog HDLs* (p. 382). Upper Saddle River, NJ: Prentice Hall/Pearson Education.

Ciletti, M. D. (2004). *Starter's Guide to Verilog 2001* (p. 234). Upper Saddle River, NJ: Prentice Hall/Pearson Education.

Coffman, K. (2000). *Real-World FPGA Design with Verilog* (p. 289). Upper Saddle River, NJ: Prentice Hall.

Cole, B. (1995, March 20). Architectures overlap applications. *Electronic Engineering Times, 40*, 64–65.

Cotterill, R. (Ed.). (1988). *Computer Simulations in Brain Science* (p. 566). Cambridge, UK: Cambridge Univ. Press. doi:10.1017/CBO9780511983467

Cross, N. (2000). *Design Methods: Strategies for Product Design* (3rd ed., p. 224). New York, NY: Wiley.

Cusumano, M. A., & Selby, R. W. (1997, June). How Microsoft builds software. *Communications of the ACM, 40*(6), 53–61. doi:10.1145/255656.255698

De Bon, S., Wolfe, D., Chagnon, J.-Y., & Paterson, W. G. (2002). Engineering Accreditation in Canada and Its Current Challenges. In *Proc. 2002 ASEE/SEFI/TUB Colloquium*, (p. 9). Retrieved May 2007 from http://www.asee.org/conferences/international/papers/upload/Engineering-Accreditation-in-Canada-and-Its-Current-Challenges.pdf

DeGrace, P., & Stahl, L. H. (1998). *Wicket Problems, Righteous Solutions: A Catalog of Modern Engineering Paradigms* (p. 272). Upper Saddle River, NJ: Prentice Hall.

Dennett, D. C. (1991). *Consciousness Explained* (p. 528). London, UK: Allan Lane/Penguin.

Douglass, B. P. (1999). *Doing Hard Time: Developing Real-Time Systems with UML, Objects, Frameworks, and Patterns* (p. 749). Reading, MA: Addison-Wesley.

Dueck, R. K. (2001). *Digital Design with CPLD Applications and VHDL*. Stamford, CT: Thomson Learning, (p. 845). {ISBN 0-7668-1160-3, +CDROM}

Eder, W. E., & Hosnedl, S. (2008). *Design Engineering: A Manual for Enhanced Creativity* (p. 588). Boca Rayton, FL: CRC.

Ernst, R. (1998, April-June). Codesign of embedded systems: Status and trends. *IEEE Design & Test of Computers, 15*(2), 45–54. doi:10.1109/54.679207

Ford, R. M., & Coulston, C. S. (2000). *Design for Electrical and Computer Engineers: Theory, Concepts, and Practice*. New York, NY: McGraw Hill (Custom Publishing), (p. 280).

Franklin, S. (1995). *Artificial Minds* (p. 464). Cambridge, MA: MIT Press.

Gajski, D. D., Vahid, F., Narayan, S., & Gong, J. (1994). *Specification and Design of Embedded Systems* (p. 450). Englewood Cliffs, NJ: PTR Prentice Hall.

Ganek, A. G., & Corbi, T. A. (2003). The dawning of the autonomic computing era. *IBM Systems J., 42*(1), 34-42. Retrieved May 2006 from http://www.research.ibm.com/journal/sj/421/ganek.pdf

Ghezzi, C., Jazayeri, M., & Mandrioli, D. (1991). *Fundamentals of Software Engineering* (p. 573). Englewood Cliffs, NJ: Prentice Hall.

Haikonen, P. O. A. (2003). *The Cognitive Approach to Conscious Machines*. New York, NY: Academic, (p. 294). (See also http://personal.inet.fi/cool/pentti.haikonen/)

Haykin, S. (2005, February). Cognitive radio: Brain-empowered wireless communications. *IEEE Journal on Selected Areas in Communications, 23*(2), 201–220. doi:10.1109/JSAC.2004.839380

Haykin, S. (2006, January). Cognitive radar. *IEEE Signal Processing Magazine*, 30–40. doi:10.1109/MSP.2006.1593335

Haykin, S., & Chen, Z. (2005). The cocktail party problem. *Neural Computation, 17*, 1875–1902. doi:10.1162/0899766054322964

Haykin, S., & Kosko, B. (2001). *Intelligent Signal Processing* (p. 573). New York, NY: Wiley-IEEE. doi:10.1109/9780470544976

Haykin, S., Principe, J. C., Sejnowski, T. J., & McWhirter, J. (2006). *New Directions in Statistical Signal Processing* (p. 544). Cambridge, MA: MIT Press.

Henderson-Sellers, B., & Edwards, J. M. (1990, September). The object-oriented systems life cycle. *Communications of the ACM, 33*(9), 142–159. doi:10.1145/83880.84529

Hoffman, D. M., & Weiss, D. M. (2001) (Eds.). *Collected Papers by David L. Parnas*. Upper Saddle River, NJ: Addison-Wesley, (p. 664).

Hollnager, E., & Woods, D. D. (2005). *Joint Cognitive Systems: Foundation of Cognitive Systems Engineering* (p. 240). Boca Rayton, FL: CRC. doi:10.1201/9781420038194

IBM. (2006). *IBM Autonomic Computing Manifesto*. Retrieved May 2006 from http://www.research.ibm.com/autonomic/

IBM. (2007). Engineering design: Clash analysis in automotive and aerospace. Retrieved May 2007 from http://www-03.ibm.com/grid/solutions/ED_clashanalysisisautoaero.shtml

ITEA. (2007). International Technology Education Association: Glossary terms for STL and AETL and Addenda, *Report*, 30 pp. (STL –Standards for Technological Literacy; AETL –Advancing Excellence in Technological Literacy; TAA – Technology for All Americans) Retrieved June 2007 from http://www.iteaconnect.org/TAA/Publications/TAA_Publications.html

Kamal, K. (2008). *Embedded Systems: Architecture, Programming, and Design* (p. 633). New York, NY: McGraw-Hill.

Kinsner, W. (1985, July), *Computer-Aided Engineering of Printed Circuit Bords*. Technical Report DEL85-1. Winnipeg, MB: Microelectronics Centre and Department of Electrical and Computer Engineering, University of Manitoba, (p. 171).

Kinsner, W. (2005). Signal processing for autonomic computing. In *Proc. 2005 Meet. Can. Applied & Industrial Math Soc.*, CAIMS 2005 (Winnipeg, MB; June 16-18, 2005). Retrieved May 2006 from http://www.umanitoba.ca/institutes/iims/caims2005_theme_signal.shtml

Kinsner, W. (2007a). Towards cognitive machines: Multiscale measures and analysis. *International Journal of Cognitive Informatics and Natural Intelligence, 1*(1), 28–38. doi:10.4018/jcini.2007010102

Kinsner, W. (2007b). Challenges in the design of daptive, intelligent, and cognitive systems. In *Proc. 3rd IEEE Intern. Conf. on Cognitive Informatics*, ICCI07, (Lake Tahoe, CA; 6-8 August 2007) ISBN 1-4244-1327-3, (pp. 13-24).

Klivington, K. (1989). *The Science of Mind* (p. 239). Cambridge, MA: MIT Press.

Koen, B. V. (2003). *Discussion of the Method: Conducting the Engineer's Approach to Problem Solving* (p. 260). Oxford, UK: Oxford University Press.

Kurzweil, R. (1990). *The Age of Intelligent Machines* (p. 565). Cambridge, MA: MIT Press.

Labrosse, J. J. (2000). *Embedded Systems Building Blocks: Complete and Ready-to-Use Modules in C* (2nd ed., p. 611). Lawrence, KS: CMP Books.

Leonhard, (1995, December). Leonhard Center for the Advancement of Engineering Education, "World-class engineer," *Report*, The Pennsylvania State University. Retrieved June 2007 from http://www.engr.psu.edu/AboutCOE/worldclass.asp

Mallat, S. (1998). *A Wavelet Tour of Signal Processing* (p. 577). San Diego, CA: Academic Press.

Mann, S. (2001). Humanistic intelligence: WearComp as a new framework and application for intelligent signal processing. In Haykin, S., & Kosko, B. (Eds.), *Intelligent Signal Processing* (pp. 1–39). New York, NY: Wiley-IEEE. doi:10.1109/5.726784

Mann, S. (2002). *Intelligent Image Processing* (p. 342). New York, NY: Wiley/IEEE.

McConnell, S. (1996). *Rapid Development: Taming Wild Software Schedules* (p. 680). Bellevue, WA: Microsoft Press.

McConnell, S. (2006). *Software Estimation: Demistifying the Black Art* (p. 308). Bellevue, WA: Microsoft Press.

Minsky, M. (1986). *The Society of Mind* (p. 339). New York, NY: Touchstone.

Navabi, Z. (1999). *Verilog Digital System Design* (p. 453). New York, NY: McGraw Hill.

Nielsen, M. A., & Chuang, I. L. (2000). *Quantum Computation and Quantum Information* (p. 676). Cambridge, UK: Cambridge Univ. Press.

Palnitkar, S. (1996). *Verilog HDL: A Guide to Digital Design and Synthesis* (p. 396). Mountain View, CA: Sun Soft Press / Prentice Hall.

Parnas, D. L., & Clements, P. C. (2001). A rational design process: How and why to fake it. In Hoffman, D. M., & Weiss, D. M. (Eds.), *Collected Papers by David L. Parnas* (pp. 352–368). Upper Saddle River, NJ: Addison-Wesley.

Parsell, M. (2005, March). Review of P.O. Haikonen, The Cognitive Approach to Consious Machines. *Psyche, 11*(2) 1-6. Retrieved May 2006 from http://psyche.cs.monash.edu.au/book_reviews/haikonen/haikone.pdf

Pedrycz, W., & Gomide, F. (1998). *An Introduction to Fuzzy Sets: Analysis and Design* (p. 465). Cambridge, MA: MIT Press.

Penrose, R. (1989). *The Emperor's New Mind* (p. 480). Oxford, UK: Oxford Univ. Press.

Penrose, R. (1994). *The Shadows of the Mind: A Search for the Missing Science of Consciousness* (p. 457). Oxford, UK: Oxford Univ. Press.

Posner, M. (1989) (Ed.). *Foundations of Cognitive Science*. Cambridge, MA: MIT Press, (p. 888).

Royce, W. W. (1970). Managing the development of large software systems: Concepts and techniques," *1970 WESCON Technical Papers*, (Western Electronics Show and Convention; Los Angeles; August 1970) pp. A/1-1 to A/1-9. Reprinted in *Proc of the IEEE 11th International Conference on Software Engineering* (Pittsburg, PA; May 1989) (pp. 328-338).

Ruaro, M. E., Bonifazi, P., & Torre, V. (2005, March). Toward the neurocomputer: Image processing and pattern recognition with neuronal cultures. *IEEE Transactions on Bio-Medical Engineering, 52*(3), 371–383. doi:10.1109/TBME.2004.842975

Rumelhart, D. E., & McClelland, J. L. (1986). *Parallel Distributed Processing*. Vols. 1 and 2. Cambridge, MA: MIT Press, (p. 547; 611).

Schach, S. R. (1999). *Classical and Object-Oriented Software Engineering with UML and Java* (4th ed., p. 616). New York, NY: McGraw Hill.

Searle, J. R. (1980). Minds, brains and programs. *The Behavioral and Brain Sciences, 3*, 417–424. doi:10.1017/S0140525X00005756

Searle, J. R. (1992). *The Rediscovery of the Mind* (p. 288). Cambridge, MA: MIT Press.

Sienko, T., Adamatzky, A., Rambidi, N. G., & Conrad, M. (2003). *Molecular Computing* (p. 257). Cambridge, MA: MIT Press.

Smith, D. J. (1996). *HDL Chip Design* (p. 448). Madison, AL: Doone Publications.

Soloman, S. (1999). *Sensor Handbook* (p. 1486). New York, NY: McGraw-Hill.

Sommerville, I. (2006). *Software Engineering* (8th ed., p. 864). Reading, MA: Addison-Wesley.

Taylor, J. G. (2003, June 20-24). The CODAM model of attention and consciousness. In *Proc. Intern. Joint Conf. Neural Networks*, IJCNN03 Portland, *OR, 1*, 292–297.

Thomas, D. D., & Moorby, P. R. (1998). *The Verilog Hardware Description Language* (4th ed., p. 354). Boston, MA: Kluwer.

Vahid, F., & Givargis, T. (2002). *Embedded System Design: A Unified Hardware/Software Introduction* (p. 324). New York, NY: Wiley.

Valvano, J. W. (2000). *Embedded Microcomputer Systems: Real-Time Interfacing* (p. 839). Pacific Grove, CA: Brooks/Cole.

von Neumann, J. (1958). *The Computer and the Brain* (p. 82). New Haven, CT: Yale Univ. Press.

Wang, Y. (2002, October). The real-time process algebra (RTPA), *Intern. J. of Annals of Software Engineering, 14*, 235–274. doi:10.1023/A:1020561826073

Wang, Y. (2003). Cognitive informatics models of software agent systems and autonomic computing: Keynote Speech. In *Proc. Intern. Conf. Agent-Based Technologies and Systems (ATS'03)*, U of C Press, Calgary, Canada, August, (p. 25).

Wang, Y. (2004). On autonomic computing and cognitive processes: Keynote speech. In *Proc. 3rd IEEE Intern. Conf. on Cognitive Informatics, ICCI04*, (Victoria, BC; 16-17 August 2004) ISBN 0-7695-2190-8, (pp. 3-4).

Wang, Y. (2006). Cognitive Informatics - Towards the future generation computers that think and feel: Keynote speech. In *Proc. 5th IEEE Intern. Conf. Cognitive Informatics*, ICCI06, (Beijing, China; July 17-19, 2006) ISBN 1-4244-0475-4, (pp. 3-7).

Weeks, M. (2007). *Digital Signal Processing Using Matlab and Wavelets* (p. 452). Hingham, MA: Infinity Science press LLC.

Wolf, W. (2002). *Modern VLSI Design: Systems-on-Chip Design* (3rd ed., p. 640). Upper Saddle River, NJ: Prentice Hall.

Zak, S. H. (2003). *Systems and Control* (p. 704). Oxford, UK: Oxford University Press.

This work was previously published in International Journal of Software Science and Computational Intelligence, Volume 1, Issue 3, edited by Yingxu Wang, pp. 16-35, copyright 2009 by IGI Publishing (an imprint of IGI Global).

Chapter 5
On Visual Semantic Algebra (VSA):
A Denotational Mathematical Structure for Modeling and Manipulating Visual Objects and Patterns

Yingxu Wang
University of Calgary, Canada

ABSTRACT

A new form of denotational mathematics known as Visual Semantic Algebra (VSA) is presented for abstract visual object and architecture manipulations. A set of cognitive theories for pattern recognition is explored such as cognitive principles of visual perception and basic mechanisms of object and pattern recognition. The cognitive process of pattern recognition is rigorously modeled using VSA and Real-Time Process Algebra (RTPA), which reveals the fundamental mechanisms of natural pattern recognition by the brain. Case studies on VSA in pattern recognition are presented to demonstrate VAS' expressive power for algebraic manipulations of visual objects. VSA can be applied not only in machinable visual and spatial reasoning, but also in computational intelligence as a powerful man-machine language for representing and manipulating visual objects and patterns. On the basis of VSA, computational intelligent systems such as robots and cognitive computers may process and inference visual and image objects rigorously and efficiently.

INTRODUCTION[1]

Pattern recognition is a fundamental cognitive process of the brain at the higher-cognition layer according to the Layered Reference Model of the Brain (LRMB) (Wang et al., 2006). The human

natural intelligence on visual object recognition, comprehension, and processing is highly dependent on the mechanisms of pattern recognition (Biedeman, 1987; Coaen et al., 1994; Gray, 1994; Kanizsa, 1979; Marr, 1982; Payne and Wenger, 1998; Western, 1999; Wilson and Keil, 2001; Wang, 2009a). However, there is a lack of studies on the cognitive mechanisms of pattern recogni-

DOI: 10.4018/978-1-4666-0261-8.ch005

tion, particularly how the natural intelligence processes visual objects and patterns (Wang, 2008d), as well as their *denotational mathematical models* (Wang, 2008a, 2008b).

The *gestalt (holistic) principles* of visual perception were developed in Germany based on experiments conducted in the 1920s and 1930s (Gray, 1994; Westen, 1999). Five gestalt principles for object and pattern perception were elicited (Kanizsa, 1979), such as *similarity, proximity, good continuation, simplicity, closure,* and *background contrast*. The gestalt principles reveal a set of important natural tendencies of human visual perception. Another set of seven cognitive informatics principles of visual object perception is identified in (Wang, 2009c) known as *association, symmetry, perfection, abstraction, categorization, analysis,* and *appreciation*, which are used in perception and identification of human figures, physical objects, abstract structure, mathematics entities, and nature.

A variety of theories and approaches are proposed for visual object and pattern recognition. Marr proposed a method for object recognition in the algorithmic approach known as the *computational method* (Marr, 1982). Biederman developed a method for object recognition in the analytic approach called *recognition by components* (Biedeman, 1987). Various methods and technologies are developed for pattern recognition in the fields of cognitive psychology (payne and Wenger, 1998; Reed, 1972; Wilson and Keil, 2001), computer science (Bender, 2000; bow, 1992; Miclet, 1986; Storer, 2002), and robotics (Horn, 1986; Murry et al., 1993). Wang presents a cognitive theory of visual information processing as well as the unified framework of human visual processing systems (Wang, 2009c) in the development of cognitive informatics – a formal theory for explaining the natural and computational intelligence (Wang, 2002a, 2003, 2007b; Wang and Kinsner, 2006; Wang et al., 2002, 2008b, 2009a, 2009b). A set of denotational mathematics (Wang, 2006, 2008a), such as concept algebra (Wang, 2008c),

system algebra (Wang, 2008d), Real-Time Process Algebra (RTPA) (Wang, 2002b, 2007a, 2008b), and granular algebra (Wang, 2009d), are created in order to rigorously manipulate complex mental processes and computational intelligence.

This paper presents the cognitive process of pattern recognition and the denotational mathematical means known as Visual Semantic Algebra (VSA). The cognitive informatics theories for pattern recognition are explored such as cognitive principles of visual perception and basic mechanisms of object and pattern recognition. A generic denotational mathematical means, VSA, is developed to manipulate basic geometric shapes and figures, as well as their compositions by a set of algebraic operations. A number of case studies are provided to explain the expressive power of VSA and its applications.

COGNITIVE INFORMATICS THEORIES FOR PATTERN RECOGNITION

It is recognized that the brain tends to perform inference and reasoning using abstract semantic objects rather than direct visual (diagram-based) objects (Coaen et al., 1994; Wang, 2009c). This is evidenced by that the brain cannot carry out concrete image inference in Short-Term Memory (STM) without looking at them in external media such as figures or pictures on paper, because this cognitive process requires too large memory beyond the capacity of STM in the brain

Basic Mechanisms of Object Recognition

Definition 1. *Object recognition is a special type of pattern recognition where the patterns are frequently used 2-D shapes, 3-D solid figures, and their compositions.*

A number of cognitive tendencies of the brain are identified in visual objects recognition, such as:

- The tendency to go beyond the obtained information by subjective perception.
- The tendency to derive a whole picture from partially given information.
- The tendency to reduce complex visual objects to simple and basic ones by decomposition.
- The tendency to use abstract semantic objects to represent real-world visual entities, particularly their basic and common components.

The Algorithmic Method

Marr proposed a method for object recognition in the algorithmic approach known as the *computational method* [Marr, 1982], which develops a set of mathematical algorithms to model how the perceptual intelligence identifies objects based on the sensational information.

The algorithmic method represents image object information in three types called the primal, the 2.5-D and the 3-D sketches: a) The *primal sketch* is a 2-D representation of an object in the retina, in which the information of contours, edges, and blobs/closures may be elicited; b) The *2.5-D sketch* is the additional information about depth, orientation, binocular disparity, texture, motion, and shading, which can be derived based on the primal sketch; and c) The 3-D sketch is reconstructed internal image representation of the external object such as its shape and spatial positions.

The Component Analysis Method

Biederman develop a method for object recognition in the component analysis approach called *recognition by components* (Biederman, 1987). The method states that objects can be decomposed into a relatively small set of basic components

and then the whole object can be denoted by the relations of these basic components.

The component analysis method introduces the notion of basic features of images known as the *nonaccidental properties* such as colinearity, curvilinearity, symmetry, parallel curves, vertices in both 2-D plane and 3-D space. Biederman identified 36 geometrical ions, shortly called *geons*, which are common 3-D solids such as cubs, cylinders, cones, and wedges (Biederman, 1987). Each geon can be discriminated by the given set of nonaccidental properties. It is assumed that if all geons may be identified in a given object, then the object can be described by the spatial relations of these interconnected common components.

Pattern Recognition

Definition 2. *Pattern recognition is a higher cognitive process of the brain that identifies an object or a composition of multiple objects, and denotes it by an internal concept and structure.*

Object and word recognition are typical recognition process related to knowledge representation, learning, perception, and memory. One of the major problems that must be solved in visual object recognition is the building of a representation of visual information, which allows recognition to occur relatively independently of size, contrast, spatial frequency, position on the retina, and angle of view, etc.

Various methods and technologies are proposed for pattern recognition (Bender, 2000; Bow, 1992; Horn, 1986; Miclet, 1986; Murry et al., 1993; Payne and Wenger, 1998; Reed, 1972; Wang, 2009c; Wilson and Keil, 2001). The basic approaches to pattern recognition are *holism* and *analytism*. The former treats a given pattern as a whole and tries to recognize by holistic matches; while the latter deals with common features and attributes of a set of given patterns and relates a certain set of features to the recognition of a particular pattern. The holistic approach to pattern recognition may be used for small sets and most frequently needed patterns and objects, which are aurally wired in a perceptual layer of the brain. The analytic approach to pattern recognition is more suitable and generic to non-common and contingent patterns and objects, particularly for machine recognition, where more efficient and adaptive methods are required under various constraints. In complex situations, the combinations of both approaches may result in more powerful solutions.

The following subsections describe two paradigms of the holistic and analytic approaches to pattern recognition. They are Neisser's template matching method (Neisser, 1967) and Wang's feature analysis method (Wang, 2008e).

The Template Matching Method

Definition 3. *The template matching method is a holistic comparison method in pattern recognition, which compares an image of stimulus with a set of pre-established images known as the templates in memory. The most matched template is the result of recognition.*

Neisser proposed the template matching method in 1967 (Neisser, 1967) for pattern recognition, where an image of stimulus in STM is directly compared with the pre-established images or patterns in Long-Term Memory (LTM) known as the templates in order to find the most matched pairs. The advances of the template matching method in pattern recognition are its simplicity and intuition for regularly appearing objects. However, the method is not adaptive and flexible to process varying objects in terms of positions, sizes, and orientations.

The Feature Analysis Method

Definition 4. *The feature analysis method is a characteristic attribute recognition method in pattern recognition, which first identifies the* *elementary features of a pattern by analysis, then synthesizes all identified features in order to reconstruct the pattern internally.*

The first feature analysis method was proposed by Selfridge in 1959 called the *pandemonium model* (Selfridge, 1959). In Selfridge's model for letter recognition, pattern recognition is divided into two stages known as feature analysis and cognitive decision. One of the advantages of the feature analysis method is its flexibility and adaptability that it can deal with all the difficulties found in the template matching method as described in preceding subsection. It also enables more efficient pattern recognition for complex objects and systems that share a set of elementary features at a lower level. Considering that there are always fewer common features than their compositions in various patterns, the feature analysis method is more adaptive and powerful in pattern recognition.

The feature analysis method takes an analysis-synthesis approach (Wang, 2008e). Its central idea is both the identification of all elementary features of a set of potential forms of patterns and the synthetic relations that demonstrated how each recognized pattern related to a certain set of predefined features. A feature analysis model for electronic digits recognition is shown in Figure 1. In this model, the features of all ten digits are identified by the set of attributes of the 7-segments in different places of the entire pattern. The synthetic relations between the cognitive results and the features are represented by the ten sets of links, which uniquely determine a specific cognition result in an applied digit pattern recognition.

VISUAL SEMANTIC ALGEBRA

The *physical space* can be formally modeled by *Euclidean space* that is a collection of the set of all abstract points in the three coordinates. Therefore, the spatial properties of abstract objects, shapes, and their interrelations can be formally studied by

Figure 1. Illustration of the feature analysis method

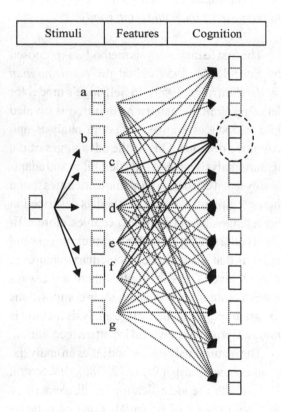

Euclidean geometry, which can be classified into *plane geometry* and *solid geometry*. The former studies the geometric figures in a plane; while the latter studies the geometric objects known as solids in the three-dimensional space. The advanced 4-D space-time model may be referred to (Minkowski, 1908; Einstein, 1995; Wang, 2009b).

In order to efficiently model the abstract visual objects, their semantic representations, and their rigorous compositions and manipulations, a new denotational mathematics known as Visual Semantic Algebra (VSA) is introduced in this section for pattern recognition and processing.

Definition 5. *Visual Semantic Algebra (VSA) is a denotational mathematical structure that formally manipulates visual objects by algebraic operations*

on symbolic or semantic objects in geometric analyses and compositions, i.e.:

$$VSA \triangleq (O, \bullet_{VSA}) \tag{1}$$

where O is a finite set of basic abstract visual objects and $\bullet_{VSA}$ is a finite set of algebraic operations on O.

The following subsections extend the algebraic system of VSA into detailed definitions and mathematical models.

Basic Abstract Visual Objects in VSA

The basic geometric shapes (2-D) and solids (3-D), known collectively *geons*, have been studies in cognitive psychology (Biedeman, 1987), computational intelligence, and robotics (Horn, 1986; Murry et al., 1993).

A set of 26 typical visual semantic objects are summarized in Figure 2 in four categories known as those of *plane geometry, solid geometry, generic figures,* and *abstract spatial limits*. In Figure 2, each abstract visual object is rigorously defined as given in the corresponding mathematical model.

Definition 6. *The abstract visual objects O, or geons, in VSA are set of 26 basic 2-D shapes H, 3-D solids S, generic figures F, and abstract spatial limits L as summarized in Figure 2, i.e.:*

$$O \triangleq \{H \cup S \cup F \cup L\} \tag{2}$$

where the four categories of abstract objects can be identified as follows, respectively:

$$H \triangleq \{\bullet, -, \angle, \frown, \triangle, \square, \square, \square, \Diamond, \bigcirc, \bigcirc\} \tag{3}$$

$$S \triangleq \{C_u, R_s, C_y, S_p, C_o, P_y\} \tag{4}$$

Figure 2. The Abstract Visual Objects in VSA

No.	Category	Basic Geon	Symbol	Mathematical model
1	Plane geometry (H)	Point	·	$\cdot \triangleq (x, y)$
2		Line	—	$- \triangleq ((x_1, y_1), (x_2, y_2)), \; l = \sqrt{(x_2 - x_1)^2 + (y_2 - y_1)^2}$
3		Angle	∠	$\angle \triangleq (((x_1, y_1), (x_2, y_2)), ((x_1, y_1), (x_3, y_3)))$
4		Arc	⌒	$\frown \triangleq ((x, y), r, \alpha_1, \alpha_2)$
5		Triangle	△	$\triangle \triangleq ((x_1, y_1), (x_2, y_2), (x_3, y_3))$
6		Square	□	$\square \triangleq ((x_1, y_1), (x_2, y_2), (x_3, y_3), (x_4, y_4)), \; |x_2 - x_1| = |y_2 - y_1|, \; \alpha_1 = \alpha_2 = 90°$
7		Rectangle	▭	$\square \triangleq ((x_1, y_1), (x_2, y_2), (x_3, y_3), (x_4, y_4)), \; |x_2 - x_1| \neq |y_2 - y_1|, \; \alpha_1 = \alpha_2 = 90°$
8		Parallelogram	▱	$\square \triangleq ((x_1, y_1), (x_2, y_2), (x_3, y_3), (x_4, y_4)), \; |x_2 - x_1| \neq |y_2 - y_1|, \; \alpha_1 \neq \alpha_2$
9		Rhomb	◇	$\diamondsuit \triangleq ((x_1, y_1), (x_2, y_2), (x_3, y_3), (x_4, y_4)), \; |x_2 - x_1| \neq |y_2 - y_1|, \; \alpha_1 \neq \alpha_2$
10		Circle	○	$\bigcirc \triangleq ((x_0, y_0), r)$
11		Ellipse	⬭	$\bigcirc \triangleq ((x_1, y_1), (x_2, y_2), r_x, r_y), \; |x_1| \; = \; |x_2| \; = \sqrt{r_x^2 - r_y^2}$
12	Solid geometry (S)	Cube		$C_u \triangleq ((x_1, y_1, z_1), (x_1, y_1, z_2), (x_1, y_2, z_1), (x_1, y_2, z_2), (x_2, y_1, z_1), (x_2, y_1, z_2), (x_2, y_2, z_1), (x_2, y_2, z_2)), \; |x_2 - x_1| = |y_2 - y_1| = |z_2 - z_1|, \; \alpha_1 = \alpha_2 = \alpha_3 = 90°$
13		Rectangular solid		$R_s \triangleq ((x_1, y_1, z_1), (x_1, y_1, z_2), (x_1, y_2, z_1), (x_1, y_2, z_2), (x_2, y_1, z_1), (x_2, y_1, z_2), (x_2, y_2, z_1), (x_2, y_2, z_2)), \; |x_2 - x_1| \neq |y_2 - y_1| \neq |z_2 - z_1|, \; \alpha_1 = \alpha_2 = \alpha_3 = 90°$
14		Cylinder		$C_y \triangleq ((x_1, y_1, z_1), (x_2, y_2, z_2), r, h), \; h = |z_2 - z_1|$
15		Sphere		$S_p \triangleq ((x_0, y_0, z_0), r), \; \sqrt{(x - x_0)^2 + (y - y_0)^2 + (z - z_0)^2} \equiv r$
16		Cone		$C_o \triangleq ((x_0, y_0, z_0), (x_v, y_v, z_v), r, h), \; h = |z_v - z_0|,$ $\sqrt{(x - x_0)^2 + (y - y_0)^2} \equiv r, \; z_0 = 0$
17		Pyramid		$P_y \triangleq ((x_1, y_1, z_1), (x_2, y_2, z_2), (x_3, y_3, z_3), (x_4, y_4, z_4), (x_v, y_v, z_v), h), \; h = |z_v - z_0|$
18	Generic figures (F)	Abstract human	♀	$\dagger \triangleq (x, y, z, t), \; t$ denotes time in the space-time model
19		Abstract system/machine	§	$\S \triangleq (x, y, z, t)$
20		Abstract object	⊕	$\oplus \triangleq (x, y, z)$
21	Abstract spatial limits (L)	Ceiling	⊤	$\top \triangleq (x, y, z_{max}, t)$
22		Bottom (Ground)	⊥	$\perp \triangleq (x, y, z_{min}, t)$
23		Left limit	⊢	$\vdash \triangleq (x_{min}, y, z, t)$
24		Right limit	⊣	$\dashv \triangleq (x_{max}, y, z, t)$
25		Back limit	[	$[\triangleq (x, y_{min}, z, t)$
26		Front limit	]	$] \triangleq (x, y_{max}, z, t)$

$$F \triangleq \{ \maltese, \S, \oplus \} \tag{5}$$

$$L \triangleq \{ \top, \bot, \vdash, \dashv, [\![,]\!] \} \tag{6}$$

Algebraic Operations on the Basic Abstract Visual Objects in VSA

A set of 13 algebraic operations, as described in Table 1, is elicited from relational compositions of the 26 abstract visual objects. In Table 1, any 2-D or 3-D geometric structure can be analyzed or composed semantically using VSA.

Definition 7. *The algebraic operations,* $\bullet_{VSA}$, *in VSA are a set of 13 fundamental relational operations on the basic abstract visual objects O as summarized in Table 1, i.e.:*

$$\bullet_{VSA} \triangleq \{ \uparrow, \downarrow, \leftarrow, \rightarrow, \odot, \otimes, \boxplus, \angle, @(p), @(x,y,x), \frown, \mapsto, \underset{i\mathbf{N}=0}{\overset{n-1\mathbf{N}}{R}}(A_i \mapsto A_{i+1}) \} \tag{7}$$

APPLICATIONS OF VSA

VSA provides a neat and powerful algebraic system for rigorously manipulating visual objects and patterns. Any 2-D or 3-D visual structure or system can be analyzed or composed using VSA. A set of case studies on applications of VSA is presented below.

Example 1. *The visual pattern of the solid structures of A and B as given in Figure 3 can be expressed in VSA as follows:*

$$A \triangleq C_o \uparrow C_y \uparrow @(center)R_s \uparrow\bot \tag{8}$$

Table 1. Algebraic Operations on Abstract Visual Objects in VSA

Relational operations	Symbol	Description	Example
Above	$\uparrow$	$S_1 \uparrow S_2$	S_1 is above S_2.
Below	$\downarrow$	$S_1 \downarrow S_2$	S_1 is below S_2.
Left	$\leftarrow$	$S_1 \leftarrow S_2$	S_1 is on the left of S_2.
Right	$\rightarrow$	$S_1 \rightarrow S_2$	S_1 is on the right of S_2.
Front	e	S_1 e S_2	S_1 is in front of S_2.
Behind	$\otimes$	$S_1 \otimes S_2$	S_1 is behind S_2.
Inside	(	$S_1 (S_2$	S_1 is inside S_2.
Angle	$R(x°)$	$S_1 R(x°) S_2$	S_1 is at an $x°$ angle position related to S_2 ($0°$ is defined at the right position).
Relative position	$@(p)$	$S @(p)$	S is allocated at the position p.
Absolute position	$@(x, y, z)$	$S @(x,y,z)$	S is allocated at the position (x, y, z).
Move	Đ	$S @(p_1)$ Đ $@(p_2)$	S moves from position p_1 to p_2.
Action (Sequential)	a	$S: (Act_1$ a $Act_2)$	S executes $action_1$ then $action_2$.
Action (Repetitive)	$\underset{i\mathbf{N}=0}{\overset{n-1\mathbf{N}}{R}}(A_i \mapsto A_{i+1})$	$S : \underset{i\mathbf{N}=0}{\overset{n-1\mathbf{N}}{R}}(A_i \mapsto A_{i+1})$	S executes a set of actions, A_i, $0 \le i \le n$, in a sequence.

Figure 3. Compositions of solids in VSA

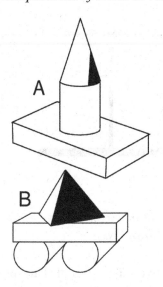

Figure 4. The desk D with five components in VSA

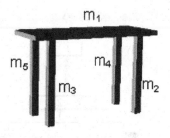

Figure 5. The thermobottle TB with three components in VSA

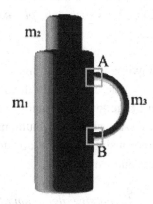

$$B \triangleq P_y \uparrow @(center)\ R_s \uparrow (C_{y1} \leftarrow C_{y2}) \uparrow \perp \tag{9}$$

where $(o) \uparrow \perp$ denotes that the object o is on the top of the ground.

Example 2. *The visual structure of a desk D as given in Figure 4 can be described in VSA as follows:*

$$D \triangleq m_1 \uparrow ((m_3\ @(LL) \odot m_5\ @(UL)) \leftarrow (m_2\ @(LR) \odot m_4\ @(UR))) \uparrow \perp \tag{10}$$

where *LL, UL, LR,* and *UR* denote the lower-left, upper-left, lower-right, and upper-right corners of m_1.

Example 3. *The visual structures of a thermobottle TB as given in Figure 5 can be described in VSA as follows:*

$$TB \triangleq m_2 \uparrow (m_1 \leftarrow @(A \wedge B)\ m_3) \uparrow \perp \tag{11}$$

where $@(A \wedge B)$ indicates the joint points between m_1 and m_3. More rigorous positions may be denoted by absolute positions with 2-D/3-D coordinates.

The *tower of Hanoi* is a well known game as described below, which may be adopted to test human's or robot's ability for complex visual object processing (Reed, 1972).

Example 4. *The layout of the tower of Hanoi, as shown in Figure 6, consists of three pegs A, B, and C, and a number of n disks of different sizes with sequential numbers from the top down, which can slide onto any peg. The initial state is set that all disks are neatly stacked on A in order of size with the smallest at the top. The objective of the game is to move the entire stack to another peg, say C, constrained by the following rules: a) Only one disk may be moved at any time; b) Each*

Figure 6. The Tower of Hanoi modeled in VSA

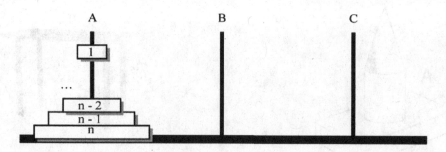

move may only slide a top disk from one peg onto another; and c) No disk may be placed on top of a smaller one.

The following two algorithms contrast the classic and VSA descriptions of the solutions to the problem of the tower of Hanoi. It is demonstrated that VSA enables both humans and machines to rigorously recognize and manipulate visual objects and patterns.

Algorithm 1. *A recursive algorithm of the tower of Hanoi enhanced from (Reed, 1972) can be described in RTPA as given in Figure 7. The time*

complexity of the algorithm is $O(2^n-1)$, where n is the number of disks.

Alternatively, the tower of Hanoi problem can be described in VSA from the point of view for visual object processing for a human or robot.

Algorithm 2. *The algorithm of the tower of Hanoi can be described in VSA as shown in Figure 8, where it encompasses the architecture (such as its layout, initial and final states), and behaviors (TOH).*

Figure 8 demonstrates how a robot handles the tower of Hanoi problem as a visual object and

Figure 7. The algorithm of the tower of Hanoi in RTPA

Algorithm 1. The Tower of Hanoi (recursive)

$TOH(n\mathbf{N}, A\mathbf{ST}, B\mathbf{ST}, C\mathbf{ST}) \triangleq$
{
$$\underset{n\mathbf{N}>0}{\overset{n\mathbf{N}=0}{R}} (\quad X\mathbf{ST} := A\mathbf{ST}$$

$\rightarrow Y\mathbf{ST} := B\mathbf{ST}$

$\rightarrow Z\mathbf{ST} := C\mathbf{ST}$

$\rightarrow TOH(n\mathbf{N}-1, X\mathbf{ST}, Y\mathbf{ST}, Z\mathbf{ST})$

$\rightarrow Move\ (d_n, X\mathbf{ST}, Z\mathbf{ST})$ // Slide disk n from peg X to Z

$\rightarrow \downarrow(n\mathbf{N})$

$\rightarrow A\mathbf{ST} := Y\mathbf{ST}$

$\rightarrow B\mathbf{ST} := X\mathbf{ST}$

)
}

pattern recognition problem using VAS. According to Algorithm 2, the robot is capable not only to carry out the behaviors for problem solving, but also to denote and recognize the architectural layout of the problem as a concrete visual pattern.

Example 5. *A more complex case is that a robot walks done stairs, as shown in Figure 9, which*

can *be formally described in VSA. The visual walk planning mechanisms and processes can be described by the walking down stairs (WDS) algorithm as given in Figure 10.*

Algorithm 3. *The algorithm of WDS algorithm can be described in VSA as shown in Figure 10. The WDS_Algorithm encompasses the architecture WDS_Architecture§, the robot behaviors*

Figure 8. The algorithm of the tower of Hanoi in VSA

```
Algorithm 2. The Tower of Hanoi (VSA)

TOH_Algorithm (nN, AST, BST, CST) ≜ ↑        §
§ TOH_Architecture (nN, AST, BST, CST) ≜
  { // Layout
      Pegs:  (AST ← BST ← CST) ↑
      Disks: (d₁↑ d₂↑ ... dₙ↑ )
   // Initial state
      (  (d₁↑ d₂↑ ... dₙ↑ ) @AST
      ‖ ∅ ↑   @BST
      ‖ ∅ ↑   @CST
      )
   // Final state
      (  ∅ ↑   @AST
      ‖ ∅ ↑   @BST
      ‖ (d₁↑ d₂↑ ... dₙ↑ ) @CST
      )
  }

↑ TOH_Behavior ≜ TOH(nN, AST, BST, CST) ::
  {
     nN = 0
    R  (  XST := AST
     nN > 0
          → YST := BST
          → ZST := CST
          → TOH(nN -1, XST, YST, ZST)
          → dₙ@XST ↷ @ZST        // Move disk n from peg X to Z
          → nN := nN +1
          → AST := YST
          → BST := XST
       )
  }
```

Figure 9. A robot walks down stairs (Honda ASIMO, from Wikipedia)

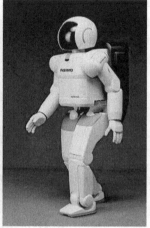

Figure 10. The algorithm of WDS in VSA

Algorithm 3. A Robot Walks Down Stairs

WDS_Algorithm $\triangleq$ **WDS_Architecture**§   **WDS_Behavior** ⭡

WDS_Architecture§ (n**N**) $\triangleq$
{ // Layout
   Stairs**ST** : $(S_0$**ST** $\odot\uparrow$ $(S_1$**ST** $\odot\uparrow$ $(S_2$**ST** $\odot\uparrow$ $(\dots$ $(S_{n-1}$**ST** $\odot\uparrow$ $)\dots))))$
 // Robot
   Robot ⭡ : (LeftFoot**ST** ‖ RightFoot**ST**)
 // Initial state
   Robot ⭡ @ ($\vdash$ Stairs**ST**.S_0**ST** $\dashv$)
 // Final state
   Robot ⭡ @ ($\vdash$ Stairs**ST**. $\dashv$)
}

WDS_Behavior ⭡ $\triangleq$ **WDS**(Robot ⭡, **WDS_Architecture**§, n**N**) ::
  {
    $\overset{n-1\mathbf{N}}{\underset{i\mathbf{N}=0}{R}}$ (Robot ⭡ .LeftFoot**ST** $\curvearrowright\otimes$ @(Stairs**ST**.$S_{i\mathbf{N}+1}$**ST**)

            $\mapsto$ Robot ⭡ .RightFoot**ST** $\curvearrowright\otimes$ @(Stairs**ST**.$S_{i\mathbf{N}+1}$**ST**
)
    $\mapsto$ Robot ⭡ .LeftFoot**ST** $\curvearrowright\otimes$ @(Stairs**ST**.)
    $\mapsto$ Robot ⭡ .RightFoot**ST** $\curvearrowright\otimes$ @(Stairs**ST**.)
  }

WDS_Behaviors ✝ *, and their interactions. WDS_ Architecture§ describes the layout, initial and final states of the system. WDS_Behaviors* ✝ *describes the actions of the robot based on its visual interpretation about the stairs' visual structures.*

The theory and case studies presented in this section demonstrate that VSA provides a new paradigm of denotational mathematical means for relational visual object manipulation. VSA can be applied not only in machine visual and spatial reasoning, but also in computational intelligence system designs as a powerful man-machine language in representing and dealing with the high-level inferences in complex visual patterns and systems. On the basis of VSA, computational intelligence systems such as robots and cognitive computers can process and reason visual and image objects and their spatial relations rigorously and efficiently at conceptual level.

CONCLUSION

This paper has introduced Visual Semantic Algebra (VSA) as a new structure of denotational mathematics for abstract visual object and architecture processing and comprehensions. Based on VSA and Real-Time Process Algebra (RTPA), the cognitive process of pattern recognition has been rigorously described. A set of cognitive theories for pattern recognition has been explored on the cognitive principles of visual perception and basic mechanisms of object/pattern recognition. VSA has provided a denotational mathematical means to manipulate basic geometric objects and visual semantic analyses/compositions by algebraic operations. A number of case studies on pattern representation and recognition have been presented to explain the expressive power of VSA.

The theory and case studies have demonstrated that VSA provides a new paradigm of denotational mathematical means for relational visual object

manipulation. SVA can be applied not only in machine visual and spatial reasoning, but also in computational intelligent system design as a powerful man-machine language in representing and dealing with visual inferences in complex geometrical and pattern systems. On the basis of VSA, computational intelligence systems such as robots and cognitive computers can process and inference visual and image objects rigorously and efficiently at the conceptual and semantic levels.

ACKNOWLEDGMENT

This work is partially sponsored by the Natural Sciences and Engineering Research Council of Canada (NSERC). The author would like to thank the anonymous reviewers for their valuable suggestions and comments on this work.

REFERENCES

Bender, E. A. (2000). *Mathematical Methods in Artificial Intelligence*. Los Alamitos, CA: IEEE CS Press.

Biedeman, I. (1987). Recognition-by-Components: A Theory of Human Image Understanding. *Psychological Review, 94*, 115–147. doi:10.1037/0033-295X.94.2.115

Bow, S. T. (1992). *Pattern Recognition and Image Preprocessing*. NY: Marcel Dekker.

Coaen, S., Ward, L. M., & Enns, J. T. (1994). *Sensation and Perception* (4th ed.). NY: Harcourt Brace College Pub.

Einstein, A. (1995). *Relativity: The Special and the General Theory*. (Reprint). Three Rivers Press.

Gray, P. (1994). *Psychology* (2nd ed.). New York: Worth Publishers, Inc.

Horn, B. K. P. (1986). *Robot Vision*. Cambridge, MA: MIT Press.

Kanizsa, G. (1979). *Organization in Vision: Essays on Gestalt Perception.* NY: Praeger.

Marr, D. (1982). *Vision.* San Francisco, CA: Freeman.

Miclet, L. (1986). *Structural Methods in Pattern Recognition.* London: North Oxford Academic.

Minkowski, H. (1908). *Space and Time.* Address, 80th Assembly of German Natural Scientists and Physicians, Cologne.

Murry, R. M., Li, Z., & Sastry, S. S. (1993). *A Mathematical Introduction to Robotic Manipulation.* Boca Raton, FL: CRC Press.

Neisser, U. (1967). *Cognitive Psychology.* Appleton, NY.

Payne, D. G., & Wenger, M. J. (1998). *Cognitive Psychology.* Boston: Houghton Mifflin Co.

Reed, S. (1972). Pattern Recognition and Categorization. *Cognitive Psychology, 3,* 383–407. doi:10.1016/0010-0285(72)90014-X

Selfridge, O. (1959). Pandemonium: A Paradigm for Learning. In *The Mechanization of Thought Processes.* London: H.M. Stationary Office.

Storer, J. A. (2002). *An Introduction to Data Structures and Algorithms.* Berlin: Springer.

Wang, Y. (2002a, August). Keynote: On Cognitive Informatics. *Proc. 1st IEEE International Conference on Cognitive Informatics* (ICCI'02) (pp. 34-42). Calgary, Canada: IEEE CS Press.

Wang, Y. (2002b). The Real-Time Process Algebra (RTPA). *Annals of Software Engineering: An International Journal, 14,* 235–274. doi:10.1023/A:1020561826073

Wang, Y. (2003, August). On Cognitive Informatics, *Brain and Mind: A Transdisciplinary Journal of Neuroscience and Neurophilosophy, 4*(3), 151-167. Kluwer Academic Publishers.

Wang, Y. (2006). Cognitive Informatics and Contemporary Mathematics for Knowledge Representation and Manipulation, Invited Plenary Talk. *Proc. 1st International Conference on Rough Set and Knowledge Technology (RSKT'06), LNAI 4062,* Springer, Chongqing, China, July, pp. 69-78.

Wang, Y. (2007a). *Software Engineering Foundations: A Software Science Perspective.* CRC Book Series in Software Engineering, Vol. II, Auerbach Publications, NY, USA.

Wang, Y. (2007b). The Theoretical Framework of Cognitive Informatics. *International Journal of Cognitive Informatics and Natural Intelligence, 1*(1), 1–27.

Wang, Y. (2007c). The OAR Model of Neural Informatics for Internal Knowledge Representation in the Brain. *International Journal of Cognitive Informatics and Natural Intelligence, 1*(3), 64–75.

Wang, Y. (2008a). On Contemporary Denotational Mathematics for Computational Intelligence. *Transactions of Computational Science, 2,* 6–29. doi:10.1007/978-3-540-87563-5_2

Wang, Y. (2008b). RTPA: A Denotational Mathematics for Manipulating Intelligent and Computational Behaviors. *International Journal of Cognitive Informatics and Natural Intelligence, 2*(2), 44–62.

Wang, Y. (2008c). On Concept Algebra: A Denotational Mathematical Structure for Knowledge and Software Modeling. *International Journal of Cognitive Informatics and Natural Intelligence, 2*(2), 1–19.

Wang, Y. (2008d). On System Algebra: A Denotational Mathematical Structure for Abstract System modeling. *International Journal of Cognitive Informatics and Natural Intelligence, 2*(2), 20–42.

Wang, Y. (2008e). The Cognitive Processes of Analysis and Synthesis in Formal Inference. *Proc. 7th IEEE International Conference on Cognitive Informatics* (ICCI'08). Stanford University, CA., USA, IEEE CS Press, August, pp. 223-231.

Wang, Y. (2009a). On Abstract Intelligence: Toward a Unified Theory of Natural, Artificial, Machinable, and Computational Intelligence. *International Journal of Software Science and Computational Intelligence*, *1*(1), 1–17.

Wang, Y. (2009b). Formal Descriptions of the Cognitive Processes of Spatiality, Time, and Motion Perceptions. *International Journal of Cognitive Informatics and Natural Intelligence*, *3*(2), 84–98.

Wang, Y. (2009c). (to appear). The Cognitive Informatics Theory and Mathematical Models of Visual Information Processing in the Brain. *International Journal of Cognitive Informatics and Natural Intelligence*, *3*(3).

Wang, Y. (2009d, June). Granular Algebra for Modeling Granular Systems and Granular Computing. *Proc. 8th IEEE International Conference on Cognitive Informatics* (ICCI'09). Hong Kong, IEEE CS Press.

Wang, Y., Johnston, R., & Smith, M. (Eds.). (2002, August). *Proc. 1st Int. Conf. of Cognitive Informatics* (ICCI'02)., Calgary, Canada: IEEE CS Press.

Wang, Y., & Kinsner, W. (2006). Recent Advances of Cognitive Informatics. *IEEE Transactions on Systems, Man, and Cybernetics*, *36*(2), 121–123. doi:10.1109/TSMCC.2006.871120

Wang, Y., Kinsner, W., Anderson, J. A., Zhang, D., Yao, Y., & Sheu, P. (2009b). A Doctrine of Cognitive Informatics. *Fundamenta Informaticae*, *90*(3), 203–228.

Wang, Y., Kinsner, W., & Zhang, D. (2009a). Contemporary Cybernetics and its Faces of Cognitive Informatics and Computational Intelligence. *IEEE Trans. on System, Man, and Cybernetics (B)*, *39*(4), 823–833. doi:10.1109/TSMCB.2009.2013721

Wang, Y., Wang, Y., Patel, S., & Patel, D. (2006). A Layered Reference Model of the Brain (LRMB). *IEEE Transactions on Systems, Man, and Cybernetics*, *36*(2), 124–133. doi:10.1109/TSMCC.2006.871126

Westen, D. (1999). *Psychology: Mind, Brain, and Culture* (2nd ed.). John Wiley & Sons, Inc.

Wilson, R. A., & Keil, F. C. (2001). *The MIT Encyclopedia of the Cognitive Sciences*. MIT Press.

This work was previously published in International Journal of Software Science and Computational Intelligence, Volume 1, Issue 1, edited by Yingxu Wang, pp. 1-28, copyright 2009 by IGI Publishing (an imprint of IGI Global).

Section 2
Cognitive Computing

Chapter 6
On Cognitive Computing

Yingxu Wang
University of Calgary, Canada

ABSTRACT

Inspired by the latest development in cognitive informatics and contemporary denotational mathematics, cognitive computing is an emerging paradigm of intelligent computing methodologies and systems, which implements computational intelligence by autonomous inferences and perceptions mimicking the mechanisms of the brain. This article presents a survey on the theoretical framework and architectural techniques of cognitive computing beyond conventional imperative and autonomic computing technologies. Theoretical foundations of cognitive computing are elaborated from the aspects of cognitive informatics, neural informatics, and denotational mathematics. Conceptual models of cognitive computing are explored on the basis of the latest advances in abstract intelligence and computational intelligence. Applications of cognitive computing are described from the aspects of autonomous agent systems and cognitive search engines, which demonstrate how machine and computational intelligence may be generated and implemented by cognitive computing theories and technologies toward autonomous knowledge processing.

INTRODUCTION

Computing as a discipline in a narrow sense, is an application of computers to solve a given computational problem by imperative instructions; while in a broad sense, it is a process to implement the instructive intelligence by a system that transfers a set of given information or instructions into expected behaviors.

According to theories of cognitive informatics (Wang, 2002a, 2003, 2006, 2007b, 2007c, 2008a, 2009a; Wang et al., 2009b), computing technologies and systems may be classified into the categories of imperative, autonomic, and cognitive from the bottom up. Imperative computing is a traditional and passive technology based

DOI: 10.4018/978-1-4666-0261-8.ch006

on stored-program controlled behaviors for data processing (Turing, 1950; von Neumann, 1946, 1958; Gersting, 1982; Mandrioli and Ghezzi, 1987; Lewis and Papadimitriou, 1998). An autonomic computing is goal-driven and self-decision-driven technologies that do not rely on instructive and procedural information (Kephart and Chess, 2003; IBM, 2006; Wang, 2004, 2007a). Cognitive computing is more intelligent technologies beyond imperative and autonomic computing, which embodies major natural intelligence behaviors of the brain such as thinking, inference, learning, and perceptions.

Definition 1. Cognitive computing is an emerging paradigm of intelligent computing methodologies and systems that implements computational intelligence by autonomous inferences and perceptions mimicking the mechanisms of the brain.

Cognitive computing systems are designed for cognitive and perceptive knowledge processing based on contemporary denotational mathematics (Zadeh, 1965; Wang, 2002b, 2007a, 2008b, 2008c, 2008d, 2008e; Wang et al, 2009a), which are centered by the parallel autonomous inference and perception mechanisms of the brain as revealed in the Layered Reference Model of the Brain (LRMB) (Wang et al., 2006). On the basis of cognitive computing, next generation cognitive computers and autonomous intelligent systems that think and feel may be designed and implemented.

This article presents the theoretical framework and architectural techniques of cognitive computing beyond conventional imperative and autonomic computing systems. Theoretical foundations of cognitive computing are elaborated from the aspects of cognitive informatics, neural informatics, and denotational mathematics. Conceptual models of cognitive computing are explored from the latest development in abstract intelligence, intelligent behaviors, and computational intel-

ligence. Applications of cognitive computing are described with an autonomous agent system and a cognitive search engine, which demonstrate how machine and computational intelligence may be generated and implemented by cognitive computing theories and technologies toward autonomous knowledge processing.

THEORETICAL FOUNDATIONS FOR COGNITIVE COMPUTING

Theories and methodologies of cognitive computing are inspired by the latest advances in cognitive informatics and denotational mathematics. This section elaborates the cognitive informatics theories and denotational mathematical structures for cognitive computing.

Cognitive Informatics for Cognitive Computing

The fundamental theories and methodologies underpinning cognitive computing are cognitive informatics (Wang, 2002a, 2003, 2006, 2007b, 2007c, 2008a, 2009a; Wang et al., 2009b). Cognitive informatics is a cutting-edge and multidisciplinary research field that tackles the fundamental problems shared by modern informatics, computation, software engineering, AI, computational intelligence, cybernetics, cognitive science, neuropsychology, medical science, systems science, philosophy, linguistics, economics, management science, and life sciences. The development and the cross fertilization between the aforementioned science and engineering disciplines have led to a whole range of emerging research areas known as cognitive informatics.

Definition 2. Cognitive informatics is a transdisciplinary enquiry of cognitive, computing, and information sciences, which studies the internal information processing mechanisms and processes of natural intelligence (the brain), the theoretical framework and denotational mathematics of abstract intelligence, and their engineering applications by cognitive computing.

The architecture of the theoretical framework of cognitive informatics (Wang, 2007b) covers the Information-Matter-Energy (IME) model (Wang, 2003), the Layered Reference Model of the Brain (LRMB) (Wang et al., 2006), the Object-Attribute-Relation (OAR) model of information representation in the brain (Wang, 2007d), the cognitive informatics model of the brain (Wang and Wang, 2006), Natural Intelligence (NI) (Wang, 2002a), Neural Informatics (NeI) (Wang, 2007b), the mechanisms of human perception processes (Wang, 2007e), and cognitive computing (Wang, 2006).

Recent studies in cognitive informatics reveal an entire set of cognitive functions of the brain (Wang, 2007b; Wang and Wang, 2006) and their cognitive process models (Wang et al., 2006) known as the LRMB model of the brain. LRMB, as shown in Figure 1, provides a reference model for the design and implementation of computational intelligence, which enables a systematic and formal description of architectures and behaviors of computational intelligence. The LRMB model explains the functional mechanisms and cognitive processes of the natural intelligence with 43 cognitive processes at seven layers known as the sensation, memory, perception, action, meta-cognitive, meta-inference, and higher cognitive layers from the bottom up. LRMB elicits the core and highly repetitive recurrent cognitive processes from a huge variety of life functions, which may shed light on the study of the fundamental mechanisms and interactions of complicated mental processes and computational intelligence, particularly the relationships and interactions between the inherited and the acquired life functions as well as those of the subconscious and conscious cognitive processes.

The seven-layer LRMB model can be refined by 43 cognitive processes as shown in Figure 2. Based LRMB, any specific life behavior in real-world is a revoke or composition of these LRMB cognitive processes interacting at different layers.

Cognitive informatics prepares a systematical theoretical foundation for the development of cognitive computing methodologies and systems. The architectural and behavioral models of cognitive computing will be developed in the next section on the basis of the theoretical framework of cognitive informatics.

Figure 1. The Layered Reference Model of the Brain (LRMB)

```
The Layered Reference Model of the Brain (LRMB)

§LRMBST ≙ §NI_Sys      // The Natural Intelligent system
       =  NI_OS         // The sub conscious NI operating system
       || NI_App        // The conscious NI applications
       = (  Layer1_Sensation_Processes
          || Layer2_Memory_Processes
          || Layer3_Perception_Processes
          || Layer4_Action_Processes
          )
       || (  Layer5_Meta_Cognitive_Processes
          || Layer6_Meta_Inference_Processes
          || Layer7_Higher_Cogntive_Processes
          )
```

Figure 2. The refined model of LRMB

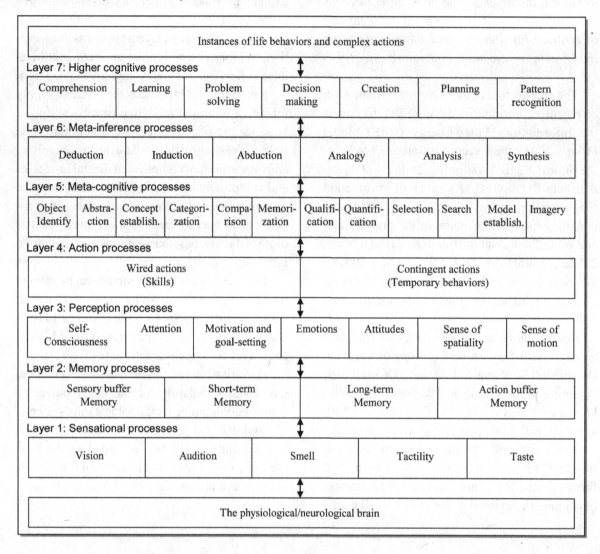

Neural Informatics for Cognitive Computing

Neural informatics (Wang, 2007b) is a branch of cognitive informatics, where memory and its neural and logical models are recognized as the foundation and platform of any form of natural or artificial intelligence (Wang and Wang, 2006).

Definition 3. *Neural Informatics is an interdisciplinary enquiry of the biological and physiological representation of information and knowledge in the brain at the neuron level and their abstract modeling in denotational mathematics.*

The major memory organ that accommodates acquired information and knowledge in the brain is the cerebrum or the cerebral cortex. In particular, the association and premotor cortex in the frontal lobe, the temporal lobe, sensory cortex in the frontal lobe, visual cortex in the occipital lobe, primary motor cortex in the frontal lobe, supplementary motor area in the frontal lobe, and procedural memory in cerebellum (Wilson and Frank, 1999; Wang and Wang, 2006).

Theorem 1. *The Cognitive Model of Memory (CMM) states that the logical architecture of human memory is parallel configured by the Sensory Buffer Memory (SBM), Short-Term Memory (STM), Conscious-Status Memory (CSM), Long-Term Memory (LTM), and Action-Buffer Memory (ABM), i.e.:*

$$
CMM\textbf{ST} \triangleq \begin{array}{l} SBM \\ \| \; STM \\ \| \; CSM \\ \| \; LTM \\ \| \; ABM \end{array} \tag{1}
$$

where $\|$ denotes a parallel relations and ST represents an abstract system structural model.

CMM provides a logical model for explaining the abstract functional partitions of memories and their roles. In Theorem 1, ABM and CSM are newly identified in (Wang and Wang, 2006), which were not modeled in literature of cognitive science, psychology, neurology, and brain science. The CMM model may be used to explain a set of fundamental mechanisms of neural informatics.

It is recognized that in contrary to the traditional *container* metaphor, the mechanisms of human memory can be described by a *relational* metaphor. The relational metaphor perceives that memory and knowledge are represented by the connections between neurons known as the synapses, rather than the neurons themselves as information containers. Therefore, the cognitive model of human memory, particularly LTM, can be described by three fundamental artefacts known as: a) Objects – an abstraction of an external entity and/or internal concept; b) *Attribute* – a sub-object that is used to denote detailed properties and characteristics of the given object; and c) *Relation* – a connection or inter-relationship

between any pair of object-object, object-attribute, and attribute-attribute.

Definition 4. *The Object-Attribute-Relation (OAR) model of LTM is described as a triple, i.e.:*

$$
OAR \, A \, (O, A, R) \tag{2}
$$

An illustration of the OAR model between two objects is shown in Figure 3. The relations between objects O_1 and O_2 can be established via pairs of object-object, object-attribute, and/or attribute-attribute. The connections could be highly complicated, while the mechanism is fairly simple that it can be reduced to the physiological links of neurons via synapses in LTM. It is noteworthy as in the OAR model that the *relations* themselves represent information and knowledge in the brain. The relational metaphor is totally different from the traditional container metaphor in neuropsychology and computer science, because the latter perceives that memory and knowledge are *stored* in individual neurons and the neurons function as containers.

Denotational Mathematics for Cognitive Computing

As that of formal logic and Boolean algebra are the mathematical foundations of von Neumann computers. The mathematical foundations of cognitive computing are based on contemporary denotational mathematics (Wang, 2008b).

Definition 5. *Denotational mathematics is a category of expressive mathematical structures that deals with high-level mathematical entities beyond numbers and simple sets, such as abstract objects, complex relations, behavioral information, concepts, knowledge, processes, intelligence, and systems.*

Figure 3. The OAR model of memory mechanisms

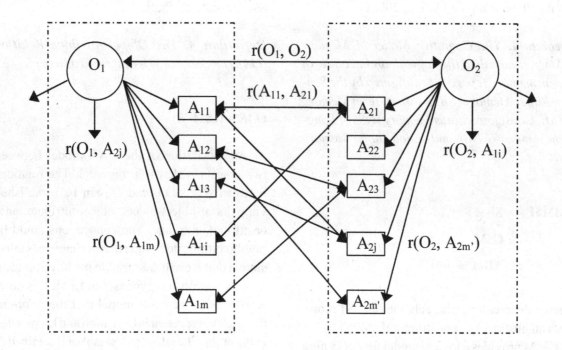

Typical paradigms of denotational mathematics are comparatively presented in Table 1, where their structures, mathematical entities, algebraic operations, and usages are contrasted. The paradigms of denotational mathematics as shown in Table 1 are concept algebra (Wang, 2008c), system algebra (Wang, 2008d; Wang et al., 2009a), and Real-Time Process Algebra (RTPA) (Wang, 2002b, 2008e). Among the three forms of denotational mathematics, concept algebra is designed to deal with the abstract mathematical structure of concepts and semantic inferences, as well as their representation and manipulation in semantic computing and knowledge engineering. System algebra is created to the rigorous treatment of abstract systems and their algebraic relations and operations. RTPA is developed to deal with series of intelligent behavioral processes of humans and systems.

The emergence of denotational mathematics is driven by the practical needs in cognitive in-

formatics, computational intelligence, computing science, software science, and knowledge engineering, because all these modern disciplines study complex human and machine behaviors and their rigorous treatments. Denotational mathematics provides a powerful mathematical means for modeling and formalizing cognitive computing systems. Not only the architectures of computational intelligent systems, but also their dynamic behaviors can be rigorously and systematically manipulated by denotational mathematics. A wide range of problems and applications have been dealt with by denotational mathematics in cognitive informatics and computational intelligence, such as autonomous machine learning (Wang, 2007f), memorization (Wang, 2009b), cognitive decision making (Wang and Ruhe, 2007), and problem solving (Wang and Chiew, 2009). The case studies in cognitive computing demonstrate that denotational mathematics is an ideal and powerful mathematical means for dealing with

Table 1. *Paradigms of denotational mathematics*

No.	Paradigm	Structure	Mathematical entities	Algebraic operations	Usage
1	Concept algebra	$CA \mathrel{\hat=} (C, OP, \Theta) = (\{O, A, R^c, R^i, R^o\}, \{\bullet_r, \bullet_c\}, \Theta_C)$	$c \mathrel{\hat=} (O, A, R^c, R^i, R^o)$	$\bullet_r \mathrel{\hat=} \{\rightarrow, \leftrightarrow, \prec, \succ, =, \cong, \sim, \triangleq\}$ $\bullet_c \mathrel{\hat=} \{\Rightarrow, \Leftrightarrow, \Rightarrow, \uplus, \in, \Leftarrow, \vdash, \dashv\}$	Algebraic manipulations on abstract concepts
2	System algebra	$SA \mathrel{\hat=} (S, OP, \Theta) = (\{C, R^c, R^i, R^o, B, \Omega\}, \{\bullet_r, \bullet_c\}, \Theta)$	$S \mathrel{\hat=} (C, R^c, R^i, R^o, B, \Omega, \Theta)$	$\bullet_r \mathrel{\hat=} \{\leftrightarrow, \leftrightarrow, \prod, =, \sqsubseteq, \sqsupseteq\}$ $\bullet_c \mathrel{\hat=} \{\Rightarrow, \Leftrightarrow, \Rightarrow, \uplus, \in, \Leftarrow, \vdash\}$	Algebraic manipulations on abstract systems
3	Real-time process algebra (RTPA)	$RTPA \mathrel{\hat=} (\mathfrak{T}, \mathfrak{P}, \mathfrak{N})$	$\mathfrak{P} \mathrel{\hat=} \{:=, \blacklozenge, \Rightarrow, \Leftarrow, \Leftarrow, \gg, \ll, \triangleright, \|, \&, @, \textcircled{}, \lfloor, \rfloor, \otimes, \boxtimes, \S\}$ $\mathfrak{T} \mathrel{\hat=} \{\mathbf{N, Z, R, S, BL, B, H, P, TI, D, DT,}$ $\mathbf{RT, ST,} @t\mathbf{TM,} @int\odot, \textcircled{S}, s\mathbf{BL}\}$	$\mathfrak{R} \mathrel{\hat=} \{\rightarrow, \curvearrowright, \|, \|\!\!\|, \cdots, R^*, R^+, R^i,$ $\circlearrowright, \rightarrow\|, \oiint, \|\!\!\|, \gg, \zeta, \downarrow, \uparrow, \downarrow, \uparrow\}$	Algebraic manipulations on abstract processes

concepts, knowledge, behavioral processes, and human/machine intelligence with real-world problems.

MODELS OF COGNITIVE COMPUTING

On the basis of cognitive informatics and denotational mathematics, new computing architectures and technologies may be developed known as cognitive computing, which adopt non-von Neumann architectures and extend traditional computing capabilities from imperative data processing to autonomous knowledge processing. The following subsections describe the abstract intelligence and behavioral models of cognitive computing.

The Abstract Intelligence Model of Cognitive Computing

According to functional reductionism, a logical model of the general form of intelligence is needed known as abstract intelligence in order to formally explain high-level mechanisms of the brain on the basis of observations at the biological, physiological, functional, and logical levels. On the basis of the logical model of abstract intelligence, the studies on the paradigms of intelligence, such as natural, artificial, machinable, and computational

intelligence, may be unified into a coherent framework (Wang, 2009a).

Definition 6. *Abstract intelligence, αI, is a human enquiry of both natural and artificial intelligence at the embody levels of neural, cognitive, functional, and logical from the bottom up.*

In the narrow sense, αI is a human or a system ability that transforms information into behaviors. While, in the broad sense, αI is any human or system ability that autonomously transfers the forms of abstract information between data, information, knowledge, and behaviors in the brain or autonomous systems. With the clarification of the intension and extension of the concept of αI, its paradigms or concrete forms in the real-world can be derived as summarized in Table 2.

It is noteworthy that all paradigms of abstract intelligence share the same cognitive informatics foundation as described in the following theorem, because they are an artificial or machine implementation of abstract intelligence. Therefore, the differences between NI, AI, MI, and CoI are only distinguishable by the means of their implementation and the extent of their intelligent capability.

Table 2. Taxonomy of abstract intelligence and its embodying forms

No.	Form of intelligence	Embodying means	Paradigms
1	Natural intelligence (NI)	Naturally grown biological and physiological organisms	Human brains and brains of other well developed species
2	Artificial intelligence (AI)	Cognitively-inspired artificial models and man-made systems	Intelligent systems, knowledge systems, decision-making systems, and distributed agent systems
3	Machinable intelligence (MI)	Complex machine and wired systems	Computers, robots, autonomic circuits, neural networks, and autonomic mechanical machines
4	Computational intelligence (CoI)	Computational methodologies and software systems	Expert systems, fuzzy systems, autonomous computing, intelligent agent systems, genetic/evolutionary systems, and autonomous learning systems

Theorem 2. *The inclusive intelligent capability states that any concrete real-world paradigm of intelligence is a subset of αI, i.e.:*

$$CoI \subseteq MI \subseteq AI \subseteq NI \subseteq \alpha I \qquad (3)$$

Theorem 2 indicates that AI, CoI, and MI are dominated by NI and αI. Therefore, one should not expect a computer or a software system to solve a problem where human cannot. In other words, no AI or computer systems may be designed and/or implemented for a given problem where there is no solution being known collectively by human beings as a whole. Further, according to Theorem 2, the development and implementation of AI rely on the understanding of the mechanisms and laws of NI.

As an embedment form of abstract intelligence, cognitive computing is a subset of αI and NI. Therefore, cognitive computing shares the LRMB reference model of the brain, which extends capabilities of CoI to the seven layers of NI. Detailed discussions will be extended in the following subsections.

The Computational Intelligence Model of Cognitive Computing

Definition 7. *Computational intelligence (CoI) is an embodying form of abstract intelligence (αI) that implements intelligent mechanisms and behaviors by computational methodologies and software systems, such as expert systems, fuzzy systems, autonomous computing, intelligent agent systems, genetic/evolutionary systems, and autonomous learning systems.*

The fundamental mechanisms of αI can be described by the Generic Abstract Intelligence Model (GAIM) (Wang, 2007c) as shown in Figure 4. In the GAIM model, different forms of intelligence are described as a driving force that transfers between a pair of abstract objects in the brain such as data (D), information (I), knowledge (K), and behavior (B). It is noteworthy that each abstract object is physically retained in a particular type of memories. This is the neural informatics foundation of natural intelligence, and the physiological evidences of why natural intelligence can be clas-

Figure 4. The Generic Abstract Intelligence Model (GAIM)

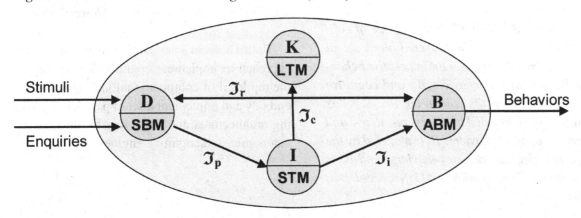

$\mathfrak{I}_p$ – *Perceptive* intelligence $\mathfrak{I}_i$ – *Instructive* intelligence

$\mathfrak{I}_c$ – *Cognitive* intelligence $\mathfrak{I}_r$ – *Reflective* intelligence

sified into four forms known as the instructive intelligence I_i, reflective intelligence I_r, cognitive intelligence I_c, and perceptive intelligence I_p.

Cognitive computing is aimed at implementing all forms of abstract intelligence in the GAIM model by imperative computing C_I, autonomic computing C_A, and cognitive computing C_C from the bottom up. The relationship between different forms of CoI and their implementation means can be elaborated as follows:

$$\begin{cases} C_I \Rightarrow \mathfrak{I}_i \\ C_A \Rightarrow \mathfrak{I}_r \\ C_C \Rightarrow \mathfrak{I}_c \cup \mathfrak{I}_p \end{cases} \tag{4}$$

where each form of cognitive computing will be specified by a set of intelligent computational behaviors in the following subsection.

The Behavioral Model of Cognitive Computing

The abstract intelligence model of cognitive computing can be refined by a behavioral model that evolves computing technologies from the conventional imperative behaviors to the autonomic and cognitive behaviors.

Definition 8. *The entire behavior space of cognitive computing, B_{CC}, is a layered hierarchical structure that encompasses the imperative behaviors B_I, autonomic behaviors B_A, and cognitive behaviors B_C from the bottom up, i.e. (see Box 1) where B_I is modeled by the event-, time-, and interrupt-driven behaviors; B_A is modeled by the goal- and decision-driven behaviors; and B_C is modeled by the perception- and inference-driven behaviors.*

On the basis of the above model, the intelligent behaviors of I_I, I_A, and I_C can be defined as follows.

Box 1.

$$\begin{aligned} B_{CC} &\triangleq (B_I, B_A, B_C) \\ &= (\quad \{B_e, B_t, B_{int}\} && // \ B_I \\ &\quad \| \{B_e, B_t, B_{int}, B_g, B_d\} && // \ B_A \\ &\quad \| \{B_e, B_t, B_{int}, B_g, B_d, B_p, B_{\inf}\} && // \ B_C \\ &\quad) \end{aligned}$$

$$\tag{5}$$

Definition 9. *The behavioral model of cognitive computing, C_C**ST**, is to implement the imperative intelligence I_I, autonomic intelligence I_A, and cognitive intelligence I_C as follows (see Box 2).*

According to Definition 9, it is obvious that the relationship among the three-level intelligence can be derived as follows.

Theorem 3. *The intelligent behaviors of cognitive computing systems are hierarchical and inclusive at the levels of imperative, autonomic, and cognitive intelligence, i.e.:*

Proof: *Directly applying Definition 9, Theorem 3 can be proven, which shows that any lower level intelligent behavior is a subset of those of a higher level. In other words, any higher layer intelligence is a natural extension of those of lower layers.*

Both Theorem 3 and Definition 9 indicate the approach to implement cognitive computing at the top level of computational intelligence is to embody and implement a set of parallel computing architectures and behaviors by imperative, autonomic, and cognitive engines.

Box 2.

$$C_C\textbf{ST} \triangleq \begin{cases} \mathfrak{I}_I = \{B_e, B_t, B_{int}\} \\ \mathfrak{I}_A = \{B_e, B_t, B_{int}, B_g, B_d\} \\ \mathfrak{I}_C = \{B_e, B_t, B_{int}, B_g, B_d, B_p, B_{\inf}\} \end{cases} \tag{6}$$

APPLICATIONS OF COGNITIVE COMPUTING

Cognitive computing as generic intelligence/knowledge processing methodology and technology can be applied to develop the next generation cognitive computers and autonomous systems. Two paradigms of cognitive computing known as autonomous agent systems and cognitive search engines are elaborated in this section, which mimic higher level intelligent capabilities of αI and NI beyond conventional imperative computing.

Autonomous Agent Systems

Definition 10. *An Autonomous Agent System (AAS) is a composition of distributed agents that possesses autonomous computing and decision making abilities as well as interactive communication capability to peers and the environment.*

An AAS may also be called an intelligent-ware, shortly intelware (Wang, 2009c), to reflect its essence and relationship with hardware and software in cognitive computing. On the basis of LRMB, an AAS can be modeled as follows.

Definition 11. *The cognitive computing model of AAS's, §AASST, is a parallel structure represented by the Agent Operating System (AOSST) and a set of agent intelligence represented by the Agent Intelligent Behaviors (AIBST), as shown in Figure 5.*

The §AASST model, denoted in RTPA (Wang, 2002b, 2008e), reveals that NI and AI share the same cognitive informatics foundations on the basis of abstract intelligence and cognitive computing. The compatible intelligent capability states that NI, AI, and AAS's, are compatible by sharing the same mechanisms of intelligent capability and behaviors. In other words, at the logical level, NI of the brain shares the same mechanisms as those of AI and computational intelligence. The differ-ences between NI and AI are only distinguishable by the means of implementation and the extent of intelligent ability. Therefore, the studies on NI and AI in general, and AAS's in particular, may be unified into a coherent framework based on cognitive informatics and cognitive computing, especially the LRMB reference model.

Cognitive Search Engines

Search is not only a basic computational application, but also a fundamental cognitive process of human brains. The study in cognitive search engines is another application paradigm of cognitive computing.

Definition 12. *Search ΣE is a cognitive process to allocate and retrieve a piece of knowledge in the memory and/or cyberspace by a given concept cST, in which an equivalent or similar concept c_iST may be found, i.e.:*

$$\mathcal{SE} \mathop{R}_{iN=1}^{nN} \triangleq cST = c_iST \lor cST \cong c_iST \tag{8}$$
$$\to c^lST = cST \uplus c_iST$$

where nN is the maximum number of elements in the designated searching space in LTM or cyberspace, and $cST = c_iST$ or $cST \cong c_iST$ denote an equivalent or similar concept according to concept algebra.

A fundamental problem in search technologies is that search is a hybrid and complex process encompassing the following three aspects: a) Queries comprehension, b) Search algorithms, and c) Results representation. An analysis and contrast of conventional search and intelligent search by cognitive computing systems on these three aspects are provided in Table 3.

It is recognized that suitable denotational mathematical means, such as concept algebra (Wang, 2008c) and visual semantic algebra (Wang,

Figure 5. The cognitive computing model of AAS

The Computational Intelligent Model of AAS

$$\S AAS\mathbf{ST} \triangleq AOS\mathbf{ST} \qquad\qquad\quad \text{// Agent operating system}$$
$$\| \; AIB\mathbf{ST} \qquad\qquad\qquad\quad \text{// Agent intelligent behaviors}$$
$$= \{ \; \text{// } AOS\mathbf{ST}$$

$$<SE\mathbf{ST}: \; \underset{ptr\mathbf{P}=0}{\overset{n-1}{R}} \; SENSORS[ptr\mathbf{P}]\mathbf{ST}> \qquad \text{// Layer 1: Sensation engine}$$

$$\| \; <ME\mathbf{ST}: \; \underset{addr\mathbf{P}=0}{\overset{5}{R}} \; MEM[addr\mathbf{P}]\mathbf{ST}> \qquad \text{// Layer 2: Memory engine}$$
$$= <SBM\mathbf{ST} \| STM\mathbf{ST} \| CSM\mathbf{ST} \| LTM\mathbf{ST} \| ABM\mathbf{ST}>$$

$$\| \; <PE\mathbf{ST}: \; \underset{i\mathbf{P}=0}{\overset{7}{R}} \; PROC[i\mathbf{N}]\mathbf{ST}> \qquad\quad \text{// Layer 3: Perception engine}$$
$$= <Attention\mathbf{ST} \| Motivation\mathbf{ST} \| Emotion\mathbf{ST} \| Attitude\mathbf{ST}$$
$$\| SensOfSpatiality\mathbf{ST} \| SensOfTime\mathbf{ST} \| SensOfMotion\mathbf{ST}>$$

$$\| \; <AE\mathbf{ST}: \; \underset{ptr\mathbf{P}=0}{\overset{n_{SERVO}\mathbf{N}-1}{R}} \; SERVOS[ptr\mathbf{P}]\mathbf{ST}> \qquad \text{// Layer 4: Action engine}$$

$$\| \; <CE\mathbf{ST}: \; \underset{i\mathbf{P}=0}{\overset{10}{R}} \; PROC[i\mathbf{N}]\mathbf{ST}> \qquad\qquad \text{// Layer 5: Meta-cognition engine}$$
$$= <ObjectIdentification\mathbf{ST} \| Abstraction\mathbf{ST} \| ConceptEstablishment\mathbf{ST}$$
$$\| Search\mathbf{ST} \| Categorization\mathbf{ST} \| Comparison\mathbf{ST} \| Memorization\mathbf{ST}$$
$$\| Qualification\mathbf{ST} \| Quantification\mathbf{ST} \| Selection\mathbf{ST}>$$

$$\| \; <IE\mathbf{ST}: \; \underset{i\mathbf{P}=0}{\overset{6}{R}} \; PROC[i\mathbf{N}]\mathbf{ST}> \qquad\qquad \text{// Layer 6: Meta-inference engine}$$
$$= <Deduction\mathbf{ST} \| Induction\mathbf{ST} \| Abduction\mathbf{ST} \| Analogy\mathbf{ST}$$
$$\| Analysis\mathbf{ST} \| Synthesis\mathbf{ST}>$$

$$\| \; <HCE\mathbf{ST}: \; \underset{i\mathbf{P}=0}{\overset{7}{R}} \; PROC[i\mathbf{N}]\mathbf{ST}> \qquad\quad \text{// Layer 7: Higher cognition engine}$$
$$= <Comprehension\mathbf{ST} \| Learning\mathbf{ST} \| Planning\mathbf{ST} \| ProblemSolving\mathbf{ST}$$
$$\| DecisionMaking\mathbf{ST} \| Creation\mathbf{ST} \| PattenRecognition\mathbf{ST}>$$
$$\| \; <\S t\mathbf{TM}> \qquad\qquad\qquad\qquad \text{// Relative clock}$$
$$\}$$

$$\| \{ \; \text{// } AIB\mathbf{ST}$$

$$\| \; < \underset{k\mathbf{N}=0}{\overset{n_e\mathbf{N}-1}{R}} \; @e_k\mathbf{S} \hookmapsto P_k\mathbf{ST}> \qquad\qquad \text{// } \textit{Event}\text{-driven behaviors } (B_e)$$

$$\| \; < \underset{k\mathbf{N}=0}{\overset{n_t\mathbf{N}-1}{R}} \; @t_k\mathbf{TM} \hookmapsto P_k\mathbf{ST}> \qquad\qquad \text{// } \textit{Time}\text{-driven behaviors } (B_t)$$

$$\| \; < \underset{k\mathbf{N}=0}{\overset{n_{int}\mathbf{N}-1}{R}} \; @int_k\odot \hookmapsto P_k\mathbf{ST}> \qquad\qquad \text{// } \textit{Interrupt}\text{-driven behaviors } (B_{int})$$

$$\| \; < \underset{k\mathbf{N}=0}{\overset{n_g\mathbf{N}-1}{R}} \; @g_k\mathbf{ST} \hookmapsto P_k\mathbf{ST}> \qquad\qquad \text{// } \textit{Goal}\text{-driven behaviors } (B_g)$$

$$\| \; < \underset{k\mathbf{N}=0}{\overset{n_t\mathbf{N}-1}{R}} \; @d_k\mathbf{ST} \hookmapsto P_k\mathbf{ST}> \qquad\qquad \text{// } \textit{Decision}\text{-driven behaviors } (B_d)$$

$$\| \; < \underset{k\mathbf{N}=0}{\overset{n_t\mathbf{N}-1}{R}} \; @p_k\mathbf{ST} \hookmapsto P_k\mathbf{ST}> \qquad\qquad \text{// } \textit{Perception}\text{-driven behaviors } (B_p)$$

$$\| \; < \underset{k\mathbf{N}=0}{\overset{n_{inf}\mathbf{N}-1}{R}} \; @inf_k\mathbf{ST} \hookmapsto P_k\mathbf{ST}> \qquad\qquad \text{// } \textit{Inference}\text{-driven behaviors } (B_{inf})$$
$$\}$$

Table 3. Comparison of search technologies

Function	Conventional Search Engines	Cognitive Search Engines
Query	Keyword-based (syntactic-oriented)	Comprehension-based (semantics-oriented)
	Symbolic guessing of user queries	Interactive semantic analysis of user queries
Search	Keyword matching (symbolic equivalence)	Semantic matching (conceptual/semantic equivalence)
	Finding all equivalent symbol strings	Finding all synonymies and related knowledge
Results representation	A list of URLs	A list of concepts with attributes and objects
	Ranking by: - Keyword frequency - Statistical or probable benchmarks	Ranking by: - Concept equivalency - Semantic similarity
	Knowledge processing: - None	Knowledge processing: - Knowledge extraction - Concept building

2009d) are required in order to support rigorous textual and visual semantic reasoning with relational linguistic/domain knowledge bases. In addition, machine learning capabilities and sophisticated computational intelligence are needed. Therefore, cognitive computing provides a set of theoretical and technical preparations for the design and implementation of next generation intelligent search engines.

CONCLUSION

Cognitive computing has been characterized as a set of autonomous and perceptive knowledge processing theories and technologies mimicking the mechanisms of the brain beyond conventional imperative data processing. This article has presented the theoretical framework of cognitive computing and recent advances in the study of cognitive computing theories and methodologies in cognitive informatics, soft computing, and computational intelligence. Conceptual and behavioral models of cognitive computing have been elaborated. A powerful mathematical means known as denotational mathematics have been introduced to deal with the design and implementation of cognitive computing systems. A wide range of applications of cognitive computing have been

identified such as autonomous agent systems and intelligent search engines. The pilot projects have demonstrated how machine and computational intelligence may be generated and implemented by cognitive computing theories and technologies toward next generation computing systems that think and feel.

ACKNOWLEDGMENT

The author would like to acknowledge the Natural Science and Engineering Council of Canada (NSERC) for its partial support to this work. The author is grateful to the IEEE ICCI'06 and ICCI'07 program committees for the invited keynotes related to this article. The author thanks the anonymous reviewers for their valuable comments and suggestions to this work.

REFERENCES

Gersting, J. L. (1982). *Mathematical Structures for Computer Science*. San Francisco: W. H. Freeman & Co.

IBM. (2006). Autonomic Computing White Paper. *An Architectural Blueprint for Autonomic Computing*, 4th ed., June, (pp. 1-37).

Kephart, J., & Chess, D. (2003). The Vision of Autonomic Computing. *IEEE Computer*, *26*(1), 41–50. doi:10.1109/MC.2003.1160055

Lewis, H. R., & Papadimitriou, C. H. (1998). *Elements of the Theory of Computation* (2nd ed.). Englewood Cliffs, NJ: Prentice Hall International.

Mandrioli, D., & Ghezzi, C. (1987). *Theoretical Foundations of Computer Science*. New York: John Wiley & Sons.

Turing, A. M. (1950). Computing Machinery and Intelligence. *Mind*, *59*, 433–460. doi:10.1093/mind/LIX.236.433

von Neumann, J. (1946). The Principles of Large-Scale Computing Machines. *Reprinted in Annals of History of Computers*, *3*(3), 263–273. doi:10.1109/MAHC.1981.10025

von Neumann, J. (1958). *The Computer and the Brain*. New Haven: Yale Univ. Press.

Wang, Y. (2002a). Keynote: On Cognitive Informatics. *Proc. 1st IEEE International Conference on Cognitive Informatics* (ICCI'02), Calgary, Canada, IEEE CS Press, August, (pp. 34-42).

Wang, Y. (2002b). The Real-Time Process Algebra (RTPA). *Annals of Software Engineering*, *14*, 235–274. doi:10.1023/A:1020561826073

Wang, Y. (2003, August). On Cognitive Informatics. *Brain and Mind: A Transdisciplinary Journal of Neuroscience and Neorophilisophy*, *4*(3), 151-167. Kluwer Academic Publishers.

Wang, Y. (2004). Keynote: On Autonomic Computing and Cognitive Processes. *Proc. 3rd IEEE International Conference on Cognitive Informatics* (ICCI'04), Victoria, Canada, IEEE CS Press, (pp. 3-4).

Wang, Y. (2006). Keynote: Cognitive Informatics - Towards the Future Generation Computers that Think and Feel. *Proc. 5th IEEE International Conference on Cognitive Informatics* (ICCI'06), Beijing, China, IEEE CS Press, (pp. 3-7).

Wang, Y. (2007a, July). *Software Engineering Foundations: A Software Science Perspective. CRC Book Series in Software Engineering*, Vol. II, Auerbach Publications, NY.

Wang, Y. (2007b). The Theoretical Framework of Cognitive Informatics. *International Journal of Cognitive Informatics and Natural Intelligence*, *1*(1), 1–27. doi:10.4018/jcini.2007010101

Wang, Y. (2007c). Keynote: Cognitive Informatics Foundations of Nature and Machine Intelligence. *Proc. 6th IEEE International Conference on Cognitive Informatics* (ICCI'07), (pp. 2-12). Lake Tahoe, CA, USA, IEEE CS Press.

Wang, Y. (2007d). The OAR Model of Neural Informatics for Internal Knowledge Representation in the Brain. *International Journal of Cognitive Informatics and Natural Intelligence*, *1*(3), 64–75. doi:10.4018/jcini.2007070105

Wang, Y. (2007e). On the Cognitive Processes of Human Perception with Emotions, Motivations, and Attitudes. *International Journal of Cognitive Informatics and Natural Intelligence*, *1*(4), 1–13. doi:10.4018/jcini.2007100101

Wang, Y. (2007f). The Theoretical Framework and Cognitive Process of Learning. *Proc. 6th International Conference on Cognitive Informatics* (ICCI'07), (pp. 470-479). IEEE CS Press.

Wang, Y. (2007g). Formal Description of the Mechanisms and Cognitive Process of Memorization. *Proc. 6th International Conference on Cognitive Informatics* (ICCI'07), (pp. 284-293). IEEE CS Press.

Wang, Y. (2008a). Keynote, On Abstract Intelligence and Its Denotational Mathematics Foundations, *Proc. 7th IEEE International Conference on Cognitive Informatics* (ICCI'08), (pp. 3-13). Stanford University, CA, USA, IEEE CS Press.

Wang, Y. (2008b). On Contemporary Denotational Mathematics for Computational Intelligence. *Transactions of Computational Science, 2*, 6–29. doi:10.1007/978-3-540-87563-5_2

Wang, Y. (2008c). On Concept Algebra: A Denotational Mathematical Structure for Knowledge and Software Modeling. *International Journal of Cognitive Informatics and Natural Intelligence, 2*(2), 1–18. doi:10.4018/jcini.2008040101

Wang, Y. (2008d). On System Algebra: A Denotational Mathematical Structure for Abstract Systems Modeling. *International Journal of Cognitive Informatics and Natural Intelligence, 2*(2), 19–40. doi:10.4018/jcini.2008040102

Wang, Y. (2008e). RTPA: A Denotational Mathematics for Manipulating Intelligent and Computational Behaviors. *International Journal of Cognitive Informatics and Natural Intelligence, 2*(2), 41–60. doi:10.4018/jcini.2008040103

Wang, Y. (2009a). On Abstract Intelligence: Toward a Unified Theory of Natural, Artificial, Machinable, and Computational Intelligence. *International Journal of Software Science and Computational Intelligence, 1*(1), 1–17. doi:10.4018/jssci.2009010101

Wang, Y. (2009b). Formal Description of the Cognitive Process of Memorization. *Transactions of Computational Science, 5*, 81–98.

Wang, Y. (2009c). A Cognitive Informatics Reference Model of Autonomous Agent Systems (AAS). *International Journal of Cognitive Informatics and Natural Intelligence, 3*(1), 1–16. doi:10.4018/jcini.2009010101

Wang, Y. (2009d). On Visual Semantic Algebra (VSA): A Denotational Mathematical Structure for Modeling and Manipulating Visual Objects and Patterns. *International Journal of Software Science and Computational Intelligence, 1*(4), 1–15. doi:10.4018/jssci.2009062501

Wang, Y., & Chiew, V. (2009). On the Cognitive Process of Human Problem Solving, *Cognitive Systems Research: An International Journal, 10*(4), Elsevier, to appear.

Wang, Y., Kinsner, W., Anderson, J. A., Zhang, D., Yao, Y. Y., & Sheu, P. (2009b). A Doctrine of Cognitive Informatics. *Fundamenta Informaticae, 90*(3), 203–228.

Wang, Y., & Ruhe, G. (2007). The Cognitive Process of Decision Making. *International Journal of Cognitive Informatics and Natural Intelligence, 1*(2), 73–85. doi:10.4018/jcini.2007040105

Wang, Y., & Wang, Y. (2006). On Cognitive Informatics Models of the Brain. *IEEE Transactions on Systems, Man and Cybernetics. Part C, Applications and Reviews, 36*(2), 16–20.

Wang, Y., Wang, Y., Patel, S., & Patel, D. (2006). A Layered Reference Model of the Brain (LRMB). *IEEE Transactions on Systems, Man and Cybernetics. Part C, Applications and Reviews, 36*(2), 124–133. doi:10.1109/TSMCC.2006.871126

Wang, Y., Zadeh, L. A., & Yao, Y. (2009a). On the System Algebra Foundations for Granular Computing. *International Journal of Software Science and Computational Intelligence, 1*(1), 64–86. doi:10.4018/jssci.2009010105

Wilson, R. A., & Frank, C. K. (Eds.). (1999). *The MIT Encyclopedia of the Cognitive Sciences.* MA: MIT Press.

Zadeh, L. A. (1965). Fuzzy Sets and Systems. In Fox, J. (Ed.), *Systems Theory* (pp. 29–37). Brooklyn, NY: Polytechnic Press.

This work was previously published in International Journal of Software Science and Computational Intelligence, Volume 1, Issue 3, edited by Yingxu Wang, pp. 1-15, copyright 2009 by IGI Publishing (an imprint of IGI Global).

Chapter 7
On the System Algebra Foundations for Granular Computing

Yingxu Wang
University of Calgary, Canada

Lotfi A. Zadeh
University of California, Berkeley, USA

Yiyu Yao
University of Regina, Canada

ABSTRACT

Granular computing studies a novel approach to computing system modeling and information process-ing. Although a rich set of work has advanced the understanding of granular computing in dealing with the "to be" and "to have" problems of systems, the "to do" aspect of system modeling and behavioral implementation has been relatively overlooked. On the basis of a recent development in denotational mathematics known as system algebra, this paper presents a system metaphor of granules and ex-plores the theoretical and mathematical foundations of granular computing. An abstract system model of granules is proposed in this paper. Rigorous manipulations of granular systems in computing are modeled by system algebra. The properties of granular systems are analyzed, which helps to explain the magnitudes and complexities of granular systems. Formal representation of granular systems for computing is demonstrated by real-world case studies, where concrete granules and their algebraic operations are explained.

DOI: 10.4018/978-1-4666-0261-8.ch007

INTRODUCTION

The term *granule* is originated from Latin *granum*, i.e., grain, to denote a small compact particle in physics and in the natural world. The *taxonomy of granules* in computing can be classified into the data granule, information granule, concept granule, computing granule, cognitive granule, and system granule (Zedeh, 1979, 2003; Lin, 1998; Skowron and Stepaniuk, 2001; Yao, 2001, 2004a; Wang, 2007a, 2008c). The study of granular computing as an emerging filed appeared in 1997 (Zadeh, 1997, 1998; Lin, 1998). Granular computing may be viewed as an umbrella term covering theories, strategies, methodologies, techniques, tools, and systems that explore multilevel granularity in information processing, knowledge manipulation, and problem solving (Yao, 2001, 2004a, 2004b, 2005).

The concept of granules in data and information modeling and its fuzzy set treatment can be traced back to the work of L.A. Zedeh in 1979 as given below (Zadeh, 1979, 2003).

Definition 1. *The data granule g is a set with the elements x as a member of a fuzzy set $\tilde{G}$ to the degree of λ, $0 \leq \lambda \leq 1$, i.e.:*

$$g \triangleq \{x \mid x \in_{\lambda} \tilde{G} \subseteq U\} \tag{1}$$

where U is the universal discourse.

Many studies investigated into granular computing based on rough sets (Lin, Yao, and Zadeh, 2002). Pawlak (1998) studied *knowledge granularity* using rough sets. Skowron and Stepaniuk (2001) proposed a rough set treatment of *information granules*. Polkowski and Skowron (1998) introduced the *granular calculus*. Lin (1998) studied *relational granules*. Pedrycz (2001) as well as Bargiela and Pedrycz (2002) suggested that granular computing may adopt a pyramid model toward various information granu-

lations. Yao developed a trarachic perspective on granular computing with the facets of philosophy, methodology, and computational implementation (Yao, 2001, 2004a, 2005), which explains the structures of granular computing by multiple levels and views. These studies have advanced the theories of granular computing in dealing with the aspects of system *"to be"* and *"to have"* problems, particularly system architectures and high-level system conceptual designs in computing, software engineering, system engineering, and cognitive informatics. Wang initiated a set of *denotational mathematics* (Wang, 2002b, 2007a, 2007c, 2007d, 2008a) known as *concept algebra* (Wang, 2008b), *system algebra* (Wang, 2008c), and *Real-Time Process Algebra* (RTPA) (Wang, 2002a, 2003b, 2007a, 2008d), which were recognized as an expressive mathematical means for modeling and manipulating all types of granules in granular computing such as the *computing, cognitive, concept, information, data granules*, and *knowledge* granules.

This article presents a new perspective on the system metaphor of granules and granular computing, which extends the conventional set metaphors (Zadeh, 1979; Klir, 1992; Wang, 2007a). The following discusses the relationships between granules/systems and granular computing/system algebra. It will demonstrate that systems may be treated rigorously as a new mathematical structure beyond conventional mathematical entities. Based on this view, the concept of granules and granular computing are discussed below.

Definition 2. *A computing granule, shortly a granule, is a basic mathematical structure that possesses a stable topology and at least a unit of computational capability or behavior.*

It is noteworthy that, comparing Definitions 1 and 2, the computing granule is not a set, but an abstract system (Wang, 2008c) with both a given structure and a set of certain behaviors. The structural and functional models of a granule will be derived in the next section.

Definition 3. *Granularity in system design is the level of abstraction or the extent of details presented in a granule and its computational behaviors in a given level of system hierarchy.*

Definition 4. *Granulation in system design is a process to partite or decompose a computing system into its smallest components step-by-step in a given system hierarchy.*

Definition 5. *Granulometric is a measurement of granularity of a computing system with a certain granulation.*

Based on the taxonomy of granules and granulation, as well as their *system metaphor*, it is naturally perceived that computational behaviors and computing systems can be design and implemented by a set of granules and a process of granulation. In this context, the concept of computing can be described as follows (Zedeh, 2003; Wang, 2007a).

Definition 6. *Computing, in a narrow sense, is an application of computers to solve a given computational problem by imperative instructions; while in a broad sense, it is a process to implement the instructive intelligence by a system that transfers a set of given information or instructions into expected behaviors.*

On the basis of Definitions 1 - 6, the concept of granular computing can be derived as follows.

Definition 7. *Granular computing is a new computational methodology that models and implements computational structures and functions by a granular system, where each granule in the system carries out a predefined function or behavior by interacting to other granules in the system.*

For instance, according to Definition 7, the Internet may be perceived as a granular system at a certain level of granularity, where each distributed computer in the web is a granule. In this Internet granular system, with an individual computer as a reference, a higher-level granularity in the system can be a Local Area Network (LAN), and a lower level granularity can be one of the threads or processes executing on a certain granular machine. This is perfectly in-line with the system philosophy (Ellis and Fred, 1962; Klir, 1992; Wang, 2007a) and models defined in system algebra (Wang, 2007a, 2008c).

This article indicates that, although a rich set of literature on granular computing exists, the implications and rigorous models of granules and granular computing are yet to be systematically studied, particularly the design and implementation of fundamental computing behaviors via granular systems. A new approach is presented in this article with a system metaphor toward granules and the theoretical and mathematical foundations of granular computing on the basis of the recent development in denotational mathematics known as system algebra. The abstract system model of granules is investigated. Rigorous manipulations of granular systems in computing are modeled by system algebra, and the properties of granular systems are qualitatively and quantitatively analyzed. Formal representation and treatment of concrete granules are explained with case studies on real-world granular systems. This article may also be perceived as a paradigm that demonstrates the generality and expressive power of system algebra and the mathematical model of abstract systems.

THE ABSTRACT SYSTEM MODEL OF GRANULES

In order to formally describe the system metaphor of granules and granular computing, the mathematical model of abstract systems and system algebra are introduced in this section.

These preparations lead to the establishment of the mathematical models of granules in system algebra, which reveal the nature and fundamental mechanisms of granular systems and granular computing.

The Mathematical Model of Abstract Systems

Systems are the most complicated entities and phenomena in abstract, physical, information, and social worlds across all science and engineering disciplines. The system concept can be traced back to the 17th Century when R. Descartes (1596-1650) noticed the interrelationships among scientific disciplines as a system. Then, the general system notion was proposed by Ludwig von Bertalanffy in the 1920s (von Bertalanffy, 1952; Ellis and Fred, 1962). The theories of system science have evolved from classic theories (Ashby, 1958, 1962; Ellis and Fred, 1962; Rapoport, 1962; Heylighen, 1989; Klir, 1992;) to contemporary theories in the mid of the 20th century such as I. Prigogine's dissipative structure theory (Prigogine et al., 1972), H. Haken's synergetics (Haken, 1977), and M. Eigen's hypercycle theory (Eigen and Schuster, 1979). Then, during late of the last century, there are proposals of complex systems theories (Zadeh, 1973; Klir, 1992), fuzzy theories (Zadeh, 1965, 1973), and chaos theories (Ford, 1986; Skarda and Freeman, 1987). Yingxu Wang found that, because of their extremely wide and frequent usability, systems may be treated rigorously as a new mathematical structure beyond conventional mathematical entities known as the *abstract systems* (Wang, 2008c). Based on this view, the concept of abstract systems and their mathematical models are introduced below.

Definition 8. An abstract system is a collection of coherent and interactive entities that has stable functions and a clear boundary with the external environment.

An abstract system forms the generic model of various real-world systems and represents the most common characteristics and properties of them. The granularity of granular computing can be explained by the following lemma in the abstract system theory.

Lemma 1. The generality principle of system abstraction states that a system can be represented as a whole in a given level k of reasoning, $1 \leq k \leq n$, without knowing the details at levels below k-1.

Definition 9. Let E be a finite nonempty set of entities, F a finite nonempty set of functions, V_E a finite nonempty set of domains of E, and V_F a finite nonempty set of domains of F, then the universal system Y, which forms the discourse of abstract systems, is denoted as a 4-tuple, i.e.:

$$\mathfrak{U} \triangleq (E, F, V_E, V_F) \tag{2}$$

Abstract systems can be classified into two categories known as the *closed* and *open* systems. Most practical and useful systems in nature are open systems in which there are interactions between the system and its environment. That is, they need to interact with external world known as the *environment* in order to exchange energy, matter, and/or information. Such systems are called open systems. Typical interactions between an open system and the environment are inputs and outputs.

Definition 10. An open system S on U, $S \sqsubseteq U$, is a 7-tuple, i.e.:

$$S \triangleq (C, R^c, R^i, R^o, B, \Omega, \Theta) \tag{3}$$

where

- $\sqsubseteq$ denotes that a set or structure (tuple) is a substructure or derivation of another structure known.

- C is a finite nonempty set of *components* of system S, $C \subseteq \text{Þ}E \sqsubseteq U$ and $C \sqsubseteq S$, where Þ denotes a power set.

- $R^c \subseteq C \times C$ is a finite nonempty set of *internal relations* between pairs of the components $C \sqsubseteq S$.

- $R^i \subseteq C_\Theta \times C$ is a finite nonempty set of *input relations*, where C_Θ is a finite nonempty set of external component, $C_\Theta \subseteq \text{Þ}E \sqsubseteq U$ and $C_\Theta \not\sqsubseteq S$.

- $R^o \subseteq C \times C_\Theta$ is a finite nonempty set of *output relations*.

- B is a finite nonempty set of *behaviors* of $C \sqsubseteq S$, $B \subseteq \text{Þ}F \sqsubseteq U$ and $B \mid S$.

- Ω is a finite nonempty set of *constraints* of C and B, $\Omega \subseteq \text{Þ}V_E \cup \text{Þ}V_F \sqsubseteq U$ and $\Omega \mid S$.

- Θ is the *environment* of S with a finite nonempty set of external components outside S, i.e., $\Theta = C_\Theta \subseteq \text{Þ}E \sqsubseteq U$ and $\Theta = C_\Theta \not\sqsubseteq S$.

It will be demonstrated throughout this article that the abstract system is an ideal model for rigorously describing both the structures and behaviors of granules in granular computing.

System Algebra

System algebra is an abstract mathematical structure for the formal treatment of abstract and general systems as well as their algebraic relations, operations, and associative rules for composing and manipulating complex systems (Wang, 2007a, 2008c).

Definition 11. *A system algebra SA on a given universal system environment U is a triple, i.e.:*

$$SA \triangleq (S, OP, \Theta) = (\{C, R^c, R^i, R^o, B, \Omega\}, \{\bullet_r, \bullet_c\}, \Theta) \tag{4}$$

where $OP = \{\bullet_r, \bullet_c\}$ are the sets of relational and compositional operations, respectively, on abstract systems as defined below (Wang, 2008c).

Definition 12. *The relational operations $\bullet_r$ in system algebra encompass 6 comparative operators for manipulating the algebraic relations between abstract systems, i.e.:*

$$\bullet_r \triangleq \{\leftrightsquigarrow, \leftrightarrow, \Pi, =, \sqsubseteq, \sqsupseteq\} \tag{5}$$

where the relational operators stand for independent, related, overlapped, equivalent, subsystem, and supersystem, respectively.

Definition 13. *The compositional operations $\bullet_c$ in system algebra encompass 9 associative operators for manipulating the algebraic compositions among abstract systems, i.e.:*

$$\bullet_c \triangleq \{\overset{-}{\Rightarrow}, \overset{+}{\Rightarrow}, \overset{\sim}{\Rightarrow}, \Rightarrow, \boxminus, \uplus, \pitchfork, \Leftarrow, \vdash\} \tag{6}$$

where the compositional operators stand for system inheritance, tailoring, extension, substitute, difference, composition, decomposition, aggregation, and specification, respectively.

System algebra provides a denotational mathematical means for algebraic manipulations of all forms of abstract systems. System algebra can be used to model, specify, and manipulate generic *"to be"* and *"to have"* type problems, particularly system architectures and high-level system designs, in computing, software engineering, system engineering, and cognitive informatics.

The Mathematical Model of Granules in System Algebra

It is recognized that any abstract or concrete granule can be formally modeled by abstract systems in system algebra. On the basis of Definition 10, an abstract granule can be formally described as follows.

Definition 14. *A computing granule G on U, G* $\sqsubseteq$ *U, is a 7-tuple, i.e.:*

$$G \triangleq S = (C, R^c, R^i, R^o, B, \Omega, \Theta) \qquad (7)$$

where

- C is a finite nonempty set of *cells* of system S, $C \subseteq \mathbb{P}E \sqsubseteq U$ and $C \mid S$, where $\mathbb{P}$ denotes a power set.
- $R^c \subseteq C \times C$ is a finite nonempty set of *internal relations* between pairs of the components $C \mid S$.
- $R^i \subseteq C_\Theta \times C$ is a finite nonempty set of *input relations*, where C_Θ is a finite nonempty set of external component, $C_\Theta \subseteq \mathbb{P}E \sqsubseteq U$ and $C_\Theta \not\sqsubseteq S$.
- $R^o \subseteq C \times C_\Theta$ is a finite nonempty set of *output relations*.
- B is a finite nonempty set of *behaviors* of $C \mid S$, $B \subseteq \mathbb{P}F \sqsubseteq U$ and $B \mid S$.
- Ω is a finite nonempty set of *constraints* of C and B, $\Omega \subseteq \mathbb{P}V_E \cup \mathbb{P}V_F \sqsubseteq U$ and $\Omega \mid S$.
- Θ is the *environment* of S with a finite nonempty set of external components outside S, i.e., $\Theta = C_\Theta \subseteq \mathbb{P}E \sqsubseteq U$. and $\Theta = C_\Theta \not\sqsubseteq S$.

A granule as an abstract open system $G(C, R^c, R^i, R^o, B, \Omega, \Theta)$ can be illustrated in Figure 1. Based on the above generic structure of the abstract system model of granules, a set of relational and compositional operations on granular systems, $OP = \{\bullet_r, \bullet_c\}$, will be rigorously defined in the next section.

It is noteworthy that system behaviors B is the most broad set of system actions implemented or embodied on the given layout of the system, including any kind of system functions, interactions, and communications. This is the major difference that distinguishes an abstract system from other static mathematical structures such as a set, lattice, group, or abstract concept (Wang, 2008b). With the structural layout of a granule as given in Definition 14, its functional model or its set of implemented behaviors can be described in RTPA (Wang, 2002a, 2003b, 2006, 2007a, 2008d) as given below.

Definition 15. *The functional model of a granule in computing is equivalent to one of the 17 meta-processes, Π, as defined in RTPA, i.e.:*

$$\mathbb{P} = \{:=, \blacklozenge, \Rightarrow, \Leftarrow, \nLeftarrow, >, <, |>, |<, \underline{@}, \triangleq, \uparrow, \downarrow, !, \otimes, \boxtimes, \S\} \quad (8)$$

where, the RTPA meta process notations stand for the processes of assignment, evaluation, addressing, memory allocation, memory release, read, write, input, output, timing, duration, increase, decrease, exception detection, skip, stop, and system, respectively.

Definition 16. *The software composing rules state that the RTPA process relation system, R, encompasses 17 fundamental algebraic and relational operations elicited from basic computing needs, i.e.:*

$$\mathfrak{R} = \{\rightarrow, \curvearrowright, |, |...|..., R^*, R^+, R^i, \circlearrowleft, \rightarrowtail, \|, \oiint, \||, », \nleftarrow, \hookrightarrow_t, \hookrightarrow_e, \hookrightarrow_i\} \qquad (9)$$

where, the RTPA relational process operators stand for those of sequence, jump, branch, switch, while-loop, repeat-loop, for-loop, recursion, function call, parallel, concurrence, interleave, pipeline, interrupt, time-driven dispatch, event-driven dispatch, and interrupt-driven dispatch (Wang, 2002a, 2003b, 2006, 2007a, 2008d).

Definition 17. *In a larger scope, the functional model of a granule may be denoted as a cognitive granule, which possesses one of the 39 basic*

Figure 1. The abstract model of a granule in granular computing

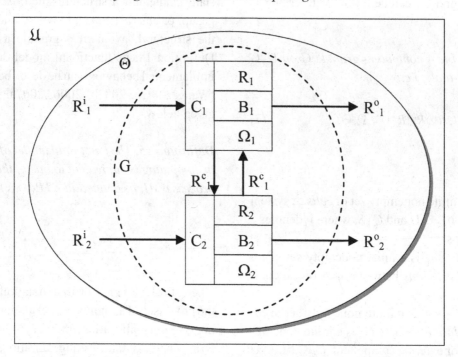

cognitive processes as identified in the Layered Reference Model of the Brain (LRMB).

According to the LRMB model (Wang et al., 2006; Wang and Wang, 2006), the 39 cognitive processes can be categorized at the layers of *sensation, memory, perception, action, meta cognitive function,* and *higher cognitive function,* such as the memorization, comprehension, and learning processes.

Definition 18. *A granular system S_G is a composition of multiple granules in a system where all granules interact with each other for a common goal of system functionality.*

Properties of granular systems obey the generic properties of abstract systems, which will be described in the fourth section of the article.

MANIPULATION OF GRANULAR SYSTEMS BY SYSTEM ALGEBRA

With the formal model of abstract granules as given in Definition 14, granular systems can be modeled and implemented using a set of relational and compositional operations in system algebra as summarized in Definitions 12 and 13, respectively.

Algebraic Relations of Granules and Granular Systems

As summarized in Definition 12, relationships between two granular systems can be independent, overlapped, related, equivalent, being subsystem, and being supersystem. The relational operations of granular systems are static and comparative operations that do not change the systems involved. These six relational operations on granular systems are described below.

Definition 19. *Two granules G_1 and G_2 are independent, denoted by $\aleph$, if both their cell sets and external relation sets are disjoint, i.e.:*

$$G_1(C_1, R_1^c, R_1^i, R_1^o, B_1, \Omega_1, \Theta_1) \nleftrightarrow$$
$$G_2(C_2, R_2^c, R_2^i, R_2^o, B_2, \Omega_2, \Theta_2)$$
$$\triangleq C_1 \cap C_2 = \varnothing \wedge R_1^i \cap R_2^i = \qquad (10)$$
$$\varnothing \wedge R_1^o \cap R_2^o = \varnothing$$

Definition 20. *Two granules G_1 and G_2 are overlapped, denoted by Π, if their cell sets are joint, i.e.*

$$G_1(C_1, R_1^c, R_1^i, R_1^o, B_1, \Omega_1, \Theta_1) \, \Pi$$
$$G_2(C_2, R_2^c, R_2^i, R_2^o, B_2, \Omega_2, \Theta_2)$$
$$\triangleq C_1 \cap C_2 \neq \varnothing \qquad (11)$$

Definition 21. *Two granules G_1 and G_2 are related, denoted by $\leftrightarrow$, if either the sets of their input or output relations are overlapped, i.e.:*

$$G_1(C_1, R_1^c, R_1^i, R_1^o, B_1, \Omega_1, \Theta_1) \leftrightarrow$$
$$G_2(C_2, R_2^c, R_2^i, R_2^o, B_2, \Omega_2, \Theta_2)$$
$$\triangleq R_1^i \cap (R_2^0)^{-1} \neq \varnothing \vee R_2^i \cap (R_1^0)^{-1} \neq \varnothing \qquad (12)$$

where $(R_1^0)^{-1}$ or $(R_2^0)^{-1}$ denotes an inverse relation, i.e., $\forall a \in C_1 \wedge b \in C_2$, $r(a, b) \in R_1^0 \Rightarrow r(b, a) \in (R_2^i) = (R_1^0)^{-1}$.

Definition 22. *Two granules G_1 and G_2 are equivalent, denoted by $=$, if all sets of cells, relations, behaviors, constraints, and environments are identical, i.e.:*

$$G_1(C_1, R_1^c, R_1^i, R_1^o, B_1, \Omega_1, \Theta_1) =$$
$$G_2(C_2, R_2^c, R_2^i, R_2^o, B_2, \Omega_2, \Theta_2) \triangleq$$
$$C_1 = C_2 \wedge R_1^c = R_2^c \wedge R_1^i = R_2^i \wedge R_1^o =$$
$$R_2^o \wedge B_1 = B_2 \wedge \Omega_1 = \Omega_2 \wedge \Theta_1 = \Theta_2$$
$$\qquad (13)$$

Definition 23. *A subgranule G' is a subsystem that is implicated in another granule G, denoted by $|$, i.e.:*

$$G'(C', R^{c'}, R^{i'}, R^{o'}, B', \Omega', \Theta') \sqsubseteq$$
$$G(C, R^c, R^i, R^o, B, \Omega, \Theta) \qquad (14)$$
$$\triangleq C' \subseteq C \wedge R^{c'} \subseteq R^c \wedge R^{i'} \subseteq R^i \wedge$$
$$R^{o'} \subseteq R^o \wedge B' \subseteq B \wedge \Omega' \subseteq \Omega \wedge \Theta' = \Theta$$

The above definition indicates that the subgranule of a given granule is a coherent part of the parent granule with all integrated cells, internal/input/output relations, behaviors, and constraints. However, they share the same environment.

Definition 24. *A supergranule G is a supersystem that consists of one or more subgranules G', denoted by $|$, i.e.:*

$$G(C, R^c, R^i, R^o, B, \Omega, \Theta) \sqsupseteq$$
$$G'(C', R^{c'}, R^{i'}, R^{o'}, B', \Omega', \Theta')$$
$$\triangleq C' \subseteq C \wedge R^{c'} \subseteq R^c \wedge R^{i'} \subseteq R^i \wedge \qquad (15)$$
$$R^{o'} \subseteq R^o \wedge B' \subseteq B \wedge \Omega' \subseteq \Omega \wedge \Theta' = \Theta$$

Compositional Operations of Granular Systems

The compositional operations on granules in system algebra are dynamic and integrative operations that manipulate all granules involved in parallel. Compositional operations on granules provide a set of fundamental mathematical means to construct complex granular systems on the basis of simple ones or to derive new granular systems on the basis of exiting ones. The compositional operations on granules as summarized in Definition 13 can be classified into the operations of reproduction, composition, and integration.

Box 1.

$$G(C,R^c,R^i,R^o,B,\Omega,\Theta) \Rightarrow G_1(C_1,R_1^c,R_1^i,R_1^o,B_1,\Omega_1,\Theta_1)$$
$$\triangleq G_1(C_1,R_1^c,R_1^i,R_1^o,B_1,\Omega_1,\Theta_1 \mid C_1 = C, R_1^c = R^c,$$
$$R^i{}_1 = R^i \cup (C \times C_1), R^o{}_1 = R^o \cup (C_1 \times C),$$
$$B_1 = B, \Omega_1 = \Omega, \Theta_1 = \Theta)$$
$$\| G(C,R^c,R^{i'},R^{o'},B,\Omega,\Theta' \mid R^{i'} = R^i \cup (C_1 \times C),$$
$$R^{o'} = R^o \cup (C \times C_1), \Theta' = \Theta \cup C_1)$$

(16)

(1) Reproduction of Granular Systems

Reproduction operations on granules are a category of composition operations in system algebra. The reproduction operations of granules encompass the algebraic manipulations of inheritance, tailoring, extension, substitution, and instantiation.

Definition 25. *The inheritance of a granule G_1 from the parent granule G, denoted by $\Rightarrow$, is the creation of the new granule G_1 by reproducing G, and the establishment of new associations between them, (see Box 1), where $\|$ denotes that a granular inheritance may create new associations between G_1 and G in parallel via*

Definition 26. *The multiple inheritance of a granule G from n parent granules G_1, G_2, ..., G_n,*

denoted by $\Rightarrow$, is an inheritance that creates the new granule G via a set of n conjoint granules and establishes new associations among them, see Box 2, where

$$\overset{n}{\underset{i=1}{R}} R_i$$

is a calculus known as the big-R notation (Wang, 2002a, 2008e), which denotes a repetitive behavior or recurrent structure as defined in RTPA (Wang, 2007a, 2008d).

Definition 27. *The tailoring of a granule G_1 from the parent granule G, denoted by $\overset{=}{\Rightarrow}$, is a special granular inheritance that creates the new granule G_1 based on G with the removal of specific subsets of cells C', behaviors B', and constraints Ω'; and*

Box 2.

$$\overset{n}{\underset{i=1}{R}} G_i \Rightarrow G(C,R^c,R^i,R^o,B,\Omega,\Theta)$$

$$\triangleq G(C,R^c,R^i,R^o,B,\Omega,\Theta \mid C = \bigcup_{i=1}^{n} C_i, R^c = \bigcup_{i=1}^{n} R^c{}_i, R^i = \bigcup_{i=1}^{n} R^i{}_i \cup \{\overset{n}{\underset{i=1}{R}}(C_i \times C)\},$$

$$R^o = \bigcup_{i=1}^{n} R^o{}_i \cup \{\overset{n}{\underset{i=1}{R}}(C \times C_i)\}, B = \bigcup_{i=1}^{n} B_i, \Omega = \bigcup_{i=1}^{n} \Omega_i, \Theta = \bigcup_{i=1}^{n} \Theta_i)$$

(17)

$$\| \overset{n}{\underset{i=1}{R}} G_i(C_i,R_i^c,R_i^i,R_i^o,B_i,\Omega_i,\Theta'_i \mid R^{i'}{}_i = R^i{}_i \cup (C \times C_i),$$

$$R^{o'}{}_i = R^o{}_i \cup (C_i \times C), \Theta'_i = \Theta_i \cup C)$$

Box 3.

$$G(C, R^c, R^i, R^o, B, \Omega, \Theta) \Rightarrow G_1(C_1, R_1^c, R_1^i, R_1^o, B_1, \Omega_1, \Theta_1)$$
$$\triangleq G_1(C_1, R_1^c, R_1^i, R_1^o, B_1, \Omega_1, \Theta_1 \mid C_1 = C \setminus C', R_1^c = R^c \setminus \{(C \times C')\},$$
$$R_1^i = R^i \cup (C \times C_1), R_1^o = R^o \cup (C_1 \times C),$$
$$B_1 = B \setminus B', \Omega_1 = \Omega \setminus \Omega', \Theta_1 = \Theta)$$
$$\| \, G(C, R^c, R^{i'}, R^{o'}, B, \Omega, \Theta' \mid R^{i'} = R^i \cup (C_1 \times C),$$
$$R^{o'} = R^o \cup (C \times C_1), \Theta' = \Theta \cup C_1)$$

(18)

Box 4.

$$G(C, R^c, R^i, R^o, B, \Omega, \Theta) \overset{+}{\Rightarrow} G_1(C_1, R_1^c, R_1^i, R_1^o, B_1, \Omega_1, \Theta_1)$$
$$\triangleq G_1(C_1, R_1^c, R_1^i, R_1^o, B_1, \Omega_1, \Theta_1 \mid C_1 = C \cup C', R_1^c = R^c \cup (C \times C')$$
$$R_1^i = R^i \cup (C \times C_1), R_1^o = R^o \cup (C_1 \times C),$$
$$B_1 = B \cup B', \Omega_1 = \Omega \cup \Omega', \Theta_1 = \Theta)$$
$$\| \, G(C, R^c, R^{i'}, R^{o'}, B, \Omega, \Theta' \mid R^{i'} = R^i \cup (C_1 \times C),$$
$$R^{o'} = R^o \cup (C \times C_1), \Theta' = \Theta \cup C_1)$$

(19)

at the same time, it establishes new associations between them, see Box 3.

Definition 28. *The extension of a granule G_1 from the parent granule G, denoted by $\overset{+}{\Rightarrow}$, is a special granular inheritance that creates the new granule G_1 based G with additional subsets of components C', behaviors B', and constraints Ω'; and at the*

same time, it establishes new associations between the two systems, see Box 4.

Definition 29. *The substitute of a granule G_1 from the parent granule G, denoted by $\overset{\sim}{\Rightarrow}$, is a flexible granular inheritance that creates the new granule G1 based on G with the new subsets of cells C'G1, behaviors B'G1, and constraint attributes Ω'_{G1} to replace the corresponding inherited ones C'_G, B'_G*

Box 5.

$$G(C, R^c, R^i, R^o, B, \Omega, \Theta) \overset{\sim}{\Rightarrow} G_1(C_1, R_1^c, R_1^i, R_1^o, B_1, \Omega_1, \Theta_1)$$
$$\triangleq G_1(C_1, R_1^c, R_1^i, R_1^o, B_1, \Omega_1, \Theta_1 \mid C_1 = (C \setminus C'_G) \cup C'_{G_1},$$
$$R_1^c = (R^c \setminus (C \times C'_G)) \cup (C \times C'_{G_1}), R_1^i = R^i \cup (C \times C_1),$$
$$R_1^o = R^o \cup (C_1 \times C), B_1 = (B \setminus B'_G) \cup B'_{G_1}, \Omega_1 = (\Omega \setminus \Omega'_G) \cup \Omega'_{G_1}, \Theta_1 = \Theta)$$
$$\| \, G(C, R^c, R^{i'}, R^{o'}, B, \Omega, \Theta' \mid R^{i'} = R^i \cup (C_1 \times C), R^{o'} = R^o \cup (C \times C_1),$$
$$\Theta' = \Theta \cup C_1)$$

(20)

and Ω'_G *that share the same identifiers; and at the same time, it establishes new associations between the two concepts, see Box 5, where* $C'_{G1} \subset C_1 \wedge C'_{G2} \subset C_2 \wedge \#C'_{G1} = \#C'_{G2}$; $B'_{G1} \subset B_1 \wedge B'_{G2} \subset B_2 \wedge \#B'_{G1} = \#B'_{G2}$; *and* $\Omega'_{G1} \subset \Omega_1 \wedge \Omega'_{G2} \subset \Omega_2 \wedge \#\Omega'_{G1} = \#\Omega'_{G2}$.

The binary tailoring, extension, and substitution can also be extended to corresponding *n*-nary operations, similar to that of inheritance as given in Definitions 25.

(2) Composition of Granular Systems

Composition operations on granules in system algebra encompass a pair of composition and decomposition operations, where decomposition is defined based on the operation of granule difference.

Definition 30. *The composition of two granules* G_1 *and* G_2, *denoted by* ®, *results in a supergranule G that is formed by the conjunction of both sets of cells and environment* $C_1 \, Y \, C_2$ *and* $\Theta_1 \, Y \, \Theta_2$, *as well as incremental unions of all sets of*

relation $R^c = R_1^{\,c} \boxplus R_2^{\,c}$, $R^i = R_1^{\,i} \boxplus R_2^{\,i}$, $R^o = R_1^{\,o} \boxplus R_2^{\,o}$, *behaviors* $B = B_1 \boxplus B_2$, *and constraints* $\Omega = \Omega_1 \boxplus \Omega_2$, *respectively, see Box 6, where the mathematical calculus of incremental union* $\boxplus$ *between sets of relations may be referred to (Wang, 2007a).*

It is noteworthy that granule compositions result in the *incremental relations* ΔR_{12}, *behaviors* (functions) ΔB_{12}, and *constraints* $\Delta \Omega_{12}$, which are solely a property of the new supergranule G, but not belong to any of the independent subgranules, i.e.:

$$\Delta R_{12} \,\mathrm{E}\, S \wedge (\Delta R_{12} \,\not\mathrm{E}\, S_1 \wedge \Delta R_{12} \,\not\mathrm{E}\, S_2) \quad (22a)$$

$$\Delta B_{12} \,\mathrm{E}\, S \wedge (\Delta B_{12} \,\not\mathrm{E}\, S_1 \wedge \Delta B_{12} \,\not\mathrm{E}\, S_2) \quad (22b)$$

$$\Delta \Omega_{12} \,\mathrm{E}\, S \wedge (\Delta \Omega_{12} \,\not\mathrm{E}\, S_1 \wedge \Delta \Omega_{12} \,\not\mathrm{E}\, S_2) \quad (22c)$$

where E denote a membership relation of a given set in a system.

Box 6.

$$G_1(C_1, R_1^{\,c}, R_1^{\,i}, R_1^{\,o}, B_1, \Omega_1, \Theta_1) \uplus G_2(C_2, R_2^{\,c}, R_2^{\,i}, R_2^{\,o}, B_2, \Omega_2, \Theta_2)$$

$$\triangleq G(C, R^c, R^i, R^o, B, \Omega, \Theta) \,|\, C = C_1 \cup C_2, R^c = R_1^{\,c} \boxplus R_2^{\,c}, R^i = R_1^{\,i} \boxplus R_2^{\,i},$$

$$R^o = R_1^{\,o} \boxplus R_2^{\,o}, B = B_1 \boxplus B_2, \Omega = \Omega_1 \boxplus \Omega_2, \Theta = \Theta_1 \cup \Theta_2)$$

$$\| \, \mathop{R}_{i=1}^{2} \, G_i(C_i, R_i^{\,c}, R_i^{\,i'}, R_i^{\,o'}, B_i, \Omega_i, \Theta'_i \,|\, R^{i'}_{\,i} = R^i_{\,i} \cup (C \times C_i),$$

$$R^{o'}_{\,i} = R^o_{\,i} \cup (C_i \times C), \Theta'_i = \Theta_i \cup C)$$

$$= G(C, R^c, R^i, R^o, B, \Omega, \Theta) \,|\, C = C_1 \cup C_2, R^c = R_1^{\,c} \cup R_2^{\,c} \cup \Delta R_{12}^{\,c},$$

$$R^i = R_1^{\,i} \cup R_2^{\,i} \cup \Delta R_{12}^{\,i}, R^o = R_1^{\,o} \cup R_2^{\,o} \cup \Delta R_{12}^{\,o},$$

$$B = B_1 \cup B_2 \cup \Delta B_{12}, \Omega = \Omega_1 \cup \Omega_2 \cup \Delta \Omega_{12}, \Theta = \Theta_1 \cup \Theta_2)$$

$$\| \, \mathop{R}_{i=1}^{2} \, G_i(C_i, R_i^{\,c}, R_i^{\,i'}, R_i^{\,o'}, B_i, \Omega_i, \Theta'_i \,|\, R^{i'}_{\,i} = R^i_{\,i} \cup (C \times C_i),$$

$$R^{o'}_{\,i} = R^o_{\,i} \cup (C_i \times C), \Theta'_i = \Theta_i \cup C)$$

(21)

The above discovery is known as the *system fusion principle* (Wang, 2008c), which reveal that the nature of granular system utilities can be rigorously explained as the newly generated relations ΔR_{12}, as well as behaviors ΔB_{12} and constraints $\Delta \Omega_{12}$, during the composition of two or more granules. The empirical awareness of this key system property has been intuitively or qualitatively described in the literature of system science (Ellis and Fred, 1962; Klir, 1992). However, the above system fusion principle provides the first mathematical explanation for the mechanism of system gains during granular system compositions.

Granule compositions as modeled in Definition 30 can be extended to *n*-nary compositions as follows.

Definition 31. *The composition of multiple granules, denoted by*

$$\biguplus_{i=1}^{n} G_i,$$

is an iterative integration of a pair of them, which cumulatively creates the new supergranules G, see Box 7.

According to Definitions 30 and 31, a granular system can be integrated from the bottom up by a series of compositions level-by-level in a system hierarchy.

Definition 32. *The difference between a granule G and a subgranule of it G_1, denoted by $\ni$, results in another subgranule G_2 that is formed by the difference of sets of cells and I/O relations (C_1, R_1^i, $R^o{}_1$), and the differences of the internal relations, behaviors, and constraints ($R^c{}_1$, B_1, Ω_1) with their incremental counterparts ($\Delta R^c{}_{12}$, ΔB_{12}, $\Delta \Omega_{12}$), see Box 8.*

Box 7.

$$G(C, R^c, R^i, R^o, B, \Omega, \Theta) \triangleq \biguplus_{i=1}^{n} G_i(C_i, R_i^c, R_i^i, R_i^o, B_i, \Omega_i, \Theta_i)$$

$$= G(C, R^c, R^i, R^o, B, \Omega, \Theta \mid C = \bigcup_{i=1}^{n} C_i, R^c = \boxplus_{i=1}^{n} R^c{}_i, R^i = \boxplus_{i=1}^{n} R^i{}_i,$$

$$R^o = \boxplus_{i=1}^{n} R^o{}_i, B = \boxplus_{i=1}^{n} B_i, \ \Omega = \boxplus_{i=1}^{n} \Omega_i, \Theta = \bigcup_{i=1}^{n} \Theta_i) \tag{23}$$

$$\| \underset{i=1}{\overset{n}{R}} \ G_i(C_i, R_i^c, R_i^{i'}, R_i^{o'}, B_i, \Omega_i, \Theta'_i \mid R^{i'}{}_i = R^i{}_i \cup (C \times C_i),$$

$$R^{o'}{}_i = R^o{}_i \cup (C_i \times C), \Theta'{}_i = \Theta_i \cup C)$$

Box 8.

$$G(C, R^c, R^i, R^o, B, \Omega, \Theta) \boxminus G_1(C_1, R_1^c, R_1^i, R_1^o, B_1, \Omega_1, \Theta_1)$$

$$\triangleq G_2(C_2, R_2^c, R_2^i, R_2^o, B_2, \Omega_2, \Theta_2 \mid C_2 = C \setminus C_1,$$

$$R_2^c = R^c \setminus (R_1^c \cup \Delta R_{12}^c), R_2^i = R^i \setminus R_1^i, \tag{24}$$

$$R_2^o = R^o \setminus R_1^o, B_2 = B \setminus (B_1 \cup \Delta B_{12}),$$

$$\Omega_2 = \Omega \setminus (\Omega_1 \cup \Delta \Omega_{12}), \Theta_2 = \Theta_1)$$

Box 9.

$$G(C,R^c,R^i,R^o,B,\Omega,\Theta) \overset{n}{\underset{i=1}{\bigsqcap}} G_i(C_i,R_i^c,R_i^i,R_i^o,B_i,\Omega_i,\Theta_i)$$

$$\triangleq \overset{n}{\underset{i=1}{R}} \{ \ G_i(C_i,R_i^c,R_i^{i'},R_i^{o'},B_i,\Omega_i,\Theta'_i \mid R_i^{i'} = R_i^i \cup (C \times C_i),$$

$$R_i^{o'} = R_i^o \cup (C_i \times C), \Theta'_i = \Theta_i \cup C) \tag{25}$$

$$\| \ G(C,R^c,R^i,R^o,B,\Omega,\Theta) \boxminus G_i(C_i,R_i^c,R_i^i,R_i^o,B_i,\Omega_i,\Theta_i)$$

$$\}$$

A granular system decomposition is an inverse operation of granule composition that breaks up a given granule into two or more subgranules. Granule decomposition can be described based on the concept of granule difference. The latter is an inversed operation of the incremental union of sets as given in Eq. 21.

Definition 33. *The decomposition of a granule G, denoted by ©, is to break up G into two or more subgranules at the same level of the system hierarchy lower than the current granule by a series of iterative difference operations, see Box 9.*

As specified in Definition 33, the decomposition operation results in the removal of all the incremental internal relations $\Delta R_{ij}^c = C_i \times C_j, 1 \le i,j \le n$ that are no longer belong to any of its subgranules.

(3) Integration of Granular Systems

Integration operations on granules are a category of composition operations in system algebra. The integration operations of granules encompass a pair of algebraic manipulations of granules known as aggregation and specification.

Definition 34. *The aggregation of a granule G from a set of n peer granules S_p, $1 \le i \le n$, denoted by ⊃, is an aggregation of G with the elicitation*

Box 10.

$$G(C,R^c,R^i,R^o,B,\Omega,\Theta) \ \Leftarrow \ \overset{n}{\underset{i=1}{R}} \ G_i(C_i,R_i^c,R_i^i,R_i^o,B_i,\Omega_i,\Theta_i)$$

$$\triangleq G(C,R^c,R^i,R^o,B,\Omega,\Theta \mid C = \bigcup_{i=1}^{n} C'_i \subseteq C_i, R^c = C \times C,$$

$$R^i = \bigcup_{i=1}^{n}(R_i^i \cup (C_i \times C)), R^o = \bigcup_{i=1}^{n}(R_i^o \cup (C \times C_i)), \tag{26}$$

$$B = \bigcup_{i=1}^{n} B'_i \subseteq B_i, \ \Omega = \bigcup_{i=1}^{n} C'_i \subseteq C_i, \ \Theta \subseteq C_\Theta \cup \bigcup_{i=1}^{n} \Theta_i)$$

$$\| \ \overset{n}{\underset{i=1}{R}} \ G_i(C_i,R_i^c,R_i^{i'},R_i^{o'},B_i,\Omega_i,\Theta'_i \mid R_i^{i'} = R_i^i \cup (C \times C_i),$$

$$R_i^{o'} = R_i^o \cup (C_i \times C), \Theta'_i = \Theta_i \cup C)$$

of interested subsets of cells C'$_i$, behaviors B'$_i$, and constraints Ω'$_i$; and at the same time, it establishes new associations among all aggregated granules, see Box 10.

Granule aggregation is also known as granule *elicitation*. According to Definitions 30 and 34, the difference between granule composition and aggregation is that the former constructs a new granule by integrating a set of subgranules as a whole; while the latter constructs a new granule by eliciting interested subsets of cells, behaviors, and/or constraints from a set of individual and independent subgranules.

A granule specification is an inverse operation of granule aggregation. A granular system specification is usually operated by a series of refinements.

Definition 35. The specification of a granule G by a set of n refined granules G$_i$, 1 ≤ i ≤ n, denoted by □, is a specification of G with a total order of a series of refinements by increasingly specific and detailed cells C$_i$, behaviors B$_i$, and constraints Ω$_{ij}$; and at the same time, it establishes new associations among all refining systems, see Box 11.

Granule specification is a refinement process where more specific and detailed cells, behaviors, and constraints are developed in a consistent and coherent top-down hierarchy. The major tasks of granule specifications are system architecture (component) and behavior specifications, which can be further refined by the *Component Logical Models* (CLMs) and *processes* as provided in RTPA (Wang, 2002a, 2007a, 2008d).

PROPERTIES OF GRANULAR SYSTEMS

Based on the abstract system models of granules and granular computing, the topological properties of granules and the granularity of granular systems can be rigorously analyzed in this section.

Topological Properties of Granular Systems

Theorem 1. A granule G(C, R^c, R^i, R^o, B, Ω, Θ) on Y is an asymmetric and reflective system because its relations R^c, R^i, and R^o, are constrained by the following rules:

(a) Internally asymmetric:

Box 11.

$$(G_n \vdash ... \vdash G_2 \vdash G_1) \vdash G_0(C_0, R_0^c, R_0^i, R_0^o, B_0, \Omega_0, \Theta_0)$$

$$\triangleq G_0(C_0, R_0^c, R_0^i, R_0^o, B_0, \Omega_0, \Theta_0 \mid C_0 = \mathop{R}_{i=1}^{n}(C_{i-1} \subset C_i), R_0^c = (C_0 \times C_0),$$

$$R_0^i = \bigcup_{i=1}^{n}(R_i^i \cup (C_i \times C_0)), R_0^o = \bigcup_{i=1}^{n}(R_i^o \cup (C_0 \times C_i)),$$

$$B_0 = \mathop{R}_{i=1}^{n}(B_{i-1} \subset B_i), \ \Omega_0 = \mathop{R}_{i=1}^{n}(B_{i-1} \subset B_i), \ \Theta_0 = \Theta_1 = \Theta_2 = ... = \Theta_n)$$

$$\| \mathop{R}_{i=1}^{n} G_i(C_i, R_i^c, R_i^{i'}, R_i^{o'}, B_i, \Omega_i, \Theta_i' \mid R_i^{i'} = R_i^i \cup (C_0 \times C_i),$$

$$R_i^{o'} = R_i^o \cup (C_i \times C_o), \Theta_i' = \Theta_i \cup C_0))$$

(27)

$$\forall a, b \in C \wedge a \neq b \wedge r \in R^c, r(a,b) \downarrow r(b,a)$$
$$(28)$$

(b) Externally asymmetric:

$$\forall a \in C \wedge \forall x \in C_\Theta \wedge r \in R^i \vee r \in R^o, r(x,a) \downarrow$$
$$r(a,x) \qquad (29)$$

(c) Reflective:

$$\forall c \in C, r(c, c) \in R^c \qquad (30)$$

Corollary 1. *The maximum number of binary relations n_r in a granule $G(C, R^c, R^i, R^o, B, \Omega, \Theta)$ is determined by the numbers of internal relations R^c as well as external relations R^i and R^o, i.e.:*

$$n_r(S) = \# R^c + \# R^i + \# R^o = n_c^2 + 2(n_c \bullet n_{c_\Theta})$$
$$= n_c(n_c + 2n_{c_\Theta})$$
$$(31)$$

Corollary 2. *If all reflective self-relations are not considered among each cells in a granule, then the maximum number of binary relations n'_r is:*

$$n'_r(S) = n_r(S) - n_c = n_c \bullet (n_c + 2n_{c_\Theta}) - n_c$$
$$= n_c \bullet (n_c + 2n_{c_\Theta} - 1)$$
$$(32)$$

According to Corollaries 1 and 2, it is apparent that a simple granule system may result in a huge number of relations n_r and the exponential increases of complexity, when the number of cells possessed in it is considerably large. Therefore, system algebra is introduced to formally and efficiently manipulate the complex abstract and concrete granular systems.

Granularity of Granular Systems

The study on system magnitudes (Wang, 2007a) can be adopted to classify the size properties of granular systems and their relationship with other basic system attributes. This results in a set of measures on the sizes, magnitudes, and complexities of granular systems as described below.

Definition 36. *The size of a granule G, S_G is the number of cells encompassed in the granule, i.e.:*

$$S_G = \# C = n_c \qquad (33)$$

Definition 37. *The magnitude of a granule G, M_G, is the number of asymmetric binary relations among the n_c components of the granule including the reflexive relations, i.e.:*

$$M_G = \# R = n_r = \#(C \times C) = n_c^2 \qquad (34)$$

If all self-reflective relations are ruled out in n_r, the pure number of binary relations M'_G in the given granular system is determined as follows:

$$M'_G = M_s - n_c = n_c^2 - n_c = n_c(n_c - 1) \qquad (35)$$

Corollary 3. *The pure number of binary relations M'_G in a granule equals to exactly two times of the number of pairwise combinations among n_c, i.e.:*

$$M'_G = n_c(n_c - 1) = 2 \bullet \frac{n_c(n_c - 1)}{2} = 2 \bullet C_{n_c}^2$$
$$(36)$$

where the factor 2 represents the asymmetric binary relation r among all cells in the granule, i.e., arb $\neq$ bra.

The magnitude of a granule determines its complexity. The complicities of a granular system can be classified based on if they are fully or partially connected. The former is the theoretical upper-bound complexity of a granule in which all cells are potentially interconnected with each other in all *n*-nary ways, $1 \leq n \leq n_c = \# C$. The latter is the more typical complexity of a granule where cells are only pairwisely connected.

Definition 38. *The complexity of a fully connected granular system C_{max} is a closure of all possible n-nary relations R^*, $1 \leq n \leq n_c$, among all components of the given granule $n_c = \#C$, i.e.:*

$$C_{max} = R^* = 2 \sum_{k=0}^{n_r} \mathbf{C}_{n_r}^k \approx 2 \bullet 2^{n_r} \qquad (37)$$
$$= 2^{n_r+1} = 2^{n_c^2+1} = 2^{M_G+1}$$

where C_{max} is also called the maximum complexity of a granular system.

According to Definition 38, the closure of all possible n-nary relations R^* may easily result in an extremely huge degree of complexity for a granule system with a few cells. For example, when $n_c = 10$, $C_{max} = 2^{101}$. This indicates that a granular system would be too hard to be modeled and handled by conventional modeling techniques.

It is noteworthy that almost all functioning systems are partially connected, because a fully connected system may not represent or provide anything meaningful. Therefore, the complexity of partially connected systems can be simplified as follows on the basis of Definition 38.

Definition 39. *The complexity of a partially connected granular system C_r is determined by the number of asymmetric binary relations M'_G of the given granule, i.e.:*

$$C_r = M'_G = 2 \bullet \mathbf{C}_{n_c}^2 = n_c(n_c-1) \qquad (38)$$

where C_r can be referred to be the relational complexity of a granular system.

It is recognized that the extent of granule magnitudes can be classified at seven levels known as the *empty, small, medium, large, giant, immense,* and *infinite* granule systems from the bottom up. A summary of the relationships between granule magnitudes, sizes, internal relations, and complexities can be described in the *granule magnitude model* as shown in Table 1.

Table 1 indicates that the complexity of a small granule system may easily be out of control of human cognitive manageability. This leads to the following principle.

Theorem 2. *The holism complexity of granular systems states that within the 7-level scale of the granule magnitude model, almost all granular systems are too complicated to be cognitively understood or mentally handled as a whole, except small granule systems or those that can be decomposed into small granule systems.*

Table 1. The magnitude model of abstract granular systems

Level	Category	Size of granule $(S_s = n_c)$	Magnitude of granule $(M_s = n_r = n_c^2)$	Relational complexity of granule $(C_r = n_c(n_c - 1))$	Maximum complexity of granule $(C_{max} = 2^{n_c^2})$
1	The empty granule (O)	0	0	0	-
2	Small granule	[1, 10]	[1, 10²]	[0, 90]	[2, 2¹⁰⁰]
3	Medium granule	(10, 10²]	(10², 10⁴]	(90, 0.99 • 10⁴]	(2¹⁰⁰, 2¹⁰,⁰⁰⁰]
4	Large granule	(10², 10³]	(10⁴, 10⁶]	(0.99 • 10⁴, 0.999 • 10⁶]	∞
5	Giant granule	(10³, 10⁴]	(10⁶, 10⁸]	(0.999 • 10⁶, 0.9999 • 10⁸]	∞
6	Immense granule	(10⁴, 10⁵]	(10⁸, 10¹⁰]	(0.9999 • 10⁸, 0.99999 •10¹⁰]	∞
7	The infinite granule (U)	∞	∞	∞	∞

According to Theorem 2, the basic principle for dealing with complicated granular systems is system decomposition or modularity, in which the complexity of a lower-level granule must be small enough to be cognitively manageable. Details of granular system decomposition methods have been provided in Definition 33.

REPRESENTATION OF GRANULAR SYSTEMS

The abstract system model of granules and granular computing, developed in preceding sections enable the formal representation of both abstract and concrete granular systems. A case study on a digital clock is presented in this section to demonstrate the representation of computing granules and granular systems, as well as the expressive power of the abstract system models of granules and system algebra.

Concrete Models of Granules in Granular Computing

Two concrete real-world granular systems in granular computing, the *Clock* and *Alarm*, are described below for illustrating how the generic abstract granule models and their algebraic operations may be applied in granule-based system design and modeling based on system algebra.

Figure 2. The Clock granule

The Clock Granule $G_1(C_1, R^c{}_1, R^i{}_1, R^o{}_1, B_1, \Omega_1, \Theta_1)$

- The set of cells:
  $C_1 = \{Processor, Keypad, LEDs, ClockPulse\}$

- The set of internal relations:
  $R^c{}_1 \subseteq C_1 \times C_1 = \{Input\ (Keypad,\ Processor),$
  $Tick\ (ClockPulse,\ Processor),$
  $Output\ (Processor,\ LEDs)\}$

- The set of input relations:
  $R^i{}_1 \subseteq C_{\Theta 1} \times C_1 = \{SetTime\ (User,\ Keypad)\}$

- The set of output relations:
  $R^o{}_1 \subseteq C_1 \times C_{\Theta 1} = \{ShowTime\ (LEDs,\ User)\}$

- The set of behaviors:
  $B_1 = \{SetTime, ShownTime, Tick\}$

- The set of constraints:
  $\Omega_1 = \{Time = \text{hh} \times \text{mm} \times \text{ss}\}$

- The environment:
  $\Theta_1 = \{User\}$

Example 1. A digital clock, Clock, can be described as a granule, or a granular system, G_1, as follows:

$$Clock \triangleq\, < G_1(C_1, R^c_1, R^i_1, R^o_1, B_1, \Omega_1, \Theta_1) \tag{39}$$

where the configuration of the Clock granule is given in Figure 2.

In Figure 2, the behaviors of the clock granule defined in B_1 can be further refined by a set of processes in RTPA.

Example 2. The alarm subsystem for the digital clock, Alarm, can be described as another granule G_2 as follows:

$$Alarm \triangleq\, G_2(C_2, R^c_2, R^i_2, R^o_2, B_2, \Omega_2, \Theta_2) \tag{40}$$

Figure 3. The Alarm granule

where the configuration of the Alarm granule is given in Figure 3.

In Figure 3, the behaviors of the alarm granule defined in B_2 can be further refined by a set of processes in RTPA.

Granular System Composition in Granular Computing

The composition of two concrete granules in real-world system design for granular computing are described below, which illustrates how the generic abstract granule composition operation may be implemented in real-world granule-based system design and modeling.

Example 3. According to Definition 30, the composition of the two granules G_1(Clock) and G_2(Alarm)

The Alarm Granule $G_2(C_2, R^c_2, R^i_2, R^o_2, B_2, \Omega_2, \Theta_2)$

- The set of cells:
  $C_2 = \{Processor, Keypad, LEDs, Bell\}$

- The set of internal relations:
  $R^c_2 \subseteq C_2 \times C_2 = \{Input\ (Keypad, Processor),$
  $AlarmCheck\ (Time, Alarm),$
  $AlarmRelease\ (Keypad, Processor),$
  $Output\ (Processor, LEDs),$
  $Ring\ (Processor, Bell)\}$

- The set of input relations:
  $R^i_2 \subseteq C_{\Theta 2} \times C_2 = \{SetAlarm\ (User, Keypad)\}$

- The set of output relations:
  $R^o_2 \subseteq C_2 \times C_{\Theta 2} = \{ShowAlarm\ (LEDs, User)\}$

- The set of behaviors:
  $B_2 = \{SetAlarm, ShownAlarm, CheckAlarm, Ring, AlarmRelease\}$

- The set of constraints:
  $\Omega_2 = \{Alarm = hh \times mm\}$

- The environment:
  $\Theta_2 = \{User\}$

Figure 4. The Alarm_Clock granule: $G(C, R^c, R^i, R^o, B, \Omega, \Theta) \triangleq G_1 \uplus G_2$

The Composed Alarm_Clock Granule $G(C, R^c, R^i, R^o, B, \Omega, \Theta)$

- The set of cells:

$C = C_1 \cup C_2$

= *{Processor, Keypad, LEDs, ClockPulse}* $\cup$

{Processor, Keypad, LEDs, Bell}

= *{Processor, Keypad, LEDs, ClockPulse, Bell}*

- The set of internal relations:

$R^c = R^c_1 \cup R^c_2 \cup \Delta R^c_{12}$

= *{Input(Keypad, Processor), Tick(ClockPulse, Processor),*

Output(Processor, LEDs)} $\cup$

{Input(Keypad, Processor), AlarmCheck(Time, Alarm),

AlarmRelease(Keypad, Processor), Output(Processor, LEDs),

Ring(Processor, Bell)} $\cup$

{Select(Clock, Alarm)}   // ΔR^c_{12}

= *{Input(Keypad, Processor), Tick(ClockPulse, Processor),*

AlarmCheck(Time, Alarm),

AlarmRelease(Keypad, Processor),

Output(Processor, LEDs), Ring(Processor, Bell),

Select(Clock, Alarm)}

- The set of input relations:

$R^i = R^i_1 \cup R^i_2$

= *{SetTime(User, Keypad), SetAlarm(User, Keypad)}*

- The set of output relations:

$R^o = R^o_1 \cup R^o_2$

= *{ShowTime(LEDs, User), ShowAlarm(LEDs, User)}*

- The set of behaviors:

$B = B_1 \cup B_2 \cup \Delta B_{12}$

= *{SetTime, ShownTime, tick}* $\cup$

{SetAlarm, ShownAlarm, CheckAlarm, Ring, AlarmRelease} $\cup$

{SelectClock, SelectAlarm}   // ΔB_{12}

- The set of constraints:

$\Omega = \Omega_1 \cup \Omega_2$

= *{Time = hh × mm × ss, Alarm = hh × mm}*

- The environment:

$\Theta = \Theta_1 \cup \Theta_2$

= *{User}*

Box 12.

$$G_1(C_1, R_1^c, R_1^i, R_1^o, B_1, \Omega_1, \Theta_1) \uplus G_2(C_2, R_2^c, R_2^i, R_2^o, B_2, \Omega_2, \Theta_2)$$
$$\triangleq G(C, R^c, R^i, R^o, B, \Omega, \Theta) \mid C = C_1 \cup C_2, R^c = R_1^c \cup R_2^c \cup \Delta R_{12}^c,$$
$$R^i = R_1^i \cup R_2^i \cup \Delta R_{12}^i, R^o = R_1^o \cup R_2^o \cup \Delta R_{12}^o,$$
$$B = B_1 \cup B_2 \cup \Delta B_{12}, \Omega = \Omega_1 \cup \Omega_2 \cup \Delta\Omega_{12}, \Theta = \Theta_1 \cup \Theta_2)$$
$$\| \mathop{R}_{i=1}^{2} G_i(C_i, R_i^c, R_i^{i'}, R_i^{o'}, B_i, \Omega_i, \Theta_i' \mid R_i^{i'} = R_i^i \cup (C \times C_i),$$
$$R_i^{o'} = R_i^o \cup (C_i \times C), \Theta_i' = \Theta_i \cup C) \tag{41}$$

as given in Examples 1 and 2 results in a new supergranule *G(Alarm_Clock)* as shown in Box 12, where the configuration of the *Alarm_Clock* granule is given in Figure 4.

Note that the newly generated relations *Select(Clock, Alarm)*, as well as the new behaviors *SelectClock* and *SelectAlarm* in the granule system *G(Alarm_Clock)* are the results of the incremental unions of systems as defined in Eq. 21. Therefore, they do not belong to either subgranule G_1*(Clock)* or G_2*(Alarm)* rather than purely the properties of the supergranule *G(Alarm_Clock)*.

Granular System Decomposition in Granular Computing

The decomposition of a concrete granule in real-world system design for granular computing is described below, which illustrates how the generic abstract granule decomposition operation may be implemented in real-world granule-based system design and modeling.

Example 4. *According to Definition 33, the decomposition of a supergranule G(AlarmClock) may result in two new subgranules G_1(Clock) and G_2(Alarm) as shown in Box 13, where the configuration of the Clock granule, G_1(Clock), is given in Figure 5.*

Box 13.

$$G(C, R^c, R^i, R^o, B, \Omega, \Theta) \mathop{\bigcap}_{i=1}^{2} G_i(C_i, R_i^c, R_i^i, R_i^o, B_i, \Omega_i, \Theta_i)$$
$$\triangleq \mathop{R}_{i=1}^{2} \{ \ G_i(C_i, R_i^c, R_i^{i'}, R_i^{o'}, B_i, \Omega_i, \Theta_i' \mid R_i^{i'} = R_i^i \cup (C \times C_i),$$
$$R_i^{o'} = R_i^o \cup (C_i \times C), \Theta_i' = \Theta_i \cup C)$$
$$\| \ G(C, R^c, R^i, R^o, B, \Omega, \Theta) \boxminus G_i(C_i, R_i^c, R_i^i, R_i^o, B_i, \Omega_i, \Theta_i)$$
$$\} \tag{42}$$

Figure 5. The Clock granule as a result of decomposition

The Decomposed Clock Granule $G_1(C_1, R^c_1, R^i_1, R^o_1, B_1, \Omega_1, \Theta_1)$

- The set of cells:
$C_1 = C \setminus C_2$
= {*Processor, Keypad, LEDs, ClockPulse, Bell*} \ {*Bell*}
= {*Processor, Keypad, LEDs, ClockPulse*}

- The set of internal relations:
$R^c_1 = R^c \setminus (R^{c}_2 \cup \Delta R^c_{12})$
= {*Input(Keypad, Processor), Tick(ClockPulse, Processor),*
AlarmCheck(Time, Alarm), AlarmRelease(Keypad, Processor),
Output(Processor, LEDs),Ring(Processor, Bell),
Select(Clock, Alarm)
} \
{*AlarmCheck(Time, Alarm),*
AlarmRelease(Keypad, Processor),
Ring(Processor, Bell)
} $\cup$
{*Select(Clock, Alarm)*}
= {*Input(Keypad, Processor), Tick(ClockPulse, Processor),*
Output(Processor, LEDs)
}

- The set of input relations:
$R^i_1 = R^i \setminus R^i_2$
= {*SetTime(User, Keypad)*}

- The set of output relations:
$R^o_1 = R^o \setminus R^o_2$
= {*ShowTime(LEDs, User)*}

- The set of behaviors:
$B_1 = B \setminus \{B_2 \cup \Delta B_{12}\}$
= {*SetTime, ShownTime, Tick, SetAlarm,*
ShownAlarm, CheckAlarm, Ring, AlarmRelease,
SelectClock, SelectAlarm
} \
{*SetAlarm, ShownAlarm, CheckAlarm, Ring, AlarmRelease,*
SelectClock, SelectAlarm
}
= {*SetTime, ShownTime, tick*}

- The set of constraints:
$\Omega_1 = \Omega \setminus \Omega_2$
= {*Time* = hh × mm × ss}

- The environment:
$\Theta_1 = \Theta \setminus \Theta'_2$
= {*User*}

Granule $G_2(Alarm)$ can be derived similarly as shown in Figure 5, which results in the second subgranule exactly as that given in Eq. 40 and Figure 3. Note that within the given supergranule G, because there is an overlap between the two subgranules G_1 and G_2, the difference operation for decomposition may only remove the disjoint subset $C'_2, R^{c'}_2$, and Θ'_2 from G. It is also noteworthy that the loss of ΔR_{12} = *Select* (*Clock*, *Alarm*) and ΔB_{12} = {*SelectClock*, *SelectAlarm*} during the operation of granular system decomposition.

CONCLUSION

A new approach to rigorously construct the theoretical foundations of granular computing has been introduced on the basis of the recent development in denotational mathematics known as system algebra. The abstract system model of granules has been developed. The rigorous treatment of granular systems in computing has been studied using system algebra. The properties of granular systems and system granularity have been formally analyzed. Case studies on concrete granules and real-world granule-based systems have been presented. A wide range of applications on the system algebra theory of granular computing have been identified in computing, software engineering, system engineering, cognitive informatics, and computational intelligence.

This paper has presented a paradigm that demonstrates the generality and expressive power of system algebra and the generic abstract systems. System algebra has been introduced as a set of relational and compositional operations for manipulating abstract systems and their composing rules. The former have been elicited as the algebraic operations of *independent, related, overlapped, equivalent, subsystem,* and *supersystem.* The latter have been identified as the algebraic operations of *inheritance, tailoring, extension, substitute, difference, composition, decomposition, aggregation,* and *specification.* The rigorous treatment of the granular computing paradigm by system algebra has established a solid foundation for granular computing and granule-based systems modeling.

ACKNOWLEDGMENT

The authors would like to acknowledge the Natural Science and Engineering Council of Canada (NSERC) for its partial support to this work. The authors would like to thank Dr. *W. Pedrycz*, Dr. *A. Skowron*, and anonymous reviewers for their valuable comments and suggestions.

REFERENCES

Ashby, W.R. (1958), Requisite Variety and Implications for Control of Complex Systems, *Cybernetica,* (1), 83-99.

Ashby, W. R. (1962), Principles of the Self-Organizing System, in von Foerster H. and Zopf G. eds, *Principles of Self-Organization*, Pergamon, Oxford, 255-278.

Bargiela, A., & Pedrycz, W. (2002). *Granular Computing: an Introduction.* Boston: Kluwer Academic Publishers.

Eigen, M., & Schuster, P. (1979). *The Hypercycle: A Principle of Natural Self-Organization.* Berlin: Springer.

Ellis, D. O., & Fred, J. L. (1962). *Systems Philosophy.* Prentice-Hall.

Ford, J. (1986). Chaos: Solving the Unsolvable, Predicting the Unpredictable. In *Chaotic Dynamics and Fractals.* Academic Press.

Haken, H. (1977). *Synergetics.* NY: Springer-Verlag.

Heylighen, F. (1989), Self-Organization, Emergence and the Architecture of Complexity, in *Proc. 1st European Conf. on System Science* (AFCET), Paris, 23-32.

Klir, G. J. (1992). *Facets of Systems Science.* New York: Plenum.

Lin, T. Y. (1998). *Granular Computing on Binary Relations (I): Data Mining and Neighborhood Systems, Proc. Rough Sets in Knowledge Discovery* (pp. 107–120). Heidelberg: Physica-Verlag.

Lin, T. Y., Yao, Y. Y., & Zadeh, L. A. (Eds.). (2002). *Data Mining*. Heidelberg: Rough Sets and Granular Computing, Physica-Verlag.

Pawlak, Z. (1987), Rough Logic, *Bulletin of the Polish Academy of Science, Technical Science*, (5-6), 253-258.

Pawlak, Z. (1998), Granularity of Knowledge, Indiscernibility and Rough Sets, *Proc. 1998 IEEE International Conference on Fuzzy Systems*, 106-110.

Pedrycz, W. (Ed.). (2001). *Granular Computing: An Emerging Paradigm*. Heidelberg: Physica-Verlag.

Polkowski, L. (2008). On Foundations and Applications of the Paradigm of Granular Rough Computing, *The International Journal of Cognitive Informatics* (IJCINI). *IGI Publishing, USA*, *2*(2), 80–94.

Polkowski, L., & Skowron, A. (1998), Towards Adaptive Calculus of Granules, *Proc. 1998 IEEE International Conference on Fuzzy Systems*, 111-116.

Prigogine, I., & Nicolis, G. (1972). Thermodynamics of Evolution. *Physics Today*, (25): 23–28. doi:10.1063/1.3071090

Rapoport, A., (1962), Mathematical Aspects of General Systems Theory, *General Systems Yearbook*, (11), 3-11.

Skarda, C. A., & Freeman, W. J. (1987). How Brains Make Chaos into Order. *The Behavioral and Brain Sciences*, 10.

Skowron, A., & Stepaniuk, J. (2001). Information Granules: Towards Foundations of Granular Computing. *International Journal of Intelligent Systems*, (16): 57–85. doi:10.1002/1098-111X(200101)16:1<57::AID-INT6>3.0.CO;2-Y

von Bertalanffy, L. (1952). *Problems of Life: An Evolution of Modern Biological and Scientific Thought*. London: C.A. Watts.

Wang, Y. (2002a), The Real-Time Process Algebra (RTPA), *Annals of Software Engineering*, Springer, (14), USA, 235-274.

Wang, Y. (2002b), Keynote: On Cognitive Informatics, *Proc. 1st IEEE International Conference on Cognitive Informatics (ICCI'02)*, Calgary, Canada, IEEE CS Press, August, 34-42.

Wang, Y. (2003a), On Cognitive Informatics, *Brain and Mind: A Transdisciplinary Journal of Neuroscience and Neurophilosophy*, 4(2), 151-167.

Wang, Y. (2003b), Using Process Algebra to Describe Human and Software System Behaviors, *Brain and Mind: A Transdisciplinary Journal of Neuroscience and Neurophilosophy*, 4(2), 199–213.

Wang, Y. (2006). On the Informatics Laws and Deductive Semantics of Software. *IEEE Transactions on Systems, Man and Cybernetics. Part C, Applications and Reviews*, *36*(2), 161–171. doi:10.1109/TSMCC.2006.871138

Wang, Y. (2007a). *Software Engineering Foundations: A Software Science Perspective, CRC Series in Software Engineering (Vol. II)*. NY, USA: Auerbach Publications.

Wang, Y. (2007b). The Theoretical Framework of Cognitive Informatics, *International Journal of Cognitive Informatics and Natural Intelligence. IGI Publishing, USA*, *1*(1), 1–27.

Wang, Y. (2007c), Keynote: On Theoretical Foundations of Software Engineering and Denotational Mathematics, *Proc. 5th Asian Workshop on Foundations of Software*, Beihang Univ. Press, Xiamen, China, 99-102.

Wang, Y. (2008a), On Contemporary Denotational Mathematics for Computational Intelligence, *Transactions on Computational Science*, (2), Springer, June, 6-29.

Wang, Y. (2008b). On Concept Algebra: A Denotational Mathematical Structure for Knowledge and Software Modeling, *International Journal of Cognitive Informatics and Natural Intelligence. IGI Publishing, USA, 2*(2), 1–19.

Wang, Y. (2008c). On System Algebra: A Denotational Mathematical Structure for Abstract Systems Modeling, *International Journal of Cognitive Informatics and Natural Intelligence. IGI Publishing, USA, 2*(2), 20–43.

Wang, Y. (2008d). RTPA: A Denotational Mathematics for Manipulating Intelligent and Computing Behaviors, *International Journal of Cognitive Informatics and Natural Intelligence. IGI Publishing, USA, 2*(2), 44–62.

Wang, Y. (2008e). On the Big-R Notation for Describing Iterative and Recursive Behaviors, *International Journal of Cognitive Informatics and Natural Intelligence. IGI Publishing, USA, 2*(1), 17–23.

Wang, Y., & Wang, Y. (2006). On Cognitive Informatics Models of the Brain. *IEEE Transactions on Systems, Man and Cybernetics. Part C, Applications and Reviews, 36*(2), 203–207. doi:10.1109/TSMCC.2006.871151

Wang, Y., Wang, Y., Patel, S., & Patel, D. (2006). A Layered Reference Model of the Brain (LRMB). *IEEE Transactions on Systems, Man and Cybernetics. Part C, Applications and Reviews, 36*(2), 124–133. doi:10.1109/TSMCC.2006.871126

Yao, Y. Y. (2001). Information Granulation and Rough Set Approximation. *International Journal of Intelligent Systems, 16*(1), 87–104. doi:10.1002/1098-111X(200101)16:1<87::AID-INT7>3.0.CO;2-S

Yao, Y. Y. (2004a). A Partition Model of Granular Computing, *Transactions on Rough Sets, 1. Springer, LNCS, 3135*, 232–253.

Yao, Y. Y. (2004b) Granular Computing, *Computer Science*, Beijing, China, (31), 1-5.

Yao, Y. Y. (2005) Perspectives of Granular Computing, *Proc. 2005 IEEE International Conference on Granular Computing*, (1), 85-90.

Yao, Y. Y., & Zhou, B. (2008). A Logic Approach to Granular Computing, *International Journal of Cognitive Informatics and Natural Intelligence. IGI Publishing, USA, 2*(2), 63–79.

Zadeh, L. A. (1965), Fuzzy Sets and Systems, in J. Fox ed., *Systems Theory*, Polytechnic Press, Brooklyn NY, 29-37.

Zadeh, L. A. (1979), Fuzzy Sets and Information Granularity, in M.M. Gupta, R. Ragade, and R. Yager eds., *Advances in Fuzzy Set Theory and Applications*, North-Holland, Amsterdam, 3-18.

Zadeh, L. A. (1997). Towards a Theory of Fuzzy Information Granulation and its Centrality in Human Reasoning and Fuzzy Logic. *Fuzzy Sets and Systems*, (19): 111–127. doi:10.1016/S0165-0114(97)00077-8

Zadeh, L. A. (1998). Some Reflections on Soft Computing, Granular Computing and Their Roles in the Conception, Design and Utilization of Information/Intelligent Systems. *Soft Computing*, (2): 23–25. doi:10.1007/s005000050030

Zadeh, L.A. (2003), Some Reflections on Information Granulation and its Centrality in Granular Computing, Computing with Words. The Computational Theory of Perceptions and Precisiated Natural Language. *Proc. Data Mining, Rough Sets and Granular Computing*, Heideberg, 1-19.

This work was previously published in International Journal of Software Science and Computational Intelligence, Volume 1, Issue 1, edited by Yingxu Wang, pp. 64-86, copyright 2009 by IGI Publishing (an imprint of IGI Global).

Chapter 8

Semantic Matching, Propagation and Transformation for Composition in Component–Based Systems

Eric Bouillet
IBM Research, USA

Zhen Liu
IBM Research, USA

Mark Feblowitz
IBM Research, USA

Anand Ranganathan
IBM Research, USA

Anton Riabov
IBM Research, USA

ABSTRACT

Composition of software applications from component parts in response to high-level goals is a long-standing and highly challenging goal. We target the problem of composition in flow-based information processing systems and demonstrate how application composition and component development can be facilitated by the use of semantically described application metadata. The semantic metadata describe both the data flowing through each application and the processing performed in the associated application code. In this paper, we explore some of the key features of the semantic model, including the matching of outputs to input requirements, and the transformation and the propagation of semantic properties by components.

Information analysts and decision-makers in many application domains face a daunting task. In order to quickly arrive at and continually update the business intelligence that informs their advice or decisions, they must collect data from many diverse sources, adapt and integrate that data and apply a variety of analytic models. For such users, the need for timely acquisition and analysis is not adequately addressed by either fixed, monolithic applications nor by queries against fixed-schema data stores. As new sources are discovered and new or evolving analyses are needed, new ap-

DOI: 10.4018/978-1-4666-0261-8.ch008

plication requirements trigger new development cycles, resulting in delayed decisions and requiring analysts to resort to manual acquisition and analysis in the interim.

Such circumstances have given rise to an important area in end-user driven computing that Cherbakov, et al, describe as *situational applications* (SAs) (Cherbakov, Bravery, & Pandya, 2007): "…situational applications describes applications built to address a particular situation, problem, or challenge. The development life cycle of these types of applications is quite different from the traditional IT-developed, SOA-based solution. SAs are usually built by casual programmers using short, iterative development life cycles that often are measured in days or weeks, not months or years."

How is it that the end user can assemble such applications? Would it be reasonable to expect that, to arrive at a desired outcome, they could identify the components needed (from a library of hundreds or thousands), know how to assemble them, and know how to prevent the seemingly sensible assembly of components into incorrect compositions? While developers can manually craft code modules and compose them into applications, how can the less knowledgeable application end users do so, without acquiring deep knowledge of the code, interface compatibility, the rules of assembly, etc.? Mashup tools such as Yahoo Pipes (Yahoo Pipes, 2007) and IBM Damia (Altinel et al, 2007) simplify the logistics of assembling situational applications, but they are limited to a relatively small and inextensible set of components. Such tools might encode interface compatibility rules, but they provide little visibility into the sometimes subtle semantics of the components' capabilities. We present a method of separately specifying *processing goals* for situational applications and the *functional capabilities* of the components to be used in addressing the goals. These specifications are used by composition tools that either

automatically provide a near-optimal solution or support the more knowledgeable user in the formulation of such a solution. We present a means of expressing processing goals using semantic expressions (graph expressions) built using terminology from the end users' problem domains. Descriptions of components' capabilities are similarly expressed. This approach is supported by SAWMILL, our semantics-based automatic flow composition middleware, as first introduced in (Bouillet et al., 2007).

The general problem of application composition is extremely challenging. To address a more tractable problem space we limit our focus to those applications described as *flow-based* information processing applications (Morrison, 1971). Flow-based applications are component assemblies arranged in a directed acyclic graph (*flow composition*) of black-box components connected by data flow links. Systems like Yahoo Pipes and IBM DAMIA support the creation of data mashups as flow-based applications. Stream processing systems like System S (Jain et al., 2006) also support flow-based applications that continuously process streaming data. Acyclic workflows in service-oriented systems can also be viewed as flow-based applications, where different services exchange messages either directly or through a coordinator service (e.g., a BPEL workflow).

In this article we describe composition of flow-based applications, describe the formal model underlying the semantic descriptions and describe how these descriptions support the composition of flow-based applications. In particular, we focus on key features of the semantic model that are particularly useful in facilitating composition. These include the matching of outputs of components to input requirements of other components, modeling the propagation of certain semantic properties by components from the inputs to the outputs, and modeling the transformation of other semantic properties by the components.

OVERVIEW: COMPONENTS AND COMPOSITION

A flow-based application is modeled as a graph—or *flow composition*—of interconnected components, describing the flow of data from one or more external data sources, through a number of software components, outputting some desired end result. In our work, the flows are described as DAGs (directed acyclic graphs). Figure 1(a) depicts a simple flow composition in the vehicle traffic analysis domain; the desired end result for this flow composition is a stream of traffic congestion levels detected at the intersection of Broadway and 42nd St in New York City.

Components are connected in the usual manner for flow-based applications: a component observes data via its inputs, performs some processing and publishes data via its outputs. Thus, a flow composition includes a collection of components—both data sources and software components—and a description of the components' interconnections, over which data published by some component can be observed by other components.[1]

Component descriptions contain all of the descriptive metadata needed to select and assemble components into flow compositions and much of the metadata needed to deploy the compositions to a target runtime environment. Descriptions of a component's inputs include metadata describing the constraints—typically constraints on input data—that must be satisfied in order for a component to be included into a flow composition. Similarly, descriptions of a component's outputs capture the characteristics of data published by the component, for observation by other components and/or by subscribers to the application's result data. For a component to be included in a flow, all of its inputs must be interconnected to other components' outputs, in a way that satisfies each of the input constraints. Outputs are typically interconnected to other components' inputs and/or are produced as result data output from the flow

composition. For a flow composition to satisfy the processing goal, each of the described results must be provided as an output from some component in the flow composition.

Descriptive metadata for software components also includes some declaration regarding the component's executable code. This can take the form of actual source or binary executable code (or reference to some repository location of either) or some specification from which the component can be generated, etc.

Consider the Video Image Sampler component in Figure 1(c). Its sole input requires VideoSegments and TimeIntervals and produces, via its sole output, Images and Times. The component also requires a SamplingFrequency rate, expressed as a configuration parameter, and is associated with the VIS.cpp source code file.

The example in this article describes a stream-oriented set of applications that provide real-time traffic information and vehicle routing services by analyzing data obtained from various sensors, web pages and other data sources. A user describes a continuous query for traffic congestion levels on a particular roadway intersection, e.g. the corner of Broadway and 42nd Street in New York City. A flow constructed for such a query might use raw data from a variety of sources. It might use video from a traffic camera at an intersection, extracting images from the video stream and examining them for alignment to visual patterns of congestion at that intersection (the upper thread in Figure 1(a)). Comparing audio data from a sound sensor at the intersection to known congestion audio patterns might be considered (the lower thread in Figure 1(a)). If combining both analyses is believed to provide a more accurate assessment of congestion, the two analytic chains can be joined using an additional component; the combined threads are depicted by the entire flow composition in Figure 1(a).[2]

Two components can be composed into a (sub) flow only if the output description of the "up-flow" component satisfies the input requirements of the

Figure 1. Example of a flow composition

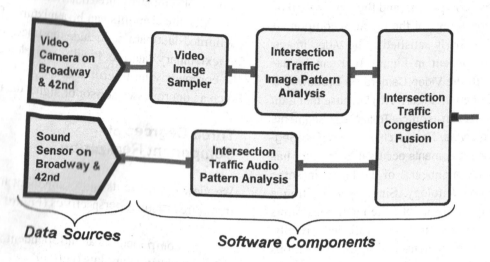

(a) Example of a flow composition

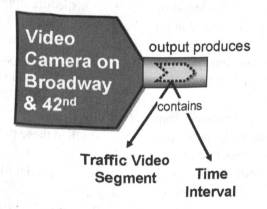

(b) Data source component

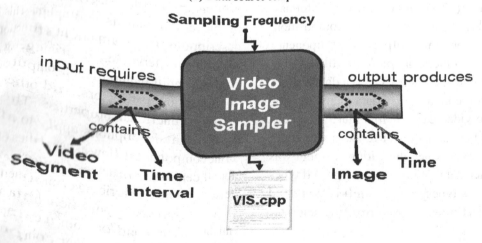

(c) Software component

"down-flow" component (and then, only if all of the input constraints of the up-flow component have been similarly satisfied). The Video Image Sampler component in Figure 1(c) can be assembled with the Video Camera on Broadway & 42nd component in Figure 1(b) because that data source produces on its output TrafficVideoSegments with TimeIntervals. The match of TrafficVideoSegments to VideoSegments occurs if the former has been declared a subclass of the latter, in some corresponding ontology. Since by definition a data source has no inputs, the input constraints on the data source (none) are satisfied trivially. Assembly of components into flow compositions is typically more involved than just a simple matching of output descriptions to input descriptions, since both inferencing and semantic propagation might come into play.

In this article, we describe any conveyance of data among components as component *interconnections*, which are generic enough to cover a variety of flow-based paradigms ranging from compositions of tightly coupled components (that interact, e.g., via direct invocation), to compositions of loosely coupled, distributed components (communicating in a publish-subscribe manner, e.g., via data streams).

At a concrete (implementation) level, information in a deployed and running flow composition is conveyed from the outputs of components to the inputs of others, in packets called FDOs (Flow Data Objects). Each FDO is a data artifact that contains a collection of data elements. For example, the video camera in Figure 1(b) conveys an FDO containing a video segment and a time interval over which the video segment was captured. Each data element has a type. All types are defined in a typesystem, which is expressed via some object-oriented programming language (e.g. Java).

This format is quite general and can be used to represent structured, semi-structured or unstructured data. In the case of structured data, each FDO can be considered to contain an element that is a tuple. For semi-structured data, like data encoded in XML, the elements can be a mixture of field-delimited data that also includes unstructured such as text, binary data, etc. Finally, each element can be completely unstructured binary or text data, such as unprocessed sensor or signal data.

Three Degrees of Component Realization

We view components and component metadata from three distinct perspectives (Figure 2):

- the component as an independent, abstract descriptive template (upper)
- a specific appearance of the component in the context of a flow assembly (middle)
- a specific concrete instance of a component, deployed onto one processing node (and operated) as part of a deployed flow composition (lower)

Each of these perspectives captures a distinct, increasing degree of component realization and each is associated with different component metadata.

The upper perspective, the *component exemplar perspective*, focuses on descriptive metadata of the component as exemplar. This includes descriptions of the component's functionality, applicability criteria, etc., describing, e.g., the component's input requirements, output capabilities, configuration parameters, and other functional and non-functional properties. These context-independent descriptions apply to all inclusions of the component in flow assemblies (middle) and for all deployed instances (lower). At the upper level, metadata describing component inputs and outputs describes hypothetical data artifacts that might flow into and/or from a component, were it interconnected with other components. More specifically, it establishes minimum constraints on data artifacts that are required on component inputs, describes minimum constraints on data

Figure 2. Software component - three degrees of realization

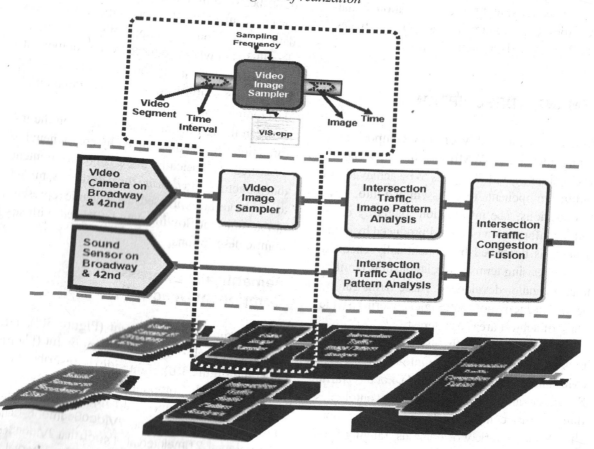

artifacts written to component outputs. Note that, without a broader context (an assembly of components), this metadata is strictly hypothetical and is likely more general than might be the case once the component is referenced into some flow composition (the *second perspective*).

The middle perspective, the *assembly perspective*, considers each inclusion of a component in each flow composition. For a given inclusion, additional metadata captures any relevant context-specific bindings for that component in that context. A specific component might appear multiple times in a flow composition—each inclusion represents a distinct context of component use, and each carries different metadata reflecting that appearance. For example, whenever the Video Image Sampler component is assembled

with a source of TrafficCameraVideoSegments (a VideoSegment takenBy a TrafficCamera), it produces only TrafficCameraImages (an Image takenBy a TrafficCamera); when paired with sources of SatelliteVideoSegments, it produces only SatelliteImages. Here, each component is placed in a specific context, likely further constraining the actual descriptions of data artifacts flowing among components.

The lower perspective, the *deployment and operation perspective*, captures the component as instantiated in a deployed and (possibly) running flow composition. Since our approach is currently limited to the deployment of fixed-topology graphs, component metadata at this level mostly describes component deployment information (e.g., assigned processing node and established interconnections) and runtime operational characteristics (e.g., resource consumption statistics, data flow rates, data quality metrics).

SEMANTIC DESCRIPTIONS

To aid in the assembly of flow compositions, our middleware, SAWMILL, relies on semantic descriptions of both the goals to be achieved by, and the components to be assembled into, flow compositions. The information sought by users and the information observed/produced by components is described by semantically encoded metadata, using terms and relationships familiar to users and/or developers. These terms can be defined in one or more ontologies covering a wide range of subject areas of interest.

SAWMILL currently uses ontologies expressed in OWL, the Web Ontology Language (McGuinness & Harmelen, 2004). For the Traffic Services example, we draw on several ontologies that describe concepts and properties (relationships) from a variety of domains, ranging from the relatively generic with concepts such as MultiMediaData and Location, to the more domain-specific with concepts like CongestionLevel and FixedPositionTrafficCamera. The depiction of the VideoImageSampler in Figure 1(b) provides only a hint of the component's data requirements or functionality, lacking in some key detail and intent. What is needed is a richer and more detailed description.

Both component descriptions and processing goals are expressed as semantic graphs, as depicted in Figure 3. Graphs describe data that is to be interchanged among components in a flow composition and data that is to be produced as *result output* from a flow composition. In the case of processing goals the semantic graphs describe constraints on the data produced by some assembled flow. A graph associated with each component input describes data required as input to a component. Similarly, a graph associated with each component output describes data that is to be output from a component. Data output from a component includes data observed on the component's inputs and/or data that is newly introduced by the component. In all three cases—inputs, outputs, and goals—the expressions establish minimum constraints on the data required or produced.

Even though the metadata describing the information observed/produced by components is described semantically, there is no requirement that the actual data *flowing through* the assembled applications be expressed in a semantic representation, nor that flowing data be tagged with semantic descriptions.

Semantically Expressed Component Descriptions

Each input of a component (Figure 3(b), left side), and each output of a component (Figure 3(a) and Figure 3(b), right side) is described by a semantic graph. Component Video Image Sampler is described as requiring an input FDO containing some VideoSegment, ?VideoSegment_1 and ing some VideoSegment, ?VideoSegment_1 and TimeInterval, ?TimeInterval_1 such that ?VideoSegment_1 was takenAt TimeInterval ?TimeInterval_1, hasSegmentWidth 0.5sec and is ofSubject some (untyped) ?Subject.

Note here that only the exemplar individuals ?VideoSegment_1 and ?TimeInterval_1 are *required* to be observed in the input FDO, as indicated by the bold arrows from the input FDO to these individuals. The other exemplar individual, ?Subject, and the data value, 0.5sec, act to constrain the actual input data, but are not explicitly referenced as being required in the input; thus neither is *required* to arrive with the required data. This descriptive metadata informs the flow composition assembler of the traits of the inputs, yet not all of the constraining metadata need be carried with the data at runtime.

The output is described as producing some FDO containing an Image, __Image_1, takenAt and a Time, __Time_1, and that the Image be ofSubject

Figure 3. Graphical depiction of semantic descriptions of a data source, a software component and a processing request

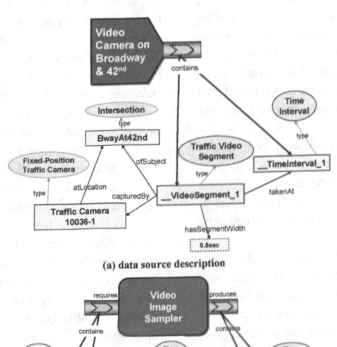

(a) data source description

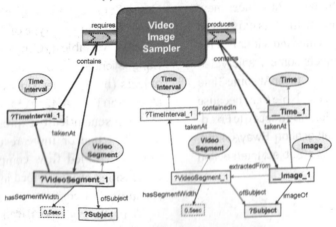

(b) component description

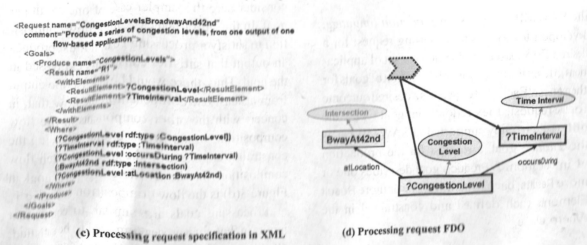

(c) Processing request specification in XML   **(d) Processing request FDO**

some ?Subject. Here, existential variables are depicted using an initial double-underscore, "__", rather than a question mark. These are variables depicting exemplar individuals that are newly introduced by this component. Making such a distinction aids the automated flow composition assembler in distinguishing the newly introduced data from variables that were inadvertently not propagated. [3]

The output data is constrained to be related to the input data in a particular way: Image__Image_1 must be extractedFrom ?VideoSegment_1, Time __Time_1 must be containedIn ?TimeInterval_1, the ?Subject of the image and the video must be the same, and so on.

Figure 3(a) depicts a special type of component, the data source. Since it introduces new data into a flow composition, all of its existential variables indicate newly created individuals. This particular data source injects some Traffic Video Segment, __VideoSegment_1, takenAt some Time Interval, __TimeInterval_1, etc. Note that, because __VideoSegment_1 is capturedBy a specific Fixed-Position Traffic Camera atLocation BwayAt42nd, the Traffic Video Segment is ofSubject Intersection BwayAt42nd.

Semantically Expressed Processing Goals

The SAWMILL *request specification language*, developed to express a processing request for a desired flow-based application (or set of applications), describes a conjoined collection of goals for the request. Each goal expresses a desired outcome for the request. The predominant goal type—the only one currently supported in SAWMILL—is the *Produce* goal, a request for the production of information. A Produce goal describes one or more Results, each containing one or more Result Elements, each defined and constrained in the Where clause.

Each described Result corresponds to one output of the application—one kind of FDO to be produced by the application. Each Result Element is represented by a single variable, which represents the exemplar individual contained in the result. Each of these variables is further described and constrained in the Where clause.

The request specification for the Congestion-LevelsBroadwayAnd42nd request, expressed in XML syntax in Figure 3(c), describes a single goal to produce CongestionLevels, with a single type of result, R1. Each result R1 would contain elements ?CongestionLevel and ?TimeInterval, as depicted in Figure 3(d).

The Where expression, expressed in a triple pattern similar to those found in the SPARQL Query Language for RDF, contains triple expressions describing the type of the object represented by each variable (?CongestionLevel is of type CongestionLevel) and relationships among the objects (the ?CongestionLevel is described to be atLocation BwayAt42nd). [4]

Each semantically expressed processing goal describes one or more result outputs of some to-be-assembled flow composition. These goal expressions are described in the same way input constraints of components are described.

While the goal specification language provides for goals that produce more than one result, we consider here the simpler case of one result per goal. In the simplified case, for a flow composition to satisfy a processing goal, it must produce an output that satisfies constraints expressed in the goal. Thus, there would be at least one output from at least one component in the flow that, in concert with the other components in the flow composition, would produce data satisfying the constraints expressed in the goal. One such flow composition for the traffic congestion goal in Figure 3(d) is the flow composition in Figure 1.

Processing goals are similar to component inputs in that, for a processing goal to be satisfied, all of the constraints described in the semantically expressed goal graph must be satisfied. Figure 3(d) depicts one such goal, the production of some CongestionLevel ?CongestionLevel atLocation BwayAt42nd for some TimeInterval ?TimeInterval. For some generated flow composition to be responsive to that goal, at least one of the outputs of that flow composition must produce data matching that description. The graph depicted in Figure 1 is one such graph. It uses two means of determining congestion and a *join* component to fuse together those analyses. If the Intersection Traffic Image Pattern Analysis and Intersection Traffic Audio Pattern Analysis components each output the desired CongestionLevel, given the goal expressed above an automated flow composition assembler could produce three alternative flow compositions, the one depicted in Figure 1, one that consists of only the upper subflow (based on video imagery), and one that consists only of the lower subflow (based on traffic noise). With appropriate quality annotations the flow composition assembler might rank the audio-only flow lowest, the video-only flow higher, and the "fused" flow as producing the highest quality result.

Note that, although the SPARQL *syntax* is used, these goal expressions are not "queries" in the traditional sense. They are not search expressions, to be executed by some query processor. Instead, they are semantically described statements of the effect(s) to be achieved by an assembled flow composition, without any required description of the operators to be used in achieving the goal. The means of achieving the goal can, and typically does, include some amount of complex processing (including, e.g., image processing, trend analysis, time-windowed statistical analyses, etc.) of stored and/or continuously streaming data. It is the job of the flow composition assembler to identify the (collection of) operators (components) needed to achieve that goal.

ASSEMBLING FLOW COMPOSITIONS: MATCHING OUTPUTS TO INPUTS

The semantic description of a component exemplar provides a general, application-independent, description of the kinds of data the component would take in and the kinds of data it would produce, were it to be included into a flow composition. Flow-based situational applications are assemblies of these components into flow compositions, compositions that are assembled such that they produce outputs matching the applications' goals. The job of the application assembler—be it a person or an automaton—is to find at least one flow composition that matches/satisfies the application's goal(s). (The SAWMILL compiler assembles a large number of alternative flow compositions and ranks them based on several metrics).

In a given application, a component's inputs are interconnected with other components' outputs, producing data artifacts that are observed via interconnections with yet other components' input ports, and so on. Data produced on any component's output port can also be observed as an application output. The assembly process is a process of matching goals to component outputs and component inputs to other components' outputs, in such a way that all goals are satisfied and all component input constraints are met.

Ultimately, the assembled flow composition matches the goal expression of the processing request. When a match occurs, the assembled flow composition is a candidate for addressing the processing request and thus a candidate as a deployable situational application. The central focus of the assembly process is the determination of which interconnections can and should be made and which data artifacts should be produced, based on the goal(s) expressed in the processing request.

Matching the Subflow Output

Automated assembly is more nuanced than simply matching a component's input descriptions to other components' output descriptions. This is because the output of any component is not simply a function of its inputs, but also a function of the entire up-flow processing context.

Consider, for example, a generic component c_1 that takes in floating point numbers and produces as output a time-windowed average of those numbers. This component is described as requiring an input stream of floating point numbers (and also a parameter indicating window size) and outputting a stream of averages. If another component c_2 were to require as input a stream of average temperature values, c_1 by itself would not match, because average temperatures are more specific than average floating point numbers. One could engineer a specific component to compute average temperatures from a stream of temperature values, but the opportunity to reuse a perfectly adequate generic component would be lost. If, on the other hand, the input to c_1 were to be a stream of temperatures, drawn from a source producing temperature values, and if the application assembler was capable of incorporating that additional contextual information into its assembly process, c_1 could be recognized as producing average temperatures and thus recognized as a suitable candidate for connection with c_2.

This additional descriptive information, drawn from the entire up-flow processing context, is supported by what we call *semantic propagation*, a key capability in SAWMILL's ability to incorporate reusable components into automatically assembled flow compositions. Semantic propagation is described in greater detail later in this article.

The output of a given component is described not merely as some locally described set of variables, but as variables whose semantics are defined/accumulated over the entirety of a subflow path. Thus, during assembly of a flow composition, a given input is matched not simply to another component's output description, but to a *subflow output*. The semantic description of a subflow output is derived from the semantic descriptions of all of the subflow's components, propagated as defined in the components' functional descriptions.

Subflow outputs are artifacts of the assembly process and thus are considered parts of the assembly perspective mentioned in section 1.1. Like a component exemplar, a subflow output is an entirely descriptive entity, not yet a concrete realization. A subflow output, which can exist even in the absence of a known subflow, represents the hypothetical output of some hypothetical subflow and is described by describing the FDOs that would be produced by that subflow, were the subflow to be populated, deployed, and operated.

The *subflow output* is perhaps the most elusive element of the assembly discussion, because it deals with a description of data that *will have been generated* by some flow composition or subflow composition. In some cases, the subflow output can clearly be identified as the output of known flow composition. But in other cases, it stands as the specification for an as-yet unassembled set of components. In this latter case, some down-flow component might need a specific output of some up-flow assembly that has not yet been assembled. This occurs when the assembler works back from a processing goal, selecting components that might achieve the goal, if only subflows producing outputs meeting the component's input criteria can be assembled. One must understand this to truly understand how the assembly process works.

The Matching

For a component to be included into a flow composition, all of its input constraints must be satisfied. This is done by identifying, for each of the component's inputs, a subflow output that satisfies the input's constraints, as expressed in an input flow pattern. A central part of the assembly process is determining whether a set of subflow outputs can be given as input to a component. This is achieved by identifying a *pattern solution* that matches the description of a subflow output to the input constraints. Once incorporated into the flow composition, the output(s) of that flow composition can offered for further interconnection.

The semantic description of a subflow output is generated by combining the output pattern describing some output o_1 of some component c_1 with the subflow outputs of each subflow matched to each of c_1's inputs. This combination occurs as a graph transformation (Baresi & Heckel, 2002). The variables in the output pattern are substituted using the substitution function, θ. In addition, other properties of the substituted values are propagated from the input to the output. A detailed explanation is found in (Baresi & Heckel, 2002).

An example is shown in Figure 4 where the VideoImageSampler component is assembled with the VideoCameraBway-42nd component. The upper part of the figure depicts the context-independent exemplar definition for two components, showing the input and output graph patterns independent of any binding. The lower part shows the specific bindings that would occur were these two components assembled in a flow composition.

In this case, the two components can be assembled because the output of the VideoCamera-Bway-42nd data source component produces data artifacts that satisfy the input constraints for component VideoImageSampler. Namely, each produced data artifact contains (at least) two elements, a VideoSegment and a TimeInterval, such that the VideoSegment was takenAt the TimeInterval, the VideoSegment hasSegmentWidth 0.5sec and the VideoSegment is ofSubject some subject (which can be any thing). Since the data source component VideoCameraBway-42nd produces a TrafficVideoSegment and a TimeInterval meeting the aforementioned criteria, and since TrafficVideoSegment is a specialization of VideoSegment, the input constraints are satisfied, an interconnection can be formed, and the various bindings can

be made. This flow assembly can be deployed, and the data artifacts that flow through it will be as described by the various descriptions with the particular bindings taken into account (assuming, that is, that the components were described correctly).[5]

In the course of matching outputs to inputs, variables can be associated with other variables or with specific individuals or literal values. _TimeInterval_1, the newly created object output from the VideoCameraBway-42nd, is associated with ?TimeInterval_1, one of the objects required by the VideoImageSampler component. The Intersection BwayAt42nd (an individual) is bound to the variable ?Subject. Any Image produced by the assembly represented in the lower part of Figure 4 would be extractedFrom a VideoSegment that is capturedBy TrafficCamera10036-1 atLocation Intersection BwayAt42nd.

Note that the data artifacts (FDOs) flowing from VideoCamera VideoCameraBway-42nd would contain the two mentioned elements, but typically do not carry any of the other referenced elements (the Fixed-PositionTrafficCamera TrafficCamera10036-1, the Intersection BwayAt42nd, the decimal measure 0.5 sec, any of the associated classes or any of the associated properties). All of these are descriptive of the two elements produced by the assembly, but are neither intended nor required to be included in the flowing data. They are, however, descriptive of the data that does flow through the components.

Also note that the semantic metadata discussed throughout this article is attached to and describes components, specifically for the purpose of guiding application assembly. It describes the data that would flow, were the components to be assembled, deployed and operated. Except in rare cases, one would not find this metadata concretely represented as annotations on flowing data. SAWMILL imposes no requirements on the representation of the data flowing through such applications. Thus, the metadata describing the components is expressed in a semantic form, but

*Figure 4. Matching the **BWay-42nd Video source** to the input pattern of* VideoImageSampler. *Dashed arrows show satisfying variable substitutions. The resulting output is also shown.*

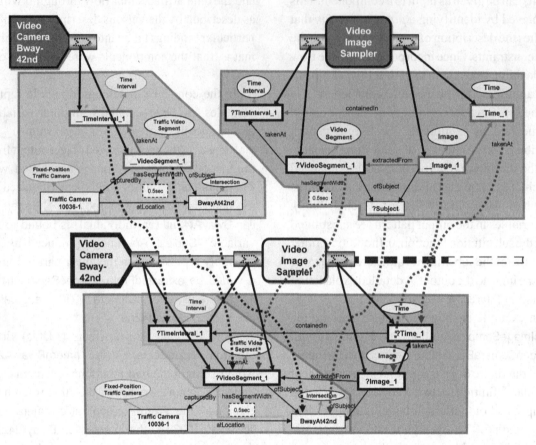

the flowing data can take any form suited to the application and its components, including structured or unstructured text, video, audio, binary data, etc. If deemed necessary or appropriate for the application the flowing data might even be expressed in a semantic representation (e.g., RDF triples or OWL), but there is no requirement that such data conform to any schema or ontology used for the component semantic metadata. It may be the case, though, that some situational application is launched to study and characterize data from a particular data source, harvesting data that might be used to describe the data source. Such introspection is possible, but should be used with caution and in a controlled engineering process, since the introduction of descriptive metadata would have an impact on application assembly.

Manual assembly and validation of these flow compositions—matching goals to outputs, outputs to inputs, and manually propagating the semantics—can be quite tedious. SAWMILL provides an automated flow assembly agent (Riabov & Liu, 05 & 06). We call this agent a "planner" rather than a "compiler," due to its roots in AI Planning and because the emphasis is more on operator-free, goal-based planning rather than on code compilation.

Semantic Propagation

The use of variables in our component model supports semantic propagation, a key advantage over other approaches, such as OWL-S. Semantic propagation is a means by which the semantic

Figure 5. Three components assembled, with propagation

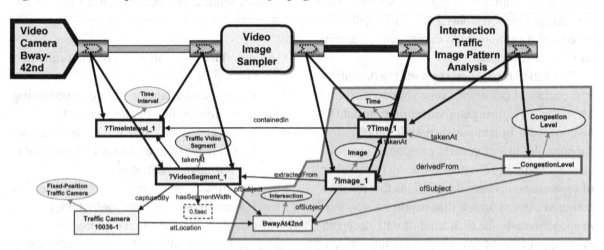

description of a component's output data artifacts depends on the semantics of the input data artifacts. Here, any interconnection between some component c_1's output o_1 to some other component c_2's input i_1 is constrained not just according to c_2's constraints on its input i_1, but also on constraints imposed on c_1's output o_2.

The description of the VideoImageSampler includes the fact that the output image (__Image_1) has the *same subject* (?Subject) as the input (?VideoSegment_1). As a result, when an interconnection containing video segments with the subject as BWayAt42nd is connected as input to this component, the output interconnection produced by the component has images with the *same* subject, BWayAt42nd. Hence, the subject information is propagated from the input to the output of the component. Were the Intersection TrafficImagePatternAnalysis component to be assembled onto this flow composition fragment (to the output of the VideoImageSampler component), all of the images processed by it would necessarily also be extractedFrom a VideoSegment that is capturedBy TrafficCamera10036-1 atLocation Intersection BwayAt42nd (Figure 5).

Consider the VideoImageSampler component in Figure 3(b). It can take in any ?VideoSegment_1 conforming to the component's input constraints.

But if the VideoImageSampler were to be assembled with the VideoCameraOnBroadwayAnd42nd component, all of the images processed by the VideoImageSampler would be extractedFrom VideoSegments capturedBy the Fixed-PositionTrafficCamera TrafficCamera10036-1. Even though component VideoImageSampler does not forward the ?VideoSegment_1 data artifact, the __Image_1 artifact that is written to the VideoImageSampler output carries with it the semantic constraint that __Image_1 was extractedFrom a VideoSegment capturedBy Fixed-PositionTrafficCamera TrafficCamera10036-1. Thus, if the processing request was for some TrafficCongestionLevel at Broadway-And42nd and that metric used the generic VideoImageSampler as part of the analysis, the data produced would be guaranteed, by the assembly constraints, to be from BroadwayAt42nd. Even though only the VideoSegment and TimeInterval flow from the VideoCameraOnBroadwayAnd42nd component to the VideoImageSampler component (and on from there...), the remainder of the semantic description constraining the VideoSegment constrains the flowing segments and images.

The primary mechanism supporting semantic propagation is the use of constrained variables (exemplar individuals). In the assembly of flow compositions, assembly of outputs to inputs associates variables in an output to similarly described variables on inputs. Later we describe the process that supports both component assembly and semantic propagation.

Semantic propagation supports the definition in metadata of constraints on component assembly, without requiring equivalent runtime data to be conveyed. In addition, semantic propagation supports the use of generic components in specific contexts, significantly reducing the number of separate component descriptions that must be authored. Any approach that requires a new VideoImageSampler for each kind of data accepted on its inputs would fail, simply due the massive proliferation (and eventual required maintenance) of mostly similar component descriptions.

Functional Fluents in Semantic Descriptions

Each component in a flow-based composition performs some kind of transformation of the data artifacts observed on its inputs to the data artifacts produced on its outputs. Thus, each component expresses what could be described as a *functional fluent*. Like fluents described in (McCarthy & Hayes, 1987) and (Welty & Fikes, 2006), functional fluents describe, strictly from a black-box perspective, the functional change that a component makes to the flowing data.

In the Video Image Sampler example, an Image __Image_1 is extractedFrom some VideoSegment ?VideoSegment_1, where __Image_1 was takenAt some Time __Time_1, which is containedIn some TimeInterval ?TimeInterval_1 and so forth. Here, the *"before"* is the state where some VideoSegment and Time, etc., are known, and as the result of applying the component's function, the *"after"* is the state where a new Image and Time, etc., are known, and known to be related to the input artifacts.

In general, a component can do any of the following:

- introduce new data elements (not found on any input)
- remove data elements (by not propagating them from an input to any output)
- establish and/or remove type associations (e.g., recognizing an Image and reclassifying it as a VehicleImage)
- establish or remove relationships (ObjectProperty or DatatypeProperty)
- establish and/or remove a property binding to a variable (either an ObjectProperty binding to an exemplar individual or a DatatypeProperty binding to a literal variable)
- establish and/or remove an equivalency (e.g., assert, via owl:sameAs, that ?Vehicle_1 on Input_1 and ?Vehicle_2 on Input_2 are the same vehicle)

Note in Figure 3(b), we explicitly separate the input constraints end and the component's outputs. However, note that the elements appearing on both the input and output sides represent the *"same"* object. The trouble is, each reference to an element on the input(s) represents the same object, but *at a different stage in the processing*.

As a simple graphical remedy, we use several visual cues to the changes the component would make to the flowing data. Objects that are newly introduced by the component are depicted both with a leading double underscore (__) and surrounded by a blue border. Newly introduced properties are depicted by blue arrows. Elements that appear on an input but not on an output are pointed to by a bold black line from the input port to the element (e.g., ?VideoSegment_1 and ?TimeInterval_1 but not pointed to by a bold black line from the output port.

RELATED WORK

Various stream query languages and stream processing architectures have been proposed in the recent past. Examples include Aurora (Abadi et al, 2003), TelegraphCQ (Chandrasekaran et al, 2003) and CQL (Arasu, Babu, & Widom, 2003). However, most existing systems focus on streams containing structured data and only consider a limited set of operators like relational and windowing operators. Hence, many of the techniques used in these systems cannot be applied for constructing plans that involve processing unstructured data in different media like audio, video, text, etc., and that use an arbitrary, extensible set of operators. While some systems allow invoking external stored procedures, such procedures have to be invoked explicitly and cannot be automatically incorporated into plans.

Various approaches have been proposed for the problem of semantic web service composition. Some of these approaches ((Narayanan & McIlraith, 2002; Berardi, Calvanese, Giacomo, Hull, & Mecella, 2005; Sirin & Parsia, 2004), etc.) work on semantic web service descriptions like OWL-S or DAML-S, including the process model of a service. They model services in terms of their preconditions and effects on the state of the world, and inputs and outputs described as concepts from an ontology. Other approaches start with a process model defined in BPEL or as transition systems to compose services (Pistore, Traverso, Bertoli, & Marconi, 2005). The main novelty of our approach is in modeling the input and output messages as instance-based graph patterns rather than concept-based models. OWL-S, DAML-S and BPEL models do not allow expressions with variables in describing inputs and outputs, or in describing constraints on data elements in a stream. Our model allows logical expressions with variables in the form of graph patterns to describe inputs and outputs, and can also relate the semantics of outputs to the semantics of inputs and allow semantic propagation. Hence, our

model is more suitable for composition of stream processing applications.

One closely related work is Semantic Streams (Whitehouse, Zhao, & Liu, 2006), which allows users to pose queries based on the semantics of sensor data. It uses a Prolog-based language and defines logic rules that describe the semantics, such as the type and location of sensor data sources, and input/output of inference units (equivalent to software components). The main difference between their approach and ours is in the choice of representation mechanism. They use predicates in Prolog, to describe sensors and inference units. While Prolog is an expressive logic programming language, queries to it may be undecidable. Our model uses OWL, based on description logics, known to be decidable. The computational advantage of OWL combined with the use of efficient planning algorithms allows our middleware to construct processing graphs quickly even when there are a large components. Besides, the choice of OWL as the representation medium enables easy utilization of the large number of domain ontologies that have been developed in the Semantic Web, such as the NCI cancer ontology (Golbeck et al., 2003) and GALEN medical ontology (Rector & Horrocks, 1997).

Subsequent approaches incorporated semantic models to improve search precision, via goal-based search (Sugumaran & Storey, 2003). Quality models were added, to enhance goal-driven retrieval with non-functional applicability criteria (Leite, Yu, Liu, Yu, & Mylopoulos, 2005). Still, the predominant focus was on specification and retrieval but not composition.

Component composition at the code level is addressed in (Reid, Flatt, Stoller, Lepreau, & Eide, 2000). More recent work proposes a dynamic hierarchical component composition (Kim, Bae, & Hong, 2007), which also emphasizes type-oriented composition models.

Web services composition is described in (Sivashanmugam, Miller, Sheth, & Verma, 04-5), and composition using UML is described in (Skogan,

Gronmo, & Solheim, 2004). Rule-based service composition is addressed in (Pu, Hristidis, & Koudas, 2006) and (Yang, Papazoglou, Orriëns, & Heuvel, 2003), semantic service composition in (Chen et al., 2003). A planner for service compositions described in (Sheshagiri, desJardins, & Finin, 2003). An approach to DL planning for service composition is described in (Qiu, Lin, Wan, & Shi, 2006). Knowledge engineering for workflow composition, (Chen et al., 2003) and ontology modeling for web service composition in (Cui, Liu, Wu, & Gu, 2004) semantic descriptions, which pose an extra burden on those describing components and on those establishing composition goals.

CONCLUSION

We have presented a semantics-based approach to describing components and application processing goals, providing support for both the manual and automated assembly of situational applications in a variety of flow-based application paradigms. We have also described the assembly of components into flow composition that produce desired result outputs. The main features of our approach are the use of expressive models for describing the semantics of structured, semi-structured or un-structured data and for describing the capabilities of components, the use of reasoning to determine semantic compatibility outputs and inputs, and the use of efficient techniques for automated assembly. We have integrated our automatic composition framework into the System S Stream Processing System (Jain et al, 2006) and have used it to construct flow-based applications in various problem domains.

While specifying component descriptions puts additional burden on developers, this extra development-time effort can pay off over time in systems with large user bases, large numbers of situational applications, and/or large numbers of components from which applications are to be assembled. By augmenting regular application engineering activities with the knowledge engineering needed to define formal component descriptions, users with little or no knowledge of the system and with little or no involvement in constructing the situational applications can consistently make optimal use of available components, even as the components evolve.

With a semantic model of components and a goal-directed means of automatically assembling these components in response to situational requests, SAWMILL simplifies the problem-solving aspects of creating situational applications, providing a means of supporting reuse of a broad class of generic components.

REFERENCES

Abadi *et al*, D. (2003). Aurora: A new model and architecture for data stream management. VLDB Journal.

Altinel., et al. M. (2007). DAMIA: A data mashup fabric for intranet applications. VLDB '07: Proceedings of the 33rd International Conference on Very Large Data Bases (1370–1373). VLDB Endowment.

Arasu, S., & Babu, S. Widom, J. (2003). The CQL continuous query language: Semantic foundations and query execution (TR-2003-67). Stanford University.

Baresi, L. Heckel, R (2002). Tutorial Introduction to graph transformation: A software engineering perspective. First International Conference on Graph Transformation.

Berardi, D., Calvanese, D., Giacomo, G. D., Hull, R. Mecella, M. (2005). Automatic composition of transition-based semantic web services with messaging. VLDB.

Bouillet, E., Feblowitz, M., Liu, Z., Ranganathan, A., & Riabov, A. Ye, F. (2007, June). A semantics-based middleware for utilizing heterogeneous sensor networks. IEEE Distributed Computing in Sensor Systems (DCOSS 2007), June 18-20, 2007. Santa Fe, New Mexico, USA.

Chandrasekaran, S., et al. (2003, January). TelegraphCQ: Continuous dataflow processing for an uncertain world. Proceedings on the First Biennial Conference on Innovative Data Systems Research (CIDR 2003).

Chen, L., Shadbolt, N., Goble, C., Tao, F., Cox, S., & Puleston, C. (2003). Towards a Knowledge-based Approach to Semantic Service Composition. The Second International Semantic Web Conference (ISWC2003).

Cherbakov, L., Bravery, A. J. F. Pandya, A. (2007). SOA meets situational applications. IBM.

Cui, J., Liu, J., & Wu, Y. Gu, N. (2004). An ontology modeling method in semantic composition of web services. CEC-EAST '04: Proceedings of the E-Commerce Technology for Dynamic E-Business, IEEE International Conference (270–273). Washington, DC.

Golbeck, J., Fragoso, G., Hartel, F., Hendler, J., Parsia, B., & Oberthaler, J. (2003). The National Cancer Institute's thesaurus and ontology. *Journal of Web Semantics, 1*(1). doi:10.1016/j.websem.2003.07.007

Jain, N., Amini, L., Andrade, H., King, R., Park, Y., & Selo, P. (2006). Design, implementation, and evaluation of the linear road benchmark on the stream processing core. SIGMOD '06: Proceedings of the 2006 ACM SIGMOD international conference on Management of data (431–442). New York, NY, USA: ACM.

Kim, I.-G., Bae, D.-H., & Hong, J.-E. (2007). A component composition model providing dynamic, flexible, and hierarchical composition of components for supporting software evolution. *Journal of Systems and Software, 80*(11), 1797–1816. doi:10.1016/j.jss.2007.02.047

Leite, J., Yu, Y., Liu, L., Yu, E., & Mylopoulos, J. (2005, January). Quality-based software reuse. *Lecture Notes in Computer Science, 3520*, 535–550. doi:10.1007/11431855_37

McCarthy, J. Hayes, P. J. (1987). Some philosophical problems from the standpoint of artificial intelligence. *Readings in nonmonotonic reasoning* 26–45, San Francisco, CA, USA: Morgan Kaufmann Publishers Inc.

McGuinness, D. Harmelen, F. van. (2004). OWL web ontology language overview. W3C Recommendation. Retrieved from the Web 5/8/2008. http://www.w3.org/TR/owl-features/

Morrison, J. P. (1971, January). Data Responsive Modular, Interleaved Task Programming System. *IBM Technical Disclosure Bulletin, 13*(8), 2425–2426.

Narayanan, S. McIlraith, S. A. (2002). Simulation, verification and automated composition of web services. WWW '02: Proceedings of the 11th International Conference on World Wide Web (77–88). New York, NY, USA: ACM.

Pistore, M., Traverso, P., & Bertoli, P. Marconi, A. (2005). Automated Synthesis of Composite BPEL4WS Web Services. ICWS '05: Proceedings of the IEEE International Conference on Web Services (293–301). Washington, DC, USA: IEEE Computer Society.

Pu, K., & Hristidis, V. Koudas, N. (2006). Syntactic Rule Based Approach to Web Service Composition. ICDE '06: Proceedings of the 22nd International Conference on Data Engineering (31). Washington, DC, USA: IEEE Computer Society.

Qiu, L., Lin, F., & Wan, C. Shi, Z. (2006). Semantic Web Services composition using AI planning of Description Logics. APSCC '06: Proceedings of the 2006 IEEE Asia-Pacific Conference on Services Computing (340–347). Washington, DC, USA: IEEE Computer Society.

Rector, A. L. Horrocks, I. R. (1997). Experience building a large, re-usable medical ontology using a description logic with transitivity and concept inclusions. Proceedings of the Fourteenth National Conference on Artificial Intelligence (AAAI'97).

Reid, A,, Flatt, M., Stoller, L., & Lepreau, J. Eide, E. (2000, October). Knit: component composition for systems software. Proc. of the 4th Operating Systems Design and Implementation (OSDI) (347–360).

Riabov, A. Liu, Z. (2005, July). Planning for stream processing systems. Proceedings of the Twentieth National Conference on Artificial Intelligence (AAAI'05).

Riabov, A. Liu, Z. (2006). Scalable planning for distributed stream processing systems. Proceedings of the Sixteenth International Conference on Automated Planning and Scheduling (ICAPS 2006).

Sheshagiri, M., & desJardins, M. Finin, T. (2003, June). A planner for composing services described in DAML-S. Proceedings of the AAMAS Workshop on Web Services and Agent-based Engineering.

Sirin, E. Parsia, B. (2004). Planning for Semantic Web Services. Semantic Web Services Workshop at the Third International Semantic Web Conference (ISWC 2004). Sivashanmugam, K., Miller, J. A., Sheth, A. P. Verma, K. (04-5). Framework for Semantic Web process composition. International Journal Electronic Commerce, 9(2), 71–106.

Skogan, D., & Gronmo, R. Solheim, I. (2004). Web Service composition in UML. EDOC '04: Proceedings of the Enterprise Distributed Object Computing Conference, Eighth IEEE International (47–57). Washington, DC, USA: IEEE Computer Society.

Sugumaran, V., & Storey, V. C. (2003). A semantic-based approach to component retrieval. *SIGMIS Database, 34*(3), 8–24. doi:10.1145/937742.937745

Welty, C. Fikes, R. (2006, November). A reusable ontology for fluents in OWL. Formal Ontology in Information Systems: Proceedings of the 4th Intl Conference (FOIS 2006), Volume 150 Frontiers in Artificial Intelligence and Applications. IOS Press.

Whitehouse, K., & Zhao, F. Liu, J. (2006). Semantic streams: A framework for composable semantic interpretation of sensor data. Proceedings of The Third European Workshop on Wireless Sensor Networks (EWSN '06).

Yahoo Pipes. (2007) Retrieved from the Web 5/8/2008. http://pipes.yahoo.com/pipes/

Yang, J., Papazoglou, M. P., & Orriëns, B. van Heuvel, W.-J. (2003). A rule based approach to the service composition life-cycle. WISE '03: Proceedings of the Fourth International Conference on Web Information Systems Engineering (295). Washington, DC, USA: IEEE Computer Society.

ENDNOTES

[1]   Some flow-based paradigms might not support the connection of a component's output to more than one input.

[2]   Other modalities, such observation and analysis of roadway loop sensor data, could also be considered where appropriate.

[3]   In cases where some exemplar individual $?X$ was described on the output of some component but not on any input, the flow

composition assembler can identify this as an error - either the author omitted a ?*X* on an input or should have referred to it as being newly introduced, by using "__*X*".

[4] The request specification language, like the OWL and SPARQL languages, makes use of XML Namespaces, to aid in term disambiguation among domain vocabularies. For brevity, examples in this article elide the namespace prefixes; only the ":" part of the prefix appears.

[5] Note here that VideoCameraBway-42nd is a data source component. As such it is the only component in simplest of all subflows, and the subflow output *is* the component output.

This work was previously published in International Journal of Software Science and Computational Intelligence, Volume 1, Issue 1, edited by Yingxu Wang, pp. 32-50, copyright 2009 by IGI Publishing (an imprint of IGI Global).

Chapter 9
Adaptive Computation Paradigm in Knowledge Representation:
Traditional and Emerging Applications

Marina L. Gavrilova
University of Calgary, Canada

ABSTRACT

The constant demand for complex applications, the ever increasing complexity and size of software systems, and the inherently complicated nature of the information drive the needs for developing radically new approaches for information representation. This drive is leading to creation of new and exciting interdisciplinary fields that investigate convergence of software science and intelligence science, as well as computational sciences and their applications. This survey article discusses the new paradigm of the algorithmic models of intelligence, based on the adaptive hierarchical model of computation, and presents the algorithms and applications utilizing this paradigm in data-intensive, collaborative environment. Examples from the various areas include references to adaptive paradigm in biometric technologies, evolutionary computing, swarm intelligence, robotics, networks, e-learning, knowledge representation and information system design. Special topics related to adaptive models design and geometric computing are also included in the survey.

INTRODUCTION

Adaptive computing focuses on the methodology and implementation of algorithms and systems that can adjust to different situations and circumstances. An adaptive system may change its own behavior depending on the goals, tasks, and other features of individual users and the environment. Adaptivity is important for ubiquitous and pervasive computing, and as it will be shown in this survey, plays an important role in a variety of traditional as well as emerging areas, such as biometric technologies, evolutionary computing, swarm intelligence, robotics, networks, e-learning, knowledge representation and information system design.

DOI: 10.4018/978-1-4666-0261-8.ch009

The constant demand for complex applications, the ever increasing complexity and size of software systems, and the inherently complicated nature of the information drive the needs for developing radically new approaches for information representation and processing. This drive is leading to creation of new and exciting interdisciplinary fields that investigate convergence of software science and intelligence science, as well as computational sciences and their applications. As can be seen from the definition, the driving force behind the need for adaptive paradigm is variety of situations, variability in backgrounds and needs of different user groups or applications. This survey article presents the new paradigm of the algorithmic models of intelligence, based on the adaptive hierarchical model of computation, and presents the algorithms and applications utilizing this paradigm in data-intensive, collaborative environment.

ADAPTIVE METHODS IN TERRAIN MODELING

For a long time, researchers were pressed with questions on how to model real-world objects realistically, while at the same time preserving efficiency, quality and operability requirements. The examples from the area of computer graphics and terrain modeling showcase the concept perfectly. Over the past twenty years, a grid, mesh, TIN, k-d trees, and Voronoi based methods for model representation were developed (Bonnefoi and Plemenos 2000, Gold and Dakowicz 2006, Cohen-Or and Levanoni 1996, Duchaineauy et. al. 1997, Franc and Skala 2002, Iglesis 2002, Kolingerová 2002). Most of these were however static methods, not suitable for rendering dynamic scenes or preserving higher level of details (see Figure 1.). In 1997, first methods for dynamic model representation: Real-time Optimally Adapting Mesh (ROAM) and Progressive Mesh (PM), were developed (Duchaineauy 1997).

However, even with the further improvements (Li et. a. 2003), these methods were not capable of dealing with large amount of complex data or significantly varied level of details (see Figure 2.). The main difference between terrain visualized using static and adaptive methods is the size and distribution of the triangles – in Figure 1, it is clearly seen that the patches of similar triangles are used throughout the various terrain features, while Figure 2 uses adaptive methods to decide on the most appropriate triangle sizes based on the curvature and distance from the viewer. However, this method is still not sufficient for dealing with all variety of terrain features, nor it is fast enough to be used in real-time.

Recently, the adaptive multi-resolution technique for real-time terrain rendering was developed (Apu and Gavrilova 2005). The method is characterized by the efficient representation of massive underlying terrain, utilizes efficient transition between detail levels, and achieves frame rate constancy ensuring visual continuity. The method is based on the adaptive loop subdivision and recursive split operation (see Figure 3.), implemented with the use of novel S-Queue operations ordering data structure.

Furthermore, a novel approach based on adaptive dynamic viewer-dependent level of details (LOD), utilizing the above strategy, was developed for real-time terrain rendering. The approach uses mesh regularity operator and LOD control parameters to achieve fast recursive seamless patch stitching, ensure geometric regularity, improve rendering quality, provide multi-resolution storage and allow for rendering and transmission of massive data sets (see Figure 4).

More formally, the process can be described as follows. A mesh M can be viewed as a piecewise linear surface. It is defined as a pair (K, V) where $V \subset P^3$ is the set of vertices and K is a simplicial complex specifying the connectivity of the mesh simplices (the adjacency of the vertices, edges and faces). A combinatorial k-simplex of K is the $(k + 1)$ element subset of K. Therefore the 0-sim-

Figure 1. A static mesh (40,000 triangles)

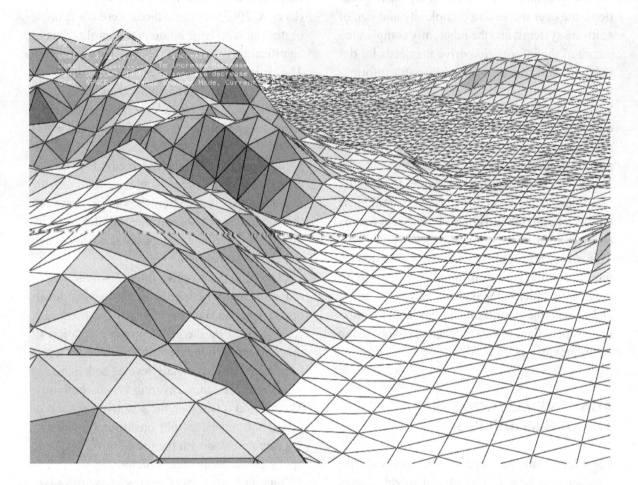

plices $\{i\} \in K$ are called vertices, the 1-simpices $\{i, j\} \in K$ are called edges, and the 2-simplices $\{i, j, l\} \in K$ are called faces.

A mesh can be considered as higher dimensional generalization of the concept of graph used in a variety of graphics applications. For instance, a mesh $M = (K, V)$ defines a graph $G = (V, \wp)$ where V is the set of vertices in M and $\wp$ is the 1-simplices of K. Therefore G is the minimum unrestricted topological realization of M. Nevertheless, higher simplices of K (i.e. faces) could be reconstructed from G by means of a convex combinatorial relationship of the transitive closure of $\wp$. For example, a triangulation of the mesh could be obtained from the transitive closure of edges defining a mesh M.

Mesh optimization is the process of reducing a mesh M_0 to a mesh M_k, where M_k contains less number of vertices and geometric primitives (i.e. triangles) than M_0. The goal is to find M_k such that the no other mesh M'_k exists, which represent a better approximation of the mesh M_0. In practical applications, it is sufficient to converge to any of the optimal solutions. There are many variations of mesh optimization techniques. Intuitively, mesh optimization is a compression method for geometric models with large details. In computer graphics, various processes such as regular tessellations, polygonized spline surfaces, polygonized parametric surfaces, polygonized implicit surfaces, range scanned surfaces and subdivision surfaces generate polygonal meshes to render or store the

Figure 2. Real-time optimally adaptive mesh (25,000 triangles)

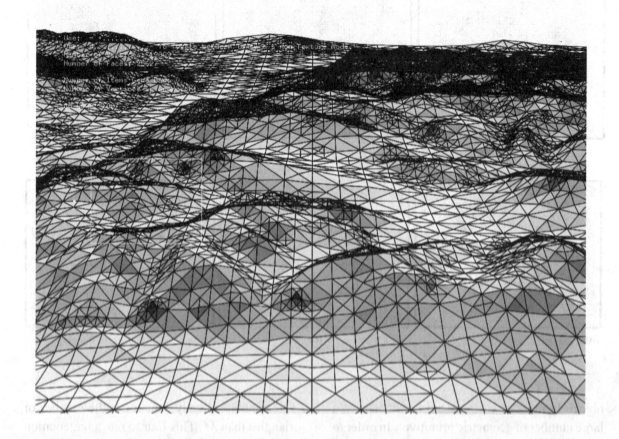

Figure 3. Adaptive loop subdivision and recursive split operations

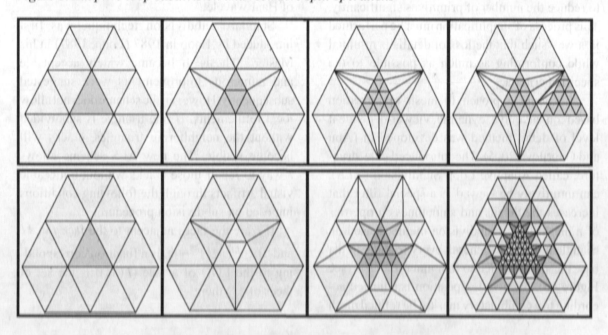

Figure 4. Varied Mesh regularity operator and LOD control parameters

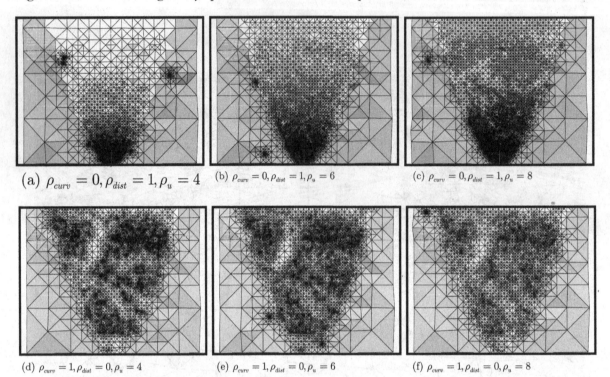

(a) $\rho_{curv} = 0, \rho_{dist} = 1, \rho_u = 4$ (b) $\rho_{curv} = 0, \rho_{dist} = 1, \rho_u = 6$ (c) $\rho_{curv} = 0, \rho_{dist} = 1, \rho_u = 8$

(d) $\rho_{curv} = 1, \rho_{dist} = 0, \rho_u = 4$ (e) $\rho_{curv} = 1, \rho_{dist} = 0, \rho_u = 6$ (f) $\rho_{curv} = 1, \rho_{dist} = 0, \rho_u = 8$

object. In most cases, these meshes consist of a large number of geometric primitives. In order to render them or store them efficiently, one needs to reduce the number of primitives significantly. This process of simplification must be performed in a way such that the loss of details is minimal while conforming as much as possible to the specified criteria.

The novel approach to mesh optimization based on adaptive dynamic viewer-dependent level of detail method was developed in (Apu and Gavrilova 2005). The introduced data structure, called Adaptive Loop Subdivision (ALS), can intuitively be viewed as a special filter that increases the details and smoothness properties of a mesh. It is a subdivision method based on triangle meshes. In general, every triangle in the base mesh M^i is split into four inner triangles (see Figure 4b). Each vertex position is adjusted according to a combinatory mask. The refined mesh

M^{i+1} contains exactly four times the number of triangles than M^i. This four to one augmentation of LOD is a direct correspondent to the refinement of Haar wavelet.

Standard subdivision technique was first introduced by Loop in 1987 (Loop, 1987) in his Master's Thesis. It became widely acceptable and numerous improvements were suggested subsequently. However, the scheme does not allow local refinements. If one triangle is subdivided without the neighboring triangles, cracks will become visible. The new ALS scheme allows a way to repair those cracks without noticeable visual artifacts through the following conditions imposed on subdivision procedure:

If f_i are the faces adjacent to the face f in M^i and $\Im : F(M^i) \to \mathbb{Z}$ is a function corresponding to the LOD of a face ($F(M_i)$) is the set of faces of M^i) then:

$$\forall i \left(\text{neighbor}(f, f_i) \rightarrow 0 \le |\Im(f) - \Im(f_i)| \le 1 \right)$$

A face *f* can be subdivided if and only if
$\aleph(f) = 1$; $\aleph : F(M^i) \rightarrow \{0,1\}$. Here,

$$\aleph(f) = \begin{cases} 0; & \text{if f is a T-face} \\ 1; & \text{otherwise} \end{cases}$$

Let $\prod$: $\Pi : F(M^i) \rightarrow F(M^{i-1})$ be the parent relationship of a face. That is $f' = \Pi(f)$ if and only if *f* in *M'* has been generated by splitting *f'*. The following condition must hold:

$$\forall f_i \forall f_j \left[\begin{array}{l} \left(\aleph(f_i) = 0 \right) \wedge \left(\aleph(f_j) = 0 \right) \wedge \text{neighbor}(f_i, f_j) \rightarrow \\ \left(\Im(f_i) \ne \Im(f_j) \right) \vee \left(\Pi(f_i) = \Pi(f_j) \right) \end{array} \right]$$

These constrains are the prime directives of the developed ALS method. They enforce the regularity of the scheme and ensures that no thin triangle is introduced. Their application leads to fine results shown in Figure 4 as well as numerous other advantages. ALS scheme was subsequently successfully used not only for terrain visualization, but in geographical information systems, motion planning and computer simulation applications.

ADAPTIVE METHODOLOGY IN TRADITIONAL APPLICATIONS

Adaptive Geometric Methods

At the same time as adaptive methods were making their way in the area of terrain rendering, the renewed interest to topology-based data structures, Voronoi diagram and Delaunay triangulation in particular, has grown significantly (Okabe et.al. 1992). The key developments on both conceptual and implementation level are regularly presented at the International Symposium on Voronoi Diagrams in Science and Engineering Conference Series. Utilization of these developments in

molecular modeling, bioinformatics and robotics promotes further stimulus to research on adaptive and dynamic problems. Thus, article (Gold and Dakowicz 2006) studies dynamic ship navigation visualization system using kinetic Voronoi diagram as an underlying concept. Utilization of the dynamic Voronoi diagram for 3D robot planning and navigation is studies in (Kolingerova 2005). Adaptive Voronoi diagram based approach to swarm simulation is presented in (Apu and Gavrilova 2006). These developments lead the way toward utilization of adaptive hierarchical models in computational geometry (see Figure 5).

Recently, some preliminary results on utilization of computational geometry techniques in biometrics began to appear, such as research on image processing using Voronoi diagrams (Asano 2006, Liang and Asano 2004), work on utilizing Voronoi diagram for fingerprint synthesis (Bebis 1999), and studies on 3D modeling of human faces using triangular mesh (Li and Jain 2005). Some interesting results were recently obtained in the BTLab, University of Calgary, through the development of topology-based feature extraction algorithms for fingerprint matching, 3D facial expression modeling and iris synthesis (Wang et. al. 2005, Wecker et. al. 2006, Bhattachariya and Gavrilova 2006).

Adaptive Image Processing and Visualization

Adaptive image processing is one of the most important techniques in visual information processing, especially in image restoration, filtering, enhancement, and segmentation. While existing literature presents some important aspects of the issue, there were no works that would treat the problem from a viewpoint that is directly linked to human perception – until the book "Adaptive Image Processing: A computational Intelligence Perspective Book" appeared (William et. al. 2001). This comprehensive collection of references treats adaptive image processing from a computational

Figure 5. Planar Voronoi diagram representation

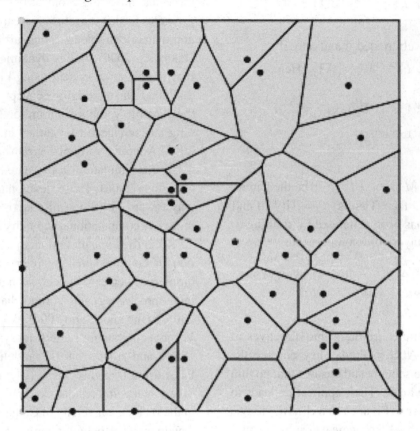

intelligence viewpoint, relating neural networks, fuzzy logic, and evolutionary computation to adaptive image processing. Based on the fundamentals of human perception, this book also gives a detailed account of computational intelligence methods and algorithms for adaptive image processing in regularization, edge detection, vision and any area where intelligent visual information processing is required.

Adaptive processing has been tightly linked not only to image processing, but to computer graphics and scientific visualization. In (Lopse et.al. 2002), authors provide an algorithm for computing a *robust adaptive polygonal approximation* of an implicit curve in the plane. The approximation is adapted to the geometry of the curve because the length of the edges varies with the curvature of the curve. Robustness is achieved by combining interval arithmetic and automatic differentiation.

Another example is adaptive visualization area of research, which is often explored in connection with geographical, urban or medical applications. A variety of engineering disciplines use large high-resolution geometric models whose computational requirements exceed current computer hardware capacities. The research presented in (Lu and Hammersley 2000) describes an *adaptive visualization* solution for interactively building such models. While adaptive visualization techniques have conventionally been applied to existing complete models, their method provides adaptive visualization of models while still under construction, through a clever utilization of multiresolution methods.

A common application of adaptive paradigm can be found in the area of medical imaging. A common active contour (*snake*) model is a popular choice for medical imaging applications, however the article by (Shen and Davatzikos 2000) goes further in exploring adaptive paradigm in this context. They propose a clever approach to geometric design and the structure of the model through *adaptive method for carrying out model deformations* in the most reliable way. Specifically, authors suggest to use an attribute vector to characterize the geometric structure around each point of the snake model, which allows to deform to nearby edges with considering geometric structure. They also provide an adaptive-focus statistical model which allows the deformation of the active contour in each stage to be influenced by the most reliable matches. Finally, they propose the deformation mechanism that is robust to local minima and is based on evaluating the snake energy function on segments of the snake at a time, instead of individual points. The approach is novel and unique, and is proven to perform very well experimentally.

Adaptive Information Systems

The current fast evolution in the areas of software, hardware and networks suggests that it will be possible to offer access to information systems through variety of interactive means, including computers, notebooks, PDA's, cellular phones, game consoles, GPS devices etc. Thus, this variety of technologies and information available required creation of a flexible environment to support adaptive interaction and services according to changing requirements, interfaces, devices, communication and user needs.

One of the research initiatives that started in 2002 was devoted specifically to this problem. The *Multichannel Adaptive Information Systems* project (MAIS) was funded by Basic Research Funds of the Italian Department of Education and involved six Universities and industry collabora-

tions. The project research areas were information systems, database systems, human computer interaction, computer networks and telecommunication, hardware design, middleware, management engineering, with the focus on adaptive computing paradigm. Adaptive e-services, adaptive portable devices and adaptive networks were at the focus of the research. The prototype applications of the methods were developed in the areas of tourism, education, and risk management in archeology.

Another relevant project is described in (Doerr 1999). Authors state that one way to increase software system adaptability is to allocate resources dynamically at run-time rather than statically at design time. For example, fine-grained run-time allocation of processor utilization and network bandwidth creates an opportunity to execute multimodal operations. Thus, this allocation strategy enhances adaptability by combining deterministic and non-deterministic functionality. Authors next showcase that adaptability is essential to improve versatility and decrease lifecycle maintenance costs for embedded real-time systems.

Adaptive Networks

As already seen from the above applications, the driving force behind the need for adaptive paradigm is variety of situations, variability in backgrounds and needs of different user groups or applications. The further expansion of Internet communications, not only for electronic exchange of ideas, but also as a means of collecting a wide range of information, has lead to a variety of other applications besides e-learning. Thus, electronic commerce, Internet transactions, collaborative newsgroups, facebooks, on-line teleconferencing are all rapidly developing. However, one of the problems is the difference in information available to network users. Network systems and services are becoming increasingly complex and diverse, and the processes involved in accessing required information are growing ever more advanced. As a result, the information disparity that arises from the presence or absence of knowledge about networks and computers is becoming a problem that cannot be overlooked. Another problem is one that is derived from changes and increases in communications traffic.

The key to dealing with the above challenges is *user adaptability* and *adaptability to changes in communication demand*. User adaptability means that the user does not conform to the conditions of the network, but rather the network adapts instantaneously to the user environment and to service needs, which change with every passing moment. Adaptability to changes in communication demand means that the network configuration and equipment functions change dynamically to absorb the introduction of new services and macrofluctuations in traffic. NTT Laboratories is one of the organizations that combines knowledge, expertise and application research in the area of *adaptive networks*, which constantly change their functions and configurations to respond immediately to changes in the environment, and to be the network platform of the Information Sharing Society of the future. Their key terms to describe the research in adaptive networks is Intellect, Evolution, and Simple & Seamless.

ADAPTIVE METHODS IN EMERGING AREAS

Biometrics and Adaptive Computing

Adaptive techniques have made their way in emerging scientific areas such as *biometric computing*. In information technology, biometric refers to a study of physical and behavioral characteristics with the purpose of person identification. In recent years, the area of biometrics has witnessed a tremendous growth, partly as a result of a pressing need for increased security, and partly as a response to the new technological advances that are literally changing the way we live. Availability of much more affordable storage

and the high resolution image capturing devices have contributed to accumulating very large datasets of biometric data. On the other hand, it also created significant challenges driven by the higher than ever volumes and the complexity of the data, that can no longer be resolved through acquisition of more memory, faster processors or optimization of existing algorithms. This justifies the need for the development of a new concept for biometric data storage and visualization based on adaptive paradigm.

It is obvious to anyone who works in the area of biometric computing that the problem is not trivial. It is not enough to simply fill the existing deficiency in data representation and visualization through application of advanced results from the areas of computational geometry and computer graphics. The backbone of the methodology is in the application of adaptive hierarchical data representation to achieve flexible and versatile data representation, fast data retrieval, reliable matching, easy updates and smooth and continuous data processing.

To achieve this objective, we suggest a novel way to represent complex biometric data (e.g. a bitmap, a graphics file, a set of vectors, a polygonal curve) through the organization of the data in a hierarchical tree-like structure. Such organization is similar to *Adaptive Memory Subdivision (AMS)* representation (see Figure 6).

AMS is a hybrid method based on the combination of traditional hierarchical tree structure with the concept of expanding or collapsing tree nodes, depending on the amount of information and level of detail (LOD) that needs to be represented. *Spatial quad-tree* is used to hold the information about the system, as well as the instructions on how to process this information. Expansion is realized through the spatial subdivision technique that refines the data and increases LOD, and collapsing is realized through the merge operation that simplifies the data representation and makes it more compact. The greedy strategy is used to optimally adapt to the best representa-

Figure 6. Adaptive Memory Subdivision (AMS) model

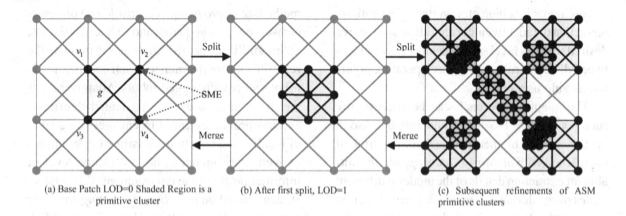

(a) Base Patch LOD=0 Shaded Region is a primitive cluster

(b) After first split, LOD=1

(c) Subsequent refinements of ASM primitive clusters

tion based on the user requirements, amount of available data and resources, and required LOD. This powerful technique enables to achieve compact data representation with required LOD. For instance, it enables to efficiently store and retrieve minor details of the facial image (e.g. scars, wrinkles) or detailed patterns of the compared irises.

Adaptive methods have been studied for increasing hand geometry reliability while new processing algorithms, such as symmetric real Gabor filters, have been used to decrease the computational cost involved in iris pattern recognition (Sanchez-Reillo et. Al. 1999). This work explores adapting these methods to small *embedded systems*, and proposes the design of new biometric systems, where the users template is stored in a portable storage media for added security. Such media could be used to store sensitive information, for instance related to user's health records, and proposed adaptive access methods are devised to avoid the reading of this data unless the biometric verification has been performed.

While the above research is aimed at increase reliability and security of biometric data, another highly interesting direction is merging *adaptive paradigm with multimodal biometric fusion*. Multimodal biometric is intended to utilize biometric information obtained by multiple sensors and from multiple sources in order to increase authentication reliability. The paper by (Veeramachaneni 2003) introduces a new Adaptive Multimodal Biometric Fusion Algorithm(AMBF) algorithm, which is a combination of *Bayesian decision fusion* technique and a *particle swarm optimization* method. A Bayesian framework is typically used to fuse decisions received from multiple biometric sensors. The optimal rule is a function of the error cost and a priori probability of an intruder. This Bayesian framework formalizes the design of a system that can adaptively increase or reduce the security level. Particle swarm optimization searches the decision and sensor operating points (i.e. thresholds) space to achieve the desired security level. The optimization function aims to minimize the cost in a Bayesian decision fusion. The particle swarm optimization algorithm results in the fusion rule and the operating points of sensors at which the system can work. The swarm algorithm can easily handle the scalability issue as the number of sensors increases and efficiently search through the highly large fusion rule search space.

The presented method successfully merges two highly interesting and important paradigms: adaptive method based on evolutionary computing and multimodal biometric system with Beyesian decision rule. As a result, it can successfully address the varying security needs and user access requirements in a biometric system. The authors report that the adaptive algorithm allows to achieve desired security level and to seemingly switch between different rules and sensor operating points for varying user needs.

The adaptive approach can be successfully sued not only for biometric modeling but also in synthesis of the biometric data. A combination of the method with *multi-resolution approach,* suitable for extracting details of the model at different scales of resolution, is a promising new direction of research which can be used to complement the missing information or to recreate the model. The method performs the high-level detail extraction and capturing of the model characteristics, and then applies this information for synthesis of new biometric data. This novel approach has shown a high potential in a recent study on iris synthesis (Wecker et.al. 2006). Moreover, *adaptive learning method can assist in* examining extracted features, retrieval patterns, and dynamic updates with the purpose of making the model more flexible.

Adaptive Methods in Robotics

Another highly important and rapidly developing area of research, that encompasses artificial intelligence, engineering, vision, geometric processing and decision-making, is robotics. *Adaptive robots* is an area of research that studies the design of robots that function in a changing environment by using high-level cognitive abilities and/or adaptive behaviors. The Dutch AIBO team, composed by research groups from the DECIS Lab and Universities of Amsterdam, Delft, Twente and Utrecht, is the leading force behind research on collaborative robot behavior and intelligent behavior of the team of robots, through robot soccer simulation and applied studies (Wong et. al. 2001). Exploring adaptive paradigm in a variety of areas essential to success of this project, including *adaptive robot vision, adaptive navigation and adaptive learning*

are just some of the examples of the current state-of-the art research related to this project. Adaptive methods to improve *self-localization* in robot soccer were devised in (Dahm and Ziegler 2003). The authors utilized adaptive strategies to improve the reliability and performance of self-localization in robot soccer with legged robots. Adaptiveness is the common feature of the presented algorithms and has proved essential to enhance the quality of localization by a new classification technique as well as to increase the confidence level of information about the environment. Cooperative strategy based on *adaptive Q-learning* for robot soccer was developed in (Hwang et.al. 2004). The strategy developed enabled robots to cooperate with each other to achieve the objectives of offense and defense. Through the mechanism of learning, the robots learned from experiences in either successes or failures, and utilized these experiences to improve the performance. The cooperative strategy is based on a hierarchical architecture. An adaptive Q-learning method showed to allow more flexibility in learning that the traditional Q-learning approach, especially in the context of cooperative strategy.

Adaptive Knowledge Representation and Learning

Adaptive Knowledge Representation and Reasoning Conference (AKRR) is one of the unique events devoted completely to the emerging paradigm of *adaptive knowledge representation*. The forum is concerned with all adaptive aspects related to knowledge representation and reasoning. Specifically, such areas as adaptive systems in economic sciences and organizational theory, new generation of semantic web, adaptive systems in medical education, research and practice, and adaptive machine translation are within the conference scope.

The idea of utilizing *adaptive methods in e-learning* is not new. One of the first articles on the subject that appeared in 1998 describes web-based educational applications that are expected to be used by very different groups of users (Brusilovsky 1998). Thus, authors argue that such a system needs to adapt to users with very different backgrounds, prior knowledge of the subject and learning goals, without human assistance. They next describe an approach for developing *adaptive electronic textbooks* and present InterBook—an authoring tool based on this approach which simplifies the development of adaptive electronic textbooks on the Web.

An extensive research in the area of adaptive learning was undertaken since that time. One example is the research on knowledge representation in the area of learning design and adaptive learning, presented in (Kravcik and Gasevic 2006). The authors deal with learning design and adaptation, and state that the procedural knowledge is highly important. They examine the degree of reusability and interoperability of procedural knowledge in the current adaptive educational hypermedia systems, and discuss several useful strategies and techniques, including informal scripts, system encoding, elicited knowledge, and standardized specifications.

Hierarchical Models in Cognitive Informatics

As it has been seen in the previous sections, adaptive computing heavily relies on hierarchical models of knowledge representing various natural and artificial phenomena. Such models can represent, for instance, complex three-dimensional terrain patterns, evolutionary behaviour of a swarm of living organisms, or an intricate structure of a web-linked virtual library. As it was recently discovered at the front line of the cognitive science and cognitive informatics research, hierarchical cognitive models can be also efficiently use to study internal information and knowledge presentation in human brains (Wang 2007).

It is commonly accepted that memory is the foundation of all forms of natural intelligence.

Neural Informatics (NeI) is a branch of cognitive informatics, where memory is recognized as the foundation and platform of any natural or artificial intelligence (Wang 2003). While traditionally the Long-Term Memory (LTM) is perceived as static and fixed in adult brains, recent discoveries in neuroscience and cognitive informatics indicate that LTM is dynamically reconfiguring, particularly at the lower levels of the neural clusters (Wang 2007). The article explains the memory establishment, enhancement, and evolution, which are typical functions of the brain, are not limited to only childhood developmental stage; thus the more complex, dynamic model is necessary to represent such functions. In order to achieve this task, the pioneering theory is presented in the article that is based on the concept of the Hierarchical Neural Cluster (HNC) Model of Memory. Furthermore, the Object-Attribute-Relation (OAR) model is introduced to formally represent the structures of internal information and knowledge acquired and learned in the brain (Wang 2007). The OAR model explains the mechanisms of internal knowledge and information representation, as well as their physical and physiological meanings, and allows to better understand learning mechanisms and help to develop more powerful algorithms for a variety of complex problems faced by scientists everyday.

CONCLUSION

The article presented a comprehensive survey of the new paradigm of the algorithmic models of intelligence, based on the adaptive hierarchical model of computation. It started with the adaptive methods for terrain modeling, and presented methodically the adaptive paradigm in geometric computing, biometric, robotics, image processing and vision, knowledge representations, information systems, e-learning and networks. Illustrations were further provided to explain some concepts related to adaptive information processing and models. Aside from the areas covered in the survey, there constantly appear a variety of new and emerging applications utilizing adaptive models of computations. It is our hope that this survey inspires readers to further in-depth study of the exciting topic of adaptive computations.

REFERENCES

Apu, R., & Gavrilova, M. L. "Adaptive Spatial Memory Representation for Real-Time Motion Planning," 3IA'2005 Int. Conf. on Comp. Graphics and Artificial Intelligence, France pp.21-32, 2005

Apu, R., & Gavrilova, M. L. (2006). *Battle Swarm: An Evolutionary Approach to Complex Swarm Intelligence,*" *3IA Int. C. Comp. Graphics and AI* (pp. 139–150). Limoges, France: Eurographics.

Asano, T. (2006). Aspect-Ratio Voronoi Diagram with Applications. In *ISVD 2006* (pp. 32–39). IEEE.

Bardis, G., Miaoulis, G., & Plemenos, D. "Learning User Preferences at the Declarative and Geometric Description Level," 3IA'2005, Limoges (France), May 11-12, 2005

Bebis, G., Deaconu, T., & Georiopoulous, M. "Fingerprint Identification using Delaunay Triangulation," ICIIS 99, Maryland, pp. 452-459, 1999

Bhattachariya, P. and Gavrilova, M.L.. "CRYSTAL - A new density-based fast and efficient clustering algorithm", IEEE-CS Press, ISVD 2006, pp. 102-111, Banff, AB, Canada, July 2006

Bonnefoi, P. F., & Plemenos, D. "Constraint satisfaction techniques for declarative scene modelling by hierarchical decomposition," 3IA'2000, Limoges (France), May 3-4, 2000

Brusilovsky, P., Eklund, J., & Schwarz, E. "Web-based education for all: a tool for development of adaptive courseware," Computer Networks and ISDN Systems, Volume 30, Issues 1-7, pp. 291-300, 1998

Capelli, R., Maio, D., & Maltoni, D. "Synthetic Fingerprint-Database Generation," ICPR 2002, Canada, vol 3, pp 369-376, 2002

Cohen-Or, D., & Levanoni, Y. (1996). *"Temporal continuity of levels of detail in Delaunay triangulated terrain,"* *Visualization '96* (pp. 37–42). IEEE Press.

Dahm, I. and Ziegler, J. "Adaptive Methods to Improve Self-localization in Robot Soccer," LNCS 2752, pps. 393-408, 2003

Doerr, B. S., Venturella, T., Jha, R., Gill, C. D., & Schmidt, D. C. "Adaptive Scheduling for Real-time, Embedded Information," in Proceedings of the 18th IEEE/AIAA Digital Avionics Systems Conference, 10 pages, 1999

Duchaineauy, M. (1997). ROAMing Terrain: Real-Time Optimally Adapting Meshes. *IEEE Visualization, 97,* 81–88.

Franc, M., & Skala, V. (2002). Fast Algorithm for Triangular Mesh Simplification Based on Vertex decimation. In *CCGM2002 Proceedings*. Lecture Notes in Computer Science Springer. doi:10.1007/3-540-46080-2_5

Gavrilova, M. L. (2008 to appear). *Computational Intelligence: A Geometry-Based Approach, Book, in series Studies in Computational Intelligence.* Springer-Verlag.

Gold, C., & Dakowicz, M. (2006). *ISVD 2006, IEEE-CS* (pp. 76–84). Banff, Canada: Kinetic Voronoi/Delaunay Drawing Tools.

Hwang, K. S., Tan, S. W., & Chen, C. C. (2004). Cooperative strategy based on adaptive Q-learning for robot soccer systems. *IEEE Transactions on Fuzzy Systems Volume, 12*(Issue: 4), 569–576. doi:10.1109/TFUZZ.2004.832523

Iglesias, A. "Computer Graphics Techniques for Realistic Modeling, Rendering, and Animation of Water. Part I: 1980-88." Int. Conf. on Computational Science (2) 2002, 181-190, 2002

Kawaharada, H., & Sugihara, K. "Compression of Arbitrary Mesh Data Using Subdivision Surfaces," IMA Conference on the Mathematics of Surfaces 2003, 99-110, 2003

Kolingerova, I. "Probabilistic Methods for Triangulated Models," 8th Int. Conference on Computer Graphics and Artificial Intelligence 3IA 2005, Limoges, France, 93-106, 2005

Kravcik, M. and Gasevic, D. "Knowledge Representation for Adaptive Learning Design," Proceedings of Adaptive Hypermedia. June, Dublin, Ireland, 11 pages, 2006

Li, S., & Jain, A. (2005). *Handbook of Face Recognition*. Springer-Verlag.

Li, S., Liu, X., & Wu, E. (2003). Feature-Based Visibility-Driven CLOD for Terrain. In *Proc. Pacific Graphics 2003* (pp. 313–322). IEEE Press.

Liang, X. F., & Asano, T. (2004). *A fast denoising method for binary fingerprint image* (pp. 309–313). Spain: IASTED.

Loop, C. T. Smooth Subdivision Surfaces Based on Triangles. Masters Thesis, University of Utah, Department of Mathematics. 1987

Lopes, H., Oliveira, J. B., & de Figueiredo, L. H. (2002). Robust adaptive polygonal approximation of implicit curves. *Computers & Graphics, 26*(Issue 6), 841–852. doi:10.1016/S0097-8493(02)00173-5

Lu, H., & Hammersley, R. "Adaptive visualization for interactive geometric modeling in geoscience," the 8th International Conference in Central Europe on Computer Graphics, Visualization and Interactive Digital Media 2000, p.1, Feb. 2000

Luo, Y. and Gavrilova, M.L.. "3D Facial model synthesis using Voronoi Approach," IEEE-CS proceedings, ISVD 2006, pp. 132-137, Banff, AB, Canada, July 2006

Medioni, G., & Waupotitsch, R. "Face recognition and modeling in 3D," IEEE Int. Workshop on Analysis and Modeling of Faces and Gestures, pp. 232-233, 2003

Moriguchi, M., & Sugihara, K. (2006). *"A new initialization method for constructing centroidal Voronoi Tessellations on Surface Meshes,"* ISVD 2006 (pp. 159–165). IEEE-CS Press.

Okabe, A., Boots, B., & Sugihara, K. (1992). *Spatial tessellation concepts and applications of Voronoi diagrams*. Chichester, England: Wiley & Sons.

Perry, S. W., Wong, H. S., & Guan, L. Adaptive Image Processing: A computational Intelligence Perspective, CRC Press, 9 volumes, 272 pages, 2001

Sanchez-Reillo, R., Sanchez-Avila, C., & Gonzalez-Marcos, A. "Multiresolution Analysis and Geometric Measures for Biometric Identification Systems," Secure Networking Proceedings, LNCS, Volume 1740, p. 783, 1999

Shen, S., & Davatzikos, C. (2000, August). An Adaptive-Focus Deformable Model Using Statistical and Geometric Information. *IEEE Transactions on Pattern Analysis and Machine Intelligence, 22*(8), 906–913. doi:10.1109/34.868689

Veeramachaneni, K., Osadciw, L. A., & Varshney, P. K. "Adaptive Multimodal Biometric Fusion Algorithm Using Particle Swarm," SPIE, vol 5099, pp. 211, Orlando, Florida, April 21-25, 2003

Wang, H., Gavrilova, M. L., Luo, Y., & Rokne, J. (2006). *"An Efficient Algorithm for Fingerprint Matching", ICPR 2006, Int. C. on Pattern Recognition.* Hong Kong: IEEE-CS.

Wang, Y. "Cognitive informatics: A new transdisciplinary research field." Brain and Mind: A Transdisciplinary Journal of Neuroscience and Neurophilosophy, 4(2), 115-127, 2003

Wang, Y. (2007, July-September). The OAR Model of Neural Informatics for Internal Knowledge Representation in the Brain. *International Journal of Cognitive Informatics and Natural Intelligence, 1*(3), 66–77. doi:10.4018/jcini.2007070105

Wecker, L., Samavati, F., & Gavrilova, M. L. "Iris Synthesis: A Multi-Resolution Approach," GRAPHITE 2005, ACM Press, in association with SIGGRAPH, pp. 121-125, 2005

Wong, C. C., Chou, M. F., Hwang, C. P., Tsai, C. H., & Shyu, S. R. "A method for obstacle avoidance and shooting action of the robot soccer," Robotics and Automation, proceedings ICRA. IEEE International Conference, pp 3778- 3782 vol.4 2001

Yanushkevich, S., Wang, P., Srihari, S., & Gavrilova, M. L. (2006). *Image Pattern Recognition: Synthesis and Analysis in Biometrics, Book.* World Scientific.

This work was previously published in International Journal of Software Science and Computational Intelligence, Volume 1, Issue 1, edited by Yingxu Wang, pp. 87-99, copyright 2009 by IGI Publishing (an imprint of IGI Global).

Chapter 10
Protoforms of Linguistic Database Summaries as a Human Consistent Tool for Using Natural Language in Data Mining

Janusz Kacprzyk
Polish Academy of Sciences, Poland

Sławomir Zadrożny
Polish Academy of Sciences, Poland

ABSTRACT

We consider linguistic database summaries in the sense of Yager (1982), in an implementable form proposed by Kacprzyk & Yager (2001) and Kacprzyk, Yager & Zadrożny (2000), exemplified by, for a personnel database, "most employees are young and well paid" (with some degree of truth) and their extensions as a very general tool for a human consistent summarization of large data sets. We advocate the use of the concept of a protoform (prototypical form), vividly advocated by Zadeh and shown by Kacprzyk & Zadrożny (2005) as a general form of a linguistic data summary. Then, we present an extension of our interactive approach to fuzzy linguistic summaries, based on fuzzy logic and fuzzy database queries with linguistic quantifiers. We show how fuzzy queries are related to linguistic summaries, and that one can introduce a hierarchy of protoforms, or abstract summaries in the sense of latest Zadeh's (2002) ideas meant mainly for increasing deduction capabilities of search engines. We show an implementation for the summarization of Web server logs.

DOI: 10.4018/978-1-4666-0261-8.ch010

INTRODUCTION

Data summarization is one of basic capabilities needed by any "intelligent" system. Since for the human being the only fully natural means of communication is natural language, a linguistic summarization would be very desirable, exemplified by, for a data set on employees, a statement (linguistic summary) "almost all young and well qualified employees are well paid".

This may clearly be an instance of a paradigm shift that is advocated in recent time whose prominent example is the so-called "computing with words (and perceptions) paradigm" introduced by Zadeh in the mid-1990s, and extensively presented in Zadeh & Kacprzyk's (1999) books.

Unfortunately, data summarization is still in general unsolved a problem. Very many techniques are available but they are not "intelligent enough", and not human-consistent, partly due to a limited use of natural language.

We show here the use of linguistic database summaries introduced by Yager (1982, 1991, 1995, 1996), and then considerably advanced by Kacprzyk (2000), Kacprzyk & Yager (2001), and Kacprzyk, Yager & Zadrożny (2000, 2001), Zadrożny & Kacprzyk (1999), and implemented in Kacprzyk & Zadrożny (1998,2000a-d, 2001a-e, 2002, 2003, 2005). We derive here linguistic data summaries as linguistically quantified propositions as, e.g., "most of the employees are young and well paid", with a degree of truth (validity), in case of a personnel database.

We employ Kacprzyk & Zadrożny's (1998, 2000a-d, 2001) interactive approach to linguistic summaries in which the determination of a class of summaries of interest is done via Kacprzyk & Zadrożny's (1994, 1995a-b, 2001b) FQUERY for Access, a fuzzy querying add-in to Microsoft Access, extended to the querying over the Internet in Kacprzyk & Zadrożny (2000b). Since a fully automatic generation of linguistic summaries is not feasible at present, an interaction with the user is assumed for the determination of a class of summaries of interest, and this is done via the above fuzzy querying add-in.

Extending Kacprzyk & Zadrożny (2002), we show that by relating various types of linguistic summaries to fuzzy queries, with various known and sought elements, we can arrive at a hierarchy of prototypical forms, or – in Zadeh's (2002) terminology – protoforms, of linguistic data summaries. This seems to be a very powerful conceptual idea.

We present an implementation of the proposed approach to the derivation of linguistic summaries for Web server logs. This implementation may be viewed as a step towards the implementation of protoforms of linguistic summaries.

LINGUISTIC SUMMARIES USING FUZZY LOGIC WITH LINGUISTIC QUANTIFIERS

In Yager's (1982) approach, we have:

- V is a quality (attribute) of interest, e.g. salary in a database of workers,
- $Y = \{y_1, ..., y_n\}$ is a set of objects (records) that manifest quality V, e.g. the set of workers; hence $V(y_i)$ are values of quality V for object y_i,
- $D = \{V(y_1), ..., V(y_n)\}$ is a set of data (the "database" on question)

    A *linguistic summary* of a data set (data base) consists of:

- a summarizer S (e.g. young),
- a quantity in agreement Q (e.g. most),
- truth T - e.g. 0.7,
- a qualifier R (optionally), i.e. another linguistic term (e.g. well-earning), determining a fuzzy subset of Y.

as, e.g., "$T(most$ of employees are *young*)=0.7". The truth T may be meant more generally as, e.g., validity.

Given a set of data D, we can hypothetize any appropriate summarizer S and any quantity in agreement Q, and the assumed measure of truth will indicate the truth of the statement that Q data items satisfy S.

We assume that the summarizer S (and qualifier R) is a linguistic expression semantically represented by a fuzzy set as, e.g., "young" would be represented as a fuzzy set in $\{1, 2, ..., 90\}$. Such a simple one-attribute summarizer serves the purpose of introducing the concept of a linguistic summary but it can readily be extended to a confluence of attribute values as, e.g, "*young* and *well paid*". Clearly, the most interesting are non-trivial, *human-consistent* summarizers (concepts) as, e.g.: *productive* workers, involving complicated *combinations of attributes*, e.g.: a hierarchy (not all attributes are of the same importance), the attribute values are ANDed and/or ORed, k out of n, *most*, etc. of them should be accounted for, etc. but they need some specific tools and techniques to be mentioned later.

Basically, two types of a linguistic quantity in agreement can be used: absolute (e.g., "about 5", "more or less 100", "several"), and relative (e.g., "a few", "more or less a half", "most", "almost all"). They are fuzzy linguistic quantifiers (cf. (Zadeh, 1983, 1985)) that can be handled by fuzzy logic.

The calculation of truth (validity) boils down to the calculation of the truth value (from $[0,1]$) of a linguistically quantified statement (e.g., "*most* of the employees are *young*") that can be done using Zadeh's (1983) calculus of linguistically quantified propositions (cf. (Zadeh & Kacprzyk, 1999)) or Yager's (1988) OWA operators [cf. (Yager & Kacprzyk, 1997)]; for a survey, see also Liu & Kerre (1998).

So, we have a linguistically quantified proposition, written "Qy's are F", where Q is a linguistic quantifier (e.g., most), $Y = \{y\}$ is a set of objects (e.g., experts), and F is a property (e.g., convinced). Importance B (later referred to with an accompanying attribute as a qualifier) may be added, yielding "QBy's are F", e.g., "most (Q) of the important (B) experts (y's) are convinced (F)".

We seek their truth values which are equal to: if F and B are fuzzy sets in Y, and a (proportional, nondecreasing) Q is assumed to be a fuzzy set in $[0,1]$ as, e.g.

$$\mu_Q(x) = \begin{cases} 1 & \text{for } x \geq 0.8 \\ 2x - 0.6 & \text{for } 0.3 < x < 0.8 \\ 0 & \text{for } x \leq 0.3 \end{cases} \qquad (1)$$

then, due to Zadeh (1983)

$$\text{truth}(Qy\text{'s are } F) = \mu_Q[\tfrac{1}{n}\textstyle\sum_{i=1}^{n} \mu_F(y_i)] \tag{2}$$

$$\text{truth}(QBy\text{'s are } F) = \mu_Q[\textstyle\sum_{i=1}^{n}(\mu_B(y_i) \wedge \mu_F(y_i)) / \sum_{i=1}^{n} \mu_B(y_i)] \tag{3}$$

The OWA operators can also be used to calculate (1) and (2) – cf. (Yager, 1988; Yager & Kacprzyk (1997)). They offer a wide array of aggregation types based on various quantifiers, both crisp and fuzzy, though they may lead to more complicated calculation formulas. In the implementation presented later the user may choose between the OWAs and Zadeh's calculus.

The basic validity criterion, i.e. the degree of truth (validity), is conceptually important but often insufficient in practice. Some other quality (validity) criteria have been proposed in Kacprzyk & Yager (2001), and Kacprzyk, Yager & Zadrożny (2000), like degrees of: imprecision, covering, and appropriateness, and the length of a summary. An optimal summary is sought which maximizes the weighted average of the particular degrees.

FUZZY QUERYING, LINGUISTIC SUMMARIES, AND THEIR PROTOFORMS

The roots of our approach are our previous papers on fuzzy logic in database querying (cf. (Kacprzyk

& Ziółkowski, 1986; Kacprzyk, Zadrożny & Ziółkowski, 1989)) in which we argued that the formulation of a precise query is often difficult for the end-user (see also (Kacprzyk et al., 2000)). For example, a customer of a real-estate agency looking for a house would rather use requirements using imprecise descriptions as *cheap, large* garden, etc. Also, to specify which combination of the criteria fulfillment would be satisfactory, one would often use, e.g., *most* or *almost all* of them. All such vague terms may be easily interpreted by fuzzy logic, hence the development of many fuzzy querying interfaces, notably our FQUERY for Access.

FQUERY for Access is an add-in that it makes possible and the following terms are available:

- fuzzy values as by *low* in "profitability is *low*",
- fuzzy relations as by *much greater than* in "income is *much greater than* spending", and
- linguistic quantifiers as by *most* in "*most* conditions have to be met".

The first two are elementary building blocks of fuzzy queries in FQUERY for Access. They are meaningful in the context of numerical fields only. There are also other fuzzy constructs allowed which may be used with scalar fields. To use a field in a query in connection with a fuzzy value, it has to be defined as an *attribute* whose definition consists of its: lower (LL) and upper (UL) limit. They set the interval which the field's values are to belong to. This interval depends on the meaning of the given field. This makes it possible to universally define fuzzy values as fuzzy sets on [-10, +10]. Then, *the matching degree md($\cdot$,$\cdot$)* of a simple condition referring to attribute AT and fuzzy value FV against a record t is calculated by $md(AT=FV,t)=\mu_{FV}(\tau(t(AT))\ md(AT=FV, t)$

$= \mu_{FV}(\tau(t(AT)))$, where: $t(AT)$ is the value of attribute AT in record t, μ_{FV} is the membership function of a fuzzy value FV, τ: $[LL_{AT},UL_{AT}] \rightarrow [-10,10]$ is a mapping from the interval defining AT onto [-10,10] so that we may use the same fuzzy values for different fields. A meaningful interpretation is secured by τ which makes it possible to treat all fields' domains as ranging over the unified interval [-10,10].

The elicitation (definition) of fuzzy sets corresponding to particular fuzzy values may be done using different methods. Normally, it involves an interface with the user(s) who provide responses to appropriate chosen questions.

Linguistic quantifiers provide for a flexible aggregation of simple conditions. In FQUERY for Access they are defined in Zadeh's (1983) sense, as fuzzy set on the [0, 10] instead of the original [0, 1]. They may be interpreted either using Zadeh's (1983) approach or via the OWA operators (Yager, 1988; or Yager & Kacprzyk, 1997); Zadeh's interpretation will be used here. The membership functions of fuzzy linguistic quantifiers are assumed piece-wise linear, hence two numbers from [0,10] are needed. Again, a mapping from [0,N], where N is the number of conditions aggregated, to [0,10] is employed to calculate the matching degree of a query. More precisely, the matching degree, $md(\cdot,\cdot)$, for *query* "*Q of N* conditions are satisfied" for record t is equal to

$$md(Q, \text{condition}_i, t) = \mu_Q[\tau(md(Q, \text{condition}_i, t)$$

$$md(Q, \text{condition}_i, t) = \mu_Q[\tau(\sum_i md(\text{condition}_i, t))]$$

(4)

We can also assign different importances to particular conditions, and the aggregation formula is equivalent to (3). Importance is given as a fuzzy set defined on [0,1], and then treated as property B in (3) leading to

$$md(QB, \text{condition}_i, t) =$$
$$= \mu_Q[\tau(\sum_i (md(\text{condition}_i, t) \land \mu_B(\text{condition}_i)) /$$
$$/ \sum_i \mu_B(\text{condition}_i))]$$

$$(5)$$

FQUERY for Access has been designed so that fuzzy queries be syntactically correct Access's queries. This has been attained by using of parameters:

[FfA_FV *fuzzy value name*] is interpreted as a fuzzy value

[FfA_FQ *fuzzy quantifier name*] - as a fuzzy quantifier

First, a fuzzy term has to be defined and stored internally. This maintenance of dictionaries of fuzzy terms defined by users, strongly supports our approach to data summarization to be discussed next. In fact, the package has a set of predefined fuzzy terms but the user may always enrich the dictionary.

When the user initiates the execution of a query it is automatically transformed and then run as a native query of Microsoft Access. Details can be found in (Kacprzyk & Zadrożny, 1994, 1995a-b, 2001b) and (Zadrożny & Kacprzyk, 1999).

In Kacprzyk & Zadrożny's (1998, 2001c) approach, *interactivity* is in the definition of summarizers (indication of attributes and their combinations), via a user interface of a fuzzy querying add-on. The queries (referring to summarizers) allowed are:

- *simple* as, e.g., "salary is *high*"
- *compound* as, e.g., "salary is *low* AND age is *old*"

- *compound with quantifier*, as, e.g., "*most* of {salary is *high*, age is *young*, ..., training is *well above average*}.

We will also use "natural" linguistic terms, i.e. (7±2!) like: *very low, low, medium, high, very high*, and also "comprehensible" quantifiers as: *most, almost all*, ..., etc.

Fuzzy queries directly correspond to summarizers in linguistic summaries. Thus, the derivation of a linguistic summary may proceed in an interactive way as follows:

- the user formulates a set of linguistic summaries of interest (relevance) using the fuzzy querying add-on described above,
- the system retrieves records from the database and calculates the validity of each summary adopted, and
- a most appropriate linguistic summary is chosen.

Fuzzy querying is very relevant because we can restate the summarization in the fuzzy querying context. First, (2) may be interpreted as:

"*Most records match query S*" (6)

where S replaces F in (2) since we refer here directly to the concept of a summarizer (this should be properly understood because S in (6) is in fact the whole condition, e.g., price = *high*, while F in (2) is just the fuzzy value, i.e. *high* in this condition; this should not lead to confusion).

Similarly, (3) may be interpreted as:

"*Most records meeting conditions B match query S*" (7)

In the database terminology, B corresponds to a (fuzzy) *filter* and (7) claims that *most* records passing through B match query S to a degree from [0,1].

Notice that the concept of a protoform in the sense of Zadeh (2002) is highly relevant here. First of all, a protoform is defined as an abstract prototype, that is, for the query (summary) (6) and (7), given as, respectively:

"Most t's are S" (8)

"Most Bt's are S" (9)

where t denotes "records", B is a filter, and S is a query.

Evidently, as protoforms may form a hierarchy, we can define higher level (more abstract) protoforms. For instance, replacing *most* by a general linguistic quantifier Q, we have:

"Qt's are S" (10)

"QBt's are S" (11)

The more abstract protoforms correspond to cases in which we assume less about summaries being sought. There are two extremes when we: (1) assume a totally abstract protoform, or (2) assume that all elements of a protoform are given on the lowest level of abstraction as specific linguistic terms. In case 1 data summarization is extremely time consuming but may produce an interesting, unexpected view on data. In case 2 the user has to guess a good candidate for a summary but the

evaluation is fairly simple, equivalent to the answering of a (fuzzy) query. Thus, case 2 refers to *ad hoc queries*. This may be shown in Table 1 in which 5 basic types of linguistic summaries are shown, corresponding to protoforms of a more and more abstract form.

Table 1 shows classifications where $S^{structure}$ denotes that attributes and their connection in a summary are known, while S^{value} denotes linguistic values that are sought and together with $S^{structure}$ fully define a summarizer.

Type 1 may be easily obtained by a simple extension of fuzzy querying. Basically, the user has to construct a query – candidate summary, and one has to determine the fraction of rows matching this query, and which linguistic quantifier best denotes this fraction. A Type 2 summary is a straightforward extension of Type 1 by adding a fuzzy filter. Type 3 summaries require much more effort. Their primary goal is to determine typical (exceptional) values of an attribute. So, query S consists of only one simple condition built of the attribute whose typical (exceptional) value is sought, the "=" relational operator and a placeholder for the value sought. For example, using the age-focused summary, S = "age=?" ("?" denotes a placeholder mentioned above) we look for a typical value of age. A Type 4 summary may produce typical (exceptional) values for some, possibly fuzzy, subset of rows. From the computational point of view, Type 5 summaries

Table 1. Classification of linguistic summaries

Type	Given	Sought	Remarks
1	S	Q	Simple summaries Through ad-hoc queries
2	$S\ B$	Q	Conditional summaries Through ad-hoc queries
3	$Q\ S^{structure}$	S^{value}	Simple value oriented Summaries
4	$Q\ S^{structure}\ B$	S^{value}	Conditional value Oriented summaries
5	nothing	$S\ B\ Q$	General fuzzy rules

represent the most general form considered here: fuzzy rules describing dependencies between specific values of particular attributes. Here the use of B is essential, while previously it was optional. The summaries of Type 1 and 3 have been implemented as an extension to Kacprzyk & Zadrożny's (2000a-d) FQUERY for Access. Two approaches to Type 5 summaries have been proposed. First, a subset of such summaries may be produced taking advantage of similarities with *association rules* and using efficient algorithms for mining them. Second, a genetic algorithm may be employed to search the space of summaries. The results of the former case are briefly presented in the next section.

The protoforms are therefore a powerful conceptual tool because we can formulate many different types of linguistic summaries in a uniform way, and devise a uniform and universal way to handle different linguistic summaries. This may be viewed to confirm Zadeh's frequent claims of the power of protoforms.

IMPLEMENTATION

As a simple illustration of Type 5 summaries, an implementation is shown for the summarization of Web server logs (cf. Zadrożny and Kacprzyk, 2007).

Each request to a Web server is recorded in one or more of its log files. The recorded information usually comprises the fields listed in Table 2 (cf. a common log file format at http://www.w3.org/Daemon/User/Config/Logging.html#common-logfile-format). There is also an extended format which includes more fields but these will be of no interest for us in this paper.

There is a lot of software available (cf. e.g., Analog at http://www.analog.cx/) that reads a log file and produces various statistics concerning the usage of a given Web server. These statistics usually include the number of requests (or requested Web pages): per month/day/hour of the week, per country or domain of the requesting computer. Often the requests from specific sources (mostly search engines) are distinguished and related statistics are generated. Also the parameters of the requesting agent, such as the browser type or the operating system may be analyzed. These statistics may be computed in terms of the number of requests and/or the number of bytes of transferred data.

These simple analyses of log files refer to particular requests or requested Web pages (which may involve a number of requests for embedded multimedia files, style files etc.) More sophisticated analyses concern sessions, i.e. the series of requests send by the same agent. This type of analysis may help to model agents' behavior, iden-

Table 2. Contents of a Web server log file

Field no.	Content
1	the requesting computer name or IP address
2	the username of the user triggering the request (often absent),
3	the user authentication data
4	the date and time of the request
5	the HTTP command related to the request which includes the path to the requested file
6	the status of the request (e.g., to determine whether a resource was correctly transferred, not found, etc.)
7	the number of bytes transferred as a result of the request
8	the software used to issue the request

tify the navigational paths and, e.g., reconstruct the Web site in order to enhance agents' experience.

It is easy to see that though those techniques, mostly involving some statistical analyses, are effective, and often powerful and efficient, their deficiency is that they are not human consistent enough. Namely, they produce numerical results that are often too voluminous and not comprehensible to an average human user who would welcome simple, intuitively appealing outcomes, possibly in a natural language. Such results are provided by linguistic summaries of data.

A Web server log file may be directly interpreted as a table of data with the columns corresponding to the fields listed in Table 2 and the rows corresponding to the requests. For instance, for the purposes of linguistic summarization attributes of requests can be as given in Table 3.

In this section we will discuss various linguistic summaries that may be derived using this data.

For efficiency, we look for a subclass of linguistic summaries that may be obtained using efficient algorithms for *association rules mining* taking into account the following correspondence between the concept of the association rule and of the linguistic summary: the condition and conclusion parts of an association rule correspond to

qualifier R and summarizer S, respectively. This essentially constraints the structure of the qualifier and summarizer to a conjunction of simple conditions. However this simplification provides for the existence of efficient algorithms for rule generation. The truth-value of the summary corresponds to the confidence measure of an association rule. Notice that we employ a restricted form of a Type 5 linguistic summary from Table 1.

The experiment was run on the log file of one of the Web servers of our institute. This is an Apache server and we used its access request log for the period of December 24, 2006 to January 16, 2007. with 352,543 requests. For extracting the data listed in Table 3, a simple Perl program was used. Then we imported the data to a Microsoft Access database and then employed our FQUERY for Access software to run the experiments by first defining a dictionary of linguistic terms. The system transformed the original access log data replacing the values of selected numerical attributes with their best matched linguistic terms (their labels or codes). Thus, in effect, a numerical attribute whose values are to be characterized in the summaries with the use of some linguistic terms is replaced with a set of binary attributes. For example, the attribute SIZE may be replaced

Table 3. Attributes of the requests used for their linguistic summarization

Attribute name	Description
Domain	Internet domain extracted from the requesting computer name (if given)
Hour	hour the request arrived; extracted from the date and time of the request
Day of the month	as above
Day of the week	as above
Month	as above
Filename	name of the requested file, including the full path, extracted from the HTTP command
Extension	extension of the requested file extracted as above
Status	Status of the request
Failure	= 1 if status code is of 4xx or 5xx form, and =0 otherwise
Success	= 1 if status code is of 2xx form, and =0 otherwise
Size	number of bytes transferred as a result of the request
Agent	name of the browser used to issue the request (name for major browsers, "other" otherwise)

by the artificial attributes: SIZEIsSmall, SIZEIs-Medium and SIZEIsLarge. The semantics of these attributes is: an attribute, e.g., SIZEIsSmall, is said to appear in a table row (transaction, in terms of association rules mining) if the value of the original attribute, i.e., SIZE, in this row belongs to the fuzzy set representing the term *Small* to a high enough degree (which is determined by a threshold value, being a parameter controlled by the user of the FQUERY for Access interface).

The values of the remaining attributes, both numerical and textual, are also coded appropriately. Then the system executes an external program that looks for association rules. In these experiments we used an efficient implementation of the Apriori algorithm by Christian Borgelt (cf. http://www.borgelt.net/apriori.html). Finally, the obtained linguistic summaries are decoded by FQUERY for Access and presented to the user.

In our experiments the following linguistic terms were defined, among others, in the dictionary of linguistic terms.

The linguistic quantifier ``most'' is defined as in (1), i.e.

$$\mu_Q(x) = \begin{cases} 1 & \text{for } x \geq 0.8 \\ 2x - 0.6 & \text{for } 0.3 < x < 0.8 \\ 0 & \text{for } x \leq 0.3 \end{cases}$$

and *small* for for the attribute *size of file* is defined by:

$$\mu_{small}(x) = \begin{cases} 1 & \text{for } x \leq 50\text{KB} \\ -\dfrac{1}{30}x + \dfrac{8}{3} & \text{for } 50 \text{ KB} < x < 80\text{KB} \\ 0 & \text{for } x \geq 80\text{KB} \end{cases}$$

In our experiments we obtained a number of interesting linguistic summaries. Due to space limitations we can only show some of them. First:

All requests with the status code 304 ("not modified"') referred to *small* files' (T=1.0)

The next summary obtained concerns scalar (non-numerical) attributes:

Most files with the "gif" extension were requested from the domain "pl" (T=0.98)

and it is worth noticing it does not hold that "*Most* files were requested from the domain 'pl'" which is true to degree 0.4 only.

We obtain more convincing summaries when we add a condition concerning the status code of the request, namely:

Most files with the "gif" extension successfully fetched (with the status code 200) were requested from the domain "pl" (T=1)

Many more interesting linguistic summaries have also been obtained which can give much insight into requests coming into the Web server.

CONCLUDING REMARKS

We presented the idea and power of the concept of a linguistic data (base) summary, originated by Yager (1982) and further developed first, in a more conventional form, by Kacprzyk & Yager (2001), and Kacprzyk, Yager & Zadrożny (2000), and then, in a more general context of Zadeh's (2002) protoforms by Kacprzyk & Zadrożny (2005), and a more implementation oriented context of its relation to fuzzy database querying by Kacprzyk & Zadrożny (1998 – 2005). These summaries are some short sequence(s) in natural language that make it possible to readily capture, even by an inexperienced and novice user, the essence of the of data,

As an application we presented the summarization of Web server logs which is a very interesting and increasingly popular research topic in data mining. Results of such analyses can be very important by helping in the reporting, advertising, and generally decision making processes in a company. For instance, the resulting knowledge may help improve navigation paths, better organize paid search advertising, personalize Web site access, better design B2B interfaces, etc.

ACKNOWLEDGMENT

This works was partially supported by the Ministry of Science and Higher Education under the T-INFO Research Network.

REFERENCES

Kacprzyk, J. (2000). Intelligent data analysis via linguistic data summaries: a fuzzy logic approach. In Decker, R., & Gaul, W. (Eds.), *Classification and Information Processing at the Turn of the Millennium* (pp. 153–161). Berlin, Heidelberg, New York: Springer-Verlag. doi:10.1007/978-3-642-57280-7_17

Kacprzyk, J., Pasi, G., Vojtaš, P., & Zadrożny, S. (2000). Fuzzy querying: issues and perspective. *Kybernetika, 36*, 605–616.

Kacprzyk, J., & Yager, R. R. (2001). Linguistic summaries of data using fuzzy logic. *International Journal of General Systems, 30*, 133–154. doi:10.1080/03081070108960702

Kacprzyk, J., Yager, R. R., & Zadrożny, S. (2000). A fuzzy logic based approach to linguistic summaries of databases. *International Journal of Applied Mathematics and Computer Science, 10*, 813–834.

Kacprzyk, J., Yager, R. R., & Zadrożny, S. (2001). Fuzzy linguistic summaries of databases for an efficient business data analysis and decision support. In Abramowicz, W., & Żurada, J. (Eds.), *Knowledge Discovery for Business Information Systems* (pp. 129–152). Boston: Kluwer. doi:10.1007/0-306-46991-X_6

Kacprzyk, J., & Zadrożny, S. (1994). Fuzzy querying for Microsoft Access. In *Proceedings of FUZZ-IEEE'94 (Orlando, USA): Vol. 1*, (pp. 167–171).

Kacprzyk, J., & Zadrożny, S. (1995a). Fuzzy queries in Microsoft Access v. 2. In *Proceedings of FUZZ-IEEE/IFES '95 (Yokohama, Japan), Workshop on Fuzzy Database Systems and Information Retrieval*, (pp. 61–66).

Kacprzyk, J., & Zadrożny, S. (1995b). FQUERY for Access: fuzzy querying for a Windows-based DBMS. In Bosc, P., & Kacprzyk, J. (Eds.), *Fuzziness in Database Management Systems* (pp. 415–433). Heidelberg: Physica-Verlag.

Kacprzyk, J., & Zadrożny, S. (1998). Data mining via linguistic summaries of data: an interactive approach. In T. Yamakawa & G. Matsumoto (Eds.), *Methodologies for the Conception, Design and Application of Soft Computing - Proceedings of IIZUKA'98 (Iizuka, Japan)*, (pp. 668–671).

Kacprzyk, J., & Zadrożny, S. (1999) The paradigm of computing with words in intelligent database querying. In L.A. Zadeh and J. Kacprzyk (Eds.): *Computing with Words in Information/Intelligent Systems.(Part 2. Foundations*, (pp. 382–398), Heidelberg and New York: Physica-Verlag (Springer-Verlag).

Kacprzyk, J., & Zadrożny, S. (2000a). On combining intelligent querying and data mining using fuzzy logic concepts. In G. Bordogna & G. Pasi (Eds.), *Recent Research Issues on the Management of Fuzziness in Databases* (pp. 67–81), Heidelberg and New York: Physica–Verlag (Springer-Verlag).

Kacprzyk, J., & Zadrożny, S. (2000b). Data mining via fuzzy querying over the Internet. In O. Pons, M.A. Vila & J. Kacprzyk (Eds.), *Knowledge Management in Fuzzy Databases* (pp. 211–233), Heidelberg and New York: Physica–Verlag (Springer-Verlag).

Kacprzyk, J., & Zadrożny, S. (2000c). On a fuzzy querying and data mining interface. *Kybernetika, 36*, 657–670.

Kacprzyk, J., & Zadrożny, S. (2000d). Computing with words: towards a new generation of linguistic querying and summarization of databases. In P. Sinčak & J. Vaščak (Eds.), *Quo Vadis Computational Intelligence?* (pp. 144 – 175), Heidelberg and New York: Physica-Verlag (Springer-Verlag).

Kacprzyk, J., & Zadrożny, S. (2001a). On linguistic approaches in flexible querying and mining of association rules. In Larsen, H. L., Kacprzyk, J., Zadrożny, S., Andreasen, T., & Christiansen, H. (Eds.), *Flexible Query Answering Systems. Recent Advances* (pp. 475–484). Heidelberg, New York: Springer-Verlag.

Kacprzyk, J., & Zadrożny, S. (2001b). Computing with words in intelligent database querying: standalone and Internet-based applications. *Information Sciences, 34*, 71–109. doi:10.1016/S0020-0255(01)00093-7

Kacprzyk, J., & Zadrożny, S. (2001c). Data mining via linguistic summaries of databases: an interactive approach. In Ding, L. (Ed.), *A New Paradigm of Knowledge Engineering by Soft Computing* (pp. 325–345). Singapore: World Scientific. doi:10.1142/9789812794604_0015

Kacprzyk, J., & Zadrożny, S. (2001d). Fuzzy linguistic summaries via association rules. In A. Kandel, M. Last & H. Bunke (Eds.), *Data Mining and Computational Intelligence*, (pp. 115 – 139), Heidelberg and New York: Physica-Verlag (Springer-Verlag).

Kacprzyk, J., & Zadrożny, S. (2001e). Using fuzzy querying over the Internet to browse through information resources. In B. Reusch and K.-H. Temme (Eds.), *Computational Intelligence in Theory and Practice* (pp. 235 – 262), Heidelberg and New York: Physica-Verlag (Springer-Verlag).

Kacprzyk, J., & Zadrożny, S. (2002). Protoforms of linguistic data summaries: towards more general natural - language - based data mining tools. In Abraham, A., Ruiz del Solar, J., & Koeppen, M. (Eds.), *Soft Computing Systems* (pp. 417–425). Amsterdam: IOS Press.

Kacprzyk, J., & Zadrożny, S. (2003). Linguistic summarization of data sets using association rules. In *Proceedings of FUZZ-IEEE '03 (St. Louis, USA)* (pp. 702 – 707).

Kacprzyk, J., & Zadrożny, S. (2005). Linguistic database summaries and their protoforms: towards natural language based knowledge discovery tools. *Information Sciences, 173*(4), 281–304. doi:10.1016/j.ins.2005.03.002

Kacprzyk, J., Zadrożny, S., & Ziółkowski, A. (1989). FQUERY III+: a 'human consistent' database querying system based on fuzzy logic with linguistic quantifiers. *Information Systems, 6*, 443–453. doi:10.1016/0306-4379(89)90012-4

Kacprzyk, J., & Ziółkowski, A. (1986). Database queries with fuzzy linguistic quantifiers. *IEEE Transactions on Systems. Man and Cybernetics, SMC, 16*, 474–479. doi:10.1109/TSMC.1986.4308982

Liu, Y., & Kerre, E. E. (1988). An overview of fuzzy quantifiers. (I) Interpretations. *Fuzzy Sets and Systems, 95*, 1–21. doi:10.1016/S0165-0114(97)00254-6

Yager, R. R. (1982). A new approach to the summarization of data. *Information Sciences, 28*, 69–86. doi:10.1016/0020-0255(82)90033-0

Yager, R. R. (1988). On ordered weighted avaraging operators in multicriteria decision making. *IEEE Transactions on Systems, Man, and Cybernetics, SMC-18*, 183–190. doi:10.1109/21.87068

Yager, R. R. (1991). On linguistic summaries of data. In Piatetsky-Shapiro, G., & Frawley, B. (Eds.), *Knowledge Discovery in Databases* (pp. 347–363). Cambridge, USA: MIT Press.

Yager, R. R. (1995). Linguistic summaries as a tool for database discovery. In *Proceedings of FUZZ-IEEE'95/IFES'95, Workshop on Fuzzy Database Systems and Information Retrieval, (Yokohama, Japan)* (pp. 79 – 82).

Yager, R. R. (1996). Database discovery using fuzzy sets. *International Journal of Intelligent Systems, 11*, 691–712. doi:10.1002/(SICI)1098-111X(199609)11:9<691::AID-INT7>3.0.CO;2-F

Yager, R. R., & Kacprzyk, J. (Eds.). (1997). *The Ordered Weighted Averaging Operators: Theory and Applications*. Boston: Kluwer. doi:10.1007/978-1-4615-6123-1

Zadeh, L. A. (1983). A computational approach to fuzzy quantifiers in natural languages. *Computers & Mathematics with Applications (Oxford, England), 9*, 149–184. doi:10.1016/0898-1221(83)90013-5

Zadeh, L. A. (1985). Syllogistic reasoning in fuzzy logic and its application to usuality and reasoning with dispositions. *IEEE Transactions on Systems, Man, and Cybernetics, SMC-15*, 754–763.

Zadeh, L. A. (2002). A prototype-centered approach to adding deduction capabilities to search engines – the concept of a protoform. In *BISC Seminar, 2002*. Berkeley: University of California. doi:10.1109/NAFIPS.2002.1018115

Zadeh, L. A., & Kacprzyk, J. (Eds.). (1999). *Computing with Words in Information/Intelligent Systems, 1. Foundations, 2. Applications*. Heidelberg and New York: Physica-Verlag (Springer-Verlag).

Zadrożny, S., & Kacprzyk, J. (1995) Fuzzy querying using the 'query-by-example' option in a Windows-based DBMS, *Proceedings of Third European Congress on Intelligent Techniques and Soft Computing - EUFIT'95 (Aachen, Germany), vol. 2 (pp. 733 – 736)*.

Zadrożny, S., & Kacprzyk, J. (1999). On database summarization using a fuzzy querying interface. In *Proceedings of IFSA'99 World Congress (Taipei, Taiwan R.O.C.), Vol. 1, (pp. 39 – 43)*.

Zadrożny, S., & Kacprzyk, J. (2007) Summarizing the contents of Web server logs: a fuzzy linguistic approach. *Proceedings of FUZZ-IEEE'2007 – The 2007 IEEE Conference on Fuzzy Systems (London, UK, July 23-26, 2007), pp. 1860 – 1865*.

This work was previously published in International Journal of Software Science and Computational Intelligence, Volume 1, Issue 1, edited by Yingxu Wang, pp. 1-28, copyright 2009 by IGI Publishing (an imprint of IGI Global).

Chapter 11
Measuring Textual Context Based on Cognitive Principles

Ning Fang
Shanghai University, China

Xiangfeng Luo
Shanghai University, China

Weimin Xu
Shanghai University, China

ABSTRACT

Based on the principle of cognitive economy, the complexity and the information of textual context are proposed to measure subjective cognitive degree of textual context. Based on minimization of Boolean complexity in human concept learning, the complexity and the difficulty of textual context are defined in order to mimic human's reading experience. Based on maximal relevance principle, the information and cognitive degree of textual context are defined in order to mimic human's cognitive sense. Experiments verify that more contexts are added, more easily the text is understood by a machine, which is consistent with the linguistic viewpoint that context can help to understand a text; furthermore, experiments verify that the author-given sentence sequence includes the less complexity and the more information than other sentence combinations, that is to say, author-given sentence sequence is more easily understood by a machine. So the principles of simplicity and maximal relevance actually exist in text writing process, which is consistent with the cognitive science viewpoint. Therefore, this chapter's measuring methods are validated from the linguistic and cognitive perspectives, and it could provide a theoretical foundation for machine-based text understanding.

DOI: 10.4018/978-1-4666-0261-8.ch011

INTRODUCTION

According to Cognitive Informatics (Wang, 2002a, 2007b), a *concept* is defined as a cognitive unit to identify and/or model a real-world concrete entity and a perceived-world abstract object. According to Wang (2006b), the formal treatment of concepts and a new mathematical structure known are defined as Concept Algebra in Cognitive Informatics. The semantic environment or context (Ganter & Wille, 1999; Hampton, 1997; Hurley, 1997; Medin & Shoben, 1988) in a given language is denoted as a triple, i.e.: a finite or infinite nonempty set of objects, a finite or infinite nonempty set of attributes, and their relations. On the basis of the Object-Attribute-Relation model and the definition of context, an abstract concept is a composition of the above three elements. Although Concept Algebra includes the operations of objects, attributes, and relations in an abstract concept, the measure of the context of textual concept is not given in Cognitive Informatics, and it is a key issue to understand the textual concept.

At present, the measure in Cognitive Informatics mainly include as follows: the theorem (Wang, 2007d) indicates that the complexities of the syntactic rules (or grammar) and of the semantic rules are inversely proportional; the cognitive complexity of software systems presented is a measure of cognitive and psychological complexity of software as a human intelligent artifact, which takes into account of both internal structures of software and the I/O data objects under processing (Wang, 2006a).

According to the Object-Attribute-Relation model (Wang, 2003, 2007b, 2007c), the semantics of a sentence may be considered having been understood when: a) The logical relations of parts of the sentence are clarified; and b) All parts of sentence are reduced to the terminal entities, which are either a real-world image or a primitive abstract concept (Wang, 2007d). Furthermore, national language is context sensitive. That is to say, context can help us to understand a textual concept.

Therefore, to understanding a textual concept, it is necessary of 1) obtaining a primitive abstract concept from textual sentences; 2) computing the weights of logical relations among sentences according to cognitive principles; 3) measuring the textual context in sentential granularity based on the weights.

Rosch (1975) indicates that *every organism hopes that the more information is acquired, the less energy is consumed in the surrounding environment*, i.e. the principle of cognitive economy. This principle enlightens us a new approach to measure textual context from subjective cognitive perspectives so as to help machine understand a text, if we regard the text understanding process as a special cognitive process. So we propose two criteria to measure textual context based on cognitive economical principle, i.e. the complexity and the information of textual context (here the complexity is considered as the energy approximately).

A *concept* in linguistics is a noun or noun-phrase that serves as the subject or object of a *to-be* statement (Hurley, 1997; Wang, 2002b, 2007a). Therefore, in this article, we only discuss concept generated from nouns in a sentence. Commonly, context refers to a wide range that includes textual semantic relations, common sense, knowledge, communication background, and culture background, etc. However, in this article we only consider simple textual context, i.e. co-text that includes textual semantic relations generated from related keywords and sentences in a text, some common sense and knowledge.

FORMULIZATION OF TEXTUAL CONTEXT

Simply speaking, textual context is constructed by sequential sentences, a sentence constructed by some significant word's combinations. If a keyword is regarded as an attribute and a sentence as an object in a text, the understanding of the text can be regarded as the process of concept learning. Therefore, the formulization of textual context is as below.

Assume that the textual context d includes m sentences (denoted by $s_1, s_2, \ldots, s_m$) and n keywords (denoted by $c_1, c_2, \ldots, c_n$). Hence, a $n \times m$ matrix can represent the distribution of keywords on sentences in textual context d, as shown in Figure 1.

Note that keyword's sign is allocated, and not considering occurrence sequence; sentence's sign is allocated according to author-given sequence.

In any sentence, a keyword includes two elementary states, '*occurrence*' and '*non-occurrence*', denoted by 1 and 0 respectively. Hence, sentences s_1, s_2, s_m (shown in Figure 1) are represented by

$$s_1 = \bigwedge_{i=1}^{n} c_i = c_1 c_2 \cdots c_n = \underbrace{11 \cdots 0}_{n}$$

$$s_2 = \bigwedge_{i=1}^{n} c_i = c_1 c_2 \cdots c_n = \underbrace{01 \cdots 0}_{n} . \qquad (1)$$

$$s_m = \bigwedge_{i=1}^{n} c_i = c_1 c_2 \cdots c_n = \underbrace{00 \cdots 1}_{n}$$

And the textual context d is represented by

$$d = \bigvee_{j=1}^{m} s_j = \bigvee_{j=1}^{m} \bigwedge_{i=1}^{n} c_i$$

$$= \underbrace{01 \cdots 0 + 11 \cdots 0 + \cdots + 00 \cdots 1}_{mn} \qquad (2)$$

where s_j denotes the jth sentence; c_i denotes the ith keyword; symbol $\wedge$ denotes 'and' combination relation between keywords in a sentence; symbol $\vee$ denotes 'or' addition relation between sentences.

In this article we do not consider the issue of extracting keyword from a text, and its related technologies include TF-IDF (Kaski, Lagus, & Honkela, et al., 1998; Salton, & Yang, 1973), mutual information (Dumais, Platt, & Heckerman, et al., 1998; Lam, Low, & Ho, 1997; Fabrizio, 2002), and TDDF (Luo, & Fang, 2008).

COMPLEXITY OF TEXTUAL CONTEXT

Text Understanding Depends on Textual Context

Let us see the following simple conversation between person A and person B.

A: Can you tell me the time?

B: The milkman has just left.

If there is no context, we never grasp the conversation. However, if the following context is added to the conversation, we should no doubt understand the conversation.

Context: The time is 6 am of the milkman leaving.

Figure 1. Distribution matrix of keywords on sentences in a text

	s_1	s_2	$\cdots$	s_m	
c_1	1	0	$\cdots$	0	c_1 exists in s_1
c_2	1	1	$\cdots$	0	c_2 exists in s_1 and s_2
$\vdots$	$\vdots$	$\vdots$	$\cdots$	$\vdots$	$\vdots$
c_n	0	0	$\cdots$	1	c_n exists in s_m

In this section, we will use mathematical computation (i.e. minimization of Boolean complexity and its related computing) to solve the problem that what degree a textual context affects the understanding of a text, and the problem is defined as the complexity of textual context and its related computation.

Related Background in Cognitive Science

According to the human concept learning in cognitive science, there is a surprisingly simple empirical 'law': the subjective difficulty of a concept is directly proportional to its Boolean complexity (Feldman, 2000, 2003b). The Boolean complexity of a propositional concept is the length of the shortest Boolean formula logically equivalent to the concept, usually expressed in terms of the number of literals (positive or negative variables). (For convenience, we write $a \wedge b$ as ab, $a \vee b$ as $a+b$, and $\neg a$ as a'.) For example, the concept $ab+ab'$ is equivalent to $a(b+b')$, and thus to a, and hence has Boolean complexity 1; whereas $ab+a'b'$ has no shorter equivalent, and hence has Boolean complexity 4. Boolean complexity is an essentially universal measure of the intrinsic mathematical complexity or 'incompressibility' of the propositional concept. Finding the shortest formula equivalent to a given formula is computationally intractable, and in practice Boolean reduction can only be achieved through approximate computational techniques (such as factorization). Here we use an available Matlab code to compute Boolean complexity (Feldman, 2006) (http://ruccs.rutgers.edu/%7ejacob/demos/algebra.html).

Now consider an arbitrary Boolean concept defined by m positive examples over n binary features. Any such concept is logically equivalent to the disjunction of its m constituent objects, each of which is a conjunction of n features, a form known as a disjunctive normal formula (DNF).

Hence, each such concept is equivalent to a DNF with $m \times n$ literals. The DNF is the completely 'uncompressed' form; it in effect lists verbatim all the objects that satisfy the concept. When each of the DNFs is compressed as much as possible (using heuristic techniques), they have lengths less and less. These Boolean complexity values predict the order of empirical difficulty precisely. Now the relation between Boolean complexity and human learning has been comprehensively tested.

Complexity and its Related Definitions of Textual Context

Definition 1. *Complexity of Textual Context.*

Assume that a textual context is constructed by m sentences and n keywords, and according to above formulization of textual context, a DNF with $m \times n$ literals can represent the textual context, and the Boolean complexity of the DNF (i.e. the shortest length of DNF) is defined as the complexity of the textual context. The length of uncompressed DNF $m \times n$ is defined as the maximal complexity of textual context.

Note that 1) we only discuss the shortest length of DNF, not conjunctive normal formula (CNF) (Bourne, 1970); 2) suppose that m sentences of n-dimension are completely different from each other, so the redundant sentences must be ignored.

Definition 2. *Difficulty of Textual Context.*

Difficulty of textual context is defined as the ratio of the complexity of textual context to its maximal complexity of textual context. The less difficulty means that the textual context has complete logical relations, so a reader understands it more easily. It is used to mimic human's reading experience and measure the degree of understanding the text in the reading process.

Definition 3. *Sum of the Complexity of Textual Context.*

Assume that a textual context is constructed by m sentences, and the sum of the complexity of textual context is defined as the sum of m complexities derived from the addition of one-by-one sequential sentences. It is used to mimic human's cognitive process and measure the energy consumed by a reader in the reading process approximately.

Computing the Complexity of Textual Context

Simple Textual Context Based on Two Keywords and Three Sentences

Example 1.

Suppose that there is a conversation between person A and person B as below,

*A: Can you tell me the **time**?*

*B: The **milkman** has just left.*

and we extract two keywords marked by bold in the conversation, i.e. time (denoted by symbol a) and milkman (denoted by symbol b). According to above background and formulization of textual context, the conversation can be represented by the polynomial ab'+a'b, its visual space state is shown in Figure 2, where a dimension denotes a feature (keyword), and a dot denotes an object (sentence). Because the polynomial cannot be compressed, its complexity of textual context is 4. Hence, its difficulty of textual context is 1. We likely grasp no meaning from the conversation, if there is no background. Now, we add the following context, i.e. background, to this conversation.

*Context: The **time** is 6 am of the **milkman** leaving.*

Then, the above conversation can be represented by the uncompressed polynomial $ab'+a'b+ab$, its visual space state is shown in Figure 3, and then, its maximal complexity of textual context is 6. By heuristic techniques its shortest polynomial is $a+b$, and then, its complexity of textual context is 2. Hence, its difficulty of textual context is 0.333.

Textual Context Based On Three Keywords and Four Sentences

Example 2.

Suppose that there is a conversation between person A and person B as below,

*A: How much **power** do you have?*

*B: I have read a lot of **books**.*

and we extract two keywords marked by bold in the conversation, i.e. power (a), book (b), and then, the conversation can be represented by the polynomial ab'+a'b, its visual space state is shown in Figure 4. Because the polynomial cannot be

Figure 2. Two keywords and two sentences

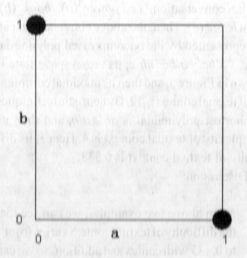

Figure 3. Two keywords and three sentences

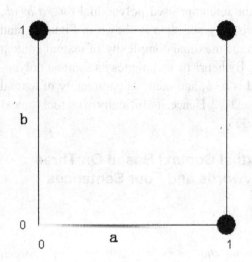

compressed, its complexity of textual context is 4. Hence, its difficulty of textual context is 1. We likely grasp no meaning from the conversation, if there is no background. Now we add the following common sense (i.e. some contexts) to this conversation.

*Common sense: There is a lot of **knowledge** in **book**s.*

*Bacon: "**knowledge** is **power**."*

And we extract three keywords marked by bold in the conversation, i.e. *power* (*a*), *book* (*b*), *knowledge* (*c*). Then, the above conversation can be represented by the uncompressed polynomial *ab'c'+a'bc'+a'bc+ab'c*, its visual space state is shown in Figure 5, and then its maximal complexity of textual context is 12. By heuristic techniques its shortest polynomial is *ab'+a'b*, and then its complexity of textual context is 4. Hence, its difficulty of textual context is 0.333.

Discussion:

1) From above two examples, we can see that the difficulty of textual context varies from 1 to 0.333 with contextual addition, so we can

conclude that textual context can decrease the difficulty of text understanding evidently, which consists with the reading experience by human.

2) In visual space state Figure 2-5, distance could reflect the close degree of semantic relation between sentences, such as the comparison of every two sentences in Figure 2 and Figure 3, and the comparison of every two sentences in Figure 4 and Figure 5. For example, one unit in visual space state represents the close relation between sentences; $\sqrt{2}$ or $\sqrt{3}$ units in visual space state represent the strange relation.

Paper's Abstract Based on Four Keywords and Five Sentences

Example 3.

In the proceedings of WWW 2005 (http://www2005. org/cdrom/contents.htm), we select a paper (paper ID is p12, and its title is "Duplicate Detection in Click Streams") and its abstract includes five sentences (denoted by $s_1, s_2, \cdots, s_5$). From the title of p12 we extract four keywords marked by bold in its abstract, i.e. duplicate (a), detection (b), click (c), and stream (d).

Since computing the complexity of textual context is the NP problem (Wegener, 1987; Garey, & Johnson, 1979), if select a lot of keywords from the context, there is extremely high computational complexity. Therefore, when we regard the title as a simple concept, and the following abstract (the title's detailed explanation) as a complete concept, we could select the few keywords from its title instead of its context in order to decrease the computational complexity.

1) We consider the problem of finding **dupli-cate**s in data **stream**s.

Figure 4. Two keywords and two sentences

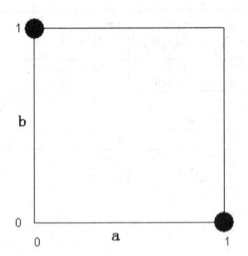

Figure 5. Three keywords and four sentences

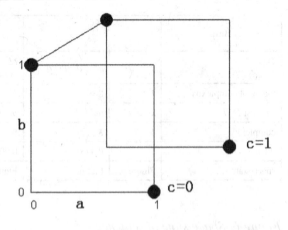

2) **Duplicate detection** in data **stream**s is utilized in various applications including fraud detection.

3) We develop a solution based on Bloom Filters, and discuss the space and time requirements for running the proposed algorithm in both the contexts of sliding, and landmark **stream** windows.

4) We run a comprehensive set of experiments, using both real and synthetic **click stream**s, to evaluate the performance of the proposed solution.

5) The results demonstrate that the proposed solution yields extremely low error rates.

In Table 1 we mimic the reading process and measure the difficulty of textual context based on the addition of one-by-one sequential sentences.

Discussion:

After reading the abstract, we conclude that sentence s_1 and sentence s_2 have close semantic relation about proposing the problem; sentence s_3 and sentence s_4 have close semantic relation about solving the problem; sentence s_5 is the conclusion.

1) According to difficulty of textual context in the above example, we conclude that the difficulty of textual context mainly decreases in the reading process, such as the comparison from state s_1 to state $s_1s_2s_3s_4s_5$.

2) In the reading process, the difficulty of textual context decreases evidently, when one explanation is illustrated completely, such as the comparison of the state s_1 and the state s_1s_2, and the comparison of the state $s_1s_2s_3$ and the state $s_1s_2s_3s_4$.

3) In the reading process, the difficulty of textual context increases slightly, when a new explanation is begun and uncompleted, such as the comparison of state s_1s_2 and state $s_1s_2s_3$, and the comparison of state $s_1s_2s_3s_4$ and state $s_1s_2s_3s_4s_5$.

4) According to visual space state, the sentences of the close semantic relation have close distance in space state, such as the distance between s_1 and s_2, and the distance between s_3 and s_4 are smaller than others, that is only one unit.

Table 1. Difficulty of textual context based on the addition of one-by-one sequential sentences in the abstract of paper 'p12'

state	s_1	$s_1 s_2$	$s_1 s_2 s_3$	$s_1 s_2 s_3 s_4$	$s_1 s_2 s_3 s_4 s_5$
DNF (*abcd*)	*ab'c'd*	*ab'c'd+abc'd*	*ab'c'd+abc'd +a'b'c'd*	*ab'c'd+abc'd +a'b'c'd+a'b'cd*	*ab'c'd+abc'd+a'b'c'd +a'b'cd+a'b'c'd'*
maximal complexity	4	8	12	16	20
shortest *DNF*	*ab'c'd*	*ac'd*	*ac'd+ b'c'd*	*a'b'd+ab'd*	*a'b'c'+a'b'd+ac'd*
complexity	4	3	6	6	9
difficulty	1	0.375	0.500	0.375	0.450
space state	Figure 6	Figure 7	Figure 8	Figure 9	Figure 10

Figure 6. Space state of sentence s_1

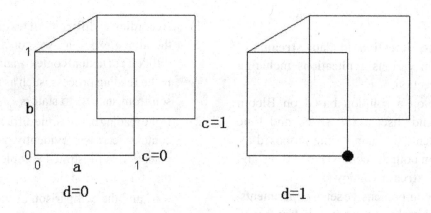

Figure 7. Space state of sentences $s_1 s_2$

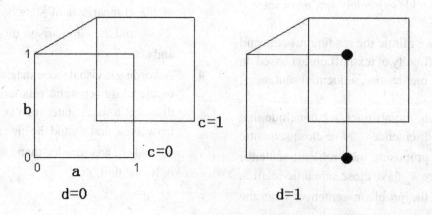

Figure 8. Space state of sentences $s_1 s_2 s_3$

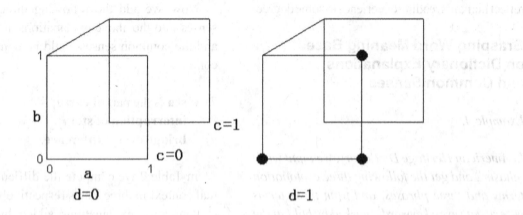

Figure 9. Space state of sentences $s_1 s_2 s_3 s_4$

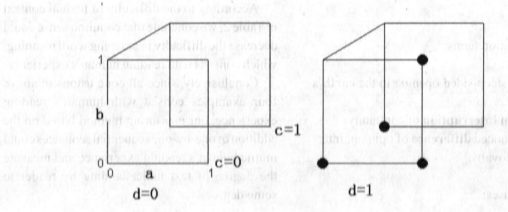

Figure 10. Space state of sentences $s_1 s_2 s_3 s_4 s_5$

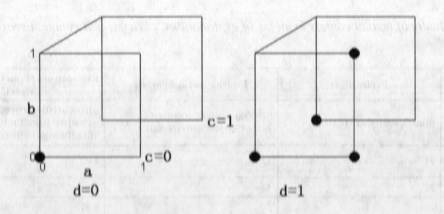

Therefore, according to above conclusions, the related computation of textual context could reflect human's reading experience to some degree.

Grasping Word Meaning Based on Dictionary Explanations and Common Senses

Example 4.

In American Heritage Dictionary, we input word 'chasm', and get the following three explanation terms and three phrases, and from these terms we extract seven keywords marked by bold in the explanations and phrases, i.e. chasm (a), earth (b), interruption (c), difference (d), sea (e), story (f), and bridge (g).

Three explanation terms:

1) A deep, steep-sided opening in the **earth**'s surface;
2) A sudden **interruption** of continuity;
3) A pronounced **difference** of opinion, interests, or loyalty.

Three phrases:

4) **sea chasm**;
5) a **chasm** in the **story**;

6) **bridge** over a **chasm**;

Now, we add the following three common senses into the above explanations and phrases, and the common senses could be considered as context.

7) **sea** is the part of **earth**;
8) **interruption** of **story**;
9) **bridge** over a **difference**.

In Table 2 we compute the difficulty of textual context in three states respectively, i.e. only explanations, explanations added by phrases, and explanations added by phrases and common senses.

Discussion:

According to the difficulty of textual context in Table 2, we conclude that common sense could decrease the difficulty in grasping word meaning, which consists with reading human's experience.

Conclusively, since all conclusions in above four examples consist with human's reading experience, our measuring method based on the addition of one-by-one sequential sentences could mimic human's reading experience and measure the degree of text understanding by reader to some degree.

Table 2. Difficulty of textual context in states of explanations, phrases, and common senses for word 'chasm'

state	Explanations	Explanations and phrases	Explanations, phrases and common senses
DNF (*abcdefg*)	0100000+0010000+0001000	0100000+0010000+0001000 +1000100+1000010+1000001	0100000+0010000+0001000 +1000100+1000010+1000001 +0100100+0010010+0001001
maximal complexity	21	42	63
complexity	21	42	39
difficulty	1	1	0.619

INFORMATION OF TEXTUAL CONTEXT

Text Understanding Depends on Textual Context

Assume that there are six illogical sentences and its meaning is confusing as below: *Jack gets a wrong rubber. The cup is new. Jack is also careless. Tom breaks the cup. The rubber is mine. Tom is careless.*

But the same six reorganized sentences have clear meaning as below: *The cup is new. Tom breaks the cup. Tom is careless. Jack is also careless. Jack gets a wrong rubber. The rubber is mine.*

After reading these two texts, why do we have such different cognitive sense? How to measure the cognitive degree of above two textual contexts? How to ensure the rationality of measurement?

Simply speaking, the cognitive degree of the textual context might be related with the set of sentences, the sentence sequence, and the cognitive logical structure. According to the principle of maximal relevance in cognitive science that *a writer always makes efforts to provide more output of textual information for readers* (Sperber, & Wilson, 1995), the information of textual context and information-based cognitive degree of textual context are proposed to measure the textual context in this section.

Cognitive Logical Structures in Textual Context

General speaking, keywords, the sentence sequences, and the logical structure between conjunctive sentences in a textual context can reflect cognitive sense to the text. Here we define three cognitive logical structures that exist in conjunctive sentences of a textual context as below.

1) Summary is Prior, Illustration Follows (SPIF), logical state map is shown by ;
2) Illustration is Prior, Summary Follows (IPSF), as shown by ;
3) Illustration is One-by-One (IOO), as shown by .

Assume that a textual context includes three sentences, denoted by s_1, s_2, s_3, and two keywords, denoted by c_1 and c_2. Thus, cognitive logical structures between conjunctive sentences are shown in Table 3.

For example, a textual context includes two keywords, i.e. *Tom* and *cup*, and three sentences as below.

1) **Tom** breaks a **cup**.
2) The **cup** is new.
3) **Tom** is careless.

Table 3. Three cognitive logical structures between conjunctive sentences

keyword	c_1	c_2	c_1	c_2	c_1	c_2
s_1	1	1	0	1	1	0
s_2	0	1	1	0	1	1
s_3	1	0	1	1	0	1
Type	SPIF		IPSF		IOO	

where 0 denotes that the corresponding keyword does not occur in the corresponding sentence; 1 denotes the occurrence of the keyword. Generally, a writer represents his paper in above three logical structures based on human's reading sense.

And their three cognitive logical structures are shown in Table 4.

Information and its Related Definitions of Textual Context

Based on three cognitive logical structures, our method provides the computation of maximal relevance between conjunctive sentences; according to the principle of the maximal relevance, we define the sum of maximal relevance as the information of textual context with which we could measure the degree of cognitive sense to textual context; in addition, based on different sentence numbers, we can transform textual context into its power spectrum in order to analyze the text conveniently.

The steps of computing the information of textual context are as below:

1) Extract keywords from the textual context, and these words mainly include nouns which have significant meaning;
2) Mark keyword's occurrence in every sentence;
3) Compute and select the maximal relevance in special sentence number based on cognitive logical structures according to the principle of maximal relevance;
4) Construct the power spectrum of textual context;

5) Compute the information of textual context through the sum of maximal relevance in all sentence numbers.

The information of textual context is related with the sentence sequence and logical structure between conjunctive sentences in a text context.

Here, we study the relevance between conjunctive sentences based on the cognitive logical structures in a textual context.

Feature of Relevance between Conjunctive Sentences

Assume that a textual context d includes m sentences, denoted by $s_1, s_2, ..., s_m$, we discuss with the following features of relevance between conjunctive sentences.

1) When a text is being read, the relevance between conjunctive sentences is related to the sentential sequence. Thus, we only discuss the relevance between sequential sentences,

i.e. $s_i \rightarrow s_{i+1}$, $s_i s_{i+1} \rightarrow s_{i+2}$,

$s_i \rightarrow s_{i+1} s_{i+2}$, $s_i \rightarrow s_{i+1} \rightarrow s_{i+2} \cdots$,

where $\rightarrow$ denotes the relation from one sentence to the next sentence. e.g. in Table 3 there are following relations,

$s_1 \rightarrow s_2$, $s_2 \rightarrow s_3$, $s_1 s_2 \rightarrow s_3$,

$s_1 \rightarrow s_2 s_3$, $s_1 \rightarrow s_2 \rightarrow s_3$;

Table 4. Three cognitive logical structures of an example

keyword	Tom	cup	Tom	cup	Tom	cup
s_1	Tom breaks a cup		A cup is new		Tom is careless	
s_2	The cup is new		Tom is careless		Tom breaks a cup	
s_3	Tom is careless		Tom breaks the cup		The cup is new	
Types	SPIF		IPSF		IOO	

2) The relevance in the type of SPIF is denoted as relation $s_i \rightarrow s_{i+1}s_{i+2}\cdots s_{i+k}$, e.g. $s_1 \rightarrow s_2 s_3$ in Table 3; the relevance in the type of IPSF is denoted as relation $s_i s_{i+1}\cdots s_{i+k-1} \rightarrow s_{i+k}$, e.g. $s_1 s_2 \rightarrow s_3$ in Table 3; the relevance in the type of IOO is denoted as relation $s_i \rightarrow s_{i+1} \rightarrow \cdots \rightarrow s_{i+k}$, e.g. $s_1 \rightarrow s_2 \rightarrow s_3$ in Table 3;

3) We define the granularity of relation between two conjunctive sentences as one order relation, denoted by $R(1)$, e.g. $(s_i \rightarrow s_{i+1}) \in R(1)$; we define the granularity of relation between three conjunctive sentences as second order relation, denoted by $R(2)$, e.g. $(s_i \rightarrow s_{i+1}s_{i+2}) \in R(2)$, $(s_i s_{i+1} \rightarrow s_{i+2}) \in R(2)$ and $(s_i \rightarrow s_{i+1} \rightarrow s_{i+2}) \in R(2)$, which correspond to type SPIF, IPSF and IOO respectively; so if a text includes m sentences, it includes $(m-1)$ order relation at most, denoted by $R(m-1)$, e.g. $(s_1 s_2 \cdots s_{m-1} \rightarrow s_m) \in R(m-1)$, $(s_1 \rightarrow s_2 \cdots s_{m-1}s_m) \in R(m-1)$ and $(s_1 \rightarrow s_2 \rightarrow \cdots \rightarrow s_m) \in R(m-1)$.

Computing Relation Weight between Conjunctive Sentences

Assume that a textual context d includes m sentences, denoted by $s_1, s_2, \ldots, s_m$, and n keywords, denoted by $c_1, c_2, \ldots, c_n$, the relevance between conjunctive sentences of three cognitive logical structures on the various order relations are defined as below.

The degree of similar relation between two sentences is defined as the ratio of common keywords to all keywords,

$$W(s_i \rightarrow s_{i+k}) = \frac{\left|\{s_i \cap s_{i+k}\}\right|}{\left|\{s_i \cup s_{i+k}\}\right|}. \tag{3}$$

where $W(s_i \rightarrow s_{i+k})$ denotes the relation weight between sentence s_i and sentence s_{i+k}; $\left|\{s_i \cap s_{i+k}\}\right|$ denotes the number of common keywords between sentence s_i and sentence s_{i+k}; $\left|\{s_i \cup s_{i+k}\}\right|$ denotes the number of all keywords in sentence s_i and sentence s_{i+k}.

Commonly, when a complicated relation is composed with several simple ones, the weakest one determines this complicate one. Therefore, the minimal one between every two sentences determines the relation weight between three sentences. The relation weights between three sentences in the types of IPSF, SPIF and IOO are below respectively.

$$W(s_i s_{i+1} \rightarrow s_{i+2}) = \arg\min\{W(s_i \rightarrow s_{i+2}), W(s_{i+1} \rightarrow s_{i+2})\} \tag{4}$$

where $W(s_i s_{i+1} \rightarrow s_{i+2})$ denotes the relation weight between three sentences in the type of IPSF.

$$W(s_i \rightarrow s_{i+1}s_{i+2}) = \arg\min\{W(s_i \rightarrow s_{i+1}), W(s_i \rightarrow s_{i+2})\} \tag{5}$$

where $W(s_i \rightarrow s_{i+1}s_{i+2})$ denotes the relation weight between three sentences in the type of SPIF.

$$W(s_i \rightarrow s_{i+1} \rightarrow s_{i+2}) = \arg\min\{W(s_i \rightarrow s_{i+1}), W(s_{i+1} \rightarrow s_{i+2})\} \tag{6}$$

where $W(s_i \rightarrow s_{i+1} \rightarrow s_{i+2})$ denotes the relation weight between three sentences in the type of IOO.

The relation weights between other numbers of sentences similarly refer to the relation weight between three sentences.

All relation weights between conjunctive sentences based on three cognitive logical structures in Table 3 are shown in Table 5.

Maximal Relevance between Conjunctive Sentences

Assume that textual context d includes m sentences, denoted by $s_1, s_2, \ldots, s_m$. Since there are the same sentences among relation $s_i \cdots s_{i+k-1} \to s_{i+k}$, $s_i \to s_{i+1} \cdots s_{i+k}$ and $s_i \to s_{i+1} \to \cdots \to s_{i+k}$, we define the similar relation between them,

$$
\begin{aligned}
&\left(s_i \cdots s_{i+k-1} \to s_{i+k}\right) \\
&\cong \left(s_i \to s_{i+1} \cdots s_{i+k}\right) \\
&\cong \left(s_i \to s_{i+1} \to \cdots \to s_{i+k}\right)
\end{aligned}
\tag{7}
$$

where $\cong$ denotes the similarity of relations between conjunctive sentences, $1 \leq i \leq i+k \leq m$.

According to the principle of maximal relevance, we select the maximal relation among similar relations as the most probable relation, and the definition is below.

$$
\begin{aligned}
&MaxRelevance\left(s_i s_{i+1} \cdots s_{i+k}\right) \\
&= \arg\max
\begin{cases}
W\left(s_i \to s_{i+1} \cdots s_{i+k}\right), \\
W\left(s_i \cdots s_{i+k-1} \to s_{i+k}\right), \\
W\left(s_i \to s_{i+1} \to \cdots \to s_{i+k}\right)
\end{cases}
\end{aligned}
\tag{8}
$$

where $MaxRelevance\left(s_i s_{i+1} \cdots s_{i+k}\right)$ denotes the most probable relation weight between $k+1$ conjunctive sentences, simply denoted as $MR\left(s_i s_{i+1} \cdots s_{i+k}\right)$.

Maximal relevance between the conjunctive sentences of three cognitive logical structures of Table 5 is shown in Table 6.

Power Spectrum

We map maximal relevance into the corresponding order number of conjunctive sentences in order to construct the power spectrum (Feldman, 2006). And the definition is below,

Table 5. Relation weight between conjunctive sentences of three cognitive logical structures in a textual context

keyword	c_1	c_2	c_1	c_2	c_1	c_2
s_1	1	1	0	1	1	0
s_2	0	1	1	0	1	1
s_3	1	0	1	1	0	1
$W\left(s_i \to s_{i+1}\right)$	$s_1 \xrightarrow{0.5} s_2$ $s_2 \xrightarrow{0} s_3$		$s_1 \xrightarrow{0} s_2$ $s_2 \xrightarrow{0.5} s_3$		$s_1 \xrightarrow{0.5} s_2$ $s_2 \xrightarrow{0.5} s_3$	
$W\left(s_i \to s_{i+2}\right)$	$s_1 \xrightarrow{0.5} s_3$		$s_1 \xrightarrow{0.5} s_3$		$s_1 \xrightarrow{0} s_3$	
$W\left(s_i s_{i+1} \to s_{i+2}\right)$	$s_1 s_2 \xrightarrow{0} s_3$		$s_1 s_2 \xrightarrow{0.5} s_3$		$s_1 s_2 \xrightarrow{0} s_3$	
$W\left(s_i \to s_{i+1} s_{i+2}\right)$	$s_1 \xrightarrow{0.5} s_2 s_3$		$s_1 \xrightarrow{0} s_2 s_3$		$s_1 \xrightarrow{0} s_2 s_3$	
$W\left(s_i \to s_{i+1} \to s_{i+2}\right)$	$s_1 \xrightarrow[\quad\quad]{0} s_2 \to s_3$		$s_1 \xrightarrow[\quad\quad]{0} s_2 \to s_3$		$s_1 \xrightarrow[\quad\quad]{0.5} s_2 \to s_3$	
logical structure	SPIF		IPSF		IOO	

Table 6. Maximal relevance between conjunctive sentences based on three cognitive logical structures

$MR(s_i s_{i+1})$	$MR(s_1 s_2) = W(s_1 \to s_2) = 0.5$ $MR(s_2 s_3) = W(s_2 \to s_3) = 0$	$MR(s_1 s_2) = W(s_1 \to s_2) = 0$ $MR(s_2 s_3) = W(s_2 \to s_3) = 0.5$	$MR(s_1 s_2) = W(s_1 \to s_2) = 0.5$ $MR(s_2 s_3) = W(s_2 \to s_3) = 0.5$
$MR(s_i s_{i+1} s_{i+2})$	$MR(s_1 s_2 s_3) = W(s_1 \to s_2 s_3) = 0.5$	$MR(s_1 s_2 s_3) = W(s_1 s_2 \to s_3) = 0.5$	$MR(s_1 s_2 s_3) = W(s_1 \to s_2 \to s_3) = 0.5$
structure	SPIF	IPSF	IOO

$$SumRelevance(k)$$
$$= \sum_{i=1}^{m-k} MaxRelevance\left(s_i s_{i+1} \cdots s_{i+k}\right) \quad (9)$$

where $SumRelevance(k)$ denotes the sum of maximal relevance on k order relation, simply denoted as $SR(k)$; m denotes the sentence number.

Power spectrums of the three cognitive logical structures of Table 6 are shown in Table 7.

Generally, a textual context is constructed as the combination of above three cognitive logical structures, and the power spectrum reflects the distribution of the maximal relevance on sentential number in a textual context.where in power spectrum the abscissa is k order relation and the ordinate is the sum of maximal relevance, denoted by $SR(k)$.

The Information

The principle of maximal relevance in cognitive mechanism indicates that *a writer always makes efforts to provide more output of textual information for readers*, i.e. represents more relevance between conjunctive sentences in his paper. The principle implies that the sum of all maximal relevance in a textual context can be defined as the information of textual context as below.

$$I(d) = \sum_{k=1}^{m-1} SumRelevance(k) \quad (10)$$

where $I(d)$ denotes the information of textual context d that includes m sentences; $SR(k)$ is the sum of maximal relevance between $(k+1)$ conjunctive sentences, i.e. the k order relation.

EXPERIMENTS IN COMPLEXITY OF TEXTUAL CONTEXT

In following experiments, the conclusion is consistent with linguistic viewpoint and cognitive science viewpoint. Therefore, the following experiments will verify our measuring method of textual context from the linguistic perspective and cognitive science perspective.

Experiment of Contextual Acquisition

Linguistics indicates that context can help us to understand a text. In this experiment we mimic the contextual acquisition of text reading process by the addition of one-by-one sequential sentences in author-given sequence.

According to the above method, we will respectively compute the difficulty of textual context in the proceedings of WWW2005 (http://www2005. org/cdrom/contents.htm). We select the abstracts of the first 14 papers, paper IDs include p2, p12, p22, p33, p43, p54, p66, p76, p86, p97, p107, p117, p128, and p138, and extract the keywords from the papers' titles respectively.

Due to the same reason mentioned above, we select the few keywords from papers' titles

Table 7. Power spectrums of textual context

$SR(k)$	$SR(1) = W(s_1 \to s_2) + W(s_2 \to s_3) = 0.5$ $SR(2) = W(s_1 \to s_2 s_3) = 0.5$	$SR(1) = W(s_1 \to s_2) + W(s_2 \to s_3) = 0.5$ $SR(2) = W(s_1 s_2 \to s_3) = 0.5$	$SR(1) = W(s_1 \to s_2) + W(s_2 \to s_3) = 1$ $SR(2) = W(s_1 \to s_2 \to s_3) = 0.5$
power spectrum	See figure 11 (a)	See figure 11 (b)	See figure 11 (c)
structure	SPIF	IPSF	IOO

instead of their contexts in order to decrease the computational complexity.

In Table 8 we mimic the reading process and compute the difficulty of textual context based on the addition of one-by-one sequential sentences in original author-given sequence.

From Table 8 most difficulties decrease with the addition of more and more context, and occasionally increase with a new explanation beginning in the abstract. Therefore, we could conclude that the difficulty of textual context mainly decline with the addition of one-by-one sequential sentences in author-given sequence for most of paper's abstracts. In other words, more contexts are added, more easily the text is understood by machine. So the textual context helps machine to understand a text, which is consistent with the linguistic viewpoint.

Experiments of Textual Presentation

Principle of Simplicity in Text Understanding

According to cognitive science, complexity minimization does indeed play a central role in

Table 8. Difficulty of textual context based on the addition of one-by-one sequential sentences in original author-given sequence for 14 abstracts

sentence number	1	2	3	4	5	6	7	8	9	10	11	12	13	14	15
p2	1	1	1	1	N	N	N	N	N	N	N	N	N	N	N
p12	1	.375	.500	.375	.45	N	N	N	N	N	N	N	N	N	N
p22	1	1	.611	.611	.667	N	N	N	N	N	N	N	N	N	N
p33	1	1	1	1	1	N	N	N	N	N	N	N	N	N	N
p43	1	1	1	.722	.778	.778	.611	N	N	N	N	N	N	N	N
p54	1	1	1	.688	.725	.438	.438	.438	.438	.500	N	N	N	N	N
p66	1	.417	.611	.667	.733	.733	N	N	N	N	N	N	N	N	N
p76	1	.429	.619	.619	.714	.543	.595	.595	.595	.595	.612	.661	.698	.614	.636
p86	1	1	1	1	.750	N	N	N	N	N	N	N	N	N	N
p97	1	1	1	1	.444	.500	.500	.200	.200	.200	N	N	N	N	N
p107	1	1	1	1	.375	.375	.500	.500	.125	N	N	N	N	N	N
p117	1	1	1	1	1	.813	N	N	N	N	N	N	N	N	N
p128	1	1	1	1	.679	.679	.679	.714	.762	N	N	N	N	N	N
p138	1	1	.429	.429	.619	.429	.543	N	N	N	N	N	N	N	N

where row denotes the paper ID; column denotes the number of reading sentences, and the symbol *N* denotes no corresponding sentence number; the values in the table denote the difficulty of textual context in the corresponding state of the reading sentences.

human concept learning. The chief finding is that subjects' ability to learn concepts depends heavily on the concepts' intrinsic complexity; more complex concepts are more difficult to learn. The principle of simplicity, that one should choose the simplest hypothesis consistent with the data, is one of the most ubiquitous laws in all fields of inference, including philosophy; in machine learning (under a variety of names, including the "minimum description length principle"). The principle seems particularly apt in the domain of concept learning, where it would dictate that we induce the simplest category consistent with the observed examples, i.e. the most parsimonious generalization available (Feldman, 2003a).

Textual writing process is just the process of concept construction by author; textual reading process is just the process of concept learning by reader. So according to the principle of simplicity, in textual writing/reading process, concept construction/learning should abide by the principle of simplicity, in other words, more simple textual presentation, more clear understanding by human.

The following experiments will verify that the principle of simplicity exists in textual writing process.

Experiment of Simple Text

Assume that there are following four illogical sentences and three keywords marked by bold, denoted as *Jack (a)*, *Tom (b)*, and *careless (c)*.

s_1 **Jack** *gets a wrong rubber.*

s_2 **Tom** *is* **careless**.

s_3 **Jack** *is also* **careless**.

s_4 **Tom** *breaks the cup.*

However, the same four sentences have a clear meaning in the different sequence, such as *Tom*

breaks the cup. ***Tom*** *is* ***careless***. ***Jack*** *gets a wrong rubber.* ***Jack*** *is also* ***careless***.

According to the above method, we compute the complexity of textual context based on the addition of one-by-one sequential sentences in all combination types that have $p_4^4 = 4! = 24$, as shown in Table 9.

Table 9. Complexity of text understanding in all combination types

sentence combination	complexity in sentence num				sum of complexity
1432	1	2	3	4	18
1423	3	6	5	4	18
1342	3	6	5	4	14
1324	3	2	5	4	14
1243	3	2	5	4	18
1234	3	6	5	4	18
4132	3	6	5	4	18
4123	3	6	5	4	18
4312	3	6	5	4	18
4321	3	6	5	4	18
4213	3	2	5	4	14
4231	3	2	5	4	14
3142	3	2	5	4	14
3124	3	2	5	4	14
3412	3	6	5	4	18
3421	3	6	5	4	18
3214	3	6	5	4	18
3241	3	6	5	4	18
2143	3	6	5	4	18
2134	3	6	5	4	18
2413	3	2	5	4	14
2431	3	2	5	4	14
2314	3	6	5	4	18
2341	3	6	5	4	18

where the row denotes all the sentence combination types; column symbols from 1 to 4 denotes the number of reading sentences; the values denote the complexity of textual context in the corresponding reading sentences; "sum of complexity" denotes the sum of complexities in the corresponding sentence combinations.

From Table 9 the sum of complexity in eight types has minimal value 14 marked in italic and bold, and with comparison of other type's ones, logical relations of eight red sentence combination types are understood more easily. So we conclude that the less sum of complexity, the more easily sentence sequence is understood. In other words, the sum of complexity of textual context could measure the cognitive sense in reading process. The experiment verifies that the sum of the complexity of textual context could be used to mimic human's cognitive process and measure the energy consumed by reader in the reading process approximately.

Experiment of the Abstract of Paper p12

According to the above example 3, there are five sentences in the abstract of paper p12, so the number of all combination types is $p_5^5 = 5! = 120$. Table 10 shows the maximal and the minimal sum of complexity in 120 sentence combination types.

In Table 10 we could see that the original author-given sentence sequence $s_1 s_2 s_3 s_4 s_5$ has the minimal sum of the complexity of textual context, so the author-given sentence sequence is understood the most easily by machine in all sentence combinations. That is to say, the principle of simplicity exists in text writing process.

Conclusively, above experiments verify that 1) more contexts are added, more easily the text is understood by machine, which is consistent with the linguistic viewpoint that context can help to understand a text; 2) author-given sentence sequence is one of the combinations most easily understood by machine in all sentence combinations, in other words, the principle of simplicity actually exists in text writing process, which is consistent with the cognitive science viewpoint. Therefore, our measuring method is validated from the perspectives of linguistics and cognitive science.

EXPERIMENTS IN INFORMATION OF TEXTUAL CONTEXT

According to the above method we will respectively compute the information in order to measure the cognitive sense to a textual context in all sentence combinations, such as in author-given sentence sequence, another random sentence sequence, and all sentence combinations. Experimental results verify that the principle of maximal relevance in cognitive science exists in text writing process, which consists with the cognitive science viewpoint. Therefore, our method of measuring the information is validated.

Experiment of Information in Author-Given (original) Sentence Sequence

In the proceedings of WWW2005, (http://www2005.org/cdrom/contents.htm), we select a paper (paper ID is p12, and its title is "*Duplicate Detection in Click Streams*"). The paper's abstract

Table 10. Maximal and minimal sum of the complexity in 120 sentence combination types for abstract of paper p12

type in sum of complexity	sum of complexity	sentence combinations
maximal sum of complexity	44	$s_4 s_2 s_5 s_1 s_3$, $s_1 s_5 s_4 s_2 s_3$ ...
minimal sum of complexity	28	$s_1 s_2 s_3 s_4 s_5$, $s_3 s_4 s_1 s_2 s_5$ ...

includes five sentences, denoted by $s_1, s_2, \cdots, s_5$, and 21 significant keywords that are bold in corresponding sentences, denoted by $c_1, c_2 \cdots c_{21}$.

1) *We consider the **problem** (c_{13}) of finding **duplicates** (c_7) in **data** (c_5) **streams** (c_{19}).*

2) ***Duplicate** (c_7) **detection** (c_6) in **data** (c_5) **streams** (c_{19}) is utilized in various **applications** (c_2) including **fraud** (c_{11}) **detection** (c_6).*

3) *We develop a **solution** (c_{17}) based on Bloom **Filters** (c_{10}), and discuss the **space** (c_{18}) and **time** (c_{20}) **requirements** (c_{15}) for running the proposed **algorithm** (c_1) in both the **contexts** (c_4) of sliding, and landmark **stream** (c_{19}) **windows** (c_{21}).*

6) *We run a comprehensive set of **experiments** (c_9), using both real and synthetic **click** (c_3) **streams** (c_{19}), to evaluate the **performance** (c_{12}) of the proposed **solution** (c_{17}).*

7) *The **results** (c_{16}) demonstrate that the proposed **solution** (c_{17}) yields extremely low **error** (c_8) **rates** (c_{14}).*

Maximal relevance, power spectrum and information in the abstract of paper p12 in original sentence sequence are computed in the following steps that refer to the above section.

1) Extract keywords;
   e.g., above 21 bold keywords are represented as

   $c_1 c_2 c_3 c_4 c_5 c_6 c_7 c_8 c_9 c_{10} c_{11} c_{12} c_{13} c_{14} c_{15} c_{16} c_{17} c_{18} c_{19} c_{20} c_{21}$

2) Mark keyword's occurrence in every sentence;
   e.g., above 5 sentences are represented as below,

   s_1 $\overset{5\ \ 7}{0000\,1\,0\,1}\overset{13}{00000\,1}\overset{19}{00000\,1\,00}$

   s_2 $\overset{2}{0\,1}\overset{5\ 6\ 7}{00\,1\,1\,1}\overset{11}{000\,1}\overset{19}{0000000\,1\,00}$

   s_3 $\overset{1\ \ \ \ 4}{1\,00\,1}\overset{10}{00000\,1}\overset{15}{0000\,1}\overset{17\,18\,19\,20\,21}{0\,1\,1\,1\,1\,1}$

3) Compute the maximal relevance between every two sentences;
   e.g., there are 4 maximal relevant relations in above 5 sentences as below,

$$MR(s_1 s_2) = \arg\max\{W(s_1 \to s_2)\} = \frac{3}{7},$$

$$MR(s_2 s_3) = \arg\max\{W(s_2 \to s_3)\} = \frac{1}{14},$$

$$MR(s_3 s_4) = \arg\max\{W(s_3 \to s_4)\} = \frac{2}{12},$$

$$MR(s_4 s_5) = \arg\max\{W(s_4 \to s_5)\} = \frac{1}{8}$$

4) Compute the maximal relevance between every three sentences;
   e.g., there are 3 maximal relevant relations in above 5 sentences as below,

$$MR(s_1 s_2 s_3) = \arg\max\begin{bmatrix} W(s_1 \to s_2 s_3), \\ W(s_1 s_2 \to s_3), \\ W(s_1 \to s_2 \to s_3) \end{bmatrix} = \frac{1}{12},$$

$$MR(s_2 s_3 s_4) = \arg\max\begin{bmatrix} W(s_2 \to s_3 s_4), \\ W(s_2 s_3 \to s_4), \\ W(s_2 \to s_3 \to s_4) \end{bmatrix} = \frac{1}{10},$$

$$MR(s_3 s_4 s_5) = \arg\max\begin{bmatrix} W(s_3 \to s_4 s_5), \\ W(s_3 s_4 \to s_5), \\ W(s_3 \to s_4 \to s_5) \end{bmatrix} = \frac{1}{8}$$

5) Compute the maximal relevance between four sentences;
   e.g., there are 2 maximal relevant relations in above 5 sentences as below,

$$MR(s_1 s_2 s_3 s_4)$$
$$= \arg\max\begin{bmatrix} W(s_1 \to s_2 s_3 s_4), \\ W(s_1 s_2 s_3 \to s_4), \\ W(s_1 \to s_2 \to s_3 \to s_4) \end{bmatrix} = \frac{1}{10},$$

$$MR(s_2 s_3 s_4 s_5)$$
$$= \arg\max\begin{bmatrix} W(s_2 \to s_3 s_4 s_5), \\ W(s_2 s_3 s_4 \to s_5), \\ W(s_2 \to s_3 \to s_4 \to s_5) \end{bmatrix} = \frac{1}{14}$$

s_4 $\overset{3}{00\,1}\overset{9}{00000\,1\,00}\overset{12}{\,1}\overset{17}{0000\,1}\overset{19}{\,0\,1\,00}$

s_5 $\overset{8}{00000000\,1}\overset{14}{00000\,1}\overset{16\,17}{\,0\,1\,1}\overset{}{\,1\,0000}$

6) Compute the maximal relevance between five sentences;

e.g., there is 1 maximal relevant relation in above 5 sentences as below,

$$MR\left(s_1 s_2 s_3 s_4 s_5\right)$$

$$= \arg\max \left\{ \begin{array}{l} W\left(s_1 \to s_2 s_3 s_4 s_5\right), \\ W\left(s_1 s_2 s_3 s_4 \to s_5\right), \\ W\left(s_1 \to s_2 \to s_3 \to s_4 \to s_5\right) \end{array} \right\} = \frac{1}{14}$$

7) Map the sum of maximal relevance into order number of relation, and construct a power spectrum;

e.g., there are 4 cognitive order numbers in above 5 sentences as below,

$$SR(1) = \frac{19}{24}, \quad SR(2) = \frac{37}{120}, \quad SR(3) = \frac{6}{35},$$

$$SR(4) = \frac{1}{14}, \text{ so the above power spec-}$$

trum of 5 sentences is given by the table shown in Figure 12.

8) Compute the information of a textual context;

e.g., information of above 5 sentences is given by

$$I\left(s_1^1 s_2^2 s_3^3 s_4^4 s_5^5\right) = \sum_{k=1}^{4} SR(k)$$

$$= \frac{19}{24} + \frac{37}{120} + \frac{6}{35} + \frac{1}{14} = 1.3429$$

Experiment of Information in a Random Sentence Sequence

Select the same abstract of paper p12 with above experiment, $s_1 s_2 s_3 s_4 s_5$ denotes the original sentential sequence and $s_1 s_5 s_4 s_2 s_3$ denotes a random

sentence sequence, denoted by $s_1^1 s_2^5 s_3^4 s_4^2 s_5^3$, where the upper symbol expresses the original sentence sequence and the lower symbol expresses new sentence sequence. Thus the power spectrum and information of the abstract in sequence $s_1^1 s_2^5 s_3^4 s_4^2 s_5^3$ is given as below.

$$I\left(s_1^1 s_2^5 s_3^4 s_4^2 s_5^3\right) = \sum_{k=1}^{4} SR(k)$$

$$= \frac{83}{280} + \frac{13}{40} + \frac{1}{14} + \frac{1}{14} = 0.7643$$

Discussion:

1) The textual information in author-given (original) sentence sequence is more than in other sequences.

According to the definition of textual information, the textual information in original sequence $s_1^1 s_2^2 s_3^3 s_4^4 s_5^5$ is 1.3429; the textual information in sequence $s_1^1 s_2^5 s_3^4 s_4^2 s_5^3$ is 0.7643. So the textual information in author-given (original) sequence $s_1^1 s_2^2 s_3^3 s_4^4 s_5^5$ is bigger than in $s_1^1 s_2^5 s_3^4 s_4^2 s_5^3$.

2) A writer always makes efforts to provide more output of textual information for readers, i.e., represents nearly maximal relevance between conjunctive sentences in his paper. Original information is generated from author-given sequence. Maximal information and minimal information are generated from 120 sequences by combinations ($p_5^5 = 5! = 120$). With the comparison of author-given information, the maximal information in sequence $s_1^5 s_2^3 s_3^4 s_4^1 s_5^2$ or sequence

Figure 11.

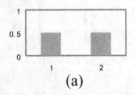

(a)

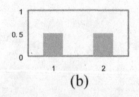

(b)

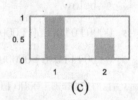

(c)

Figure 12.

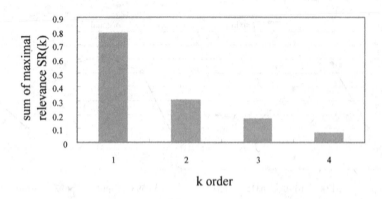

Figure 13.

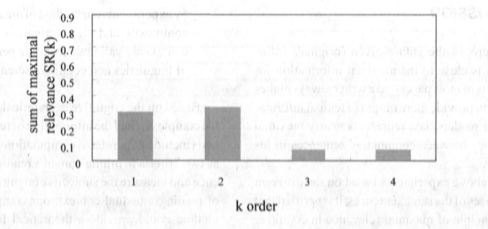

$s_1^2 s_2^1 s_3^1 s_4^3 s_5^5$ is 1.4702, and the improvement to author-given sequence is about 9.5%; minimal information in sequence $s_1^4 s_2^2 s_3^5 s_4^1 s_5^3$ or sequence $s_1^3 s_2^1 s_3^5 s_4^2 s_5^4$ is 0.6381, and the decrease to author-given sequence is about 52.5%. Then the output of textual information in author-given (original) sentential sequence is closer maximal information than in other sequences.

3) When power spectrum distributes on the lower order relations, the text is understood easily; when power spectrum distributes on the higher order relations, the text is understood difficultly.

The power spectrum in original sequence $s_1^1 s_2^2 s_3^3 s_4^4 s_5^5$ concentrates on lower order rela-

tions than in sequence $s_1^1 s_2^5 s_3^4 s_4^2 s_5^3$. Since the lower order relations reflect the fewer conjunctive sentences, i.e., the lower complexity, the concentration on the lower order relations in power spectrum means the easier understanding by a reader.

Experiment of Maximal, Minimal and Original Information

Figure 11 shows that original, maximal and minimal information for the abstracts of 11 papers that are selected at random in the proceedings of WWW2005. Due to computational complexity of the sentence combinations, we select the shorter paper's abstracts.

Figure 14. Original, maximal and minimal information for the abstracts of 11 papers

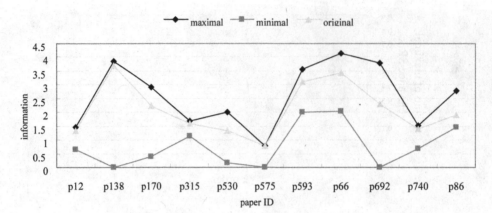

DISCUSSION

In Figure 14 the author-given (original) information is close to the maximal information for abstracts of most papers, so a writer always makes efforts to provide more output of textual information for readers, i.e., represents nearly maximal relevance between conjunctive sentences in his paper.

By above experiments based on the different sequences of the same sentences, it is verified that the principle of maximal relevance in cognitive science exists in textual writing process, so our method of computing the information based on cognitive principle is validated from the cognitive science viewpoint.

CONCLUSION

In this article, our main contributions include that:

1) based on minimization of Boolean complexity in human concept learning, the method of measuring the complexity of textual context is proposed;

2) based on the principle of maximal relevance in cognitive science, the method of measuring the information of textual context is proposed;

3) by experiments our method of measuring the complexity and the information of textual context are validated from the perspectives of linguistics and cognitive science.

Based on the cognitive economical principle, the complexity and the information of textual context (include their related computations) are used as two criteria to mimic human's reading experience and measure the subjective cognitive degree of reading a textual context, our computational method could provide a theoretical foundation for the machine-based text understanding that is a key issue in the fields of online advertisements delivery, online question-answering system, merchandise recommendation in e-Business, and knowledge discovery in e-Science, etc.

ACKNOWLEDGMENT

Research work is supported by the National Science Foundation of China, the National Basic Research Program of China, and the Graduate Innovation Foundation of Shanghai University. The authors wish to thank anonymous reviewers for helpful suggestions.

REFERENCES

Bourne, L. E. (1970). Knowing and using concepts. *Psychological Review*, (77): 546–556. doi:10.1037/h0030000

Dumais, S. T., Platt, J., Heckerman, D., et al. (1998). Inductive learning algorithms and representations for text categorization. *Proc. 7th ACM International Conference on Information and Knowledge Management* (CIKM'98), (148-155), Bethesda, MD.

Fabrizio, S. (2002). Machine learning in automated text categorization. *ACM Computing Surveys*, *34*(1), 1–47. doi:10.1145/505282.505283

Feldman, J. (2000). Minimization of Boolean complexity in human concept learning. *Nature*, *407*(5), 630–633. doi:10.1038/35036586

Feldman, J. (2003a). The Simplicity Principle in Human Concept Learning. *Current Directions in Psychological Science*, *12*(6), 227–232. doi:10.1046/j.0963-7214.2003.01267.x

Feldman, J. (2003b). A catalog of Boolean concepts. *Journal of Mathematical Psychology*, (47): 75–89. doi:10.1016/S0022-2496(02)00025-1

Feldman, J. (2006). An Algebra of human concept learning. *Journal of Mathematical Psychology*, (50): 339–368. doi:10.1016/j.jmp.2006.03.002

Ganter, B., & Wille, R. (1999). *Formal Concept Analysis*. Berlin: Springer.

Garey, M. R., & Johnson, D. S. (1979). *Computers and Intractability: A Guide to the Theory of NP-completeness*. New York: Freeman.

Hampton, J. A. (1997). *Psychological Representation of Concepts of Memory* (pp. 81-110). Hove, England: Psychology Press.

Hurley, P. J. (1997). *A Concise Introducfzon to Logic* (6th ed.). Belmony, CA: Wadsworth Pub. Co., ITP.

Kaski, S., Lagus, K., & Honkela, K., et al. (1998). Statistical aspects of the WEBSOM system in organizing document collections. *Computing Science and Statistics*, (29), 281-290.

Lam, W., Low, K. F., & Ho, C. Y. (1997). Using a Bayesian network induction approach for text categorization. *Proc. 15th International Joint Conference on Artificial Intelligence* (IJCAI-97), (pp. 745-750), Nagoya, Japan.

Luo, X. F., & Fang, N. (2008). Experimental Study on the Extraction and Distribution of Textual Domain Keywords. *Concurrency and Computation*, *20*(16), 1917–1932. doi:10.1002/cpe.1309

Medin, D. L., & Shoben, E. J. (1988). Context and Structure in Conceptual Combination. *Cognitive Psychology*, (20): 158–190. doi:10.1016/0010-0285(88)90018-7

Rosch, E. (1975). Family resemblances: studies in the internal structure of categories. *Cognitive Psychology*, (7): 23–69.

Salton, G., & Yang, C. S. (1973). On the specification of term values in automatic indexing. *The Journal of Documentation*, *29*(4), 351–372. doi:10.1108/eb026562

Sperber, D., & Wilson, D. (1995). *Relevance: Communication and Cognition* (2nd ed.). Oxford: Blackwell.

Wang, Y. (2002a, August). Keynote: On Cognitive Informatics. *Proc. 1st IEEE International Conference on Cognitive Informatics* (ICCI'02) (pp. 34-42). Calgary, Canada: IEEE CS Press.

Wang, Y. (2002b). The Real-Time Process Algebra (RTPA). *Annals of Software Engineering*, (14): 235–274. doi:10.1023/A:1020561826073

Wang, Y. (2003). On Cognitive Informatics. *Brain and Mind: A Transdisciplinary Journal of Neuroscience and Neurophilosophy*, *4*(2), 151-167.

Wang, Y. (2006a, July). Cognitive Complexity of Software and its Measurement. *Proc. 5th IEEE International Conference on Cognitive Informatics* (ICCI'06) (pp. 226-235). Beijing, China: IEEE CS Press.

Wang, Y. (2006b, July). On Concept Algebra and Knowledge Representation. *Proc. 5th IEEE International Conference on Cognitive Informatics* (ICCI'06) (pp. 320-331). Beijing, China: IEEE CS Press.

Wang, Y. (2007a). Software Engineering Foundations: A Software Science Perspective. *CRC Series in Software Engineering*, vol. II. Auerbach Publications, USA.

Wang, Y. (2007b). The Theoretical Framework of Cognitive Informatics. *International Journal of Cognitive Informatics and Natural Intelligence*, *1*(1), 1–27.

Wang, Y. (2007c, July). The OAR Model of Neural Informatics for Internal Knowledge Representation in the Brain. *International Journal of Cognitive Informatics and Natural Intelligence*, *1*(3), 64–75.

Wang, Y. (2007d). Formal Linguistic and the Deductive Grammar. *Proc. 6th IEEE International Conference on Cognitive Informatics* (ICCI'07) (pp. 43-51). Lake Tahoe, CA: IEEE CS Press.

Wegener, I. (1987). *The Complexity of Boolean Functions*. Chichester: Wiley.

This work was previously published in International Journal of Software Science and Computational Intelligence, Volume 1, Issue 4, edited by Yingxu Wang, pp. 61-89, copyright 2009 by IGI Publishing (an imprint of IGI Global).

Chapter 12
A Lexical Knowledge Representation Model for Natural Language Understanding

Ping Chen
University of Houston-Downtown, USA

Wei Ding
University of Massachusetts-Boston, USA

Chengmin Ding
IBM Business Consulting, USA

ABSTRACT

Knowledge representation is essential for semantics modeling and intelligent information processing. For decades researchers have proposed many knowledge representation techniques. However, it is a daunting problem how to capture deep semantic information effectively and support the construction of a large-scale knowledge base efficiently. This paper describes a new knowledge representation model, SenseNet, which provides semantic support for commonsense reasoning and natural language processing. SenseNet is formalized with a Hidden Markov Model. An inference algorithm is proposed to simulate human-like natural language understanding procedure. A new measurement, confidence, is introduced to facilitate the natural language understanding. The authors present a detailed case study of applying SenseNet to retrieving compensation information from company proxy filings.

INTRODUCTION

A natural language represents and models information of real world entities and relations. There exist a large number of entities in the world, and the number of relations among entities is even higher. Entities and relations together make a highly complex multiple dimensional lattices. It is not a surprise that it usually takes a lot of training for a human being to speak, write and understand a natural language even with the fact that the computation power packed in a small human brain surpasses the most powerful supercomputer in many aspects.

DOI: 10.4018/978-1-4666-0261-8.ch012

Human beings receive information through vision, hearing, smelling and touching, and send information through facial and body expressions, talking and writing. Of these communication channels, reading (from human vision), hearing, talking and writing are related to natural languages. All of them are temporally one-dimensional, and only one signal is sent out or received at a certain time point, so a natural language is communicated one dimensionally. With one-dimensional natural languages used by human being, in order to understand and describe a highly dimensional environment a series of filtering and transformations are necessary as illustrated in Figure 1. These transformations can be N-dimensional to N-dimensional or one-dimensional to N-dimensional in input process, and N-dimensional to one-dimensional or N-dimensional to N-dimensional in an output process. After these transformations information should be ready to be used by the central processing unit directly. Effectiveness and efficiency of these transformations are very important to knowledge representation and management.

A knowledge model describes structure and other properties of a knowledge base which is part of a central processing system. A knowledge representation model is simply a mirror of our world, since one important requirement for a model is its accuracy. In this sense there is hardly any intelligence in a knowledge model or a knowledge base. Instead it is the communication

process consisting of filtering and transformations that shows more intelligent behaviors. As expressed by Robert C. Berwick, et al., in a white paper of MIT Genesis project (Berwick, et. al., 2004), "The intelligence is in the I/O". As shown in Figure 1, a knowledge model may be the easiest component to start since its input has been filtered and transformed tremendously from the original format, and is ready to be stored in the knowledge base directly. On the other hand, a knowledge representation (KR) model plays a central role to any knowledge-based systems, and it eventually decides how far such a system can go. Furthermore, knowledge and experience can make the process of filtering and transformations more efficient and effective.

A KR model captures the properties of real world entities and their relationships. Enormous amounts of intervened entities constitute a highly complex multi-dimensional structure. Thus a KR method needs powerful expressiveness to model such information.

Many cognitive models of knowledge representation have been proposed in cognitive informatics. Several cognitive models are discussed in (Wang & Wang, 2006). Object-Attribute-Relation model is proposed to represent the formal information and knowledge structures acquired and learned in the brain (Wang, 2007). This model explores several interesting physical and physiological aspects of brain learning and gives a plausible estimation of

Figure 1. Communication process for a knowledge-based system

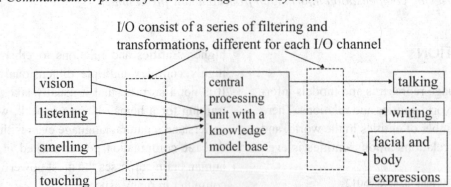

human memory capability. The cognitive foundations and processes of consciousness and attention are critical to cognitive informatics. How abstract consciousness is generated by physical and physiological organs are discussed in (Wang & Wang 2008). A nested cognitive model to explain the process of reading Chinese characters is presented in (Zheng, et. al., 2008), which indicates that there are two distinctive pathways in reading Chinese characters, and this can be employed to build reading models. Visual semantic algebra (VSA), a new form of denotational mathematics, is presented for abstract visual object and architecture manipulation (Wang, 2008). VSA can serve as a powerful man-machine interactive language for representing and manipulating visual geometrical objects in computational intelligence systems.

In Artificail Intelligence many KR techniques have been proposed since 1960's, such as semantic network, frame, scripts, logic rules etc. However, we still know little about how to capture deep semantic information effectively and support the construction of a large-scale commonsense knowledge base efficiently. Previous research focuses more on the expressiveness of KR. Recently there is an emerging interest of how to construct a large-scale knowledge base efficiently. In this paper we present a new KR model, *SenseNet*, which provides semantic support for commonsense reasoning and natural language understanding.

Our Contributions

SenseNet shares the same goal of building a large-scale commonsense knowledge base. Compared with WordNet, Cyc, and ConceptNet, our contributions are:

- We use a sense instead of a word as the building block for SenseNet, because a sense encodes semantic information more clearly.

- A relationship is defined as a probability matrix, which allows adaptive learning and leads naturally to human-like reasoning.

- Relationships among senses are formalized with a Hidden Markov Model (HMM), which gives SenseNet a solid mathematical foundation.

- A new measurement, confidence, is introduced to facilitate natural language understanding procedure.

- After the regular learning, SenseNet uses a "thinking" phase to generate new knowledge.

This paper is organized as follows. Section 2 discusses related work. We present our KR model, SenseNet, in section 3 and its inference algorithm in section 4. Section 5 shows how SenseNet can be used to model the human communication process. Section 6 describes a real world application on information extraction. Finally we conclude in section 7.

RELATED WORK

Knowledge Acquisition

A lot of research on building general-purpose or commonsense knowledge bases has recognized the importance of representing relations among words. Here we will discuss three major knowledge acquisition projects, Cyc, WordNet and ConceptNet.

WordNet is a widely used semantic resource in computational linguistics community (Fellbaum, 1998). It is a database of linked words, primarily nouns, verbs, adjectives and adverbs. These words are organized into synonym sets called synsets, and each synset represents one lexical concept. Meanings of each word are organized into "senses". Links are predefined semantic relations among words, not senses. Currently WordNet contains about 150,000 words/strings, 110,000 synsets and

200,000 word-sense pairs. Predefined relations can only satisfy some applications or domains no matter how carefully they are chosen, also lack of adaptiveness limits its learning capability.

The Cyc project emphasizes on formalization of commonsense knowledge into a logical framework (Witbrock, Baxter, & Curtis, 2003). Same as WordNet, its knowledge base is handcrafted by knowledge engineers. To use Cyc a natural language has to be transformed to a proprietary logical representation. Although a logical foundation has some nice properties, it is complex and expensive to apply Cyc to practical textual mining tasks.

ConceptNet is proposed in Open Mind Common Sense project in MIT. Comparing with WordNet and Cyc, the main advantage of ConceptNet is its unique way to acquire knowledge. Thousands of common people contribute through the Web by inputting sentences in a fill-in-the-blank fashion. Then concepts and binary-relational assertions are extracted to form ConceptNet's semantic network. At present ConceptNet contains 1.6 million edges connecting more than 300,000 nodes (Liu & Singh, 2004). Nodes are semi-structured English fragments, interrelated by an ontology of twenty predefined semantic relations.

Even with efforts of lots of people (about 14,000 people contributed to ConceptNet) in a long time (both WordNet and Cyc started almost twenty years ago), building a comprehensive knowledge base is still remote. Unstructured or general texts are still too complex for current text mining techniques. That is why a lot of research focuses only on constrained text, which is either format constrained (such as tables) or content constrained (such as extracting only location information). In the rest of this section we will discuss some techniques on named entity extraction and table analysis, which are related to our case study.

Named Entity Extraction

Named entity detection and extraction techniques try to locate and extract the entity names (such as of company, people, locations (Li, et. al., 2003), biological terms (Goutte, et. al., 2002), etc.), dates (Mckay & Cunningham, 2001), monetary amounts, references (Agichtein & Ganti, 2004) and other similar entities in unstructured text. In early systems usually a domain-specific dictionary and a pattern/rule base are built manually and tuned for a particular corpus. Extraction quality depends on the quality of these external dictionaries and bases, sufficiency of training and consistency of documents within the corpus. Recently more systems utilize context information to deal better with inconsistency among documents, which results in a more robust system. In (Cohen & Sarawagi, 2004) a semi-Markov model is proposed to make better use of external dictionaries. In (McCallum, Freitag, & Pereira, 2000) a maximum entropy Markov model is introduced to segment FAQ's. Maximum entropy (ME) is also used in (Borthwick, et. al., 1998) to combine diverse knowledge sources. Both hidden Markov model (HMM) and ME can generate statistical models of words and simple word features. Document (not the whole corpus) specific rules are learned for named entities extraction to keep more knowledge of original documents (Callan & Mitamura, 2002).

Named entity extraction focuses on extracting simple terms, hopefully to get some insights for development of general NLP techniques. However, a named entity often has semantic relations with other parts of text, and focusing on only named entities ignores these semantic connections. Instead we choose text with constrained structures, such as tables for our case study. Table is semantically complete and usually rich in information.

Table Analysis

Tables are widely used in documents, and are self-contained in semantics and structure. Unstructured text, semi-structured text (such as HTML, LATEX), structured text (such as XML), all utilize table to represent information with repeated patterns.

There exists a lot of work in table analysis, and usually they can be divided into (Zanibbi, Blostein, & Cordy, 2004):

- table detection
- table modeling
- table structure analysis
- table information extraction

After a table is detected, physical and logical structures of tables are studied. Data structures and operations are defined for more complex table processing, such as table regeneration, transformation and inferences (Wang & Wood, 1998). Then tables are decomposed with a table model, such as constraint-based table structure derivation (Hurst, 2001), graph theory based system (Amano & Asada, 2003), extraction using conditional random fields (Pinto, et. al., 2003). Even after table structure analysis, the task of table information extraction is still non-trivial. Table 2 shows that semantic information has to be considered, which may result in changes of original table model based on structure information, such as splitting or merging cells.

Recently due to the popularity of web pages, detection and analysis of tables in HTML documents get a lot of attention (Wang & Hu, 2002; Chen, Tsai, & Tsai, 2000). HTML provides table tags which often help detect and segment tables, but offers little help on semantic analysis. And due to inconsistent quality of web pages, erroneous tags become noise and require additional processing.

Most of above methods are developed for table analysis only. Instead, our work is primarily concerned with broader application of SenseNet in text mining, and entity extraction from tables is used as an application in this context. Consequently it is meaningless to compare our experimental results to those obtained by these methods designed just for table analysis, and often just for tables with specific structures and in a narrow domain. With information extraction from tables as a case study, we want to show SenseNet as a methodological study which can be applied more broadly. Additionally performing a fair comparison of our work with other entity extraction techniques is not straightforward due to the difficulty of obtaining the same set of documents and knowledge base used in their experiments and determining the effects of preprocessing performed in lots of those techniques.

SenseNet: A KNOWLEDGE REPRESENTATION MODEL

We divide the natural language understanding process into three phases:

- learning phase
- thinking phase
- testing phase

Learning or knowledge acquisition to set up a general purpose knowledge base requires large amounts of resources and time as shown by Cyc, WordNet and CommonSense projects. For SenseNet we could reuse the knowledge bases built by WordNet, but need to build semantic connections among word senses. In our case study, SenseNet is effectively applied to a specific domain, tables in financial documents. Even with this small domain, the amount of knowledge required is large. Difficulty of learning is a common and severe problem to any existing knowledge bases. Whether there exists an automatic learning method which can build a high quality, general-purpose, practical knowledge base is still an open question.

SenseNet Model

Lexicon is the knowledge of words, which includes a large amount of "character string to real entity" mappings. Memorization of these mappings is difficult for human beings. It explains why in many natural languages a word often represents multiple meanings. In computational linguistics a meaning of a word is called a sense. From the view of semantics a sense is a better choice for a knowledge base than a word because a sense encodes a single and clear meaning. Our KR model, SenseNet, uses a sense as the basic semantic unit.

An instance of SenseNet is shown in Figure 2 (a). Each node represents a word. A node has multiple attributes representing the senses of a word, and each sense represents a single unambiguous entity (meaning). *Entity* is defined as "something that has independent, separate, or self-contained existence and objective or conceptual reality" by Webster dictionary. A word $word_\alpha$ is defined as the set of all its senses $\{sense_i\}$, which is shown in the Figure 2 (b), where $i = 1, ..., n$.

A *simple edge* connects two semantically related words, for example, edge1 in Figure 2. As shown in Figure 3, a simple edge represents the semantic relationship between $word_\alpha$ and $word_\beta$, that is, the probability of $word_\alpha$ taking sense i and $word_\beta$ taking sense j at the same time. A simple edge connecting $word_\alpha$ and $word_\beta$ is defined as a probability matrix:

$$R_{n \times m} = P\{word_\alpha = sense_i, word_\beta = sense_j\}, i = 1, ..., n; j = 1, ..., m$$

R is a reflective matrix, that is, the probability of $word_\alpha$ taking the $sense_i$ if $word_\beta$ takes the $sense_j$ is equal to the probability of $word_\beta$ taking $sense_j$ and $word_\alpha$ takes $sense_i$.

A *complex edge* connects more than two words (for example, edge2 in Figure 2 connects three words, $word_2$, $word_3$, and $word_5$), which means that these words are semantically related together to express combined or more specific information. For example, to correctly analyze "give Tom a book", "give", "Tom", and "book" need to be processed together to capture the complete information. A complex edge is formally defined as:

$$R_{Nw\alpha \times Nw\beta \times ... \times Nw\gamma} = P\{word_\alpha = sense_i, word_\beta = sense_j, ..., word_\gamma = sense_k\}$$

where $sense_i$ is a sense of $word_\alpha$, $1 \leq i \leq N_{w\alpha}$, $N_{w\alpha}$ is the total number of senses of $word_\alpha$; $sense_j$ is a sense of $word_\beta$, $1 \leq j \leq N_{w\beta}$, $N_{w\beta}$ is the total number of senses of $word_\beta$; $sense_k$ is a sense of $word_\gamma$, $1 \leq k \leq N_{w\gamma}$, $N_{w\gamma}$ is the total number of senses of $word_\gamma$.

A complex edge that connects m nodes is called an *m-edge*, hence a simple edge is also a 2-edge.

Figure 2. (a) An instance of SenseNet (b) A node of SenseNet represents a word

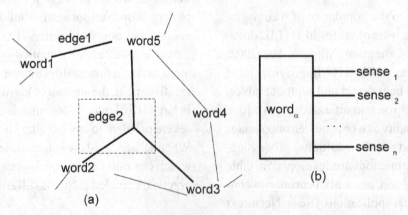

Of course, different edges will contain different probabilities reflecting different strength among connected words.

Confidence

Most machine learning algorithms discard duplicate samples during training as no new information can be gained. However, the number of these identical samples indicates how often a sample occurs and how many users agree upon them. During human learning process, duplicate samples do not give new information, but will build our confidence on the indicated information. Similarly in SenseNet we use the number of identical samples as *confidence* for that sample. We define three types of confidence: sense confidence, connection confidence and global confidence.

Suppose a word w has n senses, for each sense there exists a sense confidence. A sense confidence represents the frequency that this sense is encountered during training and is normalized to a value between 0 and 1. A connection confidence is defined on a connection between two senses. Similarly, it represents the frequency of this connection is encountered during training and is also normalized to a value between 0 and 1. Global confidence shows our overall confidence of the current SenseNet, and it serves as $C_{threshold}$ in our inference algorithm discussed in Section 4.2. Global confidence is statistically derived from sense and

connection confidence existed in a SenseNet, for example, it can be the average value, minimum, or maximum of all existing confidence. As shown in the inference algorithm (Section 4.2), if global confidence takes the minimum value, a great number of low-confidence senses will be activated, which mimics an over-confident human being.

Confidence can also be affected by the source of samples. For example, we may be very confident with word definitions in a dictionary. We thus assign a high confidence to these trusted sources directly. By this way training is shortened because the closer the confidence is to 1, the less learning is required. Just like a human being, if he is confident with his knowledge on a topic, he will not spend much time learning it.

Implication Operation

Training is expensive for most machine learning algorithms. To make the best use of training efforts we apply implication operation to generate new edges and expand the newly built SenseNet. We denote this phase as thinking phase.

Suppose that two edges are learned (Figure 4). Then through implication operation we try to determine whether an edge (semantic relationship) exists between $word_i$ and $word_j$. Implication operation is defined as:

$$R_{l \times k} = R_{l \times m} \times R_{m \times k}$$

Figure 3. An edge of SenseNet

An edge is an n×m probability matrix $R_{n \times m}$

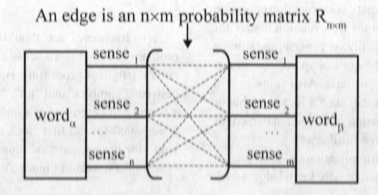

where $R_{1\times m}$ is the probability matrix between word₁ and word₂, $R_{m\times k}$ is the probability matrix between word₂ and word₃, and $R_{1\times k}$ is the calculated probability matrix between word₁ and word₃. word₁ and word₃ are not semantically related if all values in $R_{1\times k}$ are zero. Otherwise, a new edge is inserted into the SenseNet between word₁ and word₃. It is possible that there exist multiple routes connecting word₁ and word₃. In this case first we will generate multiple temporary edges from these routes, then these temporary edges are averaged to generate the new edge between two words.

The confidence of the newly generated edge is the multiplication of two original edge confidence. Because confidence values have been normalized between 0 and 1, the calculated confidence is smaller than either of the original values. This process exactly simulates the learning process of human beings, as we usually have lower confidence with indirect knowledge generated by reasoning than directly taught knowledge.

Combination Operation

After multiple simple edges connecting the same set of nodes are generated, we can combine them into a complex edge. The combination of two simple edges is defined as:

$$R_{1,k,x} = R_{1,k,1} \times R_{1,k,x} \times \theta.$$

where $R_{1,k}$ is rewritten to $R_{1,k,1}$, $R_{k,x}$ is rewritten as $R_{1,k,x}$, θ is within $[0,1]$, θ shows the decreasing confidence. As the number of nodes involved becomes large, the cost of combination operation will also go up. But the new relation matrix for combined edge is usually very sparse, and storage and processing techniques of sparse matrix can be very helpful in this case. Also some hybrid techniques can be used, such a look-up table or hash table. Combination of more than two edges can be performed in a similar way.

In summary, both implication and combination operations will generate new knowledge which

Figure 4. Implication process

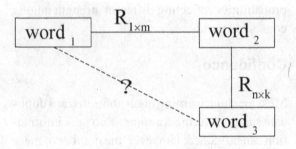

may be unique to a specific SenseNet, fortify the learning capabilities and reduce the training cost. In SenseNet both edges and nodes are learned and updated locally and flexibly. Therefore, like human intelligence, SenseNet is robust in dealing with inconsistent and incomplete data.

Disambiguation with SenseNet

According to SenseNet ambiguity arises when there is more than one way to activate the senses or edges. The following example shows how to use SenseNet to analyze word sense ambiguity. This process is formalized in section 4.2.

Example 1: A gambler lost his lot in the parking lot.

Webster dictionary defines "lot" as:

- an object used as a counter in determining a question by chance;
- a portion of land;
- a considerable quantity or extent;
- …

Which senses of "lot" should be activated? This problem is called word sense disambiguation in natural language processing. Because of the edge between "gambler" and "lot", "an object used as a counter in determining a question by chance" is activated for the first "lot", and "a portion of land" for the second "lot" due to its relation to "parking" (shown in Figure 5).

Another form of ambiguity lies in the syntactic structure of the sentence or fragment of language. In the next example it is not clear whether the adjective "small" applies to both dogs and cats or just to dogs.

Example 2: small dogs and cats

As shown in Figure 6, SenseNet has two options to activate edges, which leads to ambiguity.

The sentence below shows an example of implication ambiguity.

Example 3: The chicken is ready to eat.

For this sentence the ambiguity comes from whether to activate another node as shown in Figure 7. Although the node "people" does not appear in the sentence, but since implication or

omission is very common in communication, we may assume "people" is omitted due to simplicity. Again there are two options to activate the SenseNet, which leads to ambiguity.

Basically ambiguity arises when there are two or more ways to activate the senses, nodes or edges in a SenseNet. These examples show that flexibility and ambiguity of a natural language come from the same source. To avoid ambiguity more constraints are needed for only one activation.

NATURAL LANGUAGE UNDERSTANDING WITH SenseNet

A Hidden Markov Model (HMM) is a discrete-time finite-state automation with stochastic state transition and symbol emission (Durbin, et. al.,

Figure 5. Sense disambiguation for "lot"

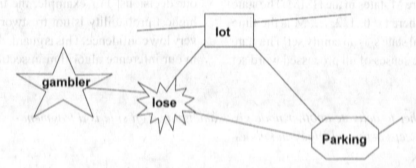

Figure 6. Left side is a fragment of SenseNet. Right side shows two options to activate edges.

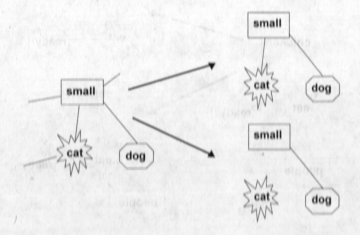

1998). Recently HMM is gaining popularity in text mining as researchers pay more attention to relations and context of entities (Seymore, McCallum, & Rosenfeld, 1999). HMM has been widely used for segmentation (Teahan, 2000), text classification (Hughes, Guttorp, & Charles, 1999), and entity extraction (Cohen & Sarawagi, 2004). For details about HMM, please refer to (Rabiner, 1989).

Formalizing Natural Language Understanding with a Hidden Markov Model

In SenseNet, the natural language understanding process is the process of selecting appropriate senses for each word in the text. To understand a document, a human being tries to determine meanings (senses) of words, which is an analysis and reasoning process. We formalize this process with a HMM using SenseNet as the knowledge base. Suppose there are M states in the HMM. The state at time t is s_t, where t = 0, 1, 2, …, M is the time index. The initial state s_0 is an empty set. The state s_t consists of the senses of all processed word set

W_t. At time t+1, we will determine the sense of next unprocessed word w_{t+1} that has connections (edges in SenseNet) with W_t. Which sense of w_{t+1} will be activated is decided by strength (probability and confidence) of edges between w_{t+1} and W_t in SenseNet. The transition from s_t to s_{t+1} is given by the conditional probability $P(s_{t+1}|W_t)$, which is specified by a state transition matrix A. Elements of A are defined as:

$$a_{ij} = P(s_{t+1} = s_t \cup w_{t+1}^j \mid W_t = W_t^i)$$

where j is the jth sense of word w_{t+1}, and W_t^i denotes the ith combination of senses of the words in W_t. Notice that $\sum_{ij} a_{ij} = 1$.

If probability is the only measure in determining word senses, we simply choose the w_{t+1}^j that has the highest probability. However, as demonstrated by human natural language understanding process, probability itself is not sufficient, thus confidence is desired to measure how confident we are with our decisions. For example, the transition with highest probability is not trustworthy if it has a very low confidence. This is guarded by the $C_{threshold}$ in our inference algorithm in section 4.2. HMM

Figure 7. Whether to activate another node gives ambiguity. Left side is a fragment of SenseNet, and right side only keeps activated edges and nodes

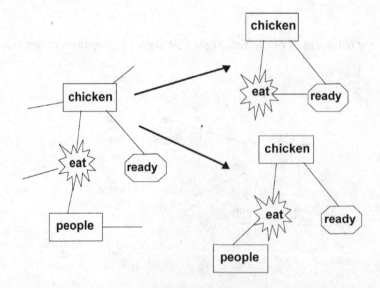

has so-called "zero-frequency problem" (Witten & Bell, 1991) if transitions of zero probability (no training samples) are activated. SenseNet solves this problem by assigning a small value to every transition as its initial probability.

In SenseNet, suppose there is a node w_i, confidence for its jth sense is denoted as c_{ij}. Suppose there are two related nodes, w_i and w_m, the confidence of probability connecting their jth and nth sense is denoted by $c_{ij,mn}$. We define that the confidence for the overall SenseNet C as average of all sense confidence and relation confidence. We use C as $C_{threshold}$ in our inference algorithm during testing phase.

Inference Algorithm for Natural Language Understanding

The inference problem of a regular HMM is to find the state with highest probability, which is efficiently solved by Viterbi algorithm (Viterbi, 1967). However, in SenseNet the goal is to find a state set S with high probability and confidence for a given document, which consists of the word sequence $W = w_1, w_2, ..., w_n$. Thus, the inference algorithm returns all states that satisfy:

$$S = \{ s_i \mid P(s_i|W) > P_{threshold}, C(s_i|W) > C_{threshold}\}$$

where $P_{threshold}$ and $C_{threshold}$ are the minimum requirements for probability and confidence. S is generated from the line 21 to 26. If S is empty, either SenseNet does not have enough knowledge or the document is semantically wrong; if S has one state, SenseNet understands the document unambiguously; if S has multiple states, there exist multiple ways to understand the document, which results in ambiguity. Ambiguity is very common in a natural language. With SenseNet we can successfully detect and analyze ambiguity. Here is the SenseNet inference algorithm for sense disambiguation. Inference $(W = w_1, w_2, ..., w_n)$ {

1. $S = \Omega$;
2. put a word with the highest confident sense into W^0, choose the first one if more than one word have the same sense confidence;
3. for each sense i of word(s) in W^0 {
4. $TBD_i = W - W^0$;
5. $S_i = W^0$;
6. for each state s_{ik} in S_i {
7. $P_{ik} = P(s_{ik})$;
8. $C_{ik} = C(s_{ik})$;
9. $TBD_{ik} = TBD_i$;
10. while TBD_{ik} is not empty {
11. choose any words in TBD_{ik} that have edges to words in s_{ik}, add them to s_{ik}, these newly added words are denoted as W', activate the senses with the highest probability;
12. $TBD_{ik} = TBD_{ik} - W'$;
13. $P_{ik} = P_{ik} \times P(newly\_added\_edges)$;
14. $C_{ik} = C_{ik} \times C(newly\_added\_edges) \times C(newly\_added\_senses)$;
15. if $C_{ik} < C_{threshold}$ or $P_{ik} < P_{threshold}$
16. remove s_{ik} from S_i, go to 6;
17. }; // end of TBD_{ik} loop
18. }; // end of S_i loop
19. $S = S \cup S_i$;
20. }; // end of W^0 loop
21. if S is empty
22. output "failure";
23. else if there is only one state in S
24. output this state as result;
25. else
26. output all states, their probabilities and confidences;
27. }

The inference algorithm simulates how a human being interprets documents. It starts with a word that owns a sense with the highest confidence (line 1 - 2). If there exist multiple such words, we choose the first one occurring in the document. Then the algorithm performs a breath-first searching of all possible paths with probability and confidence above given thresholds and save them into S (line 3 - 20). If a word in S^0 has multiple senses, all of them are enumerated by the loop starting at line 3. Within the loop TBD_i (TBD means "to be determined") saves all unprocessed words; S_i saves all partial state sequences found so far for the ith sense. Then the algorithm tries to complete each partial state sequence by activating the related senses in SenseNet (line 11). During the process, the probability and confidence for each state sequence are updated with newly added edges and senses. If either probability or confidence falls below its threshold, this state sequence is discarded (line 16). P(newly_added_edges) in line 13 is the product of probabilities of all newly added edges; C(newly_added_edges) in line 14 is the product of confidences of all newly added edges, and C(newly_added_senses) is the product of confidences of all newly added senses. Line 19 saves all qualified state sequences into S. As more words in W are processed, P_{ik} and C_{ik} become lower, which precisely mimics the process of human natural language understanding. When a human being reads a long and hard article, he feels more and more confused and less and less confident.

ANALYZING COMMUNICATION PROCESS USING SenseNet

A natural language is a very common communication tool. There are two phases in a communication process, encoding phase and decoding phase. Encoding generates texts from SenseNet, and decoding converts texts to a multiple dimensional model with help of SenseNet.

Encoding and Decoding at the Single Entity Level

Let's look at how a single entity is processed first. In the encoding phase, the language generator (either a human being or a machine) searches a vocabulary base for a word to represent the entity. Multiple matches are possible, and mismatch often exists due to the constraints of the language or insufficient learning of the language as shown in Figure 8.

In the decoding phase a receiver is able to figure out the meaning or represented entity from a single word only if the word has only one sense as shown in Figure 9.

Figure 8. Encoding process, dash-lined shape shows the original entity to be described, solid-lined shape shows the word chosen to represent it. Mismatch is possible due to language or user constraints

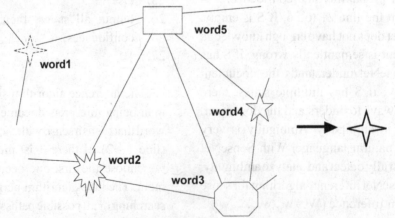

Encoding a single entity: Word 1 is chosen since one of its senses matches with the entity we want to encode

Figure 9. Decoding process, solid-lined shape shows the word a receiver gets, and mismatch can happen

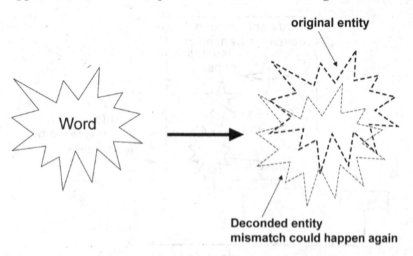

Encoding or decoding a single entity is somewhat pointless since usually more constraints are necessary to reach a decision.

Encoding and Decoding at the Scenario Level

When a scenario is to be described, usually there involve multiple entities. After choosing nodes for every entity, the language generator will organize these words together into texts as shown in Figure 10. In this organization or encoding phase, a multiple dimensional model is transformed to one dimensional text based on heuristics and syntax. During this process prepositions are used to encode time or space information, and conjunctions are used to further specify or constrain the relations among nodes.

In the decoding phase, when the receiver tries to find out what entity each word describes by performing the sense determination process described previously, and convert the one dimensional text back to multiple dimensional information modeled in SenseNet. The whole process is shown in Figure 11. It includes activation of senses, nodes and edges. And it is clear that the relations among words provide the only way for us to determine the word senses and identify the original entities.

In the scenario case, not all entities play the same roles or of the same importance. In efficient communications, such as a well-written article, there usually exist a few "core" entities which connect to lots of entities. Naturally these "core" entities can be used as keywords or for text summarization. Efficient communication is also affected by careful encoding, decoding capabilities and common knowledge shared by encoders and decoders.

Figure 10. Encoding at the scenario level

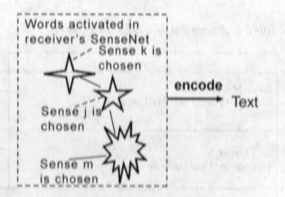

Figure 11. Decoding at the scenario level

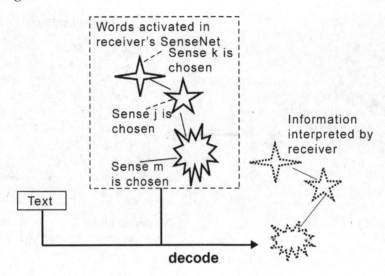

A CASE STUDY

We used a corpus of public company proxy filings retrieved from the online repository of the United States Securities and Exchange Commission (SEC). SEC names these documents as DEF 14A. Every DEF 14A contains one executive compensation table (e.g., Table 1 and Table 2). There exist a wide range of structural differences among these tables, such as different number of lines or columns for each executive entry, incomplete data. As shown in Table 1, without semantic information we cannot understand that this table describes compensation of two executives for three years. An example of ambiguity is shown in Table 2, "Jr" could be a suffix for "Ed J. Rocha", or a prefix for "CFO". Utilization of mere structural information results in a "brittle" system.

We built an Executive Compensation Retrieval System (ECRS) to extract the data fields from these tables and save them in a database. ECRS includes,

- a web crawler to download the latest DEF 14A regularly.
- a knowledge base generated from a list of personal names from the U.S. Census Bureau and a list of titles of company executives. According to the Census Bureau, this name list contains approximately 90

Table 1. A segment of a DEF 14A Form

Name	Year	Salary	Bonus	Other compensation
Edwin M. Crawford Chairman of Board and Chief Executive Officer	2003	1500000	127456	...
	2002		103203	...
	2001	1294231	207299	...
A.D. Frazier, Jr President and Chief Operating Officer	2003	1000000	450000	...
	2002	392308	418167	...
	2001	N/A	N/A	...
...				

Table 2. Another sample table from a SEC DEF 14A Form

Name and Position	Year	Salary	Other compensation
CAPITAL CORP OF THE WEST Thomas T. Hawker President/CEO	2000	181,538	...
	1999	173,115	...
	1998	170,219	...
COUNTY BANK Ed J. Rocha Jr. CFO	2000	118,750	...
	1999	104,167	...
	1998	N/A	...
...			

percent of all of the first and last names in use in the U.S. The list was partitioned by first and last name and the total number of entrees is 91,933. Each first or last name will be a node in SenseNet, and there exist one edge between each pair of first name and last name. For the company executive title list, titles were manually extracted from about 25 randomly picked financial documents. Example titles include Chief Executive Officer, CFO, Chairman, Chief, and CIO etc. We converted this list into SenseNet with each word as a node, and there are edges for words appearing in one title. We found that some words appear in both the name and title list, such as "president", "chairman". And these words have two senses and require disambiguation. Since the names and titles come from trusted sources, we assign all confidence values as 1.

- an extraction module, which locates executive compensation tables and extracts executive names, titles, salary, bonus, stock options and other data fields.
- a database that saves all the extracted information.

The experiment was conducted using randomly picked Standard and Poor's 500 companies from different industries based on Global Industry Classification Standard: 1. Automobile; 2. Bank;

3. Commercial Supply and Service; 4. Energy; 5. Food Beverage and Tobacco; 6. Health Care; 7. Insurance; 8. Pharmaceutical and Biotechnology; 9. Real Estate; 10. Software and Service; 11. Transportation. Since the only way to validate the results is by manual checking, a large-scale experiment is not feasible. Instead, we try to diversify the DEF 14A used in the experiment. At least one company of each industry was selected, and the total number of tested companies is 19. Depending on availability one to three years' reports were retrieved for each company. Total number of compensation records in these documents is 184. 149 of them are successfully extracted as shown in Table 3.

Table 3. Information extraction results

Industry	Number of years	Number of records	Extracted records
1	2	10	5
2	2	18	15
3	3	27	25
4	1	3	2
5	3	15	13
6	2	40	34
7	3	18	13
8	3	12	8
9	1	3	3
10	2	20	15
11	2	18	16

CONCLUSION AND FUTURE WORK

This paper presents a new Knowledge Representation model called SenseNet at the lexical level. We formalize SenseNet model with HMM. SenseNet models some important aspects of human reasoning in natural language understanding, can dissolve ambiguity, and simulate human communication process. We evaluate the SenseNet model by an application in table extraction. To achieve human-level intelligence there are still many open problems, e.g.,

- How to build a high-quality commonsense knowledge base automatically?
- How to build knowledge at a higher level of granularity than lexicon (such as frame)?

REFERENCES

Agichtein, E., & Ganti, V. (2004). Mining Reference Tables for Automatic Text Segmentation. *Tenth ACM International Conference on Knowledge Discovery and Data Mining*, Seattle, WA

Amano, A., & Asada, N. (2003, August). Graph Grammar Based Analysis System of Complex Table Form Document. *Seventh International Conference on Document Analysis and Recognition Volume II*, Edinburgh, Scotland.

Berwick, R., Knight, T., Shrobe, H., Sussman, G., Ullman, S., Winston, P., & Yip, K. (2004). *The Human Intelligence Enterprise*. Retrieved from http://genesis.csail.mit.edu/HIE/white.html.

Borthwick, A., Sterling, J., Agichtein, E., & Grishman, R. (1998). Exploiting diverse knowledge sources via maximum entropy in named entity recognition. *Proceedings of the Sixth Workshop on Very Large Corpora*, New Brunswick, New Jersey.

Callan, J., & Mitamura, (2002). T. Knowledge-based extraction of named entities. *Proceedings of the Eleventh International Conference on Information and Knowledge Management* (pp. 532-537). McLean, VA.

Chen, H., Tsai, S., & Tsai, J. (2000, August). Mining Tables from Large Scale HTML Texts. *18th International Conference on Computational Linguistics,* Germany.

Cohen, W., & Sarawagi, S. (2004). Exploiting dictionaries in named entity extraction: combining semi-Markov extraction processes and data integration methods. *Tenth ACM International Conference on Knowledge Discovery and Data Mining,* Seattle, WA.

Durbin, R., Eddy, S., Krogh, A., & Mitchison, G. (1998). *Biological Sequence Analysis: Probabilistic Models of Proteins and Nucleic Acids*. Cambridge UK: Cambridge University Press.

Fellbaum, C. (1998). *WordNet: An Electronic Lexical Database*. Bradfords Books, ISBN 0-262-06197-X.

Goutte, C., Déjean, H., Gaussier, E., Cancedda, N., & Renders, J. (2002). Combining labelled and unlabelled data: a case study on Fisher kernels and transductive inference for biological entity recognition. *Sixth Conference on Natural Language Learning*, Taipei, Taiwan.

Hughes, J., Guttorp, P., & Charles, S. (1999). A non-homogeneous hidden Markov model for precipitation occurrence. *Applied Statistics, 48*, 15–30. doi:10.1111/1467-9876.00136

Hurst, M. (2001, September). Layout and language: Challenges for table understanding on the web. Proceeding of International Workshop on Web Document Analysis (pp. 27-30), Seattle, USA.

Li, H., Srihari, R., Niu, C., & Li, W. (2003). Cymfony A hybrid approach to geographical references in information extraction. *Human Language Technology conference: North American chapter of the Association for Computational Linguistics annual meeting*, Edmonton, Canada.

Liu, H., & Singh, P. (2004). Commonsense reasoning in and over natural language. *Proceedings of the 8th International Conference on Knowledge-Based Intelligent Information and Engineering Systems (KES-2004)*.

McCallum, A., Freitag, D., & Pereira, F. (2000). Maximum entropy Markov models for information extraction and segmentation. *Proceedings of 17th International Conf. on Machine Learning*, San Francisco, CA.

Mckay, D., & Cunningham, S. (2001, April). Mining dates from historical documents. *The Fourth New Zealand Computer Science Research Students Conference*, New Zealand.

Pinto, D., McCallum, A., Wei, X., & Croft, W. (2003). Table extraction using conditional random fields. *Proceedings of the ACM SIGIR*.

Rabiner, L. (1989). A tutorial on hidden Markov models and selected applications in speech recognition. *Proceedings of the IEEE*, 77(2), 257–286. doi:10.1109/5.18626

Seymore, K., McCallum, A., & Rosenfeld, R. (1999). Learning hidden Markov model structure for information extraction. *AAAI Workshop on Machine Learning for Information Extraction*.

Teahan, W., Wen, Y., McNab, R., & Witten, I. (2000, September). A compression-based algorithm for Chinese word segmentation. *Computational Linguistics*, 26(3, 375–393.

Viterbi, A. (1967, April). Error bounds for convolutional codes and an asymptotically optimal decoding algorithm. *IEEE Transactions on Information Theory*, IT-13(2), 260–269. doi:10.1109/TIT.1967.1054010

Wang, X., & Wood, D. (1998). A Conceptual Model for Tables, Principles of Digital Document Processing PODDP '98. In E. Munson, C. Nicholas, & D. Wood (Eds.), *Springer-Verlag Lecture Notes in Computer Science 1481*(1998), 10-23.

Wang, Y. (2007, July). The OAR Model of Neural Informatics for Internal Knowledge Representation in the Brain. *International Journal of Cognitive Informatics and Natural Intelligence*, 1(3), 64–75.

Wang, Y. (2008). On Visual Semantic Algebra (VSA) and the cognitive process of pattern recognition. *7th IEEE International Conference on Cognitive Informatics* (pp. 384-393), Stanford, CA

Wang, Y., & Hu, J. (2002, August). Detecting Tables in HTML Documents. In D. Lopresti, J. Hu, & R. Kashi (Eds.), *Document Image Analysis System V, 5th International Workshop DAS 2002*, Princeton, NJ, USA.

Wang, Y., & Wang, Y. (2006, March). Cognitive Informatics Models of the Brain. *IEEE Transactions on Systems, Man and Cybernetics. Part C, Applications and Reviews*, 26(2), 203–207. doi:10.1109/TSMCC.2006.871151

Wang, Y., & Wang, Y. (2008). The cognitive processes of consciousness and attention. *7th IEEE International Conference on Cognitive Informatics* (pp. 30-39), Stanford, CA.

Witbrock, M., Baxter, D., & Curtis, J. (2003). An Interactive Dialogue System for Knowledge Acquisition in Cyc. *Proceedings of the Eighteenth International Joint Conference on Artificial Intelligence*, Acapulco, Mexico.

Witten, I., & Bell, T. (1991). The zero-frequency problem: Estimating the probablitiies of novel events on adaptive text compression. *IEEE Transactions on Information Theory*, 37(4), 1085–1094. doi:10.1109/18.87000

Zanibbi, R., R., Blostein, D., & Cordy, J. (2004, March). A Survey of Table Recognition: Models, Observations, Transformations, and Inferences. *International Journal of Document Analysis and Recognition*, 7(1), 1–16.

Zheng, L., Luo, F., Shan, C., & Yin, W. (2008). A novel cognitive model of reading: Neuropsychology research on internal processing of the brain. *7th IEEE International Conference on Cognitive Informatics* (pp. 122-127), Stanford, CA.

Chapter 13
A Dualism Based Semantics Formalization Mechanism for Model Driven Engineering

Yucong Duan

Capital University of Medical Sciences, China, & Pohang University of Science and Technology (POSTECH), South Korea

ABSTRACT

Firstly this article presents a thorough discussion of semantics formalization related issues in model driven engineering (MDE). Then motivated for the purpose of software implementation, and attempts to overcome the shortcomings of incompleteness and context-sensitivity in the existing models, we propose to study formalization of semantics from a cognitive background. Issues under study cover the broad scope of overlap vs. incomplete vs. complete, closed world assumption (CWA) vs. open world assumption (OWA), Y(Yes)/N(No) vs. T(True)/F(False), subjective (SUBJ) vs. objective (OBJ), static vs. dynamic, unconsciousness vs. conscious, human vs. machine aspects, and so forth. A semantics formalization approach called EID-SCE (Existence Identification Dualism-Semantics Cosmos Explosion) is designed to meet both the theoretical investigation and implementation of the proposed formalization goals. EID-SCE supports the measure/evaluation in a {complete, no overlap} manner whether a given concept or feature is an improvement. Some elementary cases are also shown to demonstrate the feasibility of EID-SCE.

INTRODUCTION

This is a revised and extended version of the work previously published in (Duan, Y., 2008c). Various languages and techniques of Model Transformations (MT) (Bar & Whittle, 2006; OMG, 2002) and Model Driven Engineering (MDE) (Atlee et al., 2002; Bézivin et al., 2006) are quickly gaining

strength and attentions with excellent application records. Many new proposals, features(Kang et al., 1990), concepts (Burmester et al., 2004; France et al., 2006) of languages of MT and MDE have been introduced and devised to further advance current practices, spanning from theoretical to industrial communities, syntax level (Bar & Whittle, 2006) to semantic level (Chitchyan et al., 2007), formal description to human-machine interactive modeling/implementation, functional

DOI: 10.4018/978-1-4666-0261-8.ch013

fulfillment to quality satisfaction (Bruel et al., 2004; Barbero et al., 2007), developers' views to system architects' artifacts, etc. However, current technologies do not provide a solution to evaluate whether a given proposal/concept/feature in a MT and MDE related system is an improvement (France et al., 2006) without writing all programs in a language, or trying out all the possible organizational environments in which software may be developed. Software engineering properties such as comprehensibility, evolvability, modularity, and analyzability, are crucial dimensions to consider in the assessment of the quality of software engineering activities and products by designers and users of MT and MDE languages and systems during the software modeling processes (Atlee et al., 2002; Bruel et al., 2004; Barbero et al., 2007).

It is a very insightful description that in the past, informatics put emphasis on external information processing while ignoring the fundamental fact that human brains are the original sources and final destinations of information and that any information must be cognized by human beings before it is understood (Wang et al.09). According to this strategy, it is reasonable to reach the conclusion that human are the original sources and final destinations of semantics. And the links among semantics and the creator of them should be given a high priority in a semantics formalization practices theoretically. This work is extended on this instructive strategy, and generally it falls into categories of Cognitive computing and Mathematical laws of software engineering of Cognitive Informatics (CI) (Wang 02; Wang 06; Wang et al 09). We propose to investigation from a new cognitive viewpoint of semantics formalization (Zhang, D., 2005; Shi, Z et al, 2006; Wang, Y.,2007a; Wang, Y.,2007b) problems of MT and MDE technologies to enable programmers to construct of a MT and MDE language with formalized semantic to help users to develop better software. The goal of the semantics formalization mechanism proposed in this article is expected to be beneficial to the design, implementation, and optimization of MT and MDE languages fundamentally. Especially it is expected to support the measure/evaluation in a {complete, no overlap} manner whether a given proposal/concept/feature in a MT and MDE related system is an improvement.

MDE SEMANTICS PROBLEM ANALYSIS

Semantics Related Scenario

There are many problems with semantics perceiving and exploring which include but not limited to the following scenario:

(a) Users have difficulty with combining their natural language (NL) semantics from their knowledge backgrounds with the semantics proposed in documents of enforcement.

(b) Users might not persuade each other (Guarino, N., 2004) with the priorities of their perceived semantics on the presumed same concept by means of pure expression techniques.

(c) Users might not convince themselves the {Yes/No, True/False} of their "self" conceived semantics in a consciously (vs. unconsciously) non-relativism, {complete, non-overlap} manner in a static or dynamic space (Block et al., 1998; Koch, C., 2004). They might not overcome/solve the beginning/first difficulty of locating/identifying themselves as an observer or insider of the target (whose?) semantics usually.

Most claimed solutions can only provide partially or empirical contributions limited to conceptual level with unsurpassable paradoxes/fallacies. This paper believes that cognitive analysis can initiate an ultimate formalization approach.

Semantics Phenomena Analysis

Most current efforts to add semantics to the systems, mathematics, etc, and support integration and transformation by means for standardization succeed or fail for the following reasons.

Analysis: Is there an existing semantics which can support itself with following restrictions?

(1) Independent: this guarantees the completeness and maintains the objectiveness of this semantics.
(2) Consistent with multiple contexts: this guarantees the essential necessary existence of semantics for communication.

From a pure philosophical thought, independent can be mapped to isolate/unique|$_{exclusive}$ |complete, and consistent can be mapped to a function of more than one variable or be abstracted to a relationship. Then they can be controversial to each other. To avoid these extremes, here we further clarify by explicitly claiming that the human are the creators of above semantics. The creation relationship of a semantics does not suffer to independent of (1).

If the answer is yes, it seems that there often lacks a sound starting semantics which goes/extends through the subsequent "human/semantics→computer/notations" consistently.

If the answer is no, a semantics must be adapted dynamically to maintain the consistency/correctness. The success of approaches/technologies of remedying the situation by explicitly introducing/"create" new concept instead of extending a existing semantics with deeper or wider context can partially be classified as an instance of this category. In a small scale, it does not differ much whether the strategy of bringing in new semantics proof to bridge the intended semantics transformations is adopted consciously or unconsciously. But from a developing view, the negative side effect of unconscious will be magnified especially in the process of formalizing semantics

for a large scale. The difficulty can eventually either getting out of the control unconsciously, or end up with some undetected inconsistencies or unnecessary overlaps of semantics. Then it seems that efficient guidelines are needed to keep formal semantics extension and validation under control in the most objective manner.

Based on above analysis, we propose that an efficient strategy/mechanism for formalizing semantics for MDE should start from exploring the creators of semantics: human. We would like to reveal a unified semantics evolution mechanism explicitly originate from its creator. Although different people have different knowledge backgrounds and {thought states, thought modes}, we believe that they can be consistently related by our semantics formalization mechanism. The final result is a formalization mechanism of semantics for the purpose of determinate by human and automation by machine with high reusability in terms of {Yes/No, True/False} as is shown in Figure 1.It is expected to provide unified/objective semantics for design, implementation, measurement, and maintenance of large project with multiple interests/concerns and stakeholders, and be effect in solving semantics problems related to immeasurable variations on efficiency, difficulty of expressing, and managing (transform/integrate) semantics, etc.

Hypotheses

(a) On thought modes: Although different people have different knowledge backgrounds and thought modes, we believe that human minds occupy or behavior in the same certain cognitive mechanism which determines the superficial variations of semantics phenomena. For this we would like to abstract and propose a role set to match the human mind states.
(b) On effort: Human spend far more efforts as a result of using informal expressions for semantics communication, and during the

Figure 1. Influence of formalization of semantics of minds

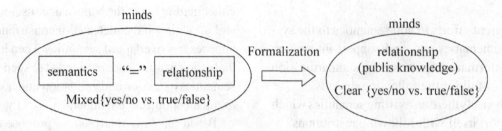

informal process of {verification, transformation, integration, adaptation}, than the actual amount of necessarily required for the sufficient but necessary semantics in formal software implementation practices. this is illustrated in Figure 2.

(c) On cognitive unconscious vs. conscious (Shi, Z. et al., 2007a): human are sometimes unconscious with the difference between their intended semantics and the semantics expressed with medias such as natural language (NL) or some programming/modeling languages, etc. Sometimes we do not have a clear/ultimate idea about the NL words/sentences/grammars which we use by ourselves. With this kind of indeterminate in semantics creators' side, there is no reason to expect the semantics accepters can remedy. We believe

that there does exist an explicit mechanism in an ultimate sense of {complete, non overlap} which supports the validation of the consciousness of expressions of intended semantics in both the final product and during the development processes. We would like to expect that such a mechanism is based on cognition investigation.

Although throughout implementation of such a mechanism may cost much more than empirical remedies in a short term especially for a small project, from a long term view for the obvious advantages of reusability brought by unified formalization will win the battle for saving human efforts for sure.

Figure 2. Analysis (cost vs. reusability) of formal vs. informal

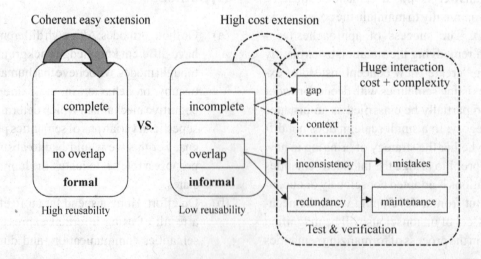

Strategy for Expression

Strategy for expression in this article: the expression used in this article follows a mitigation strategy of "informal → partially formal → formal" expression to bridge the contents and better cater for the understanding habits of readers in subsequent paragraphs.

Regardless that our intention is to proceed towards a formalization mechanism which will support refine semantics in a unified {consistent, complete} manner, anyway we (authors of this paper) have to start with NL words/sentences of which semantics are classified by us as being vague to readers. We can not use our semantics tools/mechanism without introducing it.

The feasibility of this strategy can be justified with the following reasons:

(a) Positive include: although semantics of NL terms maybe be vague depending on the individual remedy information of readers, vague|_{correct} NL semantics::= correct information|_{incomplete} or part of the correct information. It is better than without correct information or wrong information because it saves the effort towards extending to complete.

(b) Not exclude positive: semantics of NL terms does not exclude further refinement, or it is open to further modification. The readers can continuously gain more information of

the semantics which we intend to render but hindered by available techniques, through/after reading the rest parts.

The rest of the paper is organized as follows. Section 2 introduces background key issues related to the semantics formalization. Section 3 describes the EID-SCE strategy. Section 4 shows some elementary case studies on some terms of modeling with the strategy proposed in Section 3 and Section 2. Related work is discussed in Section 5. Finally, conclusion and future work are given in the last section.

PREPARATION

EID Dualism

EID dualism (Duan, Y.,2008a)::= <human/HUMAN, matter/MATTER> of both <S(static), D(dynamic)> situationsHUMAN::= <ROLEs>::=<OBS(observer), AUTR(author), READER(reader)>

The visibility of semantics of roles follows: READER →AUTR→ OBS, as is illustrated in above Figure 3.

{you, me, they} vs. {OBS, AUTR, READER}: {you, me, they} are indirect expressions for ROLEs/{OBS, AUTR, READER}. The specific map is synchronically to the specific real time

Figure 3. Human roles structure in EID

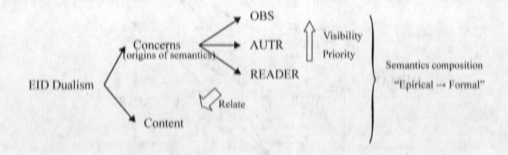

scenarios. The mapping: *{ME/WE, YOU, THEY}→{OBS, AUTR, READER}* helps the transitions from informal expressions to formal expressions in terms of {yes(Y)/no(N), truth(T)/false(F)} which is further explained in subsequent sections. Corresponding to the ROLEs of EID, the semantics modes space is illustrated in Figure 4.

Conscious vs. Unconscious of ROLEs Transformation

(1)   Human/ROLEs transformation

Human/we keep on experiencing constant ROLEs transformations of the modes of (AUTR →OBS→AUTR)|(we→AUTR)|(we→OBS), etc, consciously or unconsciously. The obsession is that with NL, we can only express from the view of READER for both <direct, indirect> observations of {OBS, AUTR, READER}. The reason of this obsession can be summarized as: the subject of observation→expression changes simultaneously with the observer/ROLEs transformation while NL does not provide a mechanism to contain/distinguish the information of changing backgrounds.

There are can be any expressions of "human in human view", but there are no such semantics of "READER in READER's view" which is the same of the semantics of the original expression scenery.

This expression involves implicit/unconscious ROLEs transformation with the first READER.

(2)   Conscious vs. unconscious of ROLEs transformation:

Theoretical unconscious: Except from the view of READER, human are theoretically "unconscious" with their behavior while playing the ROLEs of {OBS, AUTR}. This is illustrated with the priority of ROLEs in Figure 4. Most existing researches either omit the unconscious or pessimistically attribute it to something of mysterious/agnosticism. A lot of works working on the unconscious have to simply continue previously not fully rooted works of others.

The difficulty: human are not conscious with their unconsciousness of their real semantics. Sometimes we maybe wrongly presume our possessions on some of actually "non existential semantics". EID-SCE will guarantee this with a more direct and maybe deeper revelation semantics including of "ours".

(3)   Strategy for epistemological/cognitional unconsciousness

Human are always either conscious or unconscious. The general evolution mode of the cognition is as follows:

Figure 4. EID semantics modes space

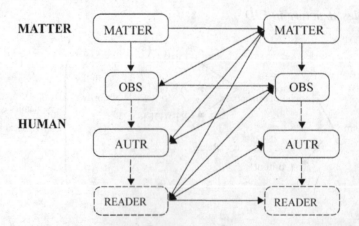

Figure 5. Conscious vs. unconscious ROLEs transformation

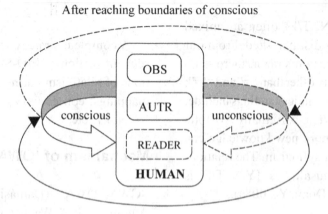

{conscious, unconscious} →*{conscious, unconscious}*

This article is not ultimate from the start, but it supports to reveal the unconscious gradually. With the aid of EID, the expected goal is to support the "*unconscious → conscious*" mitigation in the form of information replacement/clarification:

(unconscious/illusion/incorrect) →(conscious/correct)

This requires the elimination on the counter mode:

(conscious/correct expression) →(unconscious/illusion/incorrect expression)

And it is different from the usually so-called causality/"premise→effect" mode:

(conscious/correct expression)→(conscious/correct expression)

The essence of the old mode is already revealed in Aristotle's three figures of syllogism. According to the syllogism, no new knowledge will be derived outside the scope of premises. In the scope of this article, EID-SCE denies "deduction", use revelation instead of distinguishing situations of "(unconscious/illusion/incorrect) →(conscious/correct)" from situations of "(conscious/correct expression)→(conscious/correct expression)".

Figure 6. {conscious, unconscious} semantics vs. {formal, informal} expression

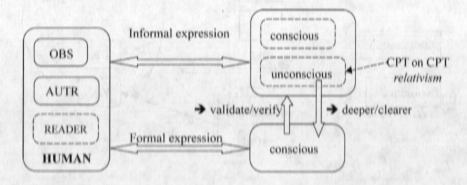

Y(Yes)/N(No) vs. T(True)/F(False)

In current logics, {Y/N, T/F} often are mixed or not capable of being distinguished. From our investigation with an occam's razor, there is no relationship like causality other than "=" and "!=":

The most accepted misunderstandings include: "causality" → (new) T/F, etc. Actually Aristotle has revealed that not more new knowledge can be derived by means of syllogism. The relationship of semantics vs. causality vs. {Y/N, T/F} is illustrated in Figure 7 (Duan, Y.,2008a).

{conscious, unconscious} →{conscious, unconscious} can be mapped to:

$\{Y/N, \ T/F\}|_{\{conscious, \ unconscious\}} \to \{Y/N, T/F\}|_{\{conscious, unconscious\}}$

(unconscious/illusion/incorrect) →(conscious/correct) can be mapped to:

$\{Y/N, T/F\}|_{unconscious} \to \{Y/N, T/F\}|_{conscious}$

(conscious/correct expression)→(conscious/correct expression) can be mapped to:

$\{Y/N, T/F\}|_{conscious} \to \{Y/N, T/F\}|_{conscious}$

The unexpected modes include:

Figure 7. Semantics vs. causality vs. {Y/N, T/F}

$\{Y/N, T/F\}|_{unconscious} \to \{Y/N, T/F\}|_{unconscious}$ and
$\{Y/N, T/F\}|_{conscious} \to \{Y/N, T/F\}|_{unconscious}$

A complete strategy is described in the subsequent section of EID-SCE covering the situations of relativism during implementation of the mappings: conscious→{Y, T} and unconscious →{N, F}, etc.

Mechanism of {OWA, CWA}

<CWA, OWA> (Damásio, C.V., Analyti, A., Antoniou, G., & Wagner, G.,2006) are helpful to illustrate the environments in a conscious manner, and to keep the ROLEs from being unconscious of ROLEs transformations.

Semantics
$::=semantic|_{ROLEs}$
$::=expression \ of \ (\{CWA, OWA\} \to \{CWA, OWA\})|_{\{OBS, AUTR, READER\}}$

The unconscious can be revealed in the following modes.

Unconscious transformations:
$OWA \to "CWA"|_{(unconscious \ mode)}$

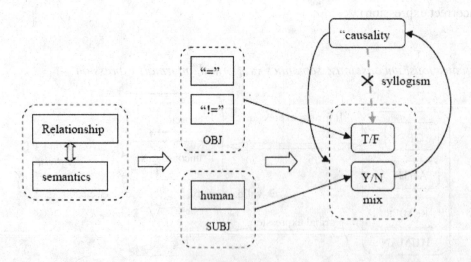

Figure 8. Evolution of ROLEs vs. observation

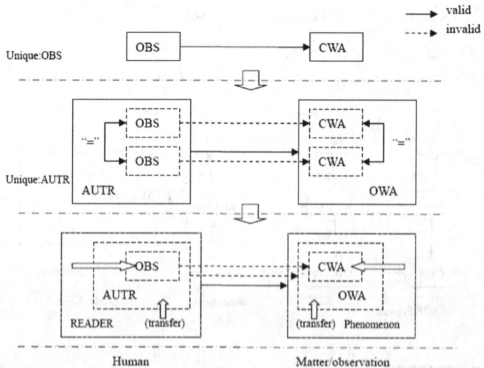

CWA→"OWA"|_(unconscious mode)

Unexpected/useless transformations:
OWA→OWA and CWA→CWA

The evolution of ROLEs vs. observation is shown in Figure 8. The essence includes: (a) for the situation of ROLEs which includes only OBS, the only observation is unique/CWA; (b) for the situation of unique AUTR, the observation is OWA which is built on the identification of "CWA$|_{AUTR}$ = CWA$|_{AUTR}$"; (c) for the situation of READER, the description objects include {CWA$|_{READER}$, OWA$|_{READER}$}.

An expected result is to extend the current practices of formal semantics based on traditional set theories and logics to a unified scope of {CWA, OWA} which flexibility cater thought modes of different stakeholders and as well as various roles of an individual. Evolutions of

ROLEs vs. observation corresponding to {OWA, CWA} are shown in Figure 8.

Following relationships (not the complete list) are proposed based on our intuition among {CWA, OWA} in the form of ({element set}|$_{(operation/relationship)}$):

$$(OWA|_{READER}, OWA|_{READER}) \rightarrow OWA|_{READER}$$
$$(OWA|_{READER}, CWA|_{READER}) \rightarrow OWA|_{READER}$$
$$(CWA|_{AUTR}, CWA|_{AUTR})\,|_{("=")} \rightarrow OWA|_{AUTR}$$
$$(CWA|_{READER}, CWA|_{READER}) \rightarrow CWA|_{READER}$$

These relationships are useful to reduce, decompose and explain the phenomena of semantics before the implementation of the formalization. They can be further revealed at subsequent sections.

Figure 9. EID-SCE strategy

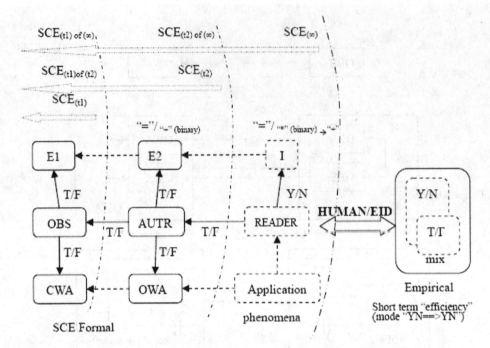

EID-SCE STRATEGY

EID-SCE Introduction

SCE::= {complete, no overlap} semantics organization mechanism based on EID (Duan, Y.,2008a; Duan, Y.,2008b).

Time=t0:
The core of SCE::= matter
matter→matter, human→{OBS},OBS→(matter$|_{OBS}$→CWA)
Time=t1:
Uniqueness/existence 1: E1
CWA::=OBS
Time=t2:
Uniqueness/existence 2: E2
OWA::=AUTR
::=CWAs
Essence: introduction of "="/"sameness"
    ::=(CWA=CWA)
Time→ *infinity(∞)*:

Phenomena (identification): I (Guarino, N., & Welty, C.,2000)
I::=READER
::=transfers (OWA→CWA(s))

Figure 9 illustrates the whole view of the layered EID-SCE strategy. It shows that {Y/N, T/F} on human side are extended into basic semantics modes corresponding to ROLEs. The modes contained in it compose rich semantics phenomena in NL semantics as well as MDE semantics.

Main steps of locating semantics with EID-SCE (phenomenon→phenomenon$|_{SCE(tx)}$) include:

(a) Decide tx.
(b) Decide CWA$|_{prime}$
(c) Decide location/ORD in dimension (CWA$|_{prime}$)

The expected semantics formalized with EID-SCE is intuitively illustrated in Figure 10 in an abstract manner (Duan, Y.,2008a).

Figure 10. Semantics formalization scheme of EID-SCE

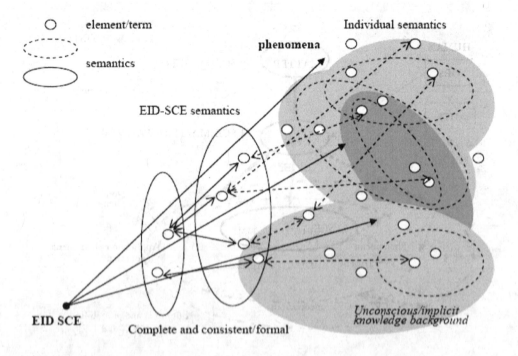

Figure 11. Y/N and T/F in SCE

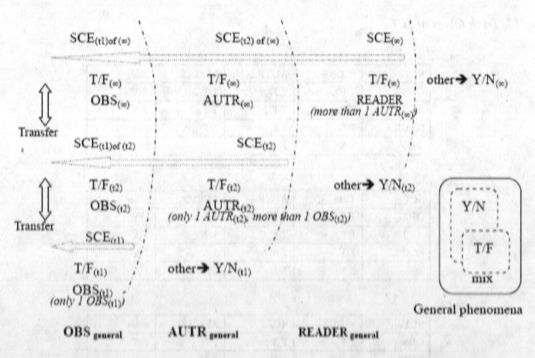

Figure 12. CE:CWA→OWA→phenomena→CWA

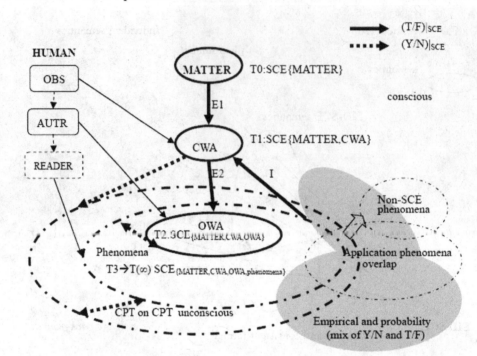

Figure 13. Truth tables of SCE

$SCE_{(\infty)}$

$SCE_{(\infty)}$	$OBS_{(\infty)}$	$AUTR_{(\infty)}$	READER	other
$OBS_{(\infty)}$	$T/F_{(\infty)}$	$T/F_{(\infty)}$	$T/F_{(\infty)}$	Y/N
$AUTR_{(\infty)}$	$T/F_{(\infty)}$	$T/F_{(\infty)}$	$T/F_{(\infty)}$	Y/N
READER	$T/F_{(\infty)}$	$T/F_{(\infty)}$	$T/F_{(\infty)}$	Y/N
other	Y/N	Y/N	Y/N	Y/N

$SCE_{(t2)}$

$SCE_{(t2)}$	$OBS_{(t1)of(t2)}$	$AUTR_{(t2)}$	READER	other
$OBS_{(t1)of(t2)}$	$T/F_{(t2)}$	$T/F_{(t2)}$	Y/N	Y/N
$AUTR_{(t2)}$	$T/F_{(t2)}$	$T/F_{(t2)}$	Y/N	Y/N
READER	Y/N	Y/N	Y/N	Y/N
other	Y/N	Y/N	Y/N	Y/N

$SCE_{(t1)}$

$SCE_{(t1)}$	$OBS_{(t1)}$	AUTR	READER	other
$OBS_{(t1)}$	$T/F_{(t1)}$	Y/N	Y/N	Y/N
AUTR	Y/N	Y/N	Y/N	Y/N
READER	Y/N	Y/N	Y/N	Y/N
other	Y/N	Y/N	Y/N	Y/N

Figure 14. Cases of {service, architecture, ...}|SCE{t1,t2,∞}

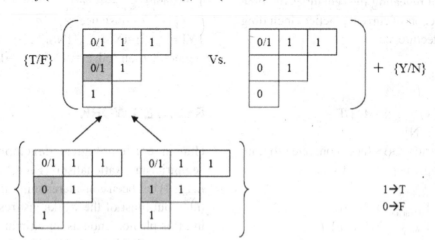

The Y/N and T/F in EID-SCE

Figure 11 reveals how the mechanism of {Y/N, T/F} are extended into EID-SCE processes, especially at the "times" of {$SCE_{(t1)}$, $SCE_{(t2)}$, $SCE_{(∞)}$}. Y/N and T/F map to states of SCE and ROLEs following the architecture of SCE expansion. Subsequently general {Y/N, T/F} semantics expressions can be revealed with a more rich set of semantics, such as with {$SCE_{(t1) of ((∞)}$, $SCE_{(t2) of ((∞)}$, $SCE_{(∞)}$}, etc.

Revisit {CWA, OWA}:
$CWA ::= T|_{OBS}$
$OWA|_{AUTR} ::= T|_{AUTR}$
$::= CWA|_{AUTR}$ "+"|"-" $CWA|_{AUTR}$
$Phenomenon ::= T|_{READER}$
$::= composition\{CWA|_{READER}, OWA|_{READER}\}$

Figure 12 reveals the semantics mechanism of SCE in terms of relationships among ROLEs and {CWA, OWA}, and its formalization in contrast to theoretical vs. empirical practices. E1 refers to the direct revelation of existence by OBS in an objective (Hill, C. O., & Rosado, H.G., 2000) manner, such as the material stone, water, etc. They are matched to $stone|_{OBS}$, $water|_{OBS}$, etc. Cases of E2 include conceptual existence of stone, water, etc.

They are matched to $stone|_{AUTR}$, $water|_{AUTR}$, etc. I further distinguishs the conceptual phenomena with an identification based on human decisions on E2 while being independent to E1, such as numbers, amount, etc. The result of semantics achieved by EID-SCE will be precisely matched with EID truth tables as is shown in Figure 13.

Some traditional terms are distinguished with the above information:

Subjective (SUBJ) vs. objective (OBJ):
$OBJ ::=$ the content of expression is mapped to $(T/F)|_{SCE}$
$SUBJ ::=$ the content of expression is mapped to $(Y/N)|_{SCE}$

Detailed processes of how $(T/F)|_{SCE}$ and $(Y/N)|_{SCE}$ values distribution are mapped to SUBJ vs. OBJ are saved here for brief.

CASE STUDY

To avoid being restricted by the relativism of semantics of natural language, phenomenal fallacies and paradoxes, EID-SCE extends its semantics revelations from its hypothesis on fundamental issues of dualism. Below feasibility of EID-SCE is illustrated in revealing the semantics of some important concepts of current practices including service, architecture, etc.

(a) Service

$SCE(READER)_{service} ::= \{ T/F_{(t1) \text{ of } (\infty)}, T_{(t2) \text{ of } (\infty)}, T_{(t1) \text{ of } (\infty)}, Y/N \}$

Possible scenarios: OBS faces concrete program codes implementation of services.

$SCE(AUTR)_{service}:$

$::= \{ T_{(t1) \text{ of } (t2)}, T_{(t2) \text{ of } (t2)}, Y/N \}$ (i)

$::= \{ F_{(t1) \text{ of } (t?)}, T_{(t?) \text{ of } (t?)}, Y/N \}$ (ii)

Possible scenarios:

For (i), AUTR abstracts services from concrete program codes.

For (ii), AUTR designs services before concrete implementation of codes.

$SCE(OBS)_{service} ::= \{ Y_{(t1)}, Y/N \}$

Possible scenarios: OBS faces concrete program codes implementation of services.

(b) Architecture

$SCE(READER)_{architecture} ::= \{ T/F_{(t1) \text{ of } (\infty)}, T_{(t2) \text{ of } (\infty)}, T_{(t1) \text{ of } (\infty)}, Y/N \}$

Possible scenarios: OBS faces concrete program codes implementation of architectures.

$SCE(AUTR)_{architecture} ::= \{ F_{(t1) \text{ of } (t2)}, T_{(t2) \text{ of } (t2)}, Y/N \}$ (i)

Possible scenarios: AUTR can only abstracts a architecture from a complete/OBS view which is not fully exchangeable in E1 layer.

$SCE(OBS)_{architecture} ::= \{ F_{(t1)}, Y/N \}$

Possible scenarios: OBS faces concrete program codes implementation of architectures.

(c) Type vs. instance

A glance of the cardinality revelation of type/class vs. instance relationship (Chen, P.P.,1976) is shown in Figure 15 within the strategy of EID-SCE.

With EID-SCE:

$T: \text{instance}|_{SCE} \rightarrow \text{type}|_{SCE}$

$F: \text{type}|_{SCE} \rightarrow \text{instance}|_{SCE}$

$TYPE|_{AUTR} ::= INS|_{AUTR} + INS|_{AUTR}$

$\text{Generalization (GL)} ::= (TYPE \leftarrow\rightarrow INS)|_{READER}$

RELATED WORK

Human epistemological development mode: "empiricism → rationalism" (Feng, Y.,1983; Kant, I.,1998) has been considered important for a long time, but most of the works just rest on accepting this phenomenon as an ultimate fact or just problems (Whitehead, N.,1925; Feyerabend et al., 1966; Kim, J.,1995; Duan, Y.,2008a). With no further analytical (Quine, W. V. O.,1951) breakthroughs are supplied in a more concrete manner on this mode, this important phenomenon is not extended to directly support issues related to semantics/understanding development in a formal manner. Empiricism (Mill, J.S.,1968) and rationalism (Kant, I.,1998) are often taken as isolated standpoints (Markie, P.,2004). Based on these unsolved problems, more alternation expressions and problems can be accumulated while inheriting related relativism and paradoxes (Quine, W. V.,1976; Sainsbury, R. M.,1995) such as, subjective vs. objective (Mill, J.S.,1968; Ellis, C. & Flaherty, M.,1992; Kant, I.,1998), conscious vs. unconscious (Shi, Z et al., 2006; Wang, Y.,2007a), truth vs. false vs. yes vs. no (Peirce, C.S.,1901; Hintikka, J., & Kulas, J.,1983), etc. Most of proposed answers are either incomplete or essentially no clearer than corresponding problems. Some answers even go to the extremes of agnosticism (Russell, B.,1970), relativism (Whitehead, N.,1925), diabetics (Hegel, G. W. F.,1807; McGreal, I.P.,1995), monist ontology e.g., materialism (Moser, P. K., & Trout, J. D.,1995), etc. To avoid the past deep-rooted misconceptions, Heidegger (Heidegger, M., 1969) believed historical way will be beneficial to philosophical inquiry. Regretfully most similar initiatives are not realized in concrete practices partially lim-

Figure 15. A revelation of type/class vs. instance

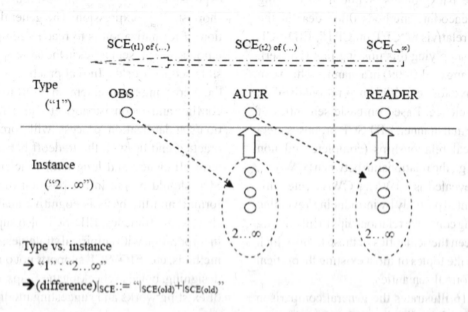

Figure 16. General comparison of semantics formalization strategies

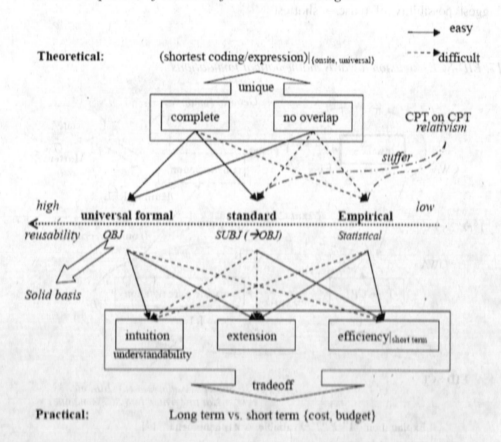

ited to time backgrounds. While most existing semantics encoding methods often deal in the manner of relativism/"CPT on CPT", EID-SCE starts with supplying this missing link (Husserl, E.,1962; Wang et al, 2009) in a manner which can be instructive for "empiricism→ rationalism" in computer science. Based on basic semantics of EID in a formal manner, EID-SCE proposes meta mathematical relationships (complete and non overlap), e.g., the relationship between "CWA vs. OWA" is revealed as "OWA:: = CWAs", etc. This is implemented partially by introducing/revealing and denoting cognitive relationships to fill missing links between the semantics of these terms which are outside the topics of most existing theoretical works on formal semantics.

Figure 16 illustrates the general comparison of semantics formalization strategies. We propose the theoretical criteria as: formal semantics → the biggest possibility of reuse→ shortest expression$|_{relative\ to\ a\ language}$; highest reuse$|_{universal}$ → shortest$|_{universal}$ expression. The general expectation of formalization is to reach <complete$|_{group}$, unique$|_{individual}$> semantics in the largest$|_{ultimate}$ possible scopes/worlds. In real practice, sometimes the increasing requirement on effort to solve the conflict and inconsistency, etc, in a formalization/standardization process will force such a practice end up with the tradeoff between short term efficiency and long term efficiency. EID-SCE should be put in the position of universal formal, and the basis is cognitive analysis. For short term efficiency, EID-SCE also supports the incorporation with empirical strategies, statistical methods, etc. EID–SCE supports not only formal designing, but also checking the {gaps, overlaps} of existing works and suggesting modification.

Figure 17. EID-SCE extension towards mathematical foundations

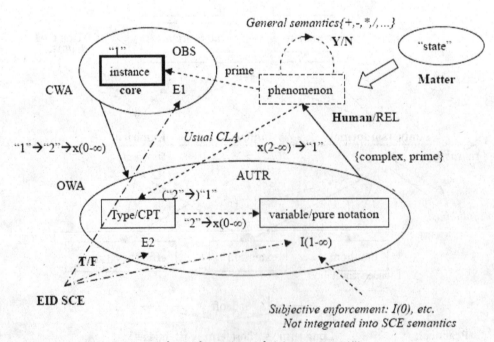

SUMMARY AND FUTURE WORK

Human always expect unifying their understandings in a consistent manner while most efforts end up in the manner of unifying the expressions instead of their understandings subjectively. EID-SCE investigates the existing obsesses of either trapped in conceptual relativism or incomplete discussion from cognition processes of human. In EID-SCE the difference among "human vs. machine" is justified by explicitly reclaiming "human" as a set of intuitive ROLEs. EID-SCE extends the valid scopes of semantics expression to more than the relativism of "CPT(concept) on CPT". In general, EID-SCE help to identify validate and integrate the existing finding of formalization works on semantics and provides the missing intuitions on semantics. Mechanisms are set up in EID-SCE to help the revelation of fundamentals such as "unconscious→conscious", "Y/N vs. T/F", "OWA vs. CWA", etc, in a formal semantics manner. By following the strategy of EID–SCE, human can guarantee and validate their expressions and their expectation/ understandings about the expressions with formal semantics. EID-SCE also supports the optimization and implementation in an on the fly manner. EID-SCE provides the foundation for starting a journey towards rebuilding semantics in an ultimate formal manner. By formulization semantics of terms and their environments, EID-SCE can be extended to support the measure/evaluation in a {complete, no overlap} manner whether a given proposal/ concept/feature in a MT and MDE related system is an improvement. Information formalized with EID-SCE has the advantages of high reusability for long term efficiency/correctness and sound extensibility, etc. Some results are also shown to demonstrate the elementary implementations. EID-SCE is expected to be beneficial to the design, implementation, and optimization of MT and MDE fundamentally.

Further investigation on the formalization of semantics is under way which involves perfecting EID-SCE with better mathematical foundations as is shown in Figure 17 (Duan, Y.,2008a). Based on EID-SCE, we propose to validate and provide formal/{complete, no unintended overlap} semantics for 4-layer UML metamodel (OMG,2007) and Logisch-Philosophische Abhandlung (Wittgenstein, L.,1921).,etc. We will also perfect EID-SCE by further fortifying the theoretical foundations and verifying with more industrial project practices.

ACKNOWLEDGMENT

This work was supported in part by a grant from the Brain Korea (BK) 21 Project. The author thanks to all lab members in SE Lab, POSTECH for precious help. The author wishes to thank deeply for the very insightful comments from anonymous reviewers.

REFERENCES

Atlee, J. M., France, R. B., Georg, G., Moreira, A., Rumpe, B., & Zschaler, B. (2007). Modeling in Software Engineering. In J. Knight, W. Emmerich & G. Rothermel (Eds.), *Software Engineering* (pp.113-114). USA: IEEE Computer Society.

Bar, T., & Whittle, J. (2006). On the Usage of Concrete Syntax in Model Transformation Rules. In I. Virbitskaite & A. Voronkov (Eds.), *Ershov Memorial Conference* (pp. 84-97). Heidelberg: Springer Press.

Barbero, M., Jouault, F., Gray, J., & Bézivin, J. (2007). A Practical Approach to Model Extension. In D.H. Akehurst, & R. F. Paige (Eds.), *Model Driven Architecture- Foundations and Applications* (pp.32-42). Heidelberg: Springer Press.

Bézivin, J., & Heckel, R. (2006). Guest Editorial to the Special Issue on Language Engineering for Model-Driven Software Development. *Software and System Modeling, 5*(3), 231–232. doi:10.1007/s10270-006-0028-6

Block, N., Flanagan, O. J., & Gzeldere, G. (1998). *The Nature of Consciousness: Philosophical Debates.* Cambridge, MA: MIT Press.

Bruel, J. M., Georg, G., Hußmann, H., Ober, I., Pohl, C., Whittle, J., & Zschaler, S. (2004). Models for Non-functional Aspects of Component-Based Software. In N. J. Nunes, B. Selic, A. R. Silva, & J. A.T. Álvarez (Eds.), *UML Modeling Languages and Applications* (pp. 62-66). Heidelberg: Springer Press.

Burmester, S., Giese, H., & Oberschelp, O. (2004). Hybrid UML Components for the Design of Complex Self-Optimizing Mechatronic Systems. In H. Araújo, A. Vieira, J. Braz, B. Encarnação, & M. Carvalho (Eds.), *International Conference on Informatics in Control, Automation and Robotics* (pp.222-229). Portugal: INSTICC Press.

Chen, P. P. (1976). The Entity-Relationship Model - Toward a Unified View of Data. *ACM Transactions on Database Systems, 1*(1), 9–36. doi:10.1145/320434.320440

Chitchyan, R., Rashid, A., Rayson, P., & Waters, R. (2007). Semantics-based composition for aspect-oriented requirements engineering. In B. M. Barry & O. Moor (Eds.), *International Conference on Aspect-Oriented Software Development* (pp.36-48). USA: ACM Press.

Damásio, C. V., Analyti, A., Antoniou, G., & Wagner, G. (2006). Supporting Open and Closed World Reasoning on the Web. In J.J. Alferes, J. Bailey, W. May, & U. Schwertel (Eds.), *Principles and Practice of Semantic Web Reasoning* (pp 149-163). Heidelberg: Springer Press.

Duan, Y. (2008a). Challenges of Model Transformation and a Solution Framework. In C. Rolland, O. Pastor, & J. L. Cavarero (Eds.), *Research Challenges in Information Science* (pp 247-252). USA: IEEE Computer Society.

Duan, Y. (2008b). A systemic approach towards recreating a unified semantics of numbers. In J.S. Pan, P. Shi, & C.S. Shieh (Eds.), Innovative Computing, Information and Control (pp 179). USA: IEEE Computer Society.

Duan, Y. (2008c). A Dualism Based Semantics Formalization Mechanism for Model Driven Engineering. In Y. Wang (Eds.), *Conference on Cognitive Informatics* (pp. 185-194). USA: IEEE Computer Society.

Duan, Y., Kang, K. C., & Gu, Y. (2008). A Solution Framework on Fundamentals in Model Transformation. In R. Y. Lee (Ed.), *Computer and Information Science* (pp. 355-360). USA: IEEE Computer Society.

Ellis, C., & Flaherty, M. (1992). *Investigating Subjectivity.* Newbury Park, CA: Sage Publications.

Feng, Y. (1983). *A History of Chinese Philosophy.* Beijing: The people's press.

Feyerabend, P. K., & Maxwell, G. (1966). *Mind, Matter and Method: Essays in Philosophy and Science in Honor of Herbert Feigl.* Minneapolis: University of Minnesota Press.

France, R. B., Bieman, J. M., & Cheng, B. H. C. (2006). Repository for Model Driven Development (ReMoDD). In T. Kühne (Ed.), *Models in Software Engineering, Workshops and Symposia at MoDELS 2006* (pp. 311-317). Heidelberg: Springer Press.

Guarino, N. (2004). Helping People (and Machines) Understanding Each Other. In R. Meersman & Z. Tari (Eds.), *On the Move to Meaningful Internet Systems* (pp. 599). Heidelberg: Springer Press.

Guarino, N., & Welty, C. (2000). Identity, Unity, and Individuation: Towards a Formal Toolkit for Ontological Analysis. In W. Horn (Ed.), *European Conference on Artificial Intelligence* (pp. 219-223). Amsterdam: IOS Press.

Hegel, G. W. F. (1807). *The Phenomenology of Mind*. Retrieved September 29, 2008, from http://www.class.uidaho.edu/mickelsen/ToC/Hegel%20Phen%20ToC.htm

Heidegger, M. (1969). *Identity and Difference*. New York: Harper & Row.

Hill, C. O., & Rosado, H. G. (2000). *Husserl or Frege? Meaning, Objectivity, and Mathematics*. Chicago: Open Court Publishing Company.

Hintikka, J., & Kulas, J. (1983). *The Game of Language: Studies in Game-Theoretical Semantics and Its Applications*. Dordrecht:D. Reidel Publishing Company.

Husserl, E. (1962). Phänomenologische Psychologie. In W. Biemel (Ed.), *Husserliana IX*. Den Haag: Martinus Nijhoff.

Kang, K. C., Cohen, S. G., Hess, J. A., Novak, W. E., & Peterson, A. S. (1990). *Feature-Oriented Domain Analysis (FODA) Feasibility Study*, SEI.

Kant, I. (1998). *Critique of Pure Reason*. P. Guyer & A.W. Wood (Trans.) (Eds.). Cambridge: Cambridge Univ. Press.

Kim, J. (1995). *Problems in the Philosophy of Mind*. Oxford Companion to Philosophy. Oxford: Oxford University Press.

Koch, C. (2004). *The Quest for Consciousness: A Neurobiological Approach*. Englewood, Colorado: Roberts and Company Publishers.

Markie, P. (2004). Rationalism vs. Empiricism. In E. N. Zalta (Ed.), *Stanford Encyclopedia of Philosophy*. Retrieved September 29, 2008, from http://plato.stanford.edu/entries/rationalism-empiricism/

McGreal, I. P. (1995). *"Gongsun Long" in Great Thinkers of the Eastern World*. New York: Harper Collins.

Mill, J. S. (1968). An Examination of Sir William Rowan Hamilton's Philosophy. In A.J. Ayer & R. Winch (Eds.), *British Empirical Philosophers*. New York: Simon and Schuster.

Moser, P. K., & Trout, J. D. (1995). *Contemporary Materialism: A Reader*. New York, Routledge.

OMG. (2002). *MOF 2.0 Query/Views/Transformation RFP*. OMG document ad/2002-04-10, from http://www.omg.org

OMG. (2007). *UML Infrastructure, v2.1.2*. Retrieved November 29, 2007, from http://www.omg.org/cgi-bin/doc?formal/07-11-03

Peirce, C. S. (1901). Truth and Falsity and Error (in part) (pp. 718–720). In J.M. Baldwin (Ed.), *Dictionary of Philosophy and Psychology* (Vol. 2). Reprinted, CP 5.565–573.

Quine, W. V. (1976). *The Ways of Paradox and Other Essays*. Cambridge: Harvard University Press.

Quine, W. V. O. (1951). Two Dogmas of Empiricism. *The Philosophical Review*, 60(1), 20–43. doi:10.2307/2181906

Russell, B. (1970). The Problem of Infinity Considered Historically. In W.C. Salmon (Ed.), *Zeno's Paradoxes*. Indianapolis/Cambridge: Hackett Publishing Co. Inc.

Sainsbury, R. M. (1995). *Paradoxes* (2nd ed.). Cambridge: Cambridge University Press.

Shi, Z., Li, Q., Shi, Z., & Shi, Z. (2006). Semantics-Biased Rapid Retrieval for Video Databases. In Y. Yao, Z. Shi, Y. Wang, & W. Kinsner (Eds.), *Conference on Cognitive Informatics* (pp. 634-639). USA: IEEE Computer Society.

Wang, Y. (2002). Keynote: On cognitive informatics. In Y. Wang et al. (Eds.), *Conference on Cognitive Informatics* (pp. 34–42). USA: IEEE Computer Society.

Wang, Y. (2006). Keynote: Cognitive informatics—Towards the future generation computers that think and feel. In Y. Yao, Z. Shi, Y. Wang, & W. Kinsner (Eds.), *Conference on Cognitive Informatics* (pp. 3-7). USA: IEEE Computer Society.

Wang, Y. (2007a). On Cognitive Informatics Foundations of Knowledge and Formal Knowledge Systems. In D. Zhang, Y. Wang, & W. Kinsner (Eds.), *Conference on Cognitive Informatics* (pp. 263-272). USA: IEEE Computer Society.

Wang, Y. (2007b). Formal Linguistics and the Deductive Grammar. In D. Zhang, Y. Wang, & W. Kinsner (Eds.), *Conference on Cognitive Informatics* (pp. 43-51). USA: IEEE Computer Society.

Wang, Y., Kinsner, W., & Zhang, D. (2009). Convergence of Cognitive Informatics and Cybernetics—Guest Editorial on Special Issue on Cybernetics and Cognitive Informatics. *IEEE Transactions on Systems, Man, and Cybernetics. Part B, Cybernetics, 39*(4), 1–5.

Whitehead, N. (1925). *Science and the Modern World.* Cambridge: Cambridge Univ. Press.

Wittgenstein, L. (1921). Logisch-Philosophische Abhandlung. In W. Ostwald (Ed.), *Annalen der Naturphilosophie* (vol. 14) (pp. 185-262).

Zhang, D. (2005). Fixpoint semantics for rule-base anomalies. In W. Kinsner, D. Zhang, Y. Wang & J. Tsai (Eds.), *Computer and Cognitive Informatics* (pp. 10-17). USA: IEEE Computer Society.

This work was previously published in International Journal of Software Science and Computational Intelligence, Volume 1, Issue 4, edited by Yingxu Wang, pp. 90-110, copyright 2009 by IGI Publishing (an imprint of IGI Global).

Section 3
Software Science

Chapter 14
Exploring the Cognitive Foundations of Software Engineering

Yingxu Wang
University of Calgary, Canada

Shushma Patel
London South Bank University, UK

ABSTRACT

It is recognized that software is a unique abstract artifact that does not obey any known physical laws. For software engineering to become a matured engineering discipline like others, it must establish its own theoretical framework and laws, which are perceived to be mainly relied on cognitive informatics and denotational mathematics, supplementing to computing science, information science, and formal linguistics. This paper analyzes the basic properties of software and seeks the cognitive informatics foundations of software engineering. The nature of software is characterized by its informatics, behavioral, mathematical, and cognitive properties. The cognitive informatics foundations of software engineering are explored on the basis of the informatics laws of software and software engineering psychology. A set of fundamental cognitive constraints of software engineering, such as intangibility, complexity, indeterminacy, diversity, polymorphism, inexpressiveness, inexplicit embodiment, and unquantifiable quality measures, is identified. The conservative productivity of software is revealed based on the constraints of human cognitive capacity.

INTRODUCTION

Software engineering is an applied discipline of software science that adopts engineering approaches, such as established methodologies, processes, architectures, measurement, tools, standards, organisation methods, management methods, quality assurance systems and the like, in the development of large-scale software seeking to result in high productivity, low cost, controllable quality, and measurable development schedule (Bauer, 1972; Dijkstra, 1976; Brooks, 1987;

DOI: 10.4018/978-1-4666-0261-8.ch014

McDermid, 1991; Perters and Pedrycz, 2000; Wang, 2007a; Wang and King, 2000). *Software Science* is a discipline that studies the theoretical framework of software as instructive and behavioral information, which can be embodied and executed by generic computers in order to create expected system behaviors and machine intelligence (Wang, 2007a, 2009a). The relationship between software science and software engineering can be described as that software science is theoretical software engineering; while software engineering is applied software science.

The object under study in software engineering and software science are software and program systems, which are a set of behavioral instructions for implementing a certain architectural layout of data objects and for embodying a set of expected behaviors on a universal computer platform for a required application. Large-scale software systems are highly complicated systems that have never been handled by mankind in engineering disciplines. It is recognized that software is a unique abstract artifact that does not obey any known physical laws (McDermid, 1991; Hartmanis. 1994; Wang, 2007a). For software engineering to become a matured engineering discipline like others, it must establish its own theoretical framework and laws, which are perceived to be mainly relied on cognitive informatics (Wang, 2002a, 2003a, 2007b) and denotational mathematics (Wang, 2008a), supplementing to computing science (Gersting, 1982; Lewis and Papadimitriou, 1998), information science (Shannon. 1948; Bell, 1953; Goldman, 1953; Wang, 2002a, 2003a), and formal linguistics (Chomsky, 1957, 1965; Wang, 2007a).

This paper explores basic properties of software and cognitive foundations of software engineering. The nature of software and software engineering is explored in the facets of the informatics, behavioral, and mathematical properties. The cognitive informatics foundations of software engineering are sought on the basis of a set of informatics laws of software. The fundamental cognitive constraints of software engineering on intangibility, complexity, indeterminacy, diversity, polymorphism, inexpressiveness, inexplicit embodiment, and unquantifiable quality measures are elaborated. Based on the basic research, a set of cognitive informatics principles for software engineering is established, such as the conservative productivity of software constrained by human cognitive capacity, the cognitive characteristics of software engineering, software engineering psychology, the cognitive mechanism of skill transformation in software engineering, the cognitive foundations of software quality theories, and the cognitive complexity of software.

BASIC PROPERTIES OF SOFTWARE AND SOFTWARE ENGINEERING

The nature of software has been perceived quite differently in research and practice of computing and software engineering. Although in the IT and software industries, software is perceived broadly as a concrete product, there are three types of metaphors in perceiving the nature of software, known as the informatics, mathematics, and intelligent behavior metaphors. With the *product* metaphor, a number of manufacturing technologies and quality assurance principles were introduced into software engineering. However, the phenomenon, which we are facing almost the same problems in software engineering as we dealt with 40 years ago, indicates a deficiency of the manufacture and mass production based metaphors on software and its development. Therefore, the nature of software and software engineering need to be systematically investigated.

The Informatics Properties of Software

Information is the third essence in modeling the natural world supplementing to matter and energy.

According to cognitive informatics theory (Wang, 2002a, 2003a, 2007b), information is any property or attribute of entities in the natural world that can be abstracted, digitally represented, and mentally processed. Software is both behavioral information to designers and instructive information to computers. With the informatics metaphor, software may be perceived as follows.

Definition 1. *Software is a kind of coded and instructive information that describes an algebraic process system of software behaviors and architectures in computing.*

The above definition indicates a new way to explain the laws and properties that govern the behavior of software. In other words, the informatics metaphor provides a new approach to study the nature and basic properties of software in software engineering, which forms an important part of the cognitive informatics foundations of software engineering.

In conventional engineering disciplines, the common approach moves from abstract to concrete, and the final product is the physical realization of an abstract design. In software engineering, however, the approach is reversed. The final software product is the virtualization and abstraction, by binary streams, of a set of original real-world requirements. The only tangible part of a software implementation is its storage media or its run-time behaviors. This is probably the most unique feature of software engineering.

There are twelve fundamental informatics properties identified in cognitive informatics, as described in Table 1, which constrain the behaviors of software and its quality (Wang, 2006). Since software is an abstract artifact that can be modeled and characterized only by information, all the informatics properties are applicable to software and its developing processes in software engineering.

The Intelligent Behavioral Properties of Software

A software system, to some extent, can be perceived as a virtual agent of human brains, because it is created to do something repeatable, to extend human capability, reachability, or memory. Conventional machines are invented to extend human physical capability, while modern information processing machines, such as computers, communication networks, and robots, are developed for extending human intelligence, memory, and the capacity for information processing. Therefore, any machine that may implement a part of human behaviors and actions in information processing is significantly important.

It is recognized (Wang, 2007b, 2009b) that the basic approaches to implement intelligent behaviors can be classified as shown in Table 2, where software for computation is the third approach to simulate and implement the natural intelligence by programmed logic. This indicates that software is a partial implementation of the natural intelligence and human behaviors, and a subset of simulated human intelligent behaviors described by programmed instructive information. Therefore, software is the simulation and execution of human behaviors, and the extension of human capability, reachability, persistency, memory, and information processing speed.

For further explain the nature of software, the following three situations where a software system is needed may be considered.

Theorem 1. *The needs for software determined by the following three conditions are necessary and sufficient:*

a.   The *repeatability:* Software is required when one needs to do something for more than once.

Table 1. The cognitive informatics properties of software

No.	Informatics properties	Description
1	Abstract artifacts	Information is an abstract artifact that can be elicited from the physical entities of the natural world. New information may be derived based on existing information.
2	Cumulativeness	Information is not conservative but cumulative, because information may be generated, reproduced, destroyed, and cumulated. The cumulativeness of information is the most significant attribute of information that human beings rely on for evolution.
3	Lossless reusable	Information is the unique artifact that can be reused by multiple users at the same time without loss in quantity and degradation in quality.
4	Dimensionless	Information has no physical size. No matter how large or small of the physical entities, their abstract representations or the cognitive visual objects occupy a similar sight frame; only the resolutions may be different.
5	Weightless:	A direct corollary based on Property 4 is that the weight of information is always zero.
6	Transformability between I-M-E	According to the I-M-E model, the three basic essences of the world are predicated to be transformable between each other. Any discovery about the unknown transformability will result in a significant evolution in software engineering and information science.
7	Multiple representation forms	Information can be represented in multiple forms by different means of abstraction.
8	Multiple carrying media	Parallel to Property 7, information can be carried by various media. It is noteworthy that a certain media may carry one or more forms of information. Correspondingly, a given form of information may be carried by different media.
9	Multiple transmission forms	The possible transmission forms of information are passing, broadcasting, gathering, and networking. The fast development of the Internet indicates that networking is the most advanced form of communications.
10	Generality of sources	The sources of information are widely generic. Information is formed by the combination between physical entities, abstract objects, and relations between them. According to the Object-Attribute-Relation (OAR) Model (Wang, 2007c), most new information can be elicited from relations among objects.
11	Conservation of information entropy and thermal entropy	In any system, the sum of the information entropy and the thermal entropy is a constant.
12	Unique quality attributes	To model the quality of software and information, a set of informatics-based quality attributes such as completeness, correctness, consistency, properly representation, clearness, feasibility, and verifiability have been identified. From this new angle, software quality can be defined as the achievement of the above inherent attributes for software architecture, static and dynamic behaviors.

b. The *flexibility* or *programmability*: Software is required when one needs to repeatedly do something not exactly the same.

c. The *run-time determinability*: Software is required when one needs to flexibly do something by a series of choices on the basis of varying sequences of events determinable only at run-time.

Theorem 1 indicates that the above three situations, namely repeatability, flexibility, and runt-time determinability, form the necessary and sufficient conditions that warrant the requirement for a software solution in computing. Although repeatability is one of the most premier needs for a software solution, it is not the only sufficient condition for requiring software, because repeatability may also be implemented by wired logic or hardware. Therefore, the flexibility and run-time determinability, particularly the latter, are necessary and sufficient for the usage of software. The third situation may be also considered as the *non-determinism* at compile-time or design-time. This feature is the fundamental issue in computation that determines the complexity of programming.

Table 2. Approaches to Implement Intelligent Behaviors

No.	Means	Approach
1	Biological organisms	Naturally grown
2	Silicon automata	Wired
3	Information processors	Programmed
4	Other means	Hybrid

The Mathematical Properties of Software

The *mathematical metaphor* of software is widely adopted in computational science in which software is perceived as a mathematical entity or a stored programmed logic on computing hardware (von Neumann, 1946; Dijkstra, 1976; Lewis and Papadimitriou, 1998; Hartmanis, 1994; Hoare, 1969, 1986; Hoare et al., 1987; Wang, 2007a, 2008f, 2008k). A powerful concept toward the understanding of the nature of software, introduced by C.A.R. Hoare, is the term *process* (Hoare, 1978), by which the behaviors of a software system can be perceived as a set of processes composed with given rules defined in an algebraic form. It is found that a process can be formally modeled by a set of embedded relational statements (Wang, 2006, 2007a). Based on them, a program can be formally modeled by a set of embedded relational processes.

Definition 2. *A process P is an embedded relational composition of a list of n meta-statements p_i and p_j, $1 \leq i < n$, $1 < j \leq m = n+1$, according to certain composing relations r_{ij}, i.e.:*

$$P = \underset{i=1}{\overset{n-1}{R}}(p_i \ r_{ij} \ p_j), j = i+1$$

$$= (...(((p_1) \ r_{12} \ p_2) \ r_{23} \ p_3) ... r_{n-1,n} \ p_n) \tag{1}$$

where the big-R notation (Wang, 2008b) is adopted that describes the nature of processes as the building blocks of programs.

With the formal process model as defined above, a generic mathematical model of programs can be derived below.

Definition 3. *A program $\wp$ is a composition of a finite set of m processes according to the time-, event-, and interrupt-based process dispatching rules of RTPA, i.e.:*

$$\wp = \underset{k=1}{\overset{m}{R}}(@ e_k \hookrightarrow P_k). \tag{2}$$

Definitions 2 and 3 indicate that a program is naturally an *embedded relational algebraic* entity, where a statement *s* in a program is an instantiation of a meta-instruction of a programming language that executes a basic unit of coherent function and leads to a predictable behavior.

Theorem 2. *The Embedded Relational Model (ERM) states that a software system or a program $\wp$ is a set of complex embedded relational processes, in which all previous processes of a given process form the context of the current process, i.e.:*

$$\wp = \underset{k=1}{\overset{m}{R}} (@ e_k \hookrightarrow P_k)$$
$$= \underset{k=1}{\overset{m}{R}} [@ e_k \hookrightarrow \underset{i=1}{\overset{n-1}{R}}(p_i(k) \ r_{ij}(k) \ p_j(k))], j = i+1 \tag{3}$$

Proof. *Theorem 2 can be directly proven on the basis of Definitions 2 and 3. Substituting P_k in Definition 3 with Eq. 1, a generic program $\wp$ obtains the form as a series of embedded relational processes as presented in Theorem 2.*

The ERM model presented in Theorem 2 reveals that a program is a finite and nonempty set of embedded binary relations between a current statement and *all previous ones* that formed the *semantic context* or environment of computing. Theorem 2 provides a unified mathematical model of software, which is a formalization of the well accepted but informal process metaphor for software systems in computing.

According to Theorem 2, a program can be reduced to the composition of a finite set of *k* processes at the component level. Then, each of the processes can be further reduced to the composition of a finite set of *n* statements at the bottom level. The definitions, syntaxes, and formal semantics of each of the meta-processes and process relations may be referred to RTPA. A complex process and a program can be derived from the meta-processes by the set of algebraic process relations.

A general taxonomy of the usages of computational mathematics can be derived on the basis of their relations with natural languages. It is recognized that languages are the basic means of thinking (Chomsky, 1957, 1965). Although they can be rich, complex, and powerfully descriptive, natural languages share the common and basic mechanisms known as *to be, to have,* and *to do* (Wang, 2007a, 2008a). All mathematical means and forms, in general, are an abstract description of these three categories of human or system behaviors and their common rules. Taking this view, mathematical logic may be perceived as the abstract means for describing 'to be' expressions, set theory for describing 'to have,' and functions for describing 'to do.' This is a fundamental view toward the formal description and modeling of human and system behaviors in general, and software behaviors in particular.

Table 3 summarizes the usages of classic and denotational mathematics, which presents a fundamental view toward the modeling and expression of natural and machine intelligence in general, and software system in particular. Table 3 also indicates that only the logic- and set-based approaches are inadequate to deal with the entire problems in complex software and intelligent systems.

FUNDAMENTAL COGNITIVE CONSTRAINTS OF SOFTWARE ENGINEERING

Software engineering is a unique and probably the most complicated engineering discipline with fundamental cognitive, organizational, and resources constraints. These constraints are inherent due to its intangibility, intricate inner connections, the cognitive difficulty of software and their dependency on systems, diversity, and human. The study on the fundamental constraints of software engineering is helpful to: a) Understand the fundamental problems in software engineering, b) Guide the development of software engineering theories and methodologies, and c) Evaluate newly proposed software engineering theories, principles, and techniques.

Definition 4. The cognitive constraints of software engineering are a set of innate cognitive attributes of software and the nature of the problems

Table 3. Basic expressive power and mathematical means in system modeling

Basic expressive power in system modeling	Mathematical means		Usage
	Classic mathematics	Denotational mathematics	
To *be*	Logic	Concept algebra	Identify *objects* and *attributes*
To *have*	Set theory	System algebra	Describe *relations* and *possession*
To *do*	Functions	RTPA	Describe *status* and *behaviors*

in software engineering that create the intricate relations of software objects and make software engineering inheritably difficult.

The following subsections identify and elaborate eight cognitive constraints of software engineering, such as intangibility, complexity, indeterminacy, diversity, polymorphism, inexpressiveness, inexplicit embodiment, and unquantifiable quality measures.

a.   Intangibility

Definition 5. *Intangibility is a basic cognitive constraint of software engineering that states software is an abstract artifact, which is not constituted by physical objects or presence, and is difficult to be defined or expressed.*

The intangibility of software refers to all aspects of software and its development. That is, none of the entire software engineering processes, such as problem representation, requirements description, design, and implementation, is tangible.

b.   Complexity

Definition 6. *Complexity is a basic cognitive constraint of software engineering that states software is innately complex and its intricate internal connections and external couplings make it extremely difficult to be expressed or cognized.*

The complexity of software refers to the complexities of its architectures, behaviors, and environments. The *architectural complexity* is the innate complexity of a software system with its data objects and their external/internal representations. The *behavioral complexity* is the complexity of a software system with its processes and their inputs/outputs. The *environmental complexity* is the complexity of a software system with its platform, related interacting processes, and users.

The most unique feature of software complexity is its intricate interconnection among components, functions, operations, and data objects. A small change in one place may result in multiple and unpredictable consequences in other places. This type of problem propagation due to intricate interconnection and coupling is a major challenge for system architects, programmers, and managers in software engineering.

The integration of a large-scale software system may easily result in a situation where no single person in the team may understand the system. During this phase, the project leader and system architect may lack sufficient detail knowledge about the implementation of the system, while individual programmers may lack the knowledge of a holistic view that treats the system as a whole with interfaces to other subsystems and components. This is a great challenge and a critical phase of human comprehension capability that often results in major failures after almost all resources have been exhausted in large-scale software projects.

c.   Indeterminacy

Definition 7. *Indeterminacy is a basic cognitive constraint of software engineering that states the events, behaviors, or their sequence of occurrence in a software system are not fully determinable on the basis of a given algorithm during design time. Instead, some of them may only be determinable until run-time.*

The indeterminacy constraint indicates that, in general, a large portion of software behaviors and/ or their sequence of occurrence are unpredictable at design time or compile time. Although the behavior space and all possible events are predictable, the order of events and the behaviors triggered by the chain of events will be greatly varying at run-time. Therefore, indeterminacy makes software design, implementation, and testing extremely difficult, because it results in a huge behavior space for a given software system, and its complete verification via testing are impossible sometimes.

Dijkstra discussed the special case of indeterminacy in automata where a given event to a finite state machine in a context may trigger no action because the machine cannot decide explicitly which action should be executed based on the given input and current state of the machine (Dijkstra, 1968b/1975). This kind of phenomena occurs in operating system, agent systems, complier design, and real-time systems, where additional information for decision making or an arbitrary decision needs to be adopted in the machine.

d. Diversity

Definition 8. *Diversity is a basic cognitive constraint of software engineering that states the great variety of software in terms of types, styles, architectures, behaviors, platforms, application domains, implementation techniques, usability, reliability, and quality.*

The extremely wide application domain of software dominates the cognitive complexity of software engineering and the knowledge requirement for architects and programmers who design and implement software systems. The diversity of software also refers to its types, which can be classified into system software, tools (compilers, code generators, communication/networking software, database management systems, and test software), and application software. The latter can be further categorized into transaction processing software, distributed software, real-time software, databases, and web-based software. It is noteworthy that there are fundamental differences between the technical, systematic, economic, organizational properties of system software and application software (Wang, 2007a).

e. Polymorphism

Definition 9. *Polymorphism is a basic cognitive constraint of software engineering that states the approaches and styles of both software design and implementation are multifaceted and polyglottic.*

Definition 9 indicates that the potential solution space of software engineering can be very large because both design and implementation have a great many options. According to the problem solving theory in cognitive informatics, software design and development is an open-end problem, which is similar to a creation process, where both possible solutions and paths that lead to one of the solutions are unknown and highly optional (Wang, 2008c; Wang and Chiew, 2008).

As that of the polysolvability for design, the polymorphism of software implementation refers to the cognitive phenomenon that approaches to implement a given design are not necessarily single. Many factors influence the solution space such as programming languages, target machine languages, coding styles, data models, memory allocations, and executing platforms. Any change among these factors may result in a different implementation of a software system.

Theorem 3. *Polymorphous solutions state that the solution space SS of software engineering for a given problem is a product of the number of all design options D and the available implementation options I, i.e.:*

$$SS = D \bullet I \tag{4}$$

Therefore, the size of *SS*, N_{ss}, is determined by the numbers of both *D* and *I*, i.e.:

$$N_{SS} = N_D \bullet N_I \tag{5}$$

On the basis of Theorem 3, a basic software engineering principle can be derived as follows.

Corollary 1. *It is hard to prove technically and/ or economically a certain software system is the* *optimal solution rather than a sound one constrained by the huge size of the solution space, which is known as the no number one principle in software engineering.*

The polymorphic characteristic of the solution space of software engineering contributes greatly to the complexity of both theories and practices of software engineering.

f.   Inexpressiveness

Software system requirements and specifications need to be essentially expressed in three aspects known as the *architecture*, *static behaviors*, and *dynamic behaviors* of the system.

Definition 10. *Inexpressiveness is a basic cognitive constraint of software engineering that states software architectures and behaviors are inherently difficult to be expressed, modeled, represented, and quantified formally and rigorously.*

Because software represents a set of instructive behavioral information, unless the behaviors and the underpinning architecture can be expressed rigorously and explicitly, no developer and machine may understand the requirement correctly and completely. Therefore, a new form of denotational mathematics (Wang, 2007a) is needed for system specification and refinement, of which typical paradigms are concept algebra (Wang, 2008g), system algebra (Wang, 2008h), and Real-Time Process Algebra (RTPA) (Wang, 2008i, 2008j).

g. Inexplicit Embodiment

Because software is intangible, the only way to make it embodied is to adopt more expressive means such as formal notations, programming languages, and visual diagrams.

Definition 11. *Inexplicit embodiment is a basic cognitive constraint of software engineering that*

states architectures and behaviors of software systems should be explicitly described by coherent symbolic notations in order to be processed and executed by computers.

According to the Hierarchical Abstraction Model (HAM) of software engineering (Wang, 2008d), any notation or diagram that cannot explicitly describe the architecture and behaviors of software systems, or that highly depends on human interpretation of implied instructions, is inadequate. According to the explicit criterion, diagram-based techniques may be useful for describing conceptual models of software systems particularly for nonprofessionals, but it is unlikely to be an expressive and rigorous basis for future automatic code generation systems, because too much design and implementation information are implied rather than explicitly expressed. Although, machines are capable of carrying out translations between explicit specifications and code in order to improve software productivity, no machine may help to extend inadequate system specifications or to comprehend inexplicit system designs implied in the software architectural and behavioral information.

h.   Unquantifiable Quality Measures

Quality is a generic measure of the degree of excellence of a product or service against a given standard. More specifically, quality is a common attribute of any product or service that characterizes the quantity of both utility and durability of the product or service. Determined by the complexity, diversity, and polymorphism constraints discussed earlier, the quality of software is a multifaceted entity and some facets of it are application specific.

Definition 12. *Unquantifiable quality measures are a basic cognitive constraint of software engineering that states the model of software quality has intricate facets and is difficult to be quantitatively modeled and measured.*

Software quality can be perceived from a relative point of view as the conformity of a software system to its specifications (design models). Therefore, software quality is inversely proportional to the differences between the behaviours and performance of a software system and those required in the specifications. However, many quality attributes of software, such as design quality, usability, implementation efficiency, and reliability, cannot be quantified, thus immeasurable.

A basic quality principle is "no measurement, no quality control." The factor that it is impossible to measure all quality attributes of a large-scale software system indicates that we are not completely in control of the development of such systems. Some qualitative or informal validation and evaluation techniques, such as review and prototyping (Boehm et al., 1984; McDermid, 1991; Arnowitz et al., 2006), are adopted in software engineering. Practitioners and users seem to be used to this situation. Therefore, measurement theories and methodologies for software systems had never been a central focus in software engineering, particularly because of its inherent difficulty in this area (Wang, 2003c).

Definition 13. *Quality Q is a generic and collective attribute of a product, a service, or a system that is proportional to both its average utility U and the available duration T of the utility, i.e.:*

$$Q = U \cdot T \; [Fh] \qquad (6)$$

where the unit of utility is function (F), and the unit of duration is hour (h), and these result in the unit of quality as Function-hour, shortly Fh.

According to Definition 13, for a given product, service, or system, there is no quality if there is a lack of either utility ($U = 0$) or availability of the utility ($T = 0$). The quality given in Definition 13 is the average quality with a static view. A more generic form of quality for representing the dynamic aspect of quality as a function of time is given below.

Definition 14. *A generic dynamic utility function U(t) is an inverse exponential function over time, i.e.:*

$$U(t) = U(1 - e^{t-T}) \; [F] \qquad (7)$$

where both U and T are a positive constant.

With the above definition of dynamic utility $U(t)$, the value of the dynamic quality can be determined by the following principle.

Theorem 4. *The integrated quality with a dynamic utility, Q(t), is an integral of the utility function U(t) over the entire lifecycle of the utility [0, T], i.e.:*

$$
\begin{aligned}
Q(t) &= \int_0^T U(t)dt \\
&= \int_0^T U(1 - e^{t-T})dt \\
&= U(e^{-T} + T - 1) \\
&= UT - U(1 - e^{-T}) \\
&= Q - U(1 - e^{-T}) \; [Fh]
\end{aligned}
\qquad (8)
$$

where U is the initial quality of a product, service, or system.

Theorem 4 shows that the integrated quality of a dissimilating utility system or product is always smaller than that of constant utility.

COGNITIVE INFORMATICS PRINCIPLES FOR SOFTWARE ENGINEERING

The cognitive constraints of software engineering as discussed in Section 3 identified the primary constraints of software engineering. On perceiving the cognitive properties of software as instructive intelligent behaviors, this section elaborates the cognitive informatics principles for software engineering, encompassing those of the conservative productivity, cognitive characteristics, software engineering psychology, cognitive skill transformation, quality assurance, and cognitive complexity of software.

The Conservative Productivity in Software Engineering

A profound discovery in software engineering is that the productivity of software development is conservative due to the cognitive mechanism in which abstract artifacts need to be represented physiologically in the brain via naturally grown neural synaptic connections in the brain (Wang and Wang, 2006). In other words, software development productivity is constrained by natural laws rather than by human subjective intentions. The fact that before any program is composed, an internal abstract model must be created inside the brain (Wang, 2007c) reveals the most fundamental constraint of software engineering, i.e., software is generated and represented in the brain before it can be transferred into the computer. Because the growth rate of the human neural system is naturally constrained, as described by the 24-hour law (Wang and Wang, 2006), it is very hard to dramatically improve the productivity of software development.

The above theory is supported by empirical data and experience. According to the statistics of software engineering literature (Albrecht, 1979; Boehm, 1987; Jones, 1981, 1986; Livermore, 2005), the average productivity of software development was about 1,300 LOC/person-year in the 1970s, 2,500 LOC/person-year in the 1980s, and 3,000 LOC/person-year in the 1990s, where management, quality assurance, and supporting activities are included, and LOC is the unit of the symbolic size of software in terms of Line of Code. It is obvious that the productivity in software engineering has not been increased remarkably in the

last four decades independent of the advances in programming languages and tools. In other words, no matter what kind of programming language is used, as long as they are for human programming, there is no difference in principle. This assertion can be proved by asking the following question: Have you ever known an author in literature who is productive because he/she writes in a particular natural language?

Productivity of software development is the key to cope with all the cognitive, time, and resources constraints in software engineering, because the other constraints may be overcome as a result of the improvement of software engineering productivity.

Lemma 1. The key approach to improve software development productivity are:

a. To explicitly express software architectures and behaviors in *denotational mathematics*;
b. To investigate the theories of rational software *engineering organization*; and
c. To develop tools that enable *automatic software code generation* based on the denotational system models.

The most significant and unique characteristic of software engineering lays on the need for the contemporary denotational mathematics in order to rigorously and explicitly model the architectures and behaviors of software systems and to reduce the cognitive complexity of software engineering, which are challenging the limitation of human cognitive capacity in large-scale software development.

The Cognitive Characteristics of Software Engineering

The following cognitive characteristics dominate the innate difficulty of software engineering: a) The inherent complexity and diversity; b) The difficulty of establishing and stabilizing requirements; c) The changeability or malleability of software; d) The abstraction and intangibility of software products; e) The requirement of varying problem domain knowledge; f) The non-deterministic and poly-solvability in design; g) The polyglotics and polymorphism in implementation; and h) The dependability of interactions between software, hardware, and human beings.

In addition to the fundamental cognitive characteristics, a set of domain specific principles of software engineering has been identified, which determine the difficulty of software development and a broad knowledge requirement for software engineers, as follows: a) Problem domain is infinite that includes all application areas of all existing science and engineering disciplines; b) Software engineering is design intensive opposed to repetitive and mass production; c) Application development is a one-off activity; d) Development processes are relatively stable and repetitive; e) A software implementation is only one of all possible solutions for a real-world problem on the basis of constraints and tradeoffs; and f) Software engineering needs new forms of denotational mathematics that are different from current analytic ones (Wang, 2007a, 2008a).

The most significant and unique characteristic of software engineering relies on the fact that its problem domain is infinite, because it encompasses almost all domains in the real world, from scientific problems and real-time control to word processing and games. It is significantly larger than any specific and limited problem domain of other engineering disciplines. This stems from the notion of a computer as a universal intelligent machine, and is a feature fundamentally dominating the complexity in engineering design and implementation of greatly varying software systems.

Software Engineering Psychology

Software engineering psychology is a transdisciplinary branch of software engineering and cognitive psychology. It is perceived that the nature of software and software engineering is in many ways closer to cognitive psychology than engineering and technology, because software is intangible and complicated abstract artifacts created by human brains and the best software often takes advantages of human creativity (Weinberg, 1971; Wang, 2007a).

A set of personality traits in software engineering psychology is identified for software engineers (Wang, 2007a), such as:

- Multilayered abstract-level thinking
- Imagination of static descriptions in terms of dynamic behaviors
- Organization capability
- Cooperative and team working attitude
- Long-term focus of attentions
- Preciseness
- Reliability
- Expressive capability in expressions and communications

Software engineering psychology identifies two types of programmers in a psychological view: the *realistic* and *idealistic* ones. The former may be suitable for coding, testing, and quality control; while the latter are good at solution seeking, Graphic User Interface (GUI) design, and carrying out tasks as system analysts.

It is interesting to contrast and analyze the differences between professionals and amateurs in software engineering. Professional software engineers are persons with professional cognitive models and knowledge on software engineering. They are trained with: a) Fundamental knowledge that governs software and software engineering practices; b) Basic principles and laws of software engineering; c) Proven algorithms; d) Problem domain knowledge; e) Problem solving experience; f) Program developing tools/environments; g) Solid programming skills in multiple programming languages; and h) A global and insightful view on system development, including its required functionalities as well as exception handling and fault-tolerance strategies. However, amateurish programmers are persons who know only one or a couple of programming languages but lack formal training characterized as follows: a) Ad hoc structure of programming knowledge; b) Limited programming experience and skills; c) Eager to try what is directly required before a system architecture is designed; and d) Tend to focus on details without a global and systematic view. Therefore, professional trainings on the foundations of software engineering are a key to improve the qualification of software engineers.

Cognitive Skill and Experience Transformation in Software Engineering

In discussing "what makes a good software engineer" in a panel, Marcia Finfer (1989) believed: "the answer, in my opinion, is simply the combination of both innate skill and significant experience in building real systems against a set of functional and performance requirements and a given budget and schedule." This shows that professional experience is a primary factor of software engineers, where an experience of problem complexity beyond 5,000LOC is a necessary benchmark (Wang, 2007a). Also, the possession of fundamental principles and laws of software engineering is essential towards excellent software engineers.

According to the cognitive informatics model (Wang, 2007c), although knowledge can be acquired indirectly in learning, experiences and skills must be obtained directly by empirical actions. The acquisition of professional skills may be described by a cognitive process. For example, in a complex building, if a newcomer is guided through once, he or she may still have difficulty

to manage to remember the ways in the beginning. Because an abstract model of the building, known as the cognitive map, has yet to be built in his/her Long-Term Memory (LTM) and which takes time according to the 24-hour law of memory (Wang and Wang, 2006). The acquisition of skills for driving is another example that explains skill acquisition according to cognitive informatics principles.

It is curious to seek what made skill and experience transfer hard in software engineering, because it is observed that programming skills and software engineering experiences cannot be transferred directly from person to person without hands on practice. The means of experience repository in software engineering can be categorized into the following types: a) Best practices; b) Know-how; c) Lessons learnt; d) Failure reports; and e) New technology trial reports. All the above items of software engineering experience seem to be hard to gain indirectly by reading because the following reasons: (a) The human brain has no direct knowledge transfer mechanism. Each brain is determined by the differences of unique individual's physiology, cognitive style, personality, and environment. Therefore, any experience or practical knowledge as new information has to be personally acquired and represented as an cognitive Object-Attribute-Relation (OAR) model in the brain (Wang, 2007c), which is linked to existing knowledge in the hierarchical neural clusters of long-term memory; (b) The only way for hand-on skill transformation is learn by doing, or trial and error; and (c) People, usually, have to experience mistakes in order to learn and remember a specific experience. In addition, it is recognized that each brain is sufficiently unique (Wang, 2007a) because of individual physiological differences, cognitive style differences, personality differences, and learning environment differences.

Therefore, although computers as external or extended memory and information processing systems for the brain provide a new possibility for people to learn things faster than ever, the internal representation of abstract knowledge or active behaviors such as skills and experiences must still rely on wired inter-connections among neural clusters in the brain.

Theoretical Foundations of Quality Assurance in Software Engineering

On the basis of various fault-tolerant measures (Wang, 2008e), the following statistical properties of human errors may be observed.

Theorem 5. *The statistical properties of human errors are as follows:*

a. *Oddness*: Although individuals make different errors in performing tasks, the chance of making a single error for a given task is most of the cases than that of multiple errors.
b. *Independence*: Different individuals have different error patterns in performing the same task.
c. *Randomness*: Different individuals do not often make the same error at the same times in performing tasks.

Properties (a) through (c) reveal the random nature of human errors on object, action, space, and time in performing tasks in a group.

Corollary 2. *The random nature of human errors in task performing in a group is determined by the statistical properties that the occurrences of same errors by different individuals are most likely at different times.*

The findings as stated in Theorem 5 and Corollary 2 form a theoretical foundation for fault-tolerance and quality assurance in software engineering. The model indicates that human errors may be prevented from happening or be corrected after their presence in a coordinative group context by means of peer reviews.

Theorem 6. *The n-fold error reduction structure states that the error rate of a work product can be reduced up to n folds from the average error rate of individuals r_e in a coordinative group via n-nary peer reviews based on the random nature of error distributions and independent nature of error patterns of individuals, i.e.:*

$$R_e = \prod_{k=1}^{n} r_e(k) \tag{9}$$

Example 1. *A software engineering project is developing by a group of four programmers. Given the individual error rates of the four group members as: $r_e(1) = 10\%$, $r_e(2) = 8\%$, $r_e(3) = 20\%$, and $r_e(4) = 5\%$, estimate the error rates of final software by adopting the following quality assurance techniques: (a) Pairwise reviews between Programmers 1 vs. 2 and Programmers 3 vs. 4; and (b) 4-nary reviews between all group members.*

a. The pairwise reviews between Programmers 1-2 and Programmers 3-4 will result in the following error rates R_{e1} and R_{e2}:

$$R_{e1} = \prod_{k=1}^{2} r_e(k)$$
$$= 10\% \cdot 8\%$$
$$= 0.8\%$$

$$R_{e2} = \prod_{k=3}^{4} r_e(k)$$
$$= 20\% \cdot 5\%$$
$$= 1.0\%$$

b. The 4-nary reviews between Programmers 1 through 4 will yield the following error rate R_{e3}:

$$R_{e3} = \prod_{k=1}^{4} r_e(k)$$
$$= 10\% \cdot 8\% \cdot 20\% \cdot 5\%$$
$$= 0.008\%$$

Theorem 6 and Example 1 explain why multiple peer reviews may greatly reduce the probability of errors in program development and software engineering. Theorem 6 is also applicable in the academic community, where peer-reviewed results may virtually prevent any mistake in a final article before its publication.

In software engineering quality assurance, a four-level quality assurance system is needed for certain critical software functions and projects as shown in Table 4.

Example 2. For a given program reviewed according to the four-level quality assurance system as shown in Table 4, assuming $r_e(10) = 10\%$, $r_e(2) = 5\%$, $r_e(3) = 2\%$, and $r_e(4) = 10\%$, estimate the quality of the final result of this program.

According to Eq. 9, the 4-nary quality assurance system may yield an expected error rate R_{e4}:

$$R_{e4} = \prod_{k=1}^{4} r_e(k)$$
$$= 10\% \cdot 5\% \cdot 2\% \cdot 10\%$$
$$= 0.001\%$$

The results indicate that the error rate of the above system has been significantly reduced from initial 100bugs/kLOC to 1bug/kLOC. This demonstrates that the hierarchical organization form for software system reviews can greatly increase the quality of software development and significantly decrease the requirement for individual capability and error rates in software engineering.

The Cognitive Complexity of Software

One of the central problems in software engineering is the inherited complexity. Software complexity may be classified into computational (time, space), symbolic (LOC), structural (control flow, cyclomatic), functional (function points, cognitive complexity), and system complexity (McCabe, 1976; Halstead, 1977; Albrecht and Gaffney, 1983; Lewis and Papadimitriou, 1998; Hartmanis, 1994; Wang, 2009c).

In cognitive informatics, it is found that the functional complexity of software can be measured by its cognitive complexity, which is determined by the internal control flows known as the Basic Control Structures (BCS's) and its input and output (2007a).

Definition 15. Basic Control Structures (BCS's) are a set of essential flow control mechanisms that are used for building logical architectures of software.

Definition 16. The cognitive weight of software is the extent of difficulty or relative time and effort for comprehending a given piece of software modeled by a set of BCS's.

Table 4. The four-level quality assurance system of software engineering

Level	Checker	Means
1	Programmer	Self checking, module-level testing
2	Senior member	Peer review, module-level testing
3	Tester/ quality engineer	System-level testing, audit, review, quality evaluation
4	Manager	Quality review, deliver evaluation, customer survey

Table 5. Definitions of BCS's and equivalent cognitive weights (W$_i$)

Category	BCS	Structure	W$_i$	RTPA notation
Sequence	Sequence (SEQ)		1	$P \rightarrow Q$
Branch	If-then-[else] (ITE)		3	$(\blacklozenge expBL = T) \rightarrow P$ $\mid (\blacklozenge\sim) \rightarrow Q$
	Case (CASE)		4	$\blacklozenge \; expRT =$ $0 \rightarrow P_0$ $\mid 1 \rightarrow P_1$ $\mid ...$ $\mid n\text{-}1 \rightarrow P_{n\text{-}1}$ $\mid else \rightarrow \varnothing$
Iteration	For-do (R$_i$)		7	$\overset{n}{\underset{i=1}{R}} (P(i))$
	Repeat-until (R$_i$)		7	$\overset{T}{\underset{exp BL=F}{R}} (P)$
	While-do (R$_o$)		8	$\overset{F}{\underset{exp BL=T}{R}} (P)$
Embedment	Function call (FC)		7	$P \downarrow F$
	Recursion (REC)		11	$P \circlearrowleft P$
Concurrency	Parallel (PAR)		15	$P \parallel Q$
	Interrupt (INT)		22	P $\parallel \odot (@eS \nearrow Q \searrow \odot)$

There are only 10 BCS's in software structures as shown in Table 5. The cognitive weight of each of the BCS's may be quantitatively measured and calibrated. In Table 5, the relative cognitive weights (W$_i$) for determining a BCS' functional-ity and complexity are calibrated based on psychological experiments and empirical studies in cognitive informatics and software engineering (Wang, 2007a).

Substantial findings in the study on the cognitive complexity properties of software have been that: a) the cognitive complexity of software in design and comprehension are dependent on three factors – internal processing structures as well as numbers of inputs and outputs; b) The cognitive complexity measure is more robust than the symbolic size measures of software (such as LOC), and independent from languages/implementations; c) Cognitive complexity provides a foundation for cross-platform analysis of complexities and sizes of both software specifications and implementations for either design or comprehension purposes in software engineering; d) Although there are similar sized software systems in term of symbolic sizes in LOC, their functional sizes in cognitive complexity would be dramatically different; and e) When the symbolic size of software systems grows above 100LOC, its cognitive complexity could be increased exponentially due to intricate interconnections of highly complicated BCS's (Wang and Shao, 2003).

CONCLUSION

Beveridge (1957) once questioned that "Elaborate apparatus plays an important part in the science of today, but I sometimes wonder if we are not inclined to forget that the most important instrument in research must always be the mind of man." Because software engineering involves intensive human creative work, the studies on the nature of software and the cognitive informatics foundations of software engineering addresses a set of central and essential problems for software engineering and software science.

This paper has explored the cognitive characteristics of software and software engineering practice. As a result, a synergy between software engineering, computer science, and cognitive informatics is established. The nature of software has been modeled by a set of properties of informatics, mathematics, and intelligent behaviors.

The cognitive informatics foundations of software engineering have been developed by a set of cognitive constraints and principles. The psychological requirements for software engineers have been identified, such as abstract-level thinking, imagination of dynamic behaviors with static descriptions, organization capability, cooperative attitude in team work, long-time focus of attentions, preciseness, reliability, and expressive capability in communications. A set of key findings in this work on the cognitive informatics foundations of software engineering has been presented, which cover the cognitive constraints of software engineering, the conservative productivity of software development, cognitive complexity of software, and the cognitive informatics theory of software quality assurance.

ACKNOWLEDGMENT

This work is partially sponsored by the Natural Sciences and Engineering Research Council of Canada (NSERC). The authors would like to thank the anonymous reviewers for their valuable suggestions and comments on this work.

REFERENCES

Albrecht, A. J. (1979), Measuring Application Development Productivity, Proc. *of IBM Applications Development Joint SHARE/GUIDE Symposium*, Oct., 83-92.

Albrecht, A. J., & Gaffney, J. E. (1983). Software Function, Source Lines of Code, and Development Effort Prediction: A Software Science Validation. *IEEE Transactions on Software Engineering*, 9(6), 639–648. doi:10.1109/TSE.1983.235271

Arnowitz, J., Arent, M., & Berger, N. (2006). *Effective Prototyping for Software Makers*. Morgan Kaufmann.

Bauer, F.L (1972), Software Engineering, *Information Processing*, 71.

Bell, D. A. (1953). *Information Theory*. London: Pitman.

Beveridge, W. I. (1957). *The Art of Scientific Investigation*. UK: Random House Trade Paperbacks.

Boehm, B. W. (1987). Improving Software Productivity. *IEEE Computer*, *20*(9), 43. doi:10.1109/MC.1987.1663694

Boehm, B. W., Gray, T. E., & Seewaldt, T. (1984). Prototyping Versus Specifying: A Multiproject Experiment. *IEEE Transactions on Software Engineering*, *10*(3), 290–302. doi:10.1109/TSE.1984.5010238

Brooks, F. P. (1987). No Silver Bullet: Essence and Accidents of Software Engineering. *IEEE Computer*, *20*(4), 10–19. doi:10.1109/MC.1987.1663532

Chomsky, N. (1957). *Syntactic Structures*. The Hague: Mouton.

Chomsky, N. (1965). *Aspects of the Theory of Syntax*. Cambridge, MA: MIT Press.

Dijkstra, E. W. (1976). *A Discipline of Programming*. Englewood Cliffs, NJ: Prentice-Hall.

Gersting, J. L. (1982). *Mathematical Structures for Computer Science*. San Francisco: W. H. Freeman & Co.

Goldman, S. (1953). *Information Theory*. Englewood Cliffs, NJ, USA: Prentice-Hall.

Halstead, M. H. (1977). *Elements of Software Science*. New York: Elsevier North -Holland.

Hartmanis, J. (1994). On Computational Complexity and the Nature of Computer Science, 1994 Turing Award Lecture. *Communications of the ACM*, *37*(10), 37–43. doi:10.1145/194313.214781

Hoare, C. A. R. (1969). An Axiomatic Basis for Computer Programming. *Communications of the ACM*, *12*(10), 576–580. doi:10.1145/363235.363259

Hoare, C. A. R. (1978). Communicating Sequential Processes. *Communications of the ACM*, *21*(8), 666–677. doi:10.1145/359576.359585

Hoare, C. A. R. (1986). *The Mathematics of Programming*. Oxford, UK: Clarendon Press.

Hoare, C. A. R., Hayes, I. J., He, J., Morgan, C. C., Roscoe, A. W., & Sanders, J. W. (1987, Aug.). Laws of programming. *Communications of the ACM*, *30*(8), 672–686. doi:10.1145/27651.27653

Jones, C. (1981). *Programming Productivity – Issues for the Eighties*. Silver Spring, MD: IEEE Press.

Jones, C. (1986). *Programming Productivity*. NY: McGraw-Hill Book Co.

Lewis, H. R., & Papadimitriou, C. H. (1998). *Elements of the Theory of Computation* (2nd ed.). Englewood Cliffs, NJ: Prentice Hall International.

McCabe, T. H. (1976). A Complexity Measure. *IEEE Transactions on Software Engineering*, *SE-2*(6), 308–320. doi:10.1109/TSE.1976.233837

McDermid, J. A. (Ed.). (1991). *Software Engineer's Reference Book*. Oxford, UK: Butterworth-Heinemann Ltd.

Peters, J. F., & Pedrycz, W. (2000). *Software Engineering: An Engineering Approach*. NY: John Wiley & Sons, Inc.

Shannon, C. E. (1948), A Mathematical Theory of Communication, *Bell System Technical Journal*, Vol.27, pp.379–423 and 623–656.

von Neumann, J. (1946). The Principles of Large-Scale Computing Machines. *IEEE Annals of the History of Computing*, *3*(3), 263–273. doi:10.1109/MAHC.1981.10025

Wang, Y. (2000). *Software Engineering Processes: Principles and Applications, CRC Software Engineering Series* (*Vol. I*). USA: CRC Press.

Wang, Y. (2002a), Keynote, On Cognitive Informatics, *Proc. 1st IEEE Int. Conf. Cognitive Informatics (ICCI'02)*, IEEE CS Press, Calgary, Canada, Aug., 34–42.

Wang, Y. (2002b), The Real-Time Process Algebra (RTPA), *Annals of Software Engineering: An International Journal*, 14, USA, Oct., 235-274.

Wang, Y. (2003a), On Cognitive Informatics, *Brain and Mind. A Transdisciplinary Journal of Neuroscience and Neurophilosophy*, 4(2), 151-167.

Wang, Y. (2003b), Using Process Algebra to Describe Human and Software System Behaviors, *Brain and Mind: A Transdisciplinary Journal of Neuroscience and Neurophilosophy*, 4(2), pp. 199–213.

Wang, Y. (2003c), The Measurement Theory for Software Engineering, *Proc. 2003 Canadian Conference on Electrical and Computer Engineering* (CCECE'03), IEEE CS Press, Montreal, Canada, May, pp.1321-1324.

Wang, Y. (2006). On the Informatics Laws and Deductive Semantics of Software. *IEEE Transactions on Systems, Man and Cybernetics. Part C, Applications and Reviews*, 36(2), 161–171. doi:10.1109/TSMCC.2006.871138

Wang, Y. (2007a), *Software Engineering Foundations: A Transdisciplinary and Rigorous Perspective*, CRC Book Series in Software Engineering, Vol. II, Auerbach Publications, NY, USA, July.

Wang, Y. (2007b). The Theoretical Framework of Cognitive Informatics. *International Journal of Cognitive Informatics and Natural Intelligence*, 1(1), 1–27. doi:10.4018/jcini.2007010101

Wang, Y. (2007c). The OAR Model of Neural Informatics for Internal Knowledge Representation in the Brain. *International Journal of Cognitive Informatics and Natural Intelligence*, 1(3), 68–82. doi:10.4018/jcini.2007070105

Wang, Y. (2008a), *On Contemporary Denotational Mathematics for Computational Intelligence, Transactions of Computational Science*, 2, Springer, August, pp. 6-29.

Wang, Y. (2008b). On the Big-R Notation for Describing Iterative and Recursive Behaviors. *International Journal of Cognitive Informatics and Natural Intelligence*, 2(1), 17–28. doi:10.4018/jcini.2008010102

Wang, Y. (2008c), On Cognitive Foundations of Creativity and the Cognitive Process of Creation, *Proc. 7th IEEE International Conference on Cognitive Informatics* (ICCI'08), Stanford University, CA, USA, IEEE CS Press, August, pp. 104-113.

Wang, Y. (2008d), A Hierarchical Abstraction Model for Software Engineering, *Proc. 30th IEEE Int'l Conf. on Software Engineering* (ICSE'08), Vol.II, 2nd Int'l Workshop on the Role of Abstraction in Software Engineering (ROA'08), Leipzig, Germany, ACM/IEEE CS Press, May, pp. 43-48.

Wang, Y. (2008e). On Cognitive Properties of Human Factors and Error Models in Engineering and Socialization. *International Journal of Cognitive Informatics and Natural Intelligence*, 2(4), 70–84. doi:10.4018/jcini.2008100106

Wang, Y. (2008f), Mathematical Laws of Software, *Transactions of Computational Science*, 2, Springer, Sept., 46-83.

Wang, Y. (2008g). On Concept Algebra: A Denotational Mathematical Structure for Knowledge and Software Modeling. *International Journal of Cognitive Informatics and Natural Intelligence*, 2(2), 1–19. doi:10.4018/jcini.2008040101

Wang, Y. (2008h). On System Algebra: A Denotational Mathematical Structure for Abstract Systems, Modeling. *International Journal of Cognitive Informatics and Natural Intelligence*, 2(2), 20–43. doi:10.4018/jcini.2008040102

Wang, Y. (2008i). RTPA: A Denotational Mathematics for Manipulating Intelligent and Computational Behaviors. *International Journal of Cognitive Informatics and Natural Intelligence*, 2(2), 44–62. doi:10.4018/jcini.2008040103

Wang, Y. (2008j). Deductive Semantics of RTPA. *International Journal of Cognitive Informatics and Natural Intelligence*, 2(2), 95–121. doi:10.4018/jcini.2008040106

Wang, Y. (2008k), *Mathematical Laws of Software, Transactions of Computational Science*, Springer, Aug., 2, 46-83.

Wang, Y. (2009a), Convergence of Software Science and Computational Intelligence: A New Transdisciplinary research Field, *International Journal of Software Science and Computational Intelligence*, IGI, USA, Jan., 1(1), i-xii.

Wang, Y. (2009b), On Abstract Intelligence: Toward a Unified Theory of Natural, Artificial, Machinable, and Computational Intelligence, *International Journal of Software Science and Computational Intelligence*, IGI, USA, Jan., 1(1), 1-17.

Wang, Y. (2009c). On the Cognitive Complexity of Software and its Quantification and Formal Measurement. *International Journal of Software Science and Computational Intelligence*, 1(2), 31–53. doi:10.4018/jssci.2009040103

Wang, Y. and V. Chiew (2008), On the Cognitive Process of Human Problem Solving, *Cognitive Systems Research: An International Journal*, 9(4), Elsevier, UK, Nov., to appear.

Wang, Y., & Shao, J. (2003), Measurement of the Cognitive Functional Complexity of Software, *Proc. 2nd IEEE International Conference on Cognitive Informatics* (ICCI'03), IEEE CS Press, London, UK, August, pp.67-74.

Wang, Y., & Wang, Y. (2006). Cognitive Informatics Models of the Brain. *IEEE Transactions on Systems, Man and Cybernetics. Part C, Applications and Reviews*, 36(2), 203–207. doi:10.1109/TSMCC.2006.871151

Wang, Y., L.A. Zadeh, and Y. Yao (2009), On the System Algebra Foundations for Granular Computing, *International Journal of Software Science and Computational Intelligence*, IGI, USA, Jan., 1(1), 64-86.

Weinberg, G. M. (1971). *The Psychology of Computer Programming*. New York: Van Nostrand Reinhold.

This work was previously published in International Journal of Software Science and Computational Intelligence, Volume 1, Issue 2, edited by Yingxu Wang, pp. 1-19, copyright 2009 by IGI Publishing (an imprint of IGI Global).

Chapter 15
Positive and Negative Innovations in Software Engineering

Capers Jones
Software Productivity Research LLC, USA

ABSTRACT

The software engineering field has been a fountain of innovation. Ideas and inventions from the software domain have literally changed the world as we know it. For software development, we have a few proven innovations. The way software is built remains surprisingly primitive. Even in 2008 major software applications are cancelled, overrun their budgets and schedules, and often have hazardously bad quality levels when released. There have been many attempts to improve software development, but progress has resembled a drunkard's walk. Some attempts have been beneficial, but others have been either ineffective or harmful. This article puts forth the hypothesis that the main reason for the shortage of positive innovation in software development methods is due to a lack of understanding of the underlying problems of the software development domain. A corollary hypothesis is that lack of understanding of the problems is due to inadequate measurement of quality, productivity, costs, and the factors that affect project outcomes.

INTRODUCTION

There are two kinds of innovations that are important to the software world: product innovations and process innovations. Product innovations involve developing new or improved products that will excite customers. Process innovations, involve developing new or improved methods of development that can shorten development times, reduce costs, or improve quality.

Innovations can be either positive or negative. Positive innovations are those that add value and have clearly defined benefits. Negative innovations are those that make situations worse, or which add to expense levels but not to perceived value.

In the software domain external product innovations and internal process innovations are at differing levels of sophistication. Even in 2008

DOI: 10.4018/978-1-4666-0261-8.ch015

very sophisticated and complex pieces of software are still constructed by manual methods with an extraordinary labor content and very distressing quality levels.

Another example of an imbalance between product innovations and process innovations can be seen in the migration of technology jobs from the United States to India, China, and other countries with low labor costs. Many sophisticated products designed in the United States are now being manufactured abroad because the U.S. has not been able to introduce internal manufacturing innovations in sufficient quantities to stay cost competitive.

However at the start of 2008, the continuing decline of the dollar against the Euro, the Yen, and other international currencies may become severe enough so that the United States becomes an outsource country with lower labor costs than most of Europe and parts of Asia. Also inflation rates abroad in much of Europe and even India are rising higher than in the United States. If these trends continue, within perhaps five years the cost advantages of international outsourcing may tip in favor of the United States.

External Product Innovation

The software domain has created scores of innovative products that have changed the way the world does business. Some examples of positive software innovations in alphabetic order include compilers, data base software, embedded software, graphical user interfaces, the internet, medical software, search engines, spreadsheets, web browsers, and word processors.

Unfortunately there have also been negative or harmful innovations. The most harmful of the external innovations from the software domain are computer viruses and spyware. Other negative innovations include pop-up ads, spam, phishing, and browser hijackers. The negative innovations have caused enormous problems and expenses for all users of computers. The negative innovations have also caused the creation of a sub-industry of anti-virus and anti-spyware companies.

Other forms of negative innovation include hacking and theft of corporate records. Identify theft is yet another form of negative innovation, and one which is becoming more and more common.

The term "phishing" has become prominent and refers to highly innovative methods of deceiving computer users into going to fraudulent web sites. The most common reason for phishing attacks is to lure users into revealing financial data, passwords, and confidential information by tricking them into thinking they are actually at the web sites of banks or government agencies when in fact the sites are merely replicas designed to look like the original, but created to route private data into the hands of identity thieves.

At the corporate level, a major negative innovation has been finding clever methods of hiding losses and exaggerating profits, as seen in the case of Enron, WorldCom, Arthur Anderson, Global Crossing and other large corporations. In recent years, negative innovations in finance and accounting have cost many billions of dollars.

Guarding against negative innovation is a major issue in the 21st century, and is likely to become even more important.

The measures and metrics for positive external innovation are standard business measures that include:

- Patents issued to employees
- Invention disclosures
- Technical publications
- Research and development spending
- Morale surveys of technical workers
- Market share
- Market growth
- Profit and revenue growth
- Customer focus group results
- Customer survey results
- Trade show editorial reviews
- Successful completion of government tests

- Loss or gain of research and development jobs
- Loss from stolen corporate data, phishing attacks, viruses, etc.
- Security costs for guarding against viruses, spyware, and hacking
- Costs of compliance with Sarbanes-Oxley legislation

The success of the software world in product innovation can also be measured by the number of billionaires and Fortune 500 companies created as a direct result of these innovations. Apple, Bose, Cisco, Hewlett Packard, IBM, Microsoft, and Oracle are excellent examples of companies built around successful product innovation. Global companies which also excel in product innovation include BMW, Honda, Mercedes Benz, SAP, Siemens, Sony, Tata, and Yamaha.

The bankruptcy and collapse of Enron and the convictions of its senior executives is a sober example of the hazards of negative innovation, as are the similar failures of more than a dozen large corporations in recent years.

Another example of the economic costs of negative innovation is the huge expense devoted to security of computer systems. In the modern computer security world of 2007, there is a race going on between the perpetrators of negative innovations and the defenders of data bases and stored information.

As of 2008 there are no standard metrics that deal with negative and harmful innovations but some informal metrics would include:

- Number of indictments of corporate executives for fraud or stock violations
- Number of hacking attempts detected by time period
- Number and value of corporate records stolen due to hacking
- Number of "phishing" scams attempted by time period

- Numbers of denial of service and viral attacks
- Rate of growth of anti-virus definitions
- Rate of growth of anti-spyware definitions
- Costs of recovery from viral or denial of service attacks
- Annual corporate budgets for security matters
- Percentages of security code and function points in software applications

One of the economic issues associated with negative innovation is that they very often lead to unbudgeted expenses. Although most modern organizations do budget funds for security purposes, some kinds of negative innovation such as denial of service attacks or indictments for stock fraud are unpredictable under normal budget processes.

Unfortunately there seems to be no central organization that keeps track of all of the negative innovations such as hacking, phishing, or viruses. Or at least there is no central organization that publishes statistics. It may be that the CIA, FBI, Homeland Security, or National Security Agency keep such statistics internally, but they are seldom reported in the literature. The major security companies such as Symantec and McAfee do publish statistics from time to time, but they cover only a portion of the overall negative innovation domain.

Internal Process Innovation

Although the software domain has been remarkably effective in external product innovation, it has not been as successful in process innovation. In fact measures of software productivity, quality, schedules, and failure rates have stayed comparatively flat between 1977 and 2008.

The following list of 30 issues is taken from the 2nd edition of the author's book Estimating Software Costs. Although the list was assembled for the 2007 edition, it would have been about the same in 1977 as it is today based on data published at approximate 10 year intervals (Jones 1977; Jones

1986; Jones 1996; Jones 2000; Jones 2006, Jones 2007. See also Brooks 1974; Boehm 1981; Kan 2003; Strassmann 97; and Yourdon 1997). The year 2008 does not promise much improvement.

Thirty Software Engineering Issues that have Stayed Constant for 30 Years

1. Initial requirements are seldom more than 50% complete.
2. Requirements grow at about 2% per calendar month during development.
3. About 20% of initial requirements are delayed until a second release.
4. Finding and fixing bugs is the most expensive software activity.
5. Creating paper documents is the second most expensive software activity.
6. Coding is the third most expensive software activity.
7. Meetings and discussions are the fourth most expensive activity.
8. Most forms of testing are less than 30% efficient in finding bugs.
9. Most forms of testing touch less than 50% of the code being tested.
10. There are more defects in requirements and design than in source code.
11. There are more defects in test cases than in the software itself.
12. Defects in requirements, design, and code average 5.0 per function point.
13. Total defect removal efficiency before release averages only about 85%.
14. About 15% of software defects are delivered to customers.
15. Delivered defects are expensive and cause customer dissatisfaction.
16. About 5% of modules in applications will contain 50% of all defects.
17. About 7% of all defect repairs will accidentally inject new defects.
18. Software reuse is only effective for materials that approach zero defects.
19. About 5% of software outsource contracts end up in litigation.
20. About 35% of projects > 10,000 function points will be cancelled.
21. About 50% of projects > 10,000 function points will be one year late.
22. The failure mode for most cost estimates is to be excessively optimistic.
23. Productivity rates in the U.S. are about 10 function points per staff month.
24. Assignment scopes for development are about 150 function points.
25. Assignment scopes for maintenance are about 750 function points.
26. Development costs about $1200 per function point in the U.S.
27. Maintenance costs about $150 per function point per calendar year.
28. After delivery applications grow at about 7% per calendar year during use.
29. Average defect repair rates are about 10 bugs or defects per month.
30. Programmers need about 10 days of annual training to stay current.

Ten new and accelerating problems since 1998:

1. Denial of service attacks are increasing in number and sophistication
2. Viruses, worms, and Trojans are increasing in number and sophistication
3. Spyware and keystroke monitors are increasing in number and sophistication
4. Theft of personal records and proprietary data is increasing
5. Phishing attempts are increasing in number and sophistication
6. Hacking into "secure" systems is increasing in number and sophistication
7. Security flaws and quality flaws appear to be related

8. Design of secure applications lags at the University level
9. Security issues are often not dealt with during development
10. Testing and normal defect removal are inadequate for security flaws

The domain of security flaws and attempts to exploit these flaws has become a major problem for the computing and software domains. As of 2008, very little personal data such as bank records, medical records, and personal information are truly secure.

There is an interesting dilemma associated with the fact that measurable progress in software productivity and quality has remained essentially flat for 30 years. Dozens of new development approaches have been created over the past 30 year period. Examples of the these include Agile development, the capability maturity model (CMM), the capability maturity model integration (CMMI), CASE tools, clean-room development, CRYSTAL development approach, dynamic system development method (DSDM), extreme programming (XP), incremental development, ISO 9000-9004 standards, iterative development, object-oriented development, pattern-based development, personal software process (PSP), rapid application development (RAD), reusability, SCRUM, six-sigma for software, spiral development, team structured process (TSP), total quality management (TQM), and the unified modeling language (UML). With all of these new methods available, why are productivity and quality results in 2008 almost the same as those in 1977?

As of 2008, the software industry has more than 700 programming languages in use. We have more than 40 different methods of designing applications. We have 38 different kinds of size metrics. We have some 26 named development methods. There are about 125 international standards that affect software. There are at least 18 different kinds of testing, and four different kinds of review and inspection method. Yet software quality and productivity levels in 2007 are hardly different from 1977.

Also in 2008 millions of programmers are locked into tasks involving the maintenance and support of millions of aging legacy applications. As time passes, the global percentage of programmers performing maintenance on aging software has steadily risen until it has become the dominant activity of the software world.

A rising percentage of software development and maintenance effort is devoted to either preventing security flaws or recovery after a security breach has been detected. Security issues will remain troublesome for the foreseeable future.

The plethora of development methodologies is a sign that none of them have actually addressed or solved all 30 of the problems shown earlier in this article. If any of the methods had solved all 30 of the problems, then it would have gradually become the standard approach for building software. It is also apparent that none of the software development methods have fully addressed the issue of security flaws and vulnerabilities. If this were not the case, then attacks on systems and data would be in decline, but in fact they are increasing.

From carrying out benchmark studies in Fortune 500 companies between 1977 and 2008, a curious phenomenon has been noted. For several years after adoption of a new software development approach productivity and quality levels do tend to improve. But when the same company is revisited after about 10 years, it often happens that the new method has been abandoned and productivity and quality results have declined back to the levels before the improvement program started. In fact one of the reasons for revisiting the same companies is that new management wants to start a new software process improvement program, since data on the earlier improvement programs has vanished or is no longer viewed as relevant.

The fact that corporations may abandon even successful process improvement methods in less than five years, and forget about them in less than 10 years, tends to occur often enough so that the phenomenon should receive additional research. What causes this "corporate memory loss?"

Another kind of innovation problem occurs from time to time in large corporations. It sometimes happens that two or more process improvement programs begin in different operating units at the same time. It often happens that each unit selects a different improvement model. For example one unit might choose the object-oriented approach, another might choose extreme programming (XP), and a third may adopt the six-sigma approach. The result is sometimes a political battle between the units, with each one striving to have its choice adopted as a corporate standard.

As of 2008, some companies are improving productivity and quality but other companies are retrogressing and losing ground. Still other companies are doing both at the same time, with improvements in some locations and regressions in others. The short-term improvements among companies upgrading their development methods are balanced by the regression of companies that are abandoning the same techniques.

There is no definitive answer for why this wave pattern of progress followed by regression occurs, but it may be related to the fact that companies don't measure software productivity or quality levels with enough detail to prove that improvements are cost justified.

In the absence of accurate measurements, organizations tend to follow the path of least resistance and abandon approaches that require continuous training. In other words, the teams that adopt new approaches eventually retire or change jobs, and their replacements are not brought up to speed in successful methods.

This brings up the related question as to why companies don't measure software productivity and software quality well enough to prove success? The first problem with accurate measurement is selecting accurate metrics.

In terms of sizing and measurement approaches, the industry is overburdened with more than a dozen function point clones, including backfired function points, Cosmic function points, engineering function points, feature points, Mark II function points, NESMA function points, object points, use-case points, and web-object points. Since there are no conversion rules among all of the disparate function point clones, there is no effective way of comparing productivity and quality between projects measured with different variations.

If you have productivity rates of 10 function points per staff month with IFPUG function points, 10 with Cosmic function points, 10 with Mark II function points, 10 with NESMA function points, 10 with web-object points, and 10 with use case points are these results the same or different? In terms of real economic productivity, which one is highest? Which one is lowest? As of 2007 there is no good answer.

The only function point method with as many as 10,000 projects measured and 30 years of historical data is that of the International Function Point Users Group (IFPUG). Even here the counting rules changed several times between 1977 and 2007. However conversion rules were established with each change. Enough projects have been measured with this metric to see that national productivity and quality levels have remained fairly constant for more than 30 years (Garmus and Herron 1995).

This is not to say that there are no differences between projects and companies. Indeed the best quality and productivity levels are more than 10 times better than the worst. There is solid evidence that organizations at or higher than level 3 on the CMM have better quality and productivity rates than those at levels 1 and 2. There is also evidence that the Agile methods have improved productivity rates for applications below 1000 function points in size (Jones 2000; Krasner 1997). But at national levels, the averages for both productivity and quality are fairly constant.

Even for the older "lines of code" metric there are too many choices. From reviewing the software literature (IEEE Software, IEEE Computing, IBM

Systems Journal, etc.) there was no consistency in the usage of lines of code metrics. About one third of the published data is based on counts of physical lines of code, about one third is based on counts of logical statements, and the remaining third uses "lines of code" without bothering to state whether physical or logical code was counted. The difference in size between physical lines and logical statements can top 500%, so this is too big a difference to ignore. There are no true international standards on source code counting.

If an application written in Objective C has a productivity rate of 750 physical lines of code per staff month while a similar application written in C++ has a productivity rate of 750 logical statements per staff month, are these two equal in terms of real economic productivity? As of 2007 there is no good answer.

Even for lines of code measures that use the same approach, the LOC metric has a major economic flaw in that it penalizes modern high-level languages and gives the false impression that older low-level languages such as assembly are more productive than they really are. This paradox was illustrated in Ed Yourdon's former American Programmer magazine (Jones 1994) in a study which showed productivity rates measured with both LOC metrics and function point metrics for 10 versions of an application written in 10 different programming languages.

The LOC metrics incorrectly showed the highest productivity rates for the lowest-level languages, and penalized modern object-oriented languages. The reason was because with modern programming languages, more than half of the work of software development goes to paperwork production or non-coding tasks. These tend to act as fixed costs, and cause LOC metrics to be inaccurate as measures of true economic productivity. Function point metrics, on the other hand, do measure economic productivity and highlight the value of modern languages.

Another aspect of the lack of solid measurements is the fact that selecting a suitable develop-

ment method is a difficult task. There are scores of competing methods. There are conflicting and ambiguous measurement methods for proving results. This leads to a paucity of empirical data. In the absence of solid data, companies tend to select the "methodology du jour" which may or may not be appropriate for the kinds of applications they build. This brings up the topic of "negative process innovation" or methods that do harm rather than adding value.

It often happens that a specific methodology was created to solve a certain kind of problem for a certain kind of software. For example the Agile approaches and extreme programming (XP) were developed to speed up the development of small projects below about 1000 function points or 100,000 logical source code statements in size. This is the size range where small teams in face to face contact are quite effective.

The Agile methods are not yet effective on large systems of 10,000 function points and 1,000,000 logical source code statements in size. In this large size range there are hundreds of developers, sometime located in different cities or even different continents. Thus the Agile approaches are a positive innovation for small projects, but sometimes negative for large systems.

The capability maturity model (CMM) on the other hand was designed specifically for large systems in the 10,000 function point or 1,000,000 source code statement size range. But the infrastructure that comes with the CMM is too massive for small projects below 1,000 function points in size. The CMM has proven to be a positive innovation for large and complex systems, but due to its extensive overhead, the CMM can be a negative innovation for small and simple programs.

This brings up the question of how should process innovations be measured? Internal innovations are subtle and sometimes difficult to measure. Because they often involve improvements in development techniques compared to prior approaches, it is necessary to have long-range measurements that cover both the "before" and "after" methodologies.

The standard economic definition of productivity is: "goods or services produced per unit of labor or expense." One of the main goals of internal innovation is to improve economic productivity. Thus a tangible improvement in economic productivity is a useful measure of internal innovation.

In the modern hi-tech world a major component of economic productivity centers on warranty repairs, recalls, and repairing defects in technical products. Therefore it is apparent that quality and reliability are also critical for successful process innovations. Some of the measures and metrics that can highlight internal innovations include:

- Time to market: inception to delivery
- Manufacturing cycle time
- Baseline studies showing improvement over time
- Benchmark studies against similar companies
- Cost of Quality measures
- Six-Sigma Quality measures
- Total cost of ownership measures
- Defect removal efficiency measures
- Scrap and rework during manufacture
- Manufacturing work hours per unit
- Manufacturing cost per unit
- Warehouse and storage cost per unit
- Distribution cost per unit
- Warranty repairs per unit
- Defect reports per unit per time period
- Defect repair rates
- Recalls of defective units
- Morale surveys of manufacturing staff
- Morale surveys of support and maintenance staff
- Litigation alleging defective products
- Government withdrawal of safety certificates
- Internal Quality Assurance reviews
- Inspection reports
- Test reports

- Customer surveys dealing with quality and reliability
- Customer surveys dealing with service and support
- Loss or gain of manufacturing jobs

As can be seen, the measurement of internal innovations includes measures of cost, measures of time to market speed, measures of quality, and measures of customer satisfaction. Success in all of these is necessary.

SUMMARY AND CONCLUSION

The software world has been a major source of exciting product innovations for more than 50 years. Unfortunately, negative innovations such as viruses and spyware have also come to light.

However the software world has continued to build large and complex applications by brute force with a high content of manual labor. Thus it is clear that the software world has not been as successful with internal process innovation as it has been with external product innovation.

A key reason for lack of tangible improvement in software development methods is because most companies have not been effective in measuring software productivity and quality. This is partly due to the competing and conflicting metrics available, and the lack of conversion rules from one metric to another.

Without solid measures that show the economic benefits of various software methods, companies have trouble selecting methods that are effective. Companies also have trouble with keeping effective methods active. This is due to lack of training of new employees in effective methods as older employees retire or change jobs.

The overall goal of corporate innovation is to have a good balance of both external and internal innovations. New and exciting products need to be coupled with efficient and reliable manufacturing steps. The software community has excelled in producing a stream of external innovations, but lags in the creation of proven internal process innovations.

The software industry needs to be much more cautious than it has been in avoiding the harmful consequences of negative innovation. All companies need to be careful about viruses, spyware, hacking, and corporate malfeasance.

In addition, the software industry needs much better proof of the effectiveness of various software development methods. Since development methods are not panaceas and are not necessarily suitable for every kind of project, the software industry needs better warnings about the limitations of various development approaches.

That brings up the final point that the software industry needs to standardize software metrics and measurement practices. The presence of scores of incompatible metrics without any conversion ratios from metric to metric is itself an example of negative innovation.

REFERENCES

Boehm, B. D. (1981). *Software Engineering Economics*. Englewood Cliffs, NJ: Prentice Hall.

Brooks, F. *The Mythical Man-Month*, Addison-Wesley, Reading, Mass., 1974, rev. 1995.

Garmus, D., & Herron, D. (1995). *Measuring the Software Process: A Practical Guide to Functional Measurement*. Englewood Cliffs, NJ: Prentice Hall.

Jones, C. (1994). *Estimating and Measuring Object-Oriented Software*. American Programmer.

Jones, C. Applied Software Measurement, 2nd edition; McGraw-Hill, New York, NY, 1996; 457 pages; 3rd edition due in the Spring of 2008.

Jones, Capers; Conflict and Litigation Between Software Clients and Developers; Version 6; Software Productivity Research, Burlington, MA; June 2006; 54 pages.

Jones, C., & the Estimating Software Costs. McGraw Hill, New York; 2nd edition, 2007; 644 pages; ISBN13: 978- 0-07-148300-1.

Jones, C., Productivity, P., McGraw, H., & York, N. ISBN 0-07-032811-0; 1986.

Jones, Capers; Program Quality and Programmer Productivity; IBM Technical Report TR 02.764, IBM San Jose, CA; January 1977.

Jones, C. Software Assessments, Benchmarks, and Best Practices. (2000). *Addison Wesley Longman*. Boston, MA.

Kan, S. H. (2003). *Metrics and Models in Software Quality Engineering* (2nd ed.). Boston, MA: Addison Wesley Longman.

Krasner, Herb; "Accumulating the Body of Evidence for the Payoff of Software Process Improvement – 1997;" Krasner Consulting, Austin, TX.

(1997). *Strassmann, Paul; The Squandered Computer*. Stamford, CT: Information Economics Press.

Yourdon, E. (1997). *Death March—The Complete Software Developer's Guide to Surviving "Mission Impossible" Projects*. Upper Saddle River, N.J.: Prentice Hall PTR.

ADDITIONAL READING

Ambler, S. (1998). *Process Patterns – Building Large-Scale Systems Using Object Technology; Cambridge University Press*. SIGS Books.

Artow, J., & Neustadt, I. (2000). *UML and the Unified Process*. Boston, MA: Addison Wesley.

Beck, K. (1999). *Extreme Programming Explained: Embrace Change*. Boston, MA: Addison Wesley.

Boehm, B. A Spiral Model of Software Development and Enhancement; Proceedings of the Int. Workshop on Software Process and Software Environments; ACM Software Engineering Notes, Aug. 1986, pp. 22-42.

(2005). *Booch, Grady; Jacobsen, Ivar, and Rumbaugh, James; The Unified Modeling Language User Guide* (2nd ed.). Boston, MA: Addison Wesley.

Capability, M. M. I. Version 1.1; Software Engineering Institute; Carnegie-Mellon Univ.; Pittsburgh, PA; March 2003; http://www.sei.cmu.edu/cmmi/

Charette, R. N. (1989). *Software Engineering Risk Analysis and Management*. New York: McGraw-Hill.

Charette, R. N. (1990). *Application Strategies for Risk Analysis*. New York: McGraw-Hill.

Chidamber, S. R., & Kemerer, C. F. (1994, June). A Metrics Suite for Object-Oriented Design. *IEEE Transactions on Software Engineering, SE20*(6), 476–493. doi:10.1109/32.295895

(2001). *Cockburn, Alistair; Agile Software Development*. Boston, MA: Addison Wesley.

Cohen, D. (2004). *Lindvall M. & Costa, P. An Introduction to agile methods; Advances in Computers* (pp. 1–66). New York: Elsevier Science.

Cohn, M., & Applied, U. S. For Agile Software Development; Addison Wesley, Boston, Ma; 2004; ISBN 0-321-20568-S. Feature Driven Development; http://en.wikipedia.org/wiki/Feature_Driven_Development.

(2005). *Cohn, Mike; Agile Estimating and Planning*. Englewood Cliffs, NJ: Prentice Hall PTR.

IFPUG Counting Practices Manual, Release 4, International Function Point Users Group, Westerville, OH; April 1995; 83 pages.

Gack G. Applying Six Sigma to Software Implementation Projects. http://software.isixsigma.com/library/content/c040915b.asp.

Gamma, E., Helm, R., Johnson, R., Vlissides, J., & Patterns, D. (1995). *Elements of Reusable Object Oriented Design*. Boston, MA: Addison Wesley.

Garmus, D., Herron, D., Analysis, F. P., & Longman, A. W. Boston, MA; 2001; ISBN 0-201-69944-3; 363 pages. Hallowell, David L.; Six Sigma Software Metrics, Part 1.; http://software.isixsigma.com/library/content/03910a.asp.

Grady, B., & Solutions, O. (1995). *Managing the Object-Oriented Project*. Reading, MA: Addison Wesley.

(2002). *Highsmith, Jim; Agile Software Development Ecosystems*. Boston, MA: Addison Wesley.

Humphrey, W. (2006). *TSP – Leading a Development Team*. Boston, MA: Addison Wesley.

(1989). *Humphrey, Watts; Managing the Software Process*. Reading, MA: Addison Wesley.

IFPUG. IT Measurement; Practical Advice from the Experts; Addison Wesley Longman, Boston, MA; 2002; 759 pages. International Organization for Standards; ISO 9000 / ISO 14000; http://www.iso.org/iso/en/iso9000-14000/index.html.

Jeffries, R. (2001). *Extreme Programming Installed*. Boston: Addison Wesley.

Jones, C. (1997). *Software Quality – Analysis and Guidelines for Success*. Boston, MA: International Thomson Computer Press.

Jones, C. (1998, December). Sizing Up Software. *Scientific American, New York, NY, 279*(6), 104–109.

Jones, C. (2003, December). Why Flawed Software Projects are not Cancelled in Time. *Cutter IT Journal*, *10*(12), 12–17.

Jones, C. (2006, June). Software Project Management Practices: Failure Versus Success. *Crosstalk*, *19*(6), 4–8.

(1995). *Jones, Capers; Patterns of Software System Failure and Success*. Boston: International Thomson Computer Press.

Kemerer, C. F. (1993). Reliability of Function Point Measurement - A Field Experiment. *Communications of the ACM*, *36*, 85–97. doi:10.1145/151220.151230

Larman, Craig & Basili, Victor; Iterative and Incremental Development – A Brief History; IEEE Computer Society; June 2003; pp 47-55.

Love, T., & Lessons, O. (1993). *SIGS Books*. New York.

McConnell. (2006). *Software Estimating: Demystifying the Black Art*. Microsoft Press.

Mertes, K. R., & the Calibration of the CHECKPOINT Model to the Space and Missile Systems Center (SMC) Software Database (SWDB). Thesis AFIT/GCA/LAS/96S-11, Air Force Institute of Technology (AFIT), Wright Patterson AFB, Ohio; September 1996; 119 pages.

Mills, H., Dyer, M., & Linger, R. (1987, Sept.). Cleanroom Software Engineering. *IEEE Software*, *4*(5), 19–25. doi:10.1109/MS.1987.231413

Park, R. E., et al. Software Cost and Schedule Estimating - A Process Improvement Initiative; Technical Report CMU/SEI 94-SR-03; Software Engineering Institute, Pittsburgh, PA; May 1994.

Park, R. E., et al., & the Checklists and Criteria for Evaluating the Costs and Schedule Estimating Capabilities of Software Organizations. Technical Report CMU/SEI 95-SR-005; Software Engineering Institute, Pittsburgh, PA; January 1995.

Perry, W. E. (1989). *Handbook of Diagnosing and Solving Computer Problems*. Blue Ridge Summit, Pa.: TAB Books.

Pressman, R. (2005). *Software Engineering – A Practitioner's Approach* (6th ed.). NY: McGraw Hill.

Putnam, L. H. (1992). *Measures for Excellence -- Reliable Software On Time, Within Budget*. Englewood Cliffs, NJ: Yourdon Press - Prentice Hall.

Putnam, Lawrence H and Myers, Ware.; Industrial Strength Software - Effective Management Using Measurement; IEEE Press, Los Alamitos, CA; ISBN 0-8186-7532-2; 1997; 320 pages. Rapid Application Development; http://en.wikipedia.org/wiki/Rapid_application_development

Roetzheim, W. H., & Beasley, R. A. Best Practices in Software Cost and Schedule Estimation. (1998). *Prentice Hall PTR*. Saddle River, NJ.

Stapleton, J. (1997). *DSDM - Dynamic System Development Method in Practice*. Boston, MA: Addison Wesley.

Stephens, M., & Rosenberg, D. Extreme Programming Refactored; The Case Against XP; APress L.P., Berkeley, CA; 2003.

Strassmann, P. Information Payoff; Information Economics Press, Stamford, Ct; 1985.

Strassmann, P. Information Productivity; Information Economics Press, Stamford, Ct; 1999.

Strassmann, P. Governance of Information Management: The Concept of an Information Constitution; 2nd edition; (eBook); Information Economics Press, Stamford, Ct; 2004.

Stukes, Sherry, Deshoretz, Jason, Apgar, Henry and Macias, Ilona; Air Force Cost Analysis Agency Software Estimating Model Analysis; TR-9545/008-2; Contract F04701-95-D-0003, Task 008; Management Consulting & Research, Inc.; Thousand Oaks, CA 91362; September 30 1996.

Symons, C. R. *Software Sizing and Estimating— Mk II FPA (Function Point Analysis),* John Wiley & Sons, Chichester, U.K., ISBN 0-471-92985-9, 1991. Wellman, Frank, *Software Costing: An Objective Approach to Estimating and Controlling the Cost of Computer Software,* Prentice Hall, Englewood Cliffs, NJ, ISBN 0-138184364, 1992.

This work was previously published in International Journal of Software Science and Computational Intelligence, Volume 1, Issue 2, edited by Yingxu Wang, pp. 20-30, copyright 2009 by IGI Publishing (an imprint of IGI Global).

Chapter 16
On the Cognitive Complexity of Software and its Quantification and Formal Measurement

Yingxu Wang
University of Calgary, Canada

ABSTRACT

The quantification and measurement of functional complexity of software are a persistent problem in software engineering. Measurement models of software complexities have been studied in two facets in computing and software engineering, where the former is machine-oriented in the small; while the latter is human-oriented in the large. The cognitive complexity of software presented in this paper is a new measurement for cross-platform analysis of complexities, functional sizes, and cognition efforts of software code and specifications in the phases of design, implementation, and maintenance in software engineering. This paper reveals that the cognitive complexity of software is a product of its architectural and operational complexities on the basis of deductive semantics. A set of ten Basic Control Structures (BCS's) are elicited from software architectural and behavioral modeling and specifications. The cognitive weights of the BCS's are derived and calibrated via a series of psychological experiments. Based on this work, the cognitive complexity of software systems can be rigorously and accurately measured and analyzed. Comparative case studies demonstrate that the cognitive complexity is highly distinguishable for software functional complexity and size measurement in software engineering.

INTRODUCTION

One of the central problems in software engineering is the inherited complexity. The quantification and measurement of functional complexity of software systems have been a persistent fundamental problem in software engineering (Hartmanis and Stearns, 1965; Basili, 1980; Kearney et al., 1986; Melton, 1996; Fenton and Pfleeger, 1998; Lewis and Papadimitriou, 1998; Wang, 2003b, 2007a). The taxonomy of the complexity and size measures of software can be classified into the categories of computational complexity (time and space) (Hartmanis, 1994; McDermid, 1991),

DOI: 10.4018/978-1-4666-0261-8.ch016

symbolic complexity (Lines of Code (LOC)) (Halstead, 1977; Albrecht and Gaffney, 1983; McDermid, 1991), structural complexity (control flow, cyclomatic) (McCabe, 1976; Zuse, 1977), functional complexity (function points, cognitive complexity) (Albrecht, 1979; Wang, 2007a; Wang and Shao, 2003).

The most simple and intuitive measure of software complexity is the symbolic complexity, which is conventionally adopted as a measure in term of Lines of Code (LOC) (Halstead, 1977; Albrecht and Gaffney, 1983; McDermid, 1991). However, the functional complexity of software is so intricate and non-linear, which is too hard to be measured or even estimated in LOC. In order to improve the accuracy and measurability, McCabe proposed the cyclomatic complexity measure (McCabe, 1976) based on Euler's theorem (Lipschutz and Lipson, 1997) in the category of structural complexity. However, it only considered the internal loop architectures of software systems without taking into account of the throughput of the system in terms of data objects and many other important internal architectures such as the sequential, branch, and embedded constructs. Because the linear blocks of code are oversimplified as one unit as in graph theory, the cyclomatic complexity is not sensitive to linear structures and external data complexity as well as their impact on the basic structures. Albrecht (1979) introduced the concept of *function point* of software (Albrecht, 1979), which is a weighted product of a set of functional characteristics of software systems. However, the physical meaning of a unit function point is not rigorously modeled except a wide range of empirical studies. The *cognitive complexity* of software systems is introduced as a measure for the functional complexity in both software design and comprehension, which consists of the architectural and operational complexities. The cognitive complexity provides a novel and profound approach to explain and measure the functional complexity of software as well as the effort in software design and comprehension.

The new approach perceives software functional complexity as a measure of cognitive complexity for human creative artifacts, which considers the effect of both internal structures of software and the I/O data objects under processing (Wang, 2007a; Wang and Shaw, 2003).

This paper presents a cognitive functional complexity of software as well as its mathematical models and formal measurement. The taxonomy and related work of software complexity measurement are explored systematically. A generic mathematical model of programs is created and the relative cognitive weights of fundamental software structures known as the Basic Control Structures (BCS's) are empirically calibrated based on a series of psychological experiments. The cognitive complexity of software systems is formally modeled as a product of the architectural and operational complexities of software. A set of comparative case studies is presented on applications of cognitive complexity in software engineering, which leads to a series of important findings on the basic properties of software cognitive complexity and its quantification and measurement.

TAXONOMY OF SOFTWARE COMPLEXITIES IN COMPUTING AND SOFTWARE ENGINEERING

The measurement models of software complexities have been studied in two facets in computing in the small and software engineering in the large. The orientation of software engineering complexity theories puts emphases on the problems of *functional complexity* that are human *cognition time* and *workload* oriented. While the computational complexity theories are focused on the problems of *high throughput complexity* that are computing *time efficiency* centered. In other words, software engineering measures system-level complexities, while computational science measures algorithmic complexities.

Although computational complexities, particularly *algorithm complexities*, are one of the focuses in computer science, software engineering is particularly interested in the *functional complexity* of large-scale and real-world software systems. The computational complexity of algorithms puts emphases on the computability and efficiency of typical algorithms of massive data processing and high throughput systems, in which computing efficiency is dependent on and dominated by the problem sizes in terms of their number of inputs such as those in sorting and searching. However, there are more generic computational problems and software systems that are not dominated by this kind of input sizes rather than by internal architectural and operational complexities such as problem solving and process dispatching. This shows the differences of focuses or problem models in the complexity theories of software engineering and computing.

In software engineering, a problem with very high computational complexity may be quite simple for human comprehension, and vice versa. For instance, according to cognitive informatics (Wang, 2002b, 2003a, 2007b), human beings may comprehend a large loop of iteration, which is the major issue of computational complexity, by looking at only the beginning and termination conditions, and one or a few arbitrary internal loops on the basis of inductive inferences. However, humans are not good at dealing with functional complexities such as a long chain of interrelated operations, very abstract data objects, and their consistency maintenance. Therefore, the system complexity of large-scale software is the focus of software engineering.

A summary of software complexity and size measures is provided in Table 1. It is noteworthy that certain measures in Table 1 are suitable only for post-coding measurement after a software system has already been developed. While the remainder are good at both pre- or post-coding measurements, which may be applied in the processes of design and organizational planning. The following subsections comparatively review and analyze typical paradigms of software complexity and size measurements, such as the computational, symbolic, structural, and cognitive complexities.

Computational Complexity

Computational complexity theory is a fundamental and well established area in computing, which studies the solvability or computational load of algorithms and computing problems (Hartmanis and Stearns, 1965; Hartmanis, 1994; McDermid, 1991; Lewis and Papadimitriou, 1998).

Definition 1. *Computational complexity is a special category of operational complexity of software that studies the taxonomy of problems in computing and their solvabilities, complexities, and efficiencies.*

Computational complexity focuses on algorithm complexities, which can be modeled by its *time* or *space* complexity, particularly the former, proportional to the sizes of computational problems.

Taxonomy of Computational Problems

The *solvable problems* in computation are those that can be computed by *polynomial-time* consumption. The *nonsolvable problems* are those that cannot be solved in any practical sense by computers due to excessive time requirements. The taxonomy of problems in computation can be classified into the following classes. The class of solvable problems that is *polynomial-time* computational by *deterministic* Turing machines are called the *class P* problems. The class of problems that is polynomial-time computational by *nondeterministic* Turing machines are called the *class NP* problems. The class of problems that their answers are complementary to the NP problems is called the *NP complementary* (coNP) problems. The subclass of NP problems

Table 1. Quantifications and measures of software complexities and sizes

No.	Category of measure	Paradigm	Measurability	Applicable process	Reference
1	Computational	Time complexity	Throughput in loops	Pre- or post-coding	(Lewis and Papadimitriou, 1998)
2		Space complexity	Source and target memory	Pre- or post-coding; language dependent	(Lewis and Papadimitriou, 1998)
3	Symbolic	Symbolic size	Lines of code (LOC)	Post coding; language dependent	(Albrecht and Gaffney, 1983)
4		Numbers of operators	Number of instructions	Post coding; language dependent	(Halstead, 1977)
5	Structural	Control flow complexity	Number of branches/loops	Pre- or post-coding	(McDermid, 1991)
6		Cyclomatic complexity	Number of control loops	Pre- or post-coding	(McCabe, 1976)
7		Architectural complexity	Number of data objects	Pre- or post-coding	(Wang, 2007a)
8	Data	Number of operands	Number of variables	Post coding; language dependent	(Halstead, 1977)
9		Information complexity	Number of I/Os	Pre- or post-coding	(Zuse, 1997)
10	Functional	Function points	Weighted sum of certain system characteristics	Pre- or post-coding	(Albrecht, 1979)
11		Operational complexity	Weighted sun of system cognitive functions	Pre- or post-coding	(Wang, 2007a)
12		Cognitive complexity	A product of system operational and architectural complexities	Pre- or post-coding	(Wang, 2007a)
13	System	System relational complexity	Number of system relations	Pre- or post-coding	(Wang, 2007a)

that serves as a meta-problem where other NP problems may be reduced to them in polynomial time, is called the *NP-complete* (NPc) problems. There is a special class of problems that can be reduced to known NP problems in polynomial time, which are usually referred to as the *NP-hard* (NPh) problems (McDermid, 1991; Lewis and Papadimitriou, 1998).

The relationship among various classes of problems in the taxonomy of computational problems can be illustrated as shown in Figure 1. It is noteworthy that there are certain classes of problems that are unsolvable or with unknown solvability in computing. However, they might be solvable by human brains on the basis of the inductive power that reduces the large or even infinitive iterative complexity of computing to a

simple or finite problem (Wang, 2007a). Therefore, software engineering complexity theories must deal with both machine-oriented computational complexities and human-oriented cognitive complexities. In many cases, these two categories of complexities are fundamentally different in theories and practice.

Time Complexity of Algorithms

The time complexity of an algorithm for a given problem in computing is measured as an estimation of its computational complexity. The time complexity of an algorithm can be measured by analyzing the number of dominant operations in the algorithm, where each of the dominant opera-

Figure 1. Taxonomy of problems in computation

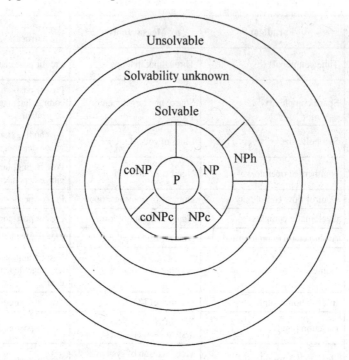

tions is assumed to take an identical unit of time in operation.

Definition 2. *The dominant operations in an algorithm are those statements within iterative structures that are proportional to the size of the problem or the number of inputs n of the algorithm.*

Definition 3. *For a given function f(x), its asymptotic function $f_a(x)$ is a function that satisfies:*

$$|f(x)| \le k|f_a(x)|, x > b \qquad (1)$$

where k and b are a positive constant.

Definition 4. *If a function f(x) has an asymptotic function $f_a(x)$, the function f(x) is said to be of order of $f_a(x)$, denoted by:*

$$f(x) = O(f_a(x)) \qquad (2)$$

where O is known as the big O notation.

Definition 5. *For a given size of a problem, n, the time complexity $C_t(n)$ of an algorithm for solving the problem is a function of the maximum required number of dominant operations $O(f_a(n))$, i.e.:*

$$C_t(n) = O(f_a(n)) \qquad (3)$$

where $f_a(n)$ is called the asymptotic function of $C_t(n)$.

It is noteworthy in Definition 5 that the maximum number of dominant operations $C_t(n)$ indicates the *worst case* scenario. An *average case* complexity is a mathematical expectation of $C_t(n)$.

Example 1. *According to Definition 5, the time complexity $C_t(n)$ of the following functions $f_1(n)$ through $f_4(n)$ can be estimated as follows:*

- $f_1(n) = 5n^3 + 2n^2 - 6 \Rightarrow C_{t1}(n) = O(f_{a1}(n)) = O(n^3)$
- $f_2(n) = 3n \Rightarrow C_{t2}(n) = O(f_{a2}(n)) = O(n)$

- $f_3(n) = 4\log_2 n + 10 \Rightarrow C_{t3}(n) = O(f_{a3}(n)) = O(\log_2 n)$
- $f_4(n) = 2 + 8 \Rightarrow C_{t4}(n) = O(f_{a4}(n)) = O(\varepsilon)$

where ε is a positive constant.

Typical asymptotic functions of algorithms and programs are shown in Figure 2, where the computational loads in term of processing time of different functions may grow polynomially or exponentially as the size of problem n, usually the number of input items, increasing. If an algorithm can be reduced to a type of function with polynomial complexity, it is always a computable problem; otherwise, it would be a very hard problem, particularly in the worst case when n is considerably large.

Space Complexity of Algorithms

Definition 6. *The space complexity of an algorithm for a given problem is the maximum required space for both working memory w and target code memory g, i.e.:*

$$C_m(n) = O(f(w+g)) \approx O(f(w)), \; w \gg g \qquad (4)$$

where w refers to the memory for data objects under processing such as input/output and intermediate variables, and g refers to the memory for executable code.

Because the target code memory is static and determinable, algorithm space complexity is focused on the dynamic part of working memory complexity.

Symbolic Complexities of Software

The most simple and direct forward complexity measure of software systems is the symbolic complexity that can be represented by the number of lines of statements in a programming language (Halstead, 1977; Albrecht and Gaffney, 1983).

Definition 7. *The symbolic complexity of a software system S, $C_s(S)$, is the linear length of its static statements measured in the unit of Lines of Code (LOC), i.e.:*

Figure 2. Typical asymptotic functions of software time complexities

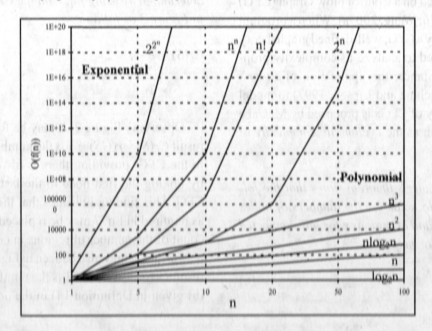

$$C_s(S) = \sum_{k=1}^{n_c} C_s(k) \quad [LOC] \tag{5}$$

where $C_s(k)$ represents the symbolic complexity of component k in S with n_c components.

It is noteworthy in measurement theory that the symbolic complexity is the measure, but LOC is the unit of the measure. It is in parallel to the measure of distance and its unit in meter. In the measure of symbolic complexity of software, variables, data objects declarations, and comments are not considered as a valid line of instructions, and an instruction separated in multiple lines is usually counted as a single line. However, there is a lack of a unified standard, and the measure is language-dependent. Therefore, only post-coding complexity and size may be measured by the symbolic complexity. The measurement of design complexity before the implementation of code is impossible.

Control Flow Complexities of Software

Another approach to measure the code complexity of software systems can be via its control structures based on a Control Flow Graph (CFG) (McCabe, 1976; Wang, 2007a). When a program is abstracted by a CFG, well-defined graph theory may be adopted to analyze its complexity properties. For instance, the application of *Euler's theorem* (Lipschutz and Lipson, 1997) to model the complexity of CFGs is proposed by McCabe in 1976 known as the *cyclomatic complexity* of software.

Theorem 1. *Euler's theorem states that the following formula holds for the numbers of nodes n, of edges e, and of regions r for any connected planar graph or map G:*

$$n - e + r = 2 \tag{6}$$

The proof of Theorem 1 may refer to Lipschutz and Lipson (1997).

The McCabe *cyclomatic complexity* (McCabe, 1976) of a software system can be determined by applying Euler's theorem onto the CFGs of software systems.

Definition 8. *The cyclomatic complexity of a software system S, Cr(S), is determined by the number of regions contained in a given CFG GS, r(GS), provided that G is connected, i.e.:*

$$Cr(S) = r(GS) = e - n + 2 \tag{7}$$

where, e is the number of edges in GS representing branches and cycles, n number of nodes in GS where a block of sequential code is reduced to a single node.

It can be observed that Eq. 7 is a derived application of Euler's theorem, which shows that the physical meaning of the McCabe cyclomatic complexity is the number of regions in a CFG for a given software system.

Example 2. *The cyclomatic complexity of the program MaxFinder as given in Figure 3 can be determined by using Eq. 7 on the CFG as shown in Figure 3 as follows:*

$$\begin{aligned} Cr(S) &= e - n + 2 \\ &= 7 - 6 + 2 \\ &= 3 \end{aligned}$$

Observing Figure 3, it may be found that the result $Cr(S) = r(GS) = 3$ is the number of regions in the CFG, providing there is always a region by linking the first node to the last node in the CFG. This finding indicates that the calculation as required in Eq. 7 may be replaced by a simple count of the number of regions in *GS*.

Further, it may also be seen in Figure 3 that the result $Cr(S) = r(GS) = 3$ is the number of BCS's (as given in Definition 14) in the program or its

Figure 3. The CFG of the program MaxFinder

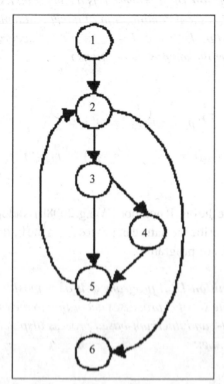

formal specification, providing a single sequential BCS is always taken into account by one. This finding reveals that the drawing of a CFG for a given program or software component is not necessary in the cyclomatic analysis. In other words, *r(CFG)* equals to the numbers of BCS's in a program (Wang, 2007a).

Incorporating the above findings with Definition 8, the following corollary is obtained.

Corollary 1. *The cyclomatic complexity of a connected software system Cr(S) can be determined by any of the following three methods:*

$$C_r(S) \triangleq e - n + 2 \qquad \text{// Method 1}$$
$$= r(CFG) \qquad \text{// Method 2} \qquad (8)$$
$$= \#(BCS) \qquad \text{// Method 3}$$

Functional Complexities of Software

In software engineering the most concerned complexity of software is the functional complexity. Functional complexity of software may be classified into two categories known as the functional points and cognitive complexity. The former is the functional complexity of software products assuming that a basic or common unit (point) of software function exist or may be definable. The latter is the functional complexity perceived by human beings in software design, implementation, and maintenance, which will be developed in the remaining sections of this paper.

Function points as a paradigm of functional size or complexity measure of software is proposed by Albrecht in 1979 (Albrecht, 1979), which is widely applied in the software industry.

Definition 9. *A function point (FP) is a virtual unit of software function that is determined by the weighted characteristic numbers of inputs, outputs, data objects, and internal processes, i.e.:*

$$S_{fp} = f(N_i, N_o, N_{if}, N_{if}, N_{if}, TCF)$$
$$= UFP * TCF$$
$$= (\sum_{k=1}^{5} w_k * N_k) * (0.65 + 0.01 \sum_{j=1}^{14} dj) \quad [FP]$$

$$(9)$$

where UFP stands for the Unjustified Function Points, TCF the Technical Correction Factors, and the characteristic numbers denote the following:

- $N_1 = N_i = \#(\text{external inputs})$, $w_1 = 4$
- $N_2 = N_o = \#(\text{external outputs})$, $w_2 = 5$
- $N_3 = N_{if} = \#(\text{internal logical files})$, $w_3 = 10$
- $N_4 = N_{if} = \#(\text{interface files})$, $w_4 = 7$
- $N_5 = N_q = \#(\text{external inquiries})$, $w_5 = 4$

According to Definition 9, function points are a subjective measure for the functional size/

complexity of software, which are affected by an individual's selection of a variety of the weights. One of the fundamental issues in the function point measurement is that its basic unit of an FP is unclear in its physical meaning, because *Sfp* is a weighted sum of all the five external I/O quantities with adjusted application area factors, the basic unit, *Sfp* = 1 [FP], has no physical sense mapping onto real-world software entities.

The survey of software complexity theories and measures in the preceding subsections indicates that more sophisticate mathematical models and measures of software functional complexity for software engineering are yet to be sought. The following sections introduce the cognitive complexity theory of software based on the generic program model and the cognitive weights of program structures in terms of BCS's.

THE COGNITIVE WEIGHTS OF FUNDAMENTAL SOFTWARE STRUCTURES BASED ON THE GENERIC MATHEMATICAL MODEL OF PROGRAMS

This section creates a generic mathematical model of programs. Based on the abstract program model, the roles of embedded process relations, particularly the BCS's, are elaborated. Then, the relative cognitive weights of BCS's are formally modeled and calibrated, which lead to the establishment of the cognitive complexity measurement of software systems in the next section.

The Mathematical Model of Programs

Despite of a rich depository of empirical knowledge on programming and software engineering, the theoretical model of programs is still unknown. This subsection presents an Embedded Relational Model (ERM) for explaining the nature of programs and software systems (Wang, 2008a, 2008d).

Definition 10. *A process P is a composed listing and a logical combination of n meta-statements p_i and p_j, $1 \leq i < n$, $1 < j \leq m = n+1$, according to certain composing relations r_{ij} i.e.:*

$$P = \mathop{R}_{i=1}^{n-1}(p_i \ r_{ij} \ p_j), j = i+1$$
$$= (...(((p_1) \ r_{12} \ p_2) \ r_{23} \ p_3) \ ... \ r_{n-1,n} \ p_n)$$

(10)

where the big-R notation (Wang, 2008b) is adopted to describe the nature of processes as the building blocks of programs.

Definition 11. *A program $\wp$ is a composition of a finite set of m processes according to the time-, event-, and interrupt-based process dispatching rules, i.e.:*

$$\wp = \mathop{R}_{k=1}^{m}(@e_k \hookrightarrow P_k)$$

(11)

The above definitions indicate that a program is an *embedded relational algebraic* entity. A *statement p* in a program is an instantiation of a meta-instruction of a programming language that executes a basic unit of coherent function and leads to a predictable behavior.

Theorem 2. *The Embedded Relational Model (ERM) states that an abstract program $\wp$ is a set of complex embedded relational processes, in which all previous processes of a given process form the context of the current process, i.e.:*

$$\wp = \mathop{R}_{k=1}^{m}(@e_k \hookrightarrow P_k)$$
$$= \mathop{R}_{k=1}^{m}[@e_k \hookrightarrow \mathop{R}_{i=1}^{n-1}(p_i(k) \ r_{ij}(k) \ p_j(k))], j = i+1$$

(12)

Proof. *Theorem 2 can be directly proved on the basis of Definitions 10 and 11. Substituting P_k as given in Definition 11 with Eq. 10, a generic program $\wp$ obtains the form as a series of embedded relational processes as presented in Theorem 2*

ERM provides a unified mathematical model of programs, which reveals that a program is a finite nonempty set of embedded binary relations between a current statement and all previous ones that forms the semantic context or environment of a program.

Theorem 3. *The sum of the cognitive weights of all rij, w(rij), in the ERM model determines the operational complexity of a software system C_{op}, i.e.:*

$$C_{op} = \sum_{i=1}^{n-1} w(r_{ij}), j = i + 1 \tag{13}$$

The EPM model of programs is developed on the basis of Real-Time Process Algebra (RTPA) (Wang, 2002a, 2007a, 2008c, 2008d, 2008e), where the definitions, syntaxes, and formal semantics of a set of meta-processes and process relational operations have been introduced. In the ERM model, a meta-process is a statement in a programming language that severs as a common and basic building block for a program, and a process relation is an algebraic composing operation between meta or complex processes.

Definition 12. *The RTPA meta-process system Π encompasses 17 fundamental computational operations elicited from the most basic computing needs, i.e.:*

$$\wp \triangleq \{:=, \blacklozenge, \Rightarrow, \Leftarrow, \Leftrightarrow, \succ, \prec, |\succ, |\prec, @, \triangleq, \uparrow, \downarrow, !, \otimes, \boxtimes, \S\} \tag{14}$$

where the meta-processes of RTPA stand for assignment, evaluation, addressing, memory allocation, memory release, read. write, input, output, timing, duration, increase, decrease, exception detection, skip, stop, and system, respectively (Wang, 2002a, 2008c).

A *complex process* can be derived from the meta-processes by the set of algebraic relational operations. Therefore, a complex process may operate on both operands and processes.

Definition 13. *The RTPA process relation system P encompasses 17 fundamental algebraic and relational operations elicited from basic computing needs, i.e.:*

$$\mathfrak{R} \triangleq \{\rightarrow, \curvearrowright, |, |\cdots|\cdots, R^*, R^+, R^i, \circlearrowleft, \rightarrowtail, \|, \oiint, \|\|, \gg, \nleftrightarrow, \hookleftarrow_t, \hookleftarrow_e, \hookleftarrow_i\} \tag{15}$$

where the relational operators of RTPA stand for sequence, jump, branch, while-loop, repeat-loop, for-loop, recursion, function call, parallel, concurrence, interleave, pipeline, interrupt, time-driven dispatch, event-driven dispatch, and interrupt-driven dispatch, respectively (Wang, 2008c).

The Role of BCS's in Software Cognitive Complexity

Definition 14. *Basic Control Structures (BCS's) are a set of essential flow control mechanisms that are used to modele logical architectures of software. The most commonly identified BCS's in computing are known as the sequential, branch, iterations, procedure call, recursion, parallel, and interrupt structures, i.e.:*

$$BCS = \{\rightarrow, |, |\cdots|, R^*, R^+, R^i, \circlearrowleft, \rightarrowtail, \| (\oiint), \nleftrightarrow\} \subset \mathfrak{R} \tag{16}$$

where $\|$ and $\oiint$ are treated as equivalent.

The ten BCS's are a subset of the most frequently used process relations P as defined in RTPA, summarized in Table 2, which provide essential compositional rules for programming. Based on the set of BCS's, any complex comput-

Table 2. BCS's and their mathematical models

Category	BCS	Structure	Definition in RTPA
Sequence	Sequence (SEQ)	(diagram)	$P \rightarrow Q$
Branch	If-then-(else) (ITE)	(diagram)	$(\blacklozenge \exp \mathbf{BL} = \mathbf{T}) \rightarrow P$ $\mid (\blacklozenge \sim) \rightarrow Q$
Branch	Case (CASE)	(diagram)	$\blacklozenge \; \exp \mathbf{RT} =$ $0 \rightarrow P_0$ $\mid 1 \rightarrow P_1$ $\mid \ldots$ $\mid n\text{-}1 \rightarrow P_{n-1}$ $\mid$ else $\rightarrow \varnothing$
Iteration	While-do (R*)	(diagram)	$\overset{F}{\underset{\exp \mathbf{BL}=\mathbf{T}}{R}} (P)$
Iteration	Repeat-until (R+)	(diagram)	$P \rightarrow \overset{F}{\underset{\exp \mathbf{BL}=\mathbf{T}}{R}} (P)$
Iteration	For-do (R^i)	(diagram)	$\overset{n}{\underset{i=1}{R}} (P(i))$
Embedment	Procedure call (PC)	(diagram)	$P \downarrow Q$
Embedment	Recursion (R$^\circlearrowleft$)	(diagram)	$P \circlearrowleft P$
Concurrency	Parallel (PAR)	(diagram)	$P \parallel Q$
Concurrency	Interrupt (INT)	(diagram)	$P \; \natural \; Q$

ing function and process may be composed on the basis of the rules of algebraic relational operations.

A formal semantics known as the *deductive semantics* of each of the above BCS's is provided in (Wang, 2006, 2008e). Since BCS's are the most highly reusable constructus in programming, according to Theorems 1 and 2, the cognitive weights of the ten fundamental BCS's play a crucial role in determining the cognitive complexity of software.

The Relative Cognitive Weights of Basic Software Structures

Definition 15. *The cognitive weight of a software system is the extent of relative difficulty or effort spent in time for comprehending the functions and semantics of the given program.*

Although it seems difficult to measure the cognitive weights of software at statement level since their variety and language dependency, it is found that it is feasible if the focus is put on the BCS's of software systems (Wang, 2007a), because there are ten BCS's only in programming no matter what kind of programming language or formal notations is used. The ten BCS's are profound architectural attributes of software systems. Therefore, their relative cognitive weights are needed to be determined in an objective approach. A set of cognitive psychological experiments for testing the relative cognitive weight of a BCS is designed (Osgood, 1953; Wang, 2005), based on the axiom that the relative time spent on comprehending the function and semantics of a BCS is proportional to the relative cognitive weight of effort for the given BCS.

Definition 16. *The relative cognitive weight of a BCS, $w_{BCS}(i)$, $1 \leq i \leq 10$, is the relative time or effort spent on comprehending the function and semantics of a BCS against that of the sequential BCS_1, i.e.:*

$$w_{BCS}(i) = \frac{t_{BCS}(i)}{t_{BCS}(1)} \ [CWU], \quad 1 \leq i \leq 10$$

(17)

where $t_{BCS}(1)$ is the relative time spent on the sequential BCS.

Definition 17. *The unit of cognitive weight of BCS's, CWU, is the relative time spent on the sequential BCS, i.e.:*

$$w_{BCS}(1) = \frac{t_{BCS}(1)}{t_{BCS}(1)}$$

$$= 1 \ [CWU]$$

(18)

Although, absolutely, different persons may comprehend the set of the ten BCS's in different speeds and efforts according to their experience and skills in a given programming language, the relative effort or the relative weight spent on each type of BCS's are statistically stable, assuming the relative weight of the *sequential* BCS is one according to Eqs. 17 and 18.

Definition 18. *The generic psychological experimental method for establishing a benchmark of the cognitive weights of the ten BCS's can be conducted in the following steps for each of the ith, $1 \leq i \leq 10$, BCS:*

a. Record the start time T_1 in mm:ss;
b. Read a given test program, Test_i, for a specific *BCS*;
c. Derive the output(s) of the given program;
d. Record the end time T_2 in mm:ss;
e. Calculate the relative cognitive weight for the given construct, BCS_i, according to Eq. 17.

A set of 126 cognitive psychological experiments as designed according to Definition 17 have been carried out among undergraduate and graduate students as well as software engineers in the industry. Based on the experiment results, the equivalent cognitive weights of the ten fundamental BCS's are statistically calibrated as summarized in Table 3 (Wang, 2005).

The calibrated cognitive weights for the ten fundamental BCS's are illustrated in Figure 4, where the relative cognitive weight of the sequential structure is defined as one unit, i.e. $w_1 = 1$ (CWU).

Table 3. Calibrated cognitive weights of BCS's

BCS	RTPA Notation	Description	Calibrated cognitive weight (w_i)
1	$\rightarrow$	Sequence	1
2	$\mid$	Branch	3
3	$\mid...\mid$	Switch	4
4	R^i	For-loop	7
5	R^*	Repeat-loop	7
6	R^*	While-loop	8
7	$\rightarrowtail$	Function call	7
8	$\circlearrowleft$	Recursion	11
9	$\parallel$ or $\oiint$	Parallel	15
10	$\lightning$	Interrupt	22

THE COGNITIVE COMPLEXITY OF SOFTWARE SYSTEMS

As reviewed in the ERM theory in Section 3, software functional complexity can be rigorously measured in a new way known as software cognitive complexity. This section develops the mathematical model and measurement methodology of cognitive complexity for software systems on the basis of software semantic structures (Wang, 2006, 2007a). A main notion is that the cognitive complexity of software is not a trivial one rather than a complex product of its operational and structural complexities.

The Operational Complexity of Software Systems

There are two structural patterns of BCS's in a given software system S: the *sequentially* and the *embedded* related BCS's. In the former, all the BCS's are in a linear layout in S, therefore the operational complexity of S is a sum of the cognitive weights of all linear BCS's. In the latter,

some BCS's are embedded in others in S, hence the operational complexity of S is a product of the cognitive weights of inner BCS's and the weights of outer layer BCS's. In general, the two types of BCS architectural relations in S may be combined in various ways. Therefore, a general method for calculating the operational complexity of software can be derived as follows.

Definition 19. *The operational complexity of a software system S, $C_{op}(S)$, is determined by the sum of the cognitive weights of its n linear blocks composed by individual BCS's, where each block may consist of q layers of embedded BCS's, and within each of the layer there are m linear BCS's, i.e.:*

$$
\begin{aligned}
C_{op}(S) &= \sum_{k=1}^{n_c} C_{op}(C_k) \\
&= \sum_{k=1}^{n_c} \left(\prod_{j=1}^{q_k} \sum_{i=1}^{m_{k,j}} w(k,j,i) \right) \quad [F]
\end{aligned}
$$
(19)

If there is no embedded BCS in any of the n_c components in Eq. 19, i.e., $q = 1$, then the operational complexity can be simplified as follows:

$$
\begin{aligned}
C_{op}(S) &= \sum_{k=1}^{n_c} C_{op}(C_k) \\
&= \sum_{k=1}^{n_c} \sum_{i=1}^{m_k} w(k,i) \quad [F]
\end{aligned}
$$
(20)

where $w(k, BCS)$ is given in Figure 4.

Definition 20. *The unit of operational complexity of software systems is a single sequential operation called a function F, i.e.:*

$$
C_{op}(S) = 1 \, [F] \Leftrightarrow \#(SeqOP(S)) = 1
$$
(21)

Figure 4. The relative cognitive weights of BCS's of software systems

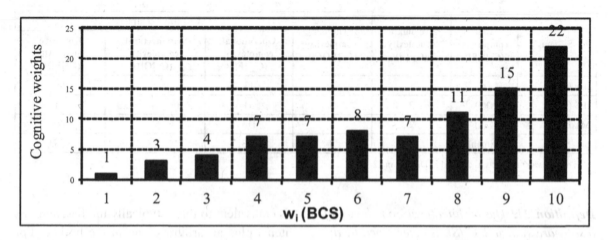

Note: 1 – sequence, 2 – branch, 3 – switch, 4 – for-loop, 5 – repeat-loop,
6 – while-loop, 7 – functional call, 8 – recursion, 9 – parallel, 10 - interrupt

With the cognitive weight of sequential process relation defined as a unit of operational function of software systems, complex process relations can be quantitatively analyzed and measured.

Example 3. *The operational complexity of the algorithm of In-Between Sum, IBS_Algorithm*ST, *as given in Figure 7, can be analyzed as follows:*

$$C_{op}(S) = \sum_{k=1}^{n_C} \left(\prod_{j=1}^{q} \sum_{i=1}^{m} w(k, i, j) \right)$$

$$= \sum_{k=1}^{n_C} \sum_{i=1}^{m} w(k, i)$$

$$= w_{BCS}(\text{SEQ}) + \{w(\text{ITE}) \cdot 2w(\text{SEQ}) + w(\text{ITE}) \cdot 2w(\text{SEQ})\}$$

$$= 1 + (3 \cdot 2 + 3 \cdot 2)$$

$$= 13 \quad [\text{F}]$$

It is noteworthy that for a fully sequential software system where only $w(\text{sequence}) = 1$ [F] is involved, its operational complexity is reduced to the symbolic complexity in LOC.

Corollary 2. *The symbolic complexity $C_s(S)$ is a special case of the operational complexity $C_{op}(S)$, where the cognitive weights of all kinds of BCS's, $w_i(BCS)$, are simplified as a constant one, i.e.:*

$$S_{op}(S) = \sum_{k=1}^{n_C} \sum_{i=1}^{m_k} w(k, i)$$

$$= C_s(S), w(k, i) \equiv 1 \qquad (22)$$

$$= C_s(S) \quad [\text{LOC}]$$

Corollary 2 presents an important finding on the relationship between conventional symbolic complexity and the operational complexity of software. It indicates that the symbolic measure in LOC is oversimplified so that it cannot represent the real functional complexities and sizes of software systems. Case studies summarized in Table 4 show that algorithms or programs with similar symbolic complexities may possess widely different functional complexities in terms of the operational and cognitive complexities.

The Architectural Complexity of Software Systems

The architectural complexity of software systems is proportional to its global and local data objects such as inputs, outputs, data structures, and internal variables.

Table 4. Comparative measurements of software system complexities

System	Time complexity (C_t [OP])	Cyclomatic complexity (C_m [-])	Symbolic complexity (C_s [LOC])	Cognitive complexity		
				Operational complexity (C_{op} [F])	Architectural complexity (C_a [O])	Cognitive complexity (C_c [FO])
IBS (a)	ε	1	7	13	5	65
IBS (b)	O(n)	2	8	34	5	170
MaxFinder	O(n)	2	5	115	5*	575
SIS_Sort	O(m+n)	5	8	163	11*	1,793

* The equivalent objects as defined in Definition 22

Definition 21. *The architectural complexity of a software system S, $C_a(S)$, is determined by the number of data objects at system and component levels, i.e.:*

$$C_a(S) = \text{OBJ}(S))$$
$$= \sum_{k=1}^{n_{CLM}} \text{OBJ}(CLM_k) + \sum_{k=1}^{n_C} \text{OBJ}(C_k) \quad [O]$$
(23)

where OBJ is a function that counts the number of data objects in a given Component Logical Model (CLM) (Wang, 2002a), which is equivalent to the number of global variables or components (number of local variables).

Definition 22. *The unit of architectural complexity of software systems is a single data object, modeled either globally or locally, called an object O, i.e.:*

$$C_a(S) = 1 \, [O] \Leftrightarrow \#(\text{OBJ}(S)) = 1 \quad (24)$$

For a high throughput system in which a large number of similar inputs and/or outputs are operated, the equivalent architectural complexity is treated as a constant *three* rather than infinitive as may be resulted in the computational complexity. This is determined on the basis of cognitive informatics where the inductive inference effort of a large even infinitive series of similar patterns

is equivalent to three, typically the first and last items plus an arbitrary one in the middle. For instance, the *equivalent number of data objects in the set* {X[1]N, X[2]N, …, X[n]N} is counted as three rather than *n*.

Example 4. *The architectural complexity of the MaxFinder algorithm as shown in Figure 9 can be determined as follows:*

$$C_a(MaxFider) = \text{OBJ}(MaxFider)$$
$$= \#(\text{inputs}) + \#(\text{outputs}) + \#(\text{local variables})$$
$$= 3+1+3$$
$$= 7 \quad [O]$$

Example 5. *The CLM SysClock ST given in Figure 5 encompasses 7 objects, therefore its architectural complexity is: $C_a(SysClock ST) = 7 \, [O]$.*

The Cognitive Complexity of Software Systems

On the basis of the elaborations of software architectural and operational complexities, the cognitive complexity of software systems is introduced as a fundamental measure of the functional complexity and sizes of software systems. It is empirically observed that the cognitive complexity of a software system is not only determined by its operational complexity, but also determined by its architectural complexity (Wang, 2006). That is, software cognitive complexity is proportional to

*Figure 5. The CLM architecture of a component: SysClock*ST

$$
\begin{aligned}
\text{SysClock}\mathbf{ST} &\triangleq \text{SysClock}\mathbf{S} :: \\
&(<\S t : \mathbf{N} \mid 0 \le \S t\mathbf{N} \le 1M>, \\
&\quad <\text{CurrentTime} : \mathbf{hh:mm:ss:ms} \mid 00:00:00:000 \le \\
&\text{CurrentTime } \mathbf{hh:mm:ss:ms} \le 23:59:59:999>, \\
&\quad <\text{Timer} : \mathbf{SS} \mid 0 \le \text{Timer}\mathbf{SS} \le 3600>, \\
&\quad <\text{MainClockPort} : \mathbf{B} \mid \text{MainClockPort}\mathbf{B} = \text{FFF0}\mathbf{H} >, \\
&\quad <\text{ClockInterval} : \mathbf{N} \mid \text{TimeInterval}\mathbf{N} = \mathbf{1ms}>, \\
&\quad <\text{InterruptCounter} : \mathbf{N} \mid 0 \le \text{InterruptCounter}\mathbf{N} \le 999> \\
&)
\end{aligned}
$$

both its operational and architectural complexities. This leads to the formal description of the cognitive complexity of software systems.

Definition 23. *The semantic function of a program $\wp$, $f_\theta(\wp)$, is a finite set of values V determined by a Cartesian product on a finite set of variables S and a finite set of executing steps T, i.e.:*

$$
\begin{aligned}
f_\theta(\wp) = f\!: T \times S \to V \\
= \begin{pmatrix}
 & s_1 & s_2 & \cdots & s_m \\
t_0 & \bot & \bot & \cdots & \bot \\
t_1 & v_{11} & v_{12} & & v_{1m} \\
\vdots & \vdots & \vdots & \ddots & \vdots \\
t_n & v_{n1} & v_{n1} & \cdots & v_{nm}
\end{pmatrix}
\end{aligned} \quad (25)
$$

where $T = \{t_0, t_1, ..., t_n\}$, $S = \{s_1, s_2, ..., s_m\}$, and V is a set of values $v(t_i, s_j)$, $0 \le i \le n$, and $1 \le j \le m$.

According to Definition 23, the semantic space of a program can be illustrated by a two dimensional plane as shown in Figure 6.

Observing Figure 6 and Eq. 25, it can be seen that the complexity of a software system, or its semantic space, is determined not only by the number of operations, but also by the number of data objects under operation.

Theorem 4. *The cognitive complexity $C_c(S)$ of a software system S is a product of the operational complexity $C_{op}(S)$ and the architectural complexity $C_a(S)$, i.e.:*

$$
\begin{aligned}
C_c(S) &= C_{op}(S) \bullet C_a(S) \\
&= \{\sum_{k=1}^{n_C} \sum_{i=1}^{\#(C_s(C_k))} w(k, i)\} \bullet \\
&\quad \{\sum_{k=1}^{n_{CLM}} \text{OBJ}(CLM_k) + \sum_{k=1}^{n_C} \text{OBJ}(C_k)\} \quad [FO]
\end{aligned} \quad (26)
$$

Corollary 3. *The cognitive complexity of a software system is proportional to both its the operational and structural complexities. That is, the more the architectural data objects and the higher the operational complicity onto these data objects, the larger the functional complexity of the system.*

Definition 24. *The unit of cognitive complexity of a software system is a single sequential operation onto a single data object called a function-object FO, i.e.:*

$$
\begin{aligned}
C_f &= C_{op} \bullet C_a \\
&= 1[F] \bullet 1[O] \\
&= 1 \quad [FO]
\end{aligned} \quad (27)
$$

According to Definition 24, the physical meaning of software cognitive complexity is how many function-object [FO] are equivalent for a given software system. The cognitive complexity as a measure enables the accurate determination of software functional sizes and design efforts in software engineering practice. It will be demonstrated in the next section that the cognitive com-

Figure 6. The semantic space of software systems

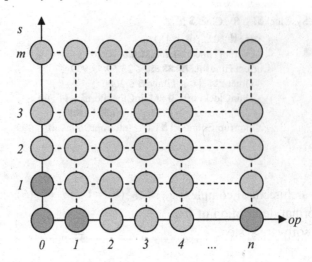

plexity is the most distinguishable and accurate measure for the inherent functional complexity of software systems.

COMPARATIVE STUDIES ON THE COGNITIVE COMPLEXITY OF SOFTWARE SYSTEMS

On the basis of the classification of software complexities and the introduction of the cognitive complexity of software systems in preceding sections, a comparatively analysis between cognitive complexity in the facets of the operational and architectural complexities, as well as conventional time, cyclomatic, and symbolic (LOC) complexities may provide useful insights. A set of case studies is carried out in order to examine the measurability and accuracy of various complexity and size measures for software systems in software engineering. The results demonstrate that cognitive complexity is the most sensitive measure for denoting the real complexities and functional sizes of software systems.

Comparative Case Studies on Different Complexity Models of Software Systems

Four sample software components in formal RTPA models are adopted to explain the comparative complexity analyses in Examples 6 through 8.

*Example 6. The formal specification of the algorithm of In-Between Sum (IBS), IBS_Algorithm*ST, *is specified in two different approaches as shown in Figures 7 and 8, respectively.*

*Example 7. An algorithm, MaxFinder*ST, *is formally described in RTPA as shown in Figure 9. Its function is to find the maximum number max*N *from a set of n inputted integers {X[1]*N, X[2]N, *..., X[n]*N}.

*Example 8. The self-index sort (SIS) algorithm, SIS*ST, *can be formally described in RTPA as shown in Figure 10. Detailed explanations of the algorithm may be referred to (Wang, 1996).*

According to the methodologies of cognitive complexity measurement, particularly Eqs. 19, 23, and 26, the cognitive complexity of these four

Figure 7. The formal model of the IBS algorithm (a) in RTPA

```
IBS_AlgorithmST ({I:: AN, BN}; {O:: ⑤IBSResultBL, IBSumN}) ≜
{ // Specification (a)
    MaxN := 65535
    → ( ◆ (0 < AN < maxN) ∧ (0 < BN < maxN) ∧ (AN < BN)
            → IBSumN := ((BN - 1) * BN) / 2) - (AN * (AN + 1) / 2)
            → ⑤IBSResultBL := T
        | ◆ ~
            → ⑤IBSResultBL := F
            → ! (@'AN and/or BN out of range, or AN ≥ BN')
        )
}
```

Figure 8. The formal model of the IBS algorithm (b) in RTPA

```
IBS_AlgorithmST ({I:: AN, BN}; {O:: ⑤IBSResultBL, IBSumN}) ≜
{ // Specification (b)
    MaxN := 65535
    → ( ◆ (0 < AN < maxN) ∧ (0 < BN < maxN) ∧ (AN < BN)
            → IBSumN := 0
```
$$\rightarrow IBSumN := \mathop{R}_{iN=AN+1}^{BN-1} (IBSumN + iN)$$
```
            → ⑤IBSResultBL := T
        | ◆ ~
            → ⑤IBSResultBL := F
            →! (@'AN and/or BN out of range, or AN ≥ BN')
        )
}
```

sample programs can be systematically analyzed as summarized in Table 4. Table 4 provides a systematical contrast of the measures of time, cyclomatic, symbolic, operational, architectural, and cognitive complexities.

Observing Table 4 it is noteworthy that the first three measurements, namely the time, cyclomatic, and symbolic complexities, cannot actually reflect the real complexity of software systems in design, representation, cognition, and/or comprehension in software engineering.

- Although the four example systems are with similar symbolic complexities, their operational and cognitive complexities are greatly different. This indicates that the symbolic complexity cannot be used to represent the operational or functional complexity of software systems.
- Symbolic complexity does not represent the throughput or the input size of problems.
- Time complexity does not work well for a system where is no loop and/or dominant operations, because theoretically in this case all statements in linear structures are treated as zero no matter how long they are. In addition, time complexity cannot distinguish the real complexities of systems with the same asymptotic function, such as in Case 2 (IBS (b)) and Case 3 (Maxfinder).

Figure 9. The formal model of the MaxFinder algorithm in RTPA

$$\text{MaxFinder}(\{I:: X[0]\mathbf{N}, X[1]\mathbf{N}, ..., X[n-1]\mathbf{N}\}; \{O:: \max\mathbf{N}\}) \triangleq$$
$$\{$$
$$\quad X\max\mathbf{N} := 0$$
$$\rightarrow \mathop{R}\limits_{i\mathbf{N}=0}^{n\mathbf{N}-1} ($$
$$\qquad\qquad \blacklozenge X[i\,\mathbf{N}]\mathbf{N} > X\max\mathbf{N}$$
$$\qquad\qquad\quad \rightarrow X\max\mathbf{N} := X[i\,\mathbf{N}]\mathbf{N}$$
$$\qquad\qquad)$$
$$\quad \rightarrow \max\mathbf{N} := X\max\mathbf{N}$$
$$\}$$

Figure 10. The Formal model of the SIS sort algorithm in RTPA

$$\text{SIS\_Sort}\mathbf{ST}(\{I:: X[i\mathbf{N}]\ \mathbf{Array}\}; \{O:: X[s_i\mathbf{N}]\ \mathbf{Array}, \text{⑤SISResult}\mathbf{BL}) \triangleq$$

$\{$ // <Input:: X[i$\mathbf{N}$] : Array | $0 \le i\mathbf{N} \le n\mathbf{N} -1$, $0 \le X[i\mathbf{N}]\,\mathbf{N} \le m\mathbf{N}-1$, $m\mathbf{N} > n\mathbf{N}$>

// <Output:: X[s_i$\mathbf{N}$] : Array | $0 \le s_i\mathbf{N} \le n\mathbf{N} -1$, $x_{s0} \le x_{s1} \le, ..., \le x_{si} \le, ..., \le x_{sn-1}$>

// <CLM:: SS[j$\mathbf{N}$] : Array | $0 \le j\mathbf{N} \le m\mathbf{N} -1$, $0 \le m\mathbf{N} \le \max\mathbf{N}$>

// Initialization
$$\mathop{R}\limits_{j=0}^{m-1} SS[j\mathbf{N}]\mathbf{N} := 0$$

// Self-index sorting
$$\rightarrow \mathop{R}\limits_{i=0}^{n-1} (\uparrow (SS[X[i\mathbf{N}]\mathbf{N}]\mathbf{N})$$

// Compression
$$\rightarrow i\mathbf{N} := 0$$

$$\rightarrow \mathop{R}\limits_{j=0}^{m-1} (\mathop{R}\limits_{ss[j]>0}^{ss[j]\le 0} (X[i\mathbf{N}]\ \mathbf{N} := j\mathbf{N}$$
$$\rightarrow \downarrow(SS[j\mathbf{N}]\mathbf{N})$$
$$\rightarrow \uparrow(i\mathbf{N})$$
$$)$$
$$)$$
$$\rightarrow \text{⑤SISResult}\mathbf{BL} := \mathbf{T}$$
$$\}$$

- The cognitive complexity is a more objective and rigorous measure of software system complexities and sizes, because it represents the real semantic complexity by integrating both the operational and architectural complexities in a coherent measure. For example, the difference between IBS(a) and IBS(b) can be successfully captured by cognitive complexity. However, symbolic and cyclomatic complexities cannot identify the functional differences very well.

The Symbolic vs. Cognitive Sizes of Software Systems

The cognitive complexity models developed so far have established a connection between the operational and architectural complexities of software. They also reveal that the symbolic complexity is only a special case of the operational complexity. The following investigation will establish another connection between the operational complexity and system relational complexity.

According to the generic system complexity theory (Wang, 2007a), when a system is treated as a black box, the relational complexity of the system can be estimated by the maximum possible pairwise relations between all components in the system.

Definition 25. *The relational complexity of software system S, $C_r(S)$, is the maximum number of relations n_r among components, i.e.:*

$$C_r(S) = n_r$$
$$= n_c(n_c - 1) \quad [R] \tag{28}$$

where the unit of the relational complexity is the number of relations R, which is equivalent to F as defined in the operational complexity.

It is noteworthy that $C_r(S)$ provides the maximum potential or the upper limit of internal relational complexity of a given software system. The relationship among the symbolic, relational, and operational complexities of software systems is plotted in Figure 11 in logarithmic scale. As shown in Figure 11, the symbolic complexity of software $C_s(S)$ is the lower bound of the functional complexity of software and it is linearly proportional to the number of statements n, i.e., $O(n)$. The relational complexity $C_r(S)$ is the upper bound of functional complexity of software in the order of $O(n^2)$. Therefore, the real cognitive functional complexity represented by the operational complexity $C_{op}(S)$ is bounded between the curves of the symbolic and relational complexities.

Figure 11 indicates that the floor of the operational complexity $C_{op}(S)$ of software systems is determined by the symbolic complexity $C_s(S)$ when only sequential relation is considered between all adjacent statements in a given program and all weights of the sequential relational operations in computing are simplified to one. The ceiling of the operational complexity $C_{op}(S)$ is determined by the relational complexity $C_r(S)$,

Figure 11. The relational and symbolic complexities as the upper/lower bounds of functional complexity of software systems

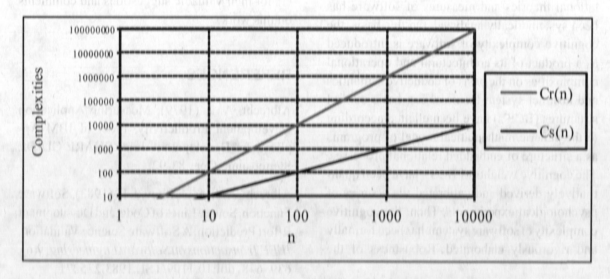

when all potential relations among the components (statements) in computing are considered.

Corollary 4. *The operational complexity $C_{op}(S)$ of a software system S is constrained by the lower bound of the symbolic complexity $C_s(S)$ and the upper bound of the relational complexity $C_r(S)$, i.e.:*

$$O(n) \leq C_{op}(S) \leq O(n^2) \qquad (29)$$

where n is the number of statements in S.

According to Corollary 4 and Figure 11 it can be seen that the real complexity and size of software systems had probably been greatly underestimated when the conventional symbolic size measurement (LOC) is adopted, because it represents the minimum functional complexity of software. Therefore, the functional size of software systems measured by the cognitive complexity as described in Theorem 3 provides a more accurate size and complexity measurement for software systems in software engineering.

CONCLUSION

This paper has presented a new approach to model and quantifying the cognitive complexity of software. A comprehensive survey of computational theories and measures of software has been systematically analyzed. On this basis, the cognitive complexity of software is introduced as a product of its architectural and operational complexities on the basis of deductive semantics and abstract system theories. Ten basic control structures (BCS's) have been elicited according to the generic mathematical model of programs as a structure of embedded relational processes. The cognitive weights of BCS's have been quantitatively derived and calibrated via a series of psychological experiments. Then, the cognitive complexity of software systems has been formally and rigorously elaborated. Robustness of the

cognitive complexity measure has been analyzed with comparative case studies.

According to the cognitive complexity theory, it is found that the traditional time, cyclomatic, and symbolic complexities cannot actually reflect the real complexity of software systems in design, representation, cognition, and/or comprehension in software engineering. More fundamentally, although it is well applied in machine oriented estimations, conventional computational complexity might not be sensitive and distinguishable for human cognitive and creative work products in software engineering. The real complexity and size of software systems might have been greatly underestimated when the conventional symbolic size measurement is adopted, because it represents only the lower bound of the functional complexity of software systems. These findings indicate that the cognitive complexity needs to be adopted for rationally measuring the functional sizes of software systems in software engineering.

ACKNOWLEDGMENT

The author would like to acknowledge the Natural Science and Engineering Council of Canada (NSERC) for its partial support to this work. The author would like to thank the anonymous reviewers for their valuable suggestions and comments on this work.

REFERENCES

Albrecht, A. J. (1979), Measuring Application Development Productivity, Proc. of IBM Applications Development Joint SHARE/GUIDE Symposium, Oct., 83-92.

Albrecht, A. J., & Gaffney, J. E. (1983). Software Function, Source Lines of Code, and Development Effort Prediction: A Software Science Validation. *IEEE Transactions on Software Engineering, 9*(6), 639–648. doi:10.1109/TSE.1983.235271

Basili, V. R. (1980). *Qualitative Software Complexity Models: A Summary in Tutorial on Models and Methods for Software Management and Engineering.* Los Alamitos, CA: IEEE Computer Society Press.

Fenton, N. E., & Pfleeger, S. L. (1998). *Software Metrics: A Rigorous and Practical Approach* (2nd ed.). Brooks/Cole Pub Co.

Halstead, M. H. (1977). *Elements of Software Science.* New York: Elsevier North – Holland.

Hartmanis, J. (1994). On Computational Complexity and the Nature of Computer Science, 1994 Turing Award Lecture. *Communications of the ACM, 37*(10), 37–43. doi:10.1145/194313.214781

Hartmanis, J., & Stearns, R. E. (1965). On the Computational Complexity of Algorithms. *Trans. AMS, 117,* 258–306. doi:10.1090/S0002-9947-1965-0170805-7

Kearney, J. K., Sedlmeyer, R. L., Thompson, W. B., Gary, M. A., & Adler, M. A. (1986). *Software Complexity Measurement* (Vol. 28, pp. 1044–1050). New York: ACM Press.

Lewis, H. R., & Papadimitriou, C. H. (1998). *Elements of the Theory of Computation* (2nd ed.). Englewood Cliffs, NJ: Prentice Hall International.

Lipschutz, S., & Lipson, M. (1997). *Schaum's Outline of Theories and Problems of Discrete Mathematics* (2nd ed.). New York, NY: McGraw-Hill Inc.

McCabe, T. H. (1976). A Complexity Measure. *IEEE Transactions on Software Engineering, SE-2*(6), 308–320. doi:10.1109/TSE.1976.233837

McDermid, J. A. (Ed.). (1991). *Software Engineer's Reference Book.* Oxford, UK: Butterworth-Heinemann Ltd.

Melton, A. (Ed.). (1996). *Software Measurement.* International Thomson Computer Press.

Osgood, C. (1953). *Method and Theory in Experimental Psychology.* UK: Oxford Univ. Press.

Wang, Y. (1996). A New Sorting Algorithm: Self-Indexed Sort. *ACM SIGPLAN, 31*(3), 28–36. doi:10.1145/227717.227725

Wang, Y. (2002a), The Real-Time Process Algebra (RTPA), *Annals of Software Engineering: An International Journal,* 14, USA, Oct., 235-274.

Wang, Y. (2002b), Keynote: *On Cognitive Informatics,* Proc. First IEEE International Conference on Cognitive Informatics (ICCI'02), Calgary, AB., Canada, IEEE CS Press, August, pp.34-42.

Wang, Y. (2003a), On Cognitive Informatics, *Brain and Mind: A Transdisciplinary Journal of Neuroscience and Neurophilosophy,* 4(2), 151-167.

Wang, Y. (2003b), The Measurement Theory for Software Engineering, *Proc. 2003 Canadian Conference on Electrical and Computer Engineering* (CCECE'03), IEEE CS Press, Montreal, Canada, May, pp.1321-1324.

Wang, Y. (2005), Keynote: Psychological Experiments on the Cognitive Complexities of Fundamental Control Structures of Software Systems, *Proc. 4th IEEE International Conference on Cognitive Informatics* (ICCI'05), IEEE CS Press, Irvin, California, USA, August, pp. 4-5.

Wang, Y. (2006). On the Informatics Laws and Deductive Semantics of Software. *IEEE Transactions on Systems, Man and Cybernetics. Part C, Applications and Reviews, 36*(2), 161–171. doi:10.1109/TSMCC.2006.871138

Wang, Y. (2007a), *Software Engineering Foundations: A Transdisciplinary and Rigorous Perspective,* CRC Book Series in Software Engineering, Vol. II, Auerbach Publications, NY, USA, July.

Wang, Y. (2007b). The Theoretical Framework of Cognitive Informatics. *International Journal of Cognitive Informatics and Natural Intelligence, 1*(1), 1–27. doi:10.4018/jcini.2007010101

Wang, Y. (2008a), *On Contemporary Denotational Mathematics for Computational Intelligence, Transactions of Computational Science, 2*, Springer, August, pp. 6-29.

Wang, Y. (2008b). On the Big-R Notation for Describing Iterative and Recursive Behaviors. *International Journal of Cognitive Informatics and Natural Intelligence, 2*(1), 17–28. doi:10.4018/jcini.2008010102

Wang, Y. (2008c). RTPA: A Denotational Mathematics for Manipulating Intelligent and Computational Behaviors. *International Journal of Cognitive Informatics and Natural Intelligence, 2*(2), 44–62. doi:10.4018/jcini.2008040103

Wang, Y. (2008d), Mathematical Laws of Software, *Transactions of Computational Science, 2*, Springer, Aug., pp. 46-83.

Wang, Y. (2008e). Deductive Semantics of RTPA. *International Journal of Cognitive Informatics and Natural Intelligence, 2*(2), 95–121. doi:10.4018/jcini.2008040106

Wang, Y., & Shao, J. (2003), Measurement of the Cognitive Functional Complexity of Software, The 2nd IEEE International Conference on Cognitive Informatics (ICCI'03), IEEE CS Press, London, UK, August, pp.67-74.

Zuse, H. (1997). *A Framework of Software Measurement*. Berlin: Walter de Gruyter & Co.

This work was previously published in International Journal of Software Science and Computational Intelligence, Volume 1, Issue 2, edited by Yingxu Wang, pp. 31-53, copyright 2009 by IGI Publishing (an imprint of IGI Global).

Chapter 17
Machine Learning and Value–Based Software Engineering

Du Zhang
California State University, USA

ABSTRACT

Software engineering research and practice thus far are primarily conducted in a value-neutral setting where each artifact in software development such as requirement, use case, test case, and defect, is treated as equally important during a software system development process. There are a number of shortcomings of such value-neutral software engineering. Value-based software engineering is to integrate value considerations into the full range of existing and emerging software engineering principles and practices. Machine learning has been playing an increasingly important role in helping develop and maintain large and complex software systems. However, machine learning applications to software engineering have been largely confined to the value-neutral software engineering setting. In this paper, the general message to be conveyed is to apply machine learning methods and algorithms to value-based software engineering. The training data or the background knowledge or domain theory or heuristics or bias used by machine learning methods in generating target models or functions should be aligned with stakeholders' value propositions. An initial research agenda is proposed for machine learning in value-based software engineering.

INTRODUCTION

Software engineering research and practice thus far are mainly conducted in a value-neutral setting where each artifact in software development such as a requirement, a use case, a test case, a defect,

and so forth, is treated as equally important during a software system development process (Boehm, 2006a). There are a number of shortcomings of such value-neutral software engineering (Biffl et al. 2006): (1) its exclusion of economics, management sciences, cognitive sciences, and humanities from the body of knowledge needed to develop successful software systems; (2) its delimitation

DOI: 10.4018/978-1-4666-0261-8.ch017

of software development by mere technical activities; and (3) its failure to explicitly recognize the fact that software systems continue to satisfy and conform to evolving human and organizational needs is to create value. Value-based software engineering (VBSE) is to integrate value considerations into the full range of existing and emerging software engineering principles and practices so as to increase the return on investment (ROI = (benefits–costs)/costs) for the stakeholders and optimize other relevant value objectives of software projects (Biffl et al. 2006; Boehm, 2006a, Wang, 2007).

Machine learning (ML) has been playing an increasingly important role in helping develop and maintain large and complex software systems. However, machine learning applications to software engineering have been largely confined to the value-neutral software engineering setting (Zhang, 2000; Zhang & Tsai, 2003; Zhang & Tsai, 2005; Zhang & Tsai, 2007, Wang, 2008). In this paper, the general message we attempt to convey is to apply ML methods beyond the value-neutral software engineering setting and to VBSE. The training data or the background knowledge or domain theory or heuristics or bias used by ML methods in generating target models or functions for software development and maintenance should be aligned with stakeholders' value propositions (SVPs) and business objectives. Even though the transition to VBSE from the traditional value-neutral setting is necessarily evolutionary because not all the theories, infrastructures, methodologies and tools for VBSE have been fully developed yet, there are a number of agenda items for VBSE (Boehm, 2006a).

The goal of the road map in VBSE is to make software development and maintenance decisions that are better for value creation (Boehm, 2006a). On the other hand, the hallmark of ML is that it results in an improved ability to make better decisions. VBSE offers a fertile ground where many software development and maintenance tasks can be formulated as ML problems and approached in terms of ML methods. The purpose of this paper is to describe an initial research agenda for ML applications to VBSE with regard to the identified areas in VBSE (value-based requirement engineering, architecting, design and development, verification and validation, planning and control, risk/quality/people managements, and a theory of VBSE (Boehm, 2006a)).

The rest of the paper is organized as follows. Section 2 offers an overview of the related work. Section 3 highlights some important concepts in VBSE. In Section 4, we describe an initial research agenda for ML applications in VBSE. Finally Section 5 concludes the paper with remark on future work.

RELATED WORK

In this section, we provide a brief account for some of the major and emerging software development paradigms which are related to the main theme of this paper. The intent is to highlight the state-of-the-art in the software development landscape and to delineate differences between the existing approaches and the one advocated in this paper.

Besides machine learning in (value-neutral) software engineering (MLSE), there are a number of related and emerging software development paradigms: search-based software engineering (SBSE), evidence-based software engineering (EBSE), model-based software engineering (MBSE), artificial intelligence in software engineering (AISE), and computational intelligence in software engineering (CISE). Figure 1 highlights their similarities and differences.

MLSE

ML falls into the following broad categories: *supervised* learning, *unsupervised* learning, *semi-supervised* learning, *analytical* learning, *reinforcement* learning, and *multi-agent* learning. Each of the categories in turn includes various

Figure 1. Emerging software development paradigms

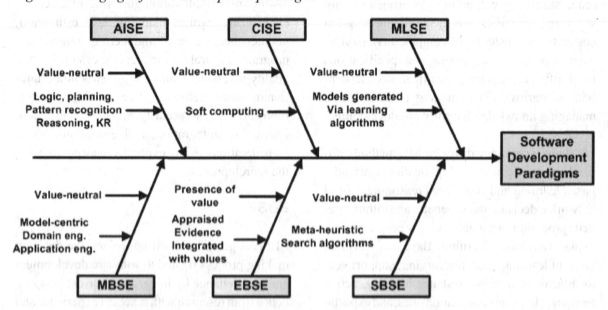

learning methods. Supervised learning deals with learning a target function from labeled examples. Unsupervised learning attempts to learn patterns and associations from a set of objects that do not have attached class labels. Semi-supervised learning is learning from a combination of labeled and unlabeled examples. Analytical learning relies on domain theory or background knowledge to learn a target function. Reinforcement learning is concerned with learning a control policy through reinforcement from an environment. Multi-agent learning is an extension to single-agent leaning. There are of course many emerging learning methods such as argument based machine learning, interactive learning, and so forth.

In software development, there are processes, products and resources (Fenton & Pfleeger, 1997). Processes are collections of software related activities, such as constructing specification, detailed design, or testing. Products refer to artifacts, deliverables, documents that result from a process activity, such as a specification document, a design document, or a segment of code. Resources are entities required by a process activity, such as personnel, software tools, or hardware. The aforementioned entities have internal and external attributes. Internal attributes describe an entity itself, whereas external attributes characterize the behavior of an entity (how the entity relates to its environment).

A partial list of ML applications in value-neutral software engineering includes (Zhang, 2000; Zhang & Tsai, 2003; Zhang & Tsai, 2005; Zhang & Tsai, 2007): (1) Predicting or estimating measurements for either internal or external attributes of software development processes, products, or resources (e.g., quality, size, cost, effort). (2) Discovering either internal or external properties of the processes, products, or resources (e.g., loop invariants, objects, normal operation boundary, equivalent mutants, process models, architecture information, aspects). (3) Transforming products to accomplish some desirable or improved external attributes (e.g., serial programs to parallel ones, improving software modularity). (4) Synthesizing or generating various products (e.g., evolutionary testing for generating test data, project management rules and schedules, design repair knowledge, design schemas, programs/scripts/agents). (5) Reusing products or processes (e.g., similarity computing, locating/adopting software to specifications, generalizing program abstractions, clustering of components). (6) Enhancing processes (e.g., extracting specifications from software, acquiring specification consistent with scenarios). (7) Managing products (e.g., managing knowledge for software development process).

There were many different ML methods utilized in the aforementioned applications (instance-based learning and case-based reasoning, neural networks, decision trees, genetic algorithms, genetic programming, inductive logic programming, explanation-based learning, Bayesian learning, concept learning, analytic learning, support vector machines, multiple instance learning, active learning, clustering, association rules, and expectation maximization) (Zhang, 2000; Zhang & Tsai, 2003; Zhang & Tsai, 2005; Zhang & Tsai, 2007). A common property in the existing ML applications is that the software engineering issues were tackled solely from technical or logical perspectives (involving mappings and transformations, for instance) without the value dimension being taken into consideration (e.g., how to increase ROI for the stakeholders and optimize other relevant value objectives of software projects). The training data or the background knowledge or domain theory or heuristics or bias used by the ML methods in generating target functions did not contain any value propositions.

SBSE

SBSE treats software development tasks as a search problem with regard to a set of constraints and a search space of possible solutions (Clark et al, 2003; Harman & Jones, 2001). It relies on evolutionary algorithms, gradient ascent/descent, particle swarm intelligence, simulated annealing, tabu search or colony optimization techniques to tackle the software development or maintenance tasks. So far its applications have included the fol-

lowing areas in software engineering: requirement engineering, project planning, cost estimation, maintenance, reverse engineering, refactoring, program comprehension, service oriented tasks, quality assessment, and testing (structural, functional, non-functional, state-based properties, robustness, stress, security, mutation, regression, interaction, integration, and exception). Value considerations are not explicitly incorporated into the search process.

EBSE

EBSE is geared toward improving the decision making process related to software development and maintenance by integrating current best evidence from research with practical experience and human values (Dyba, Kitchenham & Jorgensen, 2005; Kitchenham, Dyba & Jorgensen, 2004). There are five main steps in EBSE as delineated in (Dyba, Kitchenham & Jorgensen, 2005; Kitchenham, Dyba & Jorgensen, 2004): (1) Translate a relevant problem or need of information into an answerable question. (2) Glean the literature for the best available evidence that can be used to answer the question. (3) Assess the evidence for its validity, impact, and applicability. (4) Combine the appraised evidence with practical experience, and stakeholders' values and circumstances to make decisions. (5) Evaluate performance and find ways to improve it. One important strength of EBSE is that it does take into consideration the SVPs.

MBSE

MBSE is centered on software models, modeling, and model transformation technologies. It is a disciplined approach to developing and extending a product family. The software models provide the necessary information to support, economically and effectively, future changes to a software product family. By focusing on models that capture and consolidate developers' understanding of a family of software products, reusable assets can be developed that satisfy a wide variety of uses and can be utilized to analyze existing software to quickly compose or synthesize new solutions for subsequent products in a product family (Brown, Iyengar & Johnston, 2006; MBSE, 2008; Sendall & Kozacaynski, 2003). The goal is to achieve the benefits of reuse, shorter time to market, product maintainability and higher quality. However, value considerations are not prominently factored into the paradigm.

MBSE consists of two parallel engineering processes: domain engineering and application engineering, and sanctions the concepts of product families, a production system, and software assets (the reusable resources needed in application engineering such as domain models, software architectures, design standards, communication protocols, code components and application generators).

Domain engineering is a process of analysis, specification and implementation of software assets in a domain which are used in the development of multiple software products. Application engineering is a process that develops software products from software assets.

Many organizations have model-based development paradigm in place: Microsoft's Software Factory (Greenfield & Short, 2004), Lockheed Martin's Model Centric Software Development (Waddinggton & Lardieri 2006), and NASA JPL's Defect Detection and Prevention (Feather et al, 2008).

CISE

In CISE (or software engineering with computational intelligence), soft computing techniques such as fuzzy sets, neural networks, genetic algorithms, genetic programming and rough sets (or combinations of those individual technologies) are utilized to tackle software development issues recently [Khoshgoftaar, 2003a; Khoshgoftaar,

2003b; Lee, 2003a; Lee, 2003b; Pedrycz & Peters, 1998). The results have been largely confined to the value-neutral setting.

AISE

The application of some general artificial intelligence techniques to software engineering (AISE) has produced some encouraging results (Mendonca & Sunderhaft, 1999; Mostow, 1985; Partridge, 1998; Rich & Waters, 1986; Tsai & Weigert, 1993). Some of the successful AI techniques include: knowledge-based approach, automated reasoning, expert systems, heuristic search strategies, temporal logic, planning, and pattern recognition. Again the results thus far have been obtained in the value-neutral setting.

VBSE

The essence in VBSE is that the approach aims at aligning software development and maintenance with customer requirements and strategic business objectives. It offers a framework where SVPs are incorporated into the technical and managerial decisions made during software development and maintenance (Biffl et al. 2006; Grunbacher et al, 2006).

Value includes product, process and resource attributes. Value attributes include: profits (generated from products), strategic positioning in market share, utility, relative worth, reputation, customer loyalty, innovation technology, cost reduction, quality of life, improved productivity.

An emerging agenda of issues in VBSE has been proposed in (Boehm, 2006a), that includes the following areas:

- Value-based requirements engineering. The key objectives include recognition of success-critical stakeholders, elicitation of SVPs, and reconciliation of SVPs.

- Value-based architecturing. The goals are to iron out the discrepancy between a system's objectives and achievable architectural solutions.
- Value-based design and development. The goals are to ensure that a software system's objectives and its value considerations are embodied in the software's design and development practices.
- Value-based verification and validation. The objectives are to ascertain that a software solution meets its value objectives and that V&V tasks are sequenced and prioritized as investing activities.
- Value-based planning and control. The objectives in this area are to incorporate the value delivered to stakeholders into the product planning and control techniques.
- Value-based risk management. How to factor the value considerations into principles and practices for risk identification, analysis, prioritization, and mitigation is the main focus in this area.
- Value-based quality management. The goals are to prioritize desired software

quality considerations with respect to SVPs.

- Value-based people management. The tasks involve building stakeholder team, manage expectations, and reconcile SVPs.

A number of concepts need to be in place to facilitate ML applications in VBSE. Of the important and useful concepts is the one about Pareto modules.

Figure 2 depicts a reported study in (Bullock, 2000) where the dotted line reflects the value-neutral practice in which an automated test data generation tool assumes that all tests have the same value. The Pareto curve for the empirical data, on the other hand, displays the actual business value where one of the fifteen customer services accounted for 50% of all billing revenues.

We refer to module(s) that realizes a service of such a high positive impact on the system's ROI as *Pareto modules*. They are the most important modules of a software system with regard to its product value. How modules contribute to a product's overall value hinges on reconciled SVPs.

Figure 2. Pareto distribution for varying test case value

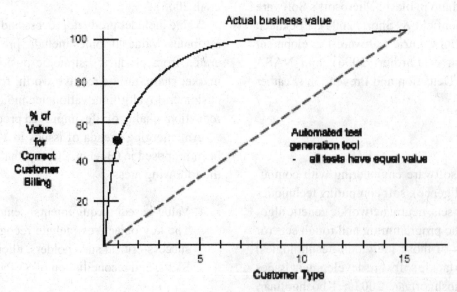

For a given software system Ω, we can define a set $\mathbf{M}_\Omega$ of modules, a valuation function υ, and a value set V as follows:

$$\mathbf{M}_\Omega = \{m_i \mid m_i \in \Omega\};$$

$$\upsilon: \mathbf{M}_\Omega \rightarrow [0, 1];$$

$$V = \{\upsilon(m_i) \mid m_i \in \mathbf{M}_\Omega\}$$

The valuation function υ can be defined by SVPs and has the following properties:

- $0 < \upsilon(m_i) \leq 1$, for all i;
- $\Sigma \upsilon(m_i) = 1$.

We define a partially ordered set $(V, \leq)$ where $\leq$ is a binary order relation on V and satisfies reflexivity, anti-symmetry and transitivity for all elements in V. We say that $\upsilon(m_p)$ is a *principal element* for $(V, \leq)$ if we have the following:

$$\forall \upsilon(m) \in V \, [\upsilon(m) \leq \upsilon(m_p)]^1$$

We use ρ to denote the *principal module* as specified by $\upsilon(m_p)$. We define a *principal-element-ordered subset* $V_{[mi, \rho]}$ of V and its cumulative value $\mu_{[mi, \rho]}$ as follows:

$$V_{[mi, \rho]} = V - \{\upsilon(m_k) \mid \upsilon(m_k) \leq \upsilon(m_i)\}$$

$$\mu_{[mi, \rho]} = \Sigma \upsilon(m_j) \in V_{[mi, \rho]}$$

Now we are in a position to formally define the concept of Pareto modules.

Definition 1. *Given a threshold value $\tau \in (0, 1]$, we identify a principal-element-ordered subset $V_{[mi, \rho]}$ such that $\tau = \mu_{[mi, \rho]}$. Modules in $V_{[mi, \rho]}$ are referred to as Pareto modules with regard to τ.*

If $\tau < \mu_{[mi, \rho]}$ but removing any m_j from $\mu_{[mi, \rho]}$ would result in $\tau > \mu_{[mi, \rho]}$, then the condition of $\tau = \mu_{[mi, \rho]}$ is relaxed to that of $\tau \leq \mu_{[mi, \rho]}$.

In practice, to identify the Pareto modules, we can apply the Pareto principle as follows: (1) arrange modules according to the descending order of their value contributions to the total product value; (2) calculate cumulative percentages of contribution with regard to all the modules; (3) draw a line graph based on the cumulative percentages and modules involved; and (4) identify the most valuable modules with regard to an established threshold value.

The next set of useful concepts pertains to modules with varying defect densities. Item four on the software defect reduction top ten list in (Boehm & Basili, 2001) indicates that "*About 80% of the defects come from 20% of the modules, and about half the modules are defect free.*" Thus, there are three types of modules here in terms of defect density measure: *defect-intensive modules* that refer to those 20% of the modules causing the bulk (80%) of defects, *defect-prone modules* that are the next 30% of modules containing the remaining 20% of defects, and *defect-free* modules that include the rest 50% of modules. In practice, there are different ways to specify the criteria for defect-intensive and defect-prone modules. Here we describe a possible way to define modules with varying defect densities that is based on the software Constructive Quality Model COQUALMO (Huang & Boehm, 2006; Steece, Chulani & Boehm, 2002).

In COQUALMO, there are two components: a defect introduction sub-model that estimates the rates at which software requirements, design and code defects are introduced, and a defect removal sub-model. Let KSLOC stand for thousand source line of code. The calibrated baseline (nominal) defect introduction rates DIR_{nom} in COQUALMO are given in Table 1 (Boehm et al, 2000; Huang & Boehm, 2006; Steece, Chulani & Boehm, 2002):

Thus the total of the nominal defect introduction rate for a software system is 60 defects/KSLOC. Multiplying the baseline rates with the size of a software system provides the total number of defects introduced in each of the three categories (requirements, design, and coding) and summing them up returns the total number of nominal defects introduced into a software system. We use NDI_Ω to denote it[2]. Scaling NDI_Ω down to the module level (e.g., if a module m has a size of 100 SLOC, then its nominal coding defects are scaled down to 3 accordingly), let NDI_m denote the nominal defects introduced into a module m and TDI_m the actual total number of defects in m. we can define defect-intensive and defect-prone modules using NDI_m as follows.

Definition 2*. A module m is defect-intensive if its defect introduction rates (in some or all three categories) are higher than the nominal rates DIR_{nom}. Therefore, we have $TDI_m > NDI_m$.*

Definition 3*. A module m is defect-prone if its defect introduction rates (in some or all three categories) are lower than the nominal rates DIR_{nom}. Therefore, we have $TDI_m \leq NDI_m$.*

There is another dimension about the nature of defects. Item five on the software defect reduction top ten list in (Boehm & Basili, 2001) states that "*About 90% of the downtime comes from, at most, 10% of the defects.*" We refer to those 10% of the defects as *impact defects*.

Definition 4*. Impact defects (or high risk defects) are those defects that result in loss of human life or high financial loss. This translates into the Required Reliability (RELY) ratings of Extra High, Very High and High according to the Constructive Cost Model (COCOMO) II (Boehm et al, 2000), and rough Mean Time Between Failures (MTBF) of one million hours, 300K hours and 10K hours, respectively (Boehm et al, 2004; Huang & Boehm, 2006).*

Definition 5*. Non-impact defects are those defects that result in moderate recoverable loss, easily recoverable loss or slight inconvenience. They have the RELY ratings of Nominal, Low and Very*

Table 1. Nominal defect introduction rates

Type of Defects	DIR_{nom}
Requirements defects	$DIR_{nom}(req) = 10/KSLOC$
Design defects	$DIR_{nom}(des) = 20/KSLOC$
Coding defects	$DIR_{nom}(cod) = 30/KSLOC$

Low, and the MTBF of 300 hours, 10 hours and 1 hour, respectively (Huang & Boehm, 2006).

The definitions of the aforementioned concepts will pave the way for ML to be utilized in various VBSE agenda issues. Further effort will be needed to fully develop concepts that accommodate comprehensive ML applications in VBSE.

RESEARCH AGENDA FOR ML IN VBSE

In this section, we first discuss some general issues on how to calibrate ML methods for VBSE tasks. Using Boehm' VBSE agenda in (Boehm, 2006a) as a roadmap, we then describe some preliminary agenda items on how ML can help with the goals, objectives and tasks in VBSE.

How to Calibrate ML Methods

ML methods formulate various general hypotheses, models and target functions through either observed training data, or some background knowledge or domain theory, or a combination of both (see Figure 3). The generalization process during leaning also hinges on certain adopted bias or heuristics.

To calibrate ML methods for VBSE tasks, the fundamental issue is how to incorporate SVPs from the business value level into the technical level details of ML model generation process. Specifically, this translates into the following issues: how to use SVPs to select data features and to group training data, how to incorporate

Figure 3. Calibrating ML methods for VBSE

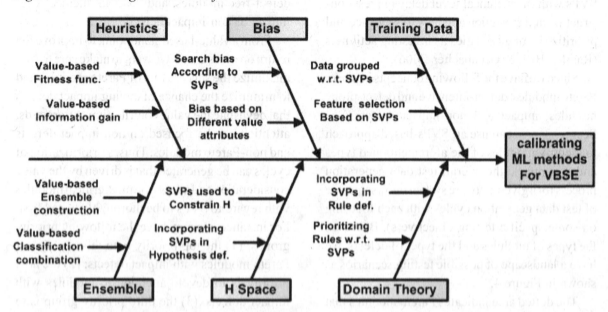

SVPs into domain knowledge representation, how to prioritize rules, based on SVPs, in domain knowledge during model generation, how to include SVPs in defining search bias, how to use different value attributes in defining domain-specific biases for the search process, how to utilize SVPs in defining hypotheses and constraining hypothesis space, how to factor SVPs into ensemble construction and classification combination process when ensemble learning is used to generate models, and how the value concept plays a role in defining ML method-specific heuristics (e.g., fitness function, information gain measure).

Value-Based Requirements Engineering

For the objectives in value-based requirements engineering, techniques such as business case analysis, requirements prioritization and release prioritization have proven to be effective (Boehm, 2006a).

ML methods can be utilized to assist business case analysis, and requirements and release

prioritization. Specifically, ML methods can be used to predict or estimate software cost, software size, software development efforts, and release prioritization and timing. These prediction, estimation or cost models would help stakeholders gain insight on what capabilities are not feasible with regard to budget, schedule and technology constraints, which features of a system are most important and attainable, and which aggregate of capabilities will meet stakeholders' critical needs given the resource constraints. This in turn will assist stakeholders in prioritizing and reconciling potential conflicting value propositions. Possible ML methods for generating the models include: decision trees, Bayesian learning, neural networks, genetic algorithms, genetic programming, case-based reasoning, and inductive logic programming.

Value-Based Verification and Validation

The key techniques in value-based V&V are value-based and risk-based testing techniques (Boehm, 2006a). Central to those techniques is how to align

SVPs with the technical level details in test construction and execution and how to sequence and prioritize testing activities as investing activities (Ramler, Biffl & Grunbacher, 2006).

Since we have the following concepts in place: Pareto modules, defect-intensive and defect-prone modules, impact and non-impact defects (see Section 3), we can use an SVPs-based approach to identify modules of the aforementioned types and decompose the overall test data generation process for a given software system into a sequence of test data generation cycles with each focusing on some specific testing objective(s). Based on the types of modules and the types of defects, we have a landscape of possible testing scenarios as shown in Figure 4.

The dotted area indicates Pareto modules that can also be defect-intensive, defect-prone, or defect-free modules, and that can intersect with impact or non-impact defects.

From a value-based standpoint, to improve the return on investment, we want to make sure to first maximize the success rate of Pareto modules and to minimize the chance of having impact defects that devastate the value contribution. Afterwards, attention can be focused on non-impact defects and non-Pareto modules. Thus, a prioritization of cycles can be generated that is driven by the value consideration and allows the most critical modules with regard to SVPs to be thoroughly tested first. For instance, we may have the following priority groups: (1) the top priority is to thoroughly test Pareto modules with impact defects; (2) the next priority is to devote attention to modules with impact defects; (3) the third priority group is to deal with Pareto modules with non-impact defects

Figure 4. Possible testing scenarios

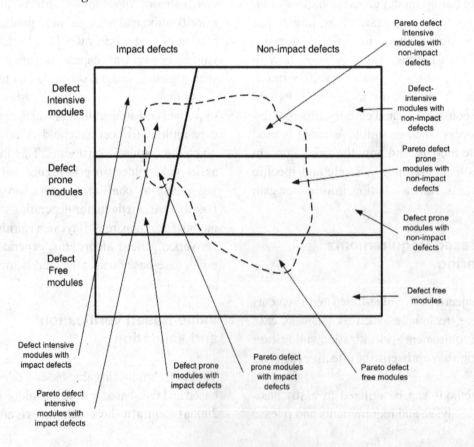

or defect-free Pareto modules; and (4) the last priority group consists of modules with non-impact defects or defect-free modules[3].

For each cycle, a number of ML methods can be utilized to generate test cases for different classes of modules. Some possible ML methods include: genetic algorithms (McMinn, 2004), genetic programming, inductive logic programming and rule-based active learning.

There are a number of issues here: how many cycles are needed, what goes to each cycle, and how cycles are prioritized.

Value-Based Risk Management

There are a number of techniques for value-based risk management: the risk-based "how-much-is-enough" techniques, the risk-based analysis for project predictability, the risk-based simulation, and the risk-based testing techniques (Boehm, 2006a).

A pivotal concept in risk management is the *risk exposure* (*RE*) involved in a prescribed course of actions. *RE* is defined as follows:

$$RE = P(L) \times S(L)$$

where $P(L)$ is the probability of loss L, and $S(L)$ is the size of loss. L can be defined based on any value attribute as discussed in Section 3. In the risk exposure profile analysis (Boehm, 2006b), there is a dichotomy between planning and market share as the value attribute: inadequate planning results in little delay to capture market share but high *RE* due to oversights and rework (RE_p in Figure 5); excessive planning reduces the chance of major problems but at the expense of high *RE* because of time-to-market delays (RE_M in Figure 5).

Figure 5. Sweet spots for different risk exposure profiles

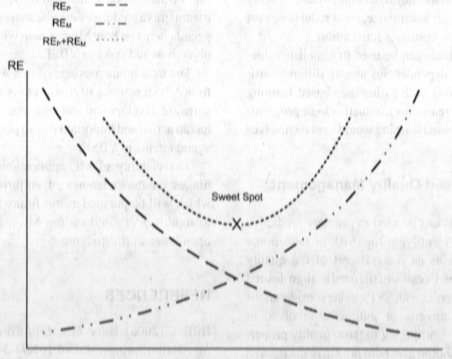

ML methods can be used to help find the "sweet spot" for different risk profiles and different risk exposure profiles (see Figure 5). Depending on the circumstances, either inductive learning, or analytical learning, or a combination of inductive and analytical learning can be deployed.

Value-Based Design and Development

To ensure that a system's objectives and its value considerations are embodied in the software's design and development practices, the software traceability techniques play an important role (Boehm, 2006a). During the software development process, many artifacts are produced and maintained: documents, requirements, design models, test scenarios, and so forth. Trace dependencies are to identify relationships among those artifacts and the quality of the trace dependencies should reflect the value of the artifacts they attempt to bridge. This is vital for a number of reasons, from documentation, program understanding, impact analysis, consistency checking, reuse, quality assurance, user acceptance, error reduction, cost estimation, to customer satisfaction.

ML methods can be used to establish value-based trace dependencies among different artifacts. Methods such as instance-based learning (case-based reasoning), inductive logic programming, rule-based learning would lend themselves to the task.

Value-Based Quality Management

ML methods can be used to generate predictive models for identifying high risk or fault prone components as an integral part of the quality management. Because of the need to align desired quality properties with SVPs, value considerations should be, directly or indirectly, involved in defining or contributing to those quality properties. SVPs should also help prioritize the desired quality factors.

ML methods that are appropriate for the task include: decision trees, genetic programming, neural networks, case-based reasoning, inductive logic programming, and concept learning.

CONCLUSION

VBSE offers a new software development paradigm that recognizes the importance of business and customer value considerations. It tackles the decision making process in software development and maintenance from a value-based perspective. In this paper, we discuss the issue of ML applications to VBSE. Because ML applications to software engineering thus far have been largely confined to the value-neutral setting, we reviewed the landscape in the field and took a closer look at the emerging agenda for VBSE to find out how ML can be positioned to play a larger role in VBSE. We propose some guideline on how to calibrate ML methods to accommodate the value considerations that are so critical in accomplishing VBSE agenda items. Using Boehm' VBSE roadmap as a guide, we describe some preliminary agenda items on how ML can help with the goals, objectives and tasks in VBSE.

The take-home message of this work is twofold: VBSE offers a ROI-conscious approach to software development and maintenance, and ML has an active and important role to play in various agenda items in VBSE.

The viability of ML applications in VBSE hinges on the outcomes of empirical studies, which will be pursued as our future work. How to solidify SVPs into various ML methods is an open issue worth studying.

REFERENCES

Biffl, S. (2006). *Value-Based Software Engineering*. Berlin: Springer. doi:10.1007/3-540-29263-2

Boehm, B. (2006a). Value-Based Software Engineering: Overview and Agenda. In Biffl, S. (Eds.), *Value-Based Software Engineering* (pp. 3–14). Berlin: Springer. doi:10.1007/3-540-29263-2_1

Boehm, B. (2006b). Value-Based Software Engineering: Seven Key Elements and Ethical Considerations. In Biffl, S. (Eds.), *Value-Based Software Engineering* (pp. 109–132). Berlin: Springer. doi:10.1007/3-540-29263-2_6

Boehm, B. (2000). *Software Cost Estimation with COCOMO II*. New Jersey: Prentice Hall.

Boehm, B. (2004). The ROI of Software Dependability: the iDAVE Model. *IEEE Software, 21*(3), 54–61. doi:10.1109/MS.2004.1293073

Boehm, B., & Basili, V. R. (2001). Software Defect Reduction Top 10 List. *IEEE Computer, 34*(1), 135–137. doi:10.1109/2.962984

Brown, A., Iyengar, S., & Johnston, S. (2006). A Rational Approach to Model-Based Development. *IBM Systems Journal, 45*(3), 463–480. doi:10.1147/sj.453.0463

Bullock, J. (2000). Calculating the Value of Testing. *Software Testing and Quality Engineering*, May/June issue, 56-62.

Clark, J. (2003). Reformulating Software Engineering as A Search Problem. *IEE Proceedings. Software, 150*(3), 161–175. doi:10.1049/ip-sen:20030559

Dyba, T., Kitchenham, B. A., & Jorgensen, M. (2005). Evidence-Based Software Engineering for Practitioners. *IEEE Software, 22*(1), 58–65. doi:10.1109/MS.2005.6

Feather, M. (2008). A Broad, Quantitative Model for Making Early Requirements Decisions. *IEEE Software, 25*(2), 49–56. doi:10.1109/MS.2008.29

Fenton, N. E., & Pfleeger, S. L. (1997). *Software Metrics*. Boston: PWS Publishing Company.

Greenfield, J., & Short, K. (2004). *Software Factories: Assembling Applications with Patterns, Models, Frameworks, and Tools*. Indianapolis, IN: Wiley Publishing.

Grunbacher, P., Koszegi, S., & Biffl, S. (2006). Stakeholder Value Proposition Elicitation and Reconciliation. In Biffl, S. (Eds.), *Value-Based Software Engineering* (pp. 133–154). Berlin: Springer. doi:10.1007/3-540-29263-2_7

Harman, M., & Jones, B. (2001). Search-Based Software Engineering. *Information and Software Technology, 43*(14), 833–839. doi:10.1016/S0950-5849(01)00189-6

Huang, L., & Boehm, B. How Much Software Investment is Enough: A Value-Based Approach. *IEEE Software, 23*(5), 88–95. doi:10.1109/MS.2006.127

Khoshgoftaar, T. (2003a). *Software Engineering with Computational Intelligence*. Berlin: Kluwer.

Khoshgoftaar, T. (2003b). Special Issue on Quality Engineering with Computational Intelligence. *Software Quality Journal, 11*(2). doi:10.1023/A:1023708325859

Kitchenham, B. A., Dyba, T., & Jorgensen, M. (2004). Evidence-Based Software Engineering. In *Proceedings of International Conference on Software Engineering*, Edinburgh, pp.273-281.

Lee, J. (2003a). *Software Engineering with Computational Intelligence*. Berlin: Springer-Verlag.

Lee, J. (2003b). Special Issue on Software Eng with Computational Intelligence. *Information and Software Technology, 45*(7). doi:10.1016/S0950-5849(03)00009-0

MBSE. (accessed 2008). http://www.sei.cmu.edu/mbse/index.html.

McMinn, P. (2004). Search-based Software Test Data Generation: A Survey. Software: Testing. *Verification and Reliability, 14*(2), 105–156. doi:10.1002/stvr.294

Mendonca, M., & Sunderhaft, N. L. (1999). Mining Software Engineering Data: A Survey. DACS State-of-the-Art Report, http://www.dacs.dtic.mil/techs/datamining/.

Mostow, J. (1985). Special issue on artificial intelligence and software engineering. *IEEE Trans. SE, 11*(11), 1253–1408.

Partridge, D. (1998). *Artificial Intelligence and Software Engineering*. Boston: AMACOM.

Pedrycz, W., & Peters, J. F. (1998). *Computational Intelligence in Software Engineering*. Singapore: World Scientific Publisher.

Ramler, R., Biffl, S., & Grunbacher, P. (2006). Value-Based Management of Software Testing. In Biffl, S. (Eds.), *Value-Based Software Engineering* (pp. 225–244). Berlin: Springer. doi:10.1007/3-540-29263-2_11

Rich, C., & Waters, R. (1986). *Readings in Artificial Intelligence and Software Engineering*. San Francisco: Morgan Kaufmann.

Sendall, S., & Kozacaynski, W. (2003). Model Transformation: the Heart and Soul of Model-Driven Software Development. *IEEE Software, 20*(5), 42–45. doi:10.1109/MS.2003.1231150

Steece, B. Chulani, S., & Boehm, B. (2002). Determining Software Quality Using COQUALMO. In *Case Studies in Reliability and Maintenance*, W. Blischke and D. Murphy (Ed.), Hoboken, NJ: John Wiley & Sons.

Tsai, J. J. P., & Weigert, T. (1993). *Knowledge-Based Software Development for Real-Time Distributed Systems*. Singapore: World Scientific Pub.

Waddinggton, D., & Lardieri, P. (2006). Model-Centric Software Development. *IEEE Computer, 39*(2), 28–29.

Wang, Y. (2007). *Software Engineering Foundations: A Software Science Perspective. CRC Book Series in Software Engineering* (*Vol. 2*). NY: Auerbach Publications.

Wang, Y. (2008). The Theoretical Framework and Cognitive Process of Learning, *ACM Transactions on Autonomous and Adaptive Systems*, 2(4), Dec.

Zhang, D. (2000). Applying Machine Learning Algorithms in Software Development. *Proceedings of Monterey Workshop on Modeling Software System Structures*, Santa Margherita Ligure, Italy, pp.275-285.

Zhang, D. (2006). Machine Learning in Value-Based Software Test Data Generation. Proceedings of the *Eighteenth IEEE International Conference on Tools with AI,* Washington DC, pp.732-736.

Zhang, D. (2008). A Value-Based Framework for Software Evolutionary Testing. Submitted for publication.

Zhang, D., & Tsai, J. J. P. (2003). Machine Learning and Software Engineering. *Software Quality Journal, 11*(2), 87–119. doi:10.1023/A:1023760326768

Zhang, D., & Tsai, J. J. P. (2005). *Machine Learning Applications in Software Engineering*. Singapore: World Scientific Publishing Co.

Zhang, D., & Tsai, J. J. P. (2007). *Advances in Machine Learning Applications in Software Engineering*. Hershey, PA: Idea Group Publishing.

ENDNOTES

[1] If there are several principal elements in V, we can use other criteria to designate one for the discussion.

2   Even though a better estimate calls for adjusting the total defect number in each category with a different calibration constant and a different quality adjustment factor (an aggregate of 22 defect introduction drivers about the characteristics of platform, product, personnel and project) (Boehm, et al. 2000), for our purpose in identifying modules with different defect density, we simply use nominal defect introduction estimate as the measure.

3   The reason to include defect-free modules (Pareto or non-Pareto) is because of the need to test for other performance related criteria.

Chapter 18
The Formal Design Model of a Telephone Switching System (TSS)

Yingxu Wang
University of Calgary, Canada

ABSTRACT

A typical real-time system, the Telephone Switching System (TSS), is a highly complicated system in design and implementation. This paper presents the formal design, specification, and modeling of the TSS system using a denotational mathematics known as Real-Time Process Algebra (RTPA). The conceptual model of the TSS system is introduced as the initial requirements for the system. Then, the architectural model of the TSS system is created using the RTPA architectural modeling methodologies and refined by a set of Unified Data Models (UDMs). The static behaviors of the TSS system are specified and refined by a set of Unified Process Models (UPMs) such as call processing and support processes. The dynamic behaviors of the TSS system are specified and refined by process priority allocation, process deployment, and process dispatching models. Based on the formal design models of the TSS system, code can be automatically generated using the RTPA Code Generator (RTPA-CG), or be seamlessly transformed into programs by programmers. The formal model of TSS may not only serve as a formal design paradigm of real-time software systems, but also a test bench of the expressive power and modeling capability of exiting formal methods in software engineering.

INTRODUCTION

Telephone Switching Systems (TSS's) are one of the typical real-time and mission-critical systems, as those of air-traffic control and banking systems, characterized by their high degree of complexity, intricate interactions with hardware devices and users, and necessary requirement for domain knowledge (Labrosse, 1999; Liu, 2000; McDermid, 1991; Ngolah et al., 2004; Wang, 2007a). All these factors warrant a TSS system as a complex but ideal design paradigm in real-world large-scale software system design in general and in real-time system modeling in particular.

DOI: 10.4018/978-1-4666-0261-8.ch018

There is no systematical and detailed repository and formal documentation of design knowledge and modeling prototypes of a TSS system nor a formal model of it in denotational mathematics and formal notation systems. This article presents the formal design, specification, and modeling of a TSS system using a denotational mathematics known as Real-Time Process Algebra (RTPA) (Wang, 2002, 2008a, 2008b). RTPA introduces only 17 meta-processes and 17 process relations to describe software system architectures and behaviors with a stepwise refinement methodology (Wang, 2007a, 2008a, 2008c, 2008d). According to the RTPA methodology for system modeling and refinement, a software system can be specified as a set of *architectural components* and *operational components*. The former are modeled by the Unified Data Models (UDMs, also known as *Component Logical Models* CLMs), which is an abstract model of the system hardware interface, an internal logic model of hardware, and/or a control structure of a system. The latter are modeled by *static* and *dynamic processes* in term of the Unified Process Models (UPMs) (Hoare, 1978; Milner, 1980; Hoare et al., 1987; Baeten and Bergstra, 1991; Corsetti and Ratto, 1991; Vereijken, 1995; Dierks, 2000; Wang, 2007a, 2008a; Wang and King, 2000).

This article develops a formal design model of the TSS system in a top-down approach on the basis of the RTPA methodology. In the remainder of this article, the conceptual model of the TSS system is described as the initial requirements of the system. The architectural model of the TSS system is created based on the conceptual model using the RTPA architectural modeling methodologies and refined by a set of CLMs. Then, the static behaviors of the TSS system are specified and refined by a set of processes. The dynamic behaviors of the TSS system are specified and refined by process priority allocation, process deployment, and process dispatching models. With the formal and rigorous models of the TSS system, code can be automatically generated by

the RTPA Code Generator (RTPA-CG) (Wang, 2007a, Wang et al., 2009), or be seamlessly transferred into programs manually. The formal model of TSS may not only serve as a formal design paradigm of real-time software systems, but also a test bench of the expressive power and modeling capability of exiting formal methods in software engineering.

THE CONCEPTUAL MODEL OF THE TSS SYSTEM

A Telephone Switching System (TSS) is a complex real-time system (Thompson, 2000; Wang, 2007a). The functional structure of the TSS system can be described by a conceptual model as illustrated in Figure 1, which consists of four subsystems known as the call processing, subscribers, routes, and signaling subsystems.

The configuration of the TSS system encompasses 1 call processor and 16 subscribers. There are 5 internal switching routes and a set of 5 signaling trunks providing the dial, busy, ringing, ring-back, and special tones. The call processor modeled by a set of functional processes operates on the line scanners, call records, digits receivers, signaling trunks, system clock, and routes in order to implement a coherent program-controlled switching functions.

The framework of the TSS system, encompassing its architecture, static behaviors, and dynamic behaviors, can be specified using RTPA as follows (Wang, 2002, 2008a):

$$§(TSS) \triangleq TSS§.Architecture\textbf{ST}$$
$$\| TSS§.StaticBehaviors\textbf{PC}$$
$$\| TSS§.DynamicBehaviors\textbf{PC}$$

$$(1)$$

where $\|$ indicates that these three subsystems related in parallel, and §, **ST**, and **PC** are type suffixes of *system*, *system structure*, and *process*, respectively.

Figure 1. Functional structure of the TSS system

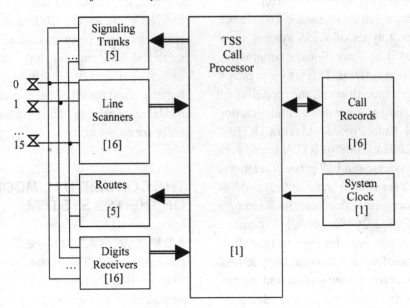

According to the RTPA methodology for system modeling, specification, and refinement (Wang, 2008a, 2008b), the top level model of any system may be specified in a similar structure as given in Equation 1. The following sections will extend and refine the top level framework of the TSS§ into detailed architectural models and behavioral models.

THE ARCHITECTURAL MODEL OF THE TSS SYSTEM

The architecture of a software system or a hybrid hardware/software system is a system framework that represents the overall structure, components, processes, and their interrelationships and interactions. The following subsections specify the architecture of TSS, TSS§.Architecture**ST**, by a high-level architecture model based on its conceptual model as developed in Figure 1. Then, each of its architectural components will be refined as a corresponding UDM.

The Architectural Framework of TSS

System architectures, at the top level, specify a list of names of UDMs and their relations. A UDM may be regarded as a predefined class of system hardware or internal control models, which can be inherited or implemented by corresponding UDM objects as specific instances in the succeeding system architectural refinement procedures.

Corresponding to the conceptual model of TSS as shown in Figure 1, the high-level specification of the architecture of TSS, TSS**§**.Architecture**ST**, is given in Figure 2 using RTPA. The high-level architectural model TSS**§**.Architecture**ST** encompasses parallel structures of CallProcessingSubsys**ST**, SubscriberSubsys**ST**, RouteSubsys**ST**, and SignalingSubsys**ST**, as well as a set of events @ Events**S** and a set of statuses &Status**BL**. The call processing subsystem CallProcessingSubsys**ST** is further refined by a set of UDMs such as a CallProcessor**ST**, a SysClock**ST**, and 16 CallRecords**ST**. Similarly, the subscriber subsystem SubscriberSubsys**ST** is refined by 16 SubscribersST and 16 LineScanners**ST**; and the signaling subsystem is refined by 16 DigitsReceivers**ST** and 5 SignalingTrunks**ST**.

The configuration of the UDMs in TSS is indicated by the numbers in the angle brackets, where each number shows how many similar devices or internal control structures are equipped that share the same UDM schema.

The UDM Structures of TSS

The UDMs of a specific system represent the abstraction and formal representation of domain knowledge and structural information. As modeled in Figure 2, the TSS system encompasses 6 kinds of UDMs for modeling system hardware interfaces and internal control structures as follows:

TSS§.UDMsST $\triangleq$ <LineScanners: **ST** | [16]>
    || <DgitsReceivers: **ST** | [16]>
    || <SignalTrunks: **ST** | [5]>
    || <SysClock: **ST** | [1]>
    || <Routes: **ST** | [5]>
    || <CallRecords: **ST** | [16]>

(2)

where the LineScanners**ST**, DgitsReceivers**ST**, SignalTrunks**ST**, and SysClock**ST** are hardware interface UDMs, while the Routes**ST** and Call-Records**ST** are internal control UDMs.

Each of the six-type system UDMs in TSS is designed and modeled in the following subsections.

a) The Line Scanners

A *line scanner* is an interface device of a telephone switching system that connects a subscriber or a pair of telephone lines to the switching system. Each telephone or subscriber is assigned a line scanner in a switching system. The schema of the line scanners, LineScanners**ST**, is designed as given in Figure 3, where all the 16 line scanners share the same structure.

Figure 2. The architectural framework of the TSS system

```
TSS§.ArchitectureST     CallProcessingSubsysST
                     || SubscriberSubsysST
                     || RouteSubsysST
                     || SignalingSubsysST
                     || <@Events : S>
                     || <  Status : BL>
= ( CallProcessorST [1]
   || SysClockST [1]
   || CallRecordsST [16]
   )
|| ( SubscribersST [16]
   || LineScannersST [16]
   )
|| RoutesST [5]
|| ( DigitsReceiversST [16]
   || SignalingTrunksST [5]
   )
|| <@EventsS>
|| <  StatusBL>
```

LineScanners**ST** encompasses five fields known as the Status**N**, PortAddress**H**, ScanInput**B**, CurrentScan**BL**, and LastScan**BL**. In the LineScanners**ST** UDM, the Status**N** denotes the operating states of the line scanner with the type of natural number; The PortAddress**H** denotes the designated addresses of a set of port interfaces in hexadecimal type; The ScanInput**B** denotes the information inputted in byte type from scanning the lines as specified by the PortAddressH; and the CurrentScan**BL** and the LastScan**BL** denote the logical line scan status in Boolean type. For each scan period, the following operations are conducted: LastScan**BL** = CurrentScan**BL** and CurrentScan**BL** = (ScanInput**B**.b_0)**BL**, i.e., (ScanInputB.b_0)**BL** := **T** when ScanInput**B**.b_0 = 1, otherwise (ScanInputB.b_0)**BL** = **F**.

Each field in the UDM, LineScanner**ST**, is declared by an RTPA type where its constraint, if any, is provided following the vertical bar. For instance, the constrains for the field Status**N** is 0 $\leq$ Status**N** $\leq$ 5, where the logical meaning of the

Figure 3. The UDM schema of line scanners

$$
\begin{aligned}
&\textbf{LineScanners}\textbf{ST} \;\; \mathop{R}_{i=0}^{15} \;\; \textbf{LineScanner(i}\textbf{N})\textbf{ST}: \\
&\quad (\textbf{PORT}\,\textbf{ST}(<\text{PortAddress} : \textbf{H} \mid \text{FF00}\textbf{H} \leq \text{PortAddress}\textbf{H} \leq \text{FF0F}\textbf{H}>, \\
&\qquad\qquad\quad <\text{ScanInput} : \textbf{B} \mid \text{ScanInput}\textbf{B} = <\text{xxxx xxxb}\textbf{B}>), \\
&\quad <\text{Status} : \textbf{N} \mid \text{Status}\textbf{N} = \{(0, \text{Idle}), (1, \text{HookOn}), (2, \text{HookOff}), (3, \text{Busy}), (4, \text{Seized}), (5, \text{Invalid})\}>, \\
&\quad <\text{CurrentScan} : \textbf{BL} \mid \textbf{T} = \text{HookOff} \wedge \textbf{F} = \text{HookOn}>, \\
&\quad <\text{LastScan} : \textbf{BL} \mid \textbf{T} = \text{HookOff} \wedge \textbf{F} = \text{HookOn}> \\
&\quad)
\end{aligned}
$$

numbers represents *idle, hook-on, hook-off, busy, seized,* and *invalid,* respectively.

The 16 refined concrete UDM objects of the line scanners can be derived as shown in Figure 4 on the basis of the abstract schema as given in Figure 3. Each concrete line scanner LineScanner(i$\textbf{N}$) $\textbf{ST}$ in Figure 4 obtains its refined physical or logical parameters.

b) The Digits Receivers

A *digital receiver* is a UDM model of the TSS system that specifies the functional requirements and mechanisms for receiving, retaining, and representing a series of numbers sent via a pair of telephone lines by a subscriber. Digital receivers monitor subscriber line close/open signals and transfer the serial pulses into digits in order to represent the numbers that the subscriber dialed. The schema of the digital receivers, DigitsReceivers$\textbf{ST}$, is designed as given in Figure 5, refined by the 16 concrete UDM objects of DigitsReceiver(i$\textbf{N}$)ST.

A digit receiver may work at one of the four statuses known as *no-dial, dial started, dialing,* and *dial completed,* which are accessed by the call processor at a designated status port. During the dialing process, dial pulses are received by the call processor from the given digit port. After processing, the pulses are transferred into decimal digits and stored in Digit1$\textbf{N}$ and Digit2$\textbf{N}$ assuming that the given TSS using two numbers. However,

it may be flexibly re-specified when it is needed for a larger system.

c) The Signaling Trunks

A *signaling trunk* of a switching system is a device that generates and sends a specific signal to a specific subscriber line. The signaling trunks can be classified into those of *dial tone, busy tone, ringing tone, ring back tone,* and *special tone.* The schema and detailed structures of the signaling trunk UDM, SignalTrunks$\textbf{ST}$, is designed as given in Figure 6. Each concrete UDM objects of SignalTrunck(i$\textbf{N}$)$\textbf{ST}$ is a logical model of the physical trunk that specifies the port address of a tone for signaling distributions.

d) The System Clock

A *system clock* is a typical real-time device for event timing, process duration manipulation, and system synchronization. The UDM model of the system clock of TSS, SysClock$\textbf{ST}$, is designed as given in Figure 7. SysClock$\textbf{ST}$ provides an *absolute* (calendar) clock CurrentTimehh:mm:ss:ms as the logical time reference of the entire system and a *relative* clock $\textbf{§t}\textbf{N}$ as a generic counter. The InterruptCounter$\textbf{N}$ is adopted to transfer the basic timing pace at 1ms into 1 second signals. The real-time system clock is updated by the process SysClock$\textbf{PC}$ as given in Figure 11.

Figure 4. The detailed UDM model of line scanners

$$\mathop{R}_{i=0}^{15} \text{LineScanner(i}\mathbf{N})\mathbf{ST} \triangleq$$

(LineScanner(0)**ST**: (PORT**ST**(PortAddress**H**, ScanInput**B**), Status**N**, CurrentScan**BL**, LastScan**BL**)
:= (FF00**H**, 0000 000b**B**, 0, **F**, **F**)

|| LineScanner(1)**ST**: (PORT**ST**(PortAddress**H**, ScanInput**B**), Status**N**, CurrentScan**BL**, LastScan**BL**)
:= (FF01**H**, 0000 00b0**B**, 0, **F**, **F**)

|| LineScanner(2)**ST**: (PORT**ST**(PortAddress**H**, ScanInput**B**), Status**N**, CurrentScan**BL**, LastScan**BL**)
:= (FF02**H**, 0000 0b00**B**, 0, **F**, **F**)

|| LineScanner(3)**ST**: (PORT**ST**(PortAddress**H**, ScanInput**B**), Status**N**, CurrentScan**BL**, LastScan**BL**)
:= (FF03**H**, 0000 b000**B**, 0, **F**, **F**)

|| LineScanner(4)**ST**: (PORT**ST**(PortAddress**H**, ScanInput**B**), Status**N**, CurrentScan**BL**, LastScan**BL**)
:= (FF04**H**, 000b 0000**B**, 0, **F**, **F**)

|| LineScanner(5)**ST**: (PORT**ST**(PortAddress**H**, ScanInput**B**), Status**N**, CurrentScan**BL**, LastScan**BL**)
:= (FF05**H**, 00b0 0000**B**, 0, **F**, **F**)

|| LineScanner(6)**ST**: (PORT**ST**(PortAddress**H**, ScanInput**B**), Status**N**, CurrentScan**BL**, LastScan**BL**)
:= (FF06**H**, 0b00 0000**B**, 0, **F**, **F**)

|| LineScanner(7)**ST**: (PORT**ST**(PortAddress**H**, ScanInput**B**), Status**N**, CurrentScan**BL**, LastScan**BL**)
:= (FF07**H**, b000 0000**B**, 0, **F**, **F**)

|| LineScanner(8)**ST**: (PORT**ST**(PortAddress**H**, ScanInput**B**), Status**N**, CurrentScan**BL**, LastScan**BL**)
:= (FF08**H**, 0000 000b**B**, 0, **F**, **F**)

|| LineScanner(9)**ST**: (PORT**ST**(PortAddress**H**, ScanInput**B**), Status**N**, CurrentScan**BL**, LastScan**BL**)
:= (FF09**H**, 0000 00b0**B**, 0, **F**, **F**)

|| LineScanner(10)**ST**: (PORT**ST**(PortAddress**H**, ScanInput**B**), Status**N**, CurrentScan**BL**, LastScan**BL**)
:= (FF0A**H**, 0000 0b00**B**, 0, **F**, **F**)

|| LineScanner(11)**ST**: (PORT**ST**(PortAddress**H**, ScanInput**B**), Status**N**, CurrentScan**BL**, LastScan**BL**)
:= (FF0B**H**, 0000 b000**B**, 0, **F**, **F**)

|| LineScanner(12)**ST**: (PORT**ST**(PortAddress**H**, ScanInput**B**), Status**N**, CurrentScan**BL**, LastScan**BL**)
:= (FF0C**H**, 000b 0000**B**, 0, **F**, **F**)

|| LineScanner(13)**ST**: (PORT**ST**(PortAddress**H**, ScanInput**B**), Status**N**, CurrentScan**BL**, LastScan**BL**)
:= (FF0D**H**, 00b0 0000**B**, 0, **F**, **F**)

|| LineScanner(14)**ST**: (PORT**ST**(PortAddress**H**, ScanInput**B**), Status**N**, CurrentScan**BL**, LastScan**BL**)
:= (FF0E**H**, 0b00 0000**B**, 0, **F**, **F**)

|| LineScanner(15)**ST**: (PORT**ST**(PortAddress**H**, ScanInput**B**), Status**N**, CurrentScan**BL**, LastScan**BL**)
:= (FF0F**H**, b000 0000**B**, 0, **F**, **F**)
)

e) The Switching Routes

A *route* of a switching system is an internal circuit or digital channel that connects a pair of subscriber lines together for conversation by a certain instruction. The required number of routes in a switching system is always far smaller than half of the number of subscribers, because not all subscribers are in use for all the time according to teletraffic theories. The schema of routes, Routes**ST**, is designed as given in Figure 8, refined by the five concrete UDM objects of Routes(i**N**) **ST**. Routes**ST** is a logical model of the physical routes that specifies the parameters of the status of a route and which pair of subscribers known as the calling and called parties are connected when it is occupied.

f) The Call Records

A *call record* is an internal logical structure in a switching system that is uniquely created for and associated to a call in order to retain detail information in its entire lifecycle. The schema of the call records, CallRecords**ST**, is designed as given in Figure 9, refined by the 16 concrete UDM objects of CallRecord(i**N**)**ST**.

Figure 5. The schema and detailed UDM models of digital receivers

```
DigitsReceiversST ≜  R  DigitsReceiver(iN)ST :
                  i=0

    (<Status : N | StatusN = {(0, NoDial), (1,DialStated), (2, Dialing), (3, DialCompleted)}>,
     PORTST(<DigitPort : N | FF10H ≤ DigitPortN ≤ FF1FH>,
              <DigitInput : B | DigitInputB = <xxxx bbbbB>),
     PORTST(<StatusPort : N | FF20H ≤ StatusPortN ≤ FF2FH>,
              <StatusInput : B | StatusInputB = <xxxx xxxbB>),
     <Digit1 : N | 0 ≤ Digit1N ≤ 9>,
     <Digit2 : N | 0 ≤ Digit2N ≤ 9>,
     <#DigitsReceived: N | 1 ≤ #DigitsReceivedN ≤ 2>,
     )
= DigitScanner(0)ST :  (StatusN, PORTST(DigitPortH, DigitInputB), PORTST(StatusPortN, StatusInputB), Digit1N, Digit2N,
                        #DigitsReceivedN) := (0, FF10H, xxxx bbbbB, FF20H, xxxx xxxbB, 0, 0, 0)
‖ DigitScanner(1)ST :  (StatusN, PORTST(DigitPortH, DigitInputB), PORTST(StatusPortN, StatusInputB), Digit1N, Digit2N,
                        #DigitsReceivedN) := (0, FF11H, xxxx bbbbB, FF21H, xxxx xxbxB, 0, 0, 0)
‖ DigitScanner(2)ST :  (StatusN, PORTST(DigitPortH, DigitInputB), PORTST(StatusPortN, StatusInputB), Digit1N, Digit2N,
                        #DigitsReceivedN) := (0, FF12H, xxxx bbbbB, FF22H, xxxx xbxxB, 0, 0, 0)
‖ DigitScanner(3)ST :  (StatusN, PORTST(DigitPortH, DigitInputB), PORTST(StatusPortN, StatusInputB), Digit1N, Digit2N,
                        #DigitsReceivedN) := (0, FF13H, xxxx bbbbB, FF23H, xxxx bxxxB, 0, 0, 0)
‖ DigitScanner(4)ST :  (StatusN, PORTST(DigitPortH, DigitInputB), PORTST(StatusPortN, StatusInputB), Digit1N, Digit2N,
                        #DigitsReceivedN) := (0, FF14H, xxxx bbbbB, FF24H, xxxb xxxxB, 0, 0, 0)
‖ DigitScanner(5)ST :  (StatusN, PORTST(DigitPortH, DigitInputB), PORTST(StatusPortN, StatusInputB), Digit1N, Digit2N,
                        #DigitsReceivedN) := (0, FF15H, xxxx bbbbB, FF25H, xxbx xxxxB, 0, 0, 0)
‖ DigitScanner(6)ST :  (StatusN, PORTST(DigitPortH, DigitInputB), PORTST(StatusPortN, StatusInputB), Digit1N, Digit2N,
                        #DigitsReceivedN) := (0, FF16H, xxxx bbbbB, FF26H, xbxx xxxxB, 0, 0, 0)
‖ DigitScanner(7)ST :  (StatusN, PORTST(DigitPortH, DigitInputB), PORTST(StatusPortN, StatusInputB), Digit1N, Digit2N,
                        #DigitsReceivedN) := (0, FF17H, xxxx bbbbB, FF27H, bxxx xxxxB, 0, 0, 0)
‖ DigitScanner(8)ST :  (StatusN, PORTST(DigitPortH, DigitInputB), PORTST(StatusPortN, StatusInputB), Digit1N, Digit2N,
                        #DigitsReceivedN) := (0, FF18H, xxxx bbbbB, FF28H, xxxx xxxbB, 0, 0, 0)
‖ DigitScanner(9)ST :  (StatusN, PORTST(DigitPortH, DigitInputB), PORTST(StatusPortN, StatusInputB), Digit1N, Digit2N,
                        #DigitsReceivedN) := (0, FF19H, xxxx bbbbB, FF29H, xxxx xxbxB, 0, 0, 00)
‖ DigitScanner(10)ST : (StatusN, PORTST(DigitPortH, DigitInputB), PORTST(StatusPortN, StatusInputB), Digit1N, Digit2N,
                        #DigitsReceivedN) := (0, FF1AH, xxxx bbbbB, FF2AH, xxxx xbxxB, 0, 0, 0)
‖ DigitScanner(11)ST : (StatusN, PORTST(DigitPortH, DigitInputB), PORTST(StatusPortN, StatusInputB), Digit1N, Digit2N,
                        #DigitsReceivedN) := (0, FF1BH, xxxx bbbbB, FF2BH, xxxx bxxxB, 0, 0, 0)
‖ DigitScanner(12)ST : (StatusN, PORTST(DigitPortH, DigitInputB), PORTST(StatusPortN, StatusInputB), Digit1N, Digit2N,
                        #DigitsReceivedN) := (0, FF1CH, xxxx bbbbB, FF2CH, xxxb xxxxB, 0, 0, 0)
‖ DigitScanner(13)ST : (StatusN, PORTST(DigitPortH, DigitInputB), PORTST(StatusPortN, StatusInputB), Digit1N, Digit2N,
                        #DigitsReceivedN) := (0, FF1DH, xxxx bbbbB, FF2DH, xxbx xxxxB, 0, 0, 0)
‖ DigitScanner(14)ST : (StatusN, PORTST(DigitPortH, DigitInputB), PORTST(StatusPortN, StatusInputB), Digit1N, Digit2N,
                        #DigitsReceivedN) := 90, FF1EH, xxxx bbbbB, FF2EH, xbxx xxxxB, 0, 0, 0)
‖ DigitScanner(15)ST : (StatusN, PORTST(DigitPortH, DigitInputB), PORTST(StatusPortN, StatusInputB), Digit1N, Digit2N,
                        #DigitsReceivedN) := (0, FF1FH, xxxx bbbbB, FF2FH, bxxx xxxxB, 0, 0, 0)
```

Figure 6. The schema and detailed UDM models of signal trunks

```
SignalTrunksST  R  SignalTrunk(iN)ST:
             i=0

        (PORTST(<SignalTrunkPort : N | FF90H ≤ SignalTrunkPortN ≤FF94H>,
                 <SignalOutput : BL | SignalOutputBL = {(T, On), (F, Off)})
        )
    = ( SignalTrunk(0)ST = PORTST(DialTonePortH, DialToneOutputBL) := (FF90H, F)
     ‖ SignalTrunk(1)ST = PORTST(BusyTonePortH, BusyToneOutputBL) := (FF91H, F)
     ‖ SignalTrunk(2)ST = PORTST(RingingTonePortH, RingingToneOutputBL) := (FF92H, F)
     ‖ SignalTrunk(3)ST = PORTST(RingBackTonePortH, RingBackToneOutputBL) := (FF93H, F)
     ‖ SignalTrunk(4)ST = PORTST(SpecialTonePortH, SpecialToneOutputBL) := (FF94H, F
     )
```

Figure 7. The schema and detailed UDM model of the system clock

SysClockST	SysClock**ST**:
	(<§t : **N** | 0 ≤ §t**N** ≤ 1M>
	<CurrentTime : **hh:mm:ss:ms** | 00:00:00:000 ≤
	CurrentTime**hh:mm:ss:ms** ≤ 23:59:59:999>
	<MainClockPort : **H** | MainClockPort**B** = F1**H**>,
	<ClockInterval : **N** | ClockInterval**N** = 1**ms**>,
	<InterruptCounter : **N** | 0 ≤ InterruptCounter**N** ≤ 999>,
	)

Figure 8. The schema and detailed UDM models of routes

$$
\textbf{RoutesST} \quad \underset{i=0}{\overset{4}{R}} \ \text{Route(i\textbf{N})\textbf{ST}}:
$$

(<Status : **BL** \| **T** = Busy ∧ **F** = Free>,
  <CallingNum : **N** \| 0 ≤ CallingNum**N** ≤ 15>,
  <CalledNum : **N** \| 0 ≤ CalledNum**N** ≤ 15>
)
= Route(0)**ST**: (Status**BL**, CallingNum**N**, CalledNum**N**) := (**F**, x, x)
‖ Route(1)**ST**: (Status**BL**, CallingNum**N**, CalledNum**N**) := (**F**, x, x)
‖ Route(2)**ST**: (Status**BL**, CallingNum**N**, CalledNum**N**) := (**F**, x, x)
‖ Route(3)**ST**: (Status**BL**, CallingNum**N**, CalledNum**N**) := (**F**, x, x)
‖ Route(4)**ST**: (Status**BL**, CallingNum**N**, CalledNum**N**) := (**F**, x, x)

The CallRecord(i**N**)**ST** in TSS models the internal control structure of calls with the information such as the CallStatus**N**, CallProcess**N**, CalledNum**N**, RouteNum**N**, Timer**N**, CallingTermination**BL**, and CalledTermination**BL**. The CallProcess**N** is a set of call process numbers defined as {(0, Idle), (1, CallOrigination), (2, Dialing), (3, CheckCalledStatus), (4, Connecting), (5, Talking), (6, CallTermination), (7, ExceptionalTermination)}. Each call record is initialized as shown in UDM objects in Figure 9.

The system architectural specification developed in this subsection provides a set of abstract object models and clear interfaces between system hardware and software. By reaching this point, the co-design of a real-time system can be separately carried out by separated hardware and software teams. It is recognized that system *architecture specification* by the means of UDMs is a fundamental and the most difficult part in software system modeling, while conventional formal methods hardly provide any support for this purpose. From the above examples in this subsection, it can be seen that RTPA provides a set of expressive notations for specifying system architectural structures and control models, including hardware, software, and their interactions. On the basis of the system architecture specification and with the work products of system architectural components (UDMs), specification of the operational components of the TSS system can be carried out directly forward, as shown in the following sections.

Figure 9. The schema and detailed UDM models of call records

$$
\textbf{CallRecordsST} \triangleq \overset{15}{\underset{i=0}{R}} \; \text{CallRecord}(i\textbf{N})\textbf{ST} :
$$

$$
\begin{aligned}
(&\; <\text{CallStatus} : \textbf{BL} \mid \textbf{T} = \text{Active} \wedge \textbf{F} = \text{Inactive}>, \\
&\; <\text{CallProcess} : \textbf{N} \mid \text{CallProcess}\textbf{N} = \{(0, \text{Idle}), (1, \text{CallOrigination}), (2, \text{Dialing}), \\
&\quad (3, \text{CheckCalledStatus}), (4, \text{Connecting}), (5, \text{Talking}), (6, \text{CallTermination}), \\
&\quad (7, \text{ExceptionalTermination})\}>, \\
&\; <\text{CalledNum} : \textbf{N} \mid 0 \leq \text{CalledNum}\textbf{N} \leq 15>, \\
&\; <\text{RouteNum} : \textbf{N} \mid 0 \leq \text{CalledNum}\textbf{N} \leq 4>, \\
&\; <\text{Timer} : \textbf{N} \mid 0 \leq \text{Timer}\textbf{N} \leq 100\textbf{ms}>, \\
&\; <\text{CallingTermination} : \textbf{BL} \mid \textbf{T} = \text{Yes} \wedge \textbf{F} = \text{No}>, \\
&\; <\text{CalledTermination} : \textbf{BL} \mid \textbf{T} = \text{Yes} \wedge \textbf{F} = \text{No}> \\
)
\end{aligned}
$$

$=$ CallRecord(0)**ST**: (CallStatus**BL**, CallProcess**N**, CalledNum**N**, RouteNum**N**, Timer**N**, CallingTermination**BL**, CalledTermination**BL**) := (**F**, 0, 0, 0, 0, **F**, **F**)

$\parallel$ CallRecord(1)**ST**: (CallStatus**BL**, CallProcess**N**, CalledNum**N**, RouteNum**N**, Timer**N**, CallingTermination**BL**, CalledTermination**BL**) := (**F**, 0, 0, 0, 0, **F**, **F**)

$\parallel$ CallRecord(2)**ST**: (CallStatus**BL**, CallProcess**N**, CalledNum**N**, RouteNum**N**, Timer**N**, CallingTermination**BL**, CalledTermination**BL**) := (**F**, 0, 0, 0, 0, **F**, **F**)

$\parallel$ CallRecord(3)**ST**: (CallStatus**BL**, CallProcess**N**, CalledNum**N**, RouteNum**N**, Timer**N**, CallingTermination**BL**, CalledTermination**BL**) := (**F**, 0, 0, 0, 0, **F**, **F**)

$\parallel$ CallRecord(4)**ST**: (CallStatus**BL**, CallProcess**N**, CalledNum**N**, RouteNum**N**, Timer**N**, CallingTermination**BL**, CalledTermination**BL**) := (**F**, 0, 0, 0, 0, **F**, **F**)

$\parallel$ CallRecord(5)**ST**: (CallStatus**BL**, CallProcess**N**, CalledNum**N**, RouteNum**N**, Timer**N**, CallingTermination**BL**, CalledTermination**BL**) := (**F**, 0, 0, 0, 0, **F**, **F**)

$\parallel$ CallRecord(6)**ST**: (CallStatus**BL**, CallProcess**N**, CalledNum**N**, RouteNum**N**, Timer**N**, CallingTermination**BL**, CalledTermination**BL**) := (**F**, 0, 0, 0, 0, **F**, **F**)

$\parallel$ CallRecord(7)**ST**: (CallStatus**BL**, CallProcess**N**, CalledNum**N**, RouteNum**N**, Timer**N**, CallingTermination**BL**, CalledTermination**BL**) := (**F**, 0, 0, 0, 0, **F**, **F**)

$\parallel$ CallRecord(8)**ST**: (CallStatus**BL**, CallProcess**N**, CalledNum**N**, RouteNum**N**, Timer**N**, CallingTermination**BL**, CalledTermination**BL**) := (**F**, 0, 0, 0, 0, **F**, **F**)

$\parallel$ CallRecord(9)**ST**: (CallStatus**BL**, CallProcess**N**, CalledNum**N**, RouteNum**N**, Timer**N**, CallingTermination**BL**, CalledTermination**BL**) := (**F**, 0, 0, 0, 0, **F**, **F**)

$\parallel$ CallRecord(10)**ST**: (CallStatus**BL**, CallProcess**N**, CalledNum**N**, RouteNum**N**, Timer**N**, CallingTermination**BL**, CalledTermination**BL**) := (**F**, 0, 0, 0, 0, **F**, **F**)

$\parallel$ CallRecord(11)**ST**: (CallStatus**BL**, CallProcess**N**, CalledNum**N**, RouteNum**N**, Timer**N**, CallingTermination**BL**, CalledTermination**BL**) := (**F**, 0, 0, 0, 0, **F**, **F**)

$\parallel$ CallRecord(12)**ST**: (CallStatus**BL**, CallProcess**N**, CalledNum**N**, RouteNum**N**, Timer**N**, CallingTermination**BL**, CalledTermination**BL**) := (**F**, 0, 0, 0, 0, **F**, **F**)

$\parallel$ CallRecord(13)**ST**: (CallStatus**BL**, CallProcess**N**, CalledNum**N**, RouteNum**N**, Timer**N**, CallingTermination**BL**, CalledTermination**BL**) := (**F**, 0, 0, 0, 0, **F**, **F**)

$\parallel$ CallRecord(14)**ST**: (CallStatus**BL**, CallProcess**N**, CalledNum**N**, RouteNum**N**, Timer**N**, CallingTermination**BL**, CalledTermination**BL**) := (**F**, 0, 0, 0, 0, **F**, **F**)

$\parallel$ CallRecord(15)**ST**: (CallStatus**BL**, CallProcess**N**, CalledNum**N**, RouteNum**N**, Timer**N**, CallingTermination**BL**, CalledTermination**BL**) := (**F**, 0, 0, 0, 0, **F**, **F**)

THE STATIC BEHAVIOR MODELS OF THE TSS SYSTEM

A static behavior is a component-level function of a given system that can be determined before run-time. On the basis of the system architecture specification and with the work products of system architectural components developed in preceding section, the operational components of the given TSS system and their behaviors can be specified as a set of behavioral processes operating on the UDMs.

The TSS static behaviors, TSS§.StaticBehaviors**PC**, encompass two subsystems known as the SysSupportProcesses**PC** and CallProcessingProcesses**PC** in parallel as specified below:

TSS§.**StaticBehaviors****PC** ≜ SysSupportPro-
cesses**PC** | [4]
‖ CallProcessingProcesses**PC** | [7]

$$(3)$$

where the former consists of 4 system support
processes and the latter consists of 7 call processing processes.

The following subsections describe how the
TSS static behaviors as specified in Equation 3 are
modeled and refined using the denotational mathematical notations and methodologies of RTPA.

Modeling System Support Processes of the TSS Static Behaviors

The static behaviors of the support processes
subsystem in TSS as specified in Equation 3 can
be further refined in the following model with
four processes:

TSS**§**.StaticBehaviors**PC**.SysSupportProcesses**PC**
≜

SysInitial**PC**
‖ SysClock**PC**
‖ LineScanning**PC**
‖ DigitsReceiving**PC**

$$(4)$$

where each of the system support processes will
be formally modeled and described in RTPA in
the following subsections.

a) The System Initialization Process

System initialization is a common support process of a real-time system that boots the system,
sets its initial environment, and preassigns the
initial values of data objects of the system such
as variables, constants, as well as architectural
(hardware interface) and control (internal) UDMs.
The *system initialization* process of TSS, SysInitial**PC**, is modeled in Figure 10, where all system
architectural and control UDMs are initialized.
Then, the system clock and timing interrupt are
set to their initial logical or calendar values.

b) The System Clock Process

The *system clock* process is a typical support
process of a real-time system that maintains
and updates an absolute (calendar) clock and a
relative clock for the system. The system clock
process of TSS, SysClock**PC**, is modeled in Figure
11. The source of the system clock is obtained
from the 1ms interrupt clock signal generated by
system hardware, by which the absolute clock
with real-time millisecond, second, minute, and
hour, SysClock**ST**.CurrentTime**hh:mm:ss:ms**, are
generated and periodically updated. The second
clock in a real-time system is the relative clock,
SysClock**ST**.§t**N**, which is usually adopted for
relative timing and duration manipulations. Both
system clocks are reset to zero at midnight each
day.

Figure 10. The behavior model of the system initialization process

```
SysInitial PC
{ Initial SytemModels ST
  → Initial ControlModels ST
  → SysClock ST .§t N := 0
  → SysClock ST .CurrentTime hh:mm:ss := hh:mm:ss
  → SysClock ST .InterruptCounter N := 0
}
```

Figure 11. The behavior model of the system clock process

```
SysClockPC
{ ↑(SysClockST.InterruptCounterN)                          // 1ms clock interrupt
  →      SysClockST.InterruptCounterN = 999                // Set to 1 second
        ( → SysClockST.InterruptCounterN = 0
            → ↑(SysClockST.§tN)
        → ↑(SysClockST.CurrentTimehh:mm:ss)
           15
        →  R (   CallRecord(iN)ST.CallStatusBL = T ∧ CallRecord(iN)ST.TimerSS ≠ 0
          i=0
                  → ↓ (CallRecord(iN)ST.TimerSS)    // Update timers in call records
               )
        → SysClockST.CurrentTimehh:mm:ss:ms = 23:59:59:999
          ( → SysClockST.CurrentTimehh:mm:ss:ms := 00:00:00:000
            → SysClockST.§tN := 0
          )
        )
}
```

Figure 12. The behavior model of the line scanning process

```
LineScanningPC ≜
{ nN := 15
        n
  →  R ( LineScanner(iN)ST.LastScanBL := LineScanner(iN)ST.CurrentScanBL
     i=1

        → PORT(LineScanner(iN)ST.PortAddressN)B |> LineScanner(iN)ST.ScanInputB

        → ( ◆ LineScanner(iN)ST.ScanInputB = 0000 0001B
              → LineScanner(iN)ST.CurrentScanBL := T
          |◆ ~
              → LineScanner(iN)ST.CurrentScanBL := F
          )
        → ( ◆ LineScanner(iN)ST.CurrentScanBL = F ∧ LineScanner(iN)ST.LastScanBL = F
              ◆ LineScanner(iN)ST.StatusN ≠ 4 ∧ LineScanner(iN)ST.StatusN ≠ 5   // Not seized or invalid
              → LineScanner(iN)ST.StatusN := 0                                   // Set idle
          | ◆ LineScanner(iN)ST.CurrentScanBL = F ∧ LineScanner(iN)ST.LastScanBL = T
              → LineScanner(iN)ST.StatusN := 1                                   // Set hook-on
          | ◆ LineScanner(iN)ST.CurrentScanBL = T ∧ LineScanner(iN)ST.LastScanBL = F
              → LineScanner(iN)ST.StatusN := 2                                   // Set hook-off
              → ( ◆ LineScanner(iN)ST.StatusN ≠ 4                                // Not a seized line
                  → CallRecord(iN)ST.CallProcessN := 1                           // Call origination
                |◆ ~
                  → CallRecord(iN)ST.CallProcessN := 0                           // Called, no dispatch
                )
          | ◆ LineScanner(iN)ST.CurrentScanBL = T ∧ LineScanner(iN)ST.LastScanBL = T
              → LineScanner(iN)ST.StatusN := 3                                   // Set busy
          )
     )
}
```

SysClock**PC** is also responsible to update all timers set in other processes by reducing its current value by one until its time out, i.e., CallRecord(i**N**) **ST**.Timer**SS** = 0. Any time-out event will be captured by the system immediately after it reaches 0.

c) The Line Scanning Process

Line scanning is a special real-time support process that monitors the line statuses of all subscribers periodically and transfers them into logical states in terms of *idle, hook-on, hook-off, busy, seized,* and *invalid*. The line scanning process of TSS, LineScanning**PC**, is modeled in Figure 12 baseed on the UDM of Linscanners**ST**. The latest status of a line is inputed into LineScanner(i**N**)**ST**.CurrentScan**BL** from LineScanner(i**N**)**ST**.ScanInput**B**, after LineScanner(i**N**)**ST**.LastScan**BL** is saved. Then the four basic operating statuses of the line can be logically determined as given in Table 1.

In Figure 12, the algorithm for line status detection in the process of line scanning can be expressed in Table 1, where the four possible line status known as idle, hook-on, hook-off, and busy, are determined by the periodical current and last scan inputs, i.e., LineScanner(i**N**)**ST**.CurrentScan**BL** ^LineScanner(i**N**)**ST**.LastScan**B**. The fourth status is set by the system when a called line is preseized for connection. The fifth status is set by the system when a given line is malfunction or out of service.

d) The Digits Receiving Process

Digital receiving is a special real-time support process that receives the called subscriber number sent by the calling subscriber in high frequency periodical interrupt cycles in order to meet its timing constraints. The digital receiving process of TSS, DigitalReceiving**PC**, is modeled in Figure 13.

This process only checks lines that its PN**N** = 2 that has progressed into the dialing process. Then, the dial status of a line DigitsReceiver(i**N**). StatusInput**B** is checked from the input of the DigitsReceiver(i**N**).StatusPort**H**. If the status is

valid, the dial pulse on the line DigitsReceiver(i**N**). DigitInput**B** is inputted from DigitsReceiver(i**N**). DigitPort**H**. According to the architectural model of the DigitsReceivers**ST** designed in Figure 5, the dial status DigitsReceiver(i**N**).Status**N** will be set to dial stated (1), first digit received (2), and all digits received (3) dependent on the progress of the dial process of a particular line.

Modeling Call-Processing Processes of the TSS Static Behaviors

The static behaviors of the TSS call processing subsystem, as modeled in Equation 3, can be further refined in the following model with seven processes:

TSS**§**.StaticBehaviors**PC**.CallProcessingPro-
    cesses**PC** ≜

        CallOrigination**PC**
        || Dialling**PC**
        || CheckCalledStatus**PC**
        || Connecting**PC**
        || Talking**PC**
        || CallTermination**PC**
        || ExceptionalTermination**PC**

                        (5)

where each of the call processing processes will be formally modeled and described in RTPA in the following subsections.

The configuration of processes of the TSS system and a set of process schemas are designed as shown in Table 2, which refine the high level model of TSS static behaviors as given in Equation 5. The process schemas of TSS provide further detailed information on each process' functionality, I/O, and its relationships with system architectural components (UDMs) and other processes.

a) The Process of Call Origination

Call origination is the first call processing process that identifies new call requests of subscribers

Figure 13. The behavior model of the digit receiving process

```
DigitsReceivingPC ≜
{ nN := 15
          n
    →  R  (◆ CallRecord(iN)ST.CallProcessN = 2                              // Dialing
         i=1
              → PORT(DigitsReceiver(iN)ST.StatusPortH)B |> DigitsReceiver(iN)ST.StatusInputB

              → ( ◆ DigitsReceiver(iN)ST.StatusInputB = 0000 0001B          // A number valid
                  → DigitsReceiver(iN)ST.StatusN := 1                       // Dial started
                  → PORT(DigitsReceiver(iN)ST.DigitPortH)B |> DigitsReceiver(iN)ST.DigitInputB

                  → ( ◆ DigitsReceiver(iN)ST.#DigitsReceivedN = 0

                      → DigitsReceiver(iN).Digit1 N:= DigitsReceiver(iN)ST.DigitInputB
                      ) DigitsReceiver(iN)ST.StatusN := 2                   // First digit received
                      → ↑ (DigitsReceiver(iN)ST.#DigitsReceivedN)
                    | ◆ ~
                      → DigitsReceiver(iN)ST.Digit2N := DigitsReceiver(iN )ST.DigitInputB
                      → DigitsReceiver(iN)ST.StatusN := 3                   // All digits received
                      → DigitsReceiver(iN)ST.#DigitsReceivedN := 0
                  )
              )
          )
}
```

Table 1. Algorithm of line status determination in TSS

No.	LineScanner(iN)ST. CurrentScanBL	LineScanner(iN)ST. LastScanBL	LineScanner(iN)ST. StatusN
1	F	F	0 – Idle
2	F	T	1 – Hook-on
3	T	F	2 – Hook-off
4	T	T	3 – Busy
5	Set by the system		4 – Seized
6	Set by the system		5 – Invalid

and creates associated internal control structures for each new call. The call origination process of TSS, CallOriginationPC, is modeled in Figure 14, where related system support processes and operated UDMs are cross referenced.

The CallOriginationPC process finds hook-off subscribers from LineScannersST and registers newly originated calls in CallRecordsST. The dial tone is sent to the subscriber which originated a new call by invoking the predesigned process ConnectDrivePC. A no-dial timer, CallRecord(iN) ST.TimerSS, is set for 5 seconds in order to monitor if the line that hears the dial tone will act to dial the called number within the given period of time. Any time out event will be detected in the next process. Then, it transfers the current call

Table 2. Specification of the TSS process schemas

PN	ProcessID**PC** ({**I**}; {**O**})	Operated CLM**ST**	Related Processes	Functional Descriptions
1	CallOrigination**PC** ({**I**:: LineNum**N**}; {**O**:: CallProcess**N**})	• LineScanners**ST** • CallRecords**ST**	• LineScanning**PC** • ConnectDrive**PC** • SysClock**PC**	• Find hook-off subscribers from LineScanners**ST** • Record originated calls in CallRecords**ST**
2	Dialing**PC** ({**I**:: LineNum**N**}; {**O**:: CallProcess**N**})	• DigitsReceivers**ST** • CallRecords**ST**	• DigitsReceiv-ing**PC** • ConnectDrive**PC** • SysClock**PC**	• Receive digits from DigitsReceivers**ST** • Record called number in CallRecords**ST**
3	CheckCalledStatus**PC** ({**I**:: LineNum**N**}; {**O**:: CallProcess**N**})	• LineScanners**ST** • CallRecords**ST** • Routes**ST**	• LineScanning**PC** • ConnectDrive**PC** • SysClock**PC**	• Check called status from callRecords**ST** • Find route from Routes**ST** • Send busy tone to calling if called's busy
4	Connecting**PC** ({**I**:: LineNum**N**}; {**O**:: CallProcess**N**})	• CallRecords**ST**	• ConnectDrive**PC** • SysClock**PC**	• Send RingbBackTone to calling • Send RingingTone to called
5	Talking**PC** ({**I**:: LineNum**N**}; {**O**:: CallProcess**N**})	• LineScanners**ST** • CallRecords**ST** • Routes**ST**	• LineScanning**PC** • ConnectDrive**PC** • SysClock**PC**	• When called answered, connect calling-called using pre-seized routes in CallRecords**ST** • Process calling give-up • Monitor call termination
6	CallTermination**PC** ({**I**:: LineNum**N**}; {**O**:: CallProcess**N**})	• LineScanners**ST** • CallRecords**ST** • Routes**ST**	• LineScanning**PC** • ConnectDrive**PC** • SysClock**PC**	• Process either party termination based on LineScanners**ST** • Release routes according to Routes**ST** • Monitor non-hook-on party in CallRecords**ST**
7	Exceptional-Termination**PC** ({**I**:: LineNum**N**}; {**O**:: CallProcess**N**})	• LineScanners**ST** • CallRecords**ST**	• LineScanning**PC** • ConnectDrive**PC** • SysClock**PC**	• Reset line status in LineScanners**ST**, if monitored party hook-on • If time-out, set line status invalid in LineScanners**ST**

process number (PN**N**), CallRecord(i**N**) **ST**.CallProcess**N**, from PN**N** = 1 (Call origination) to PN**N** = 2 (Dialing).

b) The Process of Dialing

Dialing is the second call processing process that receives digits dialed by the calling subscriber on a specific line and registers them in the associated call record. The dialing process of TSS, Dialing**PC**, is modeled in Figure 15, where related system support processes and operated UDMs are cross referenced.

The DialingPC process checks the status of dialing in the UDM DigitsReceiver(i**N**)**ST** as detected by the system. There are four status in the phase of dialing in TSS such as no dial, dial started (first digit has been received), dialing (in progress), and dial completed (all expected digits have been received) as modeled in DigitsReceiver(i**N**)**ST**.Status**N**. Based upon each status, particular actions in term of predesignated processes will be invoked as given in Figure 14. If the no dial timer, CallRecord(i**N**)**ST**.Timerss, goes off during the dialing process, the system will immediately send the busy tone to the subscriber and trigger a special process that transfers the current process to PN**N** = 7, i.e., the Exceptional Termination**PC**. When all required digits have been successfully received, the system transfers the current call process number, CallRecord(i**N**)**ST**.CallProcess**N**, from PN**N** = 2 (Dialing) to PN**N** = 3 (CheckCalledStatus).

Figure 14. The behavioral model of the call origination process

```
CallOriginationPC (<I :: LineNumN>; <O :: CallProcessN>;
                    <UDMs :: LineScannersST, CallRecordsST>)

{ // PNN = 1
  iN := LineNumN
  → LineScanner(iN)ST.StatusN := 3            // Show line is busy
    ConnectDrivePC (SubscriberLine(iN)N, DialToneN, OnBL)

  → CallRecord(iN)ST.TimerSS := 5             // Set no dial timer
  → CallRecord(iN)ST.CallStatusBL := T        // Set call record active
  → CallRecord(iN)ST.CallProcessN := 2        // To dialing
}
```

Figure 15. The behavioral model of the dialing process

```
DialingPC (<I :: LineNumN>; <O :: CallProcessN>;
           <UDMs :: DigitsReceiverST, CallRecordsST>) ≙

{ // PNN = 2
  iN := LineNumN
  → ( ◆ DigitsReceiver(iN)ST.StatusN = 0              // No dial
        → (◆ CallRecord(iN)ST.TimerSS = 0             // No dial time-out
            ↣ ConnectDrivePC (SubscriberLine(iN)N, DialToneN, OffBL)
            ↣ ConnectDrivePC (SubscriberLine(iN)N, BusyToneN, OnBL)
            → CallRecord(iN)ST.TimerSS := 10
            → CallRecord(iN)ST.CallProcessN := 7       // To exceptional termination
          )
    | ◆ DigitsReceiver(iN)ST.StatusN = 1              // Dial started
        → (◆ CallRecord(iN)ST.TimerSS = 10            // Set dial time-out timer
            ↣ ConnectDrivePC (SubscriberLine(iN)N, DialToneN, OffBL)
            → DigitalScanner(iN)ST.StatusN := 2
          )
    | ◆ DigitsReceiver(iN)ST.StatusN = 2              // Dialing
        → (◆ CallRecord(iN)ST.TimerSS = 0             // Dialing time-out
            ↣ ConnectDrivePC (SubscriberLine(iN)N, BusyToneN, OnBL)
            → CallRecord(iN)ST.CallingTerminationBL := T)
            → CallRecord(iN)ST.TimerSS := 10
            → CallRecord(iN)ST.CallProcessN := 7       // To exceptional termination
          )
    | ◆ DigitsReceiver(iN)ST.StatusN = 3              // Dial completed
        → CalledNumN := DigitalScanner(iN)ST.Digit1N * 10 +
                        DigitalScanner(iN)ST.Digit2N
        → CallRecord(iN)ST.CalledNumN := CalledNumN
        → CallRecord(iN)ST.CallProcessN := 3          // To check called status
    | ◆ ~                                             // Otherwise
        → ∅
    )
}
```

c) The Process of Check Called Status

Check called status is the third call processing process that looks into the current status of a given called subscriber, finds an available internal switching route between the calling and called parties, and sends busy tone to calling subscriber when called is busy or no route is free. The check called status process of TSS, CheckCalledStatus**PC**, is modeled in Figure 16, where related system support processes and operated UDMs are cross referenced.

The CheckCalledStatus**PC** process tests the status of the called subscriber line in order to get through the requested call. If the called line is unavailable (i.e., it is busy, just hooked-off for a new call, or invalid), the busy tone will be sent to the calling subscriber, and the call is transferred into PN**N** = 7 (Exceptional termination); Otherwise, the process goes further to seek an available internal route for connecting the pair of lines after pre-seize the called line by marking it as busy. When a free route is found, the process transfers to the next state PN**N** = 4 (Connecting). However, if there is no free route available in the system, the busy tone will be sent to the calling subscriber, the seized called line status will be released, and the process transfers to PN**N** = 7 (Exceptional termination).

d) The Process of Connecting

Connecting is the fourth call processing process that informs the called subscriber with the ringing tone, and at the same time, sends the ring back tone to the calling subscriber that is waiting for the answer of the call. The connecting process of TSS, Connecting**PC**, is modeled in Figure 17, where related system support processes and operated UDMs are cross referenced.

The Connecting**PC** process retrieves necessary information for a call such as the numbers of calling and called lines, as well as the switching route preallocated in preceding process. Then, the ringing tone and ring-back tone are sent to the called and calling subscriber lines, respectively, before the process transfers to PN**N** = 5 (Talking).

e) The Process of Talking

Talking is the fifth call processing process that physically connects both parties using pre-seized route in the dialing process when the called subscriber answered, and monitors terminations by either party. The talking process of TSS, Talking**PC**, is modeled in Figure 18, where related system support processes and operated UDMs are cross referenced.

The Talking**PC** process first detects if the called line answers the call. If the called subscriber hooks off to answer the ring while the calling party is hearing the ring back tone, the called line will be seized and marked as busy to avoid any cross connection by other calls. At the same time, signals to both parties are stopped and a physical route between the calling and called lines is then connected via the pre-seized switching route in order to make conversation. This results in a successful switching sequence and the system enters the process PN**N** = 6 (Call termination).

A possible exceptional condition in this process is that, during waiting for answer, the calling subscriber may give up before the called line hook off. This will trigger the release of the called line and the occupied route, and the cancel of both signals to the calling and called parties. Then, the system transfers to PN**N** = 0 (Ready for call origination).

It is noteworthy that the system do nothing when it enters this process if the called party has not answer the ringing signal and the calling party has remained in the waiting status by hearing the ring back tone. In this case, there is no state transition, i.e., the system remains in PN**N** = 5 (Talking) until next round processing.

Figure 16. The behavioral model of the check called status process

```
CheckCalledStatusPC (<I :: LineNumN>; <O :: CallProcessN>;
                     <UDMs :: LineScannersST, CallRecordsST, RoutesST>) ≜

{ // PNN = 3
 iN := LineNumN
 → ( CalledNumN := CallRecord(iN)ST.CalledNumN
 → ( ◆ LineScanner(CalledNumN)ST.StatusN = 2 ∨
       LineScanner(CalledNumN)ST.StatusN = 3 ∨
       LineScanner(CalledNumN)ST.StatusN = 4 ∨
       LineScanner(CalledNumN)ST.StatusN = 5        // Hook-off, busy, seized, or invalid
       → ( CallRecord(iN)ST.TimerSS := 10            // Set busy tone timer
            ⟼ ConnectDrivePC (SubscriberLine(iN)N, BusyToneN, OnBL)

            → CallRecord(iN)ST.CallingTerminationBL := T
            → CallRecord(iN)ST.TimerN := 10
            → CallRecord(iN)ST.CallProcessN := 7      // To exceptional termination
         )
    | ◆  LineScanner(CalledNumN)ST.StatusN = 0 ∨
         LineScanner(CalledNumN)ST.StatusN = 1        // Idle or hook-on
       → LineScanner(CalledNumN)ST.StatusN := 4       // Seize the line
       → LineScanner(CalledNumN)ST.CallProcessN := 0  // Mark as called without dispatching
       → RouteFoundBL := F                            // To seek a switching route
            4
       → R   ( ◆ Route(jN)ST.StatusBL = F
           jN=0
            → RouteNumN := jN
            →  RouteFoundBL := T
            → Route(jN)ST.StatusBL := T               // Seize the free route
            → ∅
         )
       → ( ◆   RouteFoundBL = T
            → CallRecord(iN)ST.RouteNumN := RouteNumN
            → CallRecord(iN)ST.CallProcessN := 4       // Connecting
          | ◆ ~
            ⟼ ConnectDrive PC (SubscriberLine(iN)N, BusyToneN, OnBL)
            → LineScanner(CalledNumN)ST.StatusN := 0   // Release called line
            → CallRecord(iN)ST.CallingTerminationBL := T
            → CallRecord(iN)ST.TimerN := 10
            → CallRecord(iN)ST.CallProcessN := 7        // To exceptional termination
         )
    ) )
}
```

f) The Process of Call Termination

Call termination is the final normal call processing process that handles call ending of either party, releases the occupied route, and immediately sends the busy tone to the party that has not hook-on. The call termination process of TSS, CallTermi-nationPC, is modeled in Figure 19, where related system support processes and operated UDMs are cross referenced.

The CallTerminationPC process handles the end of a call by monitoring the status of Calling-TerminationBL in the CallRecordST of the calling line known as *calling-party control* of call termi-

Figure 17. The behavioral model of the connecting process

```
ConnectingPC (<I :: LineNumN>; <O :: CallProcessN>;
                <UDMs :: CallRecordsST>)
{ // PNN = 4
  iN := LineNumN
   → CalledNumN := CallRecord(iN)ST.CalledNumN
     ConnectDrivePC (SubscriberLine(iN)N, RingBackToneN, OnBL)
     ConnectDrivePC (SubscriberLine(CalledNumN)N, RingingToneN, OnBL)
   → CallRecord(iN)ST.CallProcessN := 5          // To talking
}
```

Figure 18. The behavioral model of the talking process

```
TalkingPC (<I :: LineNumN>; <O :: CallProcessN>;
            <UDMs :: LineScannersST, CallRecordsST, RoutesST>) ≜
{// PNN = 5
 iN := LineNumN
  → CalledNumN := CallRecord(iN)ST.CalledNumN
  → RouteNumN := CallRecord(iN)ST.RouteNumN
  → ( ◆ LineScanner(CalledNumN)ST.StatusN = 2 ∧       // Called answers
       LineScanner(iN)ST.StatusN = 3                  // Calling is still waiting
       → LineScanner(CalledNumN)ST.Status := 3        // Show busy
       ↦ ConnectDrivePC (SubscriberLine(iN)N, RingBackToneN, OffBL)        // Stop signals
       ↦ ConnectDrivePC (SubscriberLine(CalledNumN)N, RingingToneN, OffBL)
       ↦ ConnectDrivePC (SubscriberLine(iN)N, RouteNumN, OnBL)             // Connect circuit
       ↦ ConnectDrivePC (SubscriberLine(CalledNumN)N, RouteNumN, OnBL)
       → CallRecord(iN)ST.CallingTerminationBL := T   // Set hook-on monitoring
       → CallRecord(iN)ST.CalledTerminationBL := T
       → CallRecord(iN)ST.CallProcessN := 6           // To call termination
     | ◆ LineScanner(iN)ST.StatusN = 1 ∨              // Calling give up before answer
       LineScanner(iN)ST.StatusN = 0
       → LineScanner(CalledNumN)ST.Status := 0        // Show idle
       ↦ ConnectDrivePC (SubscriberLine(iN)N, RingBackToneN, OffBL) // Stop signals
       ↦ ConnectDrive PC (SubscriberLine(CalledNumN)N, RingingToneN, OffBL)
       → Route(RouteNumN)ST.Status := F               // Free seized route
       → CallRecord(iN)ST.CallStatusBL := F           // Call gave up
       → CallRecord(iN)ST.CallProcessN := 0           // Idle
     | ◆ ~                                            // Otherwise exit
       → ∅
    )
}
```

nation. When a call termination is detected on the calling line, the subscriber and the route are immediately disconnected and released. Then, the status of the called line in the conversation is checked. If the called line has already hooked-on, it is set as free, the line status is transferred to PNN = 0 (Ready for new call origination), and the engaged call record is set to terminated. However, if the called line remains unterminated when it is hearing the busy tone, it will be transferred to PNN = 7 (Exceptional termination) after the 10 second monitoring timer is set.

Figure 19. The behavioral model of the call termination process

```
CallTerminationPC (<I :: LineNumN>; <O :: CallProcessN>;
                    <UDM:: LineScannersST, CallRecordsST, RoutesST>) ≜
{ // PNN = 6
  iN := LineNumN
  → CalledNumN := CallRecord(iN)ST.CalledNumN
  → RouteNumN := CallRecord(iN)ST.RouteNumN
  → (◆ CallRecord(iN)ST.CallingTerminationBL = T ∧
        LineScanner(iN)ST.StatusN = 1                  // Calling hook-on
        ↦ ConnectDrivePC (SubscriberLine(iN)N, RouteNumN, OffBL)  // Release route
        ↦ ConnectDrivePC (SubscriberLine(CalledNumN)N, RouteNumN, OffBL)

        ↦ ConnectDrivePC (SubscriberLine(CalledNumN)N, BusyToneN, OnBL)
        → Route(RouteNumN)ST.Status := F              // Free seized route
        → CallRecord(iN)ST.CallingTerminationBL := F
        → CallRecord(iN)ST.CallProcessN := 0          // Release calling
        → ( ◆ CallRecord(iN)ST.CalledTerminationBL = T ∧
            LineScanner(CalledNumN)ST.StatusN = 1     // Called hook-on
            → CallRecord(iN)ST.CalledTerminationBL := F
            → CallRecord(iN)ST.CallProcessN := 0      // Set idle
            → CallRecord(iN)ST.CallStatusBL := F      // Call terminated
            → CallRecord(CalledNumN)ST.CallProcessN := 0       // Release called
          | ◆ ~                                       // Set hook-on monitor for called
            → CallRecord(iN)ST.CalledTerminationBL := F
            → CallRecord(CalledNumN)ST.CallStatusBL := T
            → CallRecord(CalledNumN)ST.TimerN := 10
            → CallRecord(CalledNumN)ST.CallProcessN := 7 // To exceptional termination
          )
       )
}
```

It is noteworthy that, when a calling party controlled billing system is included in the TSS system, the starting point of billing is when the called line answers, i.e., LineScanner(CalledNumN) ST.StatusN = 2, in the TalkingPC process. However, the ending point of billing is triggered by the event CallRecord(CallingNumN) ST.CallingTerminationBL = T ∧ LineScanner(CallingNumN)ST.StatusN = 1, where the former indicates that the given line's termination status is under monitoring and the letter denotes that the line has just hooked on. In addition, the *called-party controlled* or *both-party controlled* billing techniques may be adopted in a similar approach.

g) The Process of Exceptional Termination

Exceptional termination is the seventh call processing process that handles all possible exceptional events and conditions in any previous call processing process by sending the busy tone to a given subscriber line. The exceptional termination process of TSS, ExceptionalTerminationPC, is modeled in Figure 20, where related system support processes and operated UDMs are cross referenced.

The ExceptionalTerminationPC process handles special situations in any previous call processing processes when any party does not hook-on after time out in call termination during receiving the busy tone. In the case the status of the line under monitoring for exceptional termination is detected to be hooked–on, the line will be released and the busy tone will be stopped. However, in the case of no termination after the timer is out, the line will no longer be sending the busy tone, but its status in the LineScanner**ST** will be set as invalid until the system administrator turns it back to normal services.

In the design of the TSS system, the complex call processing process, CallProcessing-Processes**PC**, is divided into seven finite state processes in which each of them is only handle a limited and timely continuous operation. This is a typical real-time technique that guarantees rigorous system timing for complicated real-time multi-threads dispatching. Further details of real-time system dispatching will be described in dynamic behaviors modeling of the TSS system. Based on the refined specifications and denotational mathematical models, code can be derived easily and rigorously, and tests of the code can be generated prior to the coding phase.

THE DYNAMIC BEHAVIOR MODEL OF THE TSS SYSTEM

Dynamic behaviors of a system are run-time process deployment and dispatching mechanisms based on the static behaviors. Because system static behaviors are a set of component processes of the system, to put the static processes into a live and interacting system at run-time, the dynamic behaviors of the system in terms of process deployment and dispatches are yet to be specified.

With the work products developed in the preceding section as a set of static behavioral processes of the TSS system, this section describes the dynamic behaviors of TSS at run-time using a three-step refinement strategy via *process priority allocation, process deployments,* and *process dispatches.*

TSS Process Priority Allocation

The process priority allocation of system dynamic behaviors is the executing and timing requirements of all static processes at run-time. In general, process priorities can be specified at 4 levels for

Figure 20. The behavioral model of the external termination process

```
ExceptionalTerminationPC (<I :: LineNumN>; <O :: CallProcessN>;
                          <CLMs :: LineScannersST, CallRecordsST>) ≙
{ // PNN = 7
  iN := LineNumN
  → ( ◆ LineScanner(iN)ST.StatusN = 1                          // Called hook-on
        → LineScanner(iN)ST.StatusN := 0                       // Set called line idle
        ↦ ConnectDrivePC (SubscriberLine(iN)N, BusyToneN, OffBL)

        → CallRecord(iN)ST.CallStatusBL := F                   // Call terminated
        → CallRecord(iN)ST.CallProcessN := 0                   // Release calling
    | ◆ LineScanner(iN)ST.StatusN = 3 ^

      CallRecord(iN)ST.TimerN = 0                              // Waiting time out
      ↦ ConnectDrivePC (SubscriberLine(iN)N, BusyToneN, OffBL)

        → LineScanner(iN)ST.StatusN := 5                       // Set to invalid
        → CallRecord(iN)ST.CallStatusBL := F
        → CallRecord(iN)ST.CallProcessN := 0
    )
}
```

real-time and nonreal-time system in an increasing priority known as: L1: *base* level processes, L2: *high* level processes, L3: *low interrupt* level processes, and L4: *high interrupt* level processes. The L1 and L2 processes are system dynamic behaviors that are executable in normal sequential manner. However, the L3 and L4 processes are executable in cyclic manner triggered by certain system timing interrupts. It is noteworthy that some of the priority levels may be omitted in modeling a particular system, except the base level processes. That is, all systems encompass at least a base level process, particularly a nonreal-time or transaction system.

According to the RTPA system modeling and refinement methodology (Wang, 2007a), the first step refinement of the dynamic behaviors of the TSS system on process priority allocation can be specified as shown in Figure 21. It may be observed that all transactional processes at run-time, such as SystemInitial**PC** and the seven call processing processes, are allocated at the base level, therefore there is no high level processes in the TSS system. However, the processes with strict timing constraints, such as LineScanning**PC**, SysClock**PC**, and Digital Receiving**PC**, are allocated as low or high level interrupt processes dependent on their timing priorities and executing frequencies.

TSS Dynamic Process Deployment

Process deployment is a dynamic behavioral model of systems at run-time, which refines the timing relations and interactions among the system, system clock, system interrupts, and all processes at different priority levels. Process deployment is a refined model of process priority allocation for time-driven behaviors of a system. On the basis of the process priority allocation model as developed in previous subsection in Figure 21, the TSS dynamic behaviors can be further refined with a process deployment model as shown in Figure 22, where precise timing relationships between different priority levels are specified.

Figure 21. Process priority allocation of TSS dynamic behaviors

```
TSS§.ProcessPriorityAllocationPC
{ // [L1: Base level processes]
  (   SystemInitialPC
   || // CallProcessingPC
      ( CallOriginationPC
      | DialingPC
      | CheckCalledStatusPC
      | ConnectingPC
      | TalkingPC
      | CallTerminationPC
      | ExceptionalTerminationPC
      )
  )
 || // [L2: High level processes]
  ...
 || // [L3: Low interrupt level processes]
  LineScanningPC
 || // [L4: High interrupt level processes]
  (   SysClockPC
   || DigitsReceivingPC
  )
}
```

Figure 22. Dynamic process deployment of the TSS system

```
TSS§.ProcessDeploymentST ≙ § →
{ // [L1: Base level processes]
  @SystemInitialS
    ↳ ( SysInitialPC
                    T
        →      R    CallProcessingPC
         SysShutdownBL=F
        → ⊠
      )
 ↯ // [L3: Low interrupt level processes]
  @SysClock100msInt®
    ↗ LineScanningPC
    ↘ ®
 ↯ // [L4: High interrupt level processes]
  @SysClock10msInt®
    ↗ (SysClockPC
       → DigitsReceivingPC
      )
    ↘ ®
} → §
```

In Figure 22, § represents the system at top level where all external, timing and interrupt events, @SystemInitial**S**, @SysClock1msInte, and @SysClock100msInte, are captured. The big-R notation indicates that, after the TSS system is initialized, the seven call processing processes collectively represented by CallProcessing**PC** are repetitively executing at the base level until Sys-Shutdown**BL** = **T**. The base level operations may be interrupted when a cyclic timing interrupt, such as SysClock1msInte and SysClock100msInte, is captured by the system, then one or a set of pre-designated interrupt level processes will be invoked. At the completion of an execution of any interrupt process, the system will return to the interrupt point e of the base level process where it was interrupted.

TSS Dynamic Process Dispatching

Process dispatch is a dynamic behavioral model of systems at run-time, which refines relations between system events and processes. Dynamic process dispatch specifies event-driven behaviors of a system. In the TSS system, the iterative call processing process, CallProcessing**PC**, is a complex process that can be further refined in a system process dispatching framework as shown in Figure 23.

The TSS process dispatching model specifies that the system iteratively handles each of the 16 subscriber requests for call processing when the *i*th CallRecord(i**N**)**ST**.CallStatus**BL** = **T**. Then, the system adopts a switch structure to handle one of the seven possible line status represented by the values of CallRecord(i**N**)**ST**.CallProcess**N**. Based on the value of the current call process number,

Figure 23. Dynamic process dispatching of the TSS system

```
CallProcessingPC ≜ § →
{
    nN := 15
                nN
    →  R  (◆ CallRecord(iN)ST.CallStatusBL = T
              N=1
                → LineNumN := iN
                → ( @CallRecord(iN)ST.CallProcessN = 0          // Idle
                      → ∅
                    | @CallRecord(iN)ST.CallProcessN = 1          // Call origination
                      ↳ CallOrigination(<I:: LineNumN>; <O:: CallProcessN>)PC
                    | @CallRecord(iN)ST.CallProcessN = 2          // Dialing
                      ↳ Dialling (<I:: LineNumN>; <O:: CallProcessN>)PC
                    | @CallRecord(iN)ST.CallProcessN = 3          // Check called status
                      ↳ CheckCalledStatus(<I:: LineNumN>; <O:: CallProcessN>)PC
                    | @CallRecord(iN)ST.CallProcessN = 4          // Connecting
                      ↳ Connecting(<I:: LineNumN>; <O:: CallProcessN>)PC
                    | @CallRecord(iN)ST.CallProcessN = 5          // Talking
                      ↳ Talking(<I:: LineNumN>; <O:: CallProcessN>)PC
                    | @CallRecord(iN)ST.CallProcessN = 6          // Call termination
                      ↳ CallTermination(<I:: LineNumN>; <O:: CallProcessN>)PC
                    | @CallRecord(iN)ST.CallProcessN = 7          // Exceptional termination
                      ↳ ExceptionalTermination(<I:: LineNumN>; <O:: CallProcessN>)PC
                  )
            )
} → §
```

a preallocated process will be dispatched except CallRecord(i**N**)**ST**.CallProcess**N** = 0.

As specified in Figure 23, the CallProcessing**PC** process is a complex process with seven state-transition processes for controlling a call from origination to termination. Because the TSS system is operating at the millisecond level, while a telephone call may last for a considerably long period, the system cannot serve and wait for the completion of a transition for a specific call for all the time. Therefore, the switching functions for an individual call are divided into seven coherent states, corresponding to the seven dispatching processes as modeled in Figure 23.

The practical formal engineering method of RTPA for system modeling and specification provides a coherent notation system and systematical methodology for large-scale software and hybrid system design and implementation. The formal design models and their refinements demonstrate a typical system modeling paradigm of the entire architectures, static behaviors, and dynamic behaviors of the TSS system according to the RTPA specification and refinement methodology. The final-level refinements of the TSS specifications provide a set of detailed and precise design blueprints for seamless code generation, system implementation, tests, and verifications.

CONCLUSION

This article has demonstrated that a complex real-time Telephone Switching System (TSS), including its architecture, static behaviors, and dynamic behaviors, can be formally and efficiently described by RTPA. On the basis of the RTPA methodologies, this article has systematically developed a formal design model of the TSS system in a top-down approach. The architectural model of the TSS system has been created using a set of UDMs. The static behaviors of the TSS system have been modeled by a set of call processing

processes. The dynamic behaviors of the TSS system have been specified and refined by a set of process priority allocation, process deployment, and dispatching models.

Based on the rigorous design models and the formal framework of the TSS system, program code can be seamlessly derived. The formal model of TSS may not only serve as a formal design paradigm of real-time software systems, but also a test bench of the expressive power and modeling capability of exiting formal methods in software engineering. Related real-world case studies on formal system modeling and refinement in RTPA may be referred to (Wang and Ngolah, 2003; Wang and Zhang, 2003; Wang et al., 2009; Tan et al., 2004; Ngolah et al., 2004). Since the equivalence between software and human behaviors, RTPA may also be use to describe human dynamic behaviors and mental processes (Wang, 2003, 2007b; Wang and Ruhe, 2007).

ACKNOWLEDGMENT

The author would like to acknowledge Natural Science and Engineering Council of Canada (NSERC) for its partial support to this work. The author would like to thank the anonymous reviewers for their invaluable comments that have greatly improved the latest version of this article.

REFERENCES

Baeten, J. C. M., & Bergstra, J. A. (1991). Real Time Process Algebra. *Formal Aspects of Computing*, *3*, 142–188. doi:10.1007/BF01898401

Corsetti, E., Montanari, A., & Ratto, E. (1991). Dealing with Different Time Granularities in Formal Specifications of Real-Time Systems. [Kluwer.]. *The Journal of Real-Time Systems*, *3*(2), 191–215. doi:10.1007/BF00365335

Dierks, H. (2000). *A Process Algebra for Real-Time Programs. LNCS #1783* (pp. 66–76). Berlin: Springer.

Hoare, C. A. R. (1978). Communicating Sequential Processes. *Communications of the ACM, 21*(8), 666–677. doi:10.1145/359576.359585

Hoare, C. A. R., Hayes, I. J., He, J., Morgan, C. C., Roscoe, A. W., & Sanders, J. W. (1987, August). Laws of Programming. *Communications of the ACM, 30*(8), 672–686. doi:10.1145/27651.27653

Labrosse, J.J. (1999, December). *MicroC/OS-II, The Real-Time Kernel*, 2nd ed., Gilroy, CA: R&D Books..

Liu, J. (2000). *Real-Time Systems*. Upper Saddle River, NJ: Prentice Hall.

McDermid, J. A. (Ed.). (1991). *Software Engineer's Reference Book*. Oxford, UK: Butterworth-Heinemann Ltd.

Milner, R. (1980). *A Calculus of Communicating Systems, LNCS 92*. Springer-Verlag.

Ngolah, C. F., Wang, Y., & Tan, X. (2004). The Real-Time Task Scheduling Algorithm of RTOS+. *IEEE Canadian Journal of Electrical and Computer Engineering, 29*(4), 237–243.

Tan, X., Wang, Y., & Ngolah, C. F. (2004). A Novel Type Checker for Software System Specifications in RTPA. *Proc. 17th Canadian Conference on Electrical and Computer Engineering* (CCECE'04), IEEE CS Press, Niagara Falls, ON, Canada, May, (pp. 1255-1258).

Thompson, R. A. (2000). *Telephone Switching Systems*. MA, USA: Artech House.

Vereijken, J. J. (1995, June). A Process Algebra for Hybrid Systems. In A. Bouajjani & O. Maler (Eds.), *Proc. 2nd European Workshop on Real-Time and Hybrid Systems*, Grenoble, France.

Wang, Y. (2002). The Real-Time Process Algebra (RTPA). *Annals of Software Engineering. International Journal (Toronto, Ont.), 14*, 235–274.

Wang, Y. (2003). Using Process Algebra to Describe Human and Software System Behaviors. *Brain and Mind, 4*(2), 199–213. doi:10.1023/A:1025457612549

Wang, Y. (2007a). *Software Engineering Foundations: A Software Science Perspective. CRC Series in Software Engineering (Vol. II)*. USA: CRC Press.

Wang, Y. (2007b). Formal Description of the Cognitive Process of Memorization. *Proc. 6th International Conference on Cognitive Informatics* (ICCI'07), IEEE CS Press, Lake Tahoe, CA., Aug., (pp. 284-293).

Wang, Y. (2008a). RTPA: A Denotational Mathematics for Manipulating Intelligent and Computational Behaviors. *International Journal of Cognitive Informatics and Natural Intelligence, 2*(2), 44–62. doi:10.4018/jcini.2008040103

Wang, Y. (2008b). Deductive Semantics of RTPA. *International Journal of Cognitive Informatics and Natural Intelligence, 2*(2), 95–121. doi:10.4018/jcini.2008040106

Wang, Y. (2008c). Mathematical Laws of Software. *Transactions of Computational Science, 2*, 46–83. doi:10.1007/978-3-540-87563-5_4

Wang, Y. (2008d). On Contemporary Denotational Mathematics for Computational Intelligence. *Transactions of Computational Science, 2*, 6–29. doi:10.1007/978-3-540-87563-5_2

Wang, Y., & King, G. (2000). *Software Engineering Processes: Principles and Applications, CRC Series in Software Engineering (Vol. I)*. USA: CRC Press.

Wang, Y., & Noglah, C. F. (2002). Formal Specification of a Real-Time Lift Dispatching System. *Proc. 2002 IEEE Canadian Conference on Electrical and Computer Engineering (CCECE'02)*, Winnipeg, Manitoba, Canada, May, (pp. 669-674).

Wang, Y., & Noglah, C. F. (2003). Formal Description of Real-Time Operating Systems using RTPA. *Proceedings of the 2003 Canadian Conference on Electrical and Computer Engineering (CCECE'03),* IEEE CS Press, Montreal, Canada, May, (pp. 1247-1250).

Wang, Y., & Ruhe, G. (2007). The Cognitive Process of Decision Making. *International Journal of Cognitive Informatics and Natural Intelligence, 1*(2), 73–85. doi:10.4018/jcini.2007040105

Wang, Y., Tan, X., & Ngolah, F. C. (2010). (to appear). Design and Implementation of Automatic Code Generators Based on RTPA. *International Journal of Software Science and Computational Intelligence, 2*(3).

Wang, Y., & Zhang, Y. (2003), Formal Description of an ATM System by RTPA, *Proc. 16th Canadian Conference on Electrical and Computer Engineering* (CCECE'03), IEEE CS Press, Montreal, Canada, May, 1255-1258.

This work was previously published in International Journal of Software Science and Computational Intelligence, Volume 1, Issue 3, edited by Yingxu Wang, pp. 92-116, copyright 2009 by IGI Publishing (an imprint of IGI Global).

Chapter 19
The Formal Design Model of a Lift Dispatching System (LDS)

Yingxu Wang
University of Calgary, Canada

Cyprian F. Ngolah
University of Calgary, Canada

Hadi Ahmadi
University of Calgary, Canada

Philip Sheu
Univ. of California, Irvine, USA

Shi Ying
Wuhan University, China

ABSTRACT

A Lift Dispatching System (LDS) is a typical real-time system that is highly complicated in design and implementation. This article presents the formal design, specification, and modeling of the LDS system using a denotational mathematics known as Real-Time Process Algebra (RTPA). The conceptual model of the LDS system is introduced as the initial requirements for the system. The architectural model of the LDS system is created using RTPA architectural modeling methodologies and refined by a set of Unified Data Models (UDMs). The static behaviors of the LDS system are specified and refined by a set of Unified Process Models (UPMs) for the lift dispatching and serving processes. The dynamic behaviors of the LDS system are specified and refined by process priority allocation and process deployment models. Based on the formal design models of the LDS system, code can be automatically generated using the RTPA Code Generator (RTPA-CG), or be seamlessly transferred into programs by programmers. The formal models of LDS may not only serve as a formal design paradigm of real-time software systems, but also a test bench of the expressive power and modeling capability of exiting formal methods in software engineering.

DOI: 10.4018/978-1-4666-0261-8.ch019

INTRODUCTION

A real-time system is characterized by event-/time-/interrupt-driven behaviours that are constrained by both its logic correctness and timing correctness. Although nonreal-time transaction processing systems may only consider the logical correctness, real-time systems have to put emphases on dynamic timing constraints with system control logics. A Lift Dispatching System (LDS) is a typical real-time control system characterized by its high degree of complexity, intricate interactions with hardware devices and users, and necessary requirements for domain knowledge (Hayes, 1985; McDermid, 1991; Chenais & Weinberger, 1992; Liu, 2000; Wang, 2002, 2007; Ngolah et al., 2004). All these factors warrant an LDS system as a complex but ideal design paradigm in large-scale software system design in general and in real-time system modeling in particular.

The lift scheduling problem has been studied as a real-time system in Chenais and Weinberger (1992) and Hamdi et al. (1995) to be NP-complete, because for n lifts, if there are p requests, then there would be upto n^p possible dispatching strategies. Further, the problem is dynamic, i.e., during executing a given dispatching plan, new requests presented inside the cabins of lifts and from the floors may often interrupt and change the current dispatching strategy. The request scheduler therefore must be able to find a suitable dispatching mechanism in order to ensure there is no request to wait for a long period before being served.

There is no systematical and detailed repository and formal documentation of design knowledge and modeling prototypes of an LDS system nor a formal model of it in denotational mathematics and formal notation systems (Wang, 2008d). This article presents the formal design, specification, and modeling of the LDS system using a denotational mathematics known as Real-Time Process Algebra (RTPA) (Wang, 2002, 2003, 2007, 2008a, 2008b). RTPA introduces only 17 meta-processes and 17 process relations to describe software system architectures and behaviors with a stepwise refinement methodology (Wang, 2007, 2008a, 2008c). According to the RTPA methodology for system modeling and refinement, a software system can be specified as a set of *architectural* and *operational components* as well as their interactions. The former is modeled by *Unified Data Models* (UDMs, also known as the component logical model (CLM)) (Wang, 2007), which is an abstract model of the system hardware interface, an internal logic model of hardware, and/or a control structure of a system. The latter is modeled by *static* and *dynamic processes* using the *Unified Process Models* (UPMs) (Hoare, 1978, 1985; Bjorner & Jones, 1982; Corsetti & Ratto, 1991; Wang, 2007, 2008a; Wang & King, 2000; Wang & Ngolah, 2002).

This article develops a formal design model of the LDS system in a top-down approach on the basis of the RTPA methodology. In the remainder of this article, the conceptual model of the LDS system is described as the initial requirements of the system. The architectural model of the LDS system is created based on the conceptual model using the RTPA architectural modeling methodologies and refined by a set of UDMs. Then, the static behaviors of the LDS system are specified and refined by a set of processes (UPMs). The dynamic behaviors of the LDS system are specified and refined by process priority allocation, process deployment, and process dispatching models. With the formal and rigorous models of the LDS system, code can be automatically generated by the RTPA Code Generator (RTPA-CG) (Wang, 2007), or be seamlessly transferred into program code manually. The formal models of LDS may not only serve as a formal design paradigm of real-time software systems, but also a test bench of the expressive power and modeling capability of exiting formal methods in software engineering.

THE CONCEPTUAL MODEL OF THE LDS SYSTEM

The Lift Dispatching System (LDS) is a real-time computer controlled system for multiple lifts in a building with multiple floors. In the conceptual model of the LDS system, as given in Figure 1, there are three lifts serving six floors. The LDS system encompasses three lifts, a controller implemented by a processor, a set of control interfaces, and a set of 30 buttons. On each floor of the building, there are three buttons corresponding to each lift in both directions, except that there are only upward buttons on floor 1 and downward buttons on floor 6. On each floor there is also an indicator of the current level of each lifts. In addition to the external equipments, the cabin of each lift consists of a bell and a set of internal buttons to control the door's open/close and to enter the expected numbers of internal requests.

Once an external button is pressed, its built-in lamp is lit up to indicate that the request is received by the system. If a button is pressed for multiple times after a request for that button has already been pended, there is no further effect. The system

also automatically set the rest buttons on the same floor with the same direction as pressed. Lights of the same group of interlinked buttons will go off when a lift arrives to serve the request. A parked lift as dispatched for serving a request at a certain floor will automatically open and then close the door of its cabin within a predesigned period except it is forced to be opened or closed by internal buttons with a higher priority.

The design constraints of the lift system and its dispatching algorithm can be informally described as follows:

1) The lift that responds to a request does so within minimum time and minimum energy consumption.

2) Only one lift should respond to a given request on a certain floor.

3) If there is no request pending, a lift should be parked on the current floor where it reached in its last dispatched destination.

4) The door of a lift remains closed except the conditions specified in item (5) is met.

5) The door of a lift keeps open when reached the floors where a current request has been

Figure 1. Conceptual model of the LDS system

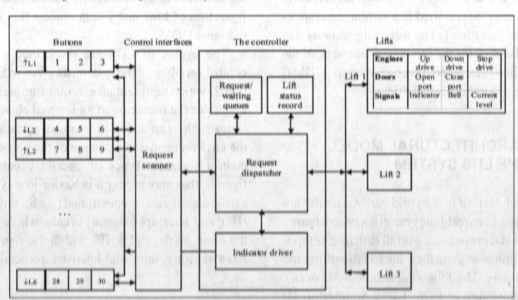

identified or the lift is in the initial state on floor 1.

6) A lift does not stop to serve a request if it is moving in the opposite direction of the pending request in a given dispatching cycle.

All design constraints and requirements for the LDS system as stated above will be rigorously specified in the formal LDS design models in the following sections, particularly the UPM of LiftDispatching**PC** and LiftServing**PC**.

The top level framework of the LDS system can be modeled by a set of architecture, static behaviors, and dynamic behaviors using RTPA (Wang, 2002, 2008a) as follows:

$$
\begin{aligned}
\S(LDS) \triangleq\ & LDS\S.Architecture\mathbf{ST} \\
& \|\ LDS\S.StaticBehaviors\mathbf{PC} \\
& \|\ LDS\S.DynamicBehaviors\mathbf{PC}
\end{aligned}
$$

(1)

where ‖ indicates that these three subsystems related in parallel, and **§**, **ST**, and **PC** are type suffixes of *system, system structure,* and *process,* respectively.

According to the RTPA methodology for system modeling, specification, and refinement (Wang, 2008a, 2008b), the top level model of any system may be specified in a similar structure as given in Equation 1. The following sections will extend and refine the top level framework of the LDS**§** into detailed architectural models (UDMs) and behavioral models (UPMs).

THE ARCHITECTURAL MODEL OF THE LDS SYSTEM

The architecture of a hybrid hardware/software system and/or a real-time system is a system framework that represents the overall structure, components, processes, and their interrelationships and interactions. The following subsections specify the architecture of LDS, LDS**§**.Architecture**ST**,

by a high-level architectural model based on its conceptual model as provided in Figure 1. Each of its architectural components will be refined as a UDM (also known as *Component Logical Model* (CLM)) (Wang, 2002a, 2007).

The Architectural Framework of LDS

System architectures, at the top level, specify a list of identifiers of UDMs and their relations. A UDM may be regarded as a predefined class of system hardware or internal control models, which can be inherited or implemented by corresponding UDM objects as specific instances in the succeeding architectural refinement for the system.

Corresponding to the conceptual model of LDS as shown in Figure 1, the high-level specification of the architecture of LDS, LDS**§**.Architecture**ST**, is given in Figure 2 in RTPA. LDS**§**.Architecture**ST** encompasses parallel structures of Lifts**ST**, Buttons**ST**, SysClock**ST**, and Controller**ST**, as well as a set of events @Events**S** and a set of statuses &Status**BL**. The controller of LDS, Controller**ST**, is a subsystem of internal control structures that may be further refined by a set of UDMs such as the RequestEvenRecord**ST**, LiftStatusRecord**ST**, LiftDispatchList**ST**, and ServiceQueues**ST**, where the numbers in angel brackets indicate the configuration of how many data objects that share the same UDM.

The events of LDS are predefined global control variables of the system, as given in Equation 2, which represent an external stimulus to a system or the occurring of an internal change of status such as an action of users, an updating of the environment, and a change of the value of a control variable. Types of general events, @Event**S**, that may trigger a behavior in a system can be classified into operational (@*e***S**), time (@*t***TM**), and interrupt (@*int*⊙) events, where @ is the *event prefix*, and **S**, **TM**, and ⊙ the type suffixes of string, time, and interrupt, respectively, i.e.:

Figure 2. The architectural framework of the LDS system

$$
\begin{aligned}
\text{LDS§.Architecture}\textbf{ST} \triangleq\ & <\text{Lifts : \textbf{ST} | [3]>} \\
\|\ & <\text{Buttons: \textbf{ST} | [30]>} \\
\|\ & <\text{SysClock: \textbf{ST} | [1]>} \\
\|\ & <\text{Controller: \textbf{ST} | [1]>} \\
\|\ & <@\text{Events\textbf{S}>} \\
\|\ & <ⓈStatus\textbf{BL}> \\
=\ & <\text{Lifts : \textbf{ST} | [3]>} \\
\|\ & <\text{Buttons: \textbf{ST} | [30]>} \\
\|\ & <\text{SysClock: \textbf{ST} | [1]>} \\
\|\ (\ & <\text{RequestEventRecord : \textbf{ST} | [30]>} \\
\|\ & <\text{LiftStatusRecord : \textbf{ST} | [3]>} \\
\|\ & <\text{LiftDispatchList : \textbf{ST} | [3]>} \\
\|\ & <\text{ServiceQueues : \textbf{ST} | [4]>} \\
) \\
\|\ & <@\text{Events\textbf{S}>} \\
\|\ & <ⓈStatus\textbf{BL}>
\end{aligned}
$$

@Events**S** ≜ @SystemInitial**S**
| @t**TM** = §thh:mm:ss
| @SysClock100msInt☉

(2)

A status denoted by Ⓢs**BL** is an abstract model of system state in Boolean type such as an operation result and an internal condition. The LDS status as a predefined global control variable is as follows:

ⓈStatus**BL** ≜ ⓈLiftFound**BL**
| ⓈSysShutDown**BL**
| ⓈUpRequestQueueEmpty**BL**
| ⓈUpRequestQueueFull**BL**
| ⓈDownRequestQueueEmpty**BL**
| ⓈDownRequestQueueFull**BL**
| ⓈUpWaitingQueueEmpty**BL**
| ⓈUpWaitingQueueFull**BL**
| ⓈDownWaitingQueueEmpty**BL**
| ⓈDownWaitingQueueFull**BL**

(3)

A UDM is a generic structural type defined in RTPA (Wang, 2002a, 2007). Mathematically, the UDM is an *n*-tuple to model a system architec-

tural component such as a hardware interface, an internal logical model, and/or a common control structure of a system. UDMs are a powerful modeling means in system architectural modeling, which can be used for unifying user defined complex data objects in system modeling, which represent the abstraction and formal representation of domain knowledge and structural information.

As modeled in Figure 2, the LDS system encompasses seven UDMs for modeling the system hardware interfaces and internal control structures as follows.

$$
\begin{aligned}
\text{LDS§.UDMs}\textbf{ST} \triangleq\ & \text{HardwareIntefaceCLMs \textbf{ST}} \\
\|\ & \text{InternalControlStructures \textbf{ST}} \\
=\ (\ & <\text{Lifts: \textbf{ST} | [3]>} \\
\|\ & <\text{Buttons: \textbf{ST} | [30]>} \\
\|\ & <\text{SysClock: \textbf{ST} | [1]>} \\
) \\
\|\ (\ & <\text{RequestEventRecord: \textbf{ST} | [30]>} \\
\|\ & <\text{LiftStatusRecord: \textbf{ST} | [3]>} \\
\|\ & <\text{LiftDispatchList: \textbf{ST} | [3]>} \\
\|\ & <\text{ServiceQueues: \textbf{ST} | [4]>} \\
)
\end{aligned}
$$

(4)

where the Lifts**ST**, Buttons**ST**, and SysClock**ST** are hardware interface UDMs, while the RequestEvenRecord**ST**, LiftStatusRecord**ST**, LiftDispatchList**ST**, and ServiceQueues**ST** are internal control UDMs.

The configuration of the UDMs in LDS is indicated by the numbers in the angle brackets in Equation 4, where each number shows how many similar devices or internal control structures are equipped that share the same UDM schema. For example, there are 3 lifts, 30 buttons, 4 service queues, and 3 lift dispatching list in the LDS system. Each of the seven type system UDMs in LDS is designed and modeled in the following subsections in the two categories of system hardware and internal control structures.

The UDM Structures of the LDS Hardware System

The hardware system of LDS and their interfaces are modeled by a set of UDMs such as Lifts**ST**, Buttons**ST**, and SysClock**ST** UDMs. Each of the three system UDMs in LDS is designed and modeled in the following subsections.

a)   The Lifts

The UDM model of lifts, Lifts**ST**, and its three derived objects Lift(i**N**)**ST**, $1 \leq$ i**N** ≤ 3, are modeled as shown in Figure 3. Lifts**ST** encompasses 18 fields known as the *engine drive ports* and *control signals* (UpDrivePort**H**, UpDriveOutput**B**; DownDrivePort**H**, DownDriveOutput**B**; StopDrivePort**H**, StopDriveOutput**B**), *door drive ports* and *control signals* (DoorOpenPort**H**, DoorOpenOutput**B**; DoorClosePort**H**, DoorClose-Output**B**; DoorBellPort**H**, DoorBellOutput**B**), and *I/O devices* (IndicatorPort**H**, IndicatorOutput**B**; CurrentLevelPort**H**, CurrentLevelInput**B**; Dest-ScanPort**H**, DestScanInput**B**). The port PORT**ST** = PORT**ST**(PortAddress**H**)**B**, as well as memory MEM**ST**, is a generic UDM model in RTPA that describes the architectural structure of system I/O

ports identified by a linear space of byte-type data identified by a hexadecimal port address. Typical operations on ports are input and output, i.e. (Wang, 2007, 2008a):

$$PORT\textbf{ST}(PortAddress\textbf{H})\textbf{B} \mid \gg PortInput\textbf{B}$$
$$PortOutput\textbf{B} \mid \ll PORT\textbf{ST}(PortAddress\textbf{H})\textbf{B}$$
$$(5)$$

Each field in Lifts**ST** is modeled by an RTPA type where its constraints, if any, are provided following the vertical bar. For instance, the constraint for the field of current level input in byte type is $1 \leq$ CurrentLevelInput**B** ≤ 6.

The three derived concrete lift models, $\overset{3}{\underset{i\textbf{N}=1}{R}}$ Lift(i**N**)**ST**, share the same structure as specified by the abstract schema Lifts**ST**. The concrete objects obtain their refined physical or logical parameters such as port addresses and initial values of the I/O signals.

b) The Buttons

The buttons of LDS, Buttons**ST**, are external keys installed on each floor for receiving service requests. As shown in the conceptual model of LDS in Figure 1, there are three buttons for each direction on each floor. Therefore, there are totally 30 button objects, Key(i**N**)**ST**, $1 \leq$ i**N** ≤ 30, that need to be modeled in LDS, which share a common UDM, Buttons**ST**, as shown in Figure 4.

The schema of Buttons**ST** models four fields with certain design constraints such as the PortAddress**H** (the physical interface of the key), Key-Input**B** (the key status information obtained from the key port where only the three most least significant bits are effective), Direction**BL** (the direction of request the key represents: **T** denotes upward and **F** downward), KeyPosition**N** (the floor number of a key represents).

The 30 derived concrete key models, $\overset{30}{\underset{i\textbf{N}=1}{R}}$ Key(i**N**)**ST**, share the same structure as specified by the abstract schema Buttons**ST**. The concrete objects obtain their refined physical or logical

Figure 3. The schema and detailed UDM model of the lifts

$$\text{Lifts} \mathbf{ST} \triangleq \mathop{\mathbf{R}}_{iN=1}^{3} \text{Lift(iN)} \mathbf{ST}:$$

(PORT**ST**(<UpDrivePort : **H** | UpDrivePort**H** ∈ {FF10**H**, FF20**H**, FF30**H**}>,
       <UpDriveOutput : **B** | UpDriveOutput**B** = {(1, On), (0, Off)}>)
| PORT**ST**(<DownDrivePort : **H** | DownDrivePort**H** ∈ {FF11**H**, FF21**H**, FF31**H**}>,
       <DownDriveOutput : **B** | DownDriveOutput**B** = {(1, On), (0, Off)}>)
| PORT**ST**(<StopDrivePort : **H** | StopDrivePort**H** ∈ {FF12**H**, FF22**H**, FF32**H**}>,
       <StopDriveOutput : **B** | StopDriveOutput**B** = {(1, On), (0, Off)}>)
| PORT**ST**(<DoorOpenPort : **H** | DoorOpenPort**H** ∈ {FF13**H**, FF23**H**, FF33**H**}>,
       <DoorOpenOutput : **B** | DoorOpenOutput**B** = {(1, On), (0, Off)}>)
| PORT**ST**(<DoorClosePort : **H** | DoorClosePort**H** ∈ {FF14**H**, FF24**H**, FF34**H**}>,
       <DoorCloseOutput : **B** | DoorCloseOutput**B** = {(1, On), (0, Off)}>)
| PORT**ST**(<DoorBellPort : **H** | DoorBellPort**H** ∈ {FF15**H**, FF25**H**, FF35**H**}>,
       <DoorBellOutput : **B** | DoorBellOutput**B** = {(1, On), (0, Off)}>)
| PORT**ST**(<IndicatorPort : **H** | IndicatorPort**H** ∈ {FF16**H**, FF26**H**, FF36**H**}>,
       <IndicatorOutput : **B** | 1 ≤ IndicatorOutput**B** ≤ 6>)
| PORT**ST**(<CurrentLevelPort : **H** | CurrentLevelPort**H** ∈ {FF17**H**, FF27**H**, FF37**H**}>,
       <CurrentLevelInput : **B** | 1 ≤ CurrentLevelInput**B** ≤ 6>)
| PORT**ST**(<DestScanPort : **H** | DestScanPort**H** ∈ {FF18**H**, FF28**H**, FF38**H**}>,
       <DestScanInput : **B** | 1 ≤ DestScanInput**N** ≤ 6>)
)
= Lift(1)**ST**: (PORT**ST**(<UpDrivePort**H** := FF10**H**>, <UpDriveOutput**B** := <0000 0000**B**>)
| PORT**ST**(<DownDrivePort**H** := FF11**H**>, <DownDriveOutput**B** := <0000 0000**B**>)
| PORT**ST**(<StopDrivePort**H** := FF12**H**>, <StopDriveOutput**B** := <0000 0001**B**>)
| PORT**ST**(<DoorOpenPort**H** := FF13**H**>, <DoorOpenOutput**B** := <0000 0001**B**>)
| PORT**ST**(<DoorClosePort**H** := FF14**H**>, <DoorCloseOutput**B** := <0000 0000**B**>)
| PORT**ST**(<DoorBellPort**H** := FF15**H**>, <DoorBellOutput**B** := <0000 0000**B**>)
| PORT**ST**(<IndicatorsPort**H** := FF16**H**>, <IndicatorOutput**B** := 1>)
| PORT**ST**(<CurrentLevelPort**H** := FF17**H**>, <CurrentLevelInput**B** := 1>)
| PORT**ST**(<DestScanPort**H** := FF18**H**>, <DestScanInput**B** := 1>)
)
|| Lift(2)**ST**: (PORT**ST**(<UpDrivePort**H** := FF20**H**>, <UpDriveOutput**B** := <0000 0000**B**>)
| PORT**ST**(<DownDrivePort**H** := FF21**H**>, <DownDriveOutput**B** := <0000 0000**B**>)
| PORT**ST**(<StopDrivePort**H** := FF22**H**>, <StopDriveOutput**B** := <0000 0001**B**>)
| PORT**ST**(<DoorOpenPort**H** := FF23**H**>, <DoorOpenOutput**B** := <0000 0001**B**>)
| PORT**ST**(<DoorClosePort**H** := FF24**H**>, <DoorCloseOutput**B** := <0000 0000**B**>)
| PORT**ST**(<DoorBellPort**H** := FF25**H**>, <DoorBellOutput**B** := <0000 0000**B**>)
| PORT**ST**(<IndicatorsPort**H** := FF26**H**>, <IndicatorOutput**B** := 1>)
| PORT**ST**(<CurrentLevelPort**H** := FF27**H**>, <CurrentLevelInput**B** := 1>)
| PORT**ST**(<DestScanPort**H** := FF28**H**>, <DestScanInput**B** := 1>)
)
|| Lift(3)**ST**: (PORT**ST**(<UpDrivePort**H** := FF30**H**>, <UpDriveOutput**B** := <0000 0000**B**>)
| PORT**ST**(<DownDrivePort**H** := FF31**H**>, <DownDriveOutput**B** := <0000 0000**B**>)
| PORT**ST**(<StopDrivePort**H** := FF32**H**>, <StopDriveOutput**B** := <0000 0001**B**>)
| PORT**ST**(<DoorOpenPort**H** := FF33**H**>, <DoorOpenOutput**B** := <0000 0001**B**>)
| PORT**ST**(<DoorClosePort**H** := FF34**H**>, <DoorCloseOutput**B** := <0000 0000**B**>)
| PORT**ST**(<DoorBellPort**H** := FF35**H**>, <DoorBellOutput**B** := <0000 0000**B**>)
| PORT**ST**(<IndicatorsPort**H** := FF36**H**>, <IndicatorOutput**B** := 1>)
| PORT**ST**(<CurrentLevelPort**H** := FF37**H**>, <CurrentLevelInput**B** := 1>)
| PORT**ST**(<DestScanPort**H** := FF38**H**>, <DestScanInput**B** := 1>)
)

Figure 4. The schema and detailed UDM model of request buttons

$$
\text{Buttons} \mathbf{ST} \triangleq \mathop{\mathbf{R}}_{iN=1}^{30} \text{Key(i}\mathbf{N})\mathbf{ST}:
$$

$$
\begin{aligned}
(\text{PORT}\mathbf{ST}(&<\text{PortAddress}: \mathbf{H} \mid \text{FF00}\mathbf{H} \le \text{PortAddress}\mathbf{H} \le \text{FF09}\mathbf{H}>, \\
&<\text{KeyInput}: \mathbf{B} \mid \text{KeyInput}\mathbf{B} = <\text{xxxx xkkk}\mathbf{B}>), \\
&<\text{Direction}: \mathbf{BL} \mid \text{Direction}\mathbf{BL} = \{(\mathbf{T}, \text{Up}), (\mathbf{F}, \text{Down})\}>, \\
&<\text{KeyPosition}: \mathbf{N} \mid 1 \le \text{KeyPosition}\mathbf{N} \le 6> \\
)
\end{aligned}
$$

= Key(1)**ST**: (PORT**ST**(PortAddress**H**, KeyInput**B**), Direction**BL**, KeyPosition**N**) := (FF00**H**, xxxx x000**B**, T, 1)
|| Key(2)**ST**: (PORT**ST**(PortAddress**H**, KeyInput**B**), Direction**BL**, KeyPosition**N**) := (FF00**H**, xxxx x000**B**, T, 1)
|| Key(3)**ST**: (PORT**ST**(PortAddress**H**, KeyInput**B**), Direction**BL**, KeyPosition**N**) := (FF00**H**, xxxx x000**B**, T, 1)

|| Key(4)**ST**: (PORT**ST**(PortAddress**H**, KeyInput**B**), Direction**BL**, KeyPosition**N**) := (FF01**H**, xxxx x000**B**, F, 2)
|| Key(5)**ST**: (PORT**ST**(PortAddress**H**, KeyInput**B**), Direction**BL**, KeyPosition**N**) := (FF01**H**, xxxx x000**B**, F, 2)
|| Key(6)**ST**: (PORT**ST**(PortAddress**H**, KeyInput**B**), Direction**BL**, KeyPosition**N**) := (FF01**H**, xxxx x000**B**, F, 2)
|| Key(7)**ST**: (PORT**ST**(PortAddress**H**, KeyInput**B**), Direction**BL**, KeyPosition**N**) := (FF02**H**, xxxx x000**B**, T, 2)
|| Key(8)**ST**: (PORT**ST**(PortAddress**H**, KeyInput**B**), Direction**BL**, KeyPosition**N**) := (FF02**H**, xxxx x000**B**, T, 2)
|| Key(9)**ST**: (PORT**ST**(PortAddress**H**, KeyInput**B**), Direction**BL**, KeyPosition**N**) := (FF02**H**, xxxx x000**B**, T, 2)

|| Key(10)**ST**: (PORT**ST**(PortAddress**H**, KeyInput**B**), Direction**BL**, KeyPosition**N**) := (FF03**H**, xxxx x000**B**, F, 3)
|| Key(11)**ST**: (PORT**ST**(PortAddress**H**, KeyInput**B**), Direction**BL**, KeyPosition**N**) := (FF03**H**, xxxx x000**B**, F, 3)
|| Key(12)**ST**: (PORT**ST**(PortAddress**H**, KeyInput**B**), Direction**BL**, KeyPosition**N**) := (FF03**H**, xxxx x000**B**, F, 3)
|| Key(13)**ST**: (PORT**ST**(PortAddress**H**, KeyInput**B**), Direction**BL**, KeyPosition**N**) := (FF04**H**, xxxx x000**B**, T, 3)
|| Key(14)**ST**: (PORT**ST**(PortAddress**H**, KeyInput**B**), Direction**BL**, KeyPosition**N**) := (FF04**H**, xxxx x000**B**, T, 3)
|| Key(15)**ST**: (PORT**ST**(PortAddress**H**, KeyInput**B**), Direction**BL**, KeyPosition**N**) := (FF04**H**, xxxx x000**B**, T, 3)

|| Key(16)**ST**: (PORT**ST**(PortAddress**H**, KeyInput**B**), Direction**BL**, KeyPosition**N**) := (FF05**H**, xxxx x000**B**, F, 4)
|| Key(17)**ST**: (PORT**ST**(PortAddress**H**, KeyInput**B**), Direction**BL**, KeyPosition**N**) := (FF05**H**, xxxx x000**B**, F, 4)
|| Key(18)**ST**: (PORT**ST**(PortAddress**H**, KeyInput**B**), Direction**BL**, KeyPosition**N**) := (FF05**H**, xxxx x000**B**, F, 4)
|| Key(19)**ST**: (PORT**ST**(PortAddress**H**, KeyInput**B**), Direction**BL**, KeyPosition**N**) := (FF06**H**, xxxx x000**B**, T, 4)
|| Key(20)**ST**: (PORT**ST**(PortAddress**H**, KeyInput**B**), Direction**BL**, KeyPosition**N**) := (FF06**H**, xxxx x000**B**, T, 4)
|| Key(21)**ST**: (PORT**ST**(PortAddress**H**, KeyInput**B**), Direction**BL**, KeyPosition**N**) := (FF06**H**, xxxx x000**B**, T, 4)

|| Key(22)**ST**: (PORT**ST**(PortAddress**H**, KeyInput**B**), Direction**BL**, KeyPosition**N**) := (FF07**H**, xxxx x000**B**, F, 5)
|| Key(23)**ST**: (PORT**ST**(PortAddress**H**, KeyInput**B**), Direction**BL**, KeyPosition**N**) := (FF07**H**, xxxx x000**B**, F, 5)
|| Key(24)**ST**: (PORT**ST**(PortAddress**H**, KeyInput**B**), Direction**BL**, KeyPosition**N**) := (FF07**H**, xxxx x000**B**, F, 5)
|| Key(25)**ST**: (PORT**ST**(PortAddress**H**, KeyInput**B**), Direction**BL**, KeyPosition**N**) := (FF08**H**, xxxx x000**B**, T, 5)
|| Key(26)**ST**: (PORT**ST**(PortAddress**H**, KeyInput**B**), Direction**BL**, KeyPosition**N**) := (FF08**H**, xxxx x000**B**, T, 5)
|| Key(27)**ST**: (PORT**ST**(PortAddress**H**, KeyInput**B**), Direction**BL**, KeyPosition**N**) := (FF08**H**, xxxx x000**B**, T, 5)
|| Key(28)**ST**: (PORT**ST**(PortAddress**H**, KeyInput**B**), Direction**BL**, KeyPosition**N**) := (FF09**H**, xxxx x000**B**, F, 6)
|| Key(29)**ST**: (PORT**ST**(PortAddress**H**, KeyInput**B**), Direction**BL**, KeyPosition**N**) := (FF09**H**, xxxx x000**B**, F, 6)
|| Key(30)**ST**: (PORT**ST**(PortAddress**H**, KeyInput**B**), Direction**BL**, KeyPosition**N**) := (FF09**H**, xxxx x000**B**, F, 6)

parameters such as port addresses and initial values of floors, directions, and the pattern of input signals of key status.

c) The System Clock

A *system clock* is a typical real-time device for event timing, process duration manipulation, and system synchronization. The UDM model of the system clock of LDS, SysClock**ST**, is designed as given in Figure 5. SysClock**ST** provides an *absolute* (calendar) clock CurrentTime**hh:mm:ss** as the logical time reference of the entire system and a *relative* clock **§t**$\mathbf{N}$ as a generic counter. The InterruptCounter$\mathbf{N}$ is adopted to transfer the basic timing ticks at 100ms interval into the second signal. The real-time system clock is updated by the process SysClock**PC**, which will be described in the following section on system static behaviors.

Figure 5. The schema and detailed UDM model of system clock

$$
\begin{aligned}
\text{SysClock}\textbf{ST} \triangleq \ (\ &<\S t : \textbf{N} \mid 0 \le \S t\textbf{N} \le 1{,}000{,}000>, \\
&<\text{CurrentTime} : \textbf{hh:mm:ss} \mid 00:00:00 \le \\
&\qquad\qquad\qquad \text{CurrentTime}\textbf{hh:mm:ss} \le 23:59:59>, \\
&<\text{MainClockPort} : \textbf{H} \mid \text{MainClockPort}\textbf{B} = \text{FFF1}\textbf{H}>, \\
&<\text{ClockInterval} : \textbf{N} \mid \text{ClockInterval}\textbf{N} = 100\textbf{ms}>, \\
&<\text{InterruptCounter} : \textbf{N} \mid 0 \le \text{InterruptCounter}\textbf{N} \le 9>, \\
)&
\end{aligned}
$$

The UDM Structures of the LDS Controller

The internal control system of LDS is modeled by a set of UDMs such as the RequestEventRecord**ST**, LiftStatusRecord**ST**, LiftDispatchList**ST**, and ServiceQueues**ST**. Each of the four internal control UDMs in LDS is designed and modeled in the following subsections.

a)   The Request Event Record

A request event record, RequestEventRecord**ST**, as shown in Figure 6 is an internal control structure that monitors and registers the current and last statuses of each of the 30 keys based on periodical scans conducted by the process RequestScanning**PC** as shown in Figure 12. Once a key press is recognized, the flag RequestEventRecord**ST**.RequestIdentified**BL** will be set to true in order to avoid redundant processing of possible repeated requests on the same key.

Each request event record, RequestRecord(i**N**)**ST**, $1 \le i\textbf{N} \le 30$ in Figure 6, is designed corresponding to a specific button in LDS, Key(i**N**)**ST**, which share the same structure of the common abstract schema as specified in RequestEventRecord**ST**.

b)   The Lift Status Record

The *lift status record*, LiftStatusRecord**ST**, is an internal structure that maintains a dynamic status of each elevator as shown in Figure 7. LiftStatusRecord**ST** records the real-time information of an elevator such as the operating status, current direction, current level, current destination, and last destination.

As modeled in Figure 7, the LDS system initializes all lifts in the idle state at floor 1 toward the upward direction. The initial current and last destinations are arbitrarily set on floor 1. By checking the information updated in LiftStatusRecord**ST**, the lift dispatching and serving processes can obtain real-time status of a lift under control.

c)   The Lift Dispatch List

The *lift dispatching list*, LiftDispatchList**ST**, is an internal structure that models the current identified and dispatched requests for each of the elevators in the LDS system. In the lift dispatching list, all requests on the same floor with the same direction will be treated as an identical service request event. Therefore, there are maximum six dispatching stops in a single way operation where certain floors will be set as Level(i**N**)**BL** = **T** by the system dispatching process.

The dynamic status of the dispatching lists is maintained in real-time. When the request on a dispatched floor i**N** is served, Level(i**N**)**BL** will be reset to **F**. An indicator, #WaitingServices**N**, is adopted to show the current total number of requests in all floors of a single way operation. #WaitingServices**N** will be synchronizely updated during operation when Level(i**N**)**BL** is set or reset.

Figure 6. The schema and detailed UDM model of request event record

$$\textbf{RequestEventRecordST} \triangleq \overset{30}{\underset{iN=1}{R}} \; \text{RequestRecord(iN)ST:}$$

(<CurrentStatus : **BL** | KeyStatus**BL** = {(**T**, Pressed), (**F**, Idle)}>,
<LastStatus : **BL** | LastStatus**BL** = {(**T**, Pressed), (**F**, Idle)}>,
<RequestIdentified : **BL** | RequestIdentified**BL** = {(**T**, Yes), (**F**, No)}>
)

= RequestRecord(1)**ST**: (CurrentStatus**BL**, LastStatus**BL**, RequestIdentified**BL**) := (F, F, F)
|| RequestRecord(2)**ST**: (CurrentStatus**BL**, LastStatus**BL**, RequestIdentified**BL**) := (F, F, F)
|| RequestRecord(3)**ST**: (CurrentStatus**BL**, LastStatus**BL**, RequestIdentified**BL**) := (F, F, F)

|| RequestRecord(4)**ST**: (CurrentStatus**BL**, LastStatus**BL**, RequestIdentified**BL**) := (F, F, F)
|| RequestRecord(5)**ST**: (CurrentStatus**BL**, LastStatus**BL**, RequestIdentified**BL**) := (F, F, F)
|| RequestRecord(6)**ST**: (CurrentStatus**BL**, LastStatus**BL**, RequestIdentified**BL**) := (F, F, F)
|| RequestRecord(7)**ST**: (CurrentStatus**BL**, LastStatus**BL**, RequestIdentified**BL**) := (F, F, F)
|| RequestRecord(8)**ST**: (CurrentStatus**BL**, LastStatus**BL**, RequestIdentified**BL**) := (F, F, F)
|| RequestRecord(9)**ST**: (CurrentStatus**BL**, LastStatus**BL**, RequestIdentified**BL**) := (F, F, F)

|| RequestRecord(10)**ST**: (CurrentStatus**BL**, LastStatus**BL**, RequestIdentified**BL**) := (F, F, F)
|| RequestRecord(11)**ST**: (CurrentStatus**BL**, LastStatus**BL**, RequestIdentified**BL**) := (F, F, F)
|| RequestRecord(12)**ST**: (CurrentStatus**BL**, LastStatus**BL**, RequestIdentified**BL**) := (F, F, F)
|| RequestRecord(13)**ST**: (CurrentStatus**BL**, LastStatus**BL**, RequestIdentified**BL**) := (F, F, F)
|| RequestRecord(14)**ST**: (CurrentStatus**BL**, LastStatus**BL**, RequestIdentified**BL**) := (F, F, F)
|| RequestRecord(15)**ST**: (CurrentStatus**BL**, LastStatus**BL**, RequestIdentified**BL**) := (F, F, F)

|| RequestRecord(16)**ST**: (CurrentStatus**BL**, LastStatus**BL**, RequestIdentified**BL**) := (F, F, F)
|| RequestRecord(17)**ST**: (CurrentStatus**BL**, LastStatus**BL**, RequestIdentified**BL**) := (F, F, F)
|| RequestRecord(18)**ST**: (CurrentStatus**BL**, LastStatus**BL**, RequestIdentified**BL**) := (F, F, F)
|| RequestRecord(19)**ST**: (CurrentStatus**BL**, LastStatus**BL**, RequestIdentified**BL**) := (F, F, F)
|| RequestRecord(20)**ST**: (CurrentStatus**BL**, LastStatus**BL**, RequestIdentified**BL**) := (F, F, F)
|| RequestRecord(21)**ST**: (CurrentStatus**BL**, LastStatus**BL**, RequestIdentified**BL**) := (F, F, F)

|| RequestRecord(22)**ST**: (CurrentStatus**BL**, LastStatus**BL**, RequestIdentified**BL**) := (F, F, F)
|| RequestRecord(23)**ST**: (CurrentStatus**BL**, LastStatus**BL**, RequestIdentified**BL**) := (F, F, F)
|| RequestRecord(24)**ST**: (CurrentStatus**BL**, LastStatus**BL**, RequestIdentified**BL**) := (F, F, F)
|| RequestRecord(25)**ST**: (CurrentStatus**BL**, LastStatus**BL**, RequestIdentified**BL**) := (F, F, F)
|| RequestRecord(26)**ST**: (CurrentStatus**BL**, LastStatus**BL**, RequestIdentified**BL**) := (F, F, F)
|| RequestRecord(27)**ST**: (CurrentStatus**BL**, LastStatus**BL**, RequestIdentified**BL**) := (F, F, F)

|| RequestRecord(28)**ST**: (CurrentStatus**BL**, LastStatus**BL**, RequestIdentified**BL**) := (F, F, F)
|| RequestRecord(29)**ST**: (CurrentStatus**BL**, LastStatus**BL**, RequestIdentified**BL**) := (F, F, F)
|| RequestRecord(30)**ST**: (CurrentStatus**BL**, LastStatus**BL**, RequestIdentified**BL**) := (F, F, F)

d) The Service Queues

Four service queues are adopted in LDS for modeling the new and waiting requests identified in the LDS system in two directions. The architecture of the service queues is a first-come-first-serve (FCFS) structure as shown in Figure 9. The instances of the ServiceQueues**ST** are the UpRequestQueue**ST**, DownRequestQueue**ST**, UpWaitingQueue**ST**, and DownWaitingQueue**ST**, where the pair of request queues contain newly identified requests and the pair of waiting queues contain requests that cannot be served in a previous dispatching cycle.

The major operational processes of the FCFS ServiceQueues**ST** are *enqueue* and *serve*, which will be described in Equation 7. The former is a process that appends an element at the end of the queue and tests if the queue is full. The latter is a process that fetches the front element of the queue, tests if the queue is empty, and shifts the remainder elements toward the front of the queue

Figure 7. The schema and detailed UDM model of lift status record

$$
\text{LiftStatusRecordST} \triangleq \mathop{R}_{iN=1}^{3} \text{LiftRecord}(iN)\text{ST}:
$$

$$
(<\text{LiftStatus}: \textbf{BL} \mid \text{LiftStatus}\textbf{BL} = \{(\textbf{T}, \text{Moving}), (\textbf{F}, \text{Idle})\}>,
$$
$$
<\text{CurrentDirection}: \textbf{BL} \mid \text{CurrentDirection}\textbf{BL} = \{(\textbf{T}, \text{Up}), (\textbf{F}, \text{Down})\}>,
$$
$$
<\text{CurrentLevel}: \textbf{N} \mid 1 \le \text{CurrentLevel}\textbf{N} \le 6>,
$$
$$
<\text{CurrentDestination}: \textbf{N} \mid 1 \le \text{CurrentDestination}\textbf{N} \le 6>,
$$
$$
<\text{LastDestination}: \textbf{N} \mid 1 \le \text{LastDestination}\textbf{N} \le 6>
$$
$$
)
$$
$$
= \text{LiftRecord}(1)\textbf{ST}: (\text{LiftStatus}\textbf{BL}, \text{CurrentDirection}\textbf{BL}, \text{CurrentLevel}\textbf{N}, \text{CurrentDestination}\textbf{N},
$$
$$
\text{LastDestination}\textbf{N}) := (F, T, 1, 1, 1)
$$
$$
\| \text{LiftRecord}(2)\textbf{ST}: (\text{LiftStatus}\textbf{BL}, \text{CurrentDirection}\textbf{BL}, \text{CurrentLevel}\textbf{N}, \text{CurrentDestination}\textbf{N},
$$
$$
\text{LastDestination}\textbf{N}) := (F, T, 1, 1, 1)
$$
$$
\| \text{LiftRecord}(3)\textbf{ST}: (\text{LiftStatus}\textbf{BL}, \text{CurrentDirection}\textbf{BL}, \text{CurrentLevel}\textbf{N}, \text{CurrentDestination}\textbf{N},
$$
$$
\text{LastDestination}\textbf{N}) := (F, T, 1, 1, 1)
$$

Figure 8. The schema and detailed UDM model of lift dispatch list

$$
\text{LiftDispatchListST} \triangleq \mathop{R}_{iN=1}^{3} \text{DispatchList}(iN)\textbf{ST}:
$$

$$
(<\#\text{WaitingService}: \textbf{N}>,
$$
$$
<\text{Level}(1): \textbf{BL} \mid \text{Level}(1)\textbf{BL} = \{(\textbf{T}, \text{ServiceRequested}), (\textbf{F}, \text{NoServiceRequest})\}>,
$$
$$
<\text{Level}(2): \textbf{BL} \mid \text{Level}(2)\textbf{BL} = \{(\textbf{T}, \text{ServiceRequested}), (\textbf{F}, \text{NoServiceRequest})\}>,
$$
$$
<\text{Level}(3): \textbf{BL} \mid \text{Level}(3)\textbf{BL} = \{(\textbf{T}, \text{ServiceRequested}), (\textbf{F}, \text{NoServiceRequest})\}>,
$$
$$
<\text{Level}(4): \textbf{BL} \mid \text{Level}(4)\textbf{BL} = \{(\textbf{T}, \text{ServiceRequested}), (\textbf{F}, \text{NoServiceRequest})\}>,
$$
$$
<\text{Level}(5): \textbf{BL} \mid \text{Level}(5)\textbf{BL} = \{(\textbf{T}, \text{ServiceRequested}), (\textbf{F}, \text{NoServiceRequest})\}>,
$$
$$
<\text{Level}(6): \textbf{BL} \mid \text{Level}(6)\textbf{BL} = \{(\textbf{T}, \text{ServiceRequested}), (\textbf{F}, \text{NoServiceRequest})\}>
$$
$$
)
$$
$$
= \text{DispatchList}(1)\textbf{ST}: (\#\text{WaitingService}\textbf{N}, \text{Level}(1)\textbf{BL}, \text{Level}(2)\textbf{BL}, \dots, \text{Level}(6)\textbf{BL}) := (0, F, F, \dots, F)
$$
$$
\| \text{DispatchList}(2)\textbf{ST}: (\#\text{WaitingService}\textbf{N}, \text{Level}(1)\textbf{BL}, \text{Level}(2)\textbf{BL}, \dots, \text{Level}(6)\textbf{BL}) := (0, F, F, \dots, F)
$$
$$
\| \text{DispatchList}(3)\textbf{ST}: (\#\text{WaitingService}\textbf{N}, \text{Level}(1)\textbf{BL}, \text{Level}(2)\textbf{BL}, \dots, \text{Level}(6)\textbf{BL}) := (0, F, F, \dots, F)
$$

Figure 9. The schema and detailed UDM model of the service queues

$$
\text{ServiceQueuesST} \triangleq \mathop{R}_{iN=1}^{4} \text{Queue}(iN)\textbf{ST}:
$$

$$
(<\text{Size}: \textbf{N} \mid \text{Size}\textbf{N} = 6>,
$$
$$
<\text{Element}: \textbf{N}>,
$$
$$
<\text{CurrentPos}: \textbf{P} \mid 0 \quad \text{CurrentPos}\textbf{P} \quad \text{Size}\textbf{N}-1>
$$
$$
<\text{Empty}: \textbf{BL} \mid \{(\textbf{T}, \text{Empty}), (\textbf{F}, \text{NonEmpty})\}>
$$
$$
<\text{Full}: \textbf{BL} \mid \{(\textbf{T}, \text{Full}), (\textbf{F}, \text{NonFull})\}>
$$
$$
)
$$
$$
= \text{Queue}(1)\textbf{ST} = \text{UpRequestQueue}\textbf{ST}: (\text{Size}\textbf{N}, \text{Element}\textbf{N}, \text{CurrentPos}\textbf{P}, \text{Empty}\textbf{BL}, \text{Full}\textbf{BL}) := (6, 0, 0, T, F)
$$
$$
\| \text{Queue}(2)\textbf{ST} = \text{DownRequestQueue}\textbf{ST}: (\text{Size}\textbf{N}, \text{Element}\textbf{N}, \text{CurrentPos}\textbf{P}, \text{Empty}\textbf{BL}, \text{Full}\textbf{BL}) := (6, 0, 0, T, F)
$$
$$
\| \text{Queue}(3)\textbf{ST} = \text{UpWaitingQueue}\textbf{ST}: (\text{Size}\textbf{N}, \text{Element}\textbf{N}, \text{CurrentPos}\textbf{P}, \text{Empty}\textbf{BL}, \text{Full}\textbf{BL}) := (6, 0, 0, T, F)
$$
$$
\| \text{Queue}(4)\textbf{ST} = \text{DownWaitingQueue}\textbf{ST}: (\text{Size}\textbf{N}, \text{Element}\textbf{N}, \text{CurrentPos}\textbf{P}, \text{Empty}\textbf{BL}, \text{Full}\textbf{BL}) := (6, 0, 0, T, F)
$$

by one place. There are also internal manipulations for the queues, such as creation, memory allocation, and release.

The system architectural models specified in this section provide a set of abstract object models and clear interfaces between system hardware and software. By reaching this point, the co-design of a real-time system can be separately carried out by separated hardware and software teams. It is recognized that system *architecture specification* by the means of UDMs is a fundamental and the most difficult part in software system modeling, while conventional formal methods hardly provide any support for this purpose. From the above examples in this subsection, it can be seen that RTPA provides a set of expressive notations for specifying system architectural structures and control models, including hardware, software, and their interactions. On the basis of the system architecture specification and with the work products of system architectural components or UDMs, specification of the operational components of the LDS system as behavioral processes can be carried out directly as elaborated in the following sections.

THE STATIC BEHAVIOR MODELS OF THE LDS SYSTEM

A static behavior is a component-level function of a given system that can be determined before run-time. On the basis of the system architecture specifications and with the UDMs of system architectural components developed in preceding section, the operational components of the given LDS system and their behaviors can be specified as a set of UPMs as behavioral processes operating on the UDMs.

The static behaviors of the LDS, LDS**§**. StaticBehaviors**PC**, can be described through operations on its architectural models. LDS**§**. StaticBehaviors**PC** encompasses the processes of SysInitial**PC**, SysClock**PC**, RequestScanning**PC**, RequestProcessing**PC**, LiftDispatching**PC**, and LiftServing**PC** in parallel as specified below:

$$
\begin{aligned}
\text{LDS§.StaticBehaviors}\mathbf{PC} \triangleq\ & \text{SysInitial}\mathbf{PC} \\
& |\ \text{SysClock}\mathbf{PC} \\
& |\ \text{RequestScanning}\mathbf{PC} \\
& |\ \text{RequestProcessing}\mathbf{PC} \\
& |\ \text{LiftDispatching}\mathbf{PC} \\
& |\ \text{LiftServing}\mathbf{PC}
\end{aligned}
$$

(6)

The following subsections describe how the LDS static behaviors as specified in Equation 6 are modeled and refined using the denotational mathematical notations and methodologies of RTPA in term of a set of UPMs.

The System Initialization Process

System initialization is a common process of a real-time system that boots the system, sets its initial environment, and preassigns the initial values of data objects of the system such as variables, constants, as well as architectural (hardware interface) and control (internal) UDMs. Initialization is crucially important for a real-time system as well as its control logic specified in the functional processes. The *system initialization* process of LDS, SysInitial**PC**, is modeled in Figure 10, where all system architectural and control UDMs are initialized as specified in their UDMs. Then, the system clock and timing interrupt are set to their initial logical or calendar values.

The initialization process sets the system control models such as the buttons, the lifts, and the system clock into given initial statuses. It also initializes the control models such as the request event records, the lift status records, and the lift dispatch lists. In the UDMs initializations, all initial values as specified in the UDM objects as given in the preceding section will be implemented in order to set the system into a correct initial state.

The System Clock Process

The *system clock* process is a support process of a real-time system that maintains and updates an absolute (calendar) clock and a relative clock for the system. The system clock process of LDS, SysClock**PC**, is modeled in Figure 11. The source of the system clock is obtained from the 100ms interrupt clock signal generated by system hardware, by which the absolute clock with real-time second, minute, and hour, SysClock**ST**.

Figure 10. The behavior model of the system initialization process

```
SysInitial(<I:: ( )>; <O:: ( )>; <UDM:: (LDS_UDMsST)>)PC ≜
{
   Initial LDS_UDMsST                    // Initialization of all UDMs
   → SysClock.§tN := 0
   → SysClock.CurrentTimehh:mm:ss := hh:mm:ss     // Real time
   → SysClock.InterruptCounterN := 0
}
```

Figure 11. The behavior model of the system clock process

```
SysClock(<I:: ( )>; <O:: ( )>; <UDM:: (SysClockST)>)PC ≜
{
   ↑ (SysClock.InterruptCounterN)
     → ◆ SysClock.InterruptCounterN = 9
        ( → SysClock.InterruptCounterN = 0
          → ↑(SysClock.§tN)
          → ↑(SysClock.CurrentTimehh:mm:ss)
          → ◆ SysClock.CurrentTimehh:mm:ss = 23:59:59
             (→ SysClock.CurrentTimehh:mm:ss := 00:00:00
                → SysClock.§tN := 0
             )
        )
}
```

Figure 12. The behavior model of the request scanning process

```
RequestScanning(<I:: ( )>; <O:: ( )>; <UDM:: (RequestRecordsST, KeysST)>)PC ≜
{
   InputMaskB = 0000 0111B
        30
   → R  ( RequestRecord(iN)ST.LastStatusBL := RequestRecord(iN)ST.CurrentStatusBL
       /N=1
        → PORT(Key(iN)ST.PortAddressH)B |≥ Key(iN)ST.KeyInputB
        → ◆ Key(iN)ST.KeyInputB ∧ InputMaskB ≠ 0
           → RequestRecord(iN)ST.CurrentStatusBL := T
        |◆ ~
           → RequestRecord(iN)ST.CurrentStatusBL := F
       )

        3
   → R  ( PORT(Lift(iN)ST.CurrentLevelPortH)B |≥ Lift(iN)ST.CurrentLevelInputB
       /N=1
        → LiftRecord(iN)ST.CurrentLevelB := Lift(iN)ST.CurrentLevelInputB
       )
}
```

339

CurrentTime**hh:mm:ss**, are generated and periodically updated. The second clock in a real-time system is the relative clock, SysClock**ST.§tN**, which is usually adopted for relative timing and duration manipulations. The relative clock is reset to zero at midnight each day in order to prevent it from overflow.

The Request Scanning Process

The request scanning process of LDS, RequestScanning**PC**, as shown in Figure 12 periodically scans the thirty buttons per 100ms in order to detect if any key is pressed on every floor. The sample period is set as 100ms based on the factor that a human key-press action is between 200ms to 500ms. If a key-press is detected, the status record flag corresponding to the button is set to true in the RequestRecord**ST**, so that this key-press will be identified if it is a new or a repeated request by the following request processing process.

According to the conceptual model of LDS in Figure 1, the request scanning process handles the buttons in 10 groups. Each group consists of 3 buttons on the same floor and with the same direction. When any key is pressed in a group, all keys in the group will be treated as pressed.

The request scanning process also periodically monitors the current level of a moving lift from the its level sensor input. Based on the input per 100ms, the current level fields in the UDMs of the lift and lift record, LiftRecord(i**N**)**ST**.CurrentLevel**B** and Lift(i**N**)**ST**.CurentLevelInput**B**, are updated at real time.

The Request Processing Process

The request processing process of LDS, RequestProcessingPC, as shown in Figure 13 is another periodical process that identifies new requests and masks repeated requests on the same floor toward the same direction. This mechanism is adopted to

Figure 13. The behavior model of the request processing process

```
RequestProcessing(<I:: ( )>; <O :: ( )>; <UDM:: (RequestRecordsST, UpRequestQueueST, DownRequestQueueST)>)PC ≜
{
        30
  →  R  ( ◆ RequestRecord(iN)ST.RequestIdentifiedBL = F                                    // New request
       iN=1
            → (◆ RequestRecord(iN)ST.CurrentStatusBL = T ∧ RequestRecord(iN).LastStatusBL = F
                → RequestRecord(iN)ST.RequestIdentifiedBL = T
                → ◆ Key(iN)ST.DirectionBL = T                                              // Upward
                    ↣ UpRequestQueueST.EnqueuePC(Key(iN)ST.KeyPositionN;
                                                 ⑤UpRequestQueueFullBL, ⑤UpRequestEnqueueSucceedBL;
                                                 UpRequestQueueST)
                    → ⑤UpRequestQueueST.EmptyBL:= F

                  | ◆ ~                                                                     // Downward
                    ↣ DownRequestQueueST.EnqueuePC(Key(iN)ST.KeyPositionN;
                                                   ⑤DownRequestQueueFullBL, ⑤DownRequestEnqueueSucceedBL;
                                                   DownRequestQueueST)
                    → ⑤DownRequestQueueST.EmptyBL:= F
                )
          )
}
```

ensure that the LDS system may only recognize multiple requests once at a certain floor for a certain direction during a given operation cycle.

The main algorithm of the request processing process is to detect if a reported key-press is a new request according to the algorithm as presented in Exhibit 1.

That is, a new request is identified by two periodical scans per 100ms where the last scan detected false (the key was unpressed) and the current scan detects true (the key is pressed). Once a new request is identified, the request processing process marks all other two buttons related to it on the same floor toward the same direction as pressed. Then, the recognized service request is registered into one of the corresponding Service-

Queues**ST** by the process Queue(i**N**)**ST**.Enqueue**PC** as specified in Equation 8.

Predefined operations on ServiceQueues**ST**, encompassing the UpRequestQueue**ST**, ncompassing DownRequestQueue**ST**, UpWaitingQueue**ST**, and DownWaitingQueue**ST**, can be specified by a set of process models as presented in Exhibit 2.

The Lift Dispatching Processes

The lift dispatching process is modeled by two similar subprocesses: a) New request dispatching, LiftDispatching_NewRequest**PC**, as shown in Figure 14; and b) Waiting request dispatching, LiftDispatching_WaitingRequest**PC**, as shown in Figure 15. Requests in waiting are given a higher

Exhibit 1.

NewRequest**BL A** RequestRecord(i**N**)**ST**.CurrentStatus**BL** = **T** $\wedge$
    RequestRecord(i**N**) ST..LastStatus**BL** = **F**

(7)

Exhibit 2.

ServiceQueues**ST**.StaticBehaviors**PC** $\triangleq$
    (Create**PC**(<**I**:: (QueueID**S**)>; <**O**:: (⊙QueueIDExisted**BL**)>; <**UDM**:: (QueueID**ST**)>)
    | Enqueue**PC**(<**I**:: (QueueID**S**, RequestFloorNum**N**)>; <**O**:: (⊙QueueIDFull**BL**,
      ⊙QueueIDEnqueueSucceed**BL**)>;<**UDM**:: (QueueID**ST**)>)
    | Serve**PC**(<**I**:: (QueueID**S**)>; <**O**:: (RequestFloorNum**N**, ⊙QueueIDEmpty**BL**,
      ⊙QueueIDServeSucceed**BL**)>; <**UDM**:: (QueueID**ST**)>)
    | Clear**PC**(<**I**:: (QueueID**S**)>; <**O**:: (⊙QueueIDEmpty**BL**)>; <**UDM**:: (QueueID**ST**)>)
    | EmptyTest**PC**(<**I**:: (QueueID**S**)>; <**O**:: (⊙QueueIDEmpty**BL**)>; <**UDM**:: (QueueID**ST**)>)
    | FullTest**PC**(<**I**:: (QueueID**S**)>; <**O**:: (⊙QueueIDFull**BL**)>; <**UDM**:: (QueueID**ST**)>)
    | Release**PC**(<**I**:: (QueueID**S**)>; <**O**:: (⊙QueueIDExisted**BL**)>; <**UDM**:: (QueueID**ST**)>)
)

(8)

where the Enqueue**PC** and Serve**PC** processes are invoked in the RequestProcessing**PC** and LiftDispatching**PC** processes, respectively. Details of these queue behavioral models may be referred to (Wang, 2007).

Figure 14. The behavior model of the lift dispatching process for new requests

```
LiftDispatching_NewRequest(<I:: ( )>; <O:: ( )>; <UDM:: (RequestRecordsST, UpRequestQueueST,
                           DownRequestQueueST, UpWaitingQueueST, DownWaitingQueueST,
                           KeysST, LiftRecordsST, DispatchListsST)>)PC ≜
{
  expBL := UpRequestQueueST.EmptyBL                                    // Process upward requests
         T
    R  (↣ UpRequestQueueST.ServePC(∅; RequestFloorNumN, ⑤UpRequestQueueEmptyBL,
  expBL=F
         ⑤UpRequestQueueServeSucceedBL; UpRequetQueueST)              // Fetch first request and
                                                                        // update queue empty status

      → MinDistanceN := 6
      → ⑤LiftFoundBL := F
         3
      → ( R  ( ◆ LiftRecord(kN)ST.LiftStatusBL = F ∨                   // Idle
          kN=1
              (LiftRecord(kN)ST.CurrentDirectionBL = T ∧              // Move up
              LiftRecord(kN)ST.CurrentLevelN ≤ RequestFloorNumN)       // Lower/equal to request floor

              → Distance(kN)N := RequestFloorNumN − LiftRecord(kN)ST.CurrentLevelN
              → ◆ Distance(kN)N < MinDistanceN
                  → MinDistanceN := Distance(kN)N
                  → AvailableLiftN := kN
                  → ⑤LiftFoundBL := T
          )
      → ( ◆ ⑤LiftFoundBL = T
              → DispatchList(AvailableLiftN)ST.Level(RequestFloorNumN)BL := T
              → ↑(DispatchList(AvailableLiftN)ST.#WaitingServiceN)
          | ◆ ~                                                        // No lift available
              ↣ UpWaitingQueueST.EnqueuePC(RequestFloorNumN; ⑤UpWaitingQueueFullBL,
                  ⑤UpWaitingEnqueueSucceedBL; UpWaitingQueueST)
              → UpWaitingQueueST.EmptyBL := F
          )
      → ◆ ⑤UpRequestQueueEmptyBL = T
          → expBL := T

  )
  → expBL := DownRequestQueueST.EmptyBL                               // Process down ward requests
         T
    R  (↣ DownRequestQueueST.ServePC(∅; RequestFloorNumN, ⑤DownRequestQueueEmptyBL,
  expBL=F
         ⑤DownRequestQueueServeSucceedBL; DownRequetQueueST)          // Fetch first request and
                                                                        // update queue empty status

      → MinDistanceN := 6
      → ⑤LiftFoundBL := F
         3
      → ( R  ( ◆ LiftRecord(kN)ST.LiftStatusBL ∨                       // Idle
          kN=1
              (LiftRecord(kN)ST.CurrentDirectionBL = F ∧              // Move down
              LiftRecord(kN)ST.CurrentLevelN ≥ RequestFloorNumN       // Higher/equal to request floor
              )
              → Distance(kN)N := LiftRecord(kN)ST.CurrentLevelN − RequestFloorNumN
              → ◆ Distance(kN)N < MinDistanceN
                  → MinDistanceN := Distance(kN)N
                  → AvailableLiftN := kN
                  → ⑤LiftFoundBL := T
          )
      → ( ◆ ⑤LiftFoundBL = T
              → DispatchList(AvailableLiftN)ST.Level(RequestFloorNumN)BL := T
              → ↑(DispatchList(AvailableLiftN)ST.#WaitingServiceN)
          | ◆ ~                                                        // No lift available
              ↣ DownWaitingQueueST.EnqueuePC(RequestFloorNumN; ⑤DownWaitingQueueFullBL,
                  ⑤DownWaitingEnqueueSucceedBL; DownWaitingQueueST)
              → DownWaitingQueueST.EmptyBL := F
          )
      → ◆ ⑤DownRequestQueueEmptyBL = T
          → expBL := T

  )
}
```

Figure 15. The behavior model of the lift dispatching process for waiting requests

```
LiftDispatching_WaitingRequest(<◁:: ( )>; <O:: ( )>; <UDM:: (RequestRecordsST, UpWaitingQueueST,
                                DownWaitingQueueST, KeysST, LiftRecordsST, DispatchListsST)>)PC ≜
{
    expBL := UpWaitingQueueST.EmptyBL                                          // Process up-waiting requests
        T
      R   (↣ UpWaitingQueueST.ServePC(∅; RequestFloorNumN, ⑤UpWaitingQueueEmptyBL,
    expBL=F
            ⑤UpWaitingQueueServeSucceedBL; UpWaitingQueueST)      // Fetch first request and
                                                                  // update queue empty status
      → MinDistanceN = 6
      → ⑤LiftFoundBL := F
          3
      → ( R  ( ◆ LiftRecord(kN)ST.LiftStatusBL = F ∨                    // Idle
            kN-1
            (LiftRecord(kN)ST.CurrentDirectionBL = T ∧             // Move up
             LiftRecord(kN)ST.CurrentLevelN ≤ RequestFloorNumN      // Lower/equal to request floor
            )
            → Distance(kN)N := RequestFloorNumN – LiftRecord(kN)ST.CurrentLevelN
            → ◆ Distance(kN)N < MinDistanceN
              → MinDistanceN := Distance(kN)N
              → AvailableLiftN := kN
              → ⑤LiftFoundBL := T
            )
      → ( ◆ ⑤LiftFoundBL = T
            → DispatchList(AvailableLiftN)ST.Level(RequestFloorNumN)BL := T
            → ↑ (DispatchList(AvailableLiftN)ST.#WaitingServiceN)
          | ◆ ~                                                           // No lift available
            ↣ UpWaitingQueueST.EnqueuePC(RequestFloorNumN; ⑤UpWaitingQueueFullBL,
                    ⑤UpWaitingEnqueueSucceedBL; UpWaitingQueueST)
            → UpWaitingQueueST.EmptyBL := F
          )
      → ◆ ⑤UpWaitingQueueEmptyBL = T
        → expBL := T
      )
    → expBL := DownWaitingQueueST.EmptyBL                                      // Down-waiting requests
        T
      R   (↣ DownWaitingQueueST.ServePC(∅; RequestFloorNumN, ⑥DownWaitingQueueEmptyBL,
    expBL=F
            ⑥DownWaitingQueueServeSucceedBL; DownWaitingQueueST)   // Fetch first request and
                                                                  // update queue empty status
      → MinDistanceN := 6
      → ⑤LiftFoundBL := F
          3
      → ( R  ( ◆ LiftRecord(kN)ST.LiftStatusBL = F ∨                    // Idle
            kN-1

            (LiftRecord(kN)ST.CurrentDirectionBL = F ∧             // Move down
             LiftRecord(kN)ST.CurrentLevelN ≥ RequestFloorNumN      // Higher/equal to request floor
            )
            → Distance(kN)N := LiftRecord(kN)ST.CurrentLevelN – RequestFloorNumN
            → ◆ Distance(kN)N < MinDistanceN
              → MinDistanceN := Distance(kN)N
              → AvailableLiftN := kN
              → ⑤LiftFoundBL := T
            )
      → ( ◆ ⑤LiftFoundBL = T
            → DispatchList(AvailableLiftN)ST.Level(RequestFloorNumN)BL := T
            → ↑ (DispatchList(AvailableLiftN)ST.#WaitingServiceN)
          | ◆ ~                                                           // No lift available
            ↣ DownWaitingQueueST.EnqueuePC(RequestFloorNumN; ⑥DownRequestQueueFullBL,
                    ⑥DownRequestEnqueueSucceedBL; DownWaitingQueueST)
            → DownWaitingQueueST.EmptyBL := F
          )
      → ◆ ⑥DownWaitingQueueEmptyBL = T
        → expBL := T
      )
}
```

priority in the dispatching algorithm in order to prevent a request from waiting for too many dispatching cycles in rush hours.

A key concept of the LDS design is the *dispatching cycle* that is a single directional serve in which the dispatched lift moves from an idle state or a U-turn state to the top/bottom floor or to a floor where it has completed all dispatched serves as listed in the current dispatching list. The operations of each lift in the LDS system are therefore divided into a series of dispatching cycles.

The lift dispatch process finds out a new or existing request when any of the UpRequestQueue**ST**, DownRequestQueue**ST**, UpWaitingQueue**ST**, or DownWaitingQueue**ST** is not empty. Then, it searches through the lift status record, LiftStatusRecord**ST**, in order to find one or multiple candidate lift(s) that either move in the same direction as the given request or are idle. If the result is positive, the distances from the requested floor to all candidate lifts are calculated, which results in the determination of an optimal dispatching with the shortest distance; otherwise the given request is sent to either UpWaitingQueue**ST** or DownWaitingQueue**ST**. It is noteworthy that any lift moving in the opposite direction is ruled out as a possible candidate in a given dispatching cycle.

a)   The Lift Dispatching Process for New Requests

The behavior model of the lift dispatching process for new requests, LiftDispatching_NewRequest**PC**, is shown in Figure 14. The lift dispatching process allocates a suitable lift to a certain request or multiple requests according to the dispatching decision-making criteria as given in the design Constraints 1 – 6 in the conceptual model of the LDS system. The dispatching algorithm can be formally specified as presented in Exhibit 3.

The algorithm in Exhibit 3 guarantees both a fast and energy-efficient serve without turning any lift in its current operating direction before it complete designated serves in a given dispatching cycle. Once the ith optimal lift is found for a new request according to the dispatching algorithm, it will be registered into the UDM DispatchingList(i**N**)**ST** for an immediate serve; Otherwise, it will be put into the UpWaitingQueue**ST** or DownWaitingQueue**ST** for a priority serve in the next dispatching cycle of the LDS system. In the latter case, the dispatching distance becomes negative, such as a request at a floor lower than all current upward serving lifts or higher than all downward serving lifts. These waiting requests will be served in the next dispatching cycle from either Floors 1 to 6 or Floors 6 to 1.

Exhibit 3.

OptimalDispatchStrategy**BL** ≜
    min(Distance(k**N**)**N** | 0 ≤ Distance(k**N**)**N** ≤ 6) ∧
                (LiftRecord(k**N**)**ST**.LiftStatus**BL** = **F** ∨
                Key(i**N**)**ST**.Direction**BL** = LiftRecord(k**N**)**ST**.CurrentDirection**BL**
)

                                                                                                            (9)

where k is the number of lifts, i the number of the key under serving, and *min* a predefined function to find the minimum of distance.

b) The Lift Dispatching Process for Waiting Requests

The behavior model of the lift dispatching process for waiting requests, LiftDispatching_WaitingRequest**PC**, is shown in Figure 15. A waiting request is one that could not be served in a previous operating cycle due to a busy state of the system or any dispatching constraint. The dispatching strategy for serving waiting request is similar to those of new requests, except that it checks UpWaitingQueue**ST** and DownWaitingQueue**ST** in order to put any existing request into the dispatching process.

The Lift Serving Processes

The lift serving process encompasses two similar subprocesses: a) Upward request serve, LiftServing_Upward**PC**, as shown in Figure 16; and b) Downward request serve, LiftServing_Downward**PC**, as shown in Figure 17. These two processes directly control all equipments of each lift such as the engine, door, indicator, bell, level sensor, and internal request buttons as illustrated in Figure 1.

a) The Lift Serving Process for Upward Requests

The behavior model of the lift serving process for upward requests, LiftServing_Upward**PC**, is shown in Figure 16. In each dispatching cycle, a lift is driven by the lift serve process to serve all requests in its way according to the pre-designated dispatching list, DispatchList**ST**, generated by the dispatching processes of the LDS system. The lift will move toward and stop on each requested floor as dispatched, light up the floor indicator, ring the bell, open the doors, clear all requests on this floor, and close the doors after a given period (8 second in this design). Then, during the lift moves to the next dispatched floor, it scans the destination information of new customers entered the cabin.

The newly identified internal request(s) are used to update the current dispatching list of this lift by updating its DispatchList**ST**. If an internal request is opposite to the current serve direction, it will be registered into the DownWaitingQueue**ST** for serving in the next dispatching cycle.

When a lift completed the serve of all dispatched requests in a dispatching cycle, it parks on the latest reached floor, remains doors open, and waits for a new dispatching list of the next dispatching cycle from the LDS system. If the parked floor is the top or bottom floor, the direction of the lift will be automatically turned.

b) The Lift Serving Process for Downward Requests

The behavior model of the lift serving process for downward requests, LiftServing_Downward**PC**, is shown in Figure 17. The downward serving process is similar to that of upward serving, except that the current direction and turning mechanism are inversed, as well as that DownWaitingQueue**ST** is replaced by UpWaitingQueue**ST**.

THE DYNAMIC BEHAVIOR MODEL OF THE LDS SYSTEM

Dynamic behaviors of systems are run-time process deployment and dispatching mechanisms based on the static behaviors modeled in UPMs. Because the static behaviors are a set of component processes of the system, to put the static processes into a live and interacting system at run-time, the dynamic behaviors of the system in terms of process priority allocation and deployment are yet to be specified.

With the UPMs developed in the preceding section as a set of static behavioral processes of the LDS system, this section describes the dynamic behaviors of the LDS system at run-time via *process priority allocation* and *process deployments*.

Figure 16. The behavior model of the lift serving process for upward requests

```
LiftServing_Upward(<I:: ( )>; <O:: ( )>; <UDM:: (LiftsST, DispatchListsST, LiftRecordsST,
              RequestRecordsST, DownWaitingQueue, KeysST)>)PC ≜

{ nN := 3
        nN
   →  R   (Lift(iN)ST.IndicatorOutputB := LiftRecord(iN)ST.CurrentLevelB          // Display current level
       iN=1

          → Lift(iN)ST.IndicatorOutputB |< PORT(Lift(iN)ST.IndicatorPortH)B
          → ◆ DispatchList(iN)ST.#WaitingServiceN > 0 ∧ LiftRecord(iN)ST.CurrentDirectionN = T
              → kN := LiftRecord(iN)ST.CurrentLevelH
              → (◆ DispatchList(iN)ST.Level(kN)BL = T                            // Serve dispatched at the floor
                  ↓ (DispatchList(iN)ST.#WaitingServiceN)
                  → DispatchList(iN)ST.Level(kN)BL := F
                  → 0000 0000 B |< PORT(Lift(iN)ST.UpDrivePortH)B                 // Release up-drive signal
                  → 0000 0001 B |< PORT(Lift(iN)ST.StopDrivePortH)B               // Stop at a dispatched floor
                  → 0000 0000 B |< PORT(Lift(iN)ST.DoorClosePortH)B               // Release close-door signal
                  → 0000 0001 B |< PORT(Lift(iN)ST.DoorOpenPortH)B                // Open doors
                  → 0000 0001 B |< PORT(Lift(iN)ST.DoorBellPortH)B                // Sound bell
                  → TimeOutBL := F
                  → @t hh:mm:ss ≜ §t hh:mm:ss + 8
                         T
                  →     R      ◆ @t hh:mm:ss = §t hh:mm:ss → TimeOutBL := T        // Delay 8s based on system clock
                      TimeOutBL=F
                  → 0000 0000 B |< PORT(Lift(iN)ST.DoorBellPortH)B                // Stop bell
                  → 0000 0000 B |< PORT(Lift(iN)ST.DoorOpenPortH)B                // Release open-door signal
                  → 0000 0001 B |< PORT(Lift(iN)ST.DoorClosePortH)B               // Close doors
                         30
                  →     R    (◆ Key(jN)ST.KeyPositionN = LiftRecord(iN)ST.CurrentLevelN ∧
                      jN=1
                              Key(jN)ST.DirectionBL = LiftRecord(iN)ST.CurrentDirectionBL

                              → RequestRecord(jN)ST.RequestIdentifiedBL := F       // Clear requests on the same level
                      )
                         6
                  →     R    (PORT(Lift(iN)ST.DestScanPort(jN)H)B |> DestScanInputB  // Scan new destination level(s)
                      jN=1
                              → ( ◆ DestScanInputB > LiftRecord(iN)ST.CurrentLevelH ∧
                                    DispatchList(iN)ST.Level(DestScanInputB)BL = F
                                    → DispatchList(iN)ST.Level(DestScanInputB)BL := T
                                    → ↑ (DispatchList(iN)ST.#WaitingServiceN)
                                 |◆ DestScanInputB < LiftRecord(iN)ST.CurrentLevelH
                                    ↣ DownWaitingQueueST.EnqueuePC(DestScanInputB; ⑤DownWaitingQueueFullBL,
                                       ⑤DownWaitingEnqueueSucceedBL; DownWaitingQueueST)
                                    → DownWaitingQueueST.EmptyBL := F
                              )
                      )
                  → ◆ DispatchList(iN)ST.#WaitingServiceN > 0
                      → 0000 0000 B |< PORT(Lift(iN).StopDrivePortH)B              // Clear stop drive
                      → 0000 0001 B |< PORT(Lift(iN).UpDrivePortH)B               // Move up
                  |◆ ~                                                            // No service at the floor
                  → ( ◆ LiftRecord(iN)ST.CurrentLevelH ≠ 6                        // Reached a middle floor
                      → 0000 0001 B |< PORT(Lift(iN).UpDrivePortH)B               // Up drive
                   |◆ ~                                                           // Reached the top floor
                      → 0000 0000 B |< PORT(Lift(iN)ST.UpDrivePortH)B             // Release up-drive signal
                      → 0000 0001 B |< PORT(Lift(iN)ST.StopDrivePortH)B           // Stop
                      → LiftRecord(iN)ST.CurrentDirectionN := F                   // Change direction
                  )
}
```

LDS Process Priority Allocation

The process priority allocation of system dynamic behaviors is the executing and timing requirements of all static processes at run-time. In general, process priorities can be specified at 4 levels for real-time and nonreal-time systems in an increasing priority known as: L1: *base* level processes, L2: *high* level processes, L3: *low interrupt* level processes, and L4: *high interrupt* level processes.

Figure 17. The behavior model of the lift serving process for downward requests

```
LiftServing_Downward(<I:: ( )>; <O:: ( )>; <UDM:: (LiftsST, DispatchListsST, LiftRecordsST,
                 RequestRecordsST, UpWaitingQueueST, KeysST)>)PC ≙
{ nN := 3
   nN
→ R    (Lift(iN)ST.IndicatorOutputB := LiftRecord(iN)ST.CurrentLevelB              // Display current level
   iN=1
       → Lift(iN)ST.IndicatorOutputB |< PORT(Lift(iN)ST.IndicatorPortH)B
         → ◆ DispatchList(iN)ST.#WaitingServiceN > 0 ∧ LiftRecord(iN)ST.CurrentDirectionN = F
            → kN := LiftRecord(iN)ST.CurrentLevelH
            → (◆ DispatchList(iN)ST.Level(kN)BL = T                                // Serve dispatched at the floor
                 ↓ (DispatchList(iN)ST.#WaitingServiceN)
               → DispatchList(iN)ST.Level(kN)BL := F
               → 0000 0000B |< PORT(Lift(iN)ST.DownDrivePortH)B                    // Release down-drive signal
               → 0000 0001B |< PORT(Lift(iN)ST.StopDrivePortH)B                    // Stop at a dispatched floor
               → 0000 0000B |< PORT(Lift(iN)ST.DoorClosePortH)B                    // Release close-door signal
               → 0000 0001B |< PORT(Lift(iN)ST.DoorOpenPortH)B                     // Open doors
               → 0000 0001B |< PORT(Lift(iN)ST.DoorBellPortH)B                     // Sound bell
             → TimeOutBL = F
             → @t hh:mm:ss ≙ §t hh:mm:ss + 8
                T
             →      R      ◆ @t hh:mm:ss = § hh:mm:ss → TimeOutBL := T             // Delay 8s based on system clock
                 TimeOutBL=F
               → 0000 0000B |< PORT(Lift(iN)ST.DoorBellPortH)B                     // Stop bell
               → 0000 0000B |< PORT(Lift(iN)ST.DoorOpenPortH)B                     // Release open-door signal
               → 0000 0001B |< PORT(Lift(iN)ST.DoorClosePortH)B                    // Close doors
                      30
               → R    (◆ Key(jN)ST.KeyPositionN = LiftRecord(iN)ST.CurrentLevelN ∧
                  jN=1

                        Key(jN)ST.DirectionBL = LiftRecord(iN)ST.CurrentDirectionBL

                     → RequestRecord(iN)ST.RequestIdentifiedBL := F                // Clear requests on the same level
                  )
                      6
               → R    (PORT(Lift(iN)ST.DestScanPort(jN)H)B |> DestScanInputB       // Scan new destination level(s)
                  jN=1

                  → ( ◆ DestScanInputB < LiftRecord(iN)ST.CurrentLevelH ∧
                        DispatchList(iN)ST.Level(DestScanInputB)BL = F
                      → DispatchList(iN)ST.Level(DestScanInputB)BL := T
                      → ↑ (DispatchList(iN)ST.#WaitingServiceN)
                    | ◆ DestScanInputB > LiftRecord(iN)ST.CurrentLevelH
                      → UpWaitingQueueST.EnqueuePC(DestScanInputB; @UpWaitingQueueFullBL,
                            @UpWaitingEnqueueSucceedBL; UpWaitingQueueST)
                      → UpWaitingQueueST.EmptyBL := F

                  )
               → ◆ DispatchList(iN)ST.#WaitingServiceN > 0
                 → 0000 0000B |< PORT(Lift(iN).StopDrivePortH)B                     // Clear stop drive
                 → 0000 0001B |< PORT(Lift(iN).DownDrivePortH)B                     // Move down
               | ◆ ~                                                               // No service at the floor
               → ( ◆ LiftRecord(iN)ST.CurrentLevelH ≠ 6                            // Reached a middle floor
                   → 0000 0001B |< PORT(Lift(iN).DownDrivePortH)B                   // Down drive
                 | ◆ ~                                                             // Reached the ground floor
                   → 0000 0000B |< PORT(Lift(iN)ST.DownDrivePortH)B                 // Release up-drive signal
                   → 0000 0001B |< PORT(Lift(iN)ST.StopDrivePortH)B                 // Stop
                   → LiftRecord(iN)ST.CurrentDirectionN := T                        // Change direction
                 )
}
```

The L1 and L2 processes are system dynamic behaviors that are executable in normal sequential manner. However, the L3 and L4 processes are executable in periodical manner triggered by certain system timing interrupts. It is noteworthy that some of the priority levels may be omitted in modeling a particular system, except the base level processes. That is, any system encompasses at least a base level process, particularly for a nonreal-time or transaction processing system.

According to the RTPA system modeling and refinement methodology (Wang, 2007), the first step refinement of the dynamic behaviors of the LDS system on process priority allocation can be specified as shown in Figure 18. It may be observed that all non-periodical processes at run-time, such as SystemInitial**PC**, LiftDispatching_WaitingRequest**PC**, LiftDispatching_NewRequest**PC**, LiftServicing_Upward**PC**, and LiftServicing_Downward**PC**, are allocated at the base level, therefore there is no high level processes in the LDS system. However, the processes with strict timing constraints, such as SysClock**PC**, RequestScanning**PC**, and RequestProcessing**PC**, are allocated as periodical interrupt processes.

LDS Dynamic Process Deployment and Dispatching

Process deployment is a dynamic behavioral model of systems at run-time, which refines the timing relations and interactions among the system, system clock, system interrupts, and all processes at different priority levels. Process deployment is a refined model of process priority allocation for time-driven behaviors of a system. On the basis of the process priority allocation model as developed in previous subsection in Figure 18, the LDS dynamic behaviors can be further refined with a process deployment model as shown in Figure 19, where precise timing relationships between different priority levels are specified.

Figure 18. Process priority allocation of LDS dynamic behaviors

LDS**§**.ProcessPriorityAllocation**PC** ≜
{ // [L1: Base level processes]
  (SystemInitial**PC**
   | LiftDispatching_WaitingRequest**PC**
   | LiftDispatching_NewRequest**PC**
   | LiftServicing_Upward**PC**
   | LiftServicing_Downward**PC**
)
 || // [L2: Interrupt level processes]
  (SysClock**PC**
   | RequestScanning**PC**
   | RequestProcessing**PC**
)
}

The dynamic behaviors of the lift dispatching system can be described by the interactions of parallel categories of processes at the base and interrupt levels, which are triggered by the event @SystemInitial**S** or @SysClock100msInst⊙. The LDS system repeatedly executes the LiftDispatching**PC** and LiftServing**PC** processes at base level until the event SysShutDown**BL** = **T** is captured by the system (**§**). When the interrupt-level processes occurs per 100ms during run-time of base level processes, the system switches priority scheduling to the interrupt level processes, such as SysClock**PC**, RequestScanning**PC**, and RequestProcessing**PC**. Once completion, the interrupt-level processes hand over control to the system in order to resume the interrupted base-level functions.

The formal design models of the LDS system and their refinements demonstrate a typical system modeling paradigm of the entire architectures, static behaviors, and dynamic behaviors according to the RTPA specification and refinement methodology. The practical formal engineering method of RTPA for system modeling and specification provides a coherent notation system and systematical methodology for large-scale software

Figure 19. Dynamic process deployment of the LDS system

```
LDS§.ProcessDeploymentST ≙ § →
{ // [L1: Base level processes]
  @SystemInitialS
    ↳ (SysInitialPC
                    T
      →          R              (↦ LiftDispatching_WaitingRequestPC
          SysShutdownBL = F
                                ↦ LiftDispatching_NewRequestPC
                                ↦ LiftServicing_UpwardPC
                                ↦ LiftServicing_DownwardPC
                                )
              → ⊠
      )
  ↯ // [L2: Interrupt level processes]
  @SysClock100msInt
    ↗ (SysClockPC
        ↦ RequestScanningPC
        ↦ RequestProcessingPC
        )
    ↘
} → §
```

and hybrid system design and implementation. The final-level refinements of the LDS specifications provide a set of detailed and precise design blueprints for seamless code generation, system implementation, tests, and verifications.

CONCLUSION

This article has demonstrated that a complex real-time Lift Dispatching System (LDS), including its architecture, static behaviors, and dynamic behaviors, can be formally and efficiently described by RTPA. On the basis of the RTPA methodologies, this article has systematically developed a formal design model of the LDS system in a top-down approach. The architectural model of the LDS system has been created using a set of UDMs. The static behaviors of the LDS system have been modeled by a set of UPMs. The dynamic behaviors of the LDS system have been specified by a set of process priority allocation and process deployment models.

The formal model of the LDS system has provided a universal and flexible design of LDS systems. The LDS system allows the design and implementation of the system be easily extended to a complex building with more floors and more elevators by changing the UDM models of LDS. The UPMs of all the behavioral processes of LDS will mainly remain unchanged. Additional functions may be added into the LDS system, such as those of special priority users for maintenance, door sensors for safe closing, and overweight detection/processing.

Based on the rigorous design models and the formal framework of the LDS system, program code can be seamlessly derived. The formal model of LDS may not only serve as a formal design paradigm of real-time software systems, but also a test bench of the expressive power and modeling capability of exiting formal methods in software engineering. Related real-world case studies on formal system modeling and refinement in RTPA may be referred to (Wang, 2009; Wang and Ngolah, 2002; Wang and Zhang, 2003; Ngolah et al., 2002, 2004). Since the equivalence between software and human behaviors, RTPA may also be use to describe human dynamic behaviors and mental processes (Wang, 2003, 2008d; Wang and Ruhe, 2007).

ACKNOWLEDGMENT

The authors would like to acknowledge Natural Science and Engineering Council of Canada (NSERC) and an IIST/UNU fellowship for their partial support to this work. The authors would like to thank the anonymous reviewers for their invaluable comments that have greatly improved the latest version of this article.

REFERENCES

Bjorner, D., & Jones, C. B. (1982). Formal Specification and Software Development. Prentice Hall.

Chenais, P., & Weinberger, K. (1992, May). New Approach in the Development of Elevator Group Control Algorithms. Amsterdam. *ELEVCON, 4,* 48–57.

Corsetti, E., Montanari, A., & Ratto, E. (1991). Dealing with Different Time Granularities in Formal Specifications of Real-Time Systems. *The Journal of Real-Time Systems, 3*(2), 191–215. doi:10.1007/BF00365335

Hamdi, M., Mulvaney, D.J., & Sillitoe, I.P. (1995). An Intelligent Real-time Lift Scheduling System. *Workshop of the UK Planning and Scheduling Special Interest Group, 14.*

Hayes, I. (1985). Applying Formal Specifications to Software Development in Industry. *IEEE Transactions on Software Engineering, 11*(2), 169–178. doi:10.1109/TSE.1985.232191

Hoare, C. A. R. (1978). Communicating Sequential Processes. *Communications of the ACM, 21*(8), 666–677. doi:10.1145/359576.359585

Hoare, C. A. R. (1985). *Communicating Sequential Processes.* Prentice-Hall Inc.

Liu, J. (2000). *Real-Time Systems.* Upper Saddle River, NJ: Prentice Hall.

McDermid, J. A. (1991). *Software Engineer's Reference Book.* Oxford, UK: Butterworth-Heinemann Ltd.

Ngolah, C. F., Wang, Y., & Tan, X. (2004). The Real-Time Task Scheduling Algorithm of RTOS+. *IEEE Canadian Journal of Electrical and Computer Engineering, 29*(4), 237–243.

Wang, Y. (2002). The Real-Time Process Algebra (RTPA). *Annals of Software Engineering, 14,* 235–274. doi:10.1023/A:1020561826073

Wang, Y. (2003). Using Process Algebra to Describe Human and Software System Behaviors. *Brain and Mind, 4*(2), 199–213. doi:10.1023/A:1025457612549

Wang, Y. (2007, July). *Software Engineering Foundations: A Software Science Perspective.* CRC Series in Software Engineering (Vol. II). Auerbach Publications, USA.

Wang, Y. (2008a, April). RTPA: A Denotational Mathematics for Manipulating Intelligent and Computational Behaviors. *International Journal of Cognitive Informatics and Natural Intelligence, 2*(2), 44–62.

Wang, Y. (2008b). Deductive Semantics of RTPA. *International Journal of Cognitive Informatics and Natural Intelligence, 2*(2), 95–121.

Wang, Y. (2008c). Mathematical Laws of Software. *Transactions of Computational Science, 2,* 46–83. doi:10.1007/978-3-540-87563-5_4

Wang, Y. (2008d). On Contemporary Denotational Mathematics for Computational Intelligence. *Transactions of Computational Science, 2,* 6–29. doi:10.1007/978-3-540-87563-5_2

Wang, Y. (2009). (to appear). The Formal Design Model of a Telephone Switching System (TSS). *International Journal of Software Science and Computational Intelligence, 1*(3).

Wang, Y., & King, G. (2000). Software Engineering Processes: Principles and Applications. *CRC Series in Software Engineering* (Vol. I). CRC Press, USA.

Wang, Y., King, G., Fayad, M., Patel, D., Court, I., Staples, G., & Ross, M. (2000, March). On Built-in Tests Reuse in Object-Oriented Framework Design. *ACM Journal on Computing Surveys, 32*(1es), 7–12. doi:10.1145/351936.351943

Wang, Y., & Noglah, C. F. (2002, May). Formal Specification of a Real-Time Lift Dispatching System. *Proc. 2002 IEEE Canadian Conference on Electrical and Computer Engineering (CCECE'02)* (pp. 669-674). Winnipeg, Manitoba, Canada.

Wang, Y., & Ruhe, G. (2007). The Cognitive Process of Decision Making. *International Journal of Cognitive Informatics and Natural Intelligence, 1*(2), 73–85.

Wang, Y., & Zhang, Y. (2003, May). Formal Description of an ATM System by RTPA. *Proc. 16th Canadian Conference on Electrical and Computer Engineering* (CCECE'03) (pp. 1255-1258). Montreal, Canada: IEEE CS Press.

This work was previously published in International Journal of Software Science and Computational Intelligence, Volume 1, Issue 4, edited by Yingxu Wang, pp. 111-137, copyright 2009 by IGI Publishing (an imprint of IGI Global).

Chapter 20
A Theory of Program Comprehension:
Joining Vision Science and Program Comprehension

Yann-Gaël Guéhéneuc
École Polytechnique de Montréal and Université de Montréal, Canada

ABSTRACT

There exists an extensive literature on vision science, on the one hand, and on program comprehension, on the other hand. However, these two domains of research have been so far rather disjoint. Indeed, several cognitive theories have been proposed to explain program comprehension. These theories explain the processes taking place in the software engineers' minds when they understand programs. They explain how software engineers process available information to perform their tasks but not how software engineers acquire this information. Vision science provides explanations on the processes used by people to acquire visual information from their environment. Joining vision science and program comprehension provides a more comprehensive theoretical framework to explain facts on program comprehension, to predict new facts, and to frame experiments. We join theories in vision science and in program comprehension; the resulting theory is consistent with facts on program comprehension and helps in predicting new facts, in devising experiments, and in putting certain program comprehension concepts in perspective.

In theory, there is no difference between theory and practice. But, in practice, there is. —Jan L. A. van de Snepscheut

INTRODUCTION

Joining vision science and program comprehension provides a theoretical framework to explain how software engineers understand programs and, thus, to explain known facts, to predict new facts, and to set up experiments on program comprehension.

In the recent year, the domain of cognitive informatics as emerged to study the internal processing mechanisms of the human brain and their applications in computing. Cognitive informatics is intrinsically multi-disciplinary and unites researchers in several domain of research such

DOI: 10.4018/978-1-4666-0261-8.ch020

as cognitive science, cybernetics, and software engineering. In particular in software engineering, it could bring interesting advances that could explain the mechanisms trough which software engineers understand, write, and debug programs. Therefore, it encompasses the domain of program comprehension.

Program comprehension is the domain of software engineering that seeks to explain how software engineers understand programs (Rugaber, S., 1995), how they obtain a mental representation of a program structure and function (Navarro-Prieto, R., 1998). Facts and laws of program comprehension lie at the heart of almost every software related activities, from development to maintenance, deployment, and use. Many studies on program comprehension have been published in the literature. However, understanding program comprehension requires more than just knowing facts; it requires a theory.

Our research concerns situations in which expert software engineers readily recognise well-known patterns (*any* kind of patterns) in a program model, while novice software engineers only perceive their constituents. Figure 1 shows a subset of a class diagram. (We cloud class names for the sake of explanation). The question is: What is the structure and function that an expert software engineer recognises instantly in that diagram and that a novice software engineer does not? (The curious reader may take few seconds to study the class diagram.) An expert software engineer could recognise that the classes follow the solution of the Composite design pattern (Gamma, E., Helm, R., Johnson, R., & Vlissides, J., 1994), thus assigning the function of representing part–whole hierarchies, while a novice software engineer only sees a hierarchy of four classes, some operations, and an aggregation relationship. (Compare with the solution of the Composite design pattern in Figure 4). We attempt to explain this difference in comprehension between expert and novice software engineers with a theory.

Existing cognitive theories[1], such as Brooks' (1978), von Mayrhauser's (1995) Pennington's (1987), Soloway, E., Pinto, J., Letovsky, S., Littman, D., & Lampert, R. (1998), provide explanations on the short-, long-, and working-memories used, on the cognitive internal processes at play, and on the internal and external knowledge incorporated and constructed during program comprehension. Other authors, such as Minsky (1974), Rich and Waters (1990), and Soloway (1986) theorise the cognitive internal representation of knowledge through the concepts of frames, plans, and chunks. However, no existing theory of program comprehension explains well the difference between expert and novice software engineers, in particular wrt. the use of patterns.

Our approach to explain the previous difference recognises the importance of sight during program comprehension and consists in describing the information flow from graphical program models (texts or diagrams) to cognitive internal processes and memories, using vision science. Vision science is an interdisciplinary domain of cognitive science, which provides a framework for understanding vision in terms of phenomena of visual perception, the nature of optical information, and the physiology of the visual nervous system (Palmer, S. E., 1999). It does not "analyse the sociocultural basis of the staggering amount of functional information people learn about familiar" items[2] but focuses "on the more perceptually relevant question of how sighted people manage to perceive an [item]'s functional significance by looking" (Palmer, S. E., 1999). Theories of vision science explain the capabilities of the human visual system to acquire visual information and to provide this information to cognitive internal processes and memories. Therefore, we develop a theory of program comprehension including the processes of acquiring and comprehending information through sight, by drawing inspiration from theories of vision science and of program comprehension. This vision–comprehension theory relates vision processes, cognitive internal

Figure 1. What is the structure and function that an expert software engineer recognises instantly in this subset of a class diagram of a well-known program and that a novice software engineer does not? How does the recognition happen?

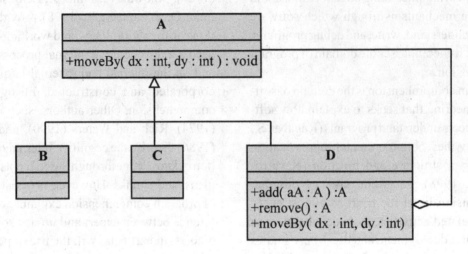

processes, and memories, during program comprehension, and brings together data and methodology of program comprehension and vision science. We show that this theory is consistent with known facts, we explain certain trends in program comprehension, and we propose possible theoretical and experimental falsification studies.

In Section 2, we introduce related work on theories of software engineering, of program comprehension, and of vision science. In Section 3, we present the rationale for developing a theory of program comprehension. In Section 4, we detail the theory and its philosophy, premises, context, and scope. In Section 5, we show that the theory explains known facts, while in Section 6 we discuss trends in program comprehension. In Section 4, we propose falsification experiments. Finally, in Section 7, we conclude and introduce future work.

RELATED WORK

What are Theories?

A theory is an integrated set of statements—hypotheses—about the principles that organises and explains known facts and that makes predictions about new facts possible. It must be an internally consistent minimal set of hypotheses from which to derive explanations of known facts and testable predictions of new facts. A theory helps in understanding a domain by explaining a list of "Why is it so?" questions Endres, A., & Rombach, D., 2003; Newell, A., 1973).

Theories in Software Engineering

The domain of software engineering possesses theories but existing theories (Endres, A. Et al., 2003) do not explain well known facts, due to the relatively recent existence of this domain, the complexity of the phenomena, and the lack of agreed upon formalisms and notations. Endres and Rombach (Endres, A. Et al., 2003) gather many facts, laws, and theories. However, we disagree with the authors calling their findings "theories".

Indeed, their theories are more like laws, because they only explain one (or few) facts at a time, they do not generalise well, and they use many hypotheses with respect to the principle of Ocam's razor.

Empirical studies are recognised as essential to understand phenomena with which software engineering deals, thanks to the work of precursors, such as Vic Basili (Boehm, B., Rombach, H. D., & Zelkowitz, M. V., 2005). Empirical studies are based on the classical cycle: observations (facts), laws, theories. Many facts have been recorded through empirical studies and some laws have been proposed. Yet, few theories have been derived to explain these facts and laws and to predict news facts. Some researchers argue that current empirical studies focus too much on generalisation and not enough on theory building (Jørgensen, M., & Sjøberg, D. I., 2004).

Another reason for the inadequacy of theories is the lack of frameworks in which to set up experiments and with which to interpret results. Indeed, theories are an invaluable help in setting up experiments to observe facts (dis)proving the laws and theories. (For example, since Albert Einstein proposed his theories of quantum physics, physicists used this framework to set up experiments to prove or to disprove the theories, to obtain and to explain new facts.)

Theories in Program Comprehension

We decompose the domain of program comprehension in three lines of research: (1) acquisition of data from programs, for example through static or dynamic or documentation analyses; (2) study of the broader context in which program comprehension takes place, the software engineers' activities, the organisational and social contexts of their activities; and, (3) development of theories based on the understanding of the software engineers' use of extracted data in a given context.

Data Acquisition

The rich literature on program comprehension focused early on the problems of obtaining data from software artifacts (static and dynamic data, features, documentation and other repositories), see for example Aho, A. V., Hopcroft, J. E., & Ullman, J. D., 1974; Spinellis, D. It also tackles the means to represent and to communicate this data, using various techniques from text-based editors to 3D interactive dynamic environments, such as (Simon, F., Steinbrückner, F., & Lewerentz, C., 2001). This literature is essential to understand what kind of data software engineers have at their disposal to comprehend programs.

Context

Less work study the contexts in which the program comprehension activity takes place. Murphy et al. (2005) attempt to distinguish, to describe, and to identify recurring patterns in the software engineers daily activities. Although not related to program comprehension explicitly, their work brings insight in the program comprehension activity, because program comprehension is part of all but the most basic software engineering activities. Thus, this line of research is important to generalise claims in program comprehension. Indeed, generalising claims is difficult because no complete taxonomy of the software engineers' activities exist. However, the authors do not frame their experiments in a particular theory of software development and, thus, run the risk to perform unfocused experiments.

Theories

Few theories of program comprehension have been proposed in the literature. We introduce two theories which are compared in more details with our theory in Section 6. The first theory, proposed by Brooks (1978) describes program comprehension as a process of building a sequence of knowledge domains, bridging the gap between problem domain and program execution. A succession of knowledge domains describes a software engineer's comprehension of a program.

The second theory, developed by von Mayrhauser (1995), is an integrated theory describing the processes taking place in the software engineers' minds during program comprehension, as a combination of top-down and bottom-up comprehension processes, working with a common knowledge base. This integrated theory accounts for the dynamics of forming and of abstracting a mental representation of a program.

These precursor theories are invaluable and we draw much inspiration from their insights. However, none of these theories explain and use the processes of acquisition of the information by the software engineers through their senses.

Theories in Vision Science

Vision science is the domain of computing science interested in the understanding of people's vision system. Vision science collects facts on vision, formulate laws from these facts, and devise theories explaining these laws and facts. With these theories, vision scientists have been able to predict new facts successfully and to refine their theories.

Vision science possesses many theories to explain colour vision, spatial vision, perception of motion and events, as well as eye movements, visual memory, and visual awareness. To the best of our knowledge, Palmer's book presents the most complete and in-depth coverage of vision theories, cast in the information processing paradigm (Palmer, S. E., 1999). For the sake of brevity, we introduce theories of vision science along with relevant references while presenting the vision–comprehension theory in Section 4.

RATIONALE OF THE THEORY

Our theory recognises software engineers as human beings. We believe that the physical and cognitive characteristics of software engineers are important because they use all of their senses and cognitive capabilities when they comprehend a program, in particular sight. Indeed, when comprehending a program, software engineers read documentation and source code and they visualise all kinds of program models. The preeminence of sight is corroborated by the extensive literature on visualisation for program comprehension. Yet, to the best of our knowledge, no previous theory of program comprehension recognised the importance of sight explicitly.

We build on vision science and on program comprehension theories to propose a theory of program comprehension accounting for the acquisition and for the use of visual information by software engineers. This theory is based on theories in vision science but does not contradict existing theories of program comprehension, such as Brooks' (1978) and von Mayrhauser's (1995): It extends these existing theories to provide explanations on the acquisition of information.

Section 2 highlights the importance of theories to explain known facts and to predict new facts. In addition, a theory is useful to frame efforts to automate the program comprehension activity. Indeed, as Marr points out, once a "theory for a process has been formulated, algorithms for implementing it may be designed, and their performance compared with that of the human" processor (Marr, D., 1982). Thus, our theory could help in devising (semi-)automated algorithms to comprehend programs and to help software engineers in comprehending programs.

Finally, our theory will help in devising experiments to answer questions related to the program comprehension activity through sight. Without theories on program comprehension, "the danger is that questions are not asked in relation to a clear [theory]." (Marr, D., 1982) and, thus, provide answers lacking focus and generality.

VISION–COMPREHENSION THEORY

Philosophy

The program comprehension activity requires information contained in a program source code and documentation. But this information is not sufficient for comprehending a program. The tasks at hand (why is the program being studied), the context of the activity (where, for what purpose is the program studied), and the experience of the software engineers (with software engineering, program comprehension, and the studied program) are required additional sources of information. Thus, software engineers contribute information during the program comprehension activity. We take a *constructivist* stance, like C. Floyd (1992) for software development, in which comprehension is constructed from external and internal information, without emphasising formalisation at the expense of communication, learning, and evolution.

Premises

We cast our theory within the information processing paradigm, in which the human brain is seen as a computational processor. This paradigm is built on the similarity between cognitive psychology and computers and belongs to the objectivist tradition (Lachman, R., Lachman, J. L., & Butterfield, E. C., 1979).

We use the meta-theoretical analysis of the information processing paradigm proposed by Palmer and Kimchi (1987), which makes different assumptions on the informational description, the recursive decomposition, and the physical embodiment of cognitive processes in the human brain: Cognitive processes, such as visual perception or program comprehension, are processes trans-

forming input information in output information. They can be decomposed in a number of cognitive processes linked by a flow diagram. They are embodied in the behaviour of the *physical* human brain in which they take place.

Thus, assume that software engineers focus their attention on the program model that they comprehend and we describe visual perception and the program comprehension activity with processes acting on different representations of information from the program model.

We also consider a theory of reinforcement learning (Sutton, R. S., & Barto, A. G., 1998) to explain the behaviour of certain processes with respect to the amount of processing required to perform the program comprehension activity.

Context

We develop our theory in the context of a growing need to understand program comprehension to reduce maintenance cost and to develop tools to support program comprehension, see for example the extensive literature on software visualisation.

Our theory relates to on-going research on alternative visualisation techniques to represent program models graphically, for example using adjacency matrices (Ghoniem, M., Fekete, J-D., & Castagliola, P., 2004) or 3D representations (Simon, F. Et al., 2001) to map and to ensure the traceability of mappings between source code and higher-level abstractions, such as design patterns (Albin-Amiot, H., Cointe, P., Guéhéneuc, Y-G., & Jussien, N., 2001) or features (Antoniol, G., & Guéhéneuc, Y-G., 2005).

Scope

We limit the scope of our theory to software engineers engaged in a program comprehension activity. Software engineers must be using sight in normal functional conditions to comprehend program models, other modalities are not accounting for (although they might influence the

Figure 2. Theory of program comprehension through vision

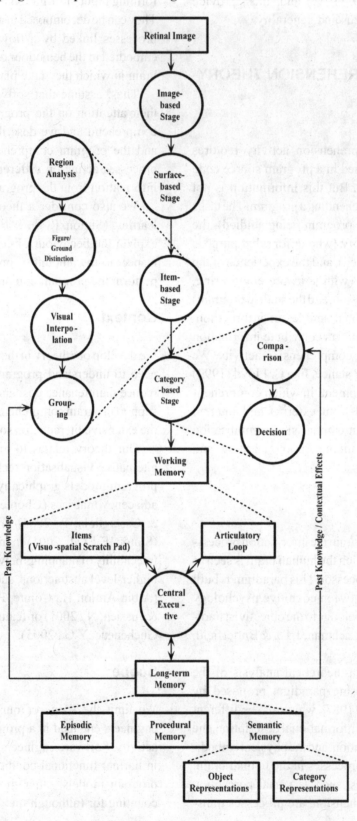

activity). The program models can be represented in any form, either textual, graphical (bi- or tri-dimensional), including static, dynamic, and–or other kinds of data.

DEFINITION

We decompose the recognition of items during program comprehension in several processes acting on different representations[3] of a program model. Figure 2 shows the sequence of processes and the flow of data among these.

Although we believe that the following theory provides a source of explanations for the program comprehension activity, beyond its details, this theory is interesting for bridging vision science and program comprehension and for integrating early stages of comprehension (vision) with later stages (cognition [Brooks, R., 1978; Mayrhauser, A. v., 1975], see also Section 6).:

- **Retinal Image.** The program comprehension activity begins with a retinal image of a program model which a software engineer is observing. The retinal image may originate from any program model, either a textual representation, a -like diagram…
- **Image-based Stage.** The retinal image is analysed to extract spatial features from its structure, such as edges, lines, and textures. This process produces a set of visual elements: edges, bars, and blobs (Marr, D., 1982). -1

Boxes represent image representations, circles are processes, arrows describe information flow, dotted lines show decompositions. Absence of representations between processes does not preclude existence but simplifies the flow:

1. **Surface-based Stage.** The visual elements from the previous process are interpreted in terms of visible surfaces in a 3D space. The process produces local pieces of oriented surface (Marr, D., 1978).

2. **Item-based Stage.** This process concerns the perceptual organisation of the visual elements (including local pieces of oriented surface) in items, see (Palmer, S. E. Et al., 1987). We decompose this process in four sub-processes:
   - **Region Analysis.** This sub-process analyses visual elements to identify regions in the image structure. A region is a bounded 2D area that constitutes a subset of the image. Different principles direct region analysis, such as connectedness, segmentation, and texture segregation.
   - **Figure/Ground Distinction.** Once regions are identified, this sub-process decomposes regions in two categories: figures and ground. Figures are parts of the image close to the observer, with a bounded contour defining their shapes. Ground is the part of the image farther from the observer, extending behind and not shaped by a contour.
   - **Visual Interpolation.** This sub-process interpolates the hidden parts of identified regions from their visible parts to allow the visual system to perceive partly-occluded visual elements.
   - **Grouping.** This sub-process groups previously identified visual elements in coherent items. It uses laws of grouping, such as proximity, similarities of colour, size, orientation, and common fate. It also uses past knowledge stored in long-term memory to perform the grouping: From now on, the reader shall always see the use of the Composite design pattern in Figure 1.

3. **Category-based Stage.** Grouping visual elements in items is not yet sufficient to allow comprehension. The items must be categorised to distinguish their different functions. We follow the theoretical approach of indirect perception of function, which decomposes in two sub-processes: Comparison and Decision. Following Rosch's theory (Rosch, E. H., 1973), we assume that memory stores exemplars of items, represented by prototypes, with which to assign identified items to categories.

   ◦ **Comparison.** This sub-process uses past knowledge and contextual effects to compare identified items with known items, accounting for the context in which items are identified. Items may belong to several categories (or to no category).

   ◦ **Decision.** Then, this sub-process decides the categories to which the items belong, typically using a maximum-over-threshold rule.

4. **Working Memory.** The previous processes produce a representation in which the various items composing the program model have been identified and categorised. This representation is handled by the Working Memory, which is similar to short-term memory but possesses an important internal structure (Baddeley, A. D., & Hitch, G., 1974). The Working Memory decomposes in a Central Executive process interacting with the Visuo-spatial Scratch Pad, the Articulatory Loop, and the Long-term Memory.

   ◦ **Central Executive.** The central executive process performs cognitive tasks, such as comprehension, problem solving, and memorisation tasks. It works closely with the two following memories.

   ◦ **Visuo-spatial Scratch Pad and Articulatory Memories.** This visuo-spatial scratch pad stores visual/spatial information while the articulatory loop stores verbal information. Other kinds of memories may exist for other modalities. These memories play the role of cache with respect to long-term memory, being faster and easier to access by the Central Executive.

   ◦ **Long-term Memory.** The central executive process also interacts with long-term memory. Long-term memory is composed of three memories: episodic, procedural, and semantic, which we describe in the context of program comprehension.

   ◦ **Episodic Memory.** The episodic memory stores information on items and events part of the software engineer's life history. It stores domain and functional knowledge learned by the software engineer during apprenticeship and program knowledge learned during program comprehension.

   ◦ **Procedural Memory.** The procedural memory stores information about skills and procedures to perform actions. It contains the software engineer's knowledge about programming and strategies for program comprehension (Mayrhauser, A. v., 1994).

   ◦ **Semantic Memory.** Finally, the semantic memory stores information concerning knowledge of concepts, such as in an encyclopedia. This memory stores the visual appearances of prototypical objects and categories, such as architectural, design, and implementation prototypes. It also stores knowledge domains (Brooks, R., 1978) (acquired through sight or built by the Central Executive).

This theory describes the program comprehension activity from a Retinal Image generated by a graphical representation of a program model to the Central Executive, which performs the comprehension activity. Before discussing the theory in Section 6, we use it to explain some known facts.

EXPLANATIONS OF KNOWN FACTS

Why are Patterns so Important?

Patterns, such as idioms (Coplien, J. O., 1997) design patterns (Gamma, E. Et al., 1994), or architectural patterns (Lévy, N., & Losavio, F., 1998), have been quickly and widely adopted by the software engineering community. In particular, the design patterns described by Gamma et al. (1994) stirred much interest in the software engineering community as a way to document and to reuse good practices in design (Coplien, J. O., 1997).

The development of a "pattern community" led to a large body of literature on pattern categorisation, formalisation, application, and identification. In this literature, many claims about patterns have been made, in particular regarding the usefulness of patterns to ease program comprehension. The claim on the usefulness of patterns is the main assumption (although often implicit) in research on pattern recovery, in particular design pattern recovery, including work by this author. This claim states that patterns ease program comprehension because software engineers recognise immediately certain patterns in program models as performing functions. Although this claim is sensible, it has never been explained theoretically. We provide an explanation, with our theory, on the usefulness of two kinds of patterns as examples: idioms and design patterns.

Idioms are patterns at the programming language level. Recovery of idioms, grouping program statements in idioms, has been subject of many work very early, for example the Programmer's Apprentice (Rich, C., & Waters, R. C., 1990).

The code excerpt in Figure 3 shows the Iterator idiom. A software engineer, who knows this idiom, would recognise the function of the statements instantly and would focus on the use of the list elements rather than on the means to iterate over these elements. We consider three cases to explain the recognition of the function of the statements:

- **The Software Engineer Does Not Know the Idiom.** A software engineer who has never been confronted to the Iterator idiom would be able to extract from the textual representation shown on Figure 3 its different statements through the Image- and Surface-based Stages. Without previous knowledge of the idiom, Long-term Memory would be unable to provide past knowledge to the Grouping and Comparison sub-processes. The statements composing the representation would be analysed by the Central Executive, which would infer and store their function in Semantic Memory, as Object Representation.

- **The Software Engineer Does Not Know the Idiom but Has Encountered its Use.** The software engineer would extract the statements through the Image- and Surface-based Stages. During the Item-based Stage, the Grouping sub-process would group the statements related to the idiom, based on information on the idiom previously stored as an Object Representation.

Figure 3. Example of the Iterator idiom

```
1. Idioms
final Iterator iterator = aList.iterator();
while(iterator.hasNext()) {
final Object o = iterator.next();
...
}
```

The Category-based Stage would use this information to compare the grouping with previous groupings, to decide their similarity, and to retrieve their function. Information on the function of the statements (along with information on the statements themselves) would go to Working Memory, thus easing the comprehension activity by supplying directly the Central Executive with the function of the statement. The Central Executive, on seeing the same group another time, may promote the group from Object Representation to Category Representation (Sutton, R. S. et al. 1998).

- **The Software Engineer Knows the Idiom.** Again, the software engineer would extract the statements through the Image- and Surface-based Stages. The Grouping sub-process would group the statements related to the idiom, based on the information on the idiom stored in the Semantic Memory as Category Representation. The Category-based Stage would use the grouping and information from the Category Representation to assign a function immediately, thus easing the use of the grouping during program comprehension by the Central Executive.

Thus, we explain the usefulness of idioms: The knowledge of idioms eases program comprehension by providing the Central Executive with the function of a group of statements directly, without requiring further processing from the Central Executive to identify its function.

Design Patterns

Design patterns, like idioms, are claimed to ease program comprehension. They have been specifically targeted towards software engineers to provide "good" solutions to recurring design problems (Gamma, E. et al., 1994). To the best of our knowledge, there exists no attempts to prove or disprove these claims but through case studies, see for example (Wendorff, P., 2001).

We see design motifs—solutions of design patterns—as prototypes that can be used in the progrram comprehension activity of micro-architectures—subsets of a program design—directly. We believe that design motifs are identical or closed to the prototypes in a software engineer's memory. A software engineer who knows design motifs would recognise their structure and function directly, such as in Figure 1 with the Composite design pattern. We consider three cases to explain the comprehension of micro-architectures:

- **The Software Engineer Does Not Know Design Patterns.** A software engineer with no knowledge of design patterns would extract the constituents of the micro-architecture presented in Figure 1 through the Image- and Surface-based Stages. Long-term Memory could not provide the Item- and Category-based Stages with past knowledge and, thus, Working Memory would perform a time- and resource-consuming analysis of the constituents to identify their function.
- **The Software Engineer Knows an Unused Design Pattern.** A software engineer with knowledge of design patterns not used in the micro-architecture is in a position similar to the one above. The information provided by the Long-term Memory to the Grouping and Comparison sub-processes of the Item- and Category-based Stages would help neither in grouping the constituents nor in categorising the micro-architecture. Again, the Central Executive would be responsible for inferring the function of the constituents.
- **The Software Engineer Knows the Used Design Pattern.** Knowledge of the design

pattern which motif is used to implement a micro-architecture decreases the work load on the Working Memory. A software engineer would extract the constituents of the micro-architecture through the Image- and Surface-based Stages. The Grouping sub-process would group these constituents using the knowledge of the similar prototypical design motif. Then, the Comparison sub-process would use this information and the knowledge on the prototype to provide the function of the micro-architecture to the Working Memory directly, thus easing program comprehension.

Thus, we can explain the quick and wide adoption of design patterns and the attention paid to their literary form: The synthetic, prototype-based, descriptions of design patterns are usable directly in the Item- and Category-based Stages of program comprehension through sight, decreasing the work load on the Working Memory and, thus, easing the program comprehension activity.

Practical Considerations

The statement composing an idiom or the constituents of a micro-architecture similar to a design motif might be scattered across a graphical program model and can be even in non-displayed parts of the model. It is important to identify the constituents forming these patterns and to bring these constituents visually together to help software engineers in using design motifs to comprehend the model.

Kosslyn (1973) performed several experiments validating the picture metaphor: These experiments revealed a highly linear relationship between response times and distances between pairs of items in an image. Thus, graphically grouping constituents of patterns help in understanding their functions through the Grouping and Comparison sub-processes as well as navigating in the program model by minimising the dwell time of eye movements among constituents. Kosslyn's experiments and our theory are consistent in justifying experimentally and theoretically the benefits of software visualisation techniques, in particular -like diagram layout algorithms (for example [Eichelberger, H., & von Gudenberg, J. W., 2002]) and alternative visualisation techniques (see Subsection 4)

Conclusion

Our theory explains the importance of patterns: Patterns reduce the amount of processing required by the Central Executive to comprehend the functions of subsets of program models. It provides explanations on the quick and wide adoption of patterns by practitioners due to their usefulness during the program comprehension activity.

Also, our theory provides explanations on the advantages of expert software engineers over novice software engineers: Expert software engineers have read and understood much larger quantities of information related to program implementation (source code) and design (models such as class diagrams). They increased the number of prototypical patterns stored in their Semantic Memory. Our theory provides a theoretical basis to the idea that reading and understanding other software engineers' program is beneficial.

Finally, our theory provides explanations on the importance of "good" graphical program models. Graphical models are important because they facilitate the Grouping and Comparison sub-processes. It enforces the idea of standardised models of source code (either textual or graphical), because these models are closer to the prototypical models (in kinds and in forms) stored in Semantic Memory.

Why are Packages and Composite States so Important?

Packages in graphical program models, such as class diagrams, and composite states in state diagrams are believed to ease program comprehension. Serrano et al. (2005) propose a study on packages for modelling data warehouses and Cruz-Lemus et al. (2005) a study on program comprehension using composite states, which tend to show that, indeed, packages and composite states ease program comprehension.

We can explain theoretically the results of these studies in a similar fashion as we explained the importance of patterns. Packages (composite states, respectively), when used adequately, are groups describing sets of functions. A software engineer, while studying a program model, would extract information on the packages through the Image- and Item-based Stages. The Item- and Category-based Stages would not need to use past knowledge on individual constituents because packages are recognised as a single item (in opposition to the package constituents, that would be recognised as a set of items to be grouped). Information on the packages would go to the Working Memory. The individual constituents of the packages would never be processed independently, thus reducing the required processing resource and time and easing program comprehension.

However, the usefulness of packages and of composite states has not yet been successfully proven empirically. We believe that absence of experimental proofs results from a lack of theoretical framework in which to cast experiments. Our theory provides an experimental framework in which to devise experiments based solely on studying composite states and packages during program comprehension, wrt. other factors such as tool support, software engineers' experience.

Why do Bounded Information ease Program Comprehension?

Gail et al. (2005) present a study of software engineers' tasks, based on the monitoring and recording of the tasks during daily work. Tasks are composed in task structures. The authors claim that task structures help in reducing software engineers' time and effort to find relevant information by reducing the amount of displayed data, by bounding queries, and by performing queries automatically. However, they do not cast their claims within a theoretical framework of program comprehension to justify what information software developers need, when they need it, and how they use it. Thus, they do not explain *why* well-defined task structures would actually ease software engineers' activities. The benefits of task structures remains hypothetical until generalisable empirical proofs are provided.

We can explain why the use of task structures could indeed reduce software engineers' time and effort to perform their program comprehension activity by presenting data in a readily processable way—close to prototypes that software engineers have in memory. Moreover, the data embedded in task structures could be used along with the idea of parallel processing and visual pop-out (Triesman, A., 1985), to provide software engineers with visual clues on important information.

Why do Alternative Visualisation Techniques ease Program Comprehension?

Ghoniem et al. (2004) realise an experiment on adjacency matrices, assessing their usefulness for different comprehension activities with respect to node–link diagrams.

An adjacency matrix represents the relationships between sets of items. An adjacency matrix is only limited by the characteristics of the display,

Figure 4. Original class diagram of the Composite design pattern (Gamma, E., 1984)

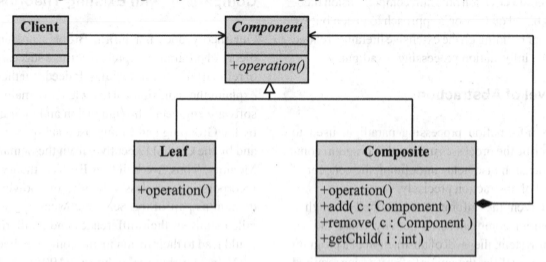

while a node–link diagram is limited also by the characteristics of the displayed network.

The authors conclude that adjacency matrices have several benefits (in time and in accuracy wrt. graph size and density) over nodes–links diagrams to estimate numbers of nodes and links, to find connected, specified, and neighbouring nodes and links, but not to find a path between nodes.

We explain the differences between adjacency matrices and nodes–links diagrams in three ways. First, estimation and finding activities requiring software engineers to distinguish nodes are performed with adjacency matrices easily because nodes–links diagrams require more processing during the Item- and Category-based Stages, in particular during Region Analysis, due to the cluttering of the diagrams.

Second, finding specific nodes and links is faster and more accurate with adjacency matrices because software engineers only need to recognise the node number, which is performed easily by the visual system or to put in correspondence two nodes, which is performed by the visual system efficiently.

Finally, finding a path between nodes is difficult for the visual system using adjacency matrices because the software engineers must focus their attention on several different parts of the matrices, thus losing their focus in the transition from one node to another, while in nodes–links diagrams, they follow links among nodes, thus keeping their focus.

DISCUSSIONS

Theoretical Bias

We postulated that we ease program comprehension by reducing the amount and the time of processing required by software engineers' minds to comprehend program models. Thus, we assume *from the start* that the information processing paradigm is correct because we assume that the program comprehension activity depends on the characteristics of the *processes* used to perform this activity.

This assumption biases our theory because we develop our theory *using* the information processing paradigm. However, to the best of our knowledge, the information processing paradigm has never been successfully challenged yet. In the domain of vision science, Gibson is the principal opponent of the information processing paradigm.

We could envision program comprehension theories based on Gibson's approach to vision but we favour building on the extensive literature related to the information processing paradigm.

Level of Abstraction

The information processing paradigm used to describe the processes involved in program comprehension also helps in defining the concept of level of abstraction precisely.

Given the information obtained through a program comprehension activity using the vision system, the level of abstraction of a program model qualifies the amount of processing required to obtain this information from the model. Thus, for a same information provided to the Central Executive, a program model at a low-level of abstraction requires more processing (including from the Central Executive) than a program model at a higher-level of abstraction.

We illustrate this definition of the level of abstraction with Figures 1 and 3. A typical implementation of the Composite design motif uses the Iterator idiom in D.moveBy(int,int) to apply recursively the A.moveBy(int,int) method on the stored instances of A (or of its subclasses). A software engineer cannot obtain easily information on the structure and function of the Composite design motif through the statements in Figure 3 (even with its complete implementation), while this information is obtained directly from the program model in Figure 1. The program model in Figure 1 is at a higher level of abstraction than that in Figure 3 because the former requires less processing to obtain a given information.

Previous work providing program models at a higher level of abstraction than source code through static, dynamic, or semantic analyses could be assessed using this definition of the level of abstraction for comparison and for evaluation of their algorithms and of the resulting program models.

Comparison with Existing Theories

Our theory does not infirm Brook's precursor theory of program comprehension as a succession of refined knowledge domains. Indeed, our theory explains the acquisition of knowledge domains by software engineers through vision and their uses by the Grouping and Comparison sub-processes and by the Central Executive, from the Semantic Memory. Thus, we build on Brooks' theory by incorporating seamlessly the idea of knowledge domain as part of the Semantic Memory. A detailed study of their differences and similarities could lead to their fusion in one complete theory.

Von Mayrhauser's theory (1995) ("integrated model" based on previous theories, such as Litovsky's) is a complete theory of program comprehension, accounting for top–down and bottom–up comprehension strategies, and program knowledge. Our theory does not challenge von Mayrhauser's theory because it provides explanations on the acquisition of program models through vision *before* any comprehension strategies is applied. It uses ideas from von Mayrhauser's theory to account for the behaviour Central Executive and for the use of past knowledge in the Grouping and Comparison sub-processes. Also, we do not assume that the objective of comprehension is to understand a program completely, as highlighted by von Mayrhauser. Thus, the two theories are complementary and explain different parts of the program comprehension activity. They could be merged to detail the complete program comprehension activity.

Falsifications

Attempts to falsify a theory are important for its refinement.

Theoretical Falsification

We propose three possible directions for falsifying our theory theoretically. First, our constructivist stance could be disputed and other philosophical stances could be used for software development and program comprehension, which would frame these activities better.

Second, we cast our theory in the information processing paradigm, but other paradigms could be envisioned to build program comprehension theories. Although we do not believe that an ecological paradigm, such as proposed by Gibson, could be used in program comprehension easily, research is needed to study other paradigms to progress in the understanding of program comprehension.

Finally, the flow of data among processes, in the definitions of the (intermediary) representations and of the processes, must be detailed. We adapted theories of vision science in one consistent whole without overloading the resulting theory with detailed explanations. We favoured a more descriptive approach to parallel the program comprehension activity and the theory. Further studies could prove parts of (or all of) our theory wrong, thus advancing the understanding of the program comprehension activity.

Experimental Falsification

Experimental falsification of our theory includes devising experiments to disprove, for example, the flow of data among processes, the use of past knowledge during the Grouping and Comparison sub-processes, or the usefulness of these sub-processes for program comprehension. Experimental falsification could be based on introspection: observation of one's own conscious experience while comprehending programs. However, cognitive psychology rejects introspection (Dunlap, K., 1912) as a valid method of investigation (except through the "think-aloud" protocol [Lewis, C., 1982]). Thus, we propose to *observe* software engineers engaged in program comprehension.

Progress in non-intrusive monitoring of human behaviour allows to monitor external activities of software engineers involved in a program com-

prehension activity. We plan to use video-based eye tracking systems to assess the pertinence of design pattern identification for program comprehension. Video-based eye tracking systems allow to follow software engineers' eye movements while looking at a program model (Guéhéneuc, Y-G. et al., 2005). We will assess design pattern identification, on the one hand, and the use of these patterns during program comprehension, on the other hand, to improve current techniques of design pattern identification and of representations of micro-architectures similar to design motifs.

First, we will use a video-based eye tracking systems to study software engineers' eye movements on the constituents of program models (for example, -like class diagrams) and the dwell time on individual constituent (classes or relationships) to assess the identification of patterns. The hypothesis is that novice software engineers do not identify patterns in program models and, thus for a set of identical comprehension tasks, navigate through the models quite differently than expert software engineers. The expected conclusion is that expert software engineers identify patterns in program models, while novice software engineers do not, thus needing more time to comprehend models.

Second, we will study the use of identified patterns. Given a program model and a set of clearly identified patterns, we will compare software engineers' eye movements when performing different program comprehension tasks, distinguishing software engineers with and without pattern knowledge. The hypothesis is that pattern knowledge eases the program comprehension activity by allowing expert software engineers to focus their attention (eye movements) on constituents *inside* or *outside* of the identified patterns instead of navigating among all their constituents. The expected conclusion is that expert software engineers benefit from their knowledge of patterns by focusing their attention relatively to these patterns. This conclusion could also be in agreement with the idea of intentionally-ignored information validated by Rock and Gutman (1981) experimentally.

CONCLUSION AND FUTURE WORK

We proposed a theory of program comprehension to explain the differences between expert and novice software engineers, in time and in effort, to perform program comprehension, in particular with patterns. This theory draws on the extensive literature in vision science and on previous theories of program comprehension. It is cast in the information processing paradigm and explains known facts on program comprehension, such as the importance of idioms, patterns, packages, composite states, and alternative graphical models, in terms of internal cognitive representations and processes. It provides a framework for concepts of program comprehension, such as level of abstraction, and for falsification studies, both theoretically and experimentally.

This theory is a step to explain the program comprehension activity and may be inadequate for some aspects of the activity. We humbly hope that our theory will foster new research as stepping stone towards more accurate explanations. Future work includes a detailed study of the internal cognitive representations used by the processes, their forms and their characteristics. It also includes a closer comparative study (and possibly fusion) of our theory with von Mayrhauser's and Brooks'. We shall also perform falsification experiments using video-based eye tracking systems. Finally, other modalities should be studied, such as hear. Other future work also includes developing our theory to integrate negative facts found in the program comprehension domain, facts that contradicted the hypotheses of the researchers that studied them. Integrating such "negative" facts would help develop a theory that is more robust to contradicting facts.

ACKNOWLEDGMENT

The author thanks Naouel Moha, Victor Ostromoukhov, and Duc-Loc Huynh deeply for the fruitful discussions.

REFERENCES

Aho, A. V., Hopcroft, J. E., & Ullman, J. D. (1974, January). *The Design and Analysis of Computer Algorithms* (1st Edition). Addison-Wesley.

Albin-Amiot, H., Cointe, P., Guéhéneuc, Y.-G., & Jussien, N. (2001, November). Instantiating and detecting design patterns: Putting bits and pieces together. In D. Richardson, M. Feather, & M. Goedicke (Eds.), *Proceedings of the 16th Conference on Automated Software Engineering*, (pp. 166–173). IEEE Computer Society Press.

Antoniol, G., & Guéhéneuc, Y.-G. (2005, September). Feature identification: A novel approach and a case study. In T. Gyimóthy & V. Rajlich (Eds.), *Proceedings of the 21st International Conference on Software Maintenance*, pages 357–366. IEEE Computer Society Press, September 2005. Best paper.

Baddeley, A. D., & Hitch, G. (1974). Working memory. In G. Bower (Ed.), *The Psychology of Learning and Motivation, 8*, 47–90. Academic Press.

Boehm, B., Rombach, H. D., & Zelkowitz, M. V. (2005). *Septmeber). Foundations of Empirical Software Engineering: The Legacy of Victor R. Basili* (1st ed.). Springer-Verlag. doi:10.1007/3-540-27662-9

Brooks, R. (1978, May). Using a behavioral theory of program comprehension in software engineering. In M. V. Wilkes, L. Belady, Y. H. Su, H. Hayman, & P. Enslow (Eds.), *Proceedings of the 3rd International Conference on Software Engineering* (pp. 196–201). IEEE Computer Society Press.

Coplien, J. O. (1997, January). Idioms and patterns as architectural literature. *IEEE Software Special Issue on Objects, Patterns, and Architectures, 14*(1), 36–42.

Cruz-Lemus, J. A., Genero, M., Manso, M. E., & Piattini, M. (2005, October). Evaluating the effect of composite states on the understandability of UML statechart diagrams. In L. Briand (Ed.), *Proceedings of the 8th International Conference on Model Driven Engineering Languages and Systems*. Springer-Verlag.

Dunlap, K. (1912). The case against introspection. *Psychological Review, 19*, 404–413. doi:10.1037/h0071571

Eichelberger, H., & von Gudenberg, J. W. (2002, May). On the visualization of Java programs. In S. Diehl (Ed.), *Proceedings of the 1st international seminar on Software Visualization*, (pp. 295–306). Springer-Verlag.

Endres, A., & Rombach, D. (2003, March). *A Handbook of Software and Systems Engineering (1ˢᵗ Ediiton)*. Addison-Wesley. edition.

Floyd, C. (1992, March). *Human Questions in Computer Science* (pp. 15–27). Springer Verlag.

Gamma, E., Helm, R., Johnson, R., & Vlissides, J. (1994). *Design Patterns – Elements of Reusable Object-Oriented Software* (1st ed.). Addison-Wesley.

Ghoniem, M., Fekete, J.-D., & Castagliola, P. (2004, October). A comparison of the readability of graphs using node-link and matrix-based representations. In M. Ward & T. Munzner (Eds.), *Proceedings of the 10th symposium on Information Visualisation*, (pp. 17–24). IEEE Computer Society Press.

Gibson, J. R. *The Perception of the Visual World*. Greenwood Publishing Group.

Guéhéneuc, Y.-G., Monnier, S., & Antoniol, G. (2005, September). Evaluating the use of design patterns during program comprehension – experimental setting. In G. Antoniol & Guéhéneuc, Y-G. (Eds.), *Proceedings of the 1st ICSM workshop in Design Pattern Theory and Practice*. IEEE Computer Society Press. In the pre-proceedings.

Jørgensen, M., & Sjøberg, D. I. (2004, May). Generalization and theory-building in software engineering research. In S. Linkman (Ed.), *Proceedings of the 8th international conference on Empirical Assessment in Software Engineering* (pp. 29–36). IEEE Computer Society Press.

Kosslyn, S. M. (1973). Scanning visual images: Some structural implications. *Perception & Psychophysics, 14*, 90–94. doi:10.3758/BF03198621

Lachman, R., Lachman, J. L., & Butterfield, E. C. (1979, June). *Cognitive Psychology and Information Processing: An Introduction* (1ˢᵗ Edition). Lawrence Erlbaum Associates, Publishers.

Lévy, N., & Losavio, F. (1998, November). Analyzing and comparing architectural styles. In R. Monge & M. Visconti (Eds.), *Proceedings of the 19ᵗʰ international Conference of the Chilean Computer Science Society*. IEEE Computer Society Press. Lewis, C. (1982). *Using the "thinking-aloud" method in cognitive interface design*. Technical Report RC9265, IBM T.J. Watson Research Center.

Marr, D. (1978). Representing visual information. In Hanson, A. R., & Riseman, E. M. (Eds.), *Computer Vision Systems* (pp. 61–80). Academic Press.

Marr, D. (1982, June). *Vision: A Computational Investigation into the Human Representation and Processing of Visual Information* (1st Edition). Henry Holt & Company.

Mayrhauser, A. v. (1995, August). Program comprehension during software maintenance and evolution. *IEEE Computer*, *28*(8), 44–55. doi:10.1109/2.402076

Minsky, M. (1974). *A framework for representing knowledge. Technical Report Memo 306*. MIT AI Laboratory.

Murphy, G. C., Kersten, M., Robillard, M. P., & Čubraniś, D. (2005, July). The emergent structure of development tasks. In A. P. Black (Ed.), *Proceedings of the 19th European Conference on Object-Oriented Programming* (pp. 33–48). Springer-Verlag.

Navarro-Prieto, R. (1998). *The Role of Imagery in Program Comprehension: Visual Programming Languages*. PhD thesis, University of Granada, Newell, A. (1973). You can't play 20 questions with nature and win. In W. G. Chase (Ed.), *Visual Information Processing*. Academic Press.

Palmer, S. E. (1999, May). *Vision Science: Photons to Phenomenology* (1st Edition). The MIT Press.

Palmer, S. E., & Kimchi, R. (1987, July). The information processing approach to cognition. (pp. 37–77). Lawrence Erlbaum Associates Publishers.

Pennington, N. (1987, July). Stimulus structures and mental representations in expert comprehension of computer programs. *Journal of Cognitive Science*, *19*(3), 295–401.

Rich, C., & Waters, R. C. (1990, January). *The Programmer's Apprentice* (1st Edition). ACM Press Frontier Series and Addison-Wesley.

Rock, I., & Gutman, D. (1981). The effect of inattention on form perception. *Journal of Experimental Psychology. Human Perception and Performance*, *7*, 275–285. doi:10.1037/0096-1523.7.2.275

Rosch, E. H. (1973). On the internal structure of perceptual and semantic categories. In Moore, T. E. (Ed.), *Cognitive Development and the Acquisition of Language* (pp. 111–144). Academic Press.

Rugaber, S. (1995). Program comprehension. *Encyclopedia of Computer Science and Technology*, *35*(20), 341–368.

Serrano, M., Romero, R., Trujillo, J. C., & Piattini, M. (2005, July). The advisability of using packages in data warehouse design. In F. B. e Abreu, C. Calero, M. Lanza, G. Poels, & H. A. Sahraoui (Eds.), *Proceedings of the 9th workshop on Quantitative Approaches in Object-Oriented Software Engineering* (pp. 118–128). Montreal: CRIM.

Simon, F., Steinbrückner, F., & Lewerentz, C. (2001, March). Metrics based refactoring. In P. Sousa & J. Ebert (Eds.), *Proceedings of the 5th Conference on Software Maintenance and Reengineering*, (pp. 30–38). IEEE Computer Society Press.

Soloway, E. (1986, September). Learning to program = Learning to construct mechanisms and explanations. *Communications of the ACM*, *29*(9), 850–858. doi:10.1145/6592.6594

Soloway, E., Pinto, J., Letovsky, S., Littman, D., & Lampert, R. (1998, November). Designing documentation to compensate for delocalized plans. *Communications of the ACM*, *31*(11), 1259–1267. doi:10.1145/50087.50088

Spinellis, D. (2003, May). *Code Reading: The Open Source Perspective* (1st Edition). Addison Wesley.

Sutton, R. S., & Barto, A. G. (1998, March). *Reinforcement Learning: An Introduction* (1st Edition). MIT Press.

Triesman, A. (1985, August). Preattentive processing in vision. *Computer Vision Graphics and Image Processing, 31*(2), 156–177. doi:10.1016/S0734-189X(85)80004-9

Wendorff, P. (2001, March). Assessment of design patterns during software reengineering: Lessons learned from a large commercial project. In P. Sousa & J. Ebert (Eds.), *Proceedings of 5th Conference on Software Maintenance and Reengineering* (pp. 77–84). IEEE Computer Society Press.

ENDNOTES

[1] We use the term "theory" instead of the occasional term "model" (see for example von Mayrhauser's integrated *model* [1995]) to prevent confusion with program models.

[2] We use the term "item" instead of the more common term "object" to distinguish between *visual* objects and objects in object-oriented programming languages.

[3] We use "representations" to denote cognitive internal representations of a program model and "models" to denote program models, such as code source text, diagrams.

This work was previously published in International Journal of Software Science and Computational Intelligence, Volume 1, Issue 2, edited by Yingxu Wang, pp. 54-72, copyright 2009 by IGI Publishing (an imprint of IGI Global).

Chapter 21
Requirements Elicitation by Defect Elimination:
An Indian Logic Perspective

G. S. Mahalakshmi
Anna University, Chennai, India

T. V. Geetha
Anna University, Chennai, India

ABSTRACT

This paper aims to develop an Indian-logic based approach for automatic generation of software requirements from a domain-specific ontology. The structure of domain ontology is adapted from Indian logic. The interactive approach proposed in this paper parses the problem statement, and the section of domain ontology, which matches the problem statement, is identified. The software generates questions to stakeholders based on the identified concepts. The answer is analysed for presence of flaws or inconsistencies. Subsequent questions are recursively generated to repair the flaw in the previous answer. These answers are populated into requirements ontology, which contains problem specific information coupled with the interests of the stakeholder. The information gathered is stored in a database, which is later segregated into functional and non-functional requirements. These requirements are classified, validated and prioritized based on combined approach of AHP and stakeholders'defined priority. Conflict between requirements is resolved by the application of cosine correlation measure.

INTRODUCTION

Requirements engineering is a part of software engineering that deals with a structured set of activities needed to create and maintain a systems requirements document (Davis 1993; Kontonya and Sommerville, 1998; Loucipoulos and Kara-

kostas, 1995; Martin, 1988). Requirements are obtained, stored, identified, classified, prioritized, traced and validated throughout the requirements engineering process. SRS (Software requirements specification) is the outcome of this process. Requirements engineering must concern itself with an understanding of beliefs of stakeholders (*episte-*

DOI: 10.4018/978-1-4666-0261-8.ch021

mology), the question of what is observable in the world (*phenomenology*), and the question of what can be agreed on as objectively true (*ontology*) (Bashar and Steve, 2000). Software requirements specification (SRS) is a complete description of the behavior of the system to be developed. The requirements are collected from the stakeholders generally through traditional techniques (Bashar and Steve, 2000), i.e. by means of questionnaires and discussions, specific to the problem domain. The answers are gathered and the initial requirements are formulated. By further exploration of the requirements, more meaningful questions emerge for which the convincing answers are collected and organized into an SRS template. Requirements elicitation and documentation are complex activities. So, not only the requirements themselves but also the people involved and the means for managing the requirements will evolve during the project (Bjorn Decker et. al., 2007).

Automation of requirements engineering involves the following activities: development of domain-specific ontology, generation of questions from the domain ontology, generation of requirements template, filling the template by answers collected from the stakeholders, requirements database generation, requirements identification, classification and prioritization, and requirements validation.

The significance of automating requirements generation with respect to cognitive informatics shall be summarized as follows: The domain knowledge (say, Banking) of the requirements analyst is tapped into the domain ontology. This domain ontology is installed with the consulting entity which is a software agent. This entity interacts with the client entity situated at the client's place in the customer environment. The client entity is also a software agent which may or may not have a previous notion about the requirements of the software (say, ATM) which is to be developed under that particular domain. While the client entity and the consulting entity

interact with one another, their interaction appears as if two humans are interacting with one another. The reason is that, the consulting entity proposes various enquiries taken from the domain ontology, into the client entity, anticipating appropriate response. To generate a proper response, the client entity should analyse it's own knowledge base, which is more similar to a system analyst at the customer site, trying to reason and answer out all the questions proposed to him with respect to the scope of the project. The responses proposed by the client entity is analysed by the consulting entity for the presence of flaws. The flaws identified are cleared by proposing further questions based on the flaws. To do this, the consulting entity executes a reasoning and inference procedure over the arriving responses, which is more identical to a requirements engineer talking to a system analyst over telephone. Therefore, the fundamental objective of the proposed idea is to provide the knowledge replica of system analyst and requirements engineer as ontologies at two different software agents and to allow them interact, reason, inference and conclude at the essential requirements needed for the software to be developed.

In this paper, we propose an ontology-based domain-specific architecture for SRS generation, for the tourism domain. We also discuss the improvement in the questions when Indian logic ontology is used for SRS generation. The paper is organized as follows: Section 2 discusses about the ontology and tools available to develop the ontology. Section 3 summarises various related literatures about requirements elicitation. Section 4 describes the motivation behind the development of this architecture. Section 5 presents the role of ontology in knowledge sharing. Section 6 defines the methodology behind defective reasoning in requirements generation. Section 7 explains the architectural design of the SRS development. Section 8 discusses the issues and open challenges with respect to our system and as well, the requirements generation process. Section 9 details the necessary results of the implemented system of automatic SRS generation.

BACKGROUND

Automation of SRS development starts from the development of domain-specific ontology. Ontology defines a common vocabulary to share information in a given domain. It includes machine-interpretable definitions of basic concepts in the domain and relations among them. Ontology can also be described as a formal explicit description of concepts; properties of each concept describing various features and attributes of the concept and restrictions on slots. Ontology together with a set of individual instances of concepts constitutes the knowledge base for the specific domain. Ontology is used in this domain-specific architecture because of the following reasons: 1.It is a medium to share common understanding of the structure of information among people who develop domain specific applications; 2.To make explicit domain assumptions. Ontology development includes defining classes in the ontology, arranging the classes in a taxonomic (subclass–super class) hierarchy, defining slots, describing allowed values for these slots and filling in the slots with various values. Many tools are used in developing the ontology. Protégé, Ontolingua, Chimaera, GATE are quite a few among ontology development tools (Lee.Y and Zhao.W, 2006). For our work, we have considered Protégé-2000 (Horridge.M et. al., 2004) for building the tourism domain ontology. It supports consistency checking, instantiation checking, and equivalence checking and plug-in for ontology visualization. Apart from ontology building, our work also insists on the use of other natural language engineering components for parsing, named entity recognition etc. for which we use the language processing components of GATE (Cunningham.H et. al., 2006). The ontology support in GATE also includes a simple viewer that can be used to navigate ontology and quickly inspects the information relating to any of the objects defined in it – Classes, instances and their properties.

Several literatures exist in the stream of domain requirements analysis. The ontology-based approach to elicit and analyze domain requirements has already been attempted (Lee.Y and Zhao.W, 2006). The given problem domain is decomposed into several sub problem domains by using subjective decomposition method. Abstract stakeholders are consulted when decomposing the problem domain and the resulting domain primitive requirements are represented as ontology. This ontology-based approach can deepen domain knowledge and eliminate gap between domain users and requirements engineers. Identifying the correct requirements from the answers of the stakeholders is still challenging because the answers are in natural language. Therefore, careful natural language analysis need to be performed over the stakeholder responses to explore the inconsistencies in the proposed requirements. Gervasi and zowghi (Gervasi.V and Zowghi.D., 2005) discuss a reasoning technique to automatically discover inconsistencies in the requirements from multiple stakeholders, using theorem proving and model checking. In (Moon.M. et. al, 2005), there is a meta-model proposed for domain requirements to identify functional and non-functional requirements and the relationship between them.

RELATED WORK

Managing requirements elicitation effectively requires detecting and handling conflicts and misunderstandings across the requirements. These problems can arise from the stakeholders' varied backgrounds and objectives, which can generate contradicting requirements or conflicts. In wiki-based stakeholder participation in requirements engineering (Bjorn Decker et. al., 2007), ways and means to handle both expressed and implicit conflicts are attempted. Explicit conflicts are handled by tagging out the areas during discussions; implicit conflicts are handled by following "edit wars" (Bjorn Decker et. al., 2007). Such methods for handling conflicts in stakeholders' requirements were possible due to clear document structure for the specifications. However, in the proposed work, we attempt to collect the abstract requirements even before creating a structured requirements document, and therefore, handling inconsistencies can be done via methods involving NLP over the stakeholders' requirements.

Industrial experience shows the need for automated support in the requirements management area (H. Kaindl, et al.,2002). Any automated support should rely purely on the original form of requirements, or unrefined natural language. Approaches using natural language processing techniques to model, validate, and help understand requirements are available in today's environment (J. Natt och Dag and V. Gervasi, 2005). Usage of NLP based techniques for Requirements Elicitation has the disadvantage of handling ambiguous and imprecise requirements (Leonid Kof, 2004); i.e. we define writing rules for stakeholders to specify necessary requirements. Moreover, these rules are given to the stakeholders by means of question templates at the time of recursive question generations. These approaches present good solutions but can't effectively cope with the large amount of requirements (J. Natt och Dag, et al, 2002; S. Park, et al., 2000). In (Johan et. al., 2005a & 2005b), the authors have attempted a linguistic engineering approach to manage large-scale requirements, using ReqSimile, an open-source tool in Java. Here, a link between a customer wish and product requirement indicates that they refer to the same software functionality. After pre-processing the initial requirements, the system internally represents each requirement using a vector of terms, according to the vector-space model. From the vectors, the system can derive how many terms the requirements have in common.

In (Philip Barry and Kathryn Laskey, 1999), the application of uncertain reasoning to requirements engineering has been attempted by System Requirement Web (SRW) approach to developing requirements specification. The methodology examines the use of Bayesian networks to translate user requirements into system requirements. Domain knowledge is modeled as Bayesian Network fragments that are combined together to form a complete view of the domain specific system requirements. More similar work on ontology based domain requirements elicitation and analysis is discussed in (Lee et. al., 2006). However, all the above approaches are dealt from the requirements perspective and not from the stakeholders' perspective. In other words, the thought process of stakeholders while they are processing or stating a requirement was never captured or followed. The use of logic in identifying and analyzing inconsistency in requirements from multiple stakeholders has been found to be effective in a number of studies (Didar et. al., 2001).

One of the goals of requirements analysis is to develop a requirements specification document of high quality. There are several methods to achieve this goal and their supporting tools are going to be used in practice, e.g., goal oriented requirements analysis methods, scenario analysis, use case modeling techniques and so on. One of the most crucial problems to automate requirements elicitation analysis is that requirements documents are usually written in natural language, e.g. English or Japanese [Haruhiko Kaiya and Motoshi Saeki, 2006]

Although techniques for natural language processing (NLP) are being advanced nowadays; it is hard to handle such requirements documents sufficiently by computer. To overcome the problem, an ontology system to develop requirements document of high quality is suggested [Haruhiko Kaiya and Motoshi Saeki, 2006]. Ontology technologies are frequently applied to many application domains nowadays.

Ontology is used in this domain-specific architecture because of the following reasons:

1. It is a medium to share common understanding of the structure of information among people who develop domain specific applications;
2. To make explicit domain assumptions.

Ontology development includes defining classes in the ontology, arranging the classes in a taxonomic (subclass–super class) hierarchy, defining slots, describing allowed values for these slots and filling in the slots with various values.

In our proposed work, we model the domain ontology and provide the stakeholders with options as to how one can proceed. Based on the answers of the stakeholder, the requirements generation process will continue further and thereby, the requirements ontology, which consists of key terms and concepts pertaining to stakeholder requirements shall be generated.

K.Saravanan and G.S.Mahalakshmi [Saravanan K. and Mahalakshmi G.S.., 2007] suggest developing an automated SRS (software requirements specification) development framework from a domain-specific ontology. The entire methodology concentrates on extracting SRS related information from the stakeholders by automatically framing questions with respect to the existing domain ontology. Through well-defined stakeholders interface, the respective answers are collected and populated into requirements ontology, which is generally a combination of sections of domain ontology coupled with the interests of the stakeholder. Mapping the requirements ontology with that of the domain ontology automatically identifies the missing information in the answers of the stakeholder. The information gathered in this fashion is stored, classified, ranked and validated to generate the draft software requirement specification. This framework provides for a set of questions that can be put forth to the stakeholders in the form of a questionnaire. Lee and Zhao [Yuqin Lee and Wenyun Zhao, 2006] suggest a system where the problem domain is decomposed into several sub problem domains by using subjective decomposition method. The top-down refinement method is used to refine each sub problem domain into primitive requirements. Abstract stakeholders are used instead of real ones when decomposing problem domain and domain primitive requirements are represented by ontology. Not only domain commonality, variability and qualities are presented, but also reasoning logic is used to detect and handle incompleteness and inconsistency of domain requirements. Existing systems only deal with automating the requirement analysis whereas, this paper [Yuqin Lee and Wenyun Zhao, 2006] proposed the generation of a validated set of requirements from the seed problem statement with the help of the domain ontology.

The focus of our work is to make the best use of the Indian logic based ontology which describes the relationships between concepts better than western ontology which is more generic in form. The structure of ontology based on Indian Logic defines a common vocabulary to share information in a given domain. According to Indian logic, the ontology is described by a quadruple consisting of the core elements of ontology, i.e. concepts, relations, qualities and values. O={C, R, Q, V}. C (Concepts) and R (Relations) are two sets, which don't intersect with each other. Q stands for qualities which form the enrichment of concepts or relations. V is the set of values (Mahalakshmi et. al., 2007a, 2007b & 2007c). Indian logic based ontology is found to be very useful in domains which have various exceptions in different levels of the domain. Indian ontology based approach provides a mechanism for defining the peculiar and intrinsic qualities of each entity (concepts) in the required domain.

MOTIVATION

Requirement gathering is generally performed manually in the software development life cycle. Requirements have to be collected by questioning the stakeholders in the problem domain (Sommerville.I and Sawyer.P, 2004). The stakeholders need to address their expectations and other related issues through formal meetings and reviews, which may lead to more abstractions in interpreting the requirements besides investing precious time and effort in collecting such requirements. Skilled persons are strictly required to carry out certain activities such as requirements identification, classification and prioritization, traceability table generation and requirements validation. Hence, there arose a need to develop architecture for automated requirements development. Existing systems deal with either automating the requirement analysis or automating the SRS generation through common (western-logic) ontologies, whereas, this paper proposes the generation of SRS from the seed problem statement with the help of the Indian-logic based domain ontology. We assume tourism domain for SRS generation; i.e. Problem statement for developing applications in the tourism domain are being fed as input to the system and the draft SRS template for the problem statement is given at the output. The actual work involves analyzing the problem statement to identify the sub-domain in the domain ontology and to pose questions with the stakeholder by referring to concepts in the sub-domain (problem domain). This question generation is a recursive process, which tries to evolve the correct requirements of the stakeholder by tracing the concepts in the answers of the stakeholders. The answers are actually analyzed and mapped with the key concepts in the domain ontology and inconsistencies are identified. By recursively framing questions out of the missing information, if any, in the respective answers, the requirements of the problem domain shall be collected. The ontology based on Indian Logic was the actual motivating factor behind the proposed work.

ONTOLOGY IN KNOWLEDGE SHARING

World knowledge used for reasoning is mostly uncertain in nature. To overcome this uncertainty, a methodology based on formal specifications of shared resources, reusable components and standard services are needed. Specifications of shared vocabulary play an important role in such a methodology. Most knowledge-based systems operate and communicate using statements in a formal knowledge representation with the domain-oriented knowledge as an input when dealing with negotiation and information exchange. Ontology is a formal mechanism of representing the world knowledge, out of which effective and easy reasoning is possible while knowledge sharing (Gruber T.R, 1993a). A specification of a representational vocabulary for a shared domain of discourse with definitions of classes, relations, functions and other objects is called an ontology (Gruber T.R, 1993b).

Lee and Zhao (Lee.Y and Zhao.W, 2006) define ontology as follows: ontology is described by a quadruple consisting of the core elements of ontology, i.e. concepts, relations, hyperspace and theorems. O={C, R, H, T}. C (Concepts) and R (Relations) are two sets, which don't intersect with each other. H stands for hyperspace consisting of concepts and relations. T is the set of ontology theorems. R indicates relations between these concepts. The relation may be an equivalence relation, the part and whole relation, system contemporary relation of two concepts, pre-condition and post-condition relation of two concepts etc. Ontological commitments are agreements that define a clear boundary of how to *view* the ontology (R. Davis et. al., 1993; Jan G. and Christine P., 2001). This means that the specification format is independent of the internal representation such that the ontological commitments are defined only at the knowledge level. In the context of multiple entities participating in knowledge sharing, a common ontology can serve as a knowledge-level specification of the ontological commitments of a set of participating entities that are involved in discussion. A common ontology defines the vocabulary with which queries and assertions are exchanged among entities involved in knowledge-sharing (Gruber T.R, 1993b). Hence, knowledge sharing deals with ontological commitments, which decides how much knowledge, is being revealed to the outside world.

METHODOLOGY OF REQUIREMENTS GENERATION

Defect Elimination

Defect Elimination is the process of eliminating inconsistencies. In the proposed work, we try to map the keywords harvested from the parsed problem statement with that of the enriched concepts of the Indian-logic based domain ontology. The answers of stakeholders that violate the ontological commitments are considered as defects and questions are raised back to stakeholders to uncover those defects. There may be more than one defects present in the response of the stakeholder, in which case, the defect or flaw with the highest score is projected at the output. The stakeholder is expected to resolve the flaw in the following response. And this continues in a recursive fashion until there are no flaws in stakeholder responses (or software requirements). The score depends on the position of the concept or word within the domain ontology, or, in other words, scores are values that qualify the significance of the sub-items or concepts within that ontology. If a more significant property of the concept is found to be inconsistent, then it means, there lies

a serious mistake in interpreting the requirements for the system to be developed and therefore, the defect elimination for that particular concept is performed.

Indian Logic Based Defect Elimination

The main objective of defect elimination is to avoid redundancy and duplication in the system requirements and also to avoid any inconsistent requirements, which are of a serious threat in terms of bugs with respect to the software. But the methodology of defect elimination and its success lies on the nature and richness of the domain ontology under consideration. Obviously, there are no specific standards for domain ontologies and one can assume any domain ontology. Therefore, evaluating and standardizing the ontologies become the major criterion. To some extent, domain information recorded may be utilized in a more efficient manner in generating more appropriate responses highlighting the most serious inconsistency. As an attempt, in this paper, we try to propose a new structure of domain ontology, which actually follows from Indian logics. This kind of ontology will have more enriched concepts and relations, thereby supporting the complex and advanced structure or meaningful repository to store the domain related information. Considering this kind of Indian logic ontologies for automated SRS enables categorized storage and retrieval of information in a more meaningful manner when compared to general western logic ontologies applied to requirements generation.

According to Indian logic, here we assume, every natural language requirement is said to be composed of concepts and relations between concepts (Mahalakshmi and Geetha, 2008), which are modeled after the syllogistic elements of Nyaya (Oetke, 2003). Every concept consists of member qualities. Quality can be mandatory, optional or exceptional and are said to describe the concept more expressively (Mahalakshmi and Geetha, 2006a). Qualities have values associated with them. Relations explain the various means by which concept categories are related to one another. Relations fall into various types (Mahalakshmi and Geetha, 2008). Relations exist not only between concepts but also between concept and its' member qualities; between qualities and their values. The relations connecting two concepts may also have quality, with which they can be differentiated (Mahalakshmi and Geetha, 2008). It can be noted (from Figure 1) that the sample section of domain ontology based on Indian logic portrays the enriched concept set for *concept: Room*, with qualities *Type* and *Class*, whereas, the representation of similar domain knowledge in western ontology classifies every detail into different concepts with *'is-a'* relations. This shows that the Indian logic approach for classifying domain information is more meaningful when compared to the general ontological classification followed by western approaches.

The invariable concomitance nature of relation existence is a major factor in identifying holes of any natural language requirement and determining its inconsistency (Virupakshananda, 1994). Invariableness is the property, which demands the existence of relating concepts simultaneously at any instant. This invariable relation between concept entities form part of the common sense knowledge base that every knowledge sharing

entity is assumed to possess. Therefore, in a natural language requirement, when a concept's existence or the value is missing, provided one of the invariably relating concepts exists, the presence of invariableness implies existence of both the relating concepts simultaneously and hence such answers are implicitly learned by the system from the Indian-logic based domain ontology. Therefore, under the circumstances of presence of invariable relation between two concepts, the stakeholder is expected to provide information about only one of the concept because, the other is assumed by default, and any further answers that violate the invariableness is just ignored. Absence of invariableness projects the necessity of taking a response from the stakeholder. Thus, the knowledge represented in Indian logic based ontology provides every benefit of analysing the natural language requirements.

The process of elicitation has three stages: problem analysis, acquisition of domain ontology and knowledge, and elicitation of requirements from stakeholders. The manipulation of requirements shall be performed with the help of domain ontologies, by discovering the interests of the stakeholders. The architecture of requirements elicitation involves all the above scenarios, which is discussed in the following section. The algorithm of requirements elicitation by Defect Elimination is given in Figure 2.

Figure 1. Tourism domain: (a) a sample section of Indian logic ontology (b) a sample section of Western ontology

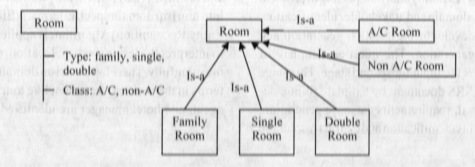

Figure 2. Algorithm of requirements elicitation by Defect Elimination

- Format the problem statement
- Tag each word (Part-of-Speech)
- Parse the tagged text
- Extract concepts
- Look for related concepts in the domain dictionary
- Identify concept clusters
- Look for potential member relations within concept clusters
- Generate questions based on member concepts of the clusters
- Capture the answers from the stakeholders. Repeat step 1

ARCHITECTURE OF ONTOLOGY BASED REQUIREMENTS ELICITATION

Roughly, the system has the following components: stakeholders Interface, tool support for ontology, requirement database (Figure.3); the system is interfaced with each stakeholder to gather requirements. The system performs parsing, named identity recognition and generates questions from the ontology by interfacing with GATE tool. Requirement database stores the requirements from the gathered information. The output of the system is the SRS document, which contains functional and non-functional requirements categorized according to the perspective of the stakeholder. The detailed architectural design diagram (Figure.4) explains the functionality of the automated SRS development, which involves two stages (Mahalakshmi and Saravanan, 2007b). First stage involves the generation of question template by feasibility analysis; parsing of problem statement, domain and stakeholder identification, ontology development, question generation and template generation. The question template of first stage is the input for second stage. This stage generates SRS document by template filling, defect removal, requirements database generation, requirements identification and conflict resolution,

requirements classification and prioritization, traceability table generation, SRS draft generation and requirements validation.

Feasibility Analysis

From the given problem statement, the system collects suggestions from various domain experts about the feasibility of the development of application by interacting through domain experts interface. The budget to develop the system, schedule to complete the development of system, effort needed to develop the application etc. is analyzed through domain expert interface. After the feasibility study, the problem statement is fed into the parser to identify the domain related terms.

Parsing of Problem Statement

System parses the problem statement with the help of GATE tool (Cunningham.H et. al., 2006) and identifies each word in the problem statement into tourism domain specific terms. NER (Named Entity Recognition) Algorithm is applied further, to interpret the terms (person, location, etc) more meaningfully. Therefore, tourism domain specific terms in the problem statement like tourist, travel agent, and hotel manager are identified.

Figure 3. General Diagram for Automated SRS development

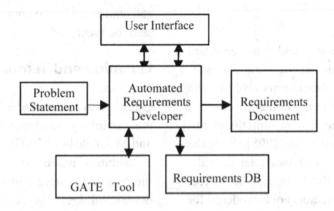

Figure 4. Architecture of requirements elicitation by defect elimination

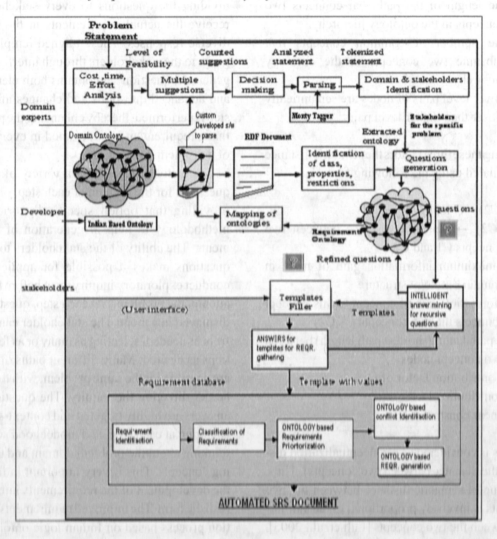

Sub-Domain and Stakeholder Identification

The sub-domain and the stakeholders are identified to develop the ontology on the particular sub-domain. The domain-related terms given by the parser is used identify the sub-domain. Semantic distance value is calculated for the initially identified set of domains [Fuli et. al., 2005].Using the semantic distance further classes related to the basic set of concepts in the domain are identified.

In our system three factors are considered for calculating semantic distance value

- the length of the path that connects two concepts in the ontology hierarchy.
- the number of common concepts that subsume two concepts in the ontology hierarchy.
- lower level pairs of nodes are semantically closer than higher level pairs

Using these three factors the semantic distance is calculated using the following formula:

$\mu(C1, C2) = C \log[(l)(I_{max} - I_c)^n]$

$\mu(C1, C2) \rightarrow$ Semantic distance between two concepts C1 and C2

$I_{max} \rightarrow$ maximum information gain of node in domain ontology structure

$I_c \rightarrow$ information gain of concept C(this concept connects the two concepts C1,C2)

$l \rightarrow$ the path length(shortest path length) between two concept nodes

$m \rightarrow$ Contribution factor of l

$n \rightarrow$ Contribution factor of $(I_{max} - I_c)$

$C \rightarrow$ linear constant

This is considered as a conceptualization distance (the distance between two concepts). Thus, the value of semantic distance between the two concepts is inversely proportional to the similarity between the two concepts [Fuli et. al., 2005].

From the identified concept set, the corresponding stakeholders who are involved in the sub domains shall be identified.

Question and Template Generation

Questions are generated in reference with the domain ontology developed in Protégé (Saravanan and Mahalakshmi, 2007). A question generation algorithm is applied to generate questions from the enriched concepts in the Indian logic based domain ontology. These questions are submitted to stakeholders in order to collect respective answers. Question templates are meaningfully aligned by dividing the questions to every stakeholder to receive the actual requirements in the form of diverse responses. These aligned templates are given to the stakeholders through interfaces. The generated question set contains both elementary and advanced questions and changes after each step is performed, thereby enhancing the potential that a requirement is understood in every aspect of a problem.

Interactively answering a variety of detailed questions for the domain at each step, or at least providing that option specifically orients the methodology to help in generation of requirements. The ability of the stakeholders to answer questions makes it possible for application to conduct exploratory inquiry even before they can attempt the problems. At each step, questions are displayed in a menu.The stakeholder can choose from as needed, selecting as many or as few questions as desired. Many different paths of inquiry are possible for the same problem, with the stakeholder directing the inquiry. The questions and answers are highly targeted and context-specific, changing at each step, and model good scientific thinking about the problem domain and underlying concepts. This is very important in fostering the development of the requirements into a more realistic form. The improved requirements generation process based on Indian logic ontologies is currently tailored as a computerized method for generating a question and answer dialogue for intelligent requirements generation, comprising creating a question-generating rule class specific for a desired type of question (optionally from a base class), generating at least one question from said question-generating rule class provided an applicability condition is satisfied, and displaying said question in a user menu, wherein the user is permitted to direct an inquiry as to which question should be asked.

Answer Mining

The answers or responses of every stakeholder are analyzed and relevant information is extracted to fill the slots of the question templates. Such filled templates are populated in parallel into the requirements ontology or business ontology, which actually describes the business needs of the stakeholder in developing an application in the tourism domain. The business ontology is incrementally developed as and when the responses to the questions match the slots of the domain template. The entire requirements ontology and the responses are later stored in a requirements database.

Inconsistency Elimination

The answers given by the stakeholders usually have inconsistencies or missing information i.e., the answers might not contain the exact information what the system needs to gather as requirements. In our work, the answers of the stakeholders are parsed and the key terms are extracted. These key terms are mapped with the concepts and relations of the domain ontology from which the questions have aroused. This mapping identifies the inconsistencies present in the requirements (or answers), which is similar to finding flaws in the stated propositions in a knowledge-sharing scenario. With the intention of collecting the exact requirement to the question proposed previously, further questions (or counter-questions) are gener-

ated (Mahalakshmi and Geetha, 2007a). To achieve this, every missing or inconsistent information of every requirement is initially grouped into an "inconsistency set"; every meaningful answer to the question deletes that particular member from the inconsistency set. In this fashion, further questions are continuously generated until the inconsistency set becomes empty, thereby, assisting the stakeholders to identify the exact software requirements.

Requirements Database Generation

System creates requirements database to store the functional and non-functional requirements of the specific application from the information given by the stakeholders. Constraints on the requirements are also collected.

Requirements Identification and Classification

Each requirement in the requirements database has to be uniquely identified. Requirement ID is given to each requirement and the type of the requirement also identified. Some requirements have conflicts because of the various answers from a group of stakeholders. One requirement may contradict another. These requirements are identified and resolved by interacting with the stakeholders. Based on their functionality, the requirements have to be classified.

An algorithm is developed to classify the requirements into separate clusters. Then for each cluster, the requirements are ranked based on the need and function of the particular requirement. Functional requirements are given highest priority and ranked first. Then Non-functional requirements have to be ranked.

Classification involves [Huang et. al., 2006]:

1. Removal of stop words
2. Porter's Stemming Algorithm-applied to set of requirements

Functional or Non-functional based on

$$\mathrm{Pr}_Q(R) = \frac{\sum_{t \in R \cap I_Q} \mathrm{Pr}_Q(t)}{\sum_{t \in I_Q} \mathrm{Pr}_Q(t)}$$

The numerator is computed as the sum of the term weights of all type Q indicator terms that are contained in R, and the denominator is the sum of the term weights for all type Q indicator terms. The probabilistic classifier for a given type Q will assign higher score PrQ(R) to a non-functional requirement, that contains several strong indicator terms for Q.

Requirements Prioritization

The requirements are prioritized based on combined approach of AHP and stakeholders' defined priority. Analytical Hierarchy Process (AHP [K.A. Khan, 2006] is based on relative assessment to prioritize software requirements. Considering n requirements, $n \times (n-1)/2$ comparisons are to be made at each hierarchy level.) Requirements are grouped together in different groups, which the stakeholders can relate to. This is also known as numerical assignment or grouping. Three groups are used namely critical, standard and optional (High, Medium, Low) depending on the requirement. These factors cumulatively constitute the weight of the requirement.

Requirements Conflict Resolution

The answers given by the stakeholders usually have inconsistencies or missing information i.e., the answers might not contain the exact information what the system needs to gather as requirements. In our work, the answers of the stakeholders are parsed and the key terms are extracted. With the intention of collecting the exact requirement to the question proposed previously, every meaningful answer to the question is analyzed and put forth to the stakeholder for verification. Conflict resolution is based on preprocessing, vector-space matrix extract, and application of the cosine correlation measure. The transformed requirements

Figure 5. User interface to get problem statement

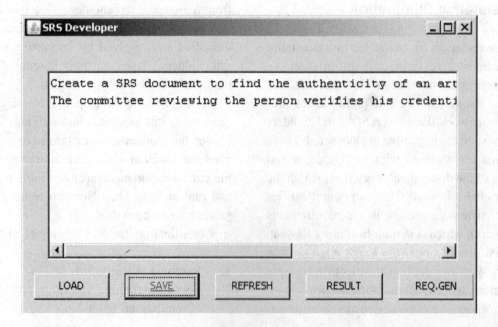

Figure 6. Semantic distance table for identification of classes

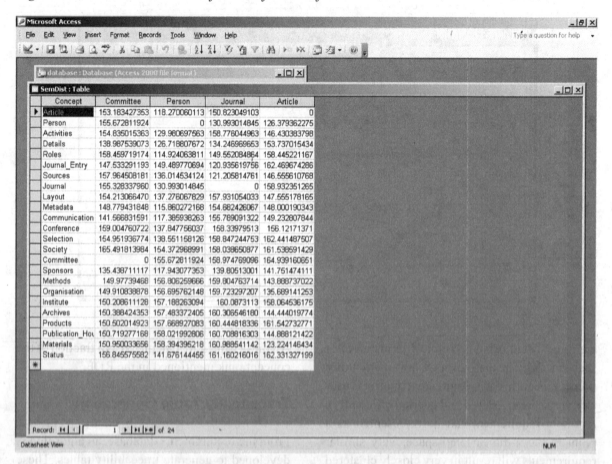

Figure 7. Sub domain and stakeholder identification

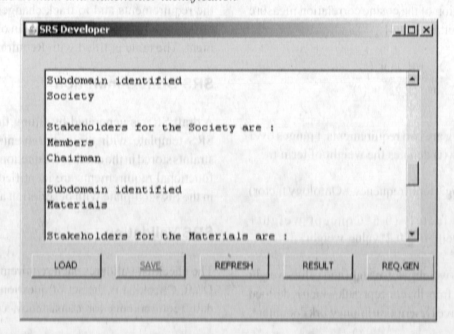

Figure 8. Questionnaire

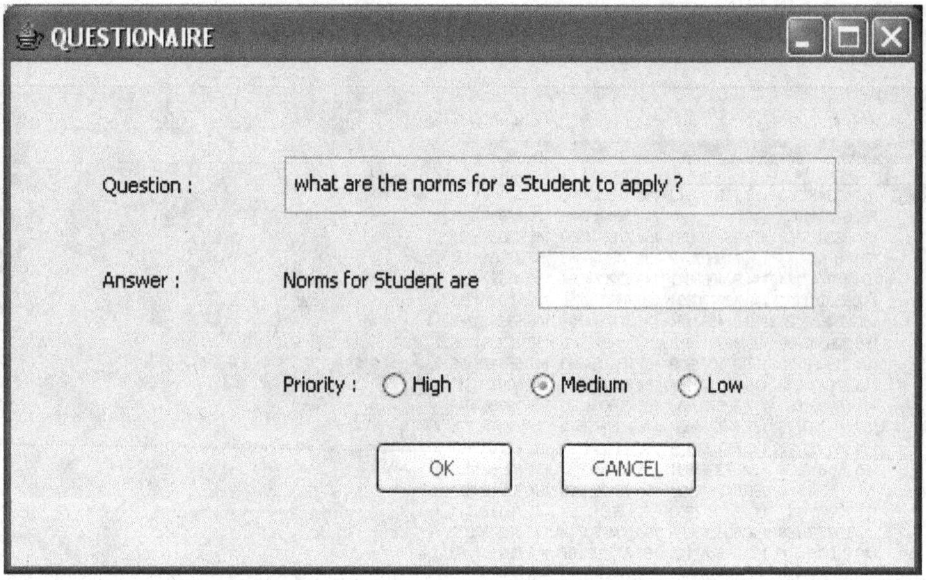

are represented using a vector of terms - vector space model. The matrix shows how many times a term appears in each requirement (matrix is usually very sparse - stored and queried efficiently). A whole requirement can be represented as a point in the n-dimensional space. Very similar requirements will result in very closely clustered points in this space.

Application of the cosine correlation measure [J. Nattoch et. al., 2004]

$$.\sigma(f,g) = \frac{\sum_t w_f(t) \cdot w_g(t)}{\sum_t w_f(t)^2 \sum_t w_g(t)^2}.$$

where f and g are two requirements, t ranges over terms, and w(t) denotes the weight of term t.

W(t) = 1 + log2(termfrequency + Ontology factor)

Ontology factor = {0.5*Concept-weight + 0.25*slot-weight + $\sum$0.2*value-weight}

Concept-weight, slot-weight and value-weight are obtained from the concept rank which is defined in the Resource Description Framework document.

All these values are calculated as a fraction of the concept rank mentioned in the RDF.

Traceability Table Generation

From the requirements database, an algorithm is developed to generate traceability tables. These tables are used to identify the relationship between the requirements and to track changes in the requirements because of the change in one requirement. The table is filled with Requirement ID.

SRS Draft Generation

A draft SRS is generated by filling the standard SRS template with the requirements and constraints stored in the database. Functional and non-functional requirements are identified and filled in the SRS template with description about them.

SRS Validation

The checklist validates each requirement in SRS Draft. Checklist is the set of questions that validate requirements for consistency, correctness, unambiguous, traceability, etc. Requirements in the template are validated against the checklist and the conflicts are resolved by stakeholder interaction. Then the system output the SRS document which has the identified, classified, ranked, traceable, validated requirements to develop the application in the corresponding domain.

ISSUES AND LIMITATIONS

In this paper, it is assumed that each stakeholder possesses the knowledge about the domain and question template filling. Each stakeholder has to be aware of the requirements engineering process in order to interact with the system effectively. Domain experts need to have the knowledge of feasibility analysis of the application. The problem statement has to be given in English language only. Since the problem statement is given in text format, the system needs to be interfaced with a language-processing tool (Cunningham.H et. al., 2006) in order to develop the ontology and parsing the problem statement. Stakeholders vary from application to application. Stakeholders interface are varied depends upon the application. Requirements database have to support object orientation since the information stored are class, object and their properties. Algorithm has to be developed for automatic generation of questions from ontology. More requirements prioritization techniques (Patrik et. al., 2006) shall be followed to generate meaningful clusters of requirements.

Figure 9. Generated set of requirements from the ontology with classification as functional or non – functional

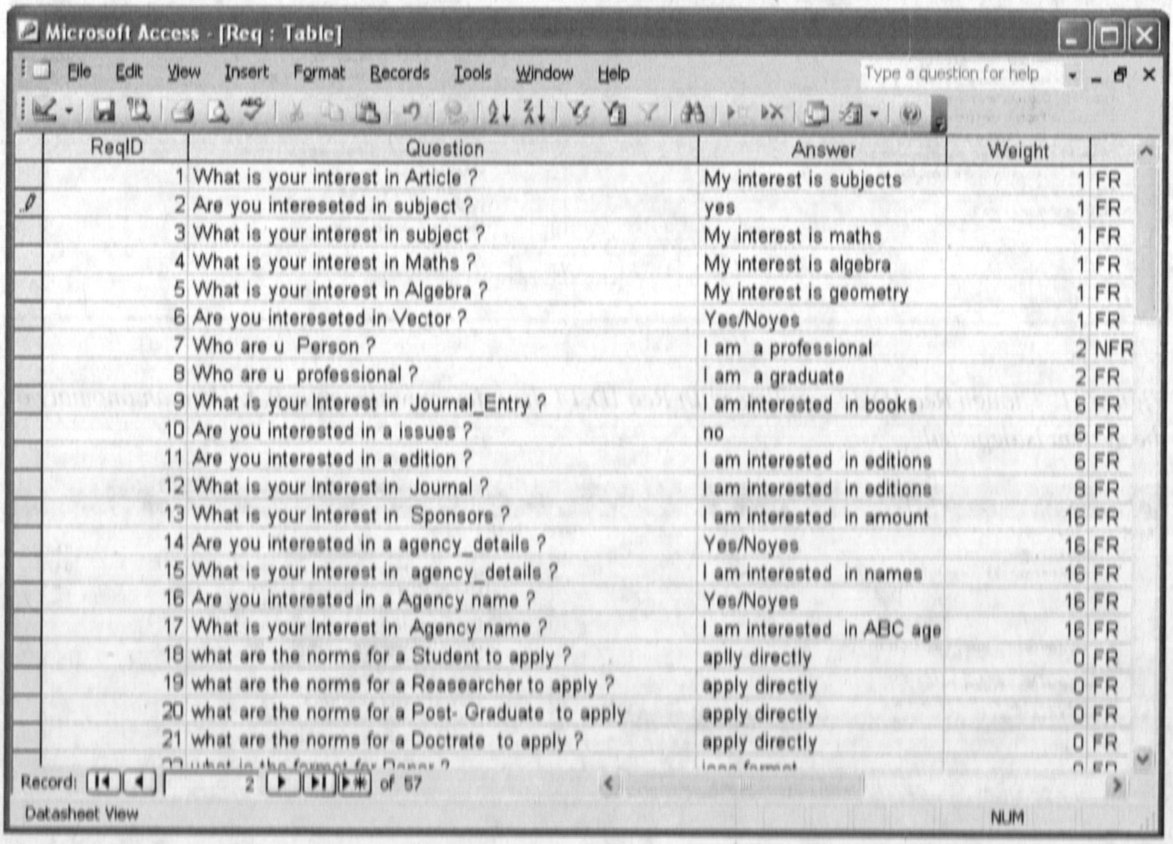

ReqID	Question	Answer	Weight	
1	What is your interest in Article ?	My interest is subjects	1	FR
2	Are you intereseted in subject ?	yes	1	FR
3	What is your interest in subject ?	My interest is maths	1	FR
4	What is your interest in Maths ?	My interest is algebra	1	FR
5	What is your interest in Algebra ?	My interest is geometry	1	FR
6	Are you intereseted in Vector ?	Yes/Noyes	1	FR
7	Who are u Person ?	I am a professional	2	NFR
8	Who are u professional ?	I am a graduate	2	FR
9	What is your Interest in Journal_Entry ?	I am interested in books	6	FR
10	Are you interested in a issues ?	no	6	FR
11	Are you interested in a edition ?	I am interested in editions	6	FR
12	What is your Interest in Journal ?	I am interested in editions	8	FR
13	What is your Interest in Sponsors ?	I am interested in amount	16	FR
14	Are you interested in a agency_details ?	Yes/Noyes	16	FR
15	What is your Interest in agency_details ?	I am interested in names	16	FR
16	Are you interested in a Agency name ?	Yes/Noyes	16	FR
17	What is your Interest in Agency name ?	I am interested in ABC age	16	FR
18	what are the norms for a Student to apply ?	aplly directly	0	FR
19	what are the norms for a Reasearcher to apply ?	apply directly	0	FR
20	what are the norms for a Post- Graduate to apply	apply directly	0	FR
21	what are the norms for a Doctrate to apply ?	apply directly	0	FR

RESULTS

To experiment the ontology-based architecture to develop SRS document, the journal publishing domain ontology was developed in protégé tool. Various sub-domains were identified and respective classes, properties, restrictions, instances for the classes were specified. Object and Data type properties for sub-domain classes have been specified. User interface to get the problem statement from the user is created.

In Figure 5, problem statement for journal sub domain is given as input to the system through user interface. The system parses the problem statement and identifies the sub domain, stakeholder belonging to the specific sub domain. An initial preliminary set of sub domains are identified. This set is then used to identify the larger set which is depicted in Figure6.

Further classes are identified through semantic distance conceptualization. Here concepts committee, article and person are the preliminary set. The extra concept identified through this methodology is materials (materials written by person and submitted to committee) and society. The stakeholders and domain information are depicted in Figure 7. The snapshot shows society and materials. Along with it Person (author), committee and article are also identified.

A series of questions are asked (Figure 8) and further questions are generated based on the answers. The answers to these questions help in determining the core requirements [Saravanan K. and Mahalakshmi G.S., 2007]. The stakeholder

Figure 10. Conflict resolution is performed after populating the database

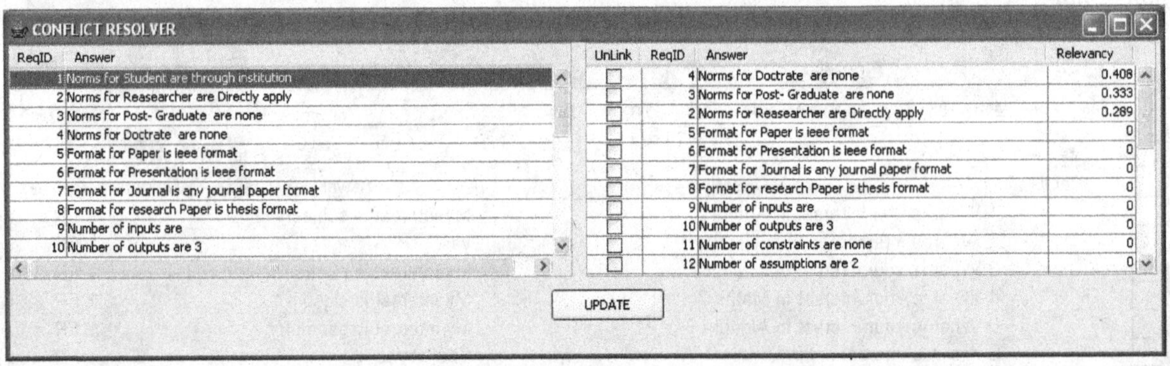

Figure 11. Though Req ID.32 conflicts with Req ID.14 the relevancy shown is 0.4. Here an anomaly of the system is depicted

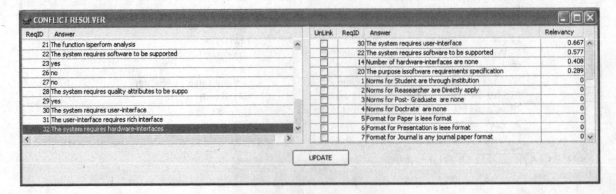

assigns a priority to each requirement. These set of classified requirements are populated in the database (Figure 9).

Here, upon selection of a particular requirement, the lists of similar requirements are retrieved with a relevancy value. Here the requirement chosen is Norms and various related norms are listed. The conflicting requirements are eliminated (Figure 10 & 11) and the unambiguous requirements are updated into the requirements database.

CONCLUSION

This paper discussed the architecture for developing a framework to automate the requirements engineering activities, generation of questions from the ontology and resolving the conflict in requirements by following Indian logic based defect elimination methodology. GATE tool is used to parse the problem statement, develop domain-specific ontology and to implement named-entity recognition. Feasibility analysis of the problem is done through domain expert interface. The domain ontology is developed using protégé tool to clearly define the domain-specific terms and their relationships. Java parser parses the developed ontology. The classes, properties are extracted from the generated owl file. Problem specific questions are generated from the extracted ontology. Further, these questions have to be assembled in prescribed templates to gather stakeholder requirements. Requirements database has to be constructed and identification, conflict resolution, classification, validation of requirements have to be performed. SRS document for the specific problem statement will be generated after these activities. However, generations of modeling diagrams such as use-case modeling, data flow diagram for the application to be developed have not been explored.

REFERENCES

Bashar Nuseibeh and Steve Easterbrook. (2000), Requirements engineering: a roadmap, In Proc. of the Conference on The Future of Software Engineering, Ireland, p.35-46.

Patrik Berander, Kashif Ahmed Khan and Laura Lehtola (2006), Towards a research framework on requirements prioritization, SERPS 06.

Cleland-Huang, R. S., & Zou, X. (2006) "The Detection and Classification of Non-Functional Requirements with Application to Early Aspects", 14th IEEE International Requirements Engineering Conference.

Cunningham.H, Maynard.D, Bontcheva.K, Tablan.V, Ursu.C, Dimitrov.M, Dowman.M, Aswani.N and Roberts.I, (2006) Developing Language Processing Components with GATE Version 3 (a User Guide), from University of Sheffield.

Davis, A. M. (1993). *Software requirements: Objects, Functions, and States*. New Jersey: Prentice Hall.

Decker, B., Ras, E., Rech, J., Jaubert, P., & Rieth, M. (2007), Wiki-Based Stakeholder Participation in Requirements Engineering, IEEE Software, Volume 24, Issue 2 pp. 28-35, ISSN:0740-7459, IEEE Computer Society Press.

Gervasi, V., & Zowghi, D. (2005). Reasoning about inconsistencies in natural Language requirements. *ACM Transactions on Software Engineering and Methodology, 14*(3), 277–330. doi:10.1145/1072997.1072999

Gruber, T. R. (1993)., Towards principles for the design of ontologies used for knowledge-sharing, in Guarino & Poli (Eds), Formal Ontology in Conceptual Analysis and Knowledge Representation, Kluwer Publishers, August 1993.

Haruhiko Kaiya and Motoshi Saeki. "Using Domain Ontology as Domain Knowledge for Requirements Elicitation", 14th IEEE International Requirements Engineering Conference (RE'06).

Horridge, M., Knublauch, H., Rector, A., Stevens, R., & Wroe, C. (2004), A Practical Guide To Building OWL Ontologies Using The Protégé-OWL Plug-in and CO-ODE Tools Edition 1.0, from University of Manchester.

J. Natt och Dag and V. Gervasi (2005a), Managing Large Repositories of Natural Language Requirements, Engineering and Managing Software Requirements, Springer-Verlag.

Jan Goossenaerts and Christine Pelletier. (2001), Ontological commitments for participative simulation, a chapter from Conceptual Modeling for New Information Systems, Lecture Notes in Computer Science, Springer Berlin / Heidelberg ISSN: 0302-9743, vol. 2465, pp. 127–140, Japan.

Johan Natt och Dag, Björn Regnell, Pär Carlshamre, Michael Andersson and Joachim Karlsson (2002), A Feasibility Study of Automated Natural Language Requirements Analysis in Market-Driven Development, Requirements Eng., vol. 7, no. 1, pp. 20–33.

Johan Natt och Dag, Vincenzo Gervasi, Sjaak Brinkkemper and Björn Regnell (2005b), A linguistic engineering approach to large-scale requirements management, IEEE Software - IEEE Software, Vol. 22, Issue 1, pp. 32-39.

Kaindl, Hermann, Brinkkemper, Sjaak, Bubenko, Janis A. Jr, Farbey, Barbara, & Greenspan, Sol J., C. L. Heitmeyer, Julio Cesar Sampaio do Prado Leite, Nancy R. Mead, J. Mylopoulos and Jawed I. A. Siddi. (2002). Requirements Engineering and Technology Transfer: Obstacles and Incentives. *Requirements Engineering*, 7(3), 113–223. doi:10.1007/s007660200008

Kashif Ahmed Khan. (2006) "A Systematic Review of Software Requirements Prioritization", Master's Thesis, Software Engineering, no: MSE-2006-18, pp:41-46.

Kontonya, G., & Sommerville, I. (1998). *Requirements Engineering: Processes and Techniques*. New York: John Wiley and Sons.

Lee, Y., & Zhao, W. (2006), An Ontology-based Approach for Domain Requirements Elicitation and Analysis, IEEE Proceedings of the First International Multi-Symposiums on Computer and Computational Sciences.

Leonid Kof. (2004), Natural Language Procesing for Requirements Engineering: Applicability to Large Requirements Documents. In Alessandra Russo, Artur Garcez, and Tim Menzies, editors, Automated Software Engineering, Proceedings of the Workshops, Linz, Austria.

Mahalakshmi, G. S., & Geetha, T. V. (2007b) Navya-Nyaya Approach to Defect Exploration in Argument Gaming for Knowledge Sharing, In proc.s of International Conference On Logic, Navya-Nyaya & Applications - A Homage To Bimal Krishna Matilal (ICLNNA '07), Jadavpur University, Calcutta, India, pp. 171-182.

Mahalakshmi, G. S., & Geetha, T. V. (2008). Reasoning and Evolution of consistent ontologies using NORM, IJAI: Special Issue on theory and applications of soft computing. *Indian Society for Development and Environment Research*, 2(No. S09), 77–94.

Mahalakshmi, G. S., & Saravanan, K. (2007a), Design And Implementation Of An Ontology Based Approach To Automate Requirements Generation, International Conf. on Soft Computing techniques in engineering, SOFTECH – 07, Avinashilingam University for Women, Coimbatore, India, pp.301-307.

Martin, C. (1988). *User-centered Requirements Analysis*. Englewook Cliffs, NJ: Prentice Hall.

Moon, M., Yeom, K., & Chae, H. S. (2005). An approach to developing domain requirements as a core asset based on commonality and variability analysis in a product line. *IEEE Transactions on Software Engineering, 31*(7), 551–569. doi:10.1109/TSE.2005.76

Nattoch, J., Dag, V. G., & Regnell, B". (2004), "Linking Customer Wishes to Product Requirements through Linguistic Engineering", Proceedings of the 12th International Requirements Engineering Conference.

C. Oetke (2003), Indian Logic and Indian Syllogism, Indo-Iranian Journal, vol. 46, no. 1, pp. 53-69(17), Kluwer Academic Publishers.

Park, S., Kim, H., Ko, Y., & Seo, J. (2000). Implementation of an Efficient Requirements-Analysis Supporting System Using Similarity Measure Techniques. *Information and Software Technology, 42*(6), 429–438. doi:10.1016/S0950-5849(99)00102-0

Philip Barry and Kathryn Laskey. (1999), An Application of Uncertain Reasoning to Requirements Engineering, Proceedings of the 15th Annual Conference on Uncertainty in Artificial Intelligence (UAI-99), Morgan Kaufmann, pp. 41-48.

Saravanan, K., & Mahalakshmi, G. S. (2007), Design And Implementation Of An Ontology Based Approach To Automate Requirements Generation, International Conference on Soft Computing techniques in engineering, SOFTECH – 07, Avinashilingam University for Women, Coimbatore, India.

Sommerville, I., & Sawyer, P. (2004). *Requirements Engineering: A Good Practice Guide* (6th ed.). Pearson Education.

Virupakshananda, S. (1994). *Tarka Samgraha*. Madras: Sri Ramakrishna Math.

Yuqin Lee and Wenyun Zhao. (2006), "An Ontology-based Approach for Domain Requirements Elicitation and Analysis", In IEEE Proc. of the First International Multi-Symposiums on Computer and Computational Sciences.

Zowghi, D., Gervasi, V., & McRae, A. (2001), Using default reasoning to discover inconsistencies in natural language requirements, Proceedings of the Eighth Asia-Pacific on Software Engineering Conference, p.133.

This work was previously published in International Journal of Software Science and Computational Intelligence, Volume 1, Issue 2, edited by Yingxu Wang, pp. 73-90, copyright 2009 by IGI Publishing (an imprint of IGI Global).

Chapter 22
Measurement of Cognitive Functional Sizes of Software

Sanjay Misra
Atilim University, Turkey

ABSTRACT

One of the major issues in software engineering is the measurement. Since traditional measurement theory has problem in defining empirical observations on software entities in terms of their measured quantities, Morasca tried to solve this problem by proposing Weak Measurement theory. Further, in calculating complexity of software, the emphasis is mostly given to the computational complexity, algorithm complexity, functional complexity, which basically estimates the time, efforts, computability and efficiency. On the other hand, understandability and compressibility of the software which involves the human interaction are neglected in existing complexity measures. Recently, cognitive complexity (CC) to calculate the architectural and operational complexity of software was proposed to fill this gap. In this paper, we evaluated CC against the principle of weak measurement theory. We find that, the approach for measuring CC is more realistic and practical in comparison to existing approaches and satisfies most of the parameters required from measurement theory.

INTRODUCTION

The key element of any engineering process is measurement. Engineers use measures to better understand and assess the quality of engineered products or systems that they built. However, absolute measures are uncommon in software engineering. Instead, software engineers attempt

DOI: 10.4018/978-1-4666-0261-8.ch022

to derive a set of indirect measures that provide an indication of quality of some representation of software. Software engineers plan 'how' an information system should be developed in order to achieve its quality objectives. The quality objectives may be listed as performance, reliability, availability and maintainability and are closely related to software complexity. Numbers of researchers have proposed variety of software complexity measures (Halstead, 1997), (Kushwaha and

Misra, 2006), (Woodward and Hennel, 1979) and (Wang, 2003, 2009). Out of the numerous proposed measures, selecting a particular complexity measure is again a problem, as every measure has its own advantages and disadvantages. There is an ongoing effort to find such a comprehensive complexity measure, which addresses most of the parameters of software. Further, complexity measurement in computer science is basically related to computational complexities which are computing the time and space complexity. On the other hand in the software engineering, the emphasis is on the functional complexity (Wang, 2003, 2007a, 2009). But in both of case, these measures do not relate the complexity due to the actual human efforts required to comprehend the software. Actually, the one facet of the complexity is the understandability of the software/ code. Understandability of the code relates to ease of comprehension. It is a cognitive process. Although, in past some efforts have been done in calculating the cognitive complexity (Rauterberg 1996, Klemola 2003) of a software, but neither they sufficient nor they cover other aspects of the complexity, like internal architecture, operational complexity, etc. (Wang, 2007a).

The cognitive complexity measures are based on cognitive informatics (Wang, 2004), which in turn help in comprehending the software characteristics. Wang and Shao (Wang and Shao, 2003) have proposed cognitive functional size (CFS) measure to calculate the cognitive complexity of a software. The measure defines the cognitive weights for the Basic Control Structures (BCS). Further, they extended and modified the CFS and presented new weight values based on empirical observations (Wang, 2005, 2009).

A newly proposed complexity measure is acceptable, only when its usefulness has been proved by a validation process. It must be validated and evaluated both formally and practically. The purpose of the validation is also to prove the usefulness of attribute, which is measured by the proposed metric. Elements of measurement theory

has been proposed and extensively discussed in literature (Briand et al., 1996), (Basili, 2007), (Fenton, 1994; 1991; 1998), (Weyuker, 1998), (Zuse, 1991; 1992) as a means to evaluate the software complexity measures. However, for formal approach of measurement theory, there is a problem: How can we recognize and describe the attribute in the empirical observation domain in order to relate its values to the proposed metric? (Misra and Kilic, 2006). Naturally, the representational measurement theory does not care about the practical difficulty of making empirical observations on the attribute and their identification. These are the underlying reasons for proposal of weak measurement theory by (Morasca, 2003). He has argued that the representation condition is very demanding for state of art of software engineering measurement. Therefore, he proposed for weakening the representation condition and developed the concept of weak measurement theory. We will discuss on it in detail in section 3.

In the present work, we applied measurement theory/weak measurement theory concepts on cognitive complexity measure. This theory for metric evaluation is more practical and useful and encompasses all the factors which are important for the evaluation of any proposed measure. It is worth mentioned that cognitive functional size has already evaluated (Misra 2004) by Weyuker's properties (Weyuker, 1998). However, satisfying Weyuker's properties is necessary, but not sufficient condition for a good complexity measure (Cherniavsky, 1991). These properties are also under several criticisms (Fenton, 1994) and (Zuse, 1991) and still the topic of research (Gursaran, 2001), (Zhang, 2002), (Sharma 2006), (Misra 2006). Further, cognitive functional size measure has been extended and improved by taking empirical observations; it is required to check its validity through measurement theory perspective. As consequences, we validate the cognitive complexity against the principles of measurement theory.

A brief introduction of cognitive complexity measure is given in section 2. We validated cognitive complexity from the perspective of weak measurement theory in section 3. We investigated the type of scale through extensive structure in section 4. The practical evaluation of cognitive complexity measure is given in section 5. The conclusion drawn is in section 6.

COGNITIVE COMPLEXITY

Cognitive complexities based on cognitive informatics are in developing phase. Actually, the credit goes to Wang, who started work on measuring the cognitive complexity of software. Earlier, cognitive (software) complexity was proposed by Rauterberg.(Rauterberg 1996) and Klemola and Rilling (Klemola, 2003). Rauterberg(Rauterberg 1996) calculates the cognitive complexity by using behaviour complexity (BC), system complexity (SC) and task complexity (TC). However, his approach was not suitable for measuring functional complexity. Klemola and Rilling (Klemola, 2003) have proposed a complexity measure based on category learning. It defines identifiers as programmer's defined labels. Based on this, identifier density (ID) can be calculated as the number of identifiers divided by line of code (LOC). Again this approach was not suitable for functional size measure. Wang et al. (Wang and Shao, 2002) proposed cognitive functional size (CFS) to measure the cognitive complexity. The measure defines the cognitive weights for the Basic Control Structures (BCS). The basic control structures sequence, branch and iteration are building blocks of software (Wang and Shao, 2002),. Four advanced BCS's have been added as recursion, parallel, function call and interrupt (Wang and Shao, 2003). The cognitive weight of software is defined as the extent of difficulty or relative time and effort for comprehending given software modeled by a number of BCS's. These cognitive weights for BCS's measure the complexity of logical structure of the software. There are two different architectures for calculating W_{bcs} i.e. the cognitive weight of BCS. Either all the BCS's are in a linear layout or some BCS's are embedded in others. For the former case, sum the weights of all n BCS's is taken and for the latter, cognitive weights of inner BCS's are multiplied with the weights of external BCS's. Further, Based on the experimental results (Wang, 2005), Wang has modified the cognitive weights and correspondingly, cognitive weights of the ten fundamental BCS's are statistically calibrated and summarized in (Wang, 2005). Further, in the natural extension of his work, he improved and modified the definition of cognitive functional size. The new definition of the *cognitive complexity Cc(S)* (Wang 2006, 2007a, 2007b, 2009) of a software system S is a product of the operational complexity *Cop(S)* and the architectural complexity *Ca(S)*. Where, The *operational complexity* of a software system S, *Cop(S)*, is determined by the sum of the cognitive weights of its *n* linear blocks composed by individual BCS's, where each block may consist of *q* layers of embedded BCS's, and within each of the layer there are *m* linear BCS's. This approach for calculating operational complexity is similar to calculate the functional complexity of software (Wang 2002). Further, the *architectural complexity* of a software system S, *Ca(S)*, is determined by the number of data objects at system and component levels. It counts the number of data objects in a given Component Logical Model (CLM) (Wang, 2002), which is equivalent to the number of global variables or components (number of local variables).

This cognitive complexity metric is demonstrated and compared with similar measures in (Wang,2009). Therefore, we are not demonstrating this metric in this paper. In the next section, we are trying to evaluate the cognitive complexity against the principle of measurement theory/Weak Measurement theory.

WEAK MEASUREMENT THEORY AND COGNITIVE COMPLEXITY

Measurement is simply the process of converting qualities to quantities. Such conversion process requires a formal description of the systems worked on. The components of the qualified system are (1) entities whose attributes are wanted to be quantified; (2) Empirical binary relations showing the intuitive knowledge about the attributes and (3) binary operations describing the production of new entities from the existing ones. Entities can either be physical objects or abstract artifacts that can be characterized or defined by a set of basic characteristics known as attribute (Wang, 2003). In the following paragraphs we describe the basic definition of measurement theory and check the validity of cognitive complexity against it. We have also shown the problem related with the empirical observations in empirical relation system.

Definition 1: *(Empirical Relational System-ERS) (Zuse, 1991). For a given attribute, an Empirical Relational System is an ordered tuple*

$ERS = <E, R_1,...,R_n, o_1,..., o_m>$ where
E: the set of entities,
$R_1, ..., R_n$ denote n empirical relations such that
   each R_i has an *arity* n_i, and $R_i \subseteq E^{n_i}$
$o_1, ..., o_m$ denote m empirical binary operations on
   the entities that produces new entities from
   the existing ones, so o_j: $E \times E \rightarrow E$ and the
   operations are represented with an infix
   notation, for example, $e_k = e_i \, o_j \, e_l$.

The components of the quantification system are the values representing the decided quantities; the binary relations showing the dependencies among them and the binary operations describing the production of new values from the existing ones. In cognitive complexity, the entities are the program bodies. The only empirical relation

is assumed to be *more_or_equal_complex* and the only empirical binary operation is the *concatenation* of program bodies. However, from practical point of view there is a major problem for the identification and possibly the existence of such empirical observations. We can explain it by a solid example. Assume that we are given a program body P and we obtain a new program body Q by simply duplicating P. Also, assume that we are given another program body R for which there is no direct clear relation between P and R. One may easily establish the relation *more_or_equal_complex* between P and Q however it may not easy to make such an empirical observation between P and R. This is due to that we may not reach a consensus on how to order P and R based on their complexity.

Definition 2: *(Numerical Relational System-NRS) A Numerical Relational System is an ordered tuple*

$NRS = <V, S_1,...,S_n, p_1,..., p_m>$ where
V: the set of values,
$S_1, ..., S_n$ denote n relations such that the arity of
   S_i is equal to the arity of R_i, and $S_i \subseteq V^{n_i}$
$p_1, ..., p_m$ denote m *numerical* binary operations
   on the values that produces new values from
   the existing ones, so p_j: $V \times V \rightarrow V$ and the
   operations are represented with an infix
   notation, for example, $v_k = v_i \, p_j \, v_l$.

For cognitive complexity, V is the set of positive integers, the binary relation is assumed to be $\geq$ and the numerical binary operation is the addition (i.e. +) of two positive integers.

Definition 3: *Measure m is a mapping of entities to the values i.e. m: $E \rightarrow V$. The measure for cognitive complexity is defined in (Wang 2009) (equation 26). Note that the measure by itself does not provide any mapping between empirical and numerical knowledge.*

Definition 4: *A measure must satisfy the following two conditions known as* **Representation Condition**

$$\forall i \in 1.n \forall <e_1,..., e_{n_i}> \in (<e_1,..., e_{n_i}> \in R_i \Leftrightarrow < m(e_1),..., m(e_{n_i})> \in S_i) \qquad (Part1)$$

$$\forall j \in 1.m \forall <e_1, e_2> \in E \times E\ (m(e_1 o_j e_2) = m(e_1)\ p_j\ m(e_2) \qquad (Part2)$$

The first part of the Representation Condition says that for a given empirically observed relation between entities, there must exist a numerical relation between corresponding measured values and vice versa. In other words, any empirical observation should be measurable and any measurement result should be empirically observable. The second part says a measured value of an entity which is obtained by the application of an empirical binary operation on two entities should be equal to the value obtained by corresponding numerical binary operation executed over individually measured values of entities. In other words complexity of the whole should be definable in terms of complexities of its parts.

For cognitive Complexity, the representation condition requires that (1) if for any two program body e_1 and e_2 are in *more_or_equal_complex* relation (i.e.$<e_1, e_2> \in$ *more_or_equal_complex*) then the measured complexity value of entity e_1 should be greater than the measured complexity value of entity e_2 (i.e. $m(e_1) > m(e_2)$) and vice versa. When we reconsider the program bodies P and Q where Q is the double of P, we can say that since cognitive complexity is based on the counting of input, output, local variable and cognitive weights of basic control structures, they also become double or vice versa. Consequently, for part (1) of the condition we can say that the empirically observed *more_or_equal_complex* rela-

tion between two program bodies leads to a numerical binary relation > among those entities or vice versa. However, part (1) is only satisfied if there is such clear empirically observable relations between program bodies for example P and Q. On the other hand, in case of P and R since we do not have any clear empirical relation between them, the requirement $\forall i \in 1.n \forall <e_1,..., e_{n_i}> \in (<m(e_1),..., m(e_{n_i})> \in S \Leftrightarrow <e_1,..., e_{n_i}> \in R_i)$ implied by part (1) may not be required anymore. The formal approach describing such relaxation is proposed by (Morasca, 2003). He has argued that the original definition of Representation Condition is very demanding for state of art of software engineering measurement. Therefore, he suggested weakening (only) the first part of the condition two way link $\Leftrightarrow$, to a one way link, $\Rightarrow$ as follows:

Definition 5: *Weak Representation Condition is defined by (Morasca, 2003).*

$$\forall i \in 1.n \forall <e_1,..., e_{n_i}> \in (<e_1,..., e_{n_i}> \in R_i \Rightarrow < m(e_1),..., m(e_{n_i})> \in S_i) \qquad (Part1)$$

$$\forall j \in 1.m \forall <e_1, e_2> \in E \times E\ (m(e_1 o_j e_2) = m(e_1)\ p_j\ m(e_2) \qquad (Part2)$$

When we consider the above example again, although we can calculate the Cognitive complexity values for P and R, this does not imply the existence of corresponding empirical relations between P and R. On the other hand, for a given *more_or_equal_complex* relation between P and Q that can be empirically observable one can always find corresponding metric values satisfying the *Weak Representation Condition*.

For part two of the Representation Condition, we can say that the complexity value of a program body which is obtained by concatenation (i.e. the empirical binary operation) of e_1 and e_2 is equal to the sum (i.e. the numerical binary operation) of their calculated complexity values. Therefore, cognitive complexity satisfies the second part of the Representation Condition. Finally, we can say that Cognitive complexity satisfies the Weak Representation condition.

Showing the cognitive complexity satisfies the Weak Representation Condition, we can investigate the type of the scale for our proposal. In order to be able to decide on the scale type we need to define the *Weak Scale* and *Weak Meaningful Statement* concepts (Morasca, 2003).

***Definition 6:** A weak scale is a triple <ERS, NRS, m>, where ERS is an Empirical Relational System, NRS is a Numerical Relational System, and m is a measure that satisfies the Weak Representation Condition.*

***Definition 7:** A statement is called Weak Meaningful Statement if its truth value does not change if a weak scale is replaced by another weak scale. Formally, if S(m) is based on measure m and S(m') is the same statement obtained by replacing m with m', we have S(m) ⇔ S(m').*

Based on the notion of weak meaningful statement we can talk about four different types of weak scales:

- **Weak nominal scale:** The meaningful statements of this class of scales are of the form $m(e_1) = m(e_2)$ for at least one pair of entities e_1 and e_2. If for one scale, $m(e_1) = m(e_2)$ is satisfied for a pair of entities e_1 and e_2 then we must have $m'(e_1) = m'(e_2)$ for all other scales m'.

- **Weak ordinal scale:** <ERS, NRS, m> is a weak ordinal scale if $m(e_1) = m(e_2)$ is a weak meaningful statement for at least one pair of entities e_1, e_2. It is not required that $m(e_1) = m(e_2)$ or $m(e_1) = m(e_2)$ be weak

meaningful statements for all pairs of entities e_1, e_2.

- **Weak interval scale:** <ERS, NRS, m> is a weak interval scale if $(m(e_1)-m(e_2))/(m(e_3)-m(e_4)) = k$ is a weak meaningful statement for at least one four-tuple of entities e_1, e_2, e_3, e_4 i.e., k is a constant value of all scales. It is not required that this statement is meaningful for all four-tuples of entities.

- **Weak ratio scale:** <ERS, NRS, m> is a weak ratio scale if $(m(e_1)-m(e_2)) = k$ is a weak meaningful statement for at least one pair of entities e_1, e_2 i.e., k is a constant value of for all scales defined by the corresponding meaningful statement. Reconsider the two program bodies P and Q above as entities e_1 and e_2 where we calculate k as 2. Then, the statement $m(Q)/m(P) = 2$ is also a Weak Meaningful Statement for LOC or Control Complexity metrics.

Therefore, we can informally say that cognitive complexity is defined on *weak ratio scale*.

A formal way of proving a given scale is a weak ratio scale or not, is done by investigating whether the scale's Empirical Relation System is a Weak Extensive Structure or not (Briand, et.al., 1996).

***Definition 8:** A hierarchy is a pair <E, R> where $R \subseteq E \times E$ is a binary relation on E such that it does not contain any cycle, i.e. any sequence of pairs {<e_1, e_2>, <e_2, e_3>, ..., <e_i, e_{i+1}>, ..., <e_n, e_{n+1}>} of any length n with $\forall i \in 1.n$ $R(e_i, e_{i+1})$ such that $e_1 = e_{n+1}$.*

WEAK EXTENSIVE STRUCTURE

***Definition 9:** Let E be a set, R be a binary relation on E, and o is a total function o: $E \times E \to E$. The relational system (E, R, o) is a Weak Extensive Structure if and only if the following axioms holds (Morasca, 2003).*

A1: $\forall e_1, e_2, e_3 \in Eq(e_1 \circ (e_2 \circ e_3)), ((e_1 \circ e_2) \circ e_3)$ where Eq is an equivalence relation defined as $Eq(e_1, e_2) \Leftrightarrow \neg R(e_1, e_2) \wedge \neg R(e_2, e_1)$ (axiom of *weak associativity*).

A2: $< E, R >$ is a hierarchy (axiom of *hierarchy*)

A3: $\forall e_1, e_2, e_3 \in E(R(e_1, e_2)) \Rightarrow \neg R(e_2 \circ e_3, e_1 \circ e_3)$ (axiom of *monotonicity*)

A4: $\forall e_1, e_2, e_3, e_4 \in E(R(e_1, e_2)) \Rightarrow \exists n \in N \neg R(ne_2 \circ e_4, ne_1 \circ e_3)$ where ne is recursively defined for any $e \in E$ as $1e = e$ and $\forall n > 1$ $ne = (n-1)e \circ e$ (*Archimedean Axiom*).

For cognitive complexity, the empirical relation R has the meaning "more or equal complex than" and the binary operation o between two objects is the "concatenation" of two program bodies. Now, we will investigate the validity of the above axioms for our empirical relation system (*ERS=<E, more_or_equal_complex, concatenation>*) defined for Cognitive complexity:

A1: When we consider the example program bodies P, Q and R, since we do not have any knowledge of relation between R and the other two, we cannot say that P concatenated with (Q concatenated with R) is *more_or_equal_complex* than (P concatenated with Q) concatenated with R. Therefore, the concatenation operator of cognitive complexity satisfies the *weak associativity* property.

A2: For any program bodies X being *more_or_equal_complex* Y and Y being *more_or_equal_complex* Z, the Z can never be *more_or_equal_complex than X*. Therefore, we can say that *<E, more_or_equal_complex>* is a *hierarchy*.

A3: When we consider the example program a body P, Q and R, having Q is *more_or_equal_complex than* P we cannot say that the same relation between Q concatenated with R and P concatenated with R because we have no knowledge of empirical relation of R and

the others. Then, *monotonicity* property is also satisfied.

A4: If entity e_1 is *more_or_equal_complex* than e_2 then for any e_3 e_4, we cannot establish a new *more_or_equal_complex* relation by any number of concatenations; say n times, of e_1 and e_2 to themselves followed by concatenation of e_3 and e_4 with them, respectively. This is because we may not have any knowledge of relation between the results of ne_2 concatenated with e_4 and ne_1 concatenated with e_3 due to unknown relation between each of e_3 and e_4 with other two. Consequently, Archimedian Axiom is also satisfied.

As a result, the ERS description of the proposed cognitive complexity is a Weak Extensive Structure. Based on the theorems "Existence of an Additive Scale for a Weak Extensive Structures" and "Weak Additive Scale and Weak Ratio Scales" given by in (Morasca, 2003). We can say that cognitive complexity is defined on W*eak Ratio Scale*. Note that among the scales defined above, the ratio scale is the highest in level. Therefore, it may be more powerful than the other scales reflect.

PRACTICAL EVALUATION OF COGNITIVE COMPLEXITY

Practical success of any proposed metric depends on the establishment of (1) its validation, (2) understandability by its users and (3) tight link between the metric and the attribute that it is intended to measure. In the previous section, we showed that the cognitive complexity is a valid measure of complexity based on evaluation from measurement theory perspective. An alternative approach to metric validation which is more practical than the formal approach is to follow the IEEE Standard 1061 as a guide. However, for both formal and practical approaches there is a problem: How can we recognize and describe the attribute in the empirical observation domain in order to relate its values to the proposed metric? Naturally, the representational measurement theory does not care about the practical difficulty of making empirical observations on the attribute and their identification. Note that, the *existence* of scale is still one of the major problems of the field. On the other hand, as pointed out by (Kaner Bond, 2004) the IEEE 1061 standard tries to solve the quantification problem by suggesting the use of *direct metric* which does not depend on a measure of any other attribute and assumed to be valid by itself. Other metrics are validated in terms of direct metrics. In (Kaner, Bond), the existence of direct metrics has been questioned through the user-dependent, subjective and not being single but multidimensional function characteristics of them. The authors have shown that the characteristic of being multidimensional function contradicts with the direct metrics' required property of being independent from the measurement of any other attribute(s).

When we look Cognitive complexity from the perspective given in (Kaner, 2004), it is an indirect metric. It is a function of three components, which contributes to the measurement of software complexity. It should be clear that cognitive complexity is neither complete nor unique measure of complexity. In the following paragraphs we evaluate cognitive complexity against the framework, which is based on the following points:

- **The purpose of the measure**: Two main purposes of cognitive complexity are to contribute to the judgment about product quality and to provide a self-assessment and improvement for the developer.
- **Scope of usage of the measure**: The cognitive complexity can be categorized as a technical metric being applicable before and after coding. Consequently, its scope of use is the software development group in design, development and testing phase.

- **Identified Attribute to measure**: The attributes measured by cognitive complexity are the quality of the product and the developer. More complex product makes it less understandable and consequently less maintainable for future development effort. In addition, the developer who can satisfy the user requirements through the usage of less number of branching and looping primitives is assumed more skillful.
- **Natural scale of the attribute**: The existence of natural scale for the attributes (but not the metrics) requires the development of a common, non-subjective view about them. We have no knowledge about the natural scale of attributes.
- **Natural variability of the attribute**: If an attribute involves human performance then we can talk about its variability. The reason behind it; although one can develop a sound approach to handle such attribute it may not be complete because of the existence of many other factors that affects the attribute's variability. The difficulty of making sound and complete empirical observations about the product results in no knowledge about the variability of the attribute.
- **Definition of metric**: The metric has been defined formally in Section 4 (Wang 2009).
- **Measuring instrument to perform the measurement**: It uses the instrument of *counting* by either human or by machine. The item to be counted is cognitive weights of different BCS's, inputs and outputs. For automated counting purpose, one can easily develop a token generator and use the string matching algorithms.
- **Natural scale for the metric**: For the natural scale for cognitive complexity, we have to go through measurement theory. When we analyze our measure, we find that, it is on the weak ratio scale.

- **The Natural variability of readings from the instrument**: Since the reading from our counting instrument is not subjective and does not require any interpretation, we can say that no variability (i.e. measurement error) on readings from the instrument can be expected. Note that, in case of automated counting, we assume that there is no bug in the devised algorithm.

- **Relationship between the attribute to the metric value**: There is a direct relation between the quality of the product and the cognitive complexity. If the cognitive complexity value increases, it is clear that the product quality will decrease since it implies inefficient use of memory and time. Note that cognitive complexity is not the unique indicator of product quality and the same argument is true for the relation between the cognitive complexity value and the developer quality attribute.

- **Natural and foreseeable side effects of using the instrument**: Once we automate the cognitive complexity calculation, it will not require considerable additional manpower workload of the company. The only cost involved is automation.

CONCLUSION

Cognitive complexity is a complexity measure based on cognitive aspects software development. Measurement process is known to be critical in both science and engineering. In order to make the software discipline more and more mature we can use the tools provided by Measurement Theory (MT). As a consequence, a proposal of new software metric can be validated through the application of MT. basics. We showed that cognitive complexity satisfies most of the parameters required by the weak measurement theory and it is also found that the proposed measure is on weak ratio scale.

In the light of the experiences we propose the future work to include the following:

1. Further researches on weak measurement theory are required. Weak measurement theory is only a partial solution to problem related to definition of a measure based on measurement theory.

2. Further extension in the cognitive complexity is possible.

3. To the best of our knowledge, complexity measures based on cognitive aspects are not tested by the practitioners. This is also a task for future work.

4. RTPA, Informatics laws, cognitive complexity may become the mile stone in software engineering because all these proposals are the efforts to solve the basic problem of software engineering (i.e. measurement). Future studies and discussion in these topics are required.

5. A tool to calculate cognitive complexity should be developed.

ACKNOWLEDGMENT

I am highly thankful to Professor K. Ibrahim Akman and Dr. Hurevren Kilic of Computer engineering department, Atilim University, for useful discussions.

REFERENCES

Basili, V. (2007). The Role of Controlled Experiments in Software Engineering Research," in *Empirical Software Engineering Issues*, LNCS 4336, pp. 33-37.

Briand, L. C., Morasca, S., & Basili, V. R. (1996). Property based Software Engineering Measurement. *IEEE Transactions on Software Engineering, 22*(1), 68–86. doi:10.1109/32.481535

Cherniavsky, J. C., & Smith, C. H. (1991). On Weyuker's Axioms for Software Complexity Measures. *IEEE Transactions on Software Engineering, 17*, 636–638. doi:10.1109/32.87287

Fenton, N. E. (1991). *Software Metrics: A Rigorous Approach*. London, UK: Chapman & Hill.

Fenton, N. E. (1994). Software Measurement: A Necessary Scientific Basis. *IEEE Transactions on Software Engineering, SE-20*(3), 199–206. doi:10.1109/32.268921

Fenton, N.E. (1998). IEEE Computer Society Standard for Software Quality Metrics Methodology. Revision IEEE Standard 1061-1998.

Gursaran, Roy,G. (2001).On the Applicability of Weyuker Property Nine to Object Oriented Structural Inheritance Complexity Metrics. *IEEE Transactions on Software Engineering, 27*, 4, (2001).pp.361-364.

Halstead, M. H. (1997). *Elements of Software Science*. New York: Elsevier North-Holland.

Kaner, C. (2004).Software Engineering Metrics: What do they Measure and how do we know? *Proc. Int. Soft. Metrics Symp*. Metrics 2004.

Klemola, T., & Rilling, J. (2003). A Cognitive complexity metric based on Category learning, *Proceedings of IEEE* (ICCI'03), pp.103-108

Kushwaha, D. S., & Misra, A. K. (2006). Robustness Analysis of Cognitive Information Complexity Measure using Weyuker's Properties. *ACM SIGSOFT Software Engineering Notes, 31*, 1–6. doi:10.1145/1108768.1108775

Misra, S. (2006). Modified Weyuker's Properties, *Proceedings of 5th IEEE International Conference on Cognitive Informatics*, pp.242-247.

Misra S. and Hurevren Kilic, (2006). Measurement theory and Validation Criteria for Software Complexity measure. *ACM SIGSOFT Software Engineering Notes*. 31,6., pp.1-3.

Misra, S., & Misra, A. K. (2004). Evaluating Cognitive Complexity Measure with Weyuker Properties. *Proceedings of IEEE (ICCI'04)*, pp.103-108.

Morasca, S. (2003). Foundations of a Weak Measurement-Theoretic Approach to Software Measurement. *Lecture Notes in Computer Science, 2621*, 200–215. doi:10.1007/3-540-36578-8_15

Rauterberg, M. (1996). How to Measure Cognitive Complexity in Human-Computer Interaction: www.idemployee.id.tue.nl/g.w.m.rauterberg/publications/EMSCR96paper.pdf

Sharma, N., Joshi, P., & Joshi, R. K. (2006). Applicability of Weyuker's Property 9 to Object Oriented Metrics. *IEEE Transactions on Software Engineering, 32*(3), 209–211. doi:10.1109/TSE.2006.21

Wang, Y. (2002), The Real-Time Process Algebra (RTPA), *Annals of Software Engineering: An International Journal*, 14, USA, Oct., pp. 235-274.

Wang, Y. (2003). The Measurement Theory for Software Engineering. *Proceedings of Canadian Conference on Electrical and Computer Engineering CCECE 2003*, pp. 1321-1324.

Wang, Y. (2004). On Cognitive Informatics: Foundation of Software Engineering. *Proceeding of the 3rd IEEE International Conference on Cognitive Informatics* (ICCI'04). IEEE CS Press. pp.22-31.

Wang, Y. (2005), Keynote: Psychological Experiments on the Cognitive Complexities of Fundamental Control Structures of Software Systems, *Proc. 4th IEEE International Conference on Cognitive Informatics* (ICCI'05), IEEE CS Press, Irvin, California, USA, August, pp. 4-5.

Wang, Y. (2006). On the Informatics Laws and Deductive Semantics of Software. *IEEE Transactions on Systems, Man and Cybernetics. Part C, Applications and Reviews, 36*(2), 161–171. doi:10.1109/TSMCC.2006.871138

Wang, Y. (2007a), *Software Engineering Foundations: A Transdisciplinary and Rigorous Perspective,* CRC Book Series in Software Engineering, Vol. II, Auerbach Publications, NY, USA, July.

Wang, Y. (2007b). The Theoretical Framework of Cognitive Informatics. *International Journal of Cognitive Informatics and Natural Intelligence, 1*(1), 1–27. doi:10.4018/jcini.2007010101

Wang, Y. (2009). On the Cognitive Complexity of Software and its Quantification and Formal Measurement. *International Journal of Software Science and Computational Intelligence, 1*(2), 31–53. doi:10.4018/jssci.2009040103

Wang, Y., & Shao, J. (2003). A New Measure of Software Complexity Based on Cognitive Weight. *Canadian Journal of Electrical and Computer Engineering,* 69–74.

Weyuker, E. J. (1988). Evaluating Software Complexity Measure. *IEEE Transactions on Software Engineering, 14,* 1357–1365. doi:10.1109/32.6178

Woodward, M. R., & Hennel, M. A. (1979). David. A Measure of Control Flow Complexity in Program Text. *IEEE Transactions on Software Engineering, 1,* 45–50. doi:10.1109/TSE.1979.226497

Zhang, L., Xie, D.(2002): Comments on 'On the Applicability of Weyuker Property Nine to Object Oriented Structural Inheritance Complexity Metrics. *IEEE Transactions on Software Engineering,* vol. 28, 5, (2002) 526-527.

Zuse, H., (1991). Software Complexity Measures and Methods. de Gruyter.

Zuse, H. (1992). Properties of Software Measures. *Software Quality Journal, 1,* 225–260. doi:10.1007/BF01885772

This work was previously published in International Journal of Software Science and Computational Intelligence, Volume 1, Issue 2, edited by Yingxu Wang, pp. 91-100, copyright 2009 by IGI Publishing (an imprint of IGI Global).

Chapter 23

Motivational Gratification:
An Integrated Work Motivation Model with Information System Design Perspective

Sugumar Mariappanadar
Australian Catholic University, Australia

ABSTRACT

Researchers in the field of information system (IS) endorse the view that there is always a discrepancy between the expressions of client's automation requirements and IS designers understanding of such requirement because of difference in the field of expertise. In this article an attempt is taken to develop a motivational gratification model (MGM) from the cognitive informatics perspective for the automation of employee motivation measurement, instead of developing a motivation theory from a management perspective and expecting the IS designers to develop a system based on the understanding of the theory that is alien to his/her field of expertise. Motivational Gratification is an integrated work motivation model which theoretically explains how employees self-regulate their effort intensity for 'production' or 'reduction' of motivational force towards future high performance, and it is developed using taxonomies of system approach from psychology and management. The practical implications of MGM in management and IS analysis and design are discussed.

INTRODUCTION

Computer applications in the field of applied psychology and management have automated many psychological applications like online psychometric testing, performance management systems, and human resource information systems. Researchers in the field of information systems have developed various techniques such as the Cognitive informatics (Wang, 2003), Object-oriented Cognitive Task Analysis and Design (OOCTAD) model (Wei & Salvendy, 2006); Cognitive Task Analysis (CTA) and Design (CTD) (Kirwan & Ainsworth 1992; Cooke 1994, Seamster et al 1997, Schraagen et al 2000); to understand cognitive activities based on human information-

DOI: 10.4018/978-1-4666-0261-8.ch023

processing theories. However, there has been very little done by researchers in the field of psychology and management to develop complex and abstract human information processing theories so that software designers and programmers are able to convert cognitive activities, such as motivation, into computer program based assessment. Hence, in this article an attempt is made to develop a new motivational gratification (MG) theory to extend the cognitive informatics theory (Wang, 2007) to understand the mechanisms of cognitive processes in employee motivation, and to develop next generation software for automating measurement of employee motivation.

The Cognitive Informatics Perspective

Wang (2003) has defined cognitive informatics "is a transdiciplinary expansion of cognitive and information sciences that into internal information processing mechanisms and processes of the natural intelligence – human brains and minds" (p.159). The cognitive informatics focuses on the nature of information processing in the brain such as information storage, categorization, retrieval, generation, representation and expression, and it effectively lends itself to cognitive foundations of software engineering. Hence, the cognitive informatics perspective provides a strong theoretical basis to develop the proposed motivational gratification model (MGM) to explain how employees self-regulate their efforts for high performance in work context, and how effectively the complex MG measure can be automated.

The Semiotic Approach

In the automation of employee motivation, it is important to be able to instruct the computer in precise, mechanical detail what exactly to do. Stamper, Liu, Hafkamp and Ades (2000) have explained how 'organizational semiotic' approach can be used in organisational analysis and infor-

mation systems design. The two basic concepts of organisational semiotic analysis in information systems design are the sign and the norm. Stamper *et al* (2000) define "a sign is anything that stands for something else for some community and a norm is a generalized disposition to the world shared by members of a community" (p. 15). Stamper et al have suggested that norms and signs are inter-related and they help to understand organisational behaviour in terms of signs and how, through norms, they are used in the automation of behaviour that is regular or capable of being anticipated (p. 16). The concept of norm lends itself to empirical study as well as develop schematic model of the fuzzy categories for the automation of behavioural processes. Hence, in this article an attempt is made to develop an integrated model of employee motivation with schema of norms, so that the computer can be used as an instrument for executing certain kinds of norms where it is more efficient to measure employee motivation. The existing motivation theories, which have been developed in the past, have very little focus to facilitate automation of organisational behaviour.

Employee Motivation and Consequentialist Assumption

Despite our commonsense understanding that what motivates employees at one point in time ceases to motivate in another point in time, the vast literature on employee motivation has no clear specifications of how to measure and understand when a subset of a hierarchy of motivators (Bagozzi, Bergami & Leone 2003; Lewis 1990) is active in imbuing effort (production) or ceases (reduction) to motivate. Many researchers in the field of psychology and management are critical of discussing employee motivation from the 'consequentialist' perspective (See Seo & Barrett 2004) of 'reduction or production' or 'wax and wane'.

The consequentialist assumption is that (1) people know all the possible outcomes and all the related probabilities and subjective values at any given moment, (2) they engage in extensive cognitive calculation, and then (3) take actions based on the calculation. However, in practice, many managers are interested in knowing more about the 'production or/and reduction' characteristics of employee motivation than the inherent complexity of consequentialist assumption. Managers also believe that employees make informed choice about what rewards/outcomes motivate them. Do we as researchers accept the criticism of consequentialist assumption of motivation and make no progress in understanding the complex cognitive calculation or use knowledge from the recent cognitive informatics theory to help understand the complex cognitive calculation of employees' motivation for the benefit of managers in companies? In this context it is important for researchers in the field of psychology and management to not only develop complex employee motivation theories with consequentialist assumption, but also include the cognitive informatics perspective for resolving the complexity of employees' motivation measurement issue for managers.

In this context, the present research attempts to achieve two objectives. Firstly, to develop a theoretical MGM, an integrated motivation model, in order to understand the complex 'production/ reduction' and 'wax/wane' effect of employee motivation from consequentialist perspective to help managers measure and understand employee motivation. Secondly, an attempt is made to explain MGM using the natural intelligent (NI) information processing system, NI-Sys (Wang & Wang, 2002) and the sign and norms of the semiotic perspective (Stamper et al., 2000) to analyse how employees cognitively internalize assigned rewards into performance outcomes and self-regulate (increase or reduce) the amount of motivational force they allocate to achieve assigned rewards for high performances. The NI-Sys of cognitive informatics and the semiotic perspectives of MGM help in designing computer program for measuring employee motivation. The aim of this article is achieved in two parts; the

first part focuses on the foundation of MGM using taxonomies of semiotic approach and NI-Sys of cognitive informatics, and also concepts from psychology and management. The second part explores the practical, empirical and theoretical implications of MG.

THE THEORETICAL FOUNDATION FOR THE PROPOSED MOTIVATIONAL GRATIFICATION MODEL

Natural Intelligent Information Processing System (NI-Sys)

The process based employee motivation theories, such as expectancy (Lawler, 1977) and Vroom's (1964) VIE theories, provide a complex understanding of an employee converts the assigned organisational (external) goals into phenomenological (internal) goals and contributes effort to achieve high performance. To effectively design an IS to handle this complex understanding of employee motivation and measurement, the NI-Sys (Wang & Wang, 2002) of cognitive informatics lends itself effectively to understand the hierarchical structure of the MGM, which is process based employee motivation. The NI-Sys suggests that the cognitive functions of the brain is based on the internal willingness-driven processes (in NI-OS), and the external event- time-driven processes (in NI-App). The MGM and the taxonomies provide a breakthrough in extending the cognitive informatics theory to understand the mechanisms of cognitive processes in employee motivation, and to develop next generation software for automating measurement of employee motivation.

Signs and Norms

Signs and norms of employee motivation semiotic are explained in this section as 'nuts and bolts' for the design of computer software of the proposed MGM. Norms lend themselves to the formation of taxonomies (Stamper *et al* 2000), and in this article the norms of employee motivation with consequentialist assumption are explained with different taxonomies from psychology and management to lay a theoretical foundation of the MGM.

Taxonomies of MGM

Locke and Latham (2004: 388) defined motivation as "the concept of motivation refers to internal factors that impel action and to external factors that can act as inducements to action". Michaelson (2005) in his response to Locke and Latham's definition of motivation highlighted that it refers to the "pulling" factor used by management to align individual motivators to organizational performance. It is commonly assumed in motivation literature that positive outcomes achieved in the past based on the 'pull' factor will tend to repeat in the future. MG attempts to introduce the consequentialist assumption in the theory development, a different perspective to this commonly held assumption, by proposing that employees self-regulate motivational force for 'assigned' goals in future action according to their 'perception of rewards/outcomes anticipated and received' contingent on performance. The proposed MGM is an integrated work motivation model that is developed based on the valid aspects of extant theories.

Tubbs and Ekeberg (1991) have discussed the processes of how 'assigned' goals (e.g. organisational rewards) influence an individual's action differently to self-determined goals. The present article is about the development of a MGM for organizational contexts where rewards that are 'assigned' for high performance stay relatively unchanged by the organisation for a certain period of time and employees have limited control over changing those 'assigned' goals/targets set by managers. Hence the other option available for the employees is to self-regulate their mo-

tivational force based on the attractiveness or non-attractiveness of organisational rewards and performance outcomes.

Self-regulation refers to the process by which people initiate, adjust, interrupt, terminate or otherwise alter actions to promote attainment of personal goals, plans or standards (Baumeister, Heatherton & Tice, 1994). Self-regulation is explained from diverse perspectives, such as volition, reinforcement, biological, cultural, social-cognitive, and self-efficacy processes (Heatherton & Baumeister, 1996), and self-determination theory (Ryan & Deci, 2000; Ryan, Kuhl & Deci, 1997). Self-regulation in the proposed MGM includes every goal-related effort (Locke & Latham, 1991; Bandura, 1991), and it is based on the principle of 'homeostasis' (drive reduction) in the control-cybernetic system (Richardson, 1991) and goal-performance discrepancy as indicated by Bandura (1991) and Austin and Vancouver (1996).

Locke and Latham's (1990b) goal setting theory explains how goals imbue motivation. Furthermore, the signs and norms of organisational semiotic proposed by Stamper *et al* (2000) is used as a basis for explaining the structure and properties of goals, goal striving processes, goal-content taxonomies process, and content framework of goals (Austin & Vancouver, 1996) so as to lay the theoretical foundation of MG in the proposed model. Austin and Vancouver explained that goals are "internal representations of desired states, where states are broadly construed as outcomes, events or processes" (p. 338). They have suggested that latent, phenomenological, and external are the three definitional perspectives used at the functional–individual level of analysis of goals. The latent perspective holds that goals define the pursuits of individuals, regardless of awareness or volition. The phenomenological is about an individual's self-perception of goals that may be simply a rationalization and an intermediate step in goal striving, and according to Locke and Latham (2004) this is the internal factor that impels action. The external perspective focuses on the external observer's view of goals being meaningful in relation to interpersonal structures and processes. The external goals are the external factors that can act as inducement to action as per Locke and Latham's definition of motivation.

The foundation for the proposed MGM is based on the assumption that the external goals imbue motivational force based on the discrepancy between achieved and desired organizational rewards to set an action hierarchy (Kuhl, 1994; Powers, 1992) of different stages or sub-systems in the MGM. The action hierarchy is about the sequence of actions in a motivation cycle (see Figure 1). For example motivational force for high job performance leads to outcomes that are contingent on job performance (Van Eerde & Thierry, 1996; Porter & Lawler, 1968; Vroom, 1964). Then, MG is interpreted based on the perception of performance outcomes (phenomenological perspective) that facilitate employees to organize goals in subsets or intention taxonomies (Lewis, 1990). These are used to self-regulate their motivational force to continue or cease in the subsequent motivation cycles.

Bagozzi, Bergami and Leone's (2003) findings suggest that employees cognitively arrange motives (rewards) in a hierarchical structure and such structure (subset or cluster) and linkages between subset of motives explain job attitudes, intentions, and commitment. However, MG is about organizing performance outcomes into a hierarchical structure based on the self-perception of goals, as an intermediate step to goal striving, to self-regulate motivational force for achieving assigned rewards.

Motivational Gratification (MG)

Motivational gratification is defined as; *an employee's self-regulation of their effort intensity for 'production' and 'reduction' of motivational force towards future high job performance is based on the dominant type of intention taxonomies of motivational gratification.* Gratified and ungratified motivational forces are the two intention taxonomies of performance outcomes that are explained as the two types of MG. Gratified Motivational Force (GMF) is *the sum of a subset of motiva-*

Figure 1. Motivational gratification model

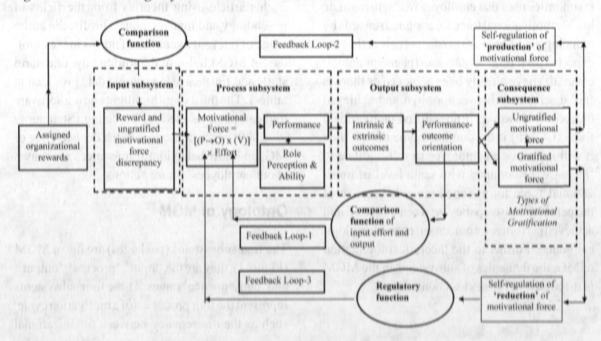

tional forces for performance outcomes that are perceived as already achieved to the anticipated outcomes for expended effort. And Ungratified Motivational Force (UGMF) is *the sum of a subset of motivational force for performance outcomes that are perceived as less than the anticipated outcomes for expended effort*.

For example, when employees achieve performance standards set by management to receive organizational rewards (external goal), certain performance outcomes are bound to follow, which might be intrinsic or extrinsic. Afterwards employees cognitively (phenomenological) organize those performance outcomes into different subsets (intention taxonomies) based on their perception of the performance outcomes achieved compared to their expectations for expended effort (i.e. GMF and UGMF). That is, the external goals of organizational rewards are translated into phenomenological goals of performance outcomes in the motivation cycle. According to the MG definition the phenomenological performance outcomes self-regulate employee's effort for future action based on either GMF or UGMF as the dominant type of MG. That is, if the GMF subset is the dominant type of MG in an employee's behaviour intention taxonomies then that employee will self-regulate his/her motivational force for assigned rewards by reducing effort because he/she perceives that the expected performance outcomes (phenomenological goals) have already been achieved or there is 'no' discrepancy between aspired and achieved outcomes. However, if ungratified motivational force (UGMF) is the dominant type of MG then it will influence an employee to self-regulate to 'increase' or continue with same level of motivational force for assigned rewards because of the perceived discrepancy between expected and achieved performance outcomes (phenomenological goals). Further to the theoretical foundation of MG, the dynamics of subsystems in the MGM is discussed in the next section.

INFORMATION FLOW BETWEEN SUBSYSTEMS IN THE MOTIVATIONAL GRATIFICATION MODEL

MEASUR and MGM

Stamper and Liu (1994) suggest that once the norms of organisational behaviour are understood then it is important to determine the relevant dynamics of the taxonomies of norms for the best result in automation of organisational behaviour. The three stages of MEASUR (Stamper, 1994) provide the basis to identify norms of the MGM, and the NI-Sys (Wang & Wang, 2002) of cognitive informatics lends itself effectively to understand the hierarchical structure of the MGM so as to automate the complex employee motivation gratification measure. The first stage, the total system of MGM is partitioned as four subsystems of norms to understand information flow between the four partitioned stages or subsystems (Vancouver, 2005) of the MGM (figure-1). Secondly, the ontology of the MGM highlights the vocabulary and the temporal relationships between subsystems, and they are explained in this article using theories from the fields of psychology and management. Thirdly, the entire range of relevant dynamics of norms in the ontology of MGM helps to determine how one norm starts and finishes using sample data provided in table-1. The third stage highlights how a software tool can be developed for modeling (Stamper *et al.*, 2000) of the consequentialist decision tree of MG, and how behavioural inferences are drawn about employees' future actions.

Ontology of MGM

The four subsystems (packages) are the of MGM (Figure 1), they are the 'input', 'process', 'output', and 'consequence' stages. These four subsystems represent the four processes of a motivation cycle, such as the discrepancy between organizational

Table 1. Sample values for motivational force, perceived-outcome orientation code and motivational gratification score

Outcome	Expectancy (P→O)	Valence (V)		[(P→O) × (V)]	Motivational Force = [(P→O) (V)] × (R')*	Perceived-outcome orientation code	Types of MG score
		(+)	(-)				
Performance bonus	1.0	+1		1.0	0.82	G	
Better income/pay raise/financial recognition	1.0	+1		1.0	0.82	G	
Interesting work	0.5	+1		0.5	0.41	G	
Job security	0.7	+1		0.7	0.57	G	
Time flexibility	0.5		0	0	0	G	
Promotion	0.7		0	0	0	G	**Total of subset of GMF outcomes = 2.62****
Recognition of job well done	0.8	+1		0.8	0.66	UG	
Increase responsibility	0.7		0	0	0	UG	
Sense of achievement/personal satisfaction	0.9	+1		0.9	0.74	UG	
Challenging task	0.6		0	0	0	UG	
Organisational growth/improving business	0.7	+1		0.7	0.57	UG	**Total of subset of UGMF outcomes = 1.97**

*Average effort probability is (R') = 0.82
**MG Score = GMF of 2.62

rewards and UGMF, motivational force, MG, and self-regulation of behaviour. The temporal cycles of the process framework of goals explain the transition of one subsystem to other based on hierarchy of actions (Kuhl, 1994; Powers, 1992) in the model. These subsystems can be used to packaging cognitive activities and classes to facilitate the use of NI-Sys of cognitive informatics (Wang & Wang, 2002) in computer programming. These four subsystems of MG are explained using structure, process and content frameworks of goals along with the hierarchy of feedback loops (Fried and Slowik, 2004; Klein, 1989). Austin and Vancouver (1996) explained, "the *structure* of goals concerns the properties, organization, and dimensions of multiple goals, within persons; *process* refers to temporal cycles of establishing, striving toward, and revising goals; and *content* pertains to classifications outcomes that individuals approach or avoid" (p. 341).

The external goals excite motivational force in the input stage of the model based on the discrepancy between desired organizational rewards (assigned goals) and UGMF. Motivational force is the 'process' stage of the MG cycle, and this is supported by expectancy theory of motivation (Porter & Lawler, 1968; Vroom, 1964). MG is the phenomenological perspective of goals and it is construed by the performance-outcome orientation, which is the 'output' subsystem of the model. Self-regulation is the 'consequence' stage of the model, where this subsystem highlights the impact of MG on employees' behaviour (Beumeister *et al.*, 1994), either to 'produce' or 'reduce' motivational force, for employees future performances.

Input Subsystem

In the proposed MGM, organizational reward and ungratified motivational force discrepancy is used as a subsystem to refer to the comparison function, which creates motivational force. This subsystem is similar to the goal-performance discrepancy phenomenon suggested by Bandura

(1991). I have chosen for simplicity to explain the function of this subsystem with a single performance outcome as an example whereas the actual measurement of MG is based on multiple performance outcomes. 'Performance bonus', which is one of the performance outcomes listed in table-1, is used here as an example to explain these four subsystems.

There might be different tiers or slabs of performance standards for obtaining performance bonuses in a company. That is, in a production context, an employee might be able to get $300, $500 or $800 as a monthly performance bonus for achieving different tiers or slabs of performance standards set by the company. Assume that an employee may have aimed for $800 of performance bonus (organisational reward/goal), but during the 'comparator' function (Vancouver, 2005; Klein, 1989) in a motivation cycle has realized that he/she has achieved only $500 of performance bonus. If this performance-outcome of $500 is perceived to be less than expected for expended effort then it is identified as one of the subsets (intention taxonomies of MG), i.e. ungratified motivational force (more details about this process of performance-outcome orientation is discussed in the 'output' subsystem section). This difference (discrepancy) created by way of comparison between aspired external goal ($800 performance bonus) and ungratified motivational force (phenomenological goal) using feedback loop-2 (see figure-1) imbues motivational force (tension) in an individual to achieve the aspired organizational rewards that have not yet been achieved. Feedback serves both to keep employee's behaviour directed towards the desired goals and to stimulate high levels of effort (Silverman, Pagson & Cober, 2005; Klein, 1989). The input subsystem from the individual employee's point of view is that it serves to satisfy a need for information about the extent to which personal goals are being met.

Process Subsystem

As per the definition of MG, employees self-regulate their future effort based on the dominant type of MG. To identify this dominant subset it is important to measure motivational force and hence it is important to discuss the measurement of motivational force apart from the concept of motivational force in the process subsystem.

Motivational force is based on the assumption that the strength of a person's motivation to perform effectively is influenced by the person's belief that effort can be converted into performance and that the net attractiveness of the outcomes is perceived to stem from good performance (Locke & Latham, 1990a; Porter & Lawler, 1968; Vroom, 1964). The motivational force has three components (Porter & Lawler, 1968); they are expectancy, valence and effort probability. The attractiveness of the outcomes is measured using expectancy, which is the probability or the likelihood of an outcome (P→O) to stem from good performance. Valence is the positive or negative or indifferent attitude towards a performance outcome. The positive valence motivates and the negative valence inhibits the individual's performance, and they are measured using +1 and −1 respectively. Effort probability (E→P) highlights the probability of effort an employee is prepared to contribute to achieve high performance.

Any high performance for assigned rewards will have contingent outcomes, which can be intrinsic or extrinsic performance outcomes for a job (see table-1). These performance outcomes can vary depending on jobs and organizations. The intrinsic and extrinsic outcomes are inter-related because any one of these performance outcomes will influence the motivational force of employees (Ryan & Deci, 2000) even when the other outcomes are sporadic in nature.

The motivational force created by the input subsystem of the motivation cycle is measured using the product of expectancies valences of each outcomes [(P→O) × (V)] and average effort probability (R'). The average effort probability (E→P) is used in the calculation of motivational force because the (E→P) is measured using multiple items and as per Porter and Lawler 1968 suggestion it is a common practice to calculate the average value of (E→P) and use it in the calculation of motivational force for each performance outcomes. As the desired level of performance has multiple outcomes related with it, firstly, the product of expectancies valences and effort-probability for each of the performance outcomes is calculated, and subsequently the sum of the product of expectancies valences and effort-probability of all outcomes (see table-1) is used to calculate motivation force. Calculation of motivational force in this stage of the MGM uses the technique suggested by the expectancy theory of motivation (Porter & Lawler, 1968; Vroom, 1964), which is considered complex because of its consequentialist assumption. Hence, in this context it is useful to calculate motivational force using a computer program instead of manual methods, so that the manager can get the benefit of measuring complex employee motivation without being concerned about the complexity involved in manual calculation of MG.

The sample data provided in table-1 are about the measure of expectancy, valence, effort and motivational force. These values are obtained based on the methods of measurement of motivational force as suggested by Porter and Lawler (1968) and subsequently supported by the meta-analysis by Van Eerde and Thierry (1996). Along with motivational force, at least two other factors, namely ability and role perception are important and essential in the process subsystem if effort is to be converted into performance. However, the focus of this article is not about the influence of these variables on self-regulation of motivational force and hence it is not dealt with in this article.

Output Subsystem

The motivational force calculated for each of the performance outcomes in the 'process' subsystem are evaluated in the output subsystem using 'performance-outcome orientation'. This cognitive evaluation of the outcomes (table-1) helps to identify (label) intention taxonomies (Lewis, 1990) or form subsets of motivational forces into two types of MG, i.e., GMF and UGMF. In this stage, the ontology of MGM provides the basis for identifying motivational force into two types of MG using deontic operators (Liu & Dix, 1997) such as 'permitted' as in the function of the output subsystem using following generic form:

whenever < condition>
if <state>
then <agent>
is <deontic operator>
to do <action>

In the following example of an employee motivation measurement, the generic form of deontic operations is explained to show how the two types of MG are identified. There are two performance-outcome orientations, affirmative and negative orientations and they are coded by alphanumeric label G and UG. Motivational force for an outcome **is** <permitted> labeled as affirmative performance-outcome orientation (label-G), **if** <state> an employee perceives that the outcome received and anticipated **is** <permitted> equal for effort expended (Mowday & Colwell, 2003; Adams, 1963) **then** <motivational force> it is clustered into the gratified motivational force type. **If** <outcome> it is perceived that the outcome received is less than anticipated for effort expended **then** <motivational force> a negative performance-outcome orientation label-UG is allocated to it and it is grouped **to** <action> ungratified motivational force type. Finally motivational forces (the product of expectancies valences and average effort-probability) for all outcomes are summed in each subset of label-G and label-UG **to** <action> obtain gratified and ungratified motivational force scores respectively (table-1). This highlights how the types of MG impact on self-regulation of motivational force to 'reduce' and/or 'produce' in the 'consequence' subsystem of the MGM, and is discussed next.

Consequence Subsystem

The MGM is considered as a non-satiating motivation cycle, the transitory phase of motivational force from one motivation cycle to another is explained using employee's self-regulation of motivational force in the 'consequence' subsystem of the model. MG denotes the 'output' subsystem of one motivation cycle and self-regulation of motivational force is the link to future actions. Hence self-regulation is labeled as the 'consequence' subsystem because it highlights the impact of the 'output' stage (MG) on input for future actions in a cycle.

The MG scores provided in table-1 reflect the translated external goal (assigned rewards) into phenomenological goals (performance outcomes) and the impact it has on self-regulation of motivational force exerted for the future achievement of assigned organizational rewards in the motivation cycle. The value of the sum of motivational force for performance outcomes clustered in the GMF type (refer to table-1) indicates the self-regulation of motivational force for assigned rewards in the subsequent cycle is activated to 'reduce' (Austin & Vancouver, 1996; Bandura, 1991; Richardson, 1991; Miller *et al.*, 1960) because of the perceived 'no' discrepancy between performance outcomes that are already attained compared to those aspired to. The sum of motivational force for outcomes in UGMF augur self-regulation of 'production' (Bandura, 1991) of motivational force for the assigned organizational rewards in the subsequent cycle because of the perceived discrepancy between performance outcomes that are aspired to compared to those already achieved.

The MG score is used as a parameter to understand an employee's motivational force 'remaining', 'produced' or 'reduced' for achievement of organizational rewards (goal). Also it indicates that an employee's higher score of the two MG types (GMF and UGMF) determines the dominant motivational force for future performance. For instance, if an employee gets a higher MG score on GMF than UGMF, then GMF is the dominant type of MG. Hence it can be assumed that the employees will self-regulate to 'reduce' his/her effort for future high performance to receive assigned rewards (external goals) because the majority of the performance outcomes (phenomenological goals) are not attractive enough to contribute 'extra' effort for high performance. This does not mean that the other type of motivational force, in this case UGMF continues to act on this employee but it signifies that it is not strong enough to influence future action compared to GMF, the dominant MG type.

The input process in 'subsequent (future) motivation cycles' is dependant on the self-regulation of motivational force using three levels of feedback loops. The first level feedback loop is based on the input and output comparator function suggested by equity theory of motivation (Adams, 1963), where employees cognitively compare the performance contingent outcomes received and anticipated (phenomenological) for effort expended. Furthermore the employees arrange GMF and UGMF (intention taxonomies) in hierarchical structures consisting of sequence of interdependent motives (Bagozzi, Begami & Leone, 2004). This hierarchical structure of motivational force is based on 'fairness' and influences their job performances through the subsequent second and third level of feedback loops.

The second level feedback loop is based on the comparison between UGMF and organisational rewards that create motivational force to continue the cycle. This motivational force created by feedback loop-2 can be either positive (the sum of effort probability and expectancies of the positively valent outcomes) or negative (the sum of effort probability and expectancies of the negatively valent outcomes). That is, if an employee aspires to be a high performer and productive on the job, based on his/her performance he/she is bound to receive intrinsic/extrinsic outcomes. If these outcomes are perceived to be UGMF and there exists a discrepancy between his/her aspiration of organizational rewards (external goals) and UGMF (phenomenological goals) then the motivation cycle continues with positive motivational force. However, an employee might still aspire for an outcome, for example promotion, but the contingent outcomes might have negative valence because of his/her negative attitude towards additional responsibilities or job transfer associated with promotion. Hence the subsequent motivational cycles are now based on the negative valence of the motivational force and that person might not contribute high effort to performance, but still perform the job as per the set performance standards because of negative regulatory focus (Tubbs & Ekeberg, 1991).

It is important to note that employee motivation is about how employees contribute high effort and not just the 'required' effort to perform the expected standard on the job and it differentiates high achievers from the average. The third level of feedback loop performs the regulatory function, and hence it self-regulates the behavioural consequences of GMF by 'reducing' motivational force for assigned organizational rewards because the performance outcomes clustered in this subset have lost their attractiveness to produce the motivational force for assigned rewards in future.

An Example of Motivational Gratification Measurement

A sample employee's MG score is explained based on the data shown in table-1. The data in the last column are the sum of scores of motivational force identified by performance-outcome orientation alphanumeric label 'G' and 'UG'. The MG as per the definition is the dominant subset of motivational force that is represented by the highest sum of motivational force in a subset identified by the performance-outcome orientation label G or UG, which can be either GMF or UGMF.

Table-1 shows that GMF is 2.62, which is the sum of six outcomes identified by performance-outcome orientation label 'G' (i.e. outcome a, b, c, d, e and f). Performance-outcome orientation label 'UG' has identified five outcomes (i.e. outcome g, h, i, j and k) and the sum of UGMF is 1.97. As per MG theory this employee's dominant type of MG is the GMF because it is higher than UGMF. Hence the dominant subset of GMF infers that the performance outcomes in this subset are not attractive enough to create further motivational force for achieving assigned rewards and hence this employee may self-regulate to 'reduce' effort to achieve assigned rewards for high performances in the future. The other type of MG, UGMF, may continue to influence the employee's behaviour but is not strong enough to impact job performance compared to GMF. So, it is useful to use the highest score of the two types as MG because it helps to understand the dominant 'subset' of motivational force of an employee for a given set of intrinsic and extrinsic performance outcomes for assigned organizational rewards. The impact of types of MG on organisational rewards that is mediated by self-regulation of motivational force is supported by the findings of a recent study by Bagozzi, Bergami and Leone (2003), where employees cognitively arrange motives in a hierarchical structure and such structure (subset or taxonomy of intentions) and linkages between subset of motives explain job attitudes, intentions, and commitment.

IMPLICATIONS

In this section the practical implications of MGM is discussed from the view of analysis and design of a computer system for the measurement of employee motivation, and subsequently the application of MG measurement to an organisational context in diagnosing and solving employee motivation issues.

Practical Implications of MGM for IS Design

The MGM, as a diagnostic model, integrates systems concepts (Vancouver, 2005; Klein, 1990), and presents a specific model to the individual employee's cognitive tasks of motivation. The MG theory is developed underpinning the organisational semiotic approach and cognitive informatics so as to facilitate computer software development for the measurement of employee motivation. Subsequently, the dynamic characteristics of the MGM, which is challenging for human brain to comprehend, can be captured using a computer program, which can be used in diagnosing and instituting changes to employee motivation.

The advantage of MG in the computer application context is that it provides a theoretical framework to measure the wane and wax effect (i.e. UGMF and GMF) of employees' persistence (motivation) in goal striving. Among a set of performance outcomes that motivates employees, a few might loose their motivator characteristics but some other in the set might continue to motivate employees for high performance. Hence, motivators normally don't stay attractive or unattractive over a period of time but MGM addresses that it continuously changes over time and using a computer system it is possible to track the dynamic nature of employees' MG.

PRACTICAL IMPLICATIONS OF MGM FOR MANAGEMENT

The practical implications of MGM for an organisational context from psychology and management perspective in diagnosing and solving employee motivation issues based on the measurement of

MG are discussed in this section. The MGM portrayed in Figure 1 can be used to diagnose motivational problems among employees using the types of MG. According to the MGM, the types of MG determine the levels of effort an employee exerts in a performance situation. That is, the two classifications of MG help to identify those aspects of a performer's perceptions and evaluation that tend to enhance motivation to work hard (UGMF), and those that tend to detract from it (GMF). By examining motivational force measurement values in each type of MG it is possible to identify the motivational problems based on multiple variables contributing to GMF and UGMF and opportunities that are inherent in the performance situation. That is, it is possible to understand motivational problems based on an employee's unrealistic aspiration of assigned organizational rewards (external goals) and also based on the metrics of different variables in MG: low motivational force either as a product of positive valence and low expectancy or a product of negative valence and high or low expectancy, and perception of outcomes (phenomenological goals i.e., GMF or UGMF) received and expected for expended effort.

Once the diagnoses of motivational problems are made using MG variables then changes can be instituted to improve the employee's motivation to work harder. Such changes (or problem solving) can involve: a) instituting new outcomes, which will be perceived as contingent of hard work, or changing the probability of existing outcomes. That is, the link between hard work and positively valued (valence) outcome is strengthened, b) weakening the link between hard work and negatively valued (valence) outcomes, or c) changing the valences of the existing outcomes. The resource-munificence model of work motivation (Klein 1990) suggests that the first alternative should be introduced at the organisation level. Nonetheless the other two alternatives are amenable to the employee behaviour level change through training.

CONCLUSION

The intention of this article is to provide a philosophical basis for the development of computer application for employee motivation measurement using semiotic assumption and cognitive informatics so that information system analysts and designers can design a good quality system. In addition it provides theoretical direction for future research on MG to add value to practice and research literature in the field of employee motivation.

The MGM illustrates that the assigned organisational rewards (external goals) set sequences of action in a motivation cycle, starting with motivational force, followed by performance outcomes and finally performance outcome orientations that facilitate employees to organize performance outcomes (phenomenological goals) into intention taxonomies of MG. These are the cognitive tasks performed by an employee in self-regulating his/her effort for high performance in a job situation. Based on the consequentialist perspective of MG theory, the practical implication of this theory in organisation context can be maximized only by using a computer program. Hence, the MG theory paves a new direction for the development of complex behavioural theories for developing software applications in the field of psychology and management. This is not to suggest that the field of information system is capable of coping with cognitive complexity in analyzing and designing computer programs. But this article highlights the small step taken to add value to the existing employee motivation and information system literature by attempting to sketch the cognitive tasks of employee motivation from 'systems' perspective by organisational behaviour researcher using organisational semiotic approach and cognitive informatics, so that it can be easily codified do develop computer software to analyse and measure complex employee motivation.

Once the complexity in the measurement of MG can by approached by designing a computer program then it is important to highlight how such measures could be used to help managers make human resource training and development decisions. Firstly, the practical implications of types of MG measures (UGMF and GMF) highlight that it helps to diagnose when employees self-regulate 'production' or 'reduction' of motivation force for assigned rewards leading to 'high' performance based on a combination of principles from external and phenomenological goals, expectancy and equity theories, and intention taxonomies. Subsequent to diagnosis, the model presents a guide to plan instituting new performance outcomes or changing the probability of existing outcomes as some of the corrective steps to enhance employees' motivation for future high performance.

Secondly, MG measures are also useful in providing alternate viewpoints to why employees' goal persistence waxes and wanes. As per the MG explanation, the UGMF and GMF intention taxonomies may contribute to the waxing and waning of goal persistence depending on the motivation cycle in which the observations of the study are made. That is, waxing or waning of goal persistence (motivation) depends on the respective dominant intention taxonomy of UGMF or GMF that influences future actions.

Thirdly, the other alternate paradigm to the commonly held negative regulatory focus explanation for why employees continue to contribute just 'required' effort, and not 'high' effort, to job performance even when majority of performance outcomes are perceived to be unattractive (GMF). MG attempts to explain that it is the 'remaining' attractive or passive motivational force (UGMF) of employee's intention taxonomies instead of punitive management action contingent on job performance (negative regulatory focus) which may influence employees to contribute the 'required' effort for job performance.

REFERENCES

Adams, S. J. (1963). Towards an understanding of inequity. *Journal of Abnormal and Social Psychology*, *67*, 422–436. doi:10.1037/h0040968

Austin, J. T., & Vancouver, J. B. (1996). Goal constructs in psychology: Structure, process and content. *Psychological Bulletin*, *120*, 338–375. doi:10.1037/0033-2909.120.3.338

Bagozzi, R, P., Bergami, M., & Leone, L. (2003). Hierarchical representation of motives in goal setting. *The Journal of Applied Psychology*, *88*, 915–943. doi:10.1037/0021-9010.88.5.915

Bagozzi, R. P., Moore, D. J., & Leone, L. (2004). Self-control and the self-regulation of dieting decisions: The role of prefactual attitudes, subjective norms, and resistance to tempatation. *Basic and Applied Social Psychology*, *26*, 199–213.

Bandura, A. (1991). Social cognitive theory of self-regulation. *Organizational Behavior and Human Decision Processes*, *50*, 248–287. doi:10.1016/0749-5978(91)90022-L

Bandura, A., & Locke, E. A. (2003). Negative self-efficacy and goal effects revisited. *The Journal of Applied Psychology*, *88*, 87–99. doi:10.1037/0021-9010.88.1.87

Baumeister, R. F., Heatherton, T. F., & Tice, D. (1994). *Losing control: How and why people fail as self-regulation*. San Diego: Academic.

Fried, Y., & Slowik, L. H. (2004). Enriching goal-setting theory with time: An integrated approach. *Academy of Management Review*, *29*, 404–422.

Heatherton, T. F., & Baumeister, R. F. (1996). Self-regulation failure: Past, Present, and Future. *Psychological Inquiry*, *7*, 90–98. doi:10.1207/s15327965pli0701_20

Kirwan, B., & Ainsworth, L. K. (1992). *A Guide to Task Analysis*. London: Taylor & Francis Ltd.

Klein, H. J. (1989). An Integrated Control Theory Model of Work Motivation. *Academy of Management Review*, *14*, 150–172.

Klein, J. I. (1990). Feasibility Theory: A Resource-Munificence Model of Work Motivation and Behavior. *Academy of Management Review*, *15*, 646–665.

Kuhl, J. (1994). Motivation and volition. In G. d'ydewalle, P. G. Eelen, & P. Bertelson (Eds.), *International perspectives on psychological science*, *2*, 311-340. (England, Drlbaum).

Lawler, E. E. (1977). Satisfaction and Behaviour. In Hackman, J. R., Lawler, E. E., & Porter, L. W. (Eds.), *Perspectives on Behavior in Organisations*. NY: McGraw-Hill.

Lewis, M. (1990). The development of intentionality and the role of consciousness. *Psychological Inquiry*, *1*, 231–247. doi:10.1207/s15327965pli0103_13

Liu, K., & Dix, A. (1997). Norm governed agens in CSCW, *The First International Workshop on Computational Semotics*, (Paris, University of De Vince).

Locke, E. A., & Latham, G. P. (1990a). Work Motivation and Satisfaction: Light at the End of the Tunnel. *Psychological Science*, *4*, 240–246. doi:10.1111/j.1467-9280.1990.tb00207.x

Locke, E. A., & Latham, G. P. (1990b). *A theory of goal setting and task performance*. NJ: Prentice-Hall.

Locke, E. A., & Latham, G. P. (1991). Self-regulation through goal setting. *Organizational Behavior and Human Decision Processes*, *50*, 212–247. doi:10.1016/0749-5978(91)90021-K

Locke, E. A., & Latham, G. P. (2004). What should we do about motivation theory? Six recommendations for the twenty-first century. *Academy of Management Review*, *29*, 388–403.

Michaelson, C. (2005). Meaningful motivation for work motivation theory. *Academy of Management Review, 30*, 235–238. doi:10.5465/AMR.2005.16387881

Miller, G. A., Galanter, E., & Pribram, K. H. (1960). *Plans and the structure of behaviour*. New York: Holt, Rinehart, and Winston. doi:10.1037/10039-000

Mowday, R., & Colwell, K. (2003). Equity Theory Predictions of Behavior in Organizations. In Bigley, G., Porter, L., & Steers, R. (Eds.), *Motivation and Work Behavior* (7th ed.). New York: Irwin-McGraw Hill.

Porter, L. W., & Lawler, E. E. (1968). *Managerial attitudes and performances*, (ILL, Irwin).

Powers, W. T. (1992). *Living control systems II*. KY: Control Systems Group.

Richardson, G. P. (1991). *Feedback thought: In social science and systems theory*. Philadelphia: University of Pennsylvania Press.

Ryan, R. M., & Deci, E. L. (2000). Self-determination theory and the facilitation of intrinsic motivation, social development, and well-being. *The American Psychologist, 55*, 68–78. doi:10.1037/0003-066X.55.1.68

Ryan, R. M., Kuhl, J., & Deci, E. l. (1997). Nature and autonomy: Organizational view of social and neurobiological aspects of self-regulation in behaviour and development. *Development and Psychopathology, 9*, 701–728. doi:10.1017/S0954579497001405

Schraagen, J. M., Chipman, S. F., & Shalin, V. L. (2000). *Cognitive Task Analysis*. London: Lawrence Erlbaum Associates.

Seamster, T. L., Redding, R. E., & Kaempf, G. L. (1997). *Applied Cognitive Task Analysis in Aviation*. Bodmin, Hartnolls Ltd.

Seo, M., & Barrett, L. R. (2004). The role of affective experience in work motivation. *Academy of Management Review, 29*, 423–439.

Silerman, S. B., Pogson, C. E., & Cober, A. B. (2005). *When employees at work don't get it: A model for enhancing individual employee change in response to performance* feedback. *The Academy of Management Executive, 19*, 135–147. doi:10.5465/AME.2005.16965190

Stamper, R. K. (1994). Social Norms in Requirements Analysis – and outline of MEASUR. In Jirotka, M., & Goguen, J. (Eds.), *Requirements Engineering: technical and social aspects*. New York: Academic Press.

Stamper, R. K., & Liu, K. (1994). Organizational dynamics, social norms and information systems. In *proceeding HICSS-27, Los Alamitos (IEEE Computer Society Press), VI*, 645-654.

Stamper, R. K., Liu, K., Hafkamp, M., & Ades, Y. (2000). Understanding the roles of signs and norms in organizations – a semiotic approach to information systems design. *Behaviour & Information Technology, 19*, 15–27. doi:10.1080/014492900118768

Tubbs, M. E., & Ekeberg, S. E. (1991). The role of intentions in work motivation: Implications for goal-setting theory and research. *Academy of Management Review, 16*, 180–199.

Van Eerde, W., & Thierry, H. (1996). Vroom's Expectancy Models and Work-Related Criteria: A Meta-Analysis. *The Journal of Applied Psychology, 81*, 575–586. doi:10.1037/0021-9010.81.5.575

Vancouver, J. B. (2005). The dept of history and explanation as benefits and bane for psychological control theories. *The Journal of Applied Psychology, 90*, 38–52. doi:10.1037/0021-9010.90.1.38

Vroom, V. H. (1964). *Work Motivation*. New York: John Wiley and Sons.

Wang, Y. (2003). On Cognitive Informatics. *Brain and Mind*, *4*(2), 151–167. doi:10.1023/A:1025401527570

Wang, Y. (2007). The Theoretical Framework of Cognitive Informatics. *International Journal of Cognitive Informatics and Natural Intelligence*, *1*(1), 1–27. doi:10.4018/jcini.2007010101

Wang, Y., & Wang, Y. (2002). Cognitive Models of the Brain. In Proceedings of the 1st IEEE International Conference on Cognitive Informatics (ICCC'02), IEEE CS Press, Calgary, Canada, August 2002, 552.

Section 4
Applications of Computational Intelligence and Cognitive Computing

Chapter 24
Supporting CSCW and CSCL with Intelligent Social Grouping Services

Jeffrey J.P. Tsai
University of Illinois-Chicago, USA

Jia Zhang
Northern Illinois University, USA

Jeff J.S. Huang
National Central University, Taiwan

Stephen J.H. Yang
National Central University, Taiwan

ABSTRACT

This article presents an intelligent social grouping service for identifying right participants to support CSCW and CSCL. We construct a three-layer hierarchical social network, in which we identify two important relationship ties – a knowledge relationship tie and a social relationship tie. We use these relationship ties as metric to measure the collaboration strength between pairs of participants in a social network. The stronger the knowledge relationship tie, the more knowledgeable the participants; the stronger the social relationship tie, the more likely the participants are willing to share their knowledge. By analyzing and calculating these relationship ties among peers using our computational models, we present a systematic way to discover collaboration peers according to configurable and customizable requirements. Experiences of social grouping services for identifying communities of practice through peer-to-peer search are also reported.

DOI: 10.4018/978-1-4666-0261-8.ch024

INTRODUCTION

Although the Internet technology has made it possible for people to collaborate effectively without staying physically together, they have led to the unintended consequence of increasing isolation among people with respect to their academic peers. In bygone times, the inconvenience of having to share resource sites (for example, computer centers and unscheduled laboratory use) afforded opportunities for developing computer-oriented social groups for virtual collaboration.

Computer Supported Cooperative Work (CSCW) provides a virtual collaboration technology that offers participants a promising option of not being physically present at cooperation. Applied to collaborative learning, CSCW techniques allow students to study in a virtual team without physically staying at a common place (Weinberger, & Fischer, 2006). Computer-Supported Collaborative Learning (CSCL) was thus coined in 1996 (Koschmann, 1996) to refer to adopting CSCW technology to provide a computer and network-supported collaborative learning platform for students to study cooperatively to acquire knowledge (Komis, Avouris, & Fidas, 2002).

While there have been significant efforts developing collaborative learning environments for existing groups, little work has been done to help people find proper partners in Internet communities. In our vision, qualitative principles and strategies from traditional higher education research and practices should be normalized and quantified into computer understandable and interpretable rules, and guide automatic formation of cooperative groups.

This research aims to promote Internet-based informal collaboration over CSCW and CSCL, by exploring the plausibility of providing system-level support and services for the forming of collaborative groups dynamically. Our outcome will lead to a plug-in into the existing Web-based platform providing intelligent social grouping services. Based on our study and surveys, we focus on exploring how to exploit knowledge and social networks on top of historical data to help students establish subgroups of cohorts that may become "communities of practice." By communities of practice, we borrow from social science and refer to a group of participants with common interests in a particular subject. By participants, we refer to the individuals who (1) possess related information, (2) can help to discover and obtain the information, or (3) are willing to exchange and share information with others.

This article presents an intelligent social grouping service empowered by social network-based peer-to-peer (P2P) search to facilitate the identification and establishment of communities of practice on the Internet. Here, peers represent individuals (participants) who are associated with the communities through knowledge and social relationships. Throughout this article, we will use the terms "peer" and "participants" interchangeably. We propose two important relationship ties, a knowledge relationship tie and a social relationship tie, as underlying metric to measure the degrees of a peer's knowledge matching and social relationships regarding a query initiated by another peer. By analyzing and calculating these relationships among peers using our computational models, we present a systematic way to discover peers based on configurable and customizable requirements. We have also conducted experiments to evaluate how our method improves the identification of communities of practice on the Interne.

The remainder of the article is organized as follows. We first review related work in section 2. We present our knowledge and social network-based P2P search framework and the methods for calculating knowledge relationship tie and social relationship tie in section 3. We present our system implementation and discuss our experiments and results in section 4, and finally, we draw conclusions in section 5.

RELATED WORK

In the literature, numerous research and practices have reported a number of instructional supporting techniques that stimulate and facilitate cooperative learning (Jonassen, 2004), in both face-to-face and computer and network-based contexts (Hron, Friedrich, 2003). Here, we concentrate on three areas most relevant to this research: CSCW and CSCL, P2P, as well as social networks.

CSCW and CSCL

Since its inception in 1984 (Grudin, Poltrock, 1997), Computer Supported Cooperative Work (CSCW) provides a virtual collaboration technology that offers participants a promising option of not being physically present at a cooperation. Applied to collaborative learning, CSCW techniques allow students to study in a virtual team without physically staying at a common place (Weinberger, & Fischer, 2006). Computer-Supported Collaborative Learning (CSCL) was thus coined in 1996 (Koschmann, 1996) to refer to adopting CSCW technology to provide a computer and network-supported collaborative learning platform for students to study cooperatively to acquire knowledge (Komis, Avouris, & Fidas, 2002). More specific, Internet-based CSCL is also referred to as Web-Based Collaborative Learning (WBCL) (Hron, Friedrich, 2003), which is the focused area of this research. Throughout this article, we will use CSCL and WBCL interchangeably. WBCL differentiates from conventional collaborative learning from several significant perspectives such as social communication situation, message exchange, cognitive load, and participation of learners (Hron, Friedrich, 2003). Kollias and others (Kollias et al., 2005) study, from a teacher's perspective, how WBCL can complement and improve classroom study. Hron and Friedrich (Hron, Friedrich, 2003) examine beyond-technique factors of WBCL. Through the development of two WBCL environments, Rubens and others (Rubens et al., 2005) summarize a set of pedagogical principles for building WBCL systems.

A CSCL-oriented software system is usually called a Collaborative Learning Environment (CLE). Some existing CLE examples are: Conversant Media (Lourdusamy et al., 2003), COMTELLA (Vassileva, 2004), EDUCOSM (Miettinen et al., 2003), EDUTELLA (Nejdl et al., 2002), Groove (Eikemeier, Lechner, 2004), and SpeakEasy (Edwards et al., 2002). Bravo and others (Bravo et al., 2006) build a learner-centered synchronous CSCL environment for students to study design. Collaboration feedbacks are also used to enhance collaborative e-learning (Zumbach, Hillers, & Reimann, 2003). A CLE can be established using all of the three aforementioned grouping approaches. For the formal learning groups and study teams approaches, a CLE provides a long-running virtual collaboration environment; for the informal learning groups approach, a CLE enables a dynamic way for students to group into a virtual learning team at run time.

Existing CSCL research focuses on how to enhance interactions (Chang, Zhang, Chang, 2006) within an already formed learning group (Zurita, Nussbaum, 2004) to improve communication, coordination, negotiation, and interactivity (Gutwin et al., 1996). In contrast to their work, our research focuses on how to form an effective learning group.

P2P for CSCL

A P2P network is a distributed networking structure that treats every participant as a peer and allows each peer to play as either a client or a server under different circumstances (Brase, Painter, 2004). P2P network is considered as a more suitable platform to build CSCL systems compared with traditional client-server model (Cuseo, 2002). Some specialized educational P2P applications have been developed and their experiences have been reported, such as COMTELLA (Vassileva, 2004), EDUCOSM (Miettinen et al., 2003),

EDUTELLA (Nejdl et al., 2002), Groove (Eike-meier, Lechner, 2004) and SpeakEasy (Edwards et al., 2002). Manlove and others (Manlove et al., 2006) conclude from a case study that P2P-based CSCL tools promote student learning in scientific inquiry learning.

Some researchers track and analyze interaction patterns in a P2P environment to guide collaborative learning (Daradoumisa et al., 2006). For example, Avouris and others (Avouris et al., 2004) design an environment for monitoring and examining group learning patterns from two aspects - activity analysis and collaboration analysis. Some other researchers focus on building powerful P2P learning environments such as Conversant Media (Lourdusamy et al., 2003) and metacognition (Dimitracopoulou, Petrou, 2005).

Compared with these related work on P2P networks, we use the P2P technology as our underlying backbone to build a hierarchical framework supporting CSCW and CSCL. We utilize the P2P technique to build both knowledge network and social network in our framework.

Social Networks

Research results and practices from the fields such as educational communications, social sciences, and psychological sciences, have provided a variety of guidelines for people to dynamically form proper teams and groups. Among others, many researchers have proven that social relationships and interactions have significant impacts on collaborative learning (Zurita, Nussbaum, 2004) (Dimitracopoulou, Petrou, 2005) (Fischer et al., 2002). Fischer and others (Fischer et al., 2002) also conclude that social relationships have an impact on knowledge acquisition in a collaboration mode. The technique of social network is thus used to represent a determinable networking structure of how people know each other (Raghavan, 2002) (Kautz et al., 1997) (Alani et al., 2003). A social network can be formalized into a net structure comprising nodes and edges. In such a network,

nodes represent individuals or organizations. Edges connecting nodes are called ties, which represent the relationships between the individuals and organizations, either directly or indirectly (Churchill, Halverson, 2005). The strength of a tie (weight of an edge) indicates the strength of the relationship.

Many kinds of ties may exist between the nodes in a social network (Churchill, Halverson, 2005). One popular tie is social interaction tie, which refers to the structural links created through social interactions between individuals in a social network (Wasko, Faraj, 2005) (Zhang, Jin, & Lin, 2005). Prior studies suggest that an individual's centrality in an electronic network of practice can be measured using the number of social ties that an individual has with others in the network (Ahuja et al., 2003). Tsai and Ghoshal (Tsai, Ghoshal, 1998) report that social interaction tie has positive impacts on the extent of inter-unit resource exchange. Wasko and Faraj (Wasko, Faraj, 2005) discover that the centrality established by the social interaction ties significantly impacts the helpfulness and the volume of knowledge contribution. Ahuja and others (Ahuja et al., 2003) suggest that an individual's centrality in an electronic network of practice be measured using the number of social ties that an individual has with others in the social network. Kreijns and others (Kreijns et al., 2005) conclude that social interactions largely affect group forming and group dynamics.

Compared with related work, we construct a social network as an integral layer of our hierarchical framework to search for potential collaborators. We exploit existing research results in the field of social network to design questionnaires to identify decision factors for calculating social interaction ties.

Social Network-based P2P Search for Intelligent Grouping

The intelligent social grouping service is empowered by a social network-based P2P search. In this research, we found P2P and social networks share many concepts in common. For example, they are both distributed networking structures; a peer in a P2P network can be viewed as an analog of a node in a social network; a link in a P2P can be viewed as an analog of a relationship tie in a social network. In contrast to most P2P researches that emphasize on search queries and protocols, our social network-based P2P search aims at reducing search time and decreasing message traffic by minimizing the number of messages circulating in the network.

Decision Factors

At the beginning of the project, we conducted a survey to identify a set of initial decision factors for group forming. We chose to recruit out of the Computer Science freshman class, so that the selected subjects possess overlapping knowledge backgrounds over generic study topics.

The survey was processed in two phases. In phase 1, a study topic was announced in the class. Students were asked to describe, in a verbose manner, how they would like to choose study partners on the Internet for the predefined study topic. They were asked to focus on the decision factors on which they form study groups and the key criteria of how they define "effective groups." After gathering students' answer sheets, we summarized and abstracted a set of decision factors and criteria. In phase 2, each student was asked to rank the obtained factors and criteria.

As shown in Figure 1, our survey revealed that students essentially count on two key factors to form a study team: knowledge possession and social relationship. The former indicates whether a student possesses relative knowledge; the latter indicates whether the student may be willing to participate. For example, a student prefers to find a partner who has some knowledge about the study topic than someone who knows nothing about the topic. Also, a student prefers to have his/her friend as a partner. In turn, we found the students ranked high the following three knowledge relationship factors: knowledge domain, proficiency, and reputation of contribution. We also found that students ranked high the following two social relationship factors: social familiarity and social reputation.

Figure 1. Decision factors

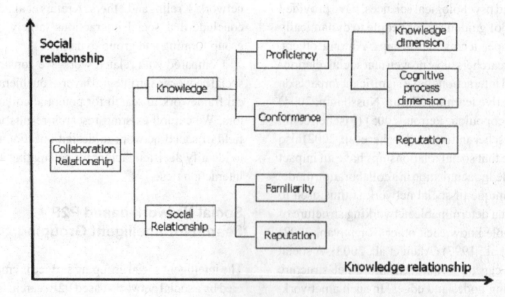

Social Network-Based P2P Framework

Based on our survey results, we decide to focus on two relationship ties on a P2P network: knowledge relationship tie and social relationship tie. A knowledge tie represents the degree of how a peer is familiar with the knowledge requested by an initiative peer. A relationship tie represents the degree of social relationship between a pair of involved peers. For simplicity, in this research we consider the social relationship between a pair of peers as a mutual relationship. In other words, in our social network is represented in an un-directional graph.

Based on the two relationship ties, we established a social network-based P2P framework for supporting group formation. As shown in Figure 2, our framework comprises three layers: a P2P knowledge net (K-net), a P2P social net (S-net), and an IM-equipped group discussion layer. Note that all users having access to the Internet form a P2P network space. Conceptually, each layer contains a P2P network, with each node denoting a peer in the P2P network space. In the first

and the lowest K-net layer, an edge represents a knowledge relationship tie. In the second S-net, an edge represents a social network tie. In the third layer, all nodes represent the search results of potential collaborators.

Our framework also shows how to dynamically create the three layers to support smart group formation. The idea is illustrated in Figure 2. For a given query requesting participants with certain knowledge, a group of potential collaborators (with strong social relationships with the initiative peer and with the requested knowledge) will be found. We will use an example shown in Figure 2 to walk readers through.

Assume that peer *Jeff* initiates a request searching for peers with knowledge about "*Software Engineering.*" For Jeff's request, a P2P K-net is dynamically generated. Available peers in the original P2P network space are examined against the requested knowledge. An edge is drawn from the requester peer to every tested peer, with a number assigned as the value of a knowledge tie. How we quantify a peer's familiarity with the requested knowledge can refer to our previous report (Yang et al., 2007). As shown in Figure 2, peers *Chris*

Figure 2. A three-layer social network-based P2P framework

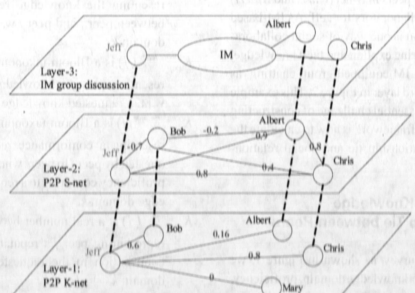

and *Albert* hold knowledge relationship ties (0.8) and (0.16) with Jeff, respectively. This means that *Chris* knows more about *"Software Engineering"* than *Albert* does. A threshold is predefined, say 0.5, to facilitate social grouping. Peers on the K-net with knowledge ties lower than the threshold will be removed from the K-net without further considerations (for example, peer *Mary*). Finally, the K-net contains peers who know enough about the knowledge. These peers form into a pool of active peers.

Then we construct a P2P S-net, as shown in Figure 2. We calculate the social relationship tie between each pair of the peers from the K-net. Our algorithm to calculate a social relationship tie will be discussed in section 4. As shown in Figure 2, *Jeff* is more familiar with *Albert* than *Chris* because the social relationship tie between *Jeff* and *Albert* is (0.9), which is greater than that between *Jeff* and *Chris* (0.8). Peers appear on S-net with negative relationships with the requester are removed (for example, *Bob*). Specific rules may be defined to decide whether all involved peers have to meet a curtain level of social relationship. For example, whether any pair of peers left cannot have negative social relationship ties between them.

The resulted peers in S-net (*Chris* and *Albert*) are potential collaborators for Jeff. As IM-based group discussion is one way of social collaboration toward sharing explicit and tacit knowledge, Jeff initiates an IM-equipped group chatting, as shown as the third layer in Figure 2. This example shows that the essential challenge of constructing this three-layer framework is how to calculate the knowledge relationship tie and social relationship tie.

Calculating Knowledge Relationship Tie between Peers

Based on our survey, as shown in Figure 1, we consider a peer's knowledge domain, proficiency, and reputation of contribution as key indicators

determining its capability to participate in collaborations. Therefore, as shown in the P2P K-net in Figure 2, we calculate a peer's knowledge relationship tie based on these three indicators.

We apply Bloom taxonomy matrix (Anderson et al., 2001) to classify a peer's domain knowledge and its proficiency in such a domain. Bloom taxonomy is a two-dimensional matrix containing Knowledge dimension and Cognitive Process dimension. The former indicates the types of knowledge; the latter indicates cognitive processing of knowledge. Each cell in the matrix is associated with a value ranging from 0 to 1, representing the level of proficiency. We adopt similar mechanism to represent a peer's reputation regarding a specific knowledge domain.

Consider peer *i* on a P2P network is requesting peer *j* whose knowledge proficiency conforms to a requested knowledge domain *k*. Peer *i*'s query can be calculated by:

$$K_{(k)}^{tie}(i, j) = K_{(k)}^{proficiency}(j) \bullet K_{(k)}^{conformance}(i)^T \bullet K_{(k)}^{reputation}(j)$$

where

$K_{(k)}^{tie}(i, j)$ is a real number between 0 and 1, representing the knowledge relationship tie between peer *i* and peer *j* w.r.t. knowledge domain *k*.

$K_{(k)}^{proficiency}(j)$ is a Bloom taxonomy matrix representing peer *j*'s knowledge proficiency w.r.t. a requested knowledge domain *k*.

$K_{(k)}^{conformance}(i)$ is a Bloom taxonomy matrix representing a conformance requirement requested by peer *i* to peers whose knowledge proficiency conforms to a requested knowledge domain *k*.

$K_{(k)}^{reputation}(j)$ is a real number between 0 and 1, representing peer *j*'s reputation regarding contribution to the requested knowledge domain *k*.

Calculating Social Relationship Tie between Peers

A social relationship tie indicates the degree of social relationships between a pair of peers on the P2P S-net. For a pair of peers, denoted by peer i and peer j, we define the social relationship tie between them as the product of their social familiarity and social reputation.

$$S^{tie}(i,j) = S^{familiarity}(i,j) \times S^{reputation}(j)$$

where,

$S^{tie}(i,j)$ is a social relationship tie between peers i and j,
$S^{familiarity}(i,j)$ is a social familiarity between peers i and j,
$S^{reputation}(j)$ is peer j's social reputation.

Social familiarity indicates the level of familiarity (for example, ranging from casual to close) between two peers. When a new peer connects to a social network, every existing peer will be notified and needs to specify his/her social familiarity with the new peer (for example, by filling forms and answering questionnaires). The default value is zero, meaning that there is no relationship with the newly joined peer. Social familiarity can be exhibited in different levels, such as friends, team-mates, organization colleagues, or virtual community members. Meanwhile, social familiarity can be either positive or negative values ranging between -1 and 1, indicating the relationship is either good or bad. To perform quantitative analysis, without losing generality, we define social familiarity between peers i and j into nine categories, represented by a lookup table (see Table 1).

Each peer has a social reputation, which is the product of the peer's social rating (Jones, Issroff, 2005) and the average of the peer's social familiarities. Social reputation represents a degree of confidence to a target peer from all other peers on a social network who know the target peer. The social reputation of peer j is computed as follows:

$$S^{reputation}(j) = AVG\left[S^{familiarity}(j)\right] \times S^{rating}(j)$$

$$= \frac{\sum_{m=1}^{NoP(m)}\left[S^{familiarity}(j,m)\right]}{NoP(j)} \times S^{rating}(j)$$

where,

$AVG\left[S^{familiarity}(j)\right]$ is an average value of peer j's social familiarities,
$S^{rating}(j)$ is peer j's social rating,
$NoP(j)$ is the number of peers connected to peer j.

System Implementation and Experiments

We have developed a P2P prototype, called SOtella as shown in Figure 3. Utilizing our social network-based P2P search, SOtella can form intelligent social grouping based on knowledge relationship tie and social relationship tie. We also conducted experiments for evaluating how well our method can facilitate intelligent social grouping.

P2P System Implementation

SOtella is implemented based on open-source software, Edutella (http://edutella.jxta.org/), which is an academic P2P framework equipped with a Resource Definition Framework (RDF)-based metadata to enhance resource description and discovery. To control the experiment scale and monitor SOtella's performance, we confine the search scope of SOtella to a small-scale network including about 56 peers within a university, from a class in Department of Computer Science. Each peer in SOtella is associated with knowledge and

Table 1.

$S^{familiarity}(i,j)$	Implications
0	*there is no relationship between peer i & j*
0~0.2	*peer i considers peer j a virtual community member with a positive relationship*
0.3~0.4	*peer i considers peer j an organization colleague with a positive relationship*
0.5~0.7	*peer i considers peer j a team-mate a with positive relationship*
0.8~1.0	*peer i considers peer j a friend with a positive relationship*
-0.8~-1.0	*peer i considers peer j a friend with a negative relationship*
-0.5~-0.7	*peer i considers peer j a team-mate with a negative relationship*
-0.3~-0.4	*peer i considers peer j an organization colleague with a negative relationship*
0~-0.2	*peer i considers peer j a virtual community member with a negative relationship*

social relationship ties as presented in the aforementioned framework.

The implementation result of the aforementioned social grouping is shown in Figure 3. The upper left part of Figure 3 shows a list of collaborative social groups categorized by their study topics. The lower left part shows the group search interface, where a peer can search using a combination of keyword, study topic, person name, email address, and organization. The right part of Figure 3 shows that a peer may browse the detail of a selected study group.

To enable adaptive group formation, we realized a rating mechanism (Jones, Issroff, 2005).

Figure 3. Screen shot of SOtella

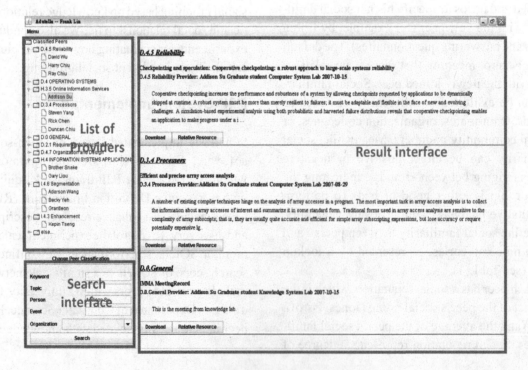

Peers may provide feedbacks to the social network by the rating mechanism, so that the calculation of knowledge and social relationship ties may be further improved. For example, after a successful collaboration, a peer may change his/her social familiarity with another peer in the formed group. This updated information can be stored and used to support future group formation.

Once potential collaborators are found, we build supporting software to facilitate collaboration. As a proof of concept, we built an IM-enabled group discussion tool. Its core component is a real-time discussion board, as shown in Figure 4. Peers can communicate with collaborators relevant to their needs and improve collaboration through such a group discussion.

As shown in Figure 4, our group discussion tool provides a roster list for each participant (Albert and Chris in this example) showing who are involved in the formed group. Participants are notified when other group members get online and can review their profiles. A participant may start discussions with a specific group member or initiate group discussions.

Our tool supports hand-writing annotation as well as voice-based annotation for text-based discussion. As shown in Figure 4, Chris asks Albert to explain the diagram, using hand-writing annotation. Albert sends back hand-writing annotation to point to the diagram and associate with a recorded annotation.

EXPERIMENTS AND DISCUSSIONS

After building the prototype system, we designed and conducted a pilot study of qualitative experiment to evaluate how well the intelligent social grouping services can be realized by our social network-based P2P framework. To understand the degree of users' satisfactions to the identified communities of practice, we arranged interviews at the end of the project for participating students to get direct and open-ended responses about how the prototype works. Every participating student was asked to complete a questionnaire to measure his/her satisfaction levels with our social network-based P2P framework.

Figure 4. Screen shots of IM-equipped group discussion

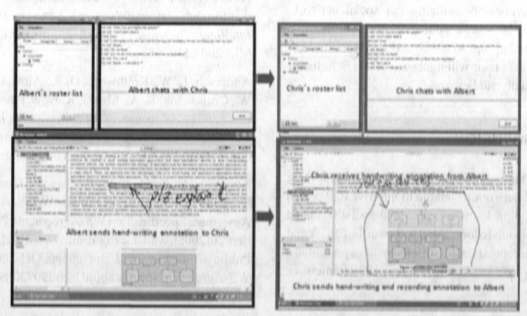

The survey reveals five findings. First, most of the participants whom found by SOtella match students' needs in terms of knowledge and social relationships. Second, students reported that even the same search option may yield different results in different trials. We found the reason is that our P2P network only searches for participants currently on line. This symptom can be alleviated since the survey shows that most of the students remain on line most of the time. Third, we found that most of the students were satisfied with the automatic identification of communities of practice. However, they still preferred to find their own participants, even though they admitted that the communities of practice identified by SOtella were knowledgeable and close to their needs. This observation suggested that we should take into account students' autonomy in addition to knowledge competence when we identify communities of practice. Fourth, most of the students emphasized the importance of user interface design of social communication and collaboration. Fifth, we perceived that students desired powerful social networking software, such as Blogs, Wikis, RSS feeds, and video podcast for synchronous discussion and file sharing.

In summary, our experiment confirmed the effectiveness of utilizing our social network-based P2P search method for the identification of social groups as a Web service. Most students expressed their willingness to utilize SOtella for their daily studies.

CONCLUSION

The major contribution of this article is applying social network technique to improve P2P search by finding knowledgeable and socially related participants to form social groups in the CSCW and CSCL context. In this article, we have presented a three-layer social network-based P2P framework equipped with the calculation methods of knowledge relationship tie and social relationship tie. Through such a framework, we demonstrated a new possibility of using social network to enhance P2P so that query can be routed to peers with strong relationship ties. Theories and models developed in support of the prototype system will also contribute to our general understanding and guide the creation of collaborative CSCW and CSCL.

We see several areas that deserve further research. Peers may have their own needs when they search for participants and interact with others; therefore, we need to conduct further study on new relationship ties and investigate special requirements from different social perspectives in addition to knowledge and social relationships.

REFERENCES

Ahuja, M., Galletta, D., & Carley, K. (2003). Individual Centrality and Performance in Virtual R&D Groups: An Empirical Study. *Management Science*, *49*(1), 21–38. doi:10.1287/mnsc.49.1.21.12756

Alani, H., Dasmahapatra, S., O'Hara, K., & Shadbolt, N. (2003). Identifying Communities of Practice through Ontology Network Analysis. *IEEE Intelligent Systems*, *18*(2), 18–25. doi:10.1109/MIS.2003.1193653

Anderson, L. W., Krathwohl, D. R., Airasian, P. W., Cruikshank, K. A., Mayer, R. E., & Pintrich, P. R. (2001). *A Taxonomy for Learning, Teaching, and Assessing: A Revision of Bloom's Taxonomy of Educational Objectives*. New York: Longman.

Andrieux, A., Czajkowski, K., Dan, A., Keahey, K., Ludwig, H., Nakata, T., et al. "Web Services Agreement Specification (WS-Agreement). 2005, Sep. 20, 2005; Available from: http://www.ggf.org/Public_Comment_Docs/Documents/Oct-2005/WS-AgreementSpecificationDraft050920.pdf.

Avouris, N., Komis, V., Margaritis, M., & Fiotakis, G. (2004). An Environment for Studying Collaborative Learning Activities. *Journal of Educational Technology & Society*, *7*(2), 34–41.

Brase, J., & Painter, M. (2004). Inferring Metadata for a Semantic Web Peer-to-Peer Environment. *Journal of Educational Technology & Society*, *7*(2), 61–67.

Bravo, C. M., Redondo, A., Ortega, M., & Verdejo, M. F. (2006). Collaborative Environments for the Learning of Design: A model and A Case Study in Domotics. *Computers & Education*, *46*, 152–173. doi:10.1016/j.compedu.2004.07.009

Chang, C. K., Zhang, J., & Chang, K. H. (2006). Survey of Computer Supported Business Collaboration in Support of Business Processes. *International Journal of Business Process Integration and Management*, *1*(2), 76–100. doi:10.1504/IJBPIM.2006.010023

Churchill, E. F., & Halverson, C. A. (2005). Social Networks and Social Networking. *IEEE Intelligent Systems*, *20*(5), 14–19.

Cuseo, J. B. (2002). *Igniting Student Involvement, Peer Interaction and Teamwork*. Stillwater, Oklahoma, USA: New Forums Press Inc.

Daradoumisa, T., Martı'nez-Mone's, A. and Xhafa, F. (2006). A Layered Framework for Evaluating On-Line Collaborative Learning Interactions. *International Journal of Human-Computer Studies*, *64*, 622–635. doi:10.1016/j.ijhcs.2006.02.001

Dimitracopoulou, A., & Petrou, A. (2005). Advanced Collaborative Distance Learning Systems for Young Students: Design Issues and Current Trends on New Cognitive and Metacognitive Tools. *Education International Journal*, *4*(11), 214–224.

Edwards, W. K., Newman, M. W., Sedivy, J. Z., Smith, T. F., Balfanz, D., Smetters, D. K., et al. (2002). Using Speakeasy for ad hoc Peer-to-Peer Collaboration. in *Proceedings of the 2002 ACM Conference on Computer Supported Cooperative Work (CSCW)*, New Orleans, LO, USA, 256-265.

Eikemeier, C., & Lechner, U. (2004). Peer-to-Peer and Group Collaboration - Do They Always Match? in *Proceedings of 13th IEEE International Workshops on Enabling Technologies: Infrastructure for Collaborative Enterprises (WET ICE)*, Jun, 101-106.

Fischer, F., Bruhn, J., Gräsel, C., & Mandl, H. (2002). Fostering Collaborative Knowledge Construction with Visualization Tools. *Learning and Instruction*, *12*, 213–232. doi:10.1016/S0959-4752(01)00005-6

Grudin, J., & Poltrock, S. (1997). Computer-supported cooperative work and groupware. *Advances in Computers*, *45*, 269–320. doi:10.1016/S0065-2458(08)60710-X

Gutwin, C., Roseman, M., & Greenberg, S. (1996). A Usability Study of Awareness Widgets in A Shared Workspace Groupware System. in *Proceedings of the 1996 ACM conference on Computer Supported Cooperative Work (CSCW)*, Boston, MA, USA, 258-267.

Hron, A., & Friedrich, H. F. (2003). A Review of Web-Based Collaborative Learning: Factors Beyond Technology. *Journal of Computer Assisted Learning*, *19*, 70–79. doi:10.1046/j.0266-4909.2002.00007.x

Jonassen, D. H. (2004). *Handbook of Research on Educational Communications and Technology: A Project of the Association for Educational Communications and Technology* (2nd ed.). Mahwah, NJ, USA: Lawrence Erlbaum Associates Inc.

Jones, A., & Issroff, K. (2005). Learning Technologies: Affective And Social Issues in Computer-Supported Collaborative Learning. *Computers & Education*, *44*, 395–408. doi:10.1016/j.compedu.2004.04.004

Kautz, H., Selman, B., & Shah, M. (1997). ReferralWeb: Combining Social Networks and Collaborative Filtering. *Communications of the ACM*, *40*(3), 27–36. doi:10.1145/245108.245123

Kollias, V., Mamalougos, N., Vamvakoussi, X., Lakkala, M., & Vosniadou, S. (2005). Teachers' Attitudes to and Beliefs about Web-Based Collaborative Learning Environments in the Context of An International Implementation. *Computers & Education*, *45*, 295–315. doi:10.1016/j.compedu.2005.04.012

Komis, V., Avouris, N., & Fidas, C. (2002). Computer-Supported Collaborative Concept Mapping: Study of Synchronous Peer Interaction. *Education and Information Technologies*, *7*(2), 169–188. doi:10.1023/A:1020309927987

Koschmann, T. (1996). Paradigm Shifts and Instructional Technology: An Introduction. In Koschmann, T. (Ed.), *CSCL: Theory and Practice of An Emerging Paradigm*. Mahwah, NJ, USA: Lawrence Erlbaum Associates.

Kreijns, K., Kirschner, P. A., Jochems, W., & Buuren, H. v. (2005). (in press). Measuring Perceived Sociability of Computer-Supported Collaborative Learning Environments. *Computers & Education*.

Lourdusamy, A., Khine, M. S., & Sipusic, M. (2003). Collaborative Learning Tool for Presenting Authentic Case Studies and Its Impact on Student Participation. *Journal of Educational Technology Systems*, *31*(4), 381–392. doi:10.2190/4GBA-UJ45-7WXU-0QVQ

Manlove, S., Lazonder, A. W., & Jong, T. (2006). Regulative Support for Collaborative Scientific Inquiry Learning. *Journal of Computer Assisted Learning*, 87–98. doi:10.1111/j.1365-2729.2006.00162.x

Miettinen, M., Kurhila, J., Nokelainen, P., Floren, P., & Tirri, H. (2003). EDUCOSM - Personalized Writable Web for Learning Communities. in *Proceedings of International Conference on Information Technology Institute of Electrical and Electronics Engineers*, 37-42.

Nejdl, W., Wolf, B., Qu, C. S., & Decker, M. Sintek, A. (2002). Naeve, M. Nilsson, M. Palmer, and T. Risch. "EDUTELLA: A P2P Networking Infrastructure Based on RDF. in *Proceedings of the ACM 11th international conference on World Wide Web (WWW)*, Honolulu, Hawaii, USA, 604-615.

Raghavan, P. (2002). Social Networks: From the Web to the Enterprise. *IEEE Internet Computing*, *6*(1), 91–94. doi:10.1109/4236.989007

Rubens, W., Emans, B., Leinonen, T., Skarmeta, A. G., & Simons, R.-J. (2005). Design of Web-Based Collaborative Learning Environments. Translating the Pedagogical Learning Principles to Human Computer Interface. *Computers & Education*, *45*, 276–294. doi:10.1016/j.compedu.2005.04.008

Tsai, W., & Ghoshal, S. (1998). Social Capital And Value Creation: The Role Of Intrafirm Networks. *Academy of Management Journal*, *41*(4), 464–476. doi:10.2307/257085

Vassileva, J. (2004). Harnessing P2P Power in the Classroom. *Intelligent Tutoring Systems (ITS'2004), Lecture Notes in Computer Science 3220*, 305-314.

Wasko, M. M., & Faraj, S. (2005). Why Should I Share? Examining Social Capital And Knowledge Contribution in Electronic Networks Of Practice. *Management Information Systems Quarterly, 29*(1), 35–57.

Weinberger, A., & Fischer, F. (2006). A Framework to Analyze Argumentative Knowledge Construction in Computer-Supported Collaborative Learning. *Computers & Education, 46*, 71–95. doi:10.1016/j.compedu.2005.04.003

Yang, S. J. H., Zhang, J., & Chen, I. Y. L. (2007). Web 2.0 Services for Identifying Communities of Practice through Social Networks. in *Proceedings of IEEE International Conference on Services Computing (SCC 2007)*, Salt Lake City, UT, USA, 130-137.

Zhang, G. Jin, Q. and Lin, M. (2005). A Framework ff Social Interaction Support for Ubiquitous Learning. in *Proceedings of the 19th International Conference on Advanced Information Networking and Applications (AINA '05)*.

Zumbach, J., Hillers, A., & Reimann, P. (2003). Supporting Distributed Problem-Based Learning: the Use of Feedback in Online Learning. In Roberts, T. (Ed.), *Online Collaborative Learning: Theory and Practice* (pp. 86–103). Hershey, PA, USA: Idea. doi:10.4018/978-1-59140-174-2.ch004

Zurita, G., & Nussbaum, M. (2004). Computer Supported Collaborative Learning using Wirelessly Interconnected Handheld Computers. *Computers & Education, 42*, 289–314. doi:10.1016/j.compedu.2003.08.005

This work was previously published in International Journal of Software Science and Computational Intelligence, Volume 1, Issue 1, edited by Yingxu Wang, pp. 51-63, copyright 2009 by IGI Publishing (an imprint of IGI Global).

Chapter 25
An Enhanced Petri Net Model to Verify and Validate a Neural-Symbolic Hybrid System

Ricardo R. Jorge
National Centre of Investigation and Technological Development, Mexico

Gerardo R. Salgado
National Centre of Investigation and Technological Development, Mexico

Vianey G. C. Sánchez
National Centre of Investigation and Technological Development, Mexico

ABSTRACT

As the Neural-Symbolic Hybrid Systems (NSHS) gain acceptance, it increases the necessity to guarantee the automatic validation and verification of the knowledge contained in them. In the past, such processes were made manually. In this article, an enhanced Petri net model is presented to the detection and elimination of structural anomalies in the knowledge base of the NSHS. In addition, a reachability model is proposed to evaluate the obtained results of the system versus the expected results by the user. The validation and verification method is divided in two stages: 1) it consists of three phases: rule normalization, rule modeling and rule verification. 2) It consists of three phases: rule modeling, dynamic modeling and evaluation of results. Such method is useful to ensure that the results of a NSHS are correct. Examples are presented to demonstrate the effectiveness of the results obtained with the method.

INTRODUCTION

Neural-Symbolic Hybrid Systems have received great attention and they have been used in application areas where the existence of faults can be expensive, such as engineering, manufacturing, science, business (Cruz, Reyes, Vergara, Perez, & Montes, 2005; Cruz, Reyes, Vergara, & Pinto, 2006; Santos, 1998) and cognitive informatics and cognitive computing (Wang, 2003, 2008). The NSHS combine symbolic knowledge (rules or frames, mainly) and connectionist (neural networks). The knowledge contained in a NSHS comes from practical and theoretical sources

DOI: 10.4018/978-1-4666-0261-8.ch025

and may contain errors. Errors occur due to data nature and to integration results from different representations (Cruz, Reyes, Vergara, Perez, & Montes, 2005; Villanueva, Cruz, Reyes, & Benítez, 2006). The previous statement is due to Rule-Based Systems (RBS) whose use is made consulting with several experts and may have conflicting experiences; on the other hand the examples of connectionist approach might be redundant due to a wrong selection. Therefore, verification and validation of extracted knowledge from a NSHS allows the knowledge engineer to make decisions in the construction of the same one (Cruz, 2004; Cruz, Reyes, Vergara, Perez, & Montes, 2005; Santos, 1998).

The validation and verification works of production rule bases have been based on the comparison of rule pairs. However, recent proposals use techniques such as Petri nets, directed graphs and directed hipergraphs (He, Chu, & Yang, 2003). In these approaches, nodes are used to represent simple clauses of a rule and directed arcs to represent causal relations.

Petri nets have been used in the study of RBS due to the possibility of capturing dynamics and structural aspects of the system. Its rule base can be verified by Petri net analysis techniques. Those techniques have been used in several works. In Yang, Lee, Chu, & Yang (1998) an error verification method in a Rule Base (RB) based in an incidence matrix is proposed. This method does not admit negated propositions. It makes a previous ordering of the RB for the verification and it does not need an initial marking of the net for the verification. In He, Chu, & Yang (2003) a reachability graph of a Petri net (PN) for structural anomalies detection in a knowledge base (KB) is presented. This technique is known as w-Net, where w indicates the amount of tokens existing in each place. Nevertheless, in this technique it is necessary to know the initial marking of the net to detect errors. In Wu & Lee (1997) a variant of classic Petri net named high level extended Petri net is proposed. This model allows the logical

negation and the use of variables and constants in the antecedent as well as consequence of the rules. Execution of the model is made by means of input conditions. It uses a reachability approach based on a color scheme for validation.

We present an enhanced Petri net model in this article. Negative relations in the rules are properly represented in this model. Errors on RB can be detected by means of an analysis of the mathematical representation of the enhanced Petri net (EPN) and the type of relation that exists between places and transitions. In validation, the inference of rules is properly represented and it considers aspects of a RBS, such as conservation of facts, refraction and closed world assumption. A color scheme for validation of the knowledge base is presented, which is raised in terms of a reachability problem.

In the following section, Neural-Symbolic Hybrid Systems are introduced. Stages of a NSHS including the validation and verification phase are presented.

NEURAL-SYMBOLIC HYBRID SYSTEMS

Neural-Symbolic Hybrid Systems are systems based on artificial neural networks that also interact with symbolic components (Cloete & Zurada, 2000). These types of systems integrate the connectionist and symbolic knowledge, in such a way that the knowledge contained in each one of these is complemented (Cruz, Reyes, Vergara, Perez, & Montes, 2005; Cruz, Reyes, Vergara, & Pinto, 2006; Negnevitsky, 2005; Santos, 1998).

NSHS transfers knowledge represented by a set of symbolic rules toward a connectionist module. The obtained neural network permits a supervised training starting from a base of examples. In the next step, an extraction algorithm is developed to obtain the knowledge of a neural network into production rule form. Finally, the rules extracted must be verified and validated to be sure that the knowledge obtained in the extracting process is suitable to solve the problem. The stages of a NSHS are shown in the Figure 1.

1. **Insertion:** In this stage, the knowledge extracted from a human expert is symbolically represented (Symbolic Module). This symbolic representation is in form of IF… THEN rules. Subsequently, it is converted to an Artificial Neural Network (ANN) named "initial" ANN. This stage is known as "rules compilation in a neural network" (Cruz, 2004).

2. **Refinement:** In this stage, a module that receives the initial ANN is implemented, which is subjected to a learning process start-ing from a base of examples. This module is named connectionist module; at the end of this stage, an artificial neural network is obtained, which is named "refined" ANN.

3. **Extraction:** In this stage, knowledge extraction contained in the refined neural network is done. At the end of the module, symbolic rules called refined rules are obtained. This process is carried out due to the necessity to interpret and to evaluate such knowledge.

4. **Verification and validation:** In this stage, the coherence of extracted knowledge in symbolic rules is verified. Just later, tests to analyze the operation of the system as a whole are done.

Figure 1. Stages of a NSHS

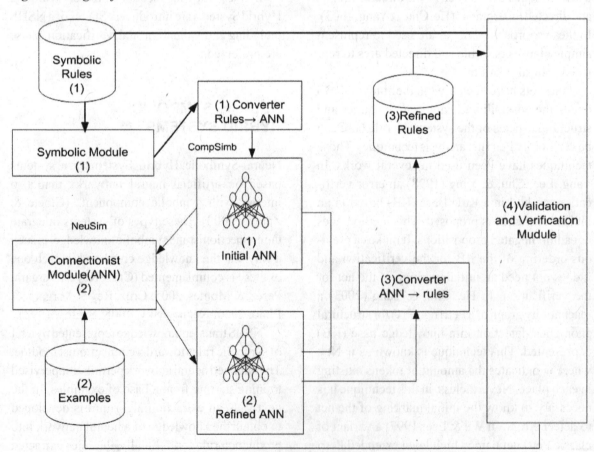

In the next section, structural errors which could arise in knowledge bases and validation problems are described.

KNOWLEDGE BASE VERIFICATION AND VALIDATION

The extracted knowledge of a NSHS is represented in production rules and stores the accessible experiences for the system. Different relations exist in the RB, for example: the conclusions of a rule can act as conditions for other rules and different rules can share common conditions. The production rules describe an IF-THEN relationship of the form $CC \Rightarrow CA$. Where CC is a collection of conditions, CA is a collection of actions or conclusions and the "$\Rightarrow$"symbol acts as a logical implication. The propositions CC can be joined by $\land \lor$ that represent the logical connectives AND/OR respectively. Propositions CA can be joined only by the connective $\land$. A negative proposition $\neg p$ in CC is true if p does not exist in the work memory. A negative proposition in CA causes elimination of p in work memory.

The main goal of verification is to obtain the consistent, complete and correct system. Because of that, anomalies on KB must be detected (Ramaswamy, Sarkar, & Chen, 1997; Ramirez & De Antonio, 2001; Tsai, Vishnuvajjala, & Zhang, 1999; Yang, Tsai, & Chen, 2003). An anomaly is referred to common fault patterns according to an analysis technique (Ramirez & De Antonio, 2007; Tsai, Vishnuvajjala, & Zhang, 1999). This KB can contain errors due to: 1) the existence of several human experts providing their experiences in the application field 2) the inserted knowledge can not be represented properly because of communication problems between human experts and the knowledge engineer, 3) the information may be missed during knowledge insertion due to matching of same one to the neural network, 4) The base of examples might be redundant due to a bad selection of samples, and 5) information

may be missed or gained during the integration process of numerical and symbolic knowledge (Cruz, Reyes, Vergara, & Pinto, 2006; He, Chu, & Yang, 2003; Santos, 1998; Villanueva, Cruz, Reyes, & Benítez, 2006). The anomalies that can be found in a KB are shown in Figure 2.

- **Redundancy:** It occurs when there are unnecessary rules in a rule base. Redundant rules increase the size of the rule base and may cause additional inferences. There are two kinds of redundancies:
  a. Duplication (equivalent rules). If $R1$: $a \land b \rightarrow c$ and $R1$: $b \land a \rightarrow c$, R1 and R2 are totally equivalents.
  b. Subsumed rules (rule contained in another one). If $R1$: $a \land c \rightarrow b$ and $R2$: $a \rightarrow b$, R1 subsumes to R2.
- **Inconsistency:** It occurs in conflictive facts. Here two types of inconsistencies are approached:

Figure 2. Anomalies that can be found in a NSHS

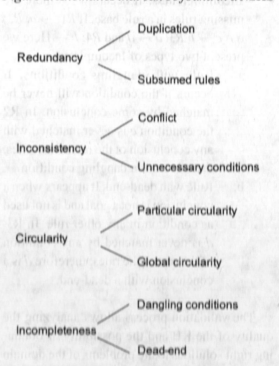

a. Conflict. A set of rules are conflicting if contrary conclusions are derived under a certain condition. An example of rules in conflict is the following: R_1: $a \rightarrow b$ and R_2: $a \rightarrow \neg b$.

b. Unnecessary conditions. A pair of rules $R, R' \in R$ has an unnecessary condition if they have the same consequent and the antecedents are only different in that some of the propositions in R are negated in R'. An example of rules with unnecessary conditions: R_1: $a \wedge b \rightarrow c$ and R_2: $a \wedge \neg b \rightarrow c$.

- **Circularity:** It occurs when several inference rules have circular dependency. Circularity can cause infinite reasoning that must be broken. The following are examples of circularity.

  a. Particular circularity. If $R1$: $a \rightarrow b$ and $R2$: $b \rightarrow a$, a cycle is formed in pairs of rules.

  b. Global circularity. If $R1$: $a \rightarrow b$, $R2$: $b \rightarrow c$, $R3$: $c \rightarrow a$ then chaining of circular rules appears.

- **Incompleteness:** It occurs when there are missing rules in a rule base. If $R1$: $\rightarrow a$, $R2$: $a \wedge c \rightarrow b$ $R3$: $a \rightarrow d$ and $R4$: $b \rightarrow$ Here we present two types of Incompleteness.

  a. Rule with dangling conditions. It occurs if the condition will never be matched by some conclusion. In R2 the condition c is never matched with any conclusion of the rest of the rules, therefore c is a dangling condition.

  b. Rule with dead-end. It appears when a conclusion is not a goal and is not used as condition in any other rule. In R3, d is never matched by any condition of the rest of the rules; therefore d is a conclusion with a dead-end.

The validation process allows analyzing the quality of the KB and the possibility of obtaining right solutions to the problems of the domain

(Knauf, Gonzalez, & Abel, 2002; Tsai, Vishnuvajjala, & Zhang, 1999).

A NSHS is only accepted when convincingly and meticulously was verified that works according to expectations.

The general evaluation frame consists of the following steps:

a. A testing criterion must be established, as reachability, reliability, safety, completeness, consistency, robustness and usability.

b. Test cases (inputs) and awaited outputs according to the selected inputs must be generated.

c. A test method to exercise the software must be applied.

d. The outputs of the software must be evaluated.

Tests are in general an intense work and a process prone to faults. Difficulties arise from different test criterions, great input and output space and legal input case generation (Knauf, Gonzalez, & Abel, 2002; Nikolopoulos, 1997; Vermesan, 1998).

- **Test criterion:** It defines the objective of comparing a system versus a specification. Different types of tests are defined according to different types of test criterions.

- **Test case generation:** Proper test inputs can be specified according to the type of problem that we can solve. It is possible to use the literature of the domain to generate the inputs as test cases.

- **Expected output generation:** An expected output consists of a response. It is possible to ask to the expert of the domain to predict the expected outputs and generate them. Furthermore, expected outputs can be generated according to explicit solution specifications, saved test cases or literature of the domain.

Test method to exercise the software. The cost of the test method not only depends on the cost of the test case generation and on the evaluation cost. It also depends on the fact that a valid result is not found. Evaluation of the software outputs. It consists on evaluating if the generated output set belongs to the expected outputs in the problem solution (Nikolopoulos, 1997).

In the following section, the concept of a Petri net and its tasks as modeling tools are described in order to introduce the validation and verification process using Petri nets.

PETRI NET AS A MODELING TOOL

A Petri net is a tool for describing and studying systems characterized for being asynchronous and concurrent. PN has been useful for modeling rule relations and PN analysis techniques can be used to analyze their actions (Ramaswamy, Sarkar, & Chen, 1997; Wu, Zhou, Wu, & Wang, 2005). A Petri net is a particular type of directed graph and it is represented graphically by a bipartite graph (there are two types of nodes) and the arcs can just connect different nodes. Nodes of a Petri net are named places and transitions. Places represent variables that define the state of the system and the transitions represent the transformer of variables. Places and transitions are connected by directed arcs (David & Alla, 2005, Murata, 1989). The graphic representation of the elements of a Petri net is shown in Figure 3.

In Figure 4, we show a Petri net with places: $P = \{P1, P2, P3, P4\}$ and transitions: $T = \{T1, T2, T3, T4\}$.

Places can be used to store "tokens". The token number contained in each place is named mark. The net marking is defined as a column vector in which the elements are the mark number contained in the places (David & Alla, 2005; Murata, 1989). In the Figure 5, the net marking is: $M=\{m_1, m_2, m_3, m_4\}$, that is: $M=[1,1,0,0]^T$.

Figure 3. Graphic representation of the Petri net elements

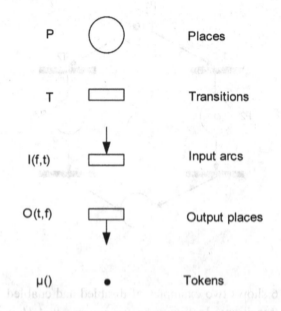

Tokens can move in the net and change the state of the same one. Tokens move from a place to other when transitions are fired.

A transition can fire if it is enabled. A transition is enabled if in each one of its input places there are, at least, the amounts of tokens as the weight of the input arcs that connect the transition (David & Alla, 2005; Murata, 1989). Figure

Figure 4. Places, transitions and arcs of a Petri net

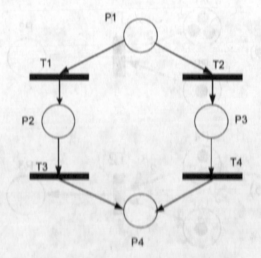

Figure 5. Net marking

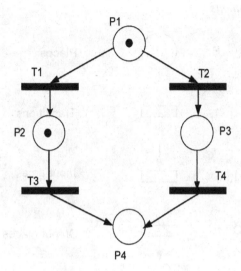

6 shows two examples of disabled and enabled transitions. In Figure 5a we can see that *t1* is enabled because of its places *P1* and *P2* comply the previous statement. In Figure 5.b, *t2* is not enabled because place *P5* does not comply with the previous statement.

The enabled transition firing permits that can be eliminated so many tokens of its input places as indicates the weight of the arcs that connect the transition. Next, it permits that can be depos-

Figure 6. Disabled and enabled transitions

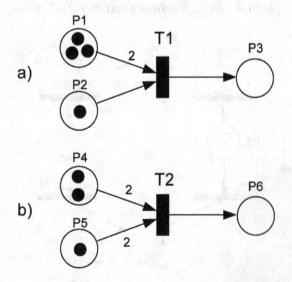

ited so many tokens in its output places as indicate the weight of the arcs that connect the transition with such output places (David & Alla, 2005; Murata, 1989).

Figure 7 shows a Petri net with two enabled transitions t1 and t3.

Figure 8 shows a Petri net after the firing of transition *t1*.

Applying Petri nets in a rule base, transitions are used to represent rules and the input and output places of transitions are used to represent conditions and conclusions of rules (Chavarría & Li, 2006; Nazareth & Kennedy, 1991). Places with tokens means the corresponding condition/conclusion is true. An enabled transition means that the conditions of the rule were satisfied and rule associated is activated. Multiple rules may be activated at the same time, but only one rule is fired at a time (Wu & Lee, 2000; Yang, Lee, Chu, & Yang, 1998; Yang, Tsai, & Chen, 2003).

Definition: *the structure of a Petri net is:* $N = \{P, T, F, W, M_0\}$

Where:

P is a set of places, *T* is a set of transitions and *F* is a set of flow relations. It means: $P \cap T = 0$, $P \cup T \neq 0$, $F \subseteq (P \times T) \cup (T \times P)$. *W* is a mapping of $F \rightarrow \{1,2,3,...\}$. It is a weight function. M_0 is

Figure 7. Petri net with enabled transitions t1 and t3

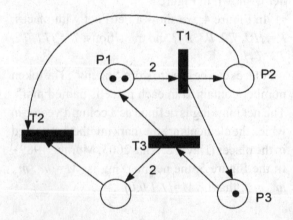

Figure 8. Petri net after the firing of t1

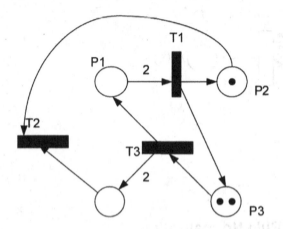

Figure 9. Elements of the EPN modeling

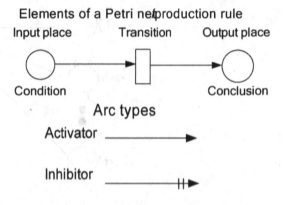

the initial marking M_0: $p \rightarrow \{0, 1, 2, 3,...\}$. It is the initial mark.

In the following section, the concept of the enhanced Petri net and the terminology used in this article about it are presented.

ENHANCED PETRI NET MODEL

Traditional Petri nets have inherent disadvantages. Some of these disadvantages are: deficiency of flexible descriptions for negative relations and necessity to formalize the original KB before beginning verification process, for example a logical system or production systems, due to the difficulty of expressing logical disjunctions (He, Chu, & Yang, 2003; Nazareth, 1993; Wu & Lee, 1997; Tsai, Vishnuvajjala, & Zhang, 1999; Yang, Lee, Chu, & Yang, 1998). In order to overcome these problems an enhanced Petri net model is proposed by us.

Definition: *An enhanced Petri net is a sextuple.*

$$N = \{P, T, F, C, I_-, I_+\}, F = F_b + F_r \qquad (1)$$

Where:

1. P is a set of places, T is a set of transitions and F contains the set of inhibitor or activator relations between CC and CA. Therefore, $F = F_b + F_r$.

2. C means that for any $p \in P$, $C(p)$ is a collection of possible colors in P. For any $t \in T$, $C(t)$ is the collection of possible colors in the transition T.

3. I_- and I_+ are negative and positive functions of PxT respectively. For any $(p,t) \in P \, x \, T$. I_- and I_+ are the previous and later transition matrices respectively.

The elements P, T, F_b, F_r are named predicate symbols (places), implications (transitions), activator arcs and inhibitor arcs, respectively. For a transition $t \in T$, a positive place $p_b \in P$ of t is a place that connects to t with an activator arc and presents a positive relation between p_b and t. A negative place $p_r \in P$ of t is a place that connects to t with an inhibitor arc and presents a negative relation between p_r and t. The elements of the EPN modeling are shown in the Figure 9.

For the rule R, t_i is its transition. The premises $C_1(r_i) \wedge C_2(r_i)... \wedge C_n(r_i)$ are *t and the conclusion $A_1(r_i)$ is t*. The representation of the rule is shown in Figure 10.

As a PN, EPN can be mathematically represented by its incidence matrix which shows the interactions between places and transitions. In an

Figure 10. EPN modeling example

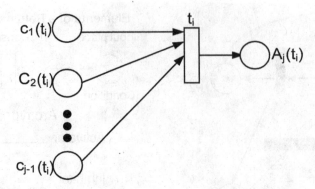

incidence matrix A_{mxn} the n columns represent places and the m rows represent transitions of N. The Table 1 shows values that can have the incidence matrix of the enhanced Petri net.

In the following section, the verification tasks are formulated as a static verification problem in a proposed Petri net.

RULE VERIFICATION PROCESS USING PETRI NETS

In this section we propose a PN based mechanism to detect and eliminate structural errors of a KB extracted from a NSHS, which consists of three phases: *rule normalization*, *rule modeling* and *rule verification.* For the rule base verification, a static analysis of the EPN model is done by means of obtaining its incidence matrix.

Rule Normalization

This step is done in order to simplify the rule base analysis. In this phase, the rules are translated into an *atomic form*:

$$R_i = C_1(r_i) \wedge C_2(r_i)... \wedge C_n(r_i) \Rightarrow A_1(r_i) \qquad (2)$$

It guarantees that each one of its parts (CC/CA) cannot be decomposed into subparts. In an atomic rule the left condition only permits the conjunction of zero or more conditional clauses and just one element as action is permitted. The kinds of rules possible to normalize are in Box 1.

In order to obtain an atomic rule, firstly, each one of the elements of production rule is transformed into disjunctive form. An element in this form consists of one or more disjunctions, each one of these being a conjunction of one or more propositions. The rules are converted to disjunctive form using the distributive property of AND over OR, the idempotency and the contradiction. It means we have to use logical equivalences. The

Table 1. Values that can have the EPN incidence matrix

Value	Means
-1	The place $p_j \in P$ is an input place to the transition $t_i \in T$.
0	There is not an arc connecting the place $p_j \in P$ with the transition $t_i \in T$ and vise versa.
1	The place $p_j \in P$ is an output place of the transition $t_i \in T$.

Box 1.

$$1.\ P_1(r_i) \wedge P_2(r_i) \wedge ... \wedge P_{j-1}(r_i) \Rightarrow P_j(r_i) \wedge P_{j+1}(r_i) \wedge ... \wedge P_k(r_i)$$
$$2.\ P_1(r_i) \vee P_2(r_i) \vee ... \vee P_{j-1}(r_i) \Rightarrow P_j(r_i) \wedge P_{j+1}(r_i) \wedge ... \wedge P_k(r_i)$$

logical equivalences that are used in this work are shown in Table 2.

Next, each subpart of the rule corresponding to each disjunction is separated. Also, a rule can have conjunctions in CA, which indicates it has multiple actions. In this way, separated rules are obtained corresponding to each action with the same set of premises that the original rule has.

In this article, we do not discuss the rules normalization with disjunctions in CA because the conclusion disjunctions do not make an explicit implication.

Rule Modeling to EPN

In this step, rule mapping of the KB to EPN modeling is shown in the section Enhanced Petri net model. The rule modeling to EPN is made once the rules were normalized to their atomic form. Mathematical representation of the EPN is also obtained.

Rule Verification

The following notations will be used during rule verification process: $CC(i)$ is a set of conditional clauses of i-th transition. $CA(i)$ is a set of conclusion clauses of i-th transition. Also:

$C_{-1,i} = \{\ P_k |\ P_k$ is the place in the j-th column in matrix A such that $A_{i,j} = -1\}$

$C_{1,i} = \{\ P_k |\ P_k$ is the place in the j-th column in matrix A such that $A_{i,j} = 1\}$

$C_{0,i} = \{\ P_k |\ P_k$ is the place in the j-th column in matrix A such that $A_{i,j} = 0\}$

Property 1. Redundancy. For t_i and t_k, $i \geq 1$, $k \leq m$; $i \neq k$; two transitions represent the rules i and k of the rule base, respectively, and execute the same action. There are two kinds of redundancy. If t_i and t_k satisfy any of the following conditions.

Table 2. Logical equivalences

Idempotency	$A \wedge A \equiv A$ $A \vee A \equiv A$
Complementary element	$A \wedge \neg A \equiv F$ $A \vee \neg A \equiv V$
Distributive	$A \vee (B \wedge C) \equiv (A \vee B) \wedge (A \vee C)$ $A \wedge (B \vee C) \equiv (A \wedge B) \vee (A \wedge C)$
Commutative	$A \vee B \equiv B \vee A$ $A \wedge B \equiv B \wedge A$

$CC(i) \subset C(k)1.$

or

$CC(i) = C(k)2.$

then the rules i and k are redundant. Duplication and subsumtion, are two kinds of redundancy.

Proof:

Property 2. *Inconsistency. For t_i and t_k $i \geq 1$, $k \leq m$, $i \neq k$; two transitions represent the rules i and k of the rule base, respectively. If t_i and t_k satisfy $CC(i) = C(k)$ and $CA(i) \neq CA(k)$ then rules i and k are conflictive rules. If t_i and t_k execute the same action and either $p_b \in C(i)$ or $p_r \in C(i)$ are not equivalent in $CC(k)$, then that condition is necessary in t_i and t_k.*

Proof:

Property 3. *Circularity. For t_p t_k,...,t_m, $i \geq 1$, $k \leq m$, $i \neq k$,..., $\neq m$; MT^*: memory work. All the transitions add their respective places to MT^* (if they were not in). In such a way if $p_b \in MT^*$ or $p_r \in TM^*$ and if it is deduced again in some transitions, then the place p causes circularity.*

Proof:

Property 4. *Incompleteness. t_i y t_k $i \geq 1$, $k \leq m$, $i \neq k$ are two transitions representing the rules i and k of the rule base, respectively; P_j is in wherever place of the transitions matrix.*

Proof: $\exists p_j \in C_{-1, i}$

1. and $\{p_b \mid p_r\} \in p_j$ for some i, such that $p_j \notin C_{-1, k}$ for all k. P_i is the condition of some rule, but it is not the conclusion of any rule. Then the corresponding rule has a dangling condition P_j.

2. $\exists p_j \in C_{-1, i}$ and $\{p_b \mid p_r\} \in p_j$ for some i, such that $p_j \notin C_{-1, k}$ for all k. P_j is the condition of some rule, but it is not matched as condition of some other rule. Besides, p_j is not a goal. The corresponding rule of p_j is a rule with dead-end.

In the following section, the task of knowledge validation is formulated as a reachability problem using a coloring scheme of the enhanced Petri net model.

RULE VALIDATION PROCESS USING PETRI NETS

In this section, we propose a mechanism to analyze the resultant rules from verification process of a NSHS. This mechanism presents a multiple color scheme in the enhanced Petri net (see section Enhanced Petri net model). The reachability of the production system is probed on the basis of the dynamic logic inference made on the enhanced Petri net. The method consists of three phases: *rule modeling to EPN, dynamic modeling of the EPN, evaluation of results.*

Rule Modeling to EPN

This step is done in order to generate the enhanced Petri net as shown in section Enhanced Petri net model. From which the verified knowledge base is received.

Firstly, The KB is mapped to the EPN model and the mathematical representation of the same one is obtained. Then, the *transposed incidence matrix* is generated, and it is represented as A^T.

The places of the enhanced Petri net model are classified into two categories: $P = \{P_C, P_R\}$. For analysis conveniences, P_C is divided into three subsets, $P_C = \{P_{CE}, P_{CI}, P_{CG}\}$ is the places collection which can obtain information through inputs by the user. P_{CI} is the places collection produced in the inference process and P_{CG} is the places collection being the conclusion of the system. On the other hand, P_R is the collection of transition places used by the model to avoid firing the same transition once the system has already fired it. It is due to the initial and deduced (in the inference process) facts are kept when the transition fire and can be used by the system has already fired it multiple rules. The reason is that input places of each transition were held as output places of the same transition (see Figure 11).

Closed world assumption. This Enhanced Petri net model works under closed world assumption, which says that if a fact is unknown, any query about it is falsified. In fact, it assumes that all positive information has been specified. Any other fact not specified is assumed as false. The negation acts as if some additional rules are added to insert all the negative information when the NSHS is consulted (Wu & Lee, 1997).

Unknown and know facts. The known facts act as input and output of the rules. The Petri net model identifies them as tokens. When the transition fires, the model deletes a token that represents an input fact from some positive input place of the transition. On the other hand, when the rule fires and it has negative propositions in the right side of a rule, it falsifies the existence of the token in that place. In order to preserve the known facts, the model must preserve the negative propositions on the left side of the rule if these exist (Wu & Lee, 1997; Wu, Zhou, Wu, & Wang 2005).

Refraction. The known facts reside in the work memory after rules fire. In order to do that, the Petri net model was modified to Enhanced Petri Net, attaching input places of a transition as well as output places of the same one (Nazareth, 993; Wu & Lee, 1997; Wu, Zhou, Wu, & Wang 2005)

Dynamic Modeling of the EPN

This step is done in order to model dynamically the EPN. This modeling is made from goals and known facts by the user.

Figure 11. Representation of the places: PCE= {P1} and PR={r1}

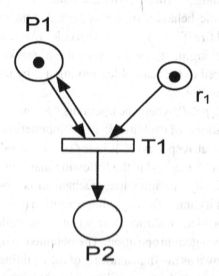

The known facts by the user act as inputs and outputs from rules. The Petri net model identifies them as tokens in the P_{CE} places. The color set: $D = \{b, r_d, r_f, f\}$ is used to the marking of the EPN and the possible tokens in places are: b, r_d, r_f and f. Color b means that the clause or conclusion represented by the place is true. Colors r_d and r_f mean that the clause or conclusion represented by the place is *deduced false* and *defaulted false*, respectively. Tokens in P_R have the color f which means that the rule has been already fired or not. Formally, the marking of the EPN is an indexed vector with respect to the places, which gives to each place p a defined *Multi-Set* (MS). The *initial marking* of the EPN is defined by using a formal notation based on sums as follows:

$$M_0 = p_1\,(1b + 1f) + p_2\,(1b + 1f).$$

The marking $M_0\,(P_R) = [1f]$, means that exist no rules fired initially.

Goals of the system are also provided by the user and they represent the P_{CG} places. They act as conclusions of the system and the goals expected by the user from the dynamic modeling.

Rules forward chaining is used to the dynamic modeling of rules. Dynamic equations control dynamic behavior of the system. A t transition could fire if it is enabled with a color $(X(t))$ under a marking μ. If t is fired then the μ' marking is changed to the reachable marking $\mu =$ by means of (see Box 2).

All $p \in P$, where the operators "+" and "-" are operations of "addition" and "subtraction" on multi-set, respectively. Where $(X(t))$ is considered a fire element and μ' the following marking of μ.

Finally, the inference mechanism is stopped when it cannot fire any other transition (there are no enabled transitions) or when some deduced fact is a goal proposition. The obtained marking is known as the final marking of the chaining and it represents the reachability of the net from initial marking to final marking. In each test, the system obtains the following data: initial facts used in the net, visited rules, fired rules, deduced facts and finally, the obtained results notification (valid or invalid results). If the final marking contains some place considered as a goal then this test is labelled as valid result. Otherwise, the test is labeled as an invalid result.

Results Evaluation

This step is done in order to evaluate all the performed tests with different initial marking. It allows evaluating the reliability of the obtained results with such initial markings.

The system is considered reliable when valid results are obtained from applied test input. If no valid results are obtained in any performed test, the quality of the input test is analyzed. In case of having applied properly test inputs, we deduce the system contains inconsistent, partially erroneous, or incomplete knowledge. In reason to, it is convenient to perform the verification process again.

In the following section, an example to demonstrate the effectiveness of our method is given.

Tests and Results

Based on our approach addressed in previous sections, the validation and verification example 1 of a KB used by a NSHS is showed.

Example 1. We propose a KB extracted from an example base which contains information about 24 patients who were examined to diagnose if they should use contact lenses according to some of their symptoms. The following data are the principal features of the example base.

Attribute information:
Age of the patient: Young, Pre-presbyopic, Presbyopic
Tear production rate: Reduced, Normal
Astigmatic: No, Yes
Spectacle prescription: Myope, Hypermetrope
Classes: Hard Contact, Soft Contact, No Contact
Distribution of the classes:
Hard Contact: 4 instances
Soft Contact: 5 instances
No Contact: 15 instances

Box 2.

$$\mu'_{b}(p) = \mu_b(p) \perp I_{b-}(p,t)(X(t)) + I_{b+}(p,t)(X(t))$$
$$\mu'_{r_d}(p) = \mu_{r_d}(p) - I_{r-}(p,t)(X(t)) + I_{r+}(p,t)(X(t))$$
$$\mu'_{r_f}(p) = \mu_{r_f}(p) - I_{b+}(p,t)(X(t)) - I_{r+}(p,t)(X(t))$$
$$-I_{b-}(p,t)(X(t)) - I_{r-}(p,t)(X(t))$$

Table 3. Results from verification process

Rule	Evaluation
2	Conflict with R12, dangling conditions
4	Conflict with R17, dangling conditions
12	Conflict with R2
17	Conflict with R4, dangling conditions
1,3,5,6,7,8,9,10, 11,13,14,15,16	Dangling conditions

The following KB was extracted from the example base mentioned above. In this case, the set of rules is normalized. It can be easily mapped into an EPN.

R1: *If -(Tear(Reduced))* **Then** *Hard_Contact*

R2: *If Astigmatic* **Then** *Hard_Contact*

R3: *If -(Spectacle(Hypermetrope)) And -(Age(Are-presbyotopic)) And -(Age(Presyopic))* **Then** *Hard_Contact*

R4: *If -(Tear(Tormal))* **Then** *Hard_Contact*

R5: *If -(Astigmatic) And -(Tear(Reduced))* **Then** *Soft_Contact*

R6: *If Spectacle(Hypermetrope) And Age(Young) And Age(Are-presbyotopic)* **Then** *Soft_Contact*

R7: *If -(Age(Presyopic)) And -(Spectacle(Myope))* **Then** *Soft_Contact*

R8: *If Tear(Tormal) And NewUnit1* **Then** *Soft_Contact*

R9: *If Tear(Reduced)* **Then** *No_Contact*

R10: *If -(Age(Young))* **Then** *No_Contact*

R11: *If -(NewUnit1)* **Then** *No_Contact*

R12: *If Astigmatic* **Then** *No_Contact*

R13: *If Spectacle(Hypermetrope)* **Then** *No_Contact*

R14: *If Age(Presyopic) And Age(Are-presbyotopic) And -(Spectacle(Myope)) And Tear(Tormal)* **Then** *No_Contact*

R15: *If Astigmatic And Age(Are-presbyotopic) And Tear(Reduced) And Spectacle(Hypermetrope)* **Then** *NewUnit1*

R16: *If -(Spectacle(Myope))* **Then** *NewUnit1*

R17: *If -(Tear(Tormal))* **Then** *NewUnit1*

Verification process results. For this analysis, the propositions: *Hard_Contact, Soft_Contact and No_Contac* were used as goals. First of all, the normalization process was made to the KB (For this case, the KB was already normalized). Next, the mapping of KB for EPN modeling and its incidence matrix was made. Finally, the veri-

Table 4. Results from validation process

Tests
Test:1   *Initial facts:* Spectacle (Hypermetrope), Age(Young), Age(Are-presbyotopic),   *Visited rules:* 1;   *Fired rules:* 1,   *Deduced facts:* Hard_Contact,   *Validate:* YES->goal: Hard_Contact
Test:2   *Initial facts:* Spectacle(Hypermetrope), Age(Young), Age(Are- presbyotopic), Tear(Reduced),   *Visited rules:* 1,2,3,4;   *Fired rules:* 4,   *Deduced facts:* Hard_Contact,   *Validate:* YES->goal: Hard_Contact
Test:3   *Initial facts:* Spectacle(Hypermetrope), Age(Young), Age(Are-presbyotopic), Tear(Reduced), Tear(Tormal),   *Visited rules:* 1,2,3,4,5,6;   *Fired rules:* 6,   *Deduced facts:* Soft_Contact,   *Validate:* YES->goal: Soft_Contact

fication process was done. The Table 3 shows the obtained results from verification process applied to the previous KB.

In this process we can see that incomplete knowledge due to dangling conditions was detected in all rules (conditions will not be matched with any conclusion).

The user makes rules elimination according to his requirements, except for duplicated rules with some other, which are eliminated automatically. The new rule base contains less rules than the original one, it is free of errors and is better structured.

Validation process results. For this analysis, each of the test used different initial facts. *Hard_Contact, Soft_Contact* and *No_Contact* were used as goal propositions. Table 4 shows the obtained results from validation process applied to the verified KB.

CONCLUSION AND FUTURE WORKS

In this article an EPN model is presented for verification and validation of a NSHS. KBs of the NSHS are expressed in production rules based on propositional logic. Such KBs can involve negative information and contain disjunctions in their production rules. These aspects can be expressed by using our EPN method, but not in a traditional Petri net. It is due to in a traditional Petri net some authors create a new place to represent a negative proposition, and use a new place to represent a set of disjunctions. Our method reduces the processing time in validation and verification processes.

Our verification method is based on incidence matrix of an EPN. This method has the advantage that it is independent from the initial marking of the net.

The validation method is based on reachability analysis of the enhanced Petri net. This analysis is executed from test cases and expected goals with such selected inputs. Important aspects of RBS such as facts conservation, refraction and closed world assumption, can be easily modelled from the color scheme here presented.

As future work we consider to include verification and validation of production rules with uncertainty factors. In order to do this, it would be necessary to redefine other verification definitions. This adaptation leads us to consider extending the redundancy and inconsistency definitions in order to detect such anomalies in a set of rules. Another promising line of work we are tackling is an extension of the proposed method that permits detecting incompleteness using submarking reachability and simulation.

REFERENCES

Chavarría, B. L., & Li, X. (2006). Structural error verification in active rule based systems using Petri nets. *Proceedings of the Fifth Mexican International Conference on Artificial Intelligence (MICAI'06)* (pp. 12 - 21), Apizaco, Mexico, Nov.

Cloete, I., & Zurada, J. (2000). *Knowledge-Based Neurocomputing* (Eds.). MIT Press, Cambridge, MA.

Cruz, S. V. G. (2004). *Neural-Symbolic Hybrid System to refine the knowledge of an Artificial Vision System.* Master Thesis, Cenidet, Cuernavaca, Morelos, Mexico.

Cruz, S. V. G., Reyes, S. G., Vergara, V. O. O., Perez, O. J., & Montes, R. A. (2005). Compilation of symbolic knowledge and integration with numeric knowledge using hybrid systems. Springer Lecture Notes In Computer Science. *Proc. 4th Mexican International Conference on Artificial Intelligence* (MICAI'05) (pp. 11−20), Monterrey, Nuevo León, México, Nov.

Cruz, S. V. G., Reyes, S. G., Vergara, V. O. O., & Pinto, E. R. (2006). A Combined Representation to Refine the Knowledge Using a Neuro-Symbolic Hybrid System applied in a Problem of Apple Classification. *Proc. 16th IEEE Int. Conf. on Electronics, Communications and Computers (CONIELECOMP-06)* (pp. 30-30). Puebla, México, Feb.

David, R., & Alla, H. (2005). *Discrete, continuous and Hybrid Petri nets.* Berlin, Heidelberg: Springer- Verlang.

He, X., Chu, W., & Yang, H. (2003). A new Approach to Verify Rule-Based System Using Petri Nets. *Information and Software Technology, 45*(10), 663–670. doi:10.1016/S0950-5849(03)00058-2

Knauf, R., Gonzalez, A. J., & Abel, T. (2002). A Framework for Validation of Rule-Based Systems. *IEEE Transactions on Systems, Man, and Cybernetics. Part B, Cybernetics, 32*(3), 281–295. doi:10.1109/TSMCB.2002.999805

Murata, T. (1989). Petri Nets: Properties, Analysis and Applications. *Proceedings of the IEEE* (pp. 541-580), Illinois, Chicago, USA, April.

Nazareth, D. L. (1993). Investigating the Applicability of Petri Nets for Rule-Based Systems Verification. *IEEE Transactions on Knowledge and Data Engineering, 4*(3), 402–415. doi:10.1109/69.224193

Nazareth, D. L., & Kennedy, M. H. (1991). Verification of Rule-Based Knowledge Using Directed Graphs. *Knowledge Acquisition, 3,* 339–360. doi:10.1016/S1042-8143(05)80024-X

Negnevitsky, M. (2005). *Artificial Intelligence. A guide to Intelligent Systems* (2nd ed.). ADDISON WESLEY.

Nikolopoulos, C. (1997). *Expert Systems*. Bradley University, Peoria Illinois. MARCEL DEKKER, INC.

Ramaswamy, M., Sarkar, S., & Chen, Y. S. (1997). Using Directed Hypergraphs to Verify Rule-Based Expert Systems. *IEEE Transactions on Knowledge and Data Engineering, 9*(2), 221–237. doi:10.1109/69.591448

Ramirez, J., & De Antonio, A. (2001). Checking Integrity Constraints in Reasoning Systems based on Propositions and Relationships. *Proceedings of the 13th International Conference on Software Engineering and Knowledge Engineering*, SEKE.01 (pp. 188-196), Buenos Aires, Argentina, June.

Ramirez, J., & De Antonio, A. (2007). Checking the Consistency of a Hybrid Knowledge Base System. *Elsevier Science. Knowledge-Based Systems, 20*(3), 225–237. doi:10.1016/j.knosys.2006.05.019

Santos, F. (1998). *INSS - Un Système Hybride Neuro-Symbolique pour l'Apprentissage Automatique Constructif,* PhD Thesis, LEIBNIZ-IMAG, Grenoble – France.

Tsai, W., Vishnuvajjala, R., & Zhang, D. (1999). Verification and Validation of Knowledge-Based Systems. *IEEE Transactions on Knowledge and Data Engineering, 11*(1), 202–212. doi:10.1109/69.755629

Vermesan, A. I. (1998). *Foundation and Application of Expert System Verification and Validation.* The Handbook of Applied Expert Systems. Ed. CRC Press LLC, (pp. 5.1–5.32).

Villanueva, T. J., Cruz, S. V. G., Reyes, S. G., & Benítez, A. (2006). Extracting Refined Rules from Hybrid Neuro-Symbolic Systems. *Proceedings of the International Joint Conference on Neural Networks (IJCNN '06)* (pp. 3021-3025). Vancouver, Canada, July.

Wang, Y. (2003). On Cognitive Informatics, *Brain and Mind: A Transdisciplinary Journal of Neuroscience and Neorophilisophy, 4*(3), 151-167, Kluwer Academic Publishers, August.

Wang, Y. (2008). On Contemporary Denotational Mathematics for Computational Intelligence. *Transactions of Computational Science, 2*, 6–29. doi:10.1007/978-3-540-87563-5_2

Wu, C., & Lee, S. (2000). A Token-Flow Paradigm for Verification of Rule-Based Expert Systems. *IEEE Trans. on Systems, Man, and Cybernetics. Part B., 30*(4), 616–624.

Wu, C. H., & Lee, S. J. (1997). Enhanced High Level Petri Nets with Multiple Colors for Knowledge Verification/Validation of Rule-Based Expert Systems. *IEEE Trans. on Systems, Man, and Cybernetics. Part B., 27*(5), 760–773.

Wu, Q., Zhou, C., Wu, J., & Wang, C. (2005). Study on Knowledge Base Verification Based on Petri Nets. *International Conference on Control and Automatization (ICCA2005)* (pp. 997–1001), Budapest, Hungry.

Yang, S. J. H., Lee, A. S., Chu, W. C., & Yang, H. (1998). Rule Base Verification Using Petri Nets. In *Proccedings 22-nd Annual Int. Computer Software and Applications Conf. (COMPSAC-98)* (pp. 476-481), Vienna, Austria, august.

Yang, S. J. H., Tsai, J. J. P., & Chen, C. C. (2003). Fuzzy Rule Base System Verification Using High-Level Petri Nets. *IEEE Transactions on Knowledge and Data Engineering, 15*(2), 457–473. doi:10.1109/TKDE.2003.1185845

This work was previously published in International Journal of Software Science and Computational Intelligence, Volume 1, Issue 3, edited by Yingxu Wang, pp. 36-52, copyright 2009 by IGI Publishing (an imprint of IGI Global).

Chapter 26
System Uncertainty Based Data-Driven Knowledge Acquisition

Jun Zhao
Chongqing University of Posts & Telecommunications, P.R. China

Guoyin Wang
Chongqing University of Posts & Telecommunications, P.R. China

ABSTRACT

In the three-layered framework for knowledge discovery, it is necessary for technique layer to develop some data-driven algorithms, whose knowledge acquiring process is characterized by and hence advantageous for the unnecessity of prior domain knowledge or external information. System uncertainty is able to conduct data-driven knowledge acquiring process. It is crucial for such a knowledge acquiring framework to measure system uncertainty reasonably and precisely. Herein, in order to find a suitable measuring method, various uncertainty measures based on rough set theory are comprehensively studied: their algebraic characteristics and quantitative relations are disclosed; their performances are compared through a series of experimental tests; consequently, the optimal measure is determined. Then, a new data-driven knowledge acquiring algorithm is developed based on the optimal uncertainty measure and the Skowron's algorithm for mining propositional default decision rules. Results of simulation experiments illustrate that the proposed algorithm obviously outperforms some other congeneric algorithms.

INTRODUCTION

Cognitive Informatics (CI) is a new transdisciplinary research field. It combines cognitive science with informatics. The combination captures both the understanding of intelligence in minds

DOI: 10.4018/978-1-4666-0261-8.ch026

and its implementation in computers. That characteristic makes CI develops rapidly in recent years (Kinsner, 2005; Wang, 2002; Wang, 2002; Wang, 2003; Wang, 2003; Wang, 2004; Wang & Kinsner, 2006; Wang, 2007). The general ideas of CI can be applied in studying related problems. In the field of knowledge discovery in databases, a three-layered framework can be accordingly established based on those ideas (Yao, 2004). The three layers, from the inner to the outer, are philosophy layer, technique layer and application layer. Different layer deals with problems in different contexts, i.e. in mind, in computer and in application, respectively. Each layer provides services for the outer ones. According to this three-layered framework, philosophy layer conceptually provides prior domain knowledge for technique layer. However, it is very possible that prior knowledge is biased or even incorrect in some real-life applications. To make matter even worse, prior knowledge is very possibly unavailable at all in some cases which have not been well explored yet. Therefore theoretically and practically speaking, it is necessary for technique layer to develop algorithms that are independent of prior knowledge. Such algorithms are completely data-driven, namely, their knowledge acquiring process can be conducted or directed by information systems themselves, and therefore prior knowledge or external information is no longer necessary for them.

Essentially, knowledge acquiring process can be regarded as a kind of knowledge transformation. In an original information system, knowledge exists in the form of primitive data. To make the knowledge more understandable and applicable, several steps may be involved in data mining process. For example, in rough set theory, a typical processing sequence includes steps such as discretization, reduction and rule acquisition. Accordingly, knowledge is sequentially transformed from original data to discretized data, reduced forms, and then ultimate decision rules or decision trees. Conceptually speaking, knowledge needs to be kept essentially undisturbed in the transforming sequence. Thus, data-driven methods have to utilize some special features of knowledge to direct its mining process. One of the most interesting issues of data-driven knowledge acquisition is to find out such reasonable features. For knowledge in different forms, those features must be commonly existed and intrinsic, and can be

quantitatively measured and comparable. System uncertainty is such a good candidate. Due to the inherent existence of various uncertain factors, system uncertainty is an intrinsic common feature of and hence becomes an essential link between information systems and their induced knowledge systems. In fact, data-driven algorithms for acquiring decision rules have already been successfully implemented based on the minimum degree of the local certainty of information systems (Wang & He, 2002; Wang & He, 2003). Obviously, a data-driven knowledge acquiring framework based on system uncertainty requires first of all, measuring and handling system uncertainty as reasonably and precisely as possible. It is obvious that the ultimate performance may be negatively influenced if an improper uncertainty measure is applied in such an algorithm.

In rough set theory, the uncertainty concerned problem is one of the hottest research topics, and some results have already been gotten: some system uncertainty measures have been proposed (Chen, Zhu, & Ji, 2001; Düntsch & Gediga, 1998; Pawlak, Grzymala-Busse, Slowinski & Ziarko, 1995; Wang, 2001; Wang, 2001; Wang & He, 2002; Wang & He, 2003); several algorithms based on system uncertainty have been implemented (Mollestad & Skowron, 1996; Wang & He, 2002; Wang & He, 2003). All these achievements paved a concrete way for the realization of data-driven knowledge acquisition based on system uncertainty. However, to my best knowledge, up to now in literature there is no thorough study or comparison on those rough set model based system uncertainty measures. Herein, to find a suitable measuring method for directing knowledge acquisition, various system uncertainty measures based on rough set theory are comprehensively studied: their algebraic characteristics and quantitative relations are theoretically analyzed; their performance is experimentally compared; and the optimal measure is then determined based on the results of the analyses and experiments. Then a new data-driven knowledge acquiring algorithm is proposed on the bases of the optimal measure for system uncertainty and the Skowron's algorithm (Mollestad & Skowron, 1996) for mining propositional default decision rules. The new algorithm is typically data-driven. Its knowledge acquiring process is completely directed by system uncertainty; and thus is independent of prior domain knowledge or external parameters. Simulation experiments illustrate that compared with other congeneric algorithms, the new algorithm can be more adaptive to the uncertainty of information systems; its comprehensive performance is improved obviously by further improving the mechanism of determining parameters for algorithms.

The rest of the article is organized as follows. Section 2 gives some relevant preliminary knowledge of rough set theory. Section 3 describes and discusses system uncertainty measures based on rough set model. Section 4 studies their algebraic characteristics and quantitative relations. Section 5 compares their performances through simulation experiments. Section 6 presents the new data-driven knowledge acquiring algorithm. Section 7 describes details of experimental comparison on the performances of the new algorithm with congeneric ones. The article is concluded with a summarization in section 8.

PRELIMINARY KNOWLEDGE

Definition 1: *A 5-tuple DS=(U, V, f, C ∪ D) is an **information system**. Where, U is a finite set of instances composing its universe; C and D determine its attribute space and are finite sets of condition attributes and decision attributes, respectively; V_a is the domain of a ∈ C ∪ D and V = ∪ V_a; f: U→V is an information function mapping its instances to attribute space.*

Information systems sometimes are more exactly called decision information systems. The value of x∈U regarding a ∈ C ∪ D is denoted by a(x), i.e. f(x, a)= a(x).

Definition 2: *Given DS = (U, V, f, C ∪ D) and A ⊆ C ∪ D, A defines an **indiscernibility relation** IND(A) on U: IND(A)={(x, y)|(x, y) ∈ U × U ∧ ∀ a ∈ A(a(x)=a(y))}.*

IND(A) is obviously an equivalence relation on U. It results in a partition on U marked by U/IND(A). By notation of $[x]_{IND(A)}$, we refer to the equivalence block of attribute set A containing instance x. Specially, X ∈ U/IND(C) is a so-called **condition class**. Y ∈ U / IND(D) is a so-called **decision class**.

Definition 3: *Given DS=(U, V, f, C ∪ D) and X ∈ U/IND(C), T_X=max({X ∩ Y | Y ∈ U /IND(D)}) is the **dominant component** of X.*

T_X includes instances of X with the most possible decision value. Thus in a sense, it can be regarded as the certain part of X. Accordingly, $|T_X|/|X|$ is the so-called **certainty ratio** of X.

For the sake of convenience, we might assume that given a DS=(U, V, f, C ∪ D), U/IND(C) = {X_1,...,X_t} and U / IND(D)={Y_1,..., Y_s}. We further assume that elements of U/IND(C) and U / IND(D) are arranged in sequences satisfying ∃$_c$ ∀$_i$ ∃$_j$(1≤ c ≤t ∧ 1 ≤i ≤c ∧ 1 ≤j ≤ s ∧ X_i ⊆ Y_j), and ∃$_{cβ}$ ∀$_i$ ∃$_j$(1 ≤ $c_β$ ≤ t ∧ 1 ≤ i ≤ $c_β$ ∧ 1 ≤ j ≤ s ∧ | T_{Xi}| / | X_i| ≥ β), where β is a threshold in (0.5, 1].

Obviously, c ≤ $c_β$, c = $c_β$ always holds when β = 1. If 1 ≤ i ≤ c, T_{Xi} = X_i.

Definition 4: *Given DS = (U, V, f, C ∪ D) and x ∈ U, if ∃ y ∈ U (y ∈ $[x]_{IND(C)}$ ∧ y ∉ $[x]_{IND(D)}$), then x is uncertain, and x is inconsistent with y; if ∀ y ∈ U (y ∈ $[x]_{IND(C)}$→y ∈ $[x]_{IND(D)}$), x is certain or deterministic.*

Inconsistent instances are accordingly with the same value regarding each condition attribute, therefore are in one condition class. However, they are with different values regarding at least one decision attribute, consequently belong to different decision classes.

A condition class is uncertain if it contains uncertain instances. An information system is uncertain if it holds at least one uncertain condition class.

Definition 5: *Given DS=(U, V, f, C∪D), $V_0 = \cup_{1 \leq i \leq c} X_i$ is the **positive region** of C with reference to D.*

Definition 6: *Given DS=(U, V, f, C ∪ D) and $0.5 < \beta \leq 1$, $V_1 = \cup_{1 \leq i \leq c\beta} X_i$ is the **β-positive region** of C with reference to D.*

Definition 7: *Given DS=(U, V, f, C ∪ D) and $0.5 < \beta \leq 1$, $V_2 = \cup_{1 \leq i \leq c\beta} T_{Xi}$ is the **modified β-positive region** of C with reference to D.*

V_0 is defined based on traditional rough set theory. V_1 and V_2 are defined based on the variable precise rough set model (Ziarko, 1993), where β, a value between 0.5 and 1, is the so-called precise threshold. Obviously, $V_0 \subseteq V_2 \subseteq V_1$.

Definition 8: *Given DS=(U, V, f, C ∪ D) and B ⊆ C ∪ D, if U/IND(B)={X_1, ..., X_n}, the **probability distribution** of B on U is: [U/IND(B):P]=*

$$\begin{bmatrix} X_1 & \cdots & X_n \\ p(X_1) & \cdots & p(X_n) \end{bmatrix}$$

where $p(X_i) =$

$$\frac{|X_i|}{|U|}, i=1, ...,n.$$

Definition 9: *Given DS=(U, V, f, C ∪ D), X ∈ U/IND(C) and Y ∈ U /IND(D), the **conditional probability** of Y to X is $p(Y|X) = |X \cap Y|/|X|$.*

Definition 10: *Given DS=(U, V, f, C ∪ D), the **information entropy** of C on U is:*

Definition 11: *Given DS=(U, V, f, C∪D), the **conditional entropy** of D on U with reference to C is $H(D|C) = -\sum_{1 \leq i \leq s} p(X_i) \sum_{1 \leq j \leq s} p(Y_j|X_i) log(p(Y_j|X_i))$.*

SYSTEM UNCERTAINTY MEASURES BASED ON ROUGH SET THEORY

Measures Based on Positive Region

Definition 12: **Given DS = (U, V, f, C ∪ D), its** *uncertainty ratio based on positive region* **is:**

$$\mu_{pos} = |U - V_0|/|U| = 1 - |V_0|/|U|.$$

Measures Based on the Certainty of Condition Classes

Totally, there are two approaches measuring system uncertainty based on the certainty of condition classes. One is **average uncertainty ratio**, the other is **whole uncertainty ratio**.

Definition 13 (Wang, 2001): **Given DS = (U, V, f, C ∪ D), its** *average uncertainty ratio* **is:**

$$\mu_{aver} = \sum_{1 \leq i \leq s} p(X_i)(|X_i - T_{Xi}|/|X_i|) = 1 - \sum_{1 \leq i \leq s} p(X_i)|T_{Xi}|/|X_i|.$$

In probability sense, μ_{aver} is the average value of the uncertainty ratios of all condition classes.

Definition 14 (Wang & He, 2003): **Given DS = (U, V, f, C ∪ D), its** *whole uncertainty ratio* **is:**

$$\mu_{whl} = 1 - (\sum_{1 \leq i \leq s} |T_{Xi}|)/|U|.$$

μ_{whl} measures system uncertainty in the way similar to μ_{pos}. The difference between them is that μ_{whl} is based on an extended concept of positive region. Essentially, μ_{whl} takes $\cup_{1 \leq i \leq s} T_{Xi}$ rather than

V_0 as the positive region of *DS*. The conclusion is obvious if the equality between $\sum_{1 \leq i \leq t} |T_{Xi}^+|$ and $|\cup_{1 \leq i \leq t} T_{Xi}|$ is noticed.

Measures Based on Information Entropy

In (Düntsch & Gediga, 1998), information systems are grouped into three types based on their capabilities of expressing their domains. Different entropy functions are defined to measure system uncertainty accordingly.

The first kind: $DS = (U, V, f, C \cup D)$ can not only express knowledge C and D, but also determine the uncertainty structure of *DS* by the interaction between C and D. Namely, *DS* provides all information about the domain space.

Definition 15: Given $DS=(U, V, f, C \cup D)$, its **knowing-it-all entropy** is $H^{loc}(C \rightarrow D) = H(C) + H(D|C)$.

Definition 16: Given $DS = (U, V, f, C \cup D)$, its **uncertainty ratio based on knowing-it-all entropy** is $\mu_{loc} = 1 - (H^{loc}(C \rightarrow D) - H(D))/(log(|U|) - H(D))$.

The second kind: $DS = (U, V, f, C \cup D)$ can express only knowledge C, that is, the mapping function from C to D is deterministic only for certain instances, but completely random for all uncertain instances.

Definition 17: Given $DS = (U, V, f, C \cup D)$, its **playing-it-safe entropy** is:

$$H^{det}(C \rightarrow D) = -\sum_{1 \leq i \leq c} p(X_i) log(p(X_i)) + log(|U|)|U - V_0|/|U|.$$

$H^{det}(C \rightarrow D)$ includes two cut parts, i.e. the entropy of positive region and the entropy of all uncertain instances. The former part is typically based on information view, while the latter is

essentially in algebra view. Thus, the concept is simultaneously with characteristics of information and algebra views. When an information system is with slight uncertainty and has few uncertain instances, $H^{det}(C \rightarrow D)$ is very possibly dominant by its characteristics of information entropy. However, with the increase of system uncertainty, the contribution of uncertain instances to $H^{det}(C \rightarrow D)$ gradually becomes more and more important, then, $H^{det}(C \rightarrow D)$ may be overwhelmed by its algebraic characteristics.

If $1 \leq i \leq c$, X_i contributes $-p(X_i)log(p(X_i))$ to $H^{det}(C \rightarrow D)$. If $c < i \leq t$, the contribution of X_i is $log(|U|)(|X_i|/|U|)=p(X_i)log(|U|)$, since $U - V_0 = \cup_{c < i \leq t} X_i$.

Definition 18: Given $DS = (U, V, f, C \cup D)$, its **uncertainty ratio based on playing-it-safe entropy** is $\mu_{det}=1-(H^{det}(C \rightarrow D)-H(D))/(log(|U|)-H(D))$.

The third kind: The first kind treats too obscurely the edge between certain and uncertain parts of an information system, while the second kind deals with that edge too abruptly. Thus, the third view handles that edge in a compromising way. It thinks that the distribution of uncertain instances can be neither completely deterministic nor completely random. Such ideas are more reasonable and realistic in real-life cases. Unfortunately, no entropy function for the third type is given in (Düntsch & Gediga, 1998).

Measures Based on Variable Precise Rough Set Model & Information Entropy

Dr. Chen et al accept the idea of **playing-it-safe entropy**, i.e. the probability distribution is deterministic for certain instances but random for uncertain ones. However, by utilizing variable precise rough set model, they extend the **positive region** of an information system from V_0 to either V_1 or V_2, so that partial uncertain instances of the system can be covered by the extended positive regions. Accordingly, two entropy functions are defined to express system uncertainty (Chen, Zhu & Ji, 2001).

Definition 19: *Given DS = (U, V, f, C ∪ D) and 0.5 < β ≤ 1, its **entropy based on β-positive region** is $H^1 (C \to D) = - \sum_{1 \leq i \leq c_\beta} p(X_i) \log(p(X_i) + \log(|U|)|U - V_1|/|U|$.*

Definition 20: *Given DS = (U, V, f, C ∪ D) and 0.5 < β ≤ 1, its **entropy based on modified β-positive region** is $H^2 (C \to D) = - \sum_{1 \leq i \leq c_\beta} p(T_{Xi}) \log(p(T_{Xi}) + \log(|U|)|U - V_2|/|U|$.*

Measures based on variable precise rough set model are more flexible, since the positive regions can be adjusted by setting proper thresholds. However, their performance depends on an external parameter, i.e. the precise threshold β. Moreover, neither $H^1(C \to D)$ nor $H^2(C \to D)$ is properly normalized, that makes incomparable their measured results on information systems with different scales.

According to the above definitions, if $1 \leq i \leq c$, each X_i contributes $-p(X_i)\log(p(X_i))$ to both H^1 $(C \to D)$ and $H^2 (C \to D)$ since $T_{Xi} = X_i$. Similarly, if $c_\beta < i \leq t$, each X_i contributes $p(X_i)\log(|U|)$ to $H^1(C \to D)$ and $H^2(C \to D)$; however, if $c < i \leq c_\beta$, each X_i contributes $-p(X_i)\log(p(X_i))$ to $H^1(C \to D)$, but $-p(T_{Xi})\log(p(T_{Xi})) + \log(|U|)p(X_i - T_{Xi})$ to $H^2(C \to D)$.

ALGEBRAIC CHARACTERISTICS OF SYSTEM UNCERTAINTY MEASURES

Theorem 1: *Given DS = (U, V, f, C ∪ D), $\mu_{aver} = \mu_{whl}$.*

Proof: *If the probability distribution of condition classes is estimated in the way of Definition 8, it is obvious that $\mu_{aver} = \mu_{whl}$.*

Theorem 2: *Given DS = (U, V, f, C ∪ D), $\mu_{whl} \leq 1 - 1/N_D$, where N_D is the number of decision classes of DS, i.e. $N_D = |U/IND(D)|$.*

Proof: $\mu_{whl} = 1 - (\sum_{1 \leq i \leq t} |T_{Xi}|)/|U| = 1 - \sum_{1 \leq i \leq t}((|T_{Xi}|/|X_i|) \times (|X_i|/|U|)) = 1 - \sum_{1 \leq i \leq t}((|T_{Xi}|/|X_i|) \times p(X_i))$

According to Definition 3, $|T_{Xi}|$ would be minimum for a given $X_i \in U/IND(C)$ if all possible decision values appear in X_i at equal probability. $|T_{Xi}|/|X_i| = 1/N_D$ under that condition. Thus, $|T_{Xi}|/|X_i| \geq 1/N_D$ holds for all $X \in U/IND(C)$. Accordingly, $\mu_{whl} \leq 1 - \sum_{1 \leq i \leq t}(1/N_D \times p(X_i)) = 1 - 1/N_D$.

Theorem 3: *Given DS = (U, V, f, C ∪ D), $\mu_{pos} \geq \mu_{whl}$.*

Proof: *It is obvious that $T_{Yi} = X_i$ if $1 \leq i \leq c$. Accordingly, $V_0 = \cup_{1 \leq i \leq c} X_i = \cup_{1 \leq i \leq c} T_{Xi} \subseteq \cup_{1 \leq i \leq t} T_{Xi}$. Then $|V_0| \leq |\cup_{1 \leq i \leq t} T_{Xi}| = \sum_{1 \leq i \leq t} |T_{Xi}|$. Thus, $\mu_{pos} \geq \mu_{whl}$.*

An approach based on either positive region or the certainty of condition classes measures system uncertainty in algebra view. The positive region based measure is relevant to only basic conceptions of traditional rough set theory. However, it may exaggerate system uncertainty to some extent, for the positive region of an information system will exclude a whole condition class even if it in fact only holds a negligible part of uncertain instances. Whereas, approaches based on the certainty of condition classes think that in a sense, a condition class always indicates a kind of certainty. The computation of the certainty of a condition class is based on an intuition that in a given condition class, the decision value which meets most instances is the most possible value, thus all instances with such decision value can be regarded as certain. With such ideas in mind, **average uncertainty ratio** gets the average value in probability sense of uncertainty ratios of all condition classes, while **whole uncertainty ratio** computes the ratio of all uncertain instances to the whole universe. However, as illustrated by Theorem 1, both methods can get the same measured results.

Theorem 4: *Given DS = (U, V, f, C ∪ D), $\mu_{loc} \geq \mu_{det}$.*

Proof: *It is proved that to DS = (U, V, f, C ∪ D), $H^{loc}(C{\rightarrow}D) \leq H^{det}(C{\rightarrow}D)$ (Düntsch, 1998). Hence, the conclusion of $\mu_{loc} \geq \mu_{det}$ holds according to Definition16 and Definition18.*

It is reasonable that $H^{loc}(C{\rightarrow}D) \leq H^{det}(C{\rightarrow}D)$, since the latter conceptually exaggerates system uncertainty to extremes. Consequently, it seems more intuitively rational that to a given information system, its uncertainty measured by $H^{det}(C{\rightarrow}D)$ should be greater than that measured by $H^{loc}(C{\rightarrow}D)$. However, as illustrated by the above theorem, the mathematical relation between μ_{det} and μ_{loc} obviously contradicts with such intuition. This fact indicates that when defining μ_{loc} and μ_{det}, the methods of utilizing $H^{loc}(C{\rightarrow}D)$ or $H^{det}(C{\rightarrow}D)$ may be further improved.

Lemma 1: *Given DS=(U, V, f, C ∪ D), if DS is certain, $V_0 = U$ and $H(D|C)=0$.*

Theorem 5: *Given DS=(U, V, f, C ∪ D), if DS is certain, $\mu_{loc}=\mu_{det}$.*

Proof: *If DS is certain, $H^{loc}(C{\rightarrow}D) = H(C)+H(D|C)$ = H(C) since H(D|C)=0; meanwhile, it is easy to see that $H^{det}(C{\rightarrow}D)=H(C)$ from Definition 17 since $V_0= U$. Then, $H^{loc}(C{\rightarrow}D) =H^{det}(C{\rightarrow}D)$. Thus, $\mu_{loc}=\mu_{det}$.*

Theorem 6: *Given DS = (U, V, f, C ∪ D), if $\mu_{pos}=1$, $\mu_{det}=0$.*

Proof: *If $\mu_{pos} = 1$, then $|V_0| = 0$ and $V_0 = \varphi$. Thus, $H^{det}(C{\rightarrow}D) = log(|U|)$. Then $\mu_{det} = 0$.*

Given DS=(U, V, f, C ∪ D), if its μ_{pos} is 1, it is natural that $H^{det}(C{\rightarrow}D)$ gets its maximum value, i.e. log(|U|), for the positive region of DS is null and all instances are uncertain. But ridiculously, μ_{det} is 0! The conclusion obviously cannot show the real uncertainty degree of DS. This suggests that the mathematical results of **uncertain ratio based on playing-it-safe entropy** cannot well

express the characteristics of information systems in some extreme cases.

Theorem 7: Given DS=(U, V, f, C ∪ D) and 0.5 < β ≤ 1, $H^{1}(C{\rightarrow}D) \leq H^{2}(C{\rightarrow}D) \leq H^{det}(C \rightarrow D)$.

Proof: *1) Firstly, prove $H^{1}(C{\rightarrow}D) \leq H^{2}(C{\rightarrow}D)$.*

If $1 \leq i \leq c$ or $c_\beta < i \leq t$, each X_i contributes the same value to $H^{1}(C{\rightarrow}D)$ and $H^{2}(C{\rightarrow}D)$; however, if $c < i \leq c_\beta$, each X_i contributes $Z_i^{1} = -p(X_i)log(p(X_i))$ to $H^{1}(C{\rightarrow}D)$, but $Z_i^{2} = -p(T_{Xi})log(p(T_{Xi}))+log(|U|)p(X_i-T_{Xi})$ to $H^{2}(C{\rightarrow}D)$. Thus, $H^{2}(C{\rightarrow}D)-H^{1}(C{\rightarrow}D) =\sum_{c<i\leq c\beta} Z_i^{2}-Z_i^{1}$.

If considering $p(X_i) = p(T_{Xi})+p(X_i-T_{Xi})$, then:

$Z_i^{2}-Z_i^{1}=p(T_{Xi})(log(p(X_i)) -log(p(T_{Xi})))+p(X_i-T_{Xi})(log(|U|)+log(p(X_i))$
$= p(T_{Xi})log(p(X_i)/p(T_{Xi}))+ p(X_i-T_{Xi}) log(|X_i|) \geq 0$

Therefore, $H^{2}(C{\rightarrow}D)-H^{1}(C{\rightarrow}D) \geq 0$ and $H^{1}(C{\rightarrow}D)\leq H^{2}(C{\rightarrow}D)$.

2) Now, prove that $H^{2}(C{\rightarrow}D) \leq H^{det}(C{\rightarrow}D)$.

Similarly, If $1 \leq i \leq c$ or $c_\beta < i \leq t$, each X_i contributes the same value to both $H^{2}(C{\rightarrow}D)$ and $H^{det}(C{\rightarrow}D)$; however, if $c < i \leq c_\beta$, each X_i contributes $Z_i^{2}= -p(T_{Xi})log(p(T_{Xi}))+log(|U|)p(X_i-T_{Xi})$ to $H^{2}(C{\rightarrow}D)$, but $Z_i^{det}= p(X_i)log(|U|)$ to $H^{det}(C{\rightarrow}D)$. Thus,

$H^{det}(C{\rightarrow}D)-H^{2}(C{\rightarrow}D)= \sum_{c<i\leq c\beta}Z_i^{det}-Z_i^{2}$

Where,

$Z_i^{det}-Z_i^{2}=p(T_{Xi}) (log(|U|)+log(p(T_{Xi})))+p(X_i-T_{Xi})(log(|U|)-log(|U|))=p(T_{Xi})log(|U|\times p(T_{Xi})) = p(T_{Xi})log(|T_{Xi}|)\geq0$. Therefore, $H^{det}(C{\rightarrow}D)-H^{2}(C{\rightarrow}D)\geq0$ and $H^{2}(C{\rightarrow}D) \leq H^{det}(C{\rightarrow}D)$.

As shown by 1) and 2), theorem 7 holds.
Given $DS = (U, V, f, C \cup D)$, $H^{1}(C{\rightarrow}D)$, $H^{2}(C{\rightarrow}D)$ and $H^{det}(C{\rightarrow}D)$ measure its uncertainty

based on the same idea, that is, the probability distribution is deterministic for its positive region but random for uncertain instances. All of them conceptually exaggerate the uncertainty of uncertain instances to extreme. The difference among them is that those three entropy functions take V_1, V_2, and V_0 as their positive regions, respectively. If the relation of $V_1 \supseteq V_2 \supseteq V_0$ is noticed, it is intuitively rational that $H^1(C{\rightarrow}D) \leq H^2(C{\rightarrow}D) \leq H^{det}(C{\rightarrow}D)$.

Theorem 8: *Given DS = (U, V, f, C ∪ D) and β = 1, $H^1(C{\rightarrow}D) = H^2(C{\rightarrow}D) = H^{det}(C{\rightarrow}D)$.*

Proof: *If β=1, c =c_β, Then $V_0 = V_1 = V_2$. Thus, Theorem 8 holds.*

PERFORMANCE OF SYSTEM UNCERTAINTY MEASURES

A series of simulation experiments are conducted to analyze and compare the above discussed system uncertainty measures based on rough set theory. In order to compare the performance of these measure methods, a large number of information systems with different scales and different uncertainty degrees are randomly generated by the following algorithm RGUS.

Algorithm RGUS //to Randomly Generate Uncertain Systems

Input: θ, |U|, C ∪ D, V // θ ∈(0, 1], *to control the system uncertainty degree*
Output: DS=(U, V, f, C ∪ D)

1. Equally divide U into 1/θ condition classes, each class has |U| × θ instances;
2. For each condition class:
   2.1 Randomly generate value vector of C for all instances;
   2.2 At the probability of θ, randomly generate value vector of D for each instance

independently. Otherwise, randomly generate value vector of D for all instances;
   //θ *indicates the probability of generating uncertain condition classes.*
3. Return generated uncertain system

Parameters of RGUS specify the scales of generated information systems. The uncertainty of a system generated by algorithm RGUS is controlled by parameter θ in two ways. The lower value θ gets, on one hand, less probably condition classes are uncertain; on the other hand, smaller granularity the universe will be partitioned into, thus, even if a condition class is uncertain, it can only slightly affect the system's comprehensive characteristics. Therefore, in probability sense, the uncertainty of generated systems tends to be more and more serious with the increase of θ.

In experiments, the cardinality of universe (|U|), cardinalities of sets of condition attributes and decision attributes and their value domains (|C|, |D| and V), are firstly given. Then 11 systems are generated when θ is set to be 0.001, 0.002, 0.004, 0.008, 0.016, 0.032, 0.064, 0.128, 0.256, 0.512 and 1, respectively. Subsequently, μ_{pos}, μ_{whl}, μ_{loc} and μ_{det} are calculated for each generated system. At last, the value variation tendencies of different measures with θ are investigated.

μ_{aver} is never taken into accounts, since $\mu_{aver}=\mu_{whl}$. Measures based on variable precise rough set (VPRS) theory are neither considered. Their performance depends on an external parameter, i.e. precise threshold. That threshold is a certain kind of prior knowledge. Thus, measures based on VPRS are not suitable for data-driven knowledge acquisition.

In experiments, more than ten system scales are investigated. For all those scales, the value tendencies of different measures with θ are quite similar. Typical results, regarding parameters |U|=2048, |C|=6, V_i={0, 1, 2, 3} where i=1, ...,

Table 1. Comparison of system uncertainty measures

θ	.001	.002	.004	.008	.016	.032	.064	.128	.256	.512	1
μ_{pos}	.167	.119	.148	.141	.188	.000	.169	.128	.744	.000	1.000
μ_{whl}	.078	.047	.059	.058	.084	.000	.077	.060	.360	.000	.498
μ_{loc}	.106	.200	.293	.391	.48	.600	.684	.787	.897	.957	1.000
μ_{det}	.093	.183	.256	.344	.405	.600	.585	.697	.230	.932	.000

6; $|D|=1$ and $V_d=\{0,1\}$, are shown in Table 1 and Figure 1.

The following conclusions can be drawn from the experiment results.

For any information system, relations of $\mu_{pos} \geq \mu_{whl}$ and $\mu_{loc} \geq \mu_{det}$ always hold. Moreover, if $\mu_{pos}=1$, then $\mu_{det}=0$. Theorems 3,4 and 6 are also validated by experiments.

μ_{pos} and μ_{whl} measure system uncertainty from the perspective of algebra view. It is very possible that neither of them can accurately measure the real system uncertainty, because their results are vulnerable being heavily affected by local characteristics of an information system. Experiments show that μ_{pos} and μ_{whl} perform poorly in some cases.

μ_{loc} is able to describe the variation tendency of system uncertainty with θ. It is sensitive to system uncertainty and can effectively distinguish systems with low, medium or high uncertainty.

When information systems are with low or even medium uncertainty, μ_{det} is also able to effectively distinguish their relative uncertainty degrees. However, if the uncertainty of information systems tends to be extremely serious, μ_{det} often fails to be coincident with the variation trend of system uncertainty.

A well-performed measure for system uncertainty would be characterized by the following features:

1. Based on the conception of information entropy. According to Shannon's information theory, information is able to reduce system uncertainty. The quantity of information is equivalent to the reduced quantity of system uncertainty. Therefore, it is consistent to

Figure 1. Comparison of system uncertainty measures (In the legend, 1, 2, 3 and 4 stand for μ_{pos}, μ_{whl}, μ_{loc} and μ_{det} respectively)

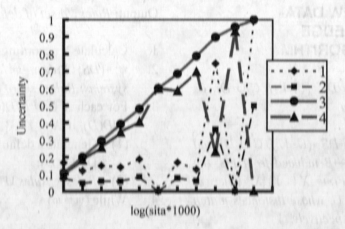

measure information and system uncertainty. Such measures are based on information entropy. In this sense, the conception of information entropy is essentially bound to system uncertainty.

2. Moderately sensitive to system uncertainty. The real uncertainty of information systems can be shown by their measured results, or at least can be discerned from each other by their relative values.

3. Appropriately to be widely applied. It can effectively distinguish information systems with low, medium or high uncertainty.

It is noticeable that a measure with higher sensitivity does not always mean it would be better, since high sensitivity may hinder its applying range. If a measure is too sensitive, its measured results vary too fast with system uncertainty and will soon reach its limits. Afterwards, it cannot further tell apart the uncertainty of more information systems.

The results of experiments disclose that among the approaches based on rough set theory, **uncertainty ratio based on knowing-it-all entropy** is the optimal, which can meet the above three requirements. In the following section, **uncertainty ratio based on knowing-it-all entropy** is applied in measuring system certainty and directing a new data-driven algorithm for knowledge acquisition.

DKAABSU: A NEW DATA-DRIVEN KNOWLEDGE ACQUIRING ALGORITHM

Definition 21: *Given DS=(U, V, f, C ∪ D), its* **certainty** *is* $\Upsilon = 1 - \mu_{loc}$.

Definition 22: *Given DS=(U, V, f, C ∪ D) and a decision rule r: A→B induced from DS, the* **confidence** *of r is CF(r)=$|X \cap Y|/|X|$, where X and Y are subsets of U, whose instances match formulas A and B, respectively.*

In a sense, the confidence of a decision rule may be regarded as its certainty.

Definition 23: *Given a knowledge system Rules containing decision rules generated from an information system, its* **certainty** *is min{CF(r) | r ∈ Rules}.*

If we allow that induced decision rules with certainty lower than that of a given information system, the rule system might performs poor, since it contains too heavy uncertainty. Considering this point, a new algorithm DKAABSU is developed based on Skowron's algorithm. DKAABSU algorithm can generate all propositional default decision rules whose confidence is no less than the certainty of a given information system.

For the sake of convenience, the conception of class descriptor is introduced here.

Definition 24: *Given DS = (U, V, f, C ∪ D) and A ⊆ C ∪ D, if X ∈ U/IND(A), the* **descriptor** *of X regarding A is the instance projection of X on A: Des(X, A) = ∧ (a, a(x)), where x ∈ X and a∈A.*

DKAABSU Algorithm

//Data-driven Knowledge acquiring Algorithm Based on System Uncertainty

Input: *DS=(U, V, f, C ∪ D)*
Output: *Rules //A set of default decision rules*

1. Calculate Υ according to Definition21;
2. ψ:={DS}; *Rules:* = φ; *//ψ: set of information systems; Rules: set of default rules.*
3. For each $X \in U/IND(C)$ and each $Y \in U/IND(D)$, if $|X \cap Y|/|X| \geq \Upsilon$, then:
   (1) Generate a default rule *r*: Des(X, C)→ Des(Y, D);
   (2) *Rules:= Rules ∪ {r};*
4. While $(\psi \neq \varphi)$

Take out one information system $DS^* = (U, V^*, f^*, C^* \cup D)$ from ψ; calculate its attribute core $Core(C^*)$;

For each $c \in Core(C^*)$ let $C_{pr} := C^* - \{c\}$. If $(C_{pr} \neq \varphi)$, then:

1. $\psi := \psi \cup \{DS'\}$, where $DS' = (U, V^*, f^*, C_{pr} \cup D)$;

2. For each $X \in U/IND(C_{pr})$ and $Y \in U/IND(D)$, if $|X \cap Y|/|X| \geq \overline{Y}$, then:

   a. Generate a default rule r: $Des(X, C_{pr}) \rightarrow Des(Y, D)$;

   b. $Rules := Rules \cup \{r\}$;

   c. For each $Z \in U/IND(C)$, if $Z \subseteq X$ and $Z \cap Y = \varphi$, generate a fact $F: Des(Z, \{c\}) \rightarrow NOT(r)$ to lock the newly generated rule r;

5. return *Rules*

Given an information system, Skowron's algorithm can generate all propositional default decision rules whose confidence is no less than a given threshold. Its performance depends on the reasonability of the threshold. The threshold is usually specified by users according to their prior domain knowledge. That makes the algorithm dependent on prior knowledge. The methodological improvement of DKAABSU algorithm over Skowron's algorithm is that DKAABSU effectively breaks such confinement. It is completely independent of any external information or prior knowledge. Namely, it is completely data-driven. In fact, another data-driven algorithm has been suggested based on ideas similar to DKAABSU, however, that algorithm takes the minimum certainty degree of condition classes as the confidence threshold (Wang & He, 2003). Such method utilizes local characteristics of an information system to direct the whole knowledge acquiring process. It emphasizes too much on extreme conditions. One can expect that algorithm DKAABSU performs better, since it is based on **uncertainty ratio based on knowing-it-all entropy**, a more rational system uncertainty measure.

EXPERIMENT TESTS ON DKAABSU AND ITS CONGENERIC ALGORITHMS

Skowron's algorithm (Mollestad & Skowron, 1996), the algorithm based on the minimum certainty of condition classes (so called "the referred algorithm" in the following) (Wang & He, 2003) and DKAABSU algorithm are tested and compared in ways similar to (Wang & He, 2003). Firstly, a training system is generated by randomly selecting half of the universe from a given information system. The uncertainty of the training system is intentionally enhanced by randomly removing some of its values of condition attributes at ratio λ. Subsequently, the training system is processed in the following steps: 1) Complete each missing value if there is any, by the average value of that attribute; 2) Discretize continuous values if there are any, by Nguyen's greedy algorithm (Nguyen, 1995); 3) Reduce attributes by Miao's MIBARK method (Miao, 1999); 4) Run algorithms of the Skowron's, the referred and the DKAABSU, respectively, and then test the rule systems generated by these three algorithms by the whole original information system to evaluate their performance. For all training systems, the confidence thresholds for Skowron's algorithm are fixed to a constant 0.5.

The three algorithms are tested over various UCI datasets. Their performance on the Balance-Scale dataset are comprehensively compared: the ratio of removing attribute values is in turn set to be 0, 0.1, 0.2, 0.3, 0.4, 0.5, 0.6, 0.7, 0.8, 0.9 to obtain 10 training systems. Then, for each resulted training system, the scales of induced rule systems, the thresholds and the learning accuracies of algorithms are compared in Table 2. For other datasets, λ is set to be 0, 0.3, 0.7, respectively. The performance of the three algorithms over each training system is compared in Table 3. In tables 2 and 3, Alg.1, Alg.2 and Alg.3 are algorithms of the Skowron's, the referred and the DKAABSU, respectively; λ is the ratio of value removal; α_c and

Table 2. Results on balance-scale

λ	Alg.1		Alg.2			Alg.3		
	N_r	η(%)	$α_C$	N_r	η(%)	ϒ	N_r	η(%)
.0	583	73.6	1	258	**88.8**	1	258	**88.8**
.1	563	60.8	.333	757	51.5	.972	212	**83.1**
.2	527	74.1	.250	753	74.1	.955	209	**79.2**
.3	450	74.7	.167	798	70.6	.936	153	**75.5**
.4	439	**72.0**	.091	832	71.0	.907	162	71.7
.5	386	71.8	.042	776	67.8	.862	152	**74.1**
.6	346	66.6	.040	720	64.2	.848	114	**72.0**
.7	336	68.2	.051	680	65.8	.802	128	**69.9**
.8	288	63.4	.021	601	58.4	.767	121	**69.9**
.9	260	65.3	.016	535	59.4	.731	117	**67.5**

ϒ are the thresholds for algorithms of the referred and the DKAABSU, respectively; N_r is the scale of a rule system; and η is the learning accuracy. An element in bold is the best in respective condition.

The complexities of the three algorithms are the same. However, simulation results illustrate those algorithms perform differently. The typical Skowron's algorithm depends on an external parameter and cannot be well adaptive to the uncertainty of information systems. The referred algorithm emphasizes too much on extreme cases of information systems. It is vulnerable generating rule systems with too large scales and too serious uncertainty. Thus, its performance is usually unsatisfactory, since it is very possible that decision rules with extremely low confidence are got in its generated rule systems. On the contrary, DKAABSU algorithm is most adaptable to system uncertainty and can generate most concise rule systems. Its performance over a given system turns out to be observably better than that of the other two algorithms.

In a certain sense, the successful application of the conception of system certainty in DKAABSU further confirms the reasonability of $μ_{loc}$ for measuring system uncertainty.

Table 3. Learning accuracies η(%) of algorithms

Data	Monk-1			Monk-2			Monk-3			Glass Identification		
λ	0.0	0.3	0.7	0.0	0.3	0.7	0.0	0.3	0.7	0.0	0.3	0.7
Alg.1	91.9	75.0	58.1	62.1	61.5	62.1	82.8	75.4	68.9	40.7	35.5	28.7
Alg.2	83.1	69.4	55.6	**83.4**	60.4	59.8	82.8	60.7	54.9	48.2	44.4	39.2
Alg.3	94.4	87.9	72.6	83.4	70.4	62.7	95.9	86.9	74.6	56.8	50.0	43.8
Data	Postoperative Patient			Thyroid Gland			Fitting Contact Lenses			Iris Plants		
λ	0.0	0.3	0.7	0.0	0.3	0.7	0.0	0.3	0.7	0.0	0.3	0.7
Alg.1	71.1	71.1	**72.2**	75.8	69.8	69.8	66.7	66.7	70.8	86.0	71.3	**76.7**
Alg.2	**81.1**	71.1	70.0	75.8	69.8	71.2	66.7	66.7	65.2	85.3	71.3	70.7
Alg.3	**81.1**	72.2	70.0	75.8	79.5	78.6	66.7	66.7	70.8	86.0	72.0	76.0

CONCLUSION AND FUTURE WORK

Three-layered model for knowledge discovery in databases based on cognitive informatics usually requires that the philosophy layer provide prior domain knowledge for technique layer. However, in some cases, prior knowledge may be biased, incorrect or even unavailable at all. Thus, data-driven knowledge acquiring algorithms are necessary theoretically and practically, since such algorithms are advantageous for their unnecessity of prior domain knowledge.

System uncertainty is an intrinsic common feature of information systems and their induced rule systems and hence can essentially link them together. Thus, data-driven knowledge acquiring process can be effectively directed by system uncertainty. The effectiveness of such data-driven knowledge acquiring framework greatly depends on the reasonability of system uncertainty measure. Herein, various system uncertainty measures based on rough set theory are introduced and discussed; their algebraic characteristics and quantitative relations are analyzed and disclosed; their performance is studied and compared by a series of experiments. From the results, we can find that the measure of **uncertainty ratio based on knowing-it-all entropy** performs best. Then a new data-driven knowledge acquiring algorithm is developed based on the optimal system uncertainty measure and the Skowron's algorithm for mining propositional default rules. Simulation experiments illustrate that compared with other congeneric algorithms, the performance of the proposed algorithm is improved obviously.

Different from data-driven knowledge acquiring methods, domain-driven approaches (Cao & Zhang, 2006; Gilbert, Kotidis, Muthukrishnan, & Strauss, 2005; Gliozzo, Magnini, & Strapparava, 2004; Gliozzo, Strapparava, & Dagan, 2004) utilize domain-specific prior knowledge to improve the performance of knowledge acquisition. Intuitively, correct and proper prior information will conduct the acquisition process more efficiently and more effectively. Thus, domain-driven approaches are more powerful in well-studied domains.

As to knowledge acquisition, no matter which algorithm is applied and whether prior knowledge is used or not, what we get are knowledge expressing potential rules, patterns or characteristics of information systems. Essentially, the knowledge is always there behind data, different results acquired through different methods present different facets of and open different viewing windows for information systems. That is the way in which data-driven and domain-driven approaches analyze information systems from different viewpoints. Though these two kinds of methods are quite different or even on the opposite, they are also well complementary to each other, and thus can be applied in knowledge acquisition jointly. It is obvious that there is a good chance that the combination of these two kinds of methods can get more reasonable results. In the near future, we will focus on the combination of domain-driven and data-driven knowledge acquiring methods.

ACKNOWLEDGMENT

This article is in partially supported by National Natural Science Funds of China (No.60773113, No.60573068), Starting Research Funds of Ministry of Education for Chinese Overseas Returnees (No.(2007)1108), Natural Science Funds of Chongqing (No.2008BA2041, No.2008BA2017), Science & Technology Research Program of the Municipal Education Committee of Chongqing (No.KJ060517, KL080510) and Science Research Funds of Chongqing University of Posts & Telecommunications (No.A2006-05).

REFERENCES

Cao, L. B., & Zhang, C. Q. (2006). Domain-driven actionable knowledge discovery in the real world. *Lecture Notes in Computer Science, 3918,* 821–830. doi:10.1007/11731139_96

Chen, X.H., Zhu, S.J., & Ji Y.D. (2001). Rule uncertainty measurement based on entropy and variable rough set. *Journal of Tsinghua University (Science & Technology Edition), 47*(3), pp.109-112.

Düntsch, I., & Gediga, G. (1998). Uncertainty measures of rough set prediction. *Artificial Intelligence, 106,* 109–137. doi:10.1016/S0004-3702(98)00091-5

Gilbert, A. C., Kotidis, Y., Muthukrishnan, S., & Strauss, M. J. (2005). Domain-driven data synopses for dynamic quantiles. *IEEE Transactions on Knowledge and Data Engineering, 17*(7), 927–938. doi:10.1109/TKDE.2005.108

Gliozzo, A., Magnini, B., & Strapparava, C. (2004). Unsupervised Domain Relevance Estimation for Word Sense Disambiguation. In D.K. Lin, & D.K. Wu (Eds.), *Proceedings of the 2004 Conference on Empirical Methods in Natural Language Processing* (pp. 25-26), Press of Association for Computational Linguistics, Barcelona, Spain.

Gliozzo, A., Strapparava, C., & Dagan, I. (2004). Unsupervised and Supervised Exploitation of Semantic Domains in Lexical Disambiguation. *Computer Speech & Language, 18*(3), 275–299. doi:10.1016/j.csl.2004.05.006

Kinsner, W. (2005). Review of Recent Development in Cognitive Informatics. In J. Tsai, Y.X. Wang, D. Zhang, & W. Kinsner (Eds.), *Proceedings of the 4th IEEE International Conference on Cognitive Informatics* (pp. 6-8), IEEE CS Press, Irvine, USA.

Miao, D. Q., & Hu, G. R. (1999). A heuristic algorithm for reduction of knowledge. *Computer Research & Development, 36*(6), 681–684.

Mollestad, T., & Skowron, A. (1996). A rough set framework for data mining of propositional default rules. *Lecture Notes in Computer Science, 1079,* 448–457.

Nguyen, H. S., & Skowron, A. (1995). Quantization of real values attributes: rough set and boolean reasoning approaches. In Wang, P.P. (Ed), *Proceedings of the Second Joint Annual Conference on Information Science* (pp. 34-37), Durham: Duke University Press.

Pawlak, Z., Grzymala-Busse, J., Slowinski, R., & Ziarko, W. (1995). Rough sets. *Communications of the ACM, 38*(11), 89–95. doi:10.1145/219717.219791

Wang, G.Y. (2001). Uncertainty measurement of decision table information systems. *Computer Science, 28*(5, Special Issue), 23-26.

Wang, G.Y. (2001). *Rough set theory and knowledge acquisition.* Xi'an, P.R. China: Press of Xi'an Jiaotong University.

Wang, G.Y., & He X. (2002). Knowledge self-learning model based on rough set theory. *Computer Science, 29*(9, Special Issue), pp.24-25.

Wang, G. Y., & He, X. (2003). A self-learning model under uncertain condition. *Journal of Software, 14*(6), 1096–1102.

Wang, Y. (2002). On Cognitive Informatics. In Y.X. Wang, R.H. Johnston, & M.R. Smith (Eds.), *Proceedings of the First IEEE International Conference on Cognitive Informatics* (pp. 34-42), IEEE CS Press, Calgary, Canada.

Wang, Y. (2002). The Latest Development on Cognitive Informatics. *Lecture Notes in Computer Science, 2452,* 3–4.

Wang, Y. (2003). On cognitive informatics. *Brain and Mind: A Transdisciplinary Journal of Neuroscience and Neuro-philosophy, 4*(2), 151-167.

Wang, Y. (2003). On the Latest Development in Cognitive Informatics. *ACM Software Engineering Notes*, *27*(2), 28.

Wang, Y. (2004). On Autonomic Computing and Cognitive Processes. In C.W. Chan, W. Kinsner, Y. Wang, & M. Miller (Eds.), *Proceedings of the 3rd IEEE International Conference on Cognitive Informatics* (pp. 3-5), IEEE CS Press, Victoria, Canada.

Wang, Y. (2007). The Theoretical Framework of Cognitive Informatics. *International Journal of Cognitive Informatics and Natural Intelligence*, *1*(1), 1–27. doi:10.4018/jcini.2007010101

Wang, Y., & Kinsner, W. (2006). Recent Advances in Cognitive Informatics. *IEEE Transactions on Systems, Man, and Cybernetics*, *36*(2), 121–123. doi:10.1109/TSMCC.2006.871120

Yao, Y. Y. (2004). Concept formation and learning: a cognitive informatics perspective. In C.W. Chan, W. Kinsner, Y. Wang, & M. Miller (Eds.), *Proceedings of the 3rd IEEE International Conference on Cognitive Informatics* (pp. 42-51), IEEE CS Press, Victoria, Canada.

Ziarko, W. (1993). Variable precision rough set model. *Artificial Intelligence*, *46*, 39–59.

This work was previously published in International Journal of Software Science and Computational Intelligence, Volume 1, Issue 3, edited by Yingxu Wang, pp. 53-66, copyright 2009 by IGI Publishing (an imprint of IGI Global).

Chapter 27
Hierarchical Function Approximation with a Neural Network Model

Luis F. de Mingo
Universidad Politécnica de Madrid, Spain

Nuria Gómez
Universidad Politécnica de Madrid, Spain

Fernando Arroyo
Universidad Politécnica de Madrid, Spain

Juan Castellanos
Universidad Politénica de Madrid, Spain

ABSTRACT

This article presents a neural network model that permits to build a conceptual hierarchy to approximate functions over a given interval. Bio-inspired axo-axonic connections are used. In these connections the signal weight between two neurons is computed by the output of other neuron. Such arquitecture can generate polynomial expressions with lineal activation functions. This network can approximate any pattern set with a polynomial equation. This neural system classifies an input pattern as an element belonging to a category that the system has, until an exhaustive classification is obtained. The proposed model is not a hierarchy of neural networks, it establishes relationships among all the different neural networks in order to propagate the activation. Each neural network is in charge of the input pattern recognition to any prototyped category, and also in charge of transmitting the activation to other neural networks to be able to continue with the approximation.

INTRODUCTION

Concepts and categories are being objects to study in practical Psychology and in Artificial Intelli-

DOI: 10.4018/978-1-4666-0261-8.ch027

gence (AI) years ago. It deals with the research of how the knowledge and meaning are represented in the memory (Tulving, 1972; Wang 2003, 2008a, 2008b). Why are concepts important? Concepts or conceptual categories are stable representations, stored in the memory, that permit to treat different samples as members of a same class; without them we will be slaves of particular (Wallace, Silverstein, Bluff, & Pipingas, 1994).

From a psychologist point of view, when dealing with objects, situations and actions as members of conceptual categories, the perceived reality is mentally being divided into different groups. A structure is imposed to the world, dividing mentally the reality (Quillian, 1968; Tulving, 1972). Categories seem to be ruled by the cognitive economy principle, this is, to extract essential things from the known world and to represent them in the most economical way in order to minimize the cognitive effort.

According to Collins and Quillian (Collins & Quillian, 1969; Quillian, 1968), the importance of a concept is not the concept by itself; it is determined by the set of relationships that are established with other different concepts. These relationships can be of two types: Subset and Property. The former type expresses the specialization of some concepts into others; it produces the categorization, allowing to mentally structuring the perceived reality.

What could be added from a connectionist point of view to the concept representation in memory? (Arroyo, Castellanos, Luengo, & Mingo, 1997). Why could not it be thought that the concepts are supported by some small sets of neural assemblies? These ones form a mix of specialized neural networks concerning the samples recognition task and they determined if a sample belongs or is classified into a concept.

Concepts are not isolated into the human cognitive system. They are immersed into a hierarchical structure that facilitates, among others, classification tasks to the human cognitive system. This conceptual hierarchy expresses a binary relationship of inclusion defined by the following criterions:

- **Inclusion criterion:** Each hierarchy node determines a domain included into domain of its father node. Each hierarchy node de-

termines a domain that includes every domain of its son nodes.

- **Generalization and Specialization criterion:** Every node in the hierarchy, has differentiating properties that make it different from its father node, if it exists, and from the others son nodes of its father, if they exist.

This Inclusion relation makes possible to keep the maximal economy criterion in the conceptual hierarchy. The defined inclusion relation makes also possible to represent a conceptual hierarchy as an acyclic directed graph in which nodes represent concepts and edges the inclusion relation among them. Edges connecting nodes establishes that the father nodes are situated in the upper hierarchical level of its son nodes. Obviously, concepts are generated in a natural manner and it will not be constrained by these formal restrictions. However, many of the classifications learnt during our school years are built using these rules. In this article, we will focus our work in this kind of hierarchies, which are learnt with a teacher or in a supervised manner.

Next sections deal with the representation of any conceptual hierarchy using a set of neural networks, permitting the complete or exhaustive classification of an input. Exhaustive classification means that an input belongs to each one of the supported concepts by the system and to their specializations. The hierarchical architecture is controlled using neural network outputs, that is, depending on the output a different neural network is activated.

PROBLEM DESCRIPTION

Let D domain of any samples. Let H a conceptual hierarchy to the elements of the domain D. Let T the tree of the conceptual hierarchy H. Each node in the tree T represents a concept in hierarchy H, and an arrow between two nodes implies that the end node is a specialization of the start node.

The nodes belonging to the first level of the tree, associated to the conceptual hierarchy, establish a partition of the input domain D in the following way.

$$D = \bigcup_{i=1}^{N} D_i \; / \; \forall_i \neq j, \, D_i \cap D_j = \emptyset$$

Where D_i are the sub concepts, corresponding the domain D of a higher level of abstraction in the conceptual hierarchy. Each point or sample in the domain could be classified as belonging to a determined concept of such a level and no other. That is:

$$\forall p \in D, \exists i \in \{1,...,n\}, j \in \{1,...,n\} \; / \; p \in D_i \wedge p \notin D_j, j \neq i$$

Once the classification of the input point $p \in D$ has been established as belonging to one concept of this level, the same classification problem arises; this time concerning the classification of p into the different sub concepts of the concept, provided that the concept had any sub concept, that is, if the following equation is verified.

$$p \in D_i \wedge D_j = \bigcup_{j=1}^{m} D_{ij}, \, D_{ik} \cap D_{il} = \emptyset, \, k \neq l$$

Then, it is verified that:

$$\exists j \in \{1,...\} \; / \; p \in D_{ij} \wedge p \notin D_{ik}, \, k \in \{1,...\} - \{j\}$$

Therefore, once an input or sample is identified into some pre-established category, into a prototype of a concept belonging to any level of the conceptual hierarchy, the process of classification can end if the recognized concept has not any sub concepts or specializations. Also, it can continue, this case the sample will form a new conceptual category.

It is said that a sample p of the domain D is exhausted classified when the degree of belonging of pattern p to each one of the concepts has been established, for all the concepts in the conceptual hierarchy. Writing this definition in terms of the associated tree, the exhaustive classification of an input $p \in D$ is defined as the path of the tree that goes from the root node to any leave node, in which the classification is ended:

$$D \rightarrow D_i \rightarrow D_{ik} \rightarrow ... \rightarrow D_{ik...l}$$

With $p \in D_i, p \in D_{ik} \cdots, p \in D_{ik...l}$.

Next section deals with the construction of a neuronal system able to solve the problem of exhaustive classification given some samples of a certain domain.

NEURAL NETWORKS MODEL

The proposed computational model assumes a dual representation in order to make easy the information process. One level is related to implement neural circuits in Artificial Neural Networks (Connectionist System) and the other one is related to maintaining of symbolic information (Aslanyan et al., 2006) about implemented concepts in Artificial Neural Circuits (Symbolic System)(Arroyo et al., 1997).

In the Connectionist System, it is possible to answer if a specific input is a member or not of one specific concept or category. Moreover, in (F.Arroyo, Castellanos, Luengo, & Mingo, 1998) it is shown how it is possible to represent a conceptual hierarchy using a supervised connectionist system in such a way that it will permit external sensorial inputs, of given perceptions, to be exhaustively classified as belonging to a whole branch of the conceptual hierarchy. Each neural network, which takes part in the system, is concerned with the association of inputs to a given category and also with the propagation of activity towards others neural networks in order to continue with the input classification. The dual representation supported by this kind of systems makes possible to process information that it is represented in a sub-symbolic or symbolic manner either (Arroyo, Luengo, Mingo, & Castellanos, 1999).

In order to represent a conceptual hierarchy into the model, it is assumed that:

- The starting domain of instances and the hierarchy tree are well defined. Hence, the differentiating properties among categories or concepts are known.
- It is possible to build sets of representative instances from every category of the conceptual tree.
- It is possible to choose representatives instances from every category. These instances will be used: (1) for training the different Artificial Neural Networks that integrate the Connectionist System and (2) for representing essential characteristics of categories in the Symbolic System.

Given an input $p \in D$ to the neural system. To exhaustively classify the input p, a path of the tree is obtained.

$$P = \{D \to D_i \to D_{ik} \to ... \to D_{ik...l}\}$$

It is true that, associated to D and to D_i's there exists a neural network responsible for giving a response concerning to which specialization of the concept the input p belongs to. Except for the end node $D_{ik...l}$ that has no specialization because it is a terminal node.

To begin with, a neural network will be design in order to admit a sample of the domain, subject to study, as an input pattern. Therefore, the number of inputs to such a neural network depend on the dimension of the samples that will be presented to the system: let say that the domain has a valid representation in R^r, so the number of inputs related with the neural networks will be r. The number

of output neurons of the neural network will be determined by the number of nodes that the tree T has as a first level, that is, the number of concepts the domain is composed by, n outputs. To identify that an input belongs to some concept the output neuron of the sub concept must be activated, in the path P it will be the i-th neuron.

Till this phase, the input p presented to the system will be propagated through the associated neural network corresponding to the domain D_i and does not to the other neural networks associated to the domains D_j with $i \neq j / i, j \in \{1, ..., n\}$. To achieve such exhaustive classification of p, it is continued treating p as a specialization of D_i, until a terminal node is reached, then the classification process of the pattern set is completed.

HIERARCHICAL MODEL

To establish these partitions over the domain is equivalent to establish a conceptual hierarchy (Luis F. Mingo, Arroyo F., M.A. Diaz and Castellanos J., 2007). Figure 1 shows the conceptual hierarchy over the domain D and its associated tree. Keeping in mind the rules stated in the previous section, the number of input neurons of all the neural networks that build the system is determined, this number is equal to 2 since this is the dimension of the input pattern domain.

Studying the associated tree to the conceptual hierarchy it can be deduced that, besides the root neural network (R_0) two more neural networks are needed in order to be able to manage the specializations of concept D_2 (R_2) and concept D_3 (R_3). Counting the number of arrows in the concepts, the number of output neurons in each one of the neural networks can be determined.

Networks (R_0) and (R_2) have three output neurons, while network (R_3) only has 2 neurons. Next step is to determine the neural network architecture, in this example a Multilayer Perceptron (MLP) has been employed.

Figure 1. Conceptual hierarchy over domain D, and the associated tree

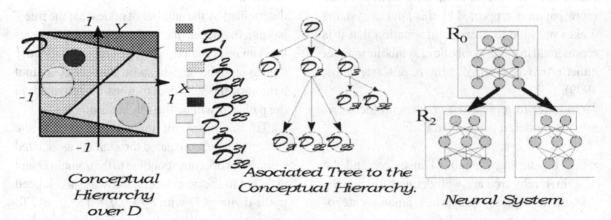

Figure 2 shows the established links among all the different neural networks in the system. Note in the figure that an excitatory response could be assimilated from a given output neuron of a neural network with the ability of transmitting current information in the system towards any network set. In this case, it could be said that, the system has neurons whose excitation is the key for transmitting the neural activity through the system.

The activation of any output neuron belonging to any neural network is interpreted as the recognition of a given input to the concept that the neuron represents. Besides, if the concept of the hierarchy has specializations, then the system will propagate the input to some neural network in order to continue with the classification process, this is what is called propagation of the neuronal activity through the system, until the exhaustive classification of the input is reached (Luis F. Mingo, Castellanos J., Arroyo F., 2006).

NUMERIC REPRESENTATION

Thanks to a neural network, see Figure 3, it is possible to predict, analyzing historical series of datasets just as with these systems but there is no need to restrict the problem or use Fourier's transform. A defect common to all those methods it is to restrict the problem setting certain hypothesis that can turn out to be wrong. We just have to train the neural network with historical series of data given by the phenomenon we are studying (Anderson & Rosenfield, 1988). Calibrating a neural network means to determinate the parameters of the connections (synapsis) through the training process. Once calibrated there is needed to test the network efficiency with known datasets, which has not been used in the learning process. There is a great number of Neural Networks (Anderson, 1995), which are substantially distinguished by: type of use, learning model (supervised/non-supervised), learning algorithm, architecture, etc.

Multilayer perceptrons (*MLPs*) are layered feed forward networks typically trained with static backpropagation. These networks have found their way into countless applications requiring static pattern classification. Their main advantage is that they are easy to use, and that they can approximate any input-output map. In principle, backpropagation provides a way to train networks with any number of hidden units arranged in any number of layers. In fact, the network does not have to be organized in layers any pattern of connectivity that permits a partial ordering of the nodes from input to output is allowed. In other words, there must be a way to order the units such that all connections go from earlier (closer to the

470

Figure 2. Neuronal system for the domain D

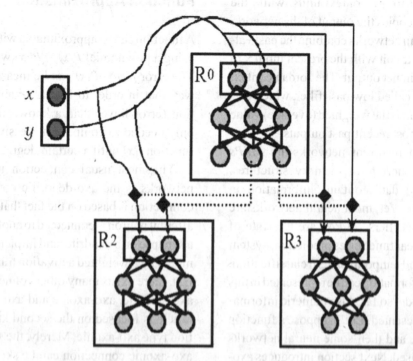

input) to later ones (closer to the output). This is equivalent to stating that their connection pattern must not contain any cycles. Networks that respect this constraint are called feed forward networks; their connection pattern forms a directed acyclic graph or dag.

Jordan and Elman networks extend the multilayer perceptron with context units, which are processing elements that remember past activity. Context units provide the network with the ability to extract temporal information from the data. In Elman networks, the activity of the first hidden

Figure 3. Multilayer perceptron architecture used in the hierarchical model

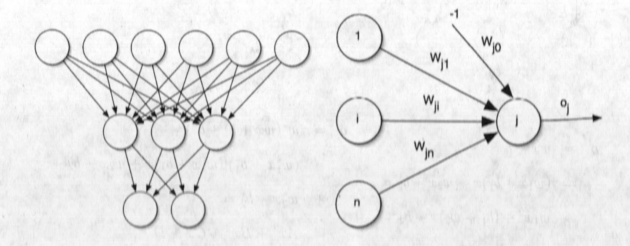

layer are copied to the context units, while the Jordan network copies the output of the network. Jordan and Elman networks combine the past values of the context unit with the present input x to obtain the present net output. The Jordan context unit acts as a so-called low pass filter, which creates an output that is the weighted (average) value of some of its most recent past outputs.

Time lagged recurrent networks are *MLPs* extended with short term memory structures. Most real-world data contains information in its time structure. Yet, most neural networks are purely static classifiers. *TLRNs* are the state of the art in nonlinear time series prediction, system identification and temporal pattern classification.

Symbolic information can be represented in this hierarchical model so far. Also numeric information can be represented. Let's suppose a function to approximate, and then some neural networks models can be used. Next section introduces axo-axonic neural networks (*ENN*) (Mingo, Aslanyan, Castellanos, Diaz, & Riazanov, 2004) that are able to perform a similar approach to Taylor series.

Function Approximation

A function can be approximated with a given error using a polynomial $P(x) = f^*(x)$ with a degree n. The error $f(x) - P(x)$ can be measured in such a way that in order to find a suitable approximation (error lower than a known threshold) it is only needed to compute successive derivates of function $f(x)$ until a certain degree n.

The most usual connection type in neural networks is the axo-dendritic connection. This connection is based on the fact that the axon of an afferent neuron is connected to another neuron via a synapse on a dendrite, and implemented in *ANN* model by a weighted activation transfer function. But, there exists many other connection types as: axo-somatic, axo-axonic and axo-synaptic. This article is focused on the second kind of connection type axo-axonic. Merely, the structure of the axo-axonic connection can be sketched by three neurons with a classical axo-dendritic connection and the synaptic axonal termination of N_3 connected to the synapse S_{12}. The principle consists

Figure 4. ENN architectures – with/without hidden layers – and output expressions

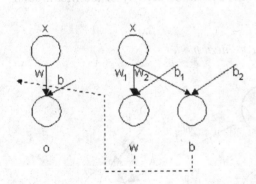

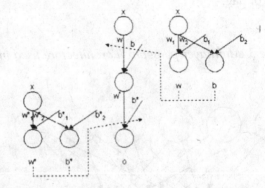

$$o = wx + b =$$
$$= (w_1x + b_1)x + w_2x + b_2 =$$
$$= w_1x^2 + (b_1 + w_2)x + b_2$$

$$o = w^*(wx + b) + b^* =$$
$$= (w_1^*x + b_1^*)[(w_1x + b_1)x + w_2x + b_2] + =$$
$$+ w_2^*x + b_2^* =$$
$$= Ax^3 + Bx^2 + Cx + D$$

Figure 5. Neural networks connections: axo-dendritic, axo-synaptic and axo-axonic (from left to right)

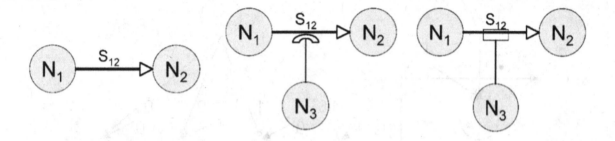

on propagating the action of neuron N_3 as synapse S_{12}, see Figure 5.

In order to model previous connection type, two neural networks are required. The first (assistant) one will compute the weight matrix of the second (principal) one. And, the second network will output a response, using the previously computed weight matrix; this architecture is named Enhanced Neural Networks *ENN*.

Enhanced Neural Networks behave as an *n*-degree polynomial approximator, depending on the number of hidden layer in the architecture. In order to obtain such behavior all activation functions of the net must be lineal function $f(x) = ax + b$.

As shown in Figure 4 and output equations, the number of hidden layers can be increased in order to increase the degree of the output polynomial, that is, the number *n* of hidden layers control, in some sense, the degree $n + 2$ of output polynomial of the net.

Table 1 shows how the degree of the output polynomial increases according to the number of hidden layers in the net.

The only condition that the learning algorithm must verified is that weights must be adjusted to values related with the successive derivates of function *f(x)* that pattern set represents. Usually such function is unknown therefore, if the network converges with a low mean squared error then all weights of the net have converged to the derivates of function *f(x)* (the pattern set unknown function), and such weights will gather some information about the function and its derivates that the pattern set represents.

As an example, function $f(x) = sin(x)cos(x)$ can be approximated using equation obtained from Taylor series, with a given point $x = 0$. Such equation can be reduced to $f^*(x) = x - 4/6 \, x^3$, using a polynomial $P(x)$ degree 3. This is a mathematical approach, but what happens if such function is the pattern set to an enhanced neural network mentioned before?

A one hidden layer neural network must be used in order to obtain a 3-degree polynomial as the output expression. Figure 6 shows such architecture, after the training stage, the final configuration is shown. Output equation of the net is $o = x - 4/6 \, x^3$, equivalent equation with $f^*(x)$.

The approximation error using net in Figure 6 can be computed using equation mentioned before, and therefore $MSE \leq |e(x)|$. Such approximation is not the only one nor the best one,

Table 1. Number of hidden layers vs. degree of output polynomial (approximation expression)

Hidden Layers	Degree P(x)	Output Polynomial
0	2	$o = a_2 x^2 + a_1 x + a_0$
1	3	$o = a_3 x^3 + a_2 x^2 + a_1 x + a_0$
...	...	...
N	n+2	$o = \sum_{i=0}^{n+2} a_i x^i$

Figure 6. Approximation of f (x) = sin(x)cos(x) with a one hidden layer

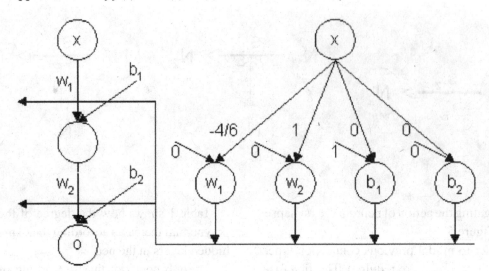

but it can be computed theoretically in order to provide the net some initial weights in order to speed up the learning process and to obtain a better approximation that the initial one with a lower error ratio. In summary, Enhanced Neural Networks can be initialized to some weights computed using the Taylor Series of the function that the pattern set defines and after this initial stage the learning algorithm must be applied in order to achieved the best solution (the one that improves the Taylor Series error).

Figure 7 shows the surface computed by a net as the number of hidden layers is increased. The mean squared error is decreasing as the number of hidden layers goes up. This figure shows that this kind of neural net is very suitable when approximating functions, a given function or a function defined by the pattern set.

Non-Linear Activation

According to previous ideas, linear *ENNs* are better than linear *MLPs*, or at least, they are able to generate complex regions in order to divide the output space. When working with a *MLP*, only hyper planes can be obtained. And moreover, the

degree of the output equation increases according to the number of hidden layers.

In order to obtain a functional basis, one constraint must be made. It consists on implementing the network architecture with lineal *PEs* except the output neurons of assistant network. These neurons must have an activation function *g(x)* which is used to computed the functional basis as the application of *g(x)* to a non lineal combination of inputs. Figure 8 shows an example of a functional basis and the main network output.

Depending on the activation function of output neurons belonging to assistant network, the main network will output an approximation function based on non-lineal combination of elements belonging to the basis. That is if a sinusoidal activation function is implemented, then a similar Fourier approximation is computed by the network; is a Ridge activation function is implemented, then a similar Ridge approximation is computed and so on.

Main advantage of this new approximation method is that is absolutely easy to implement. And moreover, a global approximation to the entire pattern set is performed. This way, if there are enough input patterns, then the generaliza-

Figure 7. Surface approximation depending on the number of hidden layers

Pattern set defined by $f(x, y) = sin(x)e^y$

   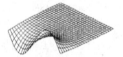

2 hidden layers   4 hidden layers   6 hidden layers   8 hidden layers

tion error will be minimized if there are enough learning iterations.

An Example

ENN obtain best performance than classical models (*MLP*, *RBF*, etc.) in order to approximate functions. But they used a global approximation schema along the whole pattern set, and in some points the mean squared error is high compared to Taylor series. Hierarchical model explained before can be used in order to perform a global-specific approximation, that is, a general net that performs a global approximation can fire up another net that performs an approximation in a given interval. This second net can fire up another net in a narrower interval an so on (see Figures 2 and 9).

A SYMBOLIC PRACTICAL CASE OF USE

In order to check the System capabilities, we have use the Zoo database from the UCI Machine Learning Repository (Blake, Keogh, & Merz, 1998). This database has the following characteristics: each record has *18* attributes, the animal name, *15* Boolean attributes corresponding to different particular values of attributes for each instance and *2* numeric attributes (one for number of legs and other for the class each animal belongs). The database has *101* instances of different classes of animal. In order to process with categorization, the database has been modified and the instances have been rearranged into a conceptual tree of categories. The Figure 10 shows the conceptual tree for this case of study.

Figure 8. Approximation with sinusoidal activation functions using basis obtained by the net –figure a) is the basis and figure b) is the result obtained combining the basis

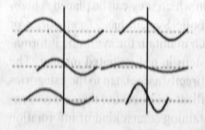 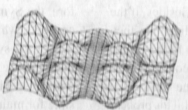 

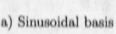

a) Sinusoidal basis   b) 3D Surfaces Approximation

Figure 9. Hierarchical Network Approximation. a) First net with a global approximation, b) Second net with an interval approximation and c) Last net with a narrow interval approximation

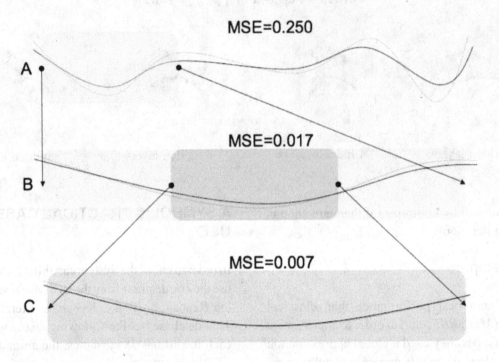

The Artificial Neural Networks chosen to represent the connectionist component for every non-terminal concept is a Multilayer Perceptron with two layers. They have been trained with the Backpropagation algorithm. Every Perceptron in the system has the same number of input neurons in order to propagate adequately the sub symbolic information in the Connectionist System. The output layer has as many output neurons as son nodes have the concept in the category tree. The activation of any output neuron belonging to any neural network in the System is interpreted as the recognition of a given input to the concept that the output neuron represents. Besides, if the concept of the hierarchy has specializations, then the system will propagate the input to the appropriate neural network in order to continue with the classification process, until the exhaustive classification of the input is reached. This process of categorization is called propagation of the neural activity through the system. Each Percep-

tron has been trained with the appropriate instances from each category independently of the other ones. In order to implement the Connectionist System, it has been needed *12* Artificial Neural Circuits, one per each category or concept with specializations; in our case of study the Neural circuit is constituted by only one Artificial Neural Network.

The symbolic component of every concept has been designed in order to keep the maximal economy criterion. Therefore, shared attributes of categories have been placed at the higher level of the hierarchy in which they can be placed. Therefore, the Symbolic System has *27* categories or concepts, which maintain the symbolic information of the system in a distributed manner. The instances are directly associated to the categories without specializations, because they are responsible for maintaining such a kind of information in the System.

Figure 10. Conceptual tree for our case of study

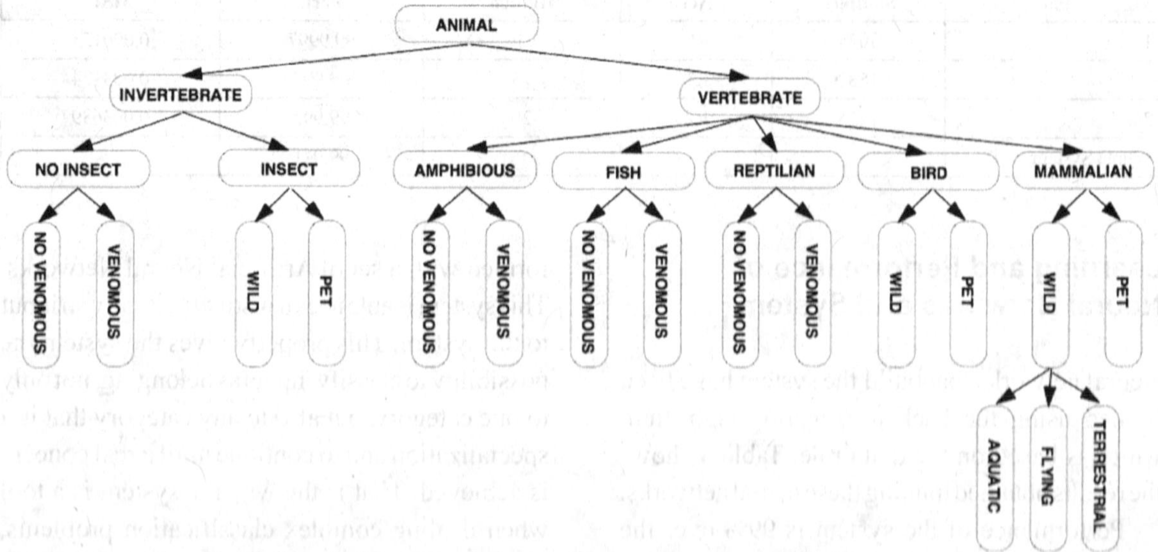

The System answers to new inputs giving an exhaustive classification for them. The exhaustive classification process presents the complete path through the conceptual tree of categories, to which the input belongs. The Connectionist System produces this classification process. Moreover, due to the duality existing in the System, it is possible to recover the input attributes from the symbolic representation of categories.

For example, if we present to the system information from an animal (e.g. clam) and this animal has never been presented to the system, the system produces the following response, see Table 2.

The new inputs presented to the System can be added to the Symbolic System be mean of this recovering process of symbolic information. Hence, if we add information from new instances to the System, it will add such information to the appropriate non-specialized category.

Table 2. System output

Attributes	
Aquatic:	0
Fins:	0
Tail:	0
Toothed:	0
Domestic:	0
Eggs:	1
Milk:	0
#Legs:	0
Hair:	0
Feathers:	0
Predator:	1
Breathes:	0
Catsize:	0
Venomous:	0
Backbone:	0
Airbourne:	0
ANIMAL INVERTEBRATE NOINSECT NO-VENOMOUS	

Table 3. Neural network performance

File	Samples	Net	Hidden	Perf.	MSE
1	3024	R0	3	99.9997	0.000154
2	1532	R1	15	99.997	0.003124
3	1275	R2	20	99.997	0.003639
Whole System				99.041	

Learning and Performance of Neural Networks and System

Neural networks that build the system have been trained using the back propagation algorithm, which is based on the delta rule. Table 3 shows the results obtained training these neural networks.

Performance of the system is 99% over the input training set. The number of patterns misclassified was *29*, and all of them were bound patterns, that is, were patterns maybe belonging to more than one class. Table 2 shows the results of the system with a test set. Performance of the system is 97% over the test set. Same as previous set, the misclassified patterns correspond to those belonging to more than one class.

CONCLUSION AND FUTURE REMARKS

This article presents a Hierarchical Connectionist - Symbolic System, which permits to insert and recover information hierarchically structured following a priory predetermined hierarchy of classification using the generalization properties from Connectionist Systems. The system not only exhaustively classifies but also recovers symbolic information from the categories of the tree, which permits to automatically insert new inputs in the appropriate non-specialized node of the hierarchy. What the System really does, is to insert new information non-previously known increasing the information about categories in the System.

This article proposes a connectionist system, inspired by the neurobiologist point of view, formed with a set of Artificial Neural Networks. This system is able to exhaustively classify an input to the system. This property gives the system the possibility to classify inputs as belonging, not only to one category, but also to any category that is a specialization and to continue until a real concept is achieved. That is the way the system is a tool when dealing complex classification problems, due to any domain features and to any information about the elements of the domain

The performance of the whole system is as good as the performance of the individual neural networks by themselves, at least in the pattern sets that have been tested. This kind of connectionist system could help in the processing of abstract information within some global system. Given an input to the system, a neural network activity turns up and this activity is propagated through the system in a total controlled way by the system.

REFERENCES

Anderson, J. A. (1995). *An introduction to neural networks*. Cambridge, Mass., USA: MIT Press.

Anderson, J. A., & Rosenfield, E. (1988). *Neurocomputing: Foundations of research*. Cambridge, Mass., USA: MIT Press.

Arroyo, F., Castellanos, J., Luengo, C., & Mingo, L. (1997). Frames neural networks for cognitive process. In *World multiconference on systemics, cypernetics and informatics* (pp. 288–295). Caracas, Venezuela.

Arroyo, F., Castellanos, J., Luengo, C., & Mingo, L. (1998). Connectionist systems for a hierarchical knowledge representation. In *1998 International conference on neural networks and brain* (pp. 471–474). Beijing, China.

Arroyo, F., Luengo, C., Mingo, F., & Castellanos, J. (1999). Evolving connectionist and symbolic processes in a hierarchical memory model. In *World multiconference on systemics, cybernetics and informatics*, 8, 255–261. Orlando, Florida, USA.

Aslanyan, L., de Mingo, L., Castellanos, J., Ryazanov, V., Chelnokov, F., & Dokukin, A. (2006). On logical correction of neural network algorithms for pattern recognition. *International Journal on Information Theories and Applications, 14*(3), 203–205.

Blake, C., Keogh, E., & Merz, C. J. (1998). *Uci repository of machine learning databases*. Available from http://www.ics.uci.edu/mlearn/MLRepository.html

Collins, A. M., & Quillian, M. R. (1969). Retrieval time from semantic memory. *Journal of Verbal Learning and Behavior, 8,* 204–247. doi:10.1016/S0022-5371(69)80069-1

Mingo, L., Arroyo, F., Diaz, M., & Castellanos, J. (2007). Hierarchical Knowledge Representation: Symbolic Conceptual Trees and Universal Approximation. *International Journal of Intelligent Control and Systems, 12*(2), 142–149.

Mingo, L., Aslanyan, L., Castellanos, J., Diaz, M., & Riazanov, V. (2004). Fourier neural networks: An approach with sinusoidal activation functions. *International Journal on Information Theories and Applications, 11*(1), 52–55.

Mingo, L., Castellanos, J., & Arroyo, F. (2006). Hierarchical Neural Networks to Approximate Functions}. *IEEE International Conference on Cognitive Informatics.* ICCI 2006. (pp. 261-267), Beijing, China.

Quillian, M. (1968). Semantic memory. In Minsky, E. (Ed.), *Semantic information processing.* Cambridge, Mass., USA: MIT Press.

Tulving, E. (1972). Episodic and semantic memory. In Tulving, E., & Donaldson, W. (Eds.), *Organization of memory.* New York, USA: Academic Press.

Wallace, J., Silverstein, R., Bluff, K., & Pipingas, A. (1994). Semantic transparency, brain monitoring and evaluation of hybrid cognitive architectures. *Connection Science, 6*(1). doi:10.1080/09540099408915709

Wang, Y. (2003, August). On Cognitive Informatics, *Brain and Mind: A Transdisciplinary Journal of Neuroscience and Neorophilisophy, 4*(3), 151-167. Kluwer Academic Publishers.

Wang, Y. (2008a). On Contemporary Denotational Mathematics for Computational Intelligence. *Transactions of Computational Science, 2,* 6–29. doi:10.1007/978-3-540-87563-5_2

Wang, Y. (2008b). On Concept Algebra: A Denotational Mathematical Structure for Knowledge and Software Modeling. *International Journal of Cognitive Informatics and Natural Intelligence, 2*(2), 1–18. doi:10.4018/jcini.2008040101

This work was previously published in International Journal of Software Science and Computational Intelligence, Volume 1, Issue 3, edited by Yingxu Wang, pp. 67-80, copyright 2009 by IGI Publishing (an imprint of IGI Global).

Chapter 28

Application of Artificial Neural Computation in Topex Waveform Data:
A Case Study on Water Ratio Regression

Bo Zhang
The Ohio State University, USA

Franklin W. Schwartz
The Ohio State University, USA

Daoqin Tong
University of Arizona, USA

ABSTRACT

Using the TOPEX radar altimeter for land cover studies has been of great interest due to the TOPEX near global coverage and its consistent availability of waveform data for about one and a half decades from 1992 to 2005. However, the complexity of the TOPEX Sensor Data Records (SDRs) makes the recognition of the radar echoes particularly difficult. In this article, artificial neural computation as one of the most powerful algorithms in pattern recognition is investigated for water ratio assessment over Lake of the Woods area using TOPEX reflected radar signals. Results demonstrate that neural networks have the capability in identifying water proportion from the TOPEX radar information, controlling the predicted errors in a reasonable range.

INTRODUCTION

Cognitive informatics (CI), a multidisciplinary study combining both modern pattern recognition technologies and biological neuropsychology theories to simulate the brain functions in infor-

mation processing has significantly improved the learning capability of human being (Wang, 2003). As one of the kernel methods in CI, artificial neural computation has been successfully performed to solve many complicated information learning problems (Shi and Shi, 2003; Cai and Shi, 2003; Yaremchuk and Dawson, 2008, *etc.*). Moreover,

DOI: 10.4018/978-1-4666-0261-8.ch028

neural networks has been widely applied in signal processing and recognition (Kinsner, *et al.*, 2003; Pernkopf *et al.*, 2009, *etc.*). Our study focuses on information learning process of the TOPEX radar signals by artificial neural computation approaches, which shows importance of CI technologies in practice for different scientific studies.

The TOPEX Radar Altimeter Satellite was launched in October 1992 by National Aeronautics and Space Administration (NASA) and French Space Agency Centre National d'Etudes Spatials (CNES). The platform of the TOPEX allows a better monitoring of ocean dynamics by providing more accurate sea level estimate with the Root Mean Square Error (RMSE) about 2.7 cm (Zieger, et al., 1991; Fu & Cazenave Eds., 2001). The satellite carries dual bands, C-band (5.3 GHz) and Ku-band (13.6 GHz) and is operated on the orbit at 1334±60 km with an inclination within 62° to 67°. The principle of the TOPEX Altimeter is to determine the range R from the sensor to the sea surface based on the overall travel time of microwave pulses with known magnitude transmitted from the sensor towards the sea surface and then reflected back to the sensor.

Although Topex Radar Altimeter was initially designed for study of Sea Surface Height (SSH), the massive data with wide coverage from latitude 66 S to 66 N and the short repeat cycle of 10 days for about 15 years can provide substantial useful information to other studies. For example, recent studies (Birkett, 1998; Birkett, 2000; Campos et al., 2001; Jekeli & Dumrongchai, 2003) have successfully demonstrated promising potentiality of the TOPEX Altimeter in detecting water level fluctuation of inland lakes and wetlands. Besides water areas, research highlighted that The TOPEX Altimeter could also be applied to examine land surfaces. For instance, Papa et al. (Papa, 2002) used the TOPEX Altimeter σ^0 (backscattering coefficient) data and successfully estimated depth of snow pack over the Northern Great Plains of the United States; Papa et al. (2003) produced the first continental σ^0 maps from the TOPEX

Altimeter and discovered interesting patterns of σ^0 values corresponding major land cover types globally. In addition, the TOPEX Altimeter can also provide great insight to rain rate estimate (Varma, et al., 1999). Hence, there are great incentives to explore capabilities of the TOPEX Altimeter further, especially in the aspect of imaging ground surfaces such as land cover. One of the most important hydrological applications in such areas is to estimate water proportion within the TOPEX footprints over land surfaces. If feasible, TOPEX data can be widely applied and extended into many other research fields such as inland lake hydrology, land change estimation, flood assessment, and etc.

However, it becomes particularly difficult to conduct water ratio estimation using data from the TOPEX Altimeter. The major factors that complicate the process include: (1), the single value of σ^0 of each ground footprint from the TOPEX Altimeter is not sufficient to identify different land cover types; (2), due to the fact that returned radar waveforms contain tremendously mixed information the data are too complex to be readily utilized as imagery data; (3), different radar reflectivity for variant land cover types and interaction of signals with terrain relieves and roughness interfere echoes received by the sensor, which, however, is not problematic for oceans as water is the only and an excellent reflector and waves on sea surfaces are assumed to follow Gaussian distributions (Fu and Cazenave Eds., 2001). Therefore, theoretical models are intractable for land surfaces. Furthermore, sizes of ground footprints of the TOPEX Altimeter are variable and depend on terrain.

Instead of relying upon theoretical models for water ratio derivation, this article examines modern pattern recognition algorithms for solution. Modern pattern recognition approaches are often powerful in discovering meaningful patterns from massive and complex dataset. In fact, machine learning algorithms such as Neural Networks have been successfully used as classification and regression methods for imagery data in remote sensing (DeFries and Chan, 2000; Tatem, et al., 2002). However, to our best knowledge, such algorithms have not been well introduced into TOPEX waveform data analysis to discover the inherent nonlinear relationships. Therefore, in this article, Neural Networks as one of the most commonly used machine learning algorithm is constructed to estimate water ratios within areas of TOPEX footprints over water and land surfaces. The objective is to provide new aspect for the TOPEX waveform data in land cover differentiation. Furthermore, these algorithms are also significant in facilitating applications of TOPEX data into research such as land cover and inland lake hydrology.

METHODOLOGY

Topex Data Description

The TOPEX altimeter provides two level data products: Geophysical Data Records (GDRs) and the Sensor Data Records (SDRs) in 10 Hz, which is delivered about every 600 m when projected onto the ground track (Remy, et al., 1996; Kruizinga, 1997). The GDRs are altimetry data for most applications in geodetics and ocean topography studies. The most important attribute of GDRs are σ^0 values, which measure the proportion of the magnitude of reflected signals per unit solid angle to the incident waves. The SDRs contain the most detailed information of radar, including waveforms. Continuous echoes are discretized into 64 bins within different time intervals (6.25 ns or 12.5 ns) (Rodriguez & Martin, 1994). Consequently, those waveforms are each represented by 64 digital numbers (DNs) in a time series. Each DN is a normalized value of the power of a reflected radar signal within the corresponding time interval.

In general, a waveform consists of three components, the thermal noise, the leading edge, and the trailing edge (Rodriguez & Martin, 1994). Over oceans, the returned waveform has a sharp, stable narrow peak making it capable of detection of the surface of ocean (Figure 1 (a)). Over land, the radar signal from the satellite is attenuated at the ground surface, providing weak power waveforms (Birkett, 1998). When water bodies become discrete, the returned waveforms broaden and typically contain multiple peaks, caused by reflection from different objects on the ground (Figure 1 (b,c, and d)) (Koblinsky, 1993). As water is an excellent reflector of radar waves, the waveform over continents should provide information of inland water areas, even though surface slope and roughness of the observing footprint complicate any analyses. Waveform data like peakiness from T/P are therefore expected to be useful in providing information on water abundance on ground tracks (Birkett, 1998).

In this study, more than 800 waveform frames for pass 169 and 178 of Topex SDRs were sampled over Lake of the Woods across Minnesota, United States, and the Canadian provinces of Ontario and Manitoba (Figure 2). This area was selected because: firstly, the lake is located at the boundary of United States and Canada, and radar echoes collected there represent typical signals of the continent of North America; Secondly, lake of the Woods is large enough to provide waveform samples for land surface as well as pure water; thirdly, the Topex satellite has two passes across over this region, providing as many data samples as possible; lastly, the terrain of this area is rather flat, which reduces interference of reflected signals from relieves of land surface. Waveforms were selected for cycle 294, 295, and 296, during September, 2002, to synchronize the Landsat image which was taken on September 16, 2002, and to avoid influence of snow and ice on radar signals. For each frame of waveforms, a circle footprint with a 6 km radius over ground was identified and water proportion was estimated by the landsat image integrated with Geographical Information System (GIS).

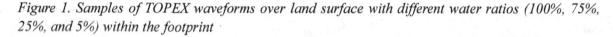

Figure 1. Samples of TOPEX waveforms over land surface with different water ratios (100%, 75%, 25%, and 5%) within the footprint

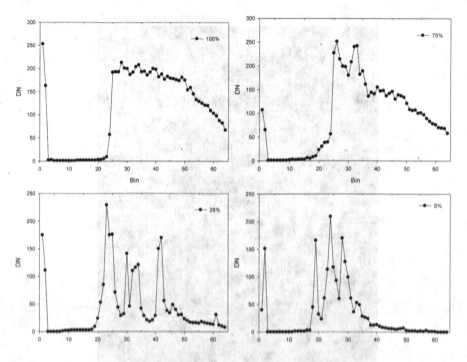

Artificial neural computation algorithms are then applied to estimate the water ratio value of each TOPEX footprint from its corresponding waveform. More specifically, in regression models the input variables are the 64 DNs of each frame of waveforms, and the corresponding target variable is the water ratio value of each footprint estimated using GIS and the Landsat image that matches the TOPEX ground tracks. The input and target data sets are as follows:

input (waveforms):   target (water ratios):

$X_1, X_2, ..., X_{64}$ (variables)

$$\begin{bmatrix} x_{1,1}, x_{1,2}, ..., x_{1,64} \\ x_{2,1}, x_{2,2}, ..., x_{2,64} \\ ...... \\ x_{N,1}, x_{N,2}, ..., x_{N,64} \end{bmatrix} \Rightarrow \begin{bmatrix} y_1 \\ y_2 \\ ...... \\ y_N \end{bmatrix}$$

where N=total number of observations

Neural Networks

Artificial neural networks are algorithms mimicking biological neural network structure and are particularly helpful to solve nonlinear problems for which linear and polynomial models are incapable of producing good predictions. The algorithms implement by linearly combining nonlinear functions of input variables to produce predictions of the target variable (Ripley, 1996). The structure of the commonly used type of neural networks, a Multilayer Perceptron (MLP) neural network with one hidden layer and 5 hidden nodes is given in Figure 3.

For this particular MLP neural network shown in Figure 3, predicted target values of Y are given in Box 1.

MLP neural networks use sigmoid such as hyperbolic tangent activation functions of input variables and thus can approximately simulate any continuous function if sufficient hidden nodes

Figure 2. Map of the sample area, Lake of the Woods, and ground track samples of the Topex waveform data

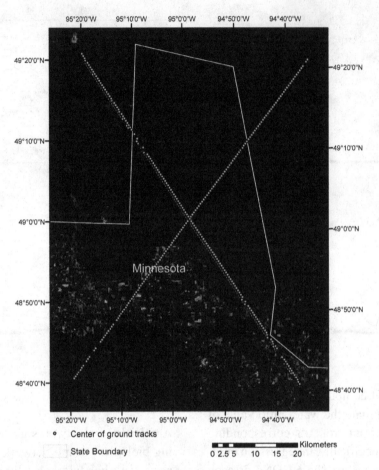

Table 1. Statistics of the neural networks from 3-fold validation

	Fit Statistic	Training	Validation
1st-fold validation	Root Average Squared Error	0.2012	0.2484
	Maximum Absolute Error	0.7163	0.6418
	Final Prediction Error	0.0620	
2nd-fold validation	Root Average Squared Error	0.2062	0.1980
	Maximum Absolute Error	0.6759	0.8636
	Final Prediction Error	0.0687	
3rd-fold validation	Root Average Squared Error	0.1849	0.1639
	Maximum Absolute Error	0.6868	0.6627
	Final Prediction Error	0.0534	

Figure 3. The structure of MLP neural networks

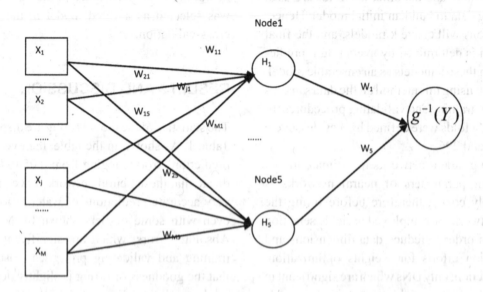

are used (Ripley, 1996). Hence the MLP neural networks were also selected for this study. $g^{-1}()$ is called link function of Y variable if Y follows a distribution in exponential family other than normal distribution. In this article, $g^{-1}()$ is logit(Y) as Y, the water ratio value is modeled as an expected value of binomial distributions.

Model Fitting

In general, three procedures are required to construct neural networks, training, validating, and testing. Consequently, the original dataset is supposed to be split into 3 independent parts,

training dataset, validating dataset, and testing dataset. Predictive models are firstly constructed from training dataset, then models are refined according to the performance for validating dataset, and finally, testing dataset is used to carry out the model assessment. However, in the case without a large number of data observations, k-fold cross-validation procedure (Ripley, 1996; Breiman, 1984) is adopted to utilize the whole dataset more sufficiently. In a k-fold cross-validation procedure, original dataset is divided into k independent folds, and k validation processes are performed to construct the best model. For each validation process, only one fold is selected for

Box 1.

$$g^{-1}(E(Y)) = w_0 + w_1 H_1 + w_2 H_2 + w_3 H_3 + w_4 H_4 + w_5 H_5$$
$$H_{i=1\ to\ 5} = \tanh(w_{0i} + w_{1i}X_1 + w_{2i}X_2 + ... + w_{Mi}X_M)\ (1)$$

where Y - target variable (Probability of water)
$X_{j=1\ to\ M}$ - varibles or attributes of data
w - weights or parameters of MLP model
$H_{i=1\ to\ 5}$ - values of hidden nodes
$\tanh(X_1, X_2,..., X_M)$ - hyperbolic tangent activation functions
$g^{-1}()$ - link function of target variables such as logit()

data validation, and the other k-1 folds are used as training data to build an initial model. Hence, k validations will create k models, and the final prediction is determined by averaging k predictions from these k models as an ensemble model. As a result, using this method all the data samples are used in training and validating procedures. In our study, 3 folds were defined by 3 cycles, cycle 294, 295 and 296.

Training neural networks to estimate model weights or parameters of neural networks is excessively costly; therefore before fitting the neural networks we employed variable selection process in order to reduce data dimensions and computation efforts for weights optimization. After selection, only DNs which are significant in χ^2 test to the target variable are retained as inputs in neural networks.

Three neural networks were built from the 3-fold cross-validation procedure. In each validation process, the neural network started with weights assigned by initial values. Quasi-Newton optimization algorithms (Ripley, 1996) were used to update the weights iteratively to obtain the minimum of the error function, because quasi-Newton optimization is one of the most robust algorithms with the fastest rate of convergence in artificial neural computation by using only first derivatives instead of second partial derivatives of error surfaces.

To avoid model overfitting due to noises of training data, iterations were terminated when the model reached the minimum error function of validating data, and a neural network with weights computed in the last iteration was selected as a fitting model. Figure 4 shows examples of the training and validating error functions for the 3-fold cross-validation. In the first plot, the error functions are from 1st-fold cross-validation using cycle 294 as validating and the other two cycles as training. Although the training error function was minimized with iterations continuously running, the smallest validating error (less than 0.1) was obtained at the 12th iteration. Therefore, the

neural network constructed at the 12th iteration was selected as a fitted model in the 1st-fold cross-validation.

RESULTS AND DISCUSSION

The statistics of the model fitting are displayed in Table 1. As shown in the table, the overall final prediction errors, ranging from 0.05 to 0.07, indicate that these neural networks have produced very accurate predictions of water ratio values, even with some outliers shown by Maximum Absolute Errors, which are significant in both training and validating processes. Also notice that the goodness of fitting is slightly dependent on data splitting. For instance, the largest Root of Average Squared Error (Root ASE) of training is 0.2062 by the 2nd-fold validation, whereas the 1st-fold validation produced the largest validation Root ASE of 0.2484.

Since the way to split original data into training and validating subsets had an effect on neural networks building, an ensemble model combining three neural networks from the 3-fold cross-validation was selected as the overall regression model. Predicted water ratio values from these three neural networks were then averaged by the ensemble model as final predictions. This averaging takes advantage of all data records in building neural networks and makes the model more robust from data splitting and overfitting noises of particular subsets.

The fitting errors for the ensemble model and 3 neural networks are shown in Table 2. Here, the

Table 2. Overall errors

Model	Root ASE
Ensemble	0.1862
1st-fold validation	0.2174
2st-fold validation	0.2035
3st-fold validation	0.1779

Figure 4. Error functions by iteration in 3-fold cross-validation

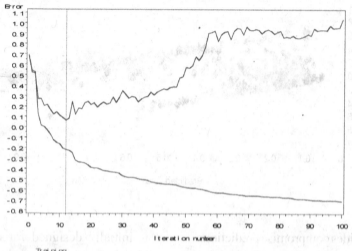

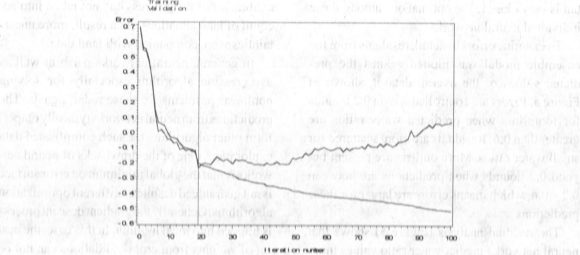

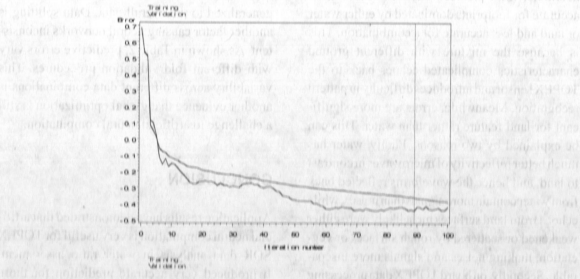

Figure 5. Residual vs. predicted value

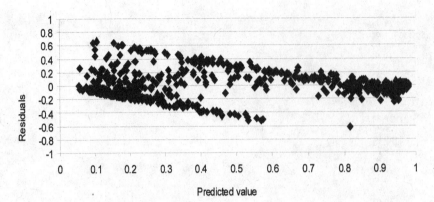

ensemble model provides compromise predictions but is very close to the optimal one among those individual neural networks.

To examine errors in detail, residuals from the ensemble model was plotted against the predicted values of the overall dataset, shown in Figure 5. Errors are controlled within 0.2 bounds for footprints when predicted water ratios are greater than 0.6. Residuals are more scattered for small water ratios. More outliers are present beyond 0.2 bounds when predictions are between 0.2 – 0.6, which means errors are larger for these predictions.

The residual analysis (Figure 5) shows that neural networks predict water ratio values more accurate for footprints dominated by either water or land and less accurate for a combination. This is because the mixture with different ground characteristics complicated echoes back to the TOPEX sensor and introduces difficulty in pattern recognition. Meanwhile, errors are more significant for land feature rather than water. This can be explained by two reasons. Firstly, water has much better reflectivity of microwaves in contrast to land, and hence the waveforms reflected back from water contain more signals than noises, while echoes from land surfaces most likely were either weakened or scattered by rough surfaces or vegetation, making noises and signals more inseparable. Secondly, on board TOPEX data processing

was initially designed for ocean surfaces, the calibration of this process had not taken into account of land situations. As a result, more uncertainties were companied with land data.

In general, neural networks perform well as a regression algorithm especially for solving nonlinear problems for these radar signals. The predictions from neural networks typically outperform other algorithms for such complicated data exploration. One of the drawbacks of neural networks is that the global minimum on error surface is not guaranteed despite of different optimization algorithms. Generally the gradient descent process is trapped into local minima. In this case, the best set of weights from cross-validations can not be generalized to the overall data. Data splitting is another factor causing neural networks inconsistent. As shown in Table 2, predictive errors vary with different fold validation procedures. This variability across different data combinations is another evidence that global optimization is still a challenge to artificial neural computation.

CONCLUSION

Application results have demonstrated that artificial neural computation is very useful for TOPEX SDR data analysis in water ratio assessment. It produced very accurate prediction for those footprints with water proportion greater than 0.6. As signal reflections deteriorated with mixture of land and water, prediction errors increased when water proportional became smaller. Further work includes incorporating more sophisticated algorithm for better predicting water-land mixed pixels and employing similar techniques for imaging the general ground surface.

ACKNOWLEDGMENT

This study was supported by the National Science Foundation, NSF Award EAR-0440007.

REFERENCES

Birkett, C. M. (1998). Contribution of the TOPEX NASA radar altimeter to the global monitoring of large rivers and wetlands. *Water Resources Research, 34*, 1223–1239. doi:10.1029/98WR00124

Birkett, C. M. (2000). Synergistic Remote Sensing of Lake Chad: Variability of Basin Inundation. *Remote Sensing of Environment, 72*, 218–236. doi:10.1016/S0034-4257(99)00105-4

Breiman, L., Friedman, J. H., Olshen, R. A., & Stone, C. J. (1984). *Classification and Regression Trees*. New York, NY: Chapman and Hall.

Cai, C., & Shi, Z. (2003). A modular neural network architecture with approximation capability and its applications. *Second IEEE International Conference on Cognitive Informatics (ICCI'03)*, August 18-20, (pp. 60- 64), London, UK.

Campos, I. O., Mercier, F., Maheu, C., Cochonneau, G., Kosuth, P., Blitzkow, D., & Cazenave, A. (2001). Temporal variations of river basin waters from Topex / Poseidon satellite altimetry: Application to the Amazon basin. *Earth and Planetary Sciences, 333*, 633–643.

DeFries, R. S., & Chan, J. C.-W. (2000). Multiple criteria for evaluating machine learning algorithms for land cover classification from satellite data. *Remote Sensing of Environment, 74*(3), 503–515. doi:10.1016/S0034-4257(00)00142-5

Fu, L. L., & Cazenave, A. (2001). *Altimetry and Earth Science. A Handbook of Techniques and Applications. (69)*. London, UK: International Geophysics Series Academic Press.

Jekeli, C., & Dumrongchai, P. (2003). On monitoring a vertical datum with satellite altimetry and water-level gauge data on large lakes. *Journal of Geodesy, 77*, 447–453. doi:10.1007/s00190-003-0345-2

Kinsner, W., Cheung, V., Cannons, K., Pear, J., & Martin, T. (2003). Signal classification through multifractal analysis and complex domain neural networks. *Second IEEE International Conference on Cognitive Informatics (ICCI'03)*, August 18-20, (pp. 41- 46), London, UK.

Koblinsky, C. J., Clarke, R. T., Brenner, A. C., & Frey, H. (1993). Measurement of river level variations with satellite altimetry. *Water Resources Research, 6*, 1839–1848. doi:10.1029/93WR00542

Kruizinga, G. (1997). *Validation and application of satellite radar altimetry*. PhD Dissertation, Univ. of Texas at Austin, Austin, TX, USA.

Papa, F., Legre'sy, B., & Re'my, F. (2003). Use of the Topex–Poseidon dual-frequency radar altimeter over land surfaces. *Remote Sensing of Environment, 87*, 136–147. doi:10.1016/S0034-4257(03)00136-6

Papa, F., Legresy, B., Mognard, N. M., Josberger, E. G., & Remy, F. (2002). Estimating Terrestrial Snow Depth with the Topex–Poseidon Altimeter and Radiometer. *IEEE Transactions on Geoscience and Remote Sensing, 40*(10), 2162–2169. doi:10.1109/TGRS.2002.802463

Pernkopf, F., Van Pham, T., Bilmes, J. A., & Pernkopf, F. (2009). Broad phonetic classification using discriminative Bayesian networks. *Speech Communication*, *51*(2), 151–166. doi:10.1016/j.specom.2008.07.003

Remy, F., Legresy, B., Bleuzen, S., Vincent, P., & Minster, J. F. (1996). Dual frequency Topex altimeter observations of Greenland. *Journal of Electromagnetic Waves and Applications*, *10*, 1507–152. doi:10.1163/156939396X00892

Ripley, B. D. (1996). *Pattern Recognition and Neural Networks*. London, UK: Cambridge University Press.

Rodriguez, E., & Martin, J. M. (1994). Assessment of the TOPEX Altimeter performance using waveform retracking. *Journal of Geophysical Research*, *99*(24), 957–969.

Shi, Z., & Shi, J. (2003). Perspectives on Cognitive Informatics. *Second IEEE International Conference on Cognitive Informatics (ICCI'03)*, August 18-20, (pp. 129-133), London, UK.

Tatem, A. J., Lewis, H. G., Atkinson, P. M., & Nixon, M. S. (2002). Super-resolution land cover pattern prediction using a Hopfield neural network. *Remote Sensing of Environment*, *79*(1), 1–14. doi:10.1016/S0034-4257(01)00229-2

Varma, A. K., Gairola, R. M., Kishtawal, C. M., Pandey, P. C., & Singh, K. P. (1999). Rain Rate Estimation From Nadir-Looking TOPEX/POSEIDON Microwave Radiometer (TMR) for Correction of Radar Altimetric Measurements. *IEEE Transactions on Geoscience and Remote Sensing*, *37*(5), 2256–2568. doi:10.1109/36.789650

Wang, Y. (2003). On Cognitive Informatics. *Brain and Mind*, *4*(3), 151–167. doi:10.1023/A:1025401527570

Yaremchuk, V., & Dawson, M. R. W. (2008). Artificial Neural Networks That Classify Musical Chords. *International Journal of Cognitive Informatics and Natural Intelligence*, *2*(3), 22–30. doi:10.4018/jcini.2008070102

Zieger, A. R., Hancock, D. W., Hayne, G. S., & Purdy, C. L. NASA (1991). Radar Altimeter for the TOPEX/POSEIDON Project. *Proceedings of the IEEE*, *79*(6), 810-826.

This work was previously published in International Journal of Software Science and Computational Intelligence, Volume 1, Issue 3, edited by Yingxu Wang, pp. 81-91, copyright 2009 by IGI Publishing (an imprint of IGI Global).

Chapter 29
A Generic Framework for Feature Representations in Image Categorization Tasks

Adam Csapo
Budapest University of Technology and Economics, Hungary

Barna Resko
Hungarian Academy of Sciences, Hungary

Morten Lind
NTNU, Dept. of Production and Quality Engineering, Norway

Peter Baranyi
Budapest University of Technology and Economics, Hungary, & Hungarian Academy of Sciences, Hungary

Domonkos Tikk
Budapest University of Technology and Economics, Hungary

ABSTRACT

The computerized modeling of cognitive visual information has been a research field of great interest in the past several decades. The research field is interesting not only from a biological perspective, but also from an engineering point of view when systems are developed that aim to achieve similar goals as biological cognitive systems. This paper introduces a general framework for the extraction and systematic storage of low-level visual features. The applicability of the framework is investigated in both unstructured and highly structured environments. In a first experiment, a linear categorization algorithm originally developed for the classification of text documents is used to classify natural images taken from the Caltech 101 database. In a second experiment, the framework is used to provide an automatically guided vehicle with obstacle detection and auto-positioning functionalities in highly structured environments. Results demonstrate that the model is highly applicable in structured environments, and also shows promising results in certain cases when used in unstructured environments.

DOI: 10.4018/978-1-4666-0261-8.ch029

The research areas inspired by cognitive science have significantly broadened and have received more attention in the last few years. Fields in engineering dealing with high-complexity intelligent systems tend to build more often on the results of cognitive science. One such example is the growing popularity of cognitive informatics based tools in modern image processing, object recognition and machine vision, designed with the motivation of cognitive science.

The algorithmic difficulties arising in computerized object recognition have been evident since the 1960s. Due to the realization that information sciences alone cannot successfully tackle the problem of object recognition, research in cognitive psychology, brain physiology and artificial intelligence have advanced hand in hand to better understand human visual processing. I. Biederman's results in the late 1980's (Biederman, 1987) - proving the indispensability of low-level visual features such as vertices and corners in the successful recognition of objects - have sparked increased interest in developing algorithms that make use of such geometrical primitives (some examples are D. Lowe's SIFT method (Lowe, 1999), A. Berg's geometric blur operator (Berg & Malik, 2001), and various works of M. Riesenhuber and T. Poggio (Riesenhuber & Poggio, 1999, 1997; Serre, Wolf, Bileschi & Riesenhuber, 2007).

Due to the increasing relative importance of cognitive inspired methods, it is important to model the processes described by cognitive science and to integrate such functions in a toolbox of cognitive informatics. This paper addresses this need by providing a general computational model of low-level feature extraction for visual information processing. The computational model - besides providing a generalized concept of visual features - allows for a highly differentiated but at the same time uniform representation of visual features. The operations defined on the visual features are all linear operations and have the advantage of requiring extremely low computational power.

The applicability of the model is demonstrated through two examples. In the first application, the proposed framework is used to generate input data structures to a linear classifier that has been shown to perform powerfully in the categorization of text documents. The method is evaluated on natural images taken from the Caltech 101 database, and is shown to yield promising results. In the second application, the representational framework is used to help automatically guided vehicles to autonomously self-locate and detect obstacles within highly structured environments.

Although the proposed framework treats all parts of images in a uniform way and does not rely on explicitly pre-determined keywords, it can be used in combination with other widespread methods within cognitive informatics, such as keyblock-based image retrieval methods (Zhu, Rao & Zhang, 2002), and various bag-of-keypoints techniques (Csurka, Dance, Fan, Willamowski & Bray, 2004; Grauman & Darrell, 2005; Lazebnik, Schmid & Ponce, 2006). In the examples given in this paper, however, we prefer to use the most naive approaches possible to demonstrate the viability of our model in the most general cases.

THE VISUAL FEATURE ARRAY

The Visual Feature Array Concept

At the heart of the proposed concept is a Visual Feature Array (VFA) model, which is a cognitive information processing model that uses the information processing structures defined in the VFA concept. The VFA model obtains information from the environment, performs various operations on it, and then supplies higher-order models of cognitive informatics with its output. The proposed VFA concept allows for the implementation of cognitive functions analogous to those performed in the primary visual cortex (Figure 1).

Figure 1. The VFA concept

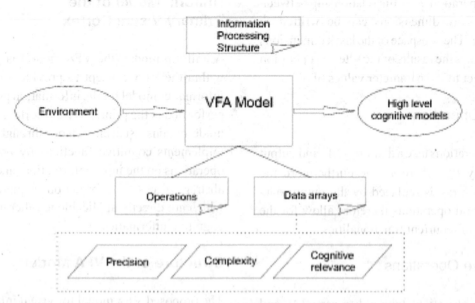

Information Processing Structures in the VFA Concept

The information processing structures of the VFA concept describe the units available and their relationships in constructing a VFA model. VFA models can be composed of data arrays and operations that can be performed on them. The models constructed in the VFA concept are functionally similar to the information processing structures in the brain, where a large number of neurons (data arrays in the concept) affect the output of other large numbers of neurons, according to the topology and strength of their connections (operations in the concept).

Data Arrays

The data arrays are multidimensional arrays whose values can be of any type. The arrays were conceived to represent the output of individual neurons responsible for visual features in the modeled neural structures. The values contained in data arrays will be subsequently referred to as (artificial) neurons or computational elements.

Operations

An operation takes a data array of n dimensions as its operand, and places its result in a data array of m dimensions. The operations of the VFA concept are of SIMD type, and each of them can have static and / or running parameters. Running parameters assume discrete values taken from a limited interval.

Let $F^{(k)}$ denote an operation, where k is the number of running parameters. Let A_n denote the input data array, and B_m the output data array, where n and m are the dimensions of A and B respectively. The performed operation can then be written as $F^{(k)}A_n = B_m$.

Three basic operation types are defined:

- Filtering operations
- Lateral operations
- Projective operations

Filtering Operations

Filtering operations take a data array A_n and output a data array B_m, where $n \leq m$. Given a filtering operation $F^{(k)}$, the relationship between the data array dimensions can be written as $m = n + k$. The subspace of the last k dimensions of B_m defines the results of the filtering operation with respect to the parameter values of $F^{(k)}$.

Lateral Operations

Lateral operations take a data array A_n and output a data array B_m, where $n = m$. Furthermore, the input data array is replaced by the output data array. Lateral operations therefore allow for the definition of recurrent functionalities.

Projective Operations

Projective operations take a data array A_n and output a data array B_m, where $m = n - k$. Such operations perform the same calculations on all values along the given k dimensions of the input data array. The result is stored in an output data array that contains all of the input data array dimensions, except for the k dimensions along which the projective operation was performed.

Uniform Model of the Primary Visual Cortex

A uniform model (the VFA model) is proposed within the VFA concept to provide a cognitive informatics model for the information processing performed in the primary visual cortex. The VFA model obtains visual information through its input, implements cognitive functions by performing operations on the input information, and outputs abstract pieces of information in matrix form, which are directly applicable to other models of cognitive informatics.

Structure of the VFA Model

The proposed VFA model for visual information processing from the retina to the primary visual cortex is shown on Figure 2. The input to the model is a greyscale image of size x-by-y, and is stored in the first 2D data array, denoted by I.

An input filtering operation $F^{(k)}$ is performed on the input image I. The number of running parameters, k, is usually 1 or 2, depending on the desired operation. The obtained result is stored in $VFA^{(k+2)}$.

Figure 2. The Visual Feature Array model. Rectangles represent data arrays, and ellipses represent operations

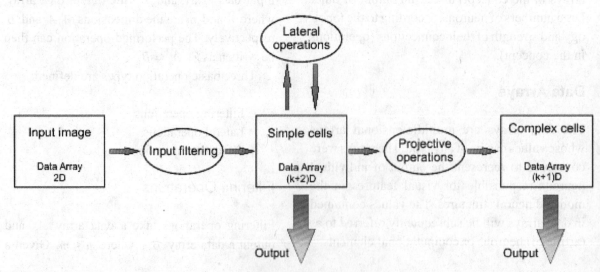

A lateral operation, L, is defined over VFA. The operation does not alter the dimensions or size of VFA, but allows for the implementation of lateral excitations and inhibitions.

Finally, a projective operation, P, is defined over the resulting array. The result is stored in data array $NMAP^{(k+1)}$.

Any of the above intermediate data arrays can be supplied as output from the VFA model, depending on the application. In the following, we briefly describe the operations $F, L,$ and P specifically used in our experiments, and it will be clear that data array VFA represents the output of cortical simple cells, while $NMAP$ represents the output of higher-order complex cells.

Modeling Simple Cells

Staying with the nomenclature from above, in our current implementation, I is an edge-detected greyscale image, and operation F consists of orientation-selective edge detection. Each element in VFA - a 3-dimensional data array - $VFA(x, y, z)$,

receives afferent input with different weighting factors from pixel (x, y) and its surroundings in image I. For each computational element in VFA, the weighting factors are determined by the following orientation-selective receptive field (Figure 3):

$$SCRF_{\lambda, \vartheta}(x, y) = \begin{cases} 0 & if \left| \dfrac{2\pi g(\vartheta)}{\lambda} \right| > 0.5\pi \\ \cos(g(\vartheta)\dfrac{2\pi}{\lambda}) & otherwise \end{cases} \quad (1)$$

where

$$g(\vartheta) = x \cos \vartheta + y \sin \vartheta \quad (2)$$

and $SCRF$ stands for Simple Cell Receptive Field.

Based on the above, k, the running parameter of $F^{(k)}$, has a single dimension, and represents the angle of orientation selectivity. $F^{(k)}$ can be applied to I by convolving I with $SCRF$ z_{max} different times, for every possible orientation.

Figure 3. Receptive field of an orientation-selective simple cell

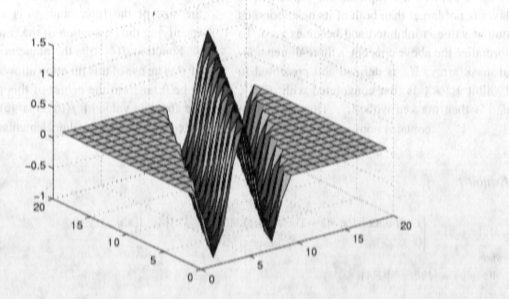

These convolutions yield z_{max} different layers, stacked up one behind another in data array *VFA*. A given point - $VFA(x, y, z)$ - therefore represents the output of a cortical simple cell whose receptive field is directed at point (x, y) of the original image, and is responsive to the orientation specified by z. Such outputs take their values from a continuous, normalized scale.

Modeling Lateral Inhibition

Inhibition Metamodel

Using the above filtering model, spurious data values are frequently obtained (for instance, when the resolution of possible angles in the operation F is high i.e., z_{max} is high, artificial neurons in neighboring layers can be active at the same time because there is so little difference between the angles they are selective to). To alleviate this problem, lateral inhibition is introduced between computational elements of each layer and their two corresponding neighbors (in neighboring iso-oriented layers), such that a computational element in a layer (after each layer has been convoluted by a filter, Filter) can only keep its output value if its two neighboring layers are less active. If the output of a computational element in a layer is not larger than both of its neighbors, its output value is inhibited and becomes zero. To formalize the above concept, a three-dimensional mask array M_F is defined and presented in Exhibit 1. *VFA* is first convoluted with *Filter*, and is then masked with M_F. Thus we obtain $V_{inhibit}$. $V_{inhibit}$ contains nonzero elements only in

layers whose orientations best correlate with the orientation of the contour elements. The measure of correlation is obtained by convolving layers of *VFA* with *Filter*. In the simplest case, *Filter* is a scalar value and is equal to 1, which means that corresponding pixel values in corresponding areas of neighboring layers are compared in a winner-take-all fashion.

VFA Inhibition Models based on the Inhibition Metamodel

The model of inhibition presented thus far, using a scalar value of 1 for *Filter*, has disturbing properties. It does not ensure, for example, that straight lines in the original image will not be divided, segment by segment, among different layers of $V_{inhibit}$.

To alleviate this problem, a wider neighborhood of each pixel can be taken into consideration by Filter. The neighborhood considered may engender a larger space, and the filter applied to each layer can also be dynamically changed based on the orientation selectivity of the given layer. In this section, two possible filters are presented in Exhibit 2 (Figures 4,5).

In $Filter_1$, the phase is ϑ, the amount of grating in the filter is specified by λ, σ correlates with the size of the filter, and γ is a shape ratio specifying the elongation of the filter.

Function $f(\vartheta)$ tilts the plane in the direction of ϑ. The use of this function allows for the filter to be 0 far from the center of this plane (where the absolute value of $f(\vartheta)$ is large). Apart from the coordinates where filter elements are 0, $Filter_1$

Exhibit 1.

$$M_F(x, y, z) = \begin{cases} 1 & if \max\left\{A(x, y, z-1), A(x, y, z), A(x, y, z+1)\right\} = A(x, y, z) \\ 0 & otherwise \end{cases} \qquad (3)$$

where

$$A(x, y, z) = (Filter * VFA)(x, y, z) \qquad (4)$$

defines a three-dimensional Gabor-function. $Filter_1$ is non-binary.

In $Filter_2$, x_0 and y_0 are the (x,y) coordinates of the point under scrutiny (the center of the filter). The first two conditions (second and third in the list) imply that only those points are considered which are in the proximity of x_0 and y_0. The third condition imposes a constraint on the bounds of constant c (thus guaranteeing that the ones in the filter form a "thick" line). The fourth constraint guarantees that the "thickness" of the line will diminish as the radius from the center grows. Finally, the sixth constraint ensures that ϑ will span through the interval $[0..\pi]$ in z_{max} steps.

Unlike $Filter_1$, $Filter_2$ is binary. However, it has the advantage of taking into consideration more points surrounding $VFA(x_0, y_0, z)$ as the radius becomes smaller and smaller.

In the remainder of this paper, data arrays VFA and $V_{inhibit}$ are often referred to as VFA. An example of how the filters work can be seen in Figures 6-7. Figure 6 shows the edge detected image used to construct the VFA and two views of the uninhibited VFA, while Figure 7 shows views of inhibited VFAs using the first and second masks, respectively.

Exhibit 2.

$$Filter_1(x,y,z) = \begin{cases} 0 & if \left| \frac{2\pi f(\vartheta)}{\lambda} + \varphi \right| > 0.5\pi \\ e^{-\frac{f(\vartheta)^2 + \gamma(-x\sin\vartheta + y\cos\vartheta)}{2\vartheta^2}} \cos(\frac{2\pi f(\vartheta)}{\lambda} + \varphi) & otherwise \end{cases} \quad (5)$$

and

$$Filter_2(x,y,z) = \begin{cases} 1 & if \exists c_{max} : \vartheta = \pi/2 \quad \frac{y - y_0 + c}{x - x_0} = \pm 15 \\ 1 & if \exists c_{max} : \frac{y - y_0 + c}{x - x_0} = \tan\theta \\ 0 & otherwise \end{cases} \quad (6)$$

where

$f(\vartheta) = 3(x\cos\vartheta + y\sin\vartheta)$

$|x - x_0| \leq c_1$

$|y - y_0| \leq c_2$

$c_3 \leq c_{max} \leq c_4$ $\quad\quad\quad (7)$

$c = \dfrac{c_{max}}{\sqrt{radius}}$

$radius = \sqrt{(x - x_0)^2 + (y - y_0)^2}$

$\vartheta = \dfrac{z\pi}{z_{max}}$

Figure 4. The figure shows the first filter for different values of θ. (a) Filter for θ = 60 (b) Filter for Θ = 90 (c) Filter for Θ = 120

Figure 4. The figure shows the first filter for different values of θ. (a) Filter for θ = 60 (b) Filter for Θ = 90 (c) Filter for Θ = 120

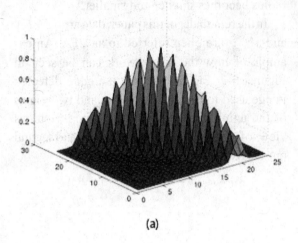

(a)

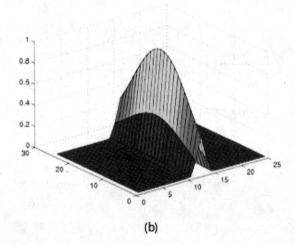

(b)

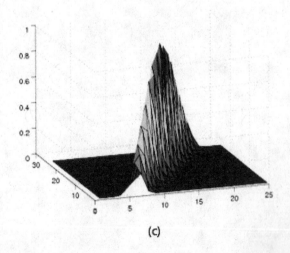

(c)

Modeling Complex Cells

The detection of crossings and corners is crucial in human visual perception, as shown in (Biederman, 1987). Even the simplest objects can become unrecognizable after the removal of only a small proportion of their characteristic nodes, while discontinuities in edges do not make object recognition impossible. Several studies have shown that the visual cortex provides an explicit mechanism for the extraction of features such as vertices and corners from visual input (Shevelev, Lazareva, Sharaev & Novikova, 1999, 1998; Hubel & Wiesel, 1968). This functionality has been proven necessary for higher-level visual processing.

Experimental evidence suggests that complex cells in visual cortex are responsible for the detection of vertices, corners and other complex forms (Hubel, 1988; Shevelev et al., 1999, 1998). Research on the cat's visual cortex proved the presence of a large variety of complex cells, each sensitive to different aspects. Some were found to be sensitive to nodes in general, some to the angle between intersecting segments, and some even to the exact orientation of an angle. In the following we present a model for the detection of line segment intersections in $V_{inhibit}$.

Detecting Intersections: When two segments intersect at a given point of the scene, they appear in different layers of the VFA (the layers corresponding to their orientations). At the point of intersection, both kinds of simple cells give increased responses. Such neurons in VFA have the same (x, y) coordinates (and only differ in their preferred angle). Consequently, line intersections can be detected by examining VFA along its third axis.

Let $VFA^{z_{max}}$ be a vector containing z_{max} elements. Values of $VFA^{z_{max}}$ correspond to the output of simple cells belonging to a given point of the image. This way, 180 degrees of orientation are covered in $(180 / z_{max})$-degree increments.

Figure 5. The figure shows the second filter used for different values of θ. Note that the filter for θ = 90 is different from filters for other values of θ because the tangent of π/ 2 radians is infinity. (a) Filter for θ = 80 (b) Filter for θ = 90 (c) Filter for Θ = 100

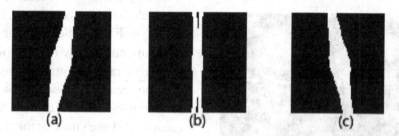

(a)   (b)   (c)

$$V_{xy} = VFA(x, y, \varphi_i)$$

$$\varphi_i = k(180/z_{max})$$

$$k = 1..z_{max} \tag{8}$$

Intersections can then be detected as follows:

$$NMAP(x, y) = signum \left\{ \sum_{j=1}^{z\,max} V_{xy}(j) - 2 \right\} \tag{9}$$

The value of $NMAP(x, y)$ will be 1 if point (x, y) contains an intersection. The neural model of the formula can be imagined as an artificial complex cell receiving inputs from all simple cells of the VFA which belong to the same point of the scene. Such a complex cell would then calculate the sum of its inputs, and compare the result to a threshold value of 2. This means that the neuron will show increased activity when stimulated by at least two of its input simple cells.

Intersections can also be differentiated based on the angles they form (depending on which layers of VFA contain high values). An example can be seen in Figure 8.

USING VFA-GENERATED INPUT FOR IMAGE CLASSIFICATION

HITEC: Introduction to the Categorization Algorithm Used

HITEC (Hierarchical Text Categorization System) was developed at the Dept. of Telecommunications and Media Informatics at the Budapest University of Technology and Economics (Tikk, Biro & Yang, 2005). HITEC was originally used for the categorization of textual documents within a taxonomy of hierarchically related categories.

In HITEC, processing units are organized into a hierarchical arrangement in a way that they have a direct, one-to-one relationship to categories in the taxonomy tree. Two processing units belonging to the same subtree in the network therefore are related through the categories they represent. An example of a taxonomy tree and a hierarchy of processing units can be seen in Figure 9.

Input vectors are fed to the top-most node, and are immediately fed to processing units on the second level. Each processing unit calculates a relevance value by applying a sigmoid function to the weighted sum of values in the input vector:

$$\varphi_{de}(v, w, \eta, \vartheta) = (1 + \eta) \tanh(\sum_{j=1}^{m} w_{ij} * v_{ij} - \vartheta) \tag{10}$$

Figure 6. Edge detected image and two views of the original VFA obtained. (a) Edge detected image (b) Front view of original VFA (c) Original VFA

(a)

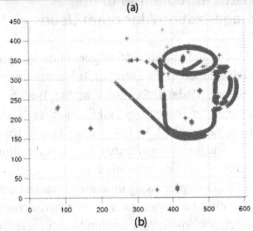

(b)

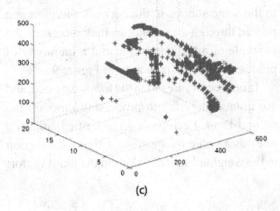

(c)

where v is the input vector, w is the weighting

vector, η and ϑ are threshold values, m is the number of nodes at a level in the hierarchy, and d and c refer to the document and the category to which the node is attributed, respectively. The use of such a function is beneficial because it grows monotonously (thus allowing the system to set up a ranking among plausible categories), and also because it is bounded, which is necessary for computational efficiency. An error value is calculated at each node in the level using the following formula:

$$e(d,c) = y(d,c) - \varphi_{dc} \qquad (11)$$

where $y(d,c)$ is the expected relevance value of document d with respect to category c. Weights are then modified based on this error value:

$$w_{ij} = \begin{cases} w_{ij} + e(d,c) * \alpha * v_{ij} & if\ e(d,c) > 0 \\ w_{ij} + e(d,c) * \beta * v_{ij} & otherwise \end{cases} \qquad (12)$$

where α is the rate of learning, and β is the rate of forgetting.

After new weights have been established, HITEC uses a relaxed greedy method to pass the input vectors down to levels lower in the hierarchy of categories. The method is greedy because it favors subtrees whose parent nodes computed relatively high relevance values, but it is relaxed because it passes input vectors down not only in the winning subtree, but also in suboptimal ones to compensate for possible errors at each level. Formally, the condition that needs to be satisfied for each subtree is:

$$\varphi_{cd} \geq \max \left\{ \lambda, \varphi_l(d), v_{\max} \right\} \qquad (13)$$

where $0 < \lambda < 1$ is a minimum threshold that needs to be exceeded by the relavance value, and $0 < v_{\max} < 1$ is the maximal deviation that can be

Figure 7. Two views of the inhibited VFA obtained using Mask1 (top row) and Mask2 (bottom row). It is clear that the use of Mask2 results in a better reduction of redundancies. (a) Front view of inhibited VFA (b) Inhibited VFA (c) Front view of inhibited VFA (d) Inhibited VFA

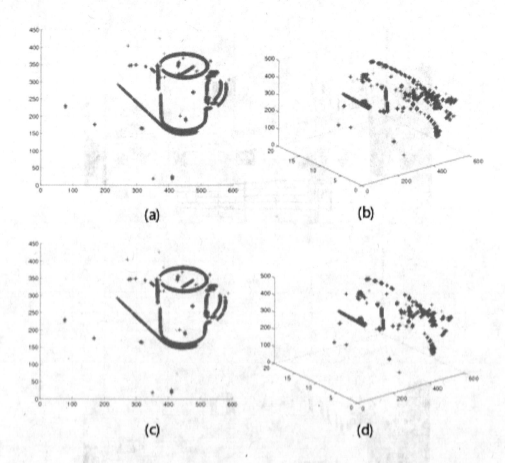

accepted between the relevance value of the given category and the largest relevance value in the layer ($\varphi_l(d)$). In this way, there is no hard limit for the number of subtrees through which the input vector is passed down, and erroneous categorizations high in the hierarchy can be compensated for at lower levels.

The Node Map Representation

An intuitive representation of images can be achieved by creating a two-dimensional map of nodes using the projective operation, P, of summation along the third dimension of VFA, without the thresholding operation at the end. Pixels where

several line segments meet will be characterized by higher values in such a map. Several experiments were conducted on the usability of such representations in image categorization. Promising results were achieved using Hierarchical Temporal Memories (HTMs) (Csapo, Baranyi & Tikk, 2007), however, very poor results were yielded using HITEC.

Generalization of the Node Map Representation

The difficulty with using a simple summation of VFA layers as input to categorization algorithms is that it does not take into consideration the

Figure 8. Intersections can be categorized in terms of the angles they define. (a) Nodes between 1ˢᵗ and 10ᵗʰ layer (b) Nodes between 10ᵗʰ and 18ᵗʰ layer

(a)

(b)

fuzziness naturally yielded by the representation used by the VFA model, and such node maps are generally useless when using linear categorization algorithms such as HITEC. An alternative approach would be to selectively apply a nonlinear function to values in different layers of VFA. Instead of summing all the layers together, without question, we may choose - for example - to take into consideration only certain orientations, and apply a weighting scheme that raises values in different layers to different powers - thus causing values on layers raised to higher powers to be less significant than other layers (given that values in the VFA are normalized to [0,1]).

Figure 9. Taxonomy tree and processing hierarchy in a HITEC network

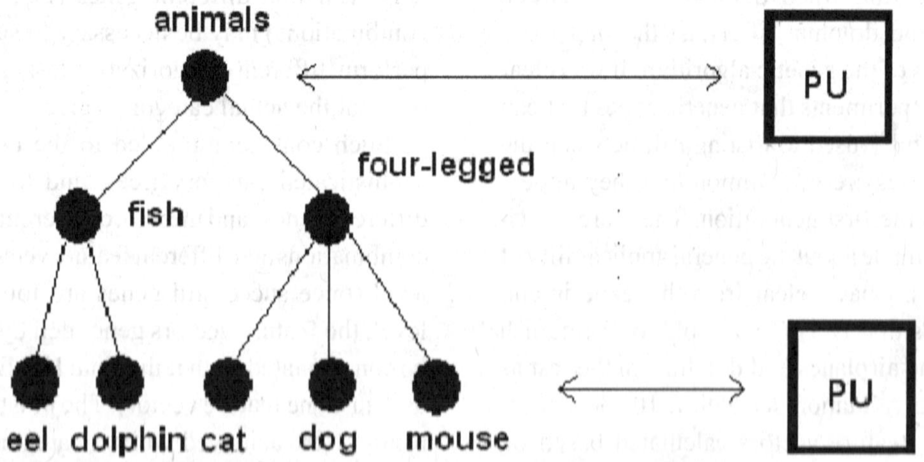

Naturally, such an approach will lead to many more possibilities than just a simple summation of layers - which is a special case of this weighting scheme - but the question arises: how can we find optimal representations so that we can check if this really works better, and also so that we can be sure that an unsuccessful categorization is not due to a poor selection of weighting functions. To answer such questions, a genetic algorithm was used to introduce competition among possible solutions.

Let $X_i, i \in 1..n$ be a layer of X_2, where n is the number of layers in VFA. A solution - represented by a gene in the genetic algorithm - is a polynomial function of these layers. Such solutions can easily be represented using binary bit sequences of coefficients, in which each position marks a certain power of values in a certain layer. If we allow powers of 3 at most, this will yield genes (i.e., bit sequences) with $3n$ dimensions.

Image Categorization Using HITEC

Distinguishing Between Two Categories

For the sake of simplicity, only two categories were used initially - airplanes and dolphins -, and the categorization system was taught to distinguish between the two. The choice of these two categories seemed justified because even though for humans, airplanes and dolphins form very different categories, this is not so for object categorization algorithms, which perceive both categories as having sleek bodies, for instance.

Images were taken from the Caltech101 database. Instead of using one training and one evaluation set, we used one training and two evaluation sets. This was necessary to prevent the genetic algorithm from learning specific characteristics of the testing set (which was used in the fitness function and therefore in the feedback to the genetic algorithm). A validation set, completely disjoint with the testing set, was used to validate the fitness of the genes. The training and testing set consisted of 20 images each, while the validation set consisted of 10 images per category.

Table 1 gives an overview of a better part of the gene population when distinguishing between airplanes and dolphins after just the first three generations of the genetic algorithm. It was clear from our experiments that genetic codes that can be successfully used to distinguish between the two categories are so common that they appear as early as the first generation. There are no assumptions made about the general applicability of these genes; what is clear from this experiment, however, is that HITEC was able to distinguish between the airplanes and dolphins in the test as well as the validation set with a 100% success rate, using feature vectors calculated based on these genes.

Distinguishing Among Several Categories

If the HTM network could not be successfully scaled up to differentiate among 10 categories (Csapo, Baranyi & Tikk, 2007), HITEC initially provided even worse results. The highest success rate that could be achieved was around 44%. The category tree used in these experiments had two layers, and all of the 10 categories were children of the same root node.

Through the experiments, it quickly became clear that the same gene could not be used to tell apart each of the 10 categories. Even intuitively, it is clear that different genes (i.e., VFA layer combinations) may be necessary to successfully perform different categorization tasks, depending on what the actual categories are.

Such considerations led to the use of more sophisticated category trees, and to the use of different genes (and therefore different VFA layer combinations and different feature vectors) at each level (once successful genes are found at each level, the feature vectors generated by them may be concatenated so that the final HITEC network uses just one feature vector). The most promising results were achieved when a category tree of n layers was used for n categories. Each node in the tree had two children; the left child contained all the remaining categories, save for one, and the right child was a leaf node, containing just one category. In this way, each level was used to decide whether the image belonged to a given category or not. Results close to or at 100% were achieved for some categories, as demonstrated in Table 2. For other categories, results were not promising at the outset. This shows clearly that further investigation is needed to prove the general applicability of the method.

A key issue with this approach is that even if all the categories could be discerned at 100% success rate, the time needed for categorization

Table 1. Best genes in gene pool after 3 generations when distinguishing between two categories. The second and fourth columns contain the percentage of genes in the test set and validation set that performed with the number of hits indicated in the first and third columns. The fifth column shows the ratio of genes within the whole gene pool that performed on the test set with the hit rate indicated in the first column, and performed at least as well on the validation set as indicated in the third column. Because the sets in the fifth column are disjoint, it can be seen that nearly half of the gene pool produced very good results.

Testing Set		Validation Set		Overlap
Number of hits/number of images	% in set	number of hits/ number of images	% in set	Number of overlaps/ number of genes
40/40	19%	20/20	35%	6/26
38/40	12%	19/20	8%	3/26
37/40	12%	18/20	4%	3/26

Table 2. Best genes in gene pool after 3 generations when distinguishing between one category and 9 others. The second and fourth columns contain the percentage of genes in the test set and validation set that performed with the number of hits indicated in the first and third columns. The fifth column shows the ratio of genes within the whole gene pool that performed on the test set with the hit rate indicated in the first column, and performed at least as well on the validation set as indicated in the third column. Because the sets in the fifth column are disjoint, it can be seen that over half of the gene pool produced very good results.

Testing Set		Validation Set		Overlap
Number of hits/number of images	% in set	number of hits/ number of images	% in set	Number of overlaps/ number of genes
200/200	50%	100/100	40%	4/10
199/200	10%	99/1009	20%	1/10
187/200	10%	93/100	10%	1/10

would not be constant when showing the network images from different categories. If, for example, an image is shown whose category resides deep inside the category tree, categorization will be much slower than if the category resides on a leaf node that is a child of the root node. Such issues were not dealt with in our research, but would provide interesting motivation for future investigations. It is perhaps an interesting coincidence that the biological visual system also shows anomalies in the recognition of different categories depending on the context; while generally, the recognition of objects is very fast and equally efficient among different categories, an object belonging to a category that is generally alien to a given environment usually increases time requirements. Such considerations are more philosophical than scientific at this point; they are not backed up by evidence in this work.

The categorization methods used with HITEC also suffer from similar problems as the categorization with HTMs did: the representations used are not scale and rotation invariant. An initial segmentation, and the use of much larger training datasets in which objects are shown at many different scales and positions, could lead to better results in the future.

VFA-BASED ROBOT GUIDING IN INDUSTRIAL ENVIRONMENTS

This section demonstrates the use of VFA representations in a structured environment to increase the stability in the localization tasks of automatically guided robots.

Formulation of Robot Guiding Problem

In production engineering, the higher the degree of flexible and agile automatization in a production system, the more cost-effective it usually is. One problem with fully automatized systems, however, is that their reconfiguration is time consuming and therefore costly, therefore, flexibility and agility are difficult to achieve. Another common concern with such systems is that their full automatization imposes constraints on the size and dimensions of the shop floor on which they are installed.

Automatically guided vehicles (AGVs) are considered to be a viable building block in solutions to such problems. With the use of AGVs, it is possible - for instance - to transport goods halfway through the production line from one conveyer to another. Because of the transportation flexibilities of the AGV, the relative location of these belts is not as constrained as it would otherwise be. Furthermore, the agility of self-navigation in free-roaming AGVs allows for obstacle avoidance and even the selection of alternative routes when obstacles appear which cannot easily be bypassed.

Such an AGV is being developed at the Dept. of Production and Quality Engineering at NTNU (Figure 10). An important goal in the project is that the AGV be built using widely available low-cost elements (therefore, expensive sensory equipment are out of the question). To this end, the AGVs are equipped with bright LEDs, and a low-cost camera system installed on the ceiling is used to track their motions.

One key issue in any automated system is how to detect unexpected situations. In normal cases, the AGV would automatically transport goods between conveyor belts, however, if its habitual path were to be suddenly blocked by an obstacle due to temporary changes in the environment (e.g., operators performing maintenance tasks, temporary storage of incoming material on the shop floor), the system would quickly run into problems.

Also interesting is the problem of automatic calibration. If an AGV suddenly loses all of its positional history (due to an unexpected restart forced by e.g. a watchdog system), or if an AGV is newly installed in the shop floor, it would hardly be cost-effective to hire an employee to guide the calibration of an otherwise automated AGV system. Also noteworthy is the case when the AGV is traversing areas where it is not lucrative to set up camera systems (such as narrow pathways) - in which case the AGV is completely on its own and needs a way to ensure that it is moving in a straight line and not deviating from its path.

The use cases to be solved are therefore the following:

- Location Plausibility Service – The AGV sends the server a message containing an image snapped at its current location, and asks the server whether or not it is plausible that it should see the given image at the current location (the location server knows the AGVs position information). If the answer is no, there is something impeding the AGV's way. The response to this question

Figure 10. The experimental AGV at NTNU, for which the Location Plausibility Service and Initial Localization Service were implmented.

should arrive back to the AGV as quickly as possible - this way the AGV needn't stop and can still be quickly alerted of possible obstacles.

- Initial Localization Service – The AGV sends a "where am I" message to the server. There are no time constraints imposed on the use case.

The two use cases are in fact two extremities across a highly granular scale of possible operations. Indeed, if one were to augment the input parameters of the above use cases with a set of descriptions of bounded areas of interest on the shop floor with corresponding probabilities (e.g., there is a 70% chance that the AGV is located in bounded area A, and a 30% chance that it is located in bounded area B), the above services would merely be two special cases of this application. In other words, when there is only a single and small bounded area of interest with a high likelihood, the query is reduced to the location plausibility problem. In contrast, when the bounded area of interest is broad, or the location probabilities attributed to the bounded areas of interest are very small, the query translates to a request to the Initial Localization server. (The data required for the determination of these bounded areas and their corresponding probabilities can be derived from a variety of sources, such as a rough location description by an operator, local inter-AGV communication and information exchange, a rough and error-prone odometric tracking device that is frequently reset during the AGV's operation, triangulation based on signal strengths of surrounding access points, etc.)

VFA-Based Feature Comparison

Using the VFA model, it is possible to construct feature representations of images as they are normally seen from different points on the shop floor at different angles. Because of its conformity to parallel computing, the VFA can be computed in a very efficient, highly parallelized way.

In the proposed algorithm, the calculation of data arrays VFA is followed by a segmentation of the images into regions (in this case, disjoint regions with fixed sizes), and an averaging or pixel values within these regions on each layer of VFA. A correlation between two such feature vectors quickly reveals discrepancies between referential and real-time images. A correlation can also be used to systematically compare the real-time image with the whole database of referential images (the initial localization problem does not involve particular time constraints).

Implementation and Test Results

In order to implement and test the above functionalities, we first set up referential and test positions in a robot laboratory at NTNU. Referential positions were set up every 2 meters on a regular grid, and test positions were created in random positions within the same grid. At each referential position, images were taken in 8 different directions (at intervals of 45 degrees).

Location Plausibility Service

The Location Plausibility server receives as input the positional information of the AGV, an image that was taken from the AGV's current location, and a threshold value used to determine how high the correlation needs to be with referential images in order for the image to be accepted as plausible. Figure 11 shows the image snapped at the test position as well as the some reference images to which it was compared to in a given request.

Initial Localization Service

The Initial Localization server receives as input an image snapped at the AGV's current location. Because it can take a long time to search through the complete database of referential images for

Figure 11. Experiments to demonstrate Location Plausibility server performance. The image snapped at the AGV's current location, shown in the top left corner, was compared to the remaining images. Only the image at the bottom right corner correlates sufficiently with the test image, at 0.99 (the second highest correlation was 0.86).

Figure 12. Three pairs of target images and resemblances found from the database using the Initial Localization Service

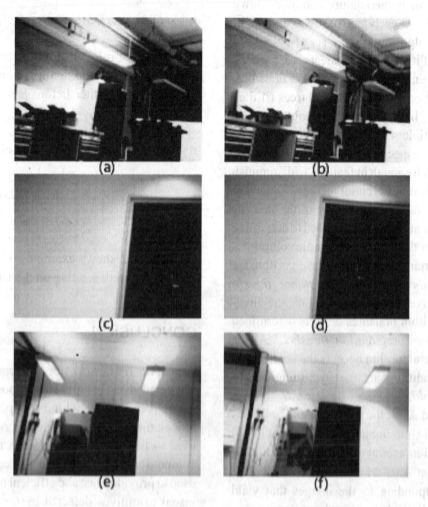

possible matches (depending on the size of the shop floor), we adopted a branch-and-bound approach to search for candidate solutions. It is also important to note that while in the location plausibility problem, the AGV was certain of its position, in this case the AGV has no idea, and therefore more strict rule sets must be used in order to be certain of the location of the AGV and to avoid false positives. In other words, a relatively high correlation between a referential image and the test image is not sufficient to convince the AGV that this is indeed the correct position. Correlations need to be very high, and need to be supported by other local evidence. If

the branch-and-bound algorithm cannot reach a unique and convincing solution, the AGV needs to be repositioned in the hopes of capturing images that are richer in features.

The branch-and-bound algorithm traverses through a binary tree of regions on the shop floor. Each node in the tree represents a region, and contains four corner points of the region as reference points. As the algorithm reaches deeper levels of the tree, smaller and smaller areas are considered. At the first level below the root of the tree, there are only two nodes (the shop floor area is divided into two partitions). In the algorithm, the first of these two is referred to as the lower branch, and the second is referred to as the upper branch. This nomenclature continues down the binary tree. At each pair of lower and upper branches, the algorithm uses a set of guidelines to determine if it should continue its search in the subtree belonging to the upper or lower branches, or if it should continue in both subtrees (if they seem equally likely to contain solutions). In this way, multiple solutions can theoretically be reached (this is especially possible if the captured image is not rich enough in features to distinguish it from most other referential images). When the algorithm reaches the final layer in the tree (its leaves), a separate set of rules is used to determine whether or not there is an acceptable solution.

Two important parameters in the algorithm are *propagation_threshold* and *acceptance_threshold*. At each layer except the final one, the direction the algorithm branches on to is determined with the help of *propagation_threshold*. At the final layer, the algorithm accepts the results only if certain conditions are met regarding *acceptance_threshold*.

Let X_1 and X_2 be the two highest correlations when the real-time image is correlated with all the referential images at all four corner points of region X. Let $Ang(X_1)$ and $Ang(X_2)$ be the angles corresponding to the images that yield correlations X_1 and X_2. Let the difference between these two angles be defined as presented in Exhibit 3.

In this case, region X is favored over region Y iff:

- $$\frac{X_1 + X_2}{2} > \frac{Y_1 + Y_2}{2}$$

Exhibit 3.

$$D(Ang(X_1), Ang(X_2)) = \begin{cases} \left| Ang(X_1) - Ang(X_2) \right| & if \left| Ang(X_1) - Ang(X_2) \right| \leq 180 \\ 360 - \left| Ang(X_1) - Ang(X_2) \right| & otherwise \end{cases}$$

- $$\frac{X_1 + X_2}{2} - \frac{Y_1 + Y_2}{2} > propagation\_threshold$$
- $$D(Ang(X_1), Ang(X_2)) \leq D(Ang(Y_1), Ang(Y_2))$$

This set of rules ensures that the algorithm is very certain of the optimality of one direction as opposed to the other before leaving out viable solutions.

In the final layer, the highest correlation at region X is considered to be a solution iff:

- $$\frac{X_1 + X_2}{2} < accep\tan ce\_threshold$$
- $$\max\{X_1, X_2\} > accep\tan ce\_threshold$$

Figure 12 shows examples of resemblances that are found depending on the target image.

CONCLUSION

A generic framework for the representation of low-level visual features was proposed. Examples were given as to what kinds of operations a VFA model might include. Lateral operations were used to filter spurious responses in the form of competitive networks. Projective operations were used to provide a fast and efficient method to filter visual primitives detected by cortical complex cells. The operations used have strong analogies with the biological vision system. In a second part of the paper we describe two applications in which the proposed framework can be used. Firstly, a categorization algorithm originally developed to evaluate text documents was used to categorize natural images. Feature vectors used for categorization were derived using projective operations in the VFA models of the images. Extremely high hit rates were achieved for pairs of categories, however the results did not scale well to a larger number of categories (better results may be achieved when using the VFA model in conjunction with higher-level cognitive models). Secondly, the VFA model was used to enhance automatically guided vehicles with auto-location and automatic calibration functionalities. Experimental results have demonstrated that the VFA model is a highly effective and computationally efficient framework to use in highly structured environments, and can also serve useful input to higher-level cognitive models in more complex, natural environments.

ACKNOWLEDGMENT

This research was supported by HUNOROB project (HU0045), a grant from Iceland, Liechtenstein and Norway through the EEA Financial Mechanism and the Hungarian National Development Agency.

REFERENCES

Berg, A. C., & Malik, J. (2001). Geometric Blur for Template Matching. In *CVPR* (pp. 607-614).

Biederman, I. (1987). Recognition-by-Components: A Theory of Human Image Understanding. *Psychological Review, 94*, 115–147. doi:10.1037/0033-295X.94.2.115

Csapo, A., Baranyi, P., & Tikk, D. (2007). Object Categorization Using VFA-generated Nodemaps and Hierarchical Temporal Memories. *Proc. Of IEEE International Conference on Computational Cybernetics* (pp. 257-262).

Csurka, G., Dance, C. R., Fan, L., Willamowski, J., & Bray, C. (2004). Visual Categorization With Bags of Keypoints. *In workshop on statistical learning in computer vision, EECV* (pp. 1-22).

Grauman, K., & Darrell, T. (2005). The Pyramid Match Kernel: Discriminative Classification with Sets of Image Features. *In ICCV* (pp. 1458-1465).

Hubel, D. (1988). *Eye, Brain and Vision.* W.H. Freeman & Co. ISBN: 0716750201.

Hubel, D., & Wiesel, T. (1968). Receptive Fields and Functional Architecture of Monkey Striate Cortex. *The Journal of Physiology, 195*, 215–243.

Lazebnik, S., Schmid, C., & Ponce, J. (2006). Beyond Bags of Features: Spatial Pyramid Matching for Recognizing Natural Scene Categories. *IEEE Conference on Computer Vision and Pattern Recognition, 2*, 1150-1157.

Lowe, D. (1999). Object Recognition From Local Scale-Invariant Features. *Proceedings of the Seventh IEEE Conference on Computer Vision, 2*, 1150-1157

Riesenhuber, M., & Poggio, T. (1997). Just One View: Invariances in Inferotemporal Cell Tuning. *Advances in Neural Information Processing Systems*, 215–221.

Riesenhuber, M., & Poggio, T. (1999). Hierarchical Models of Object Recognition in Cortex. *Nature Neuroscience, 2*, 1019–1025. doi:10.1038/14819

Serre, T., Wold, L., Bileschi, S., & Riesenhuber, M. (2007). Robust Object Recognition with Cortex-Like mechanisms. *IEEE Transactions on Pattern and Machine Intelligence, 29*(3), 411–426. doi:10.1109/TPAMI.2007.56

Shevelev, L., Lazareve, N., Sharaev, G., & Novikova, R. (1998). Second-Order Feature Extraction in the Cat Visual Cortex: Selective and Invariant Sensitivity of Neurons to the Shape and Orientation of Crosses and Corners. *Bio Systems*, *48*, 194–204. doi:10.1016/S0303-2647(98)00066-5

Shevelev, L., Lazareve, N., Sharaev, G., & Novikova, R. (1999). Interrelation of Tuning Characteristics to Bar, Cross and Corner in Striate Neurons. *Neuroscience*, *88*, 17–25. doi:10.1016/S0306-4522(98)00168-7

Tikk, D., Biro, G., & Yang, J. (2005). Experiments with a Hierarchical Text Categorization Method on WIPO Patent Collections. In *Applied Research in Uncertainty Modeling and Analysis* (pp. 283-302). Springer-Verlag.

Zhu, L., Rao, A., & Zhang, A. (2002). Theory of Keyblock-based Image Retrieval. *ACM Transactions on Information Systems*, *20*, 224–257. doi:10.1145/506309.506313

This work was previously published in International Journal of Software Science and Computational Intelligence, Volume 1, Issue 4, edited by Yingxu Wang, pp. 36-60, copyright 2009 by IGI Publishing (an imprint of IGI Global).

Compilation of References

A. Ferrero, S. Salicone, Fully comprehensive mathematical approach to the expression of uncertainty in measurement, *IEEE Transactions on Instrumentation and Measurement,* 56, 3, 2007, 706-712.

A. Gersho, R.M. Gray, *Vector Quantization and Signal Compression*, Kluwer Academic Publishers, Norwell, 1992.

Abadi *et al*, D. (2003). Aurora: A new model and architecture for data stream management. VLDB Journal.

ABET. (2006). ABET Engineering Accreditation Commission: Criteria for accreditation engineering programs. *Report*, 29 pp. Retrieved June 2007, from http://www.abet.org/forms.shtml

Adams, S. J. (1963). Towards an understanding of inequity. *Journal of Abnormal and Social Psychology*, 67, 422–436. doi:10.1037/h0040968

Agichtein, E., & Ganti, V. (2004). Mining Reference Tables for Automatic Text Segmentation. *Tenth ACM International Conference on Knowledge Discovery and Data Mining*, Seattle, WA

Aho, A. V., Hopcroft, J. E., & Ullman, J. D. (1974, January). *The Design and Analysis of Computer Algorithms* (1st Edition). Addison-Wesley.

Ahuja, M., Galletta, D., & Carley, K. (2003). Individual Centrality and Performance in Virtual R&D Groups: An Empirical Study. *Management Science*, 49(1), 21–38. doi:10.1287/mnsc.49.1.21.12756

Alani, H., Dasmahapatra, S., O'Hara, K., & Shadbolt, N. (2003). Identifying Communities of Practice through Ontology Network Analysis. *IEEE Intelligent Systems*, 18(2), 18–25. doi:10.1109/MIS.2003.1193653

Albin-Amiot, H., Cointe, P., Guéhéneuc, Y.-G., & Jussien, N. (2001, November). Instantiating and detecting design patterns: Putting bits and pieces together. In D. Richardson, M. Feather, & M. Goedicke (Eds.), *Proceedings of the 16th Conference on Automated Software Engineering*, (pp. 166–173). IEEE Computer Society Press.

Albrecht, A. J. (1979), Measuring Application Development Productivity, Proc. *of IBM Applications Development Joint SHARE/GUIDE Symposium*, Oct., 83-92.

Albrecht, A. J., & Gaffney, J. E. (1983). Software Function, Source Lines of Code, and Development Effort Prediction: A Software Science Validation. *IEEE Transactions on Software Engineering*, 9(6), 639–648. doi:10.1109/TSE.1983.235271

Albus, J. (1991). Outline for a Theory of Intelligence. *IEEE Transactions on Systems, Man, and Cybernetics*, 21(3), 473–509. doi:10.1109/21.97471

Aleksander, I. (1998). From WISARD to MAGNUS: A family of weightless neural machines. In Austin, J. (Ed.), *RAM-Based Neural Networks* (pp. 18–30). Singapore: World Scientific. doi:10.1142/9789812816849_0002

Altinel., et al. M. (2007). DAMIA: A data mashup fabric for intranet applications. VLDB '07: Proceedings of the 33rd International Conference on Very Large Data Bases (1370–1373). VLDB Endowment.

Amano, A., & Asada, N. (2003, August). Graph Grammar Based Analysis System of Complex Table Form Document. *Seventh International Conference on Document Analysis and Recognition Volume II*, Edinburgh, Scotland.

Anderson, J. A. (1995). *An introduction to neural networks*. Cambridge, Mass., USA: MIT Press.

Anderson, J. A., & Rosenfield, E. (1988). *Neurocomputing: Foundations of research*. Cambridge, Mass., USA: MIT Press.

Anderson, L. W., Krathwohl, D. R., Airasian, P. W., Cruikshank, K. A., Mayer, R. E., & Pintrich, P. R. (2001). *A Taxonomy for Learning, Teaching, and Assessing: A Revision of Bloom's Taxonomy of Educational Objectives*. New York: Longman.

Andrieux, A., Czajkowski, K., Dan, A., Keahey, K., Ludwig, H., Nakata, T., et al. "Web Services Agreement Specification (WS-Agreement). 2005, Sep. 20, 2005; Available from: http://www.ggf.org/Public_Comment_Docs/Documents/Oct-2005/WS-AgreementSpecificationDraft050920.pdf.

Antoniol, G., & Guéhéneuc, Y.-G. (2005, September). Feature identification: A novel approach and a case study. In T. Gyimóthy & V. Rajlich (Eds.), *Proceedings of the 21st International Conference on Software Maintenance*, pages 357–366. IEEE Computer Society Press, September 2005. Best paper.

Apu, R., & Gavrilova, M. L. "Adaptive Spatial Memory Representation for Real-Time Motion Planning," 3IA'2005 Int. Conf. on Comp. Graphics and Artificial Intelligence, France pp.21-32, 2005

Apu, R., & Gavrilova, M. L. (2006). *"Battle Swarm: An Evolutionary Approach to Complex Swarm Intelligence,"* 3IA Int. C. Comp. Graphics and AI (pp. 139–150). Limoges, France: Eurographics.

Arasu, S., & Babu, S. Widom, J. (2003). The CQL continuous query language: Semantic foundations and query execution (TR-2003-67). Stanford University.

Arnold, M. G. (1999). *Verilog Digital Computer Design: Algorithms into Hardware* (p. 602). Upper Saddle River, NJ: Prentice Hall.

Arnowitz, J., Arent, M., & Berger, N. (2006). *Effective Prototyping for Software Makers*. Morgan Kaufmann.

Arroyo, F., Castellanos, J., Luengo, C., & Mingo, L. (1997). Frames neural networks for cognitive process. In *World multiconference on systemics, cypernetics and informatics* (pp. 288–295). Caracas, Venezuela.

Arroyo, F., Castellanos, J., Luengo, C., & Mingo, L. (1998). Connectionist systems for a hierarchical knowledge representation. In *1998 International conference on neural networks and brain* (pp. 471–474). Beijing, China.

Arroyo, F., Luengo, C., Mingo, F., & Castellanos, J. (1999). Evolving connectionist and symbolic processes in a hierarchical memory model. In *World multiconference on systemics, cybernetics and informatics*, 8, 255–261. Orlando, Florida, USA.

Asano, T. (2006). Aspect-Ratio Voronoi Diagram with Applications. In *ISVD 2006* (pp. 32–39). IEEE.

Ashby, W. R. (1962), Principles of the Self-Organizing System, in von Foerster H. and Zopf G. eds, *Principles of Self-Organization*, Pergamon, Oxford, 255-278.

Ashby, W.R. (1958), Requisite Variety and Implications for Control of Complex Systems, *Cybernetica*, (1), 83-99.

Ashenden, P. J. (1998). *The Student's Guide To VHDLs* (p. 312). San Francisco, CA: Morgan Kaufmann.

Aslanyan, L., de Mingo, L., Castellanos, J., Ryazanov, V., Chelnokov, F., & Dokukin, A. (2006). On logical correction of neural network algorithms for pattern recognition. *International Journal on Information Theories and Applications*, *14*(3), 203–205.

Atlee, J. M., France, R. B., Georg, G., Moreira, A., Rumpe, B., & Zschaler, B. (2007). Modeling in Software Engineering. In J. Knight, W. Emmerich & G. Rothermel (Eds.), *Software Engineering* (pp.113-114). USA: IEEE Computer Society.

Austin, J. (Ed.). (1998). *RAM-Based Neural Networks* (p. 240). Singapore: World Scientific.

Austin, J. T., & Vancouver, J. B. (1996). Goal constructs in psychology: Structure, process and content. *Psychological Bulletin*, *120*, 338–375. doi:10.1037/0033-2909.120.3.338

Avouris, N., Komis, V., Margaritis, M., & Fiotakis, G. (2004). An Environment for Studying Collaborative Learning Activities. *Journal of Educational Technology & Society*, *7*(2), 34–41.

Ayad, H., & Kamel, M. Finding natural clusters using multi-cluster combiner based on shared nearest neighbors, *Proc. 4th Int. Workshop on Multiple Classifier Systems*, 2003, 166-175.

Baddeley, A. D., & Hitch, G. (1974). Working memory. In G. Bower (Ed.), *The Psychology of Learning and Motivation, 8*, 47–90. Academic Press.

Baeten, J. C. M., & Bergstra, J. A. (1991). Real Time Process Algebra. *Formal Aspects of Computing, 3*, 142–188. doi:10.1007/BF01898401

Bagozzi, R, P., Bergami, M., & Leone, L. (2003). Hierarchical representation of motives in goal setting. *The Journal of Applied Psychology, 88*, 915–943. doi:10.1037/0021-9010.88.5.915

Bagozzi, R. P., Moore, D. J., & Leone, L. (2004). Self-control and the self-regulation of dieting decisions: The role of prefactual attitudes, subjective norms, and resistance to tempatation. *Basic and Applied Social Psychology, 26*, 199–213.

Bandura, A. (1991). Social cognitive theory of self-regulation. *Organizational Behavior and Human Decision Processes, 50*, 248–287. doi:10.1016/0749-5978(91)90022-L

Bandura, A., & Locke, E. A. (2003). Negative self-efficacy and goal effects revisited. *The Journal of Applied Psychology, 88*, 87–99. doi:10.1037/0021-9010.88.1.87

Bar, T., & Whittle, J. (2006). On the Usage of Concrete Syntax in Model Transformation Rules. In I. Virbitskaite & A. Voronkov (Eds.), *Ershov Memorial Conference* (pp. 84-97). Heidelberg: Springer Press.

Barbero, M., Jouault, F., Gray, J., & Bézivin, J. (2007). A Practical Approach to Model Extension. In D.H. Akehurst, & R. F. Paige (Eds.), *Model Driven Architecture-Foundations and Applications* (pp.32-42). Heidelberg: Springer Press.

Bardis, G., Miaoulis, G., & Plemenos, D. "Learning User Preferences at the Declarative and Geometric Description Level," 3IA'2005, Limoges (France), May 11-12, 2005

Baresi, L. Heckel, R (2002). Tutorial Introduction to graph transformation: A software engineering perspective. First International Conference on Graph Transformation.

Bargiela, A., & Pedrycz, W. (2002). *Granular Computing: an Introduction*. Boston: Kluwer Academic Publishers.

Bashar Nuseibeh and Steve Easterbrook. (2000), Requirements engineering: a roadmap, In Proc. of the Conference on The Future of Software Engineering, Ireland, p.35-46.

Basili, V. (2007). The Role of Controlled Experiments in Software Engineering Research," in *Empirical Software Engineering Issues*, LNCS 4336, pp. 33-37.

Basili, V. R. (1980). *Qualitative Software Complexity Models: A Summary in Tutorial on Models and Methods for Software Management and Engineering*. Los Alamitos, CA: IEEE Computer Society Press.

Bauer, F.L (1972), Software Engineering, *Information Processing*, 71.

Baumeister, R. F., Heatherton, T. F., & Tice, D. (1994). *Losing control: How and why people fail as self-regulation*. San Diego: Academic.

Bebis, G., Deaconu, T., & Georiopoulous, M. "Fingerprint Identification using Delaunay Triangulation," ICIIS 99, Maryland, pp. 452-459, 1999

Beck, K., & Andres, C. (2004). *Extreme Programming Explained: Embrace Change* (2nd ed., p. 224). Upper Saddle River, NJ: Addison-Wesley Professional.

Bell, D. A. (1953). *Information Theory*. London: Pitman.

Bender, E. A. (2000). *Mathematical Methods in Artificial Intelligence*. Los Alamitos, CA: IEEE CS Press.

Berardi, D., Calvanese, D., Giacomo, G. D., Hull, R. Mecella, M. (2005). Automatic composition of transition-based semantic web services with messaging. VLDB.

Berg, A. C., & Malik, J. (2001). Geometric Blur for Template Matching. In *CVPR* (pp. 607-614).

Berwick, R., Knight, T., Shrobe, H., Sussman, G., Ullman, S., Winston, P., & Yip, K. (2004). *The Human Intelligence Enterprise*. Retrieved from http://genesis.csail.mit.edu/HIE/white.html.

Beveridge, W. I. (1957). *The Art of Scientific Investigation*. UK: Random House Trade Paperbacks.

Bezdek, J. C. *Pattern Recognition with Fuzzy Objective Function Algorithms*, Plenum Press, N. York, 1981.

Bézivin, J., & Heckel, R. (2006). Guest Editorial to the Special Issue on Language Engineering for Model-Driven Software Development. *Software and System Modeling*, *5*(3), 231–232. doi:10.1007/s10270-006-0028-6

Bhattachariya, P. and Gavrilova, M.L.. "CRYSTAL - A new density-based fast and efficient clustering algorithm", IEEE-CS Press, ISVD 2006, pp. 102-111, Banff, AB, Canada, July 2006

Bickel, S., & Scheffer, T. Multi-view clustering, Proc. of the 4th IEEE Int. Conf. on Data Mining, ICDM'04, 2004, 19-26.

Biedeman, I. (1987). Recognition-by-Components: A Theory of Human Image Understanding. *Psychological Review*, *94*, 115–147. doi:10.1037/0033-295X.94.2.115

Biffl, S. (2006). *Value-Based Software Engineering*. Berlin: Springer. doi:10.1007/3-540-29263-2

Binet, A. (1905). New Methods for the Diagnosis of the Intellectual Level of Subnormals. *L'Année Psychologique*, (12): 191–244.

Birkett, C. M. (1998). Contribution of the TOPEX NASA radar altimeter to the global monitoring of large rivers and wetlands. *Water Resources Research*, *34*, 1223–1239. doi:10.1029/98WR00124

Birkett, C. M. (2000). Synergistic Remote Sensing of Lake Chad: Variability of Basin Inundation. *Remote Sensing of Environment*, *72*, 218–236. doi:10.1016/S0034-4257(99)00105-4

Bishop, C. M. (1995). *Neural Networks for Pattern Recognition* (p. 482). Oxford, UK: Oxford Univ. Press.

Bjorner, D., & Jones, C. B. (1982). Formal Specification and Software Development. Prentice Hall.

Blake, C., Keogh, E., & Merz, C. J. (1998). *Uci repository of machine learning databases*. Available from http://www.ics.uci.edu/mlearn/MLRepository.html

Block, N., Flanagan, O. J., & Gzeldere, G. (1998). *The Nature of Consciousness: Philosophical Debates.* Cambridge, MA: MIT Press.

Boehm, B. (2000). *Software Cost Estimation with CO-COMO II*. New Jersey: Prentice Hall.

Boehm, B. (2004). The ROI of Software Dependability: the iDAVE Model. *IEEE Software*, *21*(3), 54–61. doi:10.1109/MS.2004.1293073

Boehm, B. (2006). Value-Based Software Engineering: Overview and Agenda. In Biffl, S. (Eds.), *Value-Based Software Engineering* (pp. 3–14). Berlin: Springer. doi:10.1007/3-540-29263-2_1

Boehm, B. (2006). Value-Based Software Engineering: Seven Key Elements and Ethical Considerations. In Biffl, S. (Eds.), *Value-Based Software Engineering* (pp. 109–132). Berlin: Springer. doi:10.1007/3-540-29263-2_6

Boehm, B. D. (1981). *Software Engineering Economics*. Englewood Cliffs, NJ: Prentice Hall.

Boehm, B. W. (1987). Improving Software Productivity. *IEEE Computer*, *20*(9), 43. doi:10.1109/MC.1987.1663694

Boehm, B. W., Gray, T. E., & Seewaldt, T. (1984). Prototyping Versus Specifying: A Multiproject Experiment. *IEEE Transactions on Software Engineering*, *10*(3), 290–302. doi:10.1109/TSE.1984.5010238

Boehm, B., & Basili, V. R. (2001). Software Defect Reduction Top 10 List. *IEEE Computer*, *34*(1), 135–137. doi:10.1109/2.962984

Boehm, B., Rombach, H. D., & Zelkowitz, M. V. (2005). *Septmeber). Foundations of Empirical Software Engineering: The Legacy of Victor R. Basili* (1st ed.). Springer-Verlag. doi:10.1007/3-540-27662-9

Bolton, W. (2003). *Mechatronics:Electronic Control Systems in Mechanical and Electrical Engineering* (3rd ed., p. 574). Edinburgh Gate, UK: Pearson Education.

Bonnefoi, P. F., & Plemenos, D. "Constraint satisfaction techniques for declarative scene modelling by hierarchical decomposition," 3IA'2000, Limoges (France), May 3-4, 2000

Borthwick, A., Sterling, J., Agichtein, E., & Grishman, R. (1998). Exploiting diverse knowledge sources via maximum entropy in named entity recognition. *Proceedings of the Sixth Workshop on Very Large Corpora*, New Brunswick, New Jersey.

Bouchon-Meunier, B. (1998). *Aggregation and Fusion of Imperfect Information*. Heidelberg: Physica-Verlag.

Bouillet, E., Feblowitz, M., Liu, Z., Ranganathan, A., & Riabov, A. Ye, F. (2007, June). A semantics-based middleware for utilizing heterogeneous sensor networks. IEEE Distributed Computing in Sensor Systems (DCOSS 2007), June 18-20, 2007. Santa Fe, New Mexico, USA.

Bourne, L. E. (1970). Knowing and using concepts. *Psychological Review*, (77): 546–556. doi:10.1037/h0030000

Bow, S. T. (1992). *Pattern Recognition and Image Pre-processing*. NY: Marcel Dekker.

Brase, J., & Painter, M. (2004). Inferring Metadata for a Semantic Web Peer-to-Peer Environment. *Journal of Educational Technology & Society*, 7(2), 61–67.

Bravo, C. M., Redondo, A., Ortega, M., & Verdejo, M. F. (2006). Collaborative Environments for the Learning of Design: A model and A Case Study in Domotics. *Computers & Education*, 46, 152–173. doi:10.1016/j.compedu.2004.07.009

Breiman, L., Friedman, J. H., Olshen, R. A., & Stone, C. J. (1984). *Classification and Regression Trees*. New York, NY: Chapman and Hall.

Briand, L. C., Morasca, S., & Basili, V. R. (1996). Property based Software Engineering Measurement. *IEEE Transactions on Software Engineering*, 22(1), 68–86. doi:10.1109/32.481535

Brooks, F. *The Mythical Man-Month*, Addison-Wesley, Reading, Mass., 1974, rev. 1995.

Brooks, R. (1978, May). Using a behavioral theory of program comprehension in software engineering. In M. V. Wilkes, L. Belady, Y. H. Su, H. Hayman, & P. Enslow (Eds.), *Proceedings of the 3rd International Conference on Software Engineering* (pp. 196–201). IEEE Computer Society Press.

Brooks, R. A. (1970), New Approaches to Robotics, *American Elsevier*, NY, (5), 3-23.

Brooks, F. P. (1987). No Silver Bullet: Essence and Accidents of Software Engineering. *IEEE Computer*, 20(4), 10–19. doi:10.1109/MC.1987.1663532

Brown, A., Iyengar, S., & Johnston, S. (2006). A Rational Approach to Model-Based Development. *IBM Systems Journal*, 45(3), 463–480. doi:10.1147/sj.453.0463

Bruel, J. M., Georg, G., Hußmann, H., Ober, I., Pohl, C., Whittle, J., & Zschaler, S. (2004). Models for Non-functional Aspects of Component-Based Software. In N. J. Nunes, B. Selic, A. R. Silva, & J. A.T. Álvarez (Eds.), *UML Modeling Languages and Applications* (pp. 62-66). Heidelberg: Springer Press.

Brusilovsky, P., Eklund, J., & Schwarz, E. "Web-based education for all: a tool for development of adaptive courseware," Computer Networks and ISDN Systems, Volume 30, Issues 1-7, pp. 291-300, 1998

Bullock, J. (2000). Calculating the Value of Testing. *Software Testing and Quality Engineering*, May/June issue, 56-62.

Burmester, S., Giese, H., & Oberschelp, O. (2004). Hybrid UML Components for the Design of Complex Self-Optimizing Mechatronic Systems. In H. Araújo, A. Vieira, J. Braz, B. Encarnação, & M. Carvalho (Eds.), *International Conference on Informatics in Control, Automation and Robotics* (pp.222-229). Portugal: INSTICC Press.

C. Oetke (2003), Indian Logic and Indian Syllogism, Indo-Iranian Journal, vol. 46, no. 1, pp. 53-69(17), Kluwer Academic Publishers.

Cai, C., & Shi, Z. (2003). A modular neural network architecture with approximation capability and its applications. *Second IEEE International Conference on Cognitive Informatics (ICCI'03)*, August 18-20, (pp. 60- 64), London, UK.

Callan, J., & Mitamura, (2002). T. Knowledge-based extraction of named entities. *Proceedings of the Eleventh International Conference on Information and Knowledge Management* (pp. 532-537), McLean, VA.

Cambridge Engineering Design Centre. (2007), Research (Report). Cambridge, UK: Cambridge Engineering Design Centre, 2007. (Retrieved June 2007 from http://www-edc.eng.cam.ac.uk/research/)

Campos, I. O., Mercier, F., Maheu, C., Cochonneau, G., Kosuth, P., Blitzkow, D., & Cazenave, A. (2001). Temporal variations of river basin waters from Topex / Poseidon satellite altimetry: Application to the Amazon basin. *Earth and Planetary Sciences*, 333, 633–643.

Cao, L. B., & Zhang, C. Q. (2006). Domain-driven actionable knowledge discovery in the real world. *Lecture Notes in Computer Science, 3918*, 821–830. doi:10.1007/11731139_96

Capelli, R., Maio, D., & Maltoni, D. "Synthetic Fingerprint-Database Generation," ICPR 2002, Canada, vol 3, pp 369-376, 2002

Castle Island. (2007). The worldwide guide to rapid prototyping. *Tutorials and Directories*. Retrieved June 2007 from http://home.att.net/~castleisland/home.html

CEAB. (2006). Canadian Engineering Accreditation Board: Accreditation criteria and procedures, (*Report*),(p. 40). Retrieved June 2007 from http://www.engineerscanda.ca/e/prog_publications_3.cfm

Cetinkunt, S. (2007). *Mechatronics*. New York, NY: Wiley.

Chalmers, D. (1997). The Conscious Mind. In *Search of a Fundamental Theory* (p. 432). Oxford, UK: Oxford Univ. Press.

Chandrasekaran, S., et al. (2003, January). TelegraphCQ: Continuous dataflow processing for an uncertain world. Proceedings on the First Biennial Conference on Innovative Data Systems Research (CIDR 2003).

Chang, C. K., Zhang, J., & Chang, K. H. (2006). Survey of Computer Supported Business Collaboration in Support of Business Processes. [IJBPIM]. *International Journal of Business Process Integration and Management, 1*(2), 76–100. doi:10.1504/IJBPIM.2006.010023

Chao, L. P., & Ishii, K. (2004, August). Design process error-proofing: Challenges and methods in quantifying design elements. In *Proc. Tenth ISSAT Intern. Conf. on Reliability and Quality in Design* (Las Vegas, NV; August 2004) 5 pp. Retrieved June 2007 from http://www-mml.standford.edu/publications/2004/ISSATquality-C04-24.pdf

Chavarría, B. L., & Li, X. (2006). Structural error verification in active rule based systems using Petri nets. *Proceedings of the Fifth Mexican International Conference on Artificial Intelligence (MICAI'06)* (pp. 12 - 21), Apizaco, Mexico, Nov.

Chen, H., Tsai, S., & Tsai, J. (2000, August). Mining Tables from Large Scale HTML Texts. *18th International Conference on Computational Linguistics,* Germany.

Chen, L., Shadbolt, N., Goble, C., Tao, F., Cox, S., & Puleston, C. (2003). Towards a Knowledge-based Approach to Semantic Service Composition. The Second International Semantic Web Conference (ISWC2003).

Chen, X.H., Zhu, S.J., & Ji Y.D. (2001). Rule uncertainty measurement based on entropy and variable rough set. *Journal of Tsinghua University (Science & Technology Edition), 47*(3), pp.109-112.

Chenais, P., & Weinberger, K. (1992, May). New Approach in the Development of Elevator Group Control Algorithms. Amsterdam. *ELEVCON, 4*, 48–57.

Chen, P. P. (1976). The Entity-Relationship Model - Toward a Unified View of Data. *ACM Transactions on Database Systems, 1*(1), 9–36. doi:10.1145/320434.320440

Cherbakov, L., Bravery, A. J. F. Pandya, A. (2007). SOA meets situational applications. IBM.

Cherniavsky, J. C., & Smith, C. H. (1991). On Weyuker's Axioms for Software Complexity Measures. *IEEE Transactions on Software Engineering, 17*, 636–638. doi:10.1109/32.87287

Chitchyan, R., Rashid, A., Rayson, P., & Waters, R. (2007). Semantics-based composition for aspect-oriented requirements engineering. In B. M. Barry & O. Moor (Eds.), *International Conference on Aspect-Oriented Software Development* (pp.36-48). USA: ACM Press.

Chomsky, N. (1957). *Syntactic Structures*. The Hague: Mouton.

Chomsky, N. (1965). *Aspects of the Theory of Syntax*. Cambridge, MA: MIT Press.

Churchill, E. F., & Halverson, C. A. (2005). Social Networks and Social Networking. *IEEE Intelligent Systems, 20*(5), 14–19.

Ciletti, M. D. (1999). *Modelling, Synthesis and Rapid Prototyping with Verilog HDL* (p. 724). Upper Saddle River, NJ: Prentice Hall/Pearson Education.

Ciletti, M. D. (2003). *Advanced Digital Design with the Verilog HDLs* (p. 382). Upper Saddle River, NJ: Prentice Hall/Pearson Education.

Ciletti, M. D. (2004). *Starter's Guide to Verilog 2001* (p. 234). Upper Saddle River, NJ: Prentice Hall/Pearson Education.

Clark, J. (2003). Reformulating Software Engineering as A Search Problem. *IEE Proceedings. Software*, *150*(3), 161–175. doi:10.1049/ip-sen:20030559

Cleland-Huang, R. S., & Zou, X. (2006) "The Detection and Classification of Non-Functional Requirements with Application to Early Aspects", 14th IEEE International Requirements Engineering Conference.

Cloete, I., & Zurada, J. (2000). *Knowledge-Based Neuro-computing* (Eds.). MIT Press, Cambridge, MA.

Coaen, S., Ward, L. M., & Enns, J. T. (1994). *Sensation and Perception* (4th ed.). NY: Harcourt Brace College Pub.

Coffman, K. (2000). *Real-World FPGA Design with Verilog* (p. 289). Upper Saddle River, NJ: Prentice Hall.

Cohen, W., & Sarawagi, S. (2004). Exploiting dictionaries in named entity extraction: combining semi-Markov extraction processes and data integration methods. *Tenth ACM International Conference on Knowledge Discovery and Data Mining*, Seattle, WA.

Cohen-Or, D., & Levanoni, Y. (1996). *"Temporal continuity of levels of detail in Delaunay triangulated terrain,"* Visualization '96 (pp. 37–42). IEEE Press.

Cole, B. (1995, March 20). Architectures overlap applications. *Electronic Engineering Times*, *40*, 64–65.

Collins, A. M., & Quillian, M. R. (1969). Retrieval time from semantic memory. *Journal of Verbal Learning and Behavior*, *8*, 204–247. doi:10.1016/S0022-5371(69)80069-1

Coplien, J. O. (1997, January). Idioms and patterns as architectural literature. *IEEE Software Special Issue on Objects, Patterns, and Architectures*, *14*(1), 36–42.

Corsetti, E., Montanari, A., & Ratto, E. (1991). Dealing with Different Time Granularities in Formal Specifications of Real-Time Systems. [Kluwer.]. *The Journal of Real-Time Systems*, *3*(2), 191–215. doi:10.1007/BF00365335

Costa da Silva, J., & Klusch, M. (2006). Inference in distributed data clustering. *Engineering Applications of Artificial Intelligence*, *19*, 363–369. doi:10.1016/j.engappai.2006.01.013

Cotterill, R. (Ed.). (1988). *Computer Simulations in Brain Science* (p. 566). Cambridge, UK: Cambridge Univ. Press. doi:10.1017/CBO9780511983467

Cross, N. (2000). *Design Methods: Strategies for Product Design* (3rd ed., p. 224). New York, NY: Wiley.

Cruz, S. V. G. (2004). *Neural-Symbolic Hybrid System to refine the knowledge of an Artificial Vision System.* Master Thesis, Cenidet, Cuernavaca, Morelos, Mexico.

Cruz, S. V. G., Reyes, S. G., Vergara, V. O. O., & Pinto, E. R. (2006). A Combined Representation to Refine the Knowledge Using a Neuro-Symbolic Hybrid System applied in a Problem of Apple Classification. *Proc. 16th IEEE Int. Conf. on Electronics, Communications and Computers (CONIELECOMP-06)* (pp. 30-30). Puebla, México, Feb.

Cruz, S. V. G., Reyes, S. G., Vergara, V. O. O., Perez, O. J., & Montes, R. A. (2005). Compilation of symbolic knowledge and integration with numeric knowledge using hybrid systems. Springer Lecture Notes In Computer Science. *Proc. 4th Mexican International Conference on Artificial Intelligence* (MICAI'05) (pp. 11 – 20), Monterrey, Nuevo León, México, Nov.

Cruz-Lemus, J. A., Genero, M., Manso, M. E., & Piattini, M. (2005, October). Evaluating the effect of composite states on the understandability of UML statechart diagrams. In L. Briand (Ed.), *Proceedings of the 8th International Conference on Model Driven Engineering Languages and Systems*. Springer-Verlag.

Csapo, A., Baranyi, P., & Tikk, D. (2007). Object Categorization Using VFA-generated Nodemaps and Hierarchical Temporal Memories. *Proc. Of IEEE International Conference on Computational Cybernetics* (pp. 257-262).

Csurka, G., Dance, C. R., Fan, L., Willamowski, J., & Bray, C. (2004). Visual Categorization With Bags of Keypoints. *In workshop on statistical learning in computer vision, EECV* (pp. 1-22).

Cui, J., Liu, J., & Wu, Y. Gu, N. (2004). An ontology modeling method in semantic composition of web services. CEC-EAST '04: Proceedings of the E-Commerce Technology for Dynamic E-Business, IEEE International Conference (270–273). Washington, DC.

Cunningham.H, Maynard.D, Bontcheva.K, Tablan.V, Ursu.C, Dimitrov.M, Dowman.M, Aswani.N and Roberts.I, (2006) Developing Language Processing Components with GATE Version 3 (a User Guide), from University of Sheffield.

Cuseo, J. B. (2002). *Igniting Student Involvement, Peer Interaction and Teamwork*. Stillwater, Oklahoma, USA: New Forums Press Inc.

Cusumano, M. A., & Selby, R. W. (1997, June). How Microsoft builds software. *Communications of the ACM, 40*(6), 53–61. doi:10.1145/255656.255698

D. B. Skillicorn, S. M. McConnell, Distributed prediction from vertically partitioned data, *Journal of Parallel and Distributed computing*, 2007.

Dahm, I. and Ziegler, J. "Adaptive Methods to Improve Self-localization in Robot Soccer," LNCS 2752, pps. 393-408, 2003

Damásio, C. V., Analyti, A., Antoniou, G., & Wagner, G. (2006). Supporting Open and Closed World Reasoning on the Web. In J.J. Alferes, J. Bailey, W. May, & U. Schwertel (Eds.), *Principles and Practice of Semantic Web Reasoning* (pp 149-163). Heidelberg: Springer Press.

Daradoumisa, T., Martı'nez-Mone's, A. and Xhafa, F. (2006). A Layered Framework for Evaluating On-Line Collaborative Learning Interactions. *International Journal of Human-Computer Studies, 64*, 622–635. doi:10.1016/j.ijhcs.2006.02.001

David, R., & Alla, H. (2005). *Discrete, continuous and Hybrid Petri nets*. Berlin, Heidelberg: Springer- Verlang.

Davis, A. M. (1993). *Software requirements: Objects, Functions, and States*. New Jersey: Prentice Hall.

De Bon, S., Wolfe, D., Chagnon, J.-Y., & Paterson, W. G. (2002). Engineering Accreditation in Canada and Its Current Challenges. In *Proc. 2002 ASEE/SEFI/TUB Colloquium*, (p. 9). Retrieved May 2007 from http://www.asee.org/conferences/international/papers/upload/Engineering-Accreditation-in-Canada-and-Its-Current-Challenges.pdf

Debenham, J. K. (1989). *Knowledge Systems Design*. NY: Prentice Hall.

Decker, B., Ras, E., Rech, J., Jaubert, P., & Rieth, M. (2007), Wiki-Based Stakeholder Participation in Requirements Engineering, IEEE Software, Volume 24, Issue 2 pp. 28-35, ISSN:0740-7459, IEEE Computer Society Press.

DeFries, R. S., & Chan, J. C.-W. (2000). Multiple criteria for evaluating machine learning algorithms for land cover classification from satellite data. *Remote Sensing of Environment, 74*(3), 503–515. doi:10.1016/S0034-4257(00)00142-5

DeGrace, P., & Stahl, L. H. (1998). *Wicket Problems, Righteous Solutions: A Catalog of Modern Engineering Paradigms* (p.272). Upper Saddle River, NJ: Prentice Hall.

Dennett, D. C. (1991). *Consciousness Explained* (p. 528). London, UK: Allan Lane/Penguin.

Dierks, H. (2000). *A Process Algebra for Real-Time Programs. LNCS #1783* (pp. 66–76). Berlin: Springer.

Dijkstra, E. W. (1976). *A Discipline of Programming*. Englewood Cliffs, NJ: Prentice Hall.

Dimitracopoulou, A., & Petrou, A. (2005). Advanced Collaborative Distance Learning Systems for Young Students: Design Issues and Current Trends on New Cognitive and Metacognitive Tools. *Education International Journal, 4*(11), 214–224.

Doerr, B. S., Venturella, T., Jha, R., Gill, C. D., & Schmidt, D. C. "Adaptive Scheduling for Real-time, Embedded Information," in Proceedings of the 18th IEEE/AIAA Digital Avionics Systems Conference, 10 pages, 1999

Douglass, B. P. (1999). *Doing Hard Time: Developing Real-Time Systems with UML, Objects, Frameworks, and Patterns* (p. 749). Reading, MA: Addison-Wesley.

Duan, Y. (2008). Challenges of Model Transformation and a Solution Framework. In C. Rolland, O. Pastor, & J. L. Cavarero (Eds.), *Research Challenges in Information Science* (pp 247-252). USA: IEEE Computer Society.

Duan, Y. (2008). A systemic approach towards recreating a unified semantics of numbers. In J.S. Pan, P. Shi, & C.S. Shieh (Eds.), Innovative Computing, Information and Control (pp 179). USA: IEEE Computer Society.

Duan, Y. (2008). A Dualism Based Semantics Formalization Mechanism for Model Driven Engineering. In Y. Wang (Eds.), *Conference on Cognitive Informatics* (pp. 185-194). USA: IEEE Computer Society.

Duan, Y., Kang, K. C., & Gu, Y. (2008). A Solution Framework on Fundamentals in Model Transformation. In R. Y. Lee (Ed.), *Computer and Information Science* (pp. 355-360). USA: IEEE Computer Society.

Duchaineauy, M. (1997). ROAMing Terrain: Real-Time Optimally Adapting Meshes. *IEEE Visualization, 97*, 81–88.

Dueck, R. K. (2001). *Digital Design with CPLD Applications and VHDL.* Stamford, CT: Thomson Learning, (p. 845). {ISBN 0-7668-1160-3, +CDROM}

Dumais, S. T., Platt, J., Heckerman, D., et al. (1998). Inductive learning algorithms and representations for text categorization. *Proc. 7th ACM International Conference on Information and Knowledge Management* (CIKM'98), (148-155), Bethesda, MD.

Dunlap, K. (1912). The case against introspection. *Psychological Review, 19*, 404–413. doi:10.1037/h0071571

Düntsch, I., & Gediga, G. (1998). Uncertainty measures of rough set prediction. *Artificial Intelligence, 106*, 109–137. doi:10.1016/S0004-3702(98)00091-5

Durbin, R., Eddy, S., Krogh, A., & Mitchison, G. (1998). *Biological Sequence Analysis: Probabilistic Models of Proteins and Nucleic Acids.* Cambridge UK: Cambridge University Press.

Dyba, T., Kitchenham, B. A., & Jorgensen, M. (2005). Evidence-Based Software Engineering for Practitioners. *IEEE Software, 22*(1), 58–65. doi:10.1109/MS.2005.6

Eder, W. E., & Hosnedl, S. (2008). *Design Engineering: A Manual for Enhanced Creativity* (p. 588). Boca Rayton, FL: CRC.

Edwards, W. K., Newman, M. W., Sedivy, J. Z., Smith, T. F., Balfanz, D., Smetters, D. K., et al. (2002). Using Speakeasy for ad hoc Peer-to-Peer Collaboration. in *Proceedings of the 2002 ACM Conference on Computer Supported Cooperative Work (CSCW)*, New Orleans, LO, USA, 256 -265.

Eichelberger, H., & von Gudenberg, J. W. (2002, May). On the visualization of Java programs. In S. Diehl (Ed.), *Proceedings of the 1st international seminar on Software Visualization,* (pp. 295–306). Springer-Verlag.

Eigen, M., & Schuster, P. (1979). *The Hypercycle: A Principle of Natural Self-Organization.* Berlin: Springer.

Eikemeier, C., & Lechner, U. (2004). Peer-to-Peer and Group Collaboration - Do They Always Match? in *Proceedings of 13th IEEE International Workshops on Enabling Technologies: Infrastructure for Collaborative Enterprises (WET ICE)*, Jun, 101-106.

Einstein, A. (1995). *Relativity: The Special and the General Theory.* (Reprint). Three Rivers Press.

Ellis, C., & Flaherty, M. (1992). *Investigating Subjectivity.* Newbury Park, CA: Sage Publications.

Ellis, D. O., & Fred, J. L. (1962). *Systems Philosophy.* Prentice-Hall.

Endres, A., & Rombach, D. (2003, March). *A Handbook of Software and Systems Engineering (1st Ediiton).* Addison-Wesley. edition.

Ernst, R. (1998, April-June). Codesign of embedded systems: Status and trends. *IEEE Design & Test of Computers, 15*(2), 45–54. doi:10.1109/54.679207

Fabrizio, S. (2002). Machine learning in automated text categorization. *ACM Computing Surveys, 34*(1), 1–47. doi:10.1145/505282.505283

Feather, M. (2008). A Broad, Quantitative Model for Making Early Requirements Decisions. *IEEE Software, 25*(2), 49–56. doi:10.1109/MS.2008.29

Feldman, J. (2000). Minimization of Boolean complexity in human concept learning. *Nature, 407*(5), 630–633. doi:10.1038/35036586

Feldman, J. (2003). The Simplicity Principle in Human Concept Learning. *Current Directions in Psychological Science, 12*(6), 227–232. doi:10.1046/j.0963-7214.2003.01267.x

Feldman, J. (2003). A catalog of Boolean concepts. *Journal of Mathematical Psychology*, (47): 75–89. doi:10.1016/S0022-2496(02)00025-1

Feldman, J. (2006). An Algebra of human concept learning. *Journal of Mathematical Psychology*, (50): 339–368. doi:10.1016/j.jmp.2006.03.002

Fellbaum, C. (1998). *WordNet: An Electronic Lexical Database*. Bradfords Books, ISBN 0-262-06197-X.

Feng, Y. (1983). *A History of Chinese Philosophy*. Beijing: The people's press.

Fenton, N.E. (1998). IEEE Computer Society Standard for Software Quality Metrics Methodology. Revision IEEE Standard 1061-1998.

Fenton, N. E. (1991). *Software Metrics: A Rigorous Approach*. London, UK: Chapman & Hill.

Fenton, N. E. (1994). Software Measurement: A Necessary Scientific Basis. *IEEE Transactions on Software Engineering, SE-20*(3), 199–206. doi:10.1109/32.268921

Fenton, N. E., & Pfleeger, S. L. (1997). *Software Metrics*. Boston: PWS Publishing Company.

Fenton, N. E., & Pfleeger, S. L. (1998). *Software Metrics: A Rigorous and Practical Approach* (2nd ed.). Brooks/Cole Pub Co.

Feyerabend, P. K., & Maxwell, G. (1966). *Mind, Matter and Method: Essays in Philosophy and Science in Honor of Herbert Feigl*. Minneapolis: University of Minnesota Press.

Fischer, F., Bruhn, J., Gräsel, C., & Mandl, H. (2002). Fostering Collaborative Knowledge Construction with Visualization Tools. *Learning and Instruction, 12*, 213–232. doi:10.1016/S0959-4752(01)00005-6

Floyd, C. (1992, March). *Human Questions in Computer Science* (pp. 15–27). Springer Verlag.

Ford, R. M., & Coulston, C. S. (2000). *Design for Electrical and Computer Engineers: Theory, Concepts, and Practice*. New York, NY: McGraw Hill (Custom Publishing), (p. 280).

Ford, J. (1986). Chaos: Solving the Unsolvable, Predicting the Unpredictable. In *Chaotic Dynamics and Fractals*. Academic Press.

France, R. B., Bieman, J. M., & Cheng, B. H. C. (2006). Repository for Model Driven Development (ReMoDD). In T. Kühne (Ed.), *Models in Software Engineering, Workshops and Symposia at MoDELS 2006* (pp. 311-317). Heidelberg: Springer Press.

Franc, M., & Skala, V. (2002). Fast Algorithm for Triangular Mesh Simplification Based on Vertex decimation. In *CCGM 2002 Proceedings*. Lecture Notes in Computer Science Springer. doi:10.1007/3-540-46080-2_5

Franklin, S. (1995). *Artificial Minds* (p. 464). Cambridge, MA: MIT Press.

Fried, G. H., & Hademenos, G. J. (1999). *Schaum's Outline of Theory and Problems of Biology* (2nd ed.). NY: McGraw-Hill.

Fried, Y., & Slowik, L. H. (2004). Enriching goal-setting theory with time: An integrated approach. *Academy of Management Review, 29*, 404–422.

Fu, L. L., & Cazenave, A. (2001). *Altimetry and Earth Science. A Handbook of Techniques and Applications. (69)*. London, UK: International Geophysics Series Academic Press.

G. Acampora, V. Loia, A proposal of ubiquitous fuzzy computing for Ambient Intelligence, *Information Sciences*, 178, 3, 2008, 631-646.

G. Campobello, M. Mantineo, G. Patanè, M. Russo, LBGS: a smart approach for very large data sets vector quantization, *Signal Processing: Image Communication*, 20, 1, 2005, 91-114.

Gajski, D. D., Vahid, F., Narayan, S., & Gong, J. (1994). *Specification and Design of Embedded Systems* (p. 450). Englewood Cliffs, NJ: PTR Prentice Hall.

Gamma, E., Helm, R., Johnson, R., & Vlissides, J. (1994). *Design Patterns – Elements of Reusable Object-Oriented Software* (1st ed.). Addison-Wesley.

Ganek, A. G., & Corbi, T. A. (2003). The dawning of the autonomic computing era. *IBM Systems J., 42*(1), 34-42. Retrieved May 2006 from http://www.research.ibm.com/journal/sj/421/ganek.pdf

Ganter, B., & Wille, R. (1999). *Formal Concept Analysis*. Berlin: Springer.

Gardner, H. (1983). *Frames of Mind: The Theory of Multiple Intelligences*. New York, NY: Basic Books.

Garey, M. R., & Johnson, D. S. (1979). *Computers and Intractability: A Guide to the Theory of NP-completeness*. New York: Freeman.

Garmus, D., & Herron, D. (1995). *Measuring the Software Process: A Practical Guide to Functional Measurement*. Englewood Cliffs, NJ: Prentice Hall.

Gavrilova, M. L. (2008to appear). *Computational Intelligence: A Geometry-Based Approach, Book, in series Studies in Computational Intelligence*. Springer-Verlag.

Gersting, J. L. (1982). *Mathematical Structures for Computer Science*. San Francisco: W. H. Freeman & Co.

Gervasi, V., & Zowghi, D. (2005). Reasoning about inconsistencies in natural Language requirements. *ACM Transactions on Software Engineering and Methodology, 14*(3), 277–330. doi:10.1145/1072997.1072999

Ghezzi, C., Jazayeri, M., & Mandrioli, D. (1991). *Fundamentals of Software Engineering* (p. 573). Englewood Cliffs, NJ: Prentice Hall.

Ghoniem, M., Fekete, J.-D., & Castagliola, P. (2004, October). A comparison of the readability of graphs using node-link and matrix-based representations. In M. Ward & T. Munzner (Eds.), *Proceedings of the 10th symposium on Information Visualisation*, (pp. 17–24). IEEE Computer Society Press.

Giarrantans, J., & Riley, G. (1989). *Expert Systems: Principles and Programming*. Boston: PWS-KENT Pub. Co.

Gibson, J. R. *The Perception of the Visual World*. Greenwood Publishing Group.

Gilbert, A. C., Kotidis, Y., Muthukrishnan, S., & Strauss, M. J. (2005). Domain-driven data synopses for dynamic quantiles. *IEEE Transactions on Knowledge and Data Engineering, 17*(7), 927–938. doi:10.1109/TKDE.2005.108

Gliozzo, A., Magnini, B., & Strapparava, C. (2004). Unsupervised Domain Relevance Estimation for Word Sense Disambiguation. In D.K. Lin, & D.K. Wu (Eds.), *Proceedings of the 2004 Conference on Empirical Methods in Natural Language Processing* (pp. 25-26), Press of Association for Computational Linguistics, Barcelona, Spain.

Gliozzo, A., Strapparava, C., & Dagan, I. (2004). Unsupervised and Supervised Exploitation of Semantic Domains in Lexical Disambiguation. *Computer Speech & Language, 18*(3), 275–299. doi:10.1016/j.csl.2004.05.006

Golbeck, J., Fragoso, G., Hartel, F., Hendler, J., Parsia, B., & Oberthaler, J. (2003). The National Cancer Institute's thesaurus and ontology. *Journal of Web Semantics, 1*(1). doi:10.1016/j.websem.2003.07.007

Gold, C., & Dakowicz, M. (2006). *ISVD 2006, IEEE-CS* (pp. 76–84). Banff, Canada: Kinetic Voronoi/Delaunay Drawing Tools.

Goldman, S. (1953). *Information Theory*. Englewood Cliffs, NJ, USA: Prentice-Hall.

Goutte, C., Déjean, H., Gaussier, E., Cancedda, N., & Renders, J. (2002). Combining labelled and unlabelled data: a case study on Fisher kernels and transductive inference for biological entity recognition. *Sixth Conference on Natural Language Learning*, Taipei, Taiwan.

Grauman, K., & Darrell, T. (2005). The Pyramid Match Kernel: Discriminative Classification with Sets of Image Features. *In ICCV* (pp. 1458-1465).

Gray, P. (1994). *Psychology* (2nd ed.). New York: Worth Publishers, Inc.

Greenfield, J., & Short, K. (2004). *Software Factories: Assembling Applications with Patterns, Models, Frameworks, and Tools*. Indianapolis, IN: Wiley Publishing.

Gruber, T. R. (1993)., Towards principles for the design of ontologies used for knowledge-sharing, in Guarino & Poli (Eds), Formal Ontology in Conceptual Analysis and Knowledge Representation, Kluwer Publishers, August 1993.

Grudin, J., & Poltrock, S. (1997). Computer-supported cooperative work and groupware. *Advances in Computers, 45*, 269–320. doi:10.1016/S0065-2458(08)60710-X

Grunbacher, P., Koszegi, S., & Biffl, S. (2006). Stakeholder Value Proposition Elicitation and Reconciliation. In Biffl, S. (Eds.), *Value-Based Software Engineering* (pp. 133–154). Berlin: Springer. doi:10.1007/3-540-29263-2_7

Guarino, N. (2004). Helping People (and Machines) Understanding Each Other. In R. Meersman & Z. Tari (Eds.), *On the Move to Meaningful Internet Systems* (pp. 599). Heidelberg: Springer Press.

Guarino, N., & Welty, C. (2000). Identity, Unity, and Individuation: Towards a Formal Toolkit for Ontological Analysis. In W. Horn (Ed.), *European Conference on Artificial Intelligence* (pp. 219-223). Amsterdam: IOS Press.

Guéhéneuc, Y.-G., Monnier, S., & Antoniol, G. (2005, September). Evaluating the use of design patterns during program comprehension – experimental setting. In G. Antoniol & Guéhéneuc, Y-G. (Eds.), *Proceedings of the 1st ICSM workshop in Design Pattern Theory and Practice*. IEEE Computer Society Press. In the pre-proceedings.

Gursaran, Roy, G. (2001). On the Applicability of Weyuker Property Nine to Object Oriented Structural Inheritance Complexity Metrics. *IEEE Transactions on Software Engineering, 27,* 4, (2001).pp.361-364.

Gutwin, C., Roseman, M., & Greenberg, S. (1996). A Usability Study of Awareness Widgets in A Shared Workspace Groupware System. in *Proceedings of the 1996 ACM conference on Computer Supported Cooperative Work (CSCW)*, Boston, MA, USA, 258-267.

Haikonen, P. O. A. (2003). *The Cognitive Approach to Conscious Machines*. New York, NY: Academic, (p. 294). (See also http://personal.inet.fi/cool/pentti.haikonen/)

Haken, H. (1977). *Synergetics*. NY: Springer-Verlag.

Halstead, M. H. (1997). *Elements of Software Science*. New York: Elsevier North-Holland.

Hamdi, M., Mulvaney, D.J., & Sillitoe, I.P. (1995). An Intelligent Real-time Lift Scheduling System. *Workshop of the UK Planning and Scheduling Special Interest Group, 14.*

Hampton, J. A. (1997). *Psychological Representation of Concepts of Memory* (pp. 81-110). Hove, England: Psychology Press.

Harman, M., & Jones, B. (2001). Search-Based Software Engineering. *Information and Software Technology, 43*(14), 833–839. doi:10.1016/S0950-5849(01)00189-6

Hartmanis, J. (1994). On Computational Complexity and the Nature of Computer Science, 1994 Turing Award Lecture. *Communications of the ACM, 37*(10), 37–43. doi:10.1145/194313.214781

Hartmanis, J., & Stearns, R. E. (1965). On the Computational Complexity of Algorithms. *Trans. AMS, 117,* 258–306. doi:10.1090/S0002-9947-1965-0170805-7

Haruhiko Kaiya and Motoshi Saeki. "Using Domain Ontology as Domain Knowledge for Requirements Elicitation", 14th IEEE International Requirements Engineering Conference (RE'06).

Hayes, I. (1985). Applying Formal Specifications to Software Development in Industry. *IEEE Transactions on Software Engineering, 11*(2), 169–178. doi:10.1109/TSE.1985.232191

Haykin, S. (1998). *Neural Networks: A Comprehensive Foundation* (2nd ed.). Upper Saddle River, NJ: Prentice Hall.

Haykin, S. (2005, February). Cognitive radio: Brain-empowered wireless communications. *IEEE Journal on Selected Areas in Communications, 23*(2), 201–220. doi:10.1109/JSAC.2004.839380

Haykin, S. (2006, January). Cognitive radar. *IEEE Signal Processing Magazine*, 30–40. doi:10.1109/MSP.2006.1593335

Haykin, S., & Chen, Z. (2005). The cocktail party problem. *Neural Computation, 17,* 1875–1902. doi:10.1162/0899766054322964

Haykin, S., & Kosko, B. (2001). *Intelligent Signal Processing* (p. 573). New York, NY: Wiley-IEEE. doi:10.1109/9780470544976

Haykin, S., Principe, J. C., Sejnowski, T. J., & McWhirter, J. (2006). *New Directions in Statistical Signal Processing* (p. 544). Cambridge, MA: MIT Press.

Heatherton, T. F., & Baumeister, R. F. (1996). Self-regulation failure: Past, Present, and Future. *Psychological Inquiry, 7,* 90–98. doi:10.1207/s15327965pli0701_20

Hegel, G. W. F. (1807). *The Phenomenology of Mind.* Retrieved September 29, 2008, from http://www.class. uidaho.edu/mickelsen/ToC/Hegel%20Phen%20ToC.htm

Heidegger, M. (1969). *Identity and Difference.* New York: Harper & Row.

Henderson-Sellers, B., & Edwards, J. M. (1990, September). The object-oriented systems life cycle. *Communications of the ACM, 33*(9), 142–159. doi:10.1145/83880.84529

Hewitt, C. (1977). Viewing Control Structures as Patterns of Passing Messages. *Artificial Intelligence, 8*(3), 323–364. doi:10.1016/0004-3702(77)90033-9

He, X., Chu, W., & Yang, H. (2003). A new Approach to Verify Rule-Based System Using Petri Nets. *Information and Software Technology, 45*(10), 663–670. doi:10.1016/ S0950-5849(03)00058-2

Heylighen, F. (1989), Self-Organization, Emergence and the Architecture of Complexity, in *Proc. 1st European Conf. on System Science* (AFCET), Paris, 23-32.

Hill, C. O., & Rosado, H. G. (2000). *Husserl or Frege? Meaning, Objectivity, and Mathematics.* Chicago: Open Court Publishing Company.

Hintikka, J., & Kulas, J. (1983). *The Game of Language: Studies in Game-Theoretical Semantics and Its Applications.* Dordrecht: D. Reidel Publishing Company.

Hoare, C. A. R. (1985). *Communicating Sequential Processes.* Prentice-Hall Inc.

Hoare, C. A. R. (1969). An Axiomatic Basis for Computer Programming. *Communications of the ACM, 12*(10), 576–580. doi:10.1145/363235.363259

Hoare, C. A. R. (1978). Communicating Sequential Processes. *Communications of the ACM, 21*(8), 666–677. doi:10.1145/359576.359585

Hoare, C. A. R. (1986). *The Mathematics of Programming.* Oxford, UK: Clarendon Press.

Hoare, C. A. R., Hayes, I. J., He, J., Morgan, C. C., Roscoe, A. W., & Sanders, J. W. (1987, Aug.). Laws of programming. *Communications of the ACM, 30*(8), 672–686. doi:10.1145/27651.27653

Hoffman, D. M., & Weiss, D. M. (2001) (Eds.). *Collected Papers by David L. Parnas.* Upper Saddle River, NJ: Addison-Wesley, (p. 664).

Hollnager, E., & Woods, D. D. (2005). *Joint Cognitive Systems: Foundation of Cognitive Systems Engineering* (p. 240). Boca Rayton, FL: CRC. doi:10.1201/9781420038194

Horn, B. K. P. (1986). *Robot Vision.* Cambridge, MA: MIT Press.

Horridge, M., Knublauch, H., Rector, A., Stevens, R., & Wroe, C. (2004), A Practical Guide To Building OWL Ontologies Using The Protégé-OWL Plug-in and CO-ODE Tools Edition 1.0, from University of Manchester.

Hron, A., & Friedrich, H. F. (2003). A Review of Web-Based Collaborative Learning: Factors Beyond Technology. *Journal of Computer Assisted Learning, 19,* 70–79. doi:10.1046/j.0266-4909.2002.00007.x

Huang, L., & Boehm, B. How Much Software Investment is Enough: A Value-Based Approach. *IEEE Software, 23*(5), 88–95. doi:10.1109/MS.2006.127

Hubel, D. (1988). *Eye, Brain and Vision.* W.H. Freeman & Co. ISBN: 0716750201.

Hubel, D., & Wiesel, T. (1968). Receptive Fields and Functional Architecture of Monkey Striate Cortex. *The Journal of Physiology, 195,* 215–243.

Hughes, J., Guttorp, P., & Charles, S. (1999). A non-homogeneous hidden Markov model for precipitation occurrence. *Applied Statistics, 48,* 15–30. doi:10.1111/1467-9876.00136

Hurley, P. J. (1997). *A Concise Introducfzon to Logic* (6th ed.). Belmony, CA: Wadsworth Pub. Co., ITP.

Hurst, M. (2001, September). Layout and language: Challenges for table understanding on the web. Proceeding of International Workshop on Web Document Analysis (pp. 27-30), Seattle, USA.

Husserl, E. (1962). Phänomenologische Psychologie. In W. Biemel (Ed.), *Husserliana IX.* Den Haag: Martinus Nijhoff.

Hwang, K. S., Tan, S. W., & Chen, C. C. (2004). Cooperative strategy based on adaptive Q-learning for robot soccer systems. *IEEE Transactions on Fuzzy Systems Volume*, *12*(Issue: 4), 569–576. doi:10.1109/TFUZZ.2004.832523

IBM. (2006), Autonomic Computing White Paper: *An Architectural Blueprint for Autonomic Computing*, 4th ed., June, 1-37.

IBM. (2006). *IBM Autonomic Computing Manifesto*. Retrieved May 2006 from http://www.research.ibm.com/autonomic/

IBM. (2007). Engineering design: Clash analysis in automotive and aerospace. Retrieved May 2007 from http://www-03.ibm.com/grid/solutions/ED_clashanalysisautoaero.shtml

Iglesias, A. "Computer Graphics Techniques for Realistic Modeling, Rendering, and Animation of Water. Part I: 1980-88." Int. Conf. on Computational Science (2) 2002, 181-190, 2002

ITEA. (2007). International Technology Education Association: Glossary terms for STL and AETL and Addenda, *Report*, 30 pp. (STL –Standards for Technological Literacy; AETL –Advancing Excellence in Technological Literacy; TAA –Technology for All Americans) Retrieved June 2007 from http://www.iteaconnect.org/TAA/Publications/TAA_Publications.html

J. Natt och Dag and V. Gervasi (2005), Managing Large Repositories of Natural Language Requirements, Engineering and Managing Software Requirements, Springer-Verlag.

Jain, N., Amini, L., Andrade, H., King, R., Park, Y., & Selo, P. (2006). Design, implementation, and evaluation of the linear road benchmark on the stream processing core. SIGMOD '06: Proceedings of the 2006 ACM SIGMOD international conference on Management of data (431–442). New York, NY, USA: ACM.

Jan Goossenaerts and Christine Pelletier. (2001), Ontological commitments for participative simulation, a chapter from Conceptual Modeling for New Information Systems, Lecture Notes in Computer Science, Springer Berlin / Heidelberg ISSN: 0302-9743, vol. 2465, pp. 127 – 140, Japan.

Jeasen, A. R. (1969). How Much can We Boost IQ and Scholastic Achievement? *Harvard Educational Review*, (39): 1–123.

Jeasen, A. R. (1987). Psychometric g as a Focus on Concerted Research Effort. *Intelligence*, (11): 193–198. doi:10.1016/0160-2896(87)90005-5

Jekeli, C., & Dumrongchai, P. (2003). On monitoring a vertical datum with satellite altimetry and water-level gauge data on large lakes. *Journal of Geodesy*, *77*, 447–453. doi:10.1007/s00190-003-0345-2

Jennings, N. R. (2000). On Agent-Based Software Engineering. *Artificial Intelligence*, *17*(2), 277–296. doi:10.1016/S0004-3702(99)00107-1

Johan Natt och Dag, Björn Regnell, Pär Carlshamre, Michael Andersson and Joachim Karlsson (2002), A Feasibility Study of Automated Natural Language Requirements Analysis in Market-Driven Development, Requirements Eng., vol. 7, no. 1, pp. 20–33.

Johan Natt och Dag, Vincenzo Gervasi, Sjaak Brinkkemper and Björn Regnell (2005), A linguistic engineering approach to large-scale requirements management, IEEE Software - IEEE Software, Vol. 22, Issue 1, pp. 32-39.

Jonassen, D. H. (2004). *Handbook of Research on Educational Communications and Technology: A Project of the Association for Educational Communications and Technology* (2nd ed.). Mahwah, NJ, USA: Lawrence Erlbaum Associates Inc.

Jones, C. Applied Software Measurement, 2nd edition; McGraw-Hill, New York, NY, 1996; 457 pages; 3rd edition due in the Spring of 2008.

Jones, C., & the Estimating Software Costs. McGraw Hill, New York; 2nd edition, 2007; 644 pages; ISBN13: 978- 0-07-148300-1.

Jones, C., Productivity, P., McGraw, H., & York, N. ISBN 0-07-032811-0; 1986.

Jones, Capers; Conflict and Litigation Between Software Clients and Developers; Version 6; Software Productivity Research, Burlington, MA; June 2006; 54 pages.

Jones, Capers; Program Quality and Programmer Productivity; IBM Technical Report TR 02.764, IBM San Jose, CA; January 1977.

Jones, A., & Issroff, K. (2005). Learning Technologies: Affective And Social Issues in Computer-Supported Collaborative Learning. *Computers & Education, 44*, 395–408. doi:10.1016/j.compedu.2004.04.004

Jones, C. (1981). *Programming Productivity – Issues for the Eighties*. Silver Spring, MD: IEEE Press.

Jones, C. (1986). *Programming Productivity*. NY: McGraw-Hill Book Co.

Jones, C. (1994). *Estimating and Measuring Object-Oriented Software*. American Programmer.

Jones, C. Software Assessments, Benchmarks, and Best Practices. (2000). *Addison Wesley Longman*. Boston, MA.

Jordan, M. I. (1999), Computational Intelligence, in Wilson, R.A. and C.K. Frank eds., *The MIT Encyclopedia of the Cognitive Sciences*, MIT Press, pp. i73-i80.

Jørgensen, M., & Sjøberg, D. I. (2004, May). Generalization and theory-building in software engineering research. In S. Linkman (Ed.), *Proceedings of the 8th international conference on Empirical Assessment in Software Engineering* (pp. 29–36). IEEE Computer Society Press.

Kacprzyk, J., & Zadrożny, S. (1994). Fuzzy querying for Microsoft Access. In *Proceedings of FUZZ-IEEE'94 (Orlando, USA): Vol. 1*, (pp. 167 – 171).

Kacprzyk, J., & Zadrożny, S. (1995). Fuzzy queries in Microsoft Access v. 2. In *Proceedings of FUZZ-IEEE/ IFES '95 (Yokohama, Japan), Workshop on Fuzzy Database Systems and Information Retrieval*, (pp. 61 – 66).

Kacprzyk, J., & Zadrożny, S. (1998). Data mining via linguistic summaries of data: an interactive approach. In T. Yamakawa & G. Matsumoto (Eds.), *Methodologies for the Conception, Design and Application of Soft Computing - Proceedings of IIZUKA '98 (Iizuka, Japan)*, (pp. 668 – 671).

Kacprzyk, J., & Zadrożny, S. (1999) The paradigm of computing with words in intelligent database querying. In L.A. Zadeh and J. Kacprzyk (Eds.): *Computing with Words in Information/Intelligent Systems.(Part 2. Foundations*, (pp. 382 – 398), Heidelberg and New York: Physica-Verlag (Springer-Verlag).

Kacprzyk, J., & Zadrożny, S. (2000). On combining intelligent querying and data mining using fuzzy logic concepts. In G. Bordogna & G. Pasi (Eds.), *Recent Research Issues on the Management of Fuzziness in Databases* (pp. 67 – 81), Heidelberg and New York: Physica – Verlag (Springer-Verlag).

Kacprzyk, J., & Zadrożny, S. (2000). Data mining via fuzzy querying over the Internet. In O. Pons, M.A. Vila & J. Kacprzyk (Eds.), *Knowledge Management in Fuzzy Databases* (pp. 211 – 233), Heidelberg and New York: Physica – Verlag (Springer-Verlag).

Kacprzyk, J., & Zadrożny, S. (2000). Computing with words: towards a new generation of linguistic querying and summarization of databases. In P. Sinčak & J. Vaščak (Eds.), *Quo Vadis Computational Intelligence?* (pp. 144 – 175), Heidelberg and New York: Physica-Verlag (Springer-Verlag).

Kacprzyk, J., & Zadrożny, S. (2001). Fuzzy linguistic summaries via association rules. In A. Kandel, M. Last & H. Bunke (Eds.), *Data Mining and Computational Intelligence*, (pp. 115 – 139), Heidelberg and New York: Physica-Verlag (Springer-Verlag).

Kacprzyk, J., & Zadrożny, S. (2001). Using fuzzy querying over the Internet to browse through information resources. In B. Reusch and K.-H. Temme (Eds.), *Computational Intelligence in Theory and Practice* (pp. 235 – 262), Heidelberg and New York: Physica-Verlag (Springer-Verlag).

Kacprzyk, J., & Zadrożny, S. (2003). Linguistic summarization of data sets using association rules. In *Proceedings of FUZZ-IEEE '03 (St. Louis, USA)* (pp. 702 – 707).

Kacprzyk, J. (2000). Intelligent data analysis via linguistic data summaries: a fuzzy logic approach. In Decker, R., & Gaul, W. (Eds.), *Classification and Information Processing at the Turn of the Millennium* (pp. 153–161). Berlin, Heidelberg, New York: Springer-Verlag. doi:10.1007/978-3-642-57280-7_17

Kacprzyk, J., Pasi, G., Vojtaš, P., & Zadrożny, S. (2000). Fuzzy querying: issues and perspective. *Kybernetika, 36*, 605–616.

Kacprzyk, J., & Yager, R. R. (2001). Linguistic summaries of data using fuzzy logic. *International Journal of General Systems, 30*, 133–154. doi:10.1080/03081070108960702

Kacprzyk, J., Yager, R. R., & Zadrożny, S. (2000). A fuzzy logic based approach to linguistic summaries of databases. *International Journal of Applied Mathematics and Computer Science, 10,* 813–834.

Kacprzyk, J., Yager, R. R., & Zadrożny, S. (2001). Fuzzy linguistic summaries of databases for an efficient business data analysis and decision support. In Abramowicz, W., & Żurada, J. (Eds.), *Knowledge Discovery for Business Information Systems* (pp. 129–152). Boston: Kluwer. doi:10.1007/0-306-46991-X_6

Kacprzyk, J., & Zadrożny, S. (1995). FQUERY for Access: fuzzy querying for a Windows-based DBMS. In Bosc, P., & Kacprzyk, J. (Eds.), *Fuzziness in Database Management Systems* (pp. 415–433). Heidelberg: Physica-Verlag.

Kacprzyk, J., & Zadrożny, S. (2000). On a fuzzy querying and data mining interface. *Kybernetika, 36,* 657–670.

Kacprzyk, J., & Zadrożny, S. (2001). On linguistic approaches in flexible querying and mining of association rules. In Larsen, H. L., Kacprzyk, J., Zadrożny, S., Andreasen, T., & Christiansen, H. (Eds.), *Flexible Query Answering Systems. Recent Advances* (pp. 475–484). Heidelberg, New York: Springer-Verlag.

Kacprzyk, J., & Zadrożny, S. (2001). Computing with words in intelligent database querying: standalone and Internet-based applications. *Information Sciences, 34,* 71–109. doi:10.1016/S0020-0255(01)00093-7

Kacprzyk, J., & Zadrożny, S. (2001). Data mining via linguistic summaries of databases: an interactive approach. In Ding, L. (Ed.), *A New Paradigm of Knowledge Engineering by Soft Computing* (pp. 325–345). Singapore: World Scientific. doi:10.1142/9789812794604_0015

Kacprzyk, J., & Zadrożny, S. (2002). Protoforms of linguistic data summaries: towards more general natural - language - based data mining tools. In Abraham, A., Ruiz del Solar, J., & Koeppen, M. (Eds.), *Soft Computing Systems* (pp. 417–425). Amsterdam: IOS Press.

Kacprzyk, J., & Zadrożny, S. (2005). Linguistic database summaries and their protoforms: towards natural language based knowledge discovery tools. *Information Sciences, 173*(4), 281–304. doi:10.1016/j.ins.2005.03.002

Kacprzyk, J., Zadrożny, S., & Ziółkowski, A. (1989). FQUERY III+: a 'human consistent' database querying system based on fuzzy logic with linguistic quantifiers. *Information Systems, 6,* 443–453. doi:10.1016/0306-4379(89)90012-4

Kacprzyk, J., & Ziółkowski, A. (1986). Database queries with fuzzy linguistic quantifiers. *IEEE Transactions on Systems. Man and Cybernetics, SMC, 16,* 474–479. doi:10.1109/TSMC.1986.4308982

Kaindl, Hermann, Brinkkemper, Sjaak, Bubenko, Janis A. Jr, Farbey, Barbara, & Greenspan, Sol J., C. L. Heitmeyer, Julio Cesar Sampaio do Prado Leite, Nancy R. Mead, J. Mylopoulos and Jawed I. A. Siddi. (2002). Requirements Engineering and Technology Transfer: Obstacles and Incentives. *Requirements Engineering, 7*(3), 113–223. doi:10.1007/s007660200008

Kamal, K. (2008). *Embedded Systems: Architecture, Programming, and Design* (p. 633). New York, NY: McGraw-Hill.

Kandel, E. R., Schwartz, J. H., & Jessell, T. M. (Eds.). (2000). *Principles of Neural Science* (4th ed.). New York: McGraw-Hill.

Kaner, C. (2004). Software Engineering Metrics: What do they Measure and how do we know? *Proc. Int. Soft. Metrics Symp.* Metrics 2004.

Kang, K. C., Cohen, S. G., Hess, J. A., Novak, W. E., & Peterson, A. S. (1990). *Feature-Oriented Domain Analysis (FODA) Feasibility Study*, SEI.

Kanizsa, G. (1979). *Organization in Vision: Essays on Gestalt Perception.* NY: Praeger.

Kan, S. H. (2003). *Metrics and Models in Software Quality Engineering* (2nd ed.). Boston, MA: Addison Wesley Longman.

Kant, I. (1998). *Critique of Pure Reason.* P. Guyer & A. W. Wood (Trans.) (Eds.). Cambridge: Cambridge Univ. Press.

Kashif Ahmed Khan. (2006) "A Systematic Review of Software Requirements Prioritization", Master's Thesis, Software Engineering, no: MSE-2006-18, pp:41-46.

Kaski, S., Lagus, K., & Honkela, K., et al. (1998). Statistical aspects of the WEBSOM system in organizing document collections. *Computing Science and Statistics*, (29), 281-290.

Kautz, H., Selman, B., & Shah, M. (1997). Referral-Web: Combining Social Networks and Collaborative Filtering. *Communications of the ACM, 40*(3), 27–36. doi:10.1145/245108.245123

Kawaharada, H., & Sugihara, K. "Compression of Arbitrary Mesh Data Using Subdivision Surfaces," IMA Conference on the Mathematics of Surfaces 2003, 99-110, 2003

Kearney, J. K., Sedlmeyer, R. L., Thompson, W. B., Gary, M. A., & Adler, M. A. (1986). *Software Complexity Measurement* (Vol. 28, pp. 1044–1050). New York: ACM Press.

Kephart, J., & Chess, D. (2003). The Vision of Autonomic Computing, IEEE. *Computer, 26*(1), 41–50. doi:10.1109/MC.2003.1160055

Khoshgoftaar, T. (2003). *Software Engineering with Computational Intelligence*. Berlin: Kluwer.

Khoshgoftaar, T. (2003). Special Issue on Quality Engineering with Computational Intelligence. *Software Quality Journal, 11*(2). doi:10.1023/A:1023708325859

Kim, J. (1995). *Problems in the Philosophy of Mind*. Oxford Companion to Philosophy. Oxford: Oxford University Press.

Kim, I.-G., Bae, D.-H., & Hong, J.-E. (2007). A component composition model providing dynamic, flexible, and hierarchical composition of components for supporting software evolution. *Journal of Systems and Software, 80*(11), 1797–1816. doi:10.1016/j.jss.2007.02.047

Kinsner, W. (1985, July), *Computer-Aided Engineering of Printed Circuit Bords*. Technical Report DEL85-1. Winnipeg, MB: Microelectronics Centre and Department of Electrical and Computer Engineering, University of Manitoba, (p. 171).

Kinsner, W. (2005). Review of Recent Development in Cognitive Informatics. In J. Tsai, Y.X. Wang, D. Zhang, & W. Kinsner (Eds.), *Proceedings of the 4th IEEE International Conference on Cognitive Informatics* (pp. 6-8), IEEE CS Press, Irvine, USA.

Kinsner, W. (2005). Signal processing for autonomic computing. In *Proc. 2005 Meet. Can. Applied & Industrial Math Soc.*, CAIMS 2005 (Winnipeg, MB; June 16-18, 2005). Retrieved May 2006 from http://www.umanitoba.ca/institutes/iims/caims2005_theme_signal.shtml

Kinsner, W. (2007). Challenges in the design of daptive, intelligent, and cognitive systems. In *Proc. 3rd IEEE Intern. Conf. on Cognitive Informatics*, ICCI07, (Lake Tahoe, CA; 6-8 August 2007) ISBN 1-4244-1327-3, (pp. 13-24).

Kinsner, W., Cheung, V., Cannons, K., Pear, J., & Martin, T. (2003). Signal classification through multifractal analysis and complex domain neural networks. *Second IEEE International Conference on Cognitive Informatics (ICCI'03)*, August 18-20, (pp. 41- 46), London, UK.

Kinsner, W. (2007). Towards cognitive machines: Multiscale measures and analysis. *International Journal of Cognitive Informatics and Natural Intelligence, 1*(1), 28–38. doi:10.4018/jcini.2007010102

Kirwan, B., & Ainsworth, L. K. (1992). *A Guide to Task Analysis*. London: Taylor & Francis Ltd.

Kitchenham, B. A., Dyba, T., & Jorgensen, M. (2004). Evidence-Based Software Engineering. In *Proceedings of International Conference on Software Engineering*, Edinburgh, pp.273-281.

Kleene, S. C. (1956), Representation of Events by Nerve Nets, in C.E. Shannon and J. McCarthy eds., *Automata Studies*, Princeton Univ. Press, 3-42.

Klein, H. J. (1989). An Integrated Control Theory Model of Work Motivation. *Academy of Management Review, 14*, 150–172.

Klein, J. I. (1990). Feasibility Theory: A Resource-Munificence Model of Work Motivation and Behavior. *Academy of Management Review, 15*, 646–665.

Klemola, T., & Rilling, J. (2003). A Cognitive complexity metric based on Category learning, *Proceedings of IEEE (ICCI'03)*, pp.103-108

Klir, G. J. (1992). *Facets of Systems Science*. New York: Plenum.

Klivington, K. (1989). *The Science of Mind* (p. 239). Cambridge, MA: MIT Press.

Knauf, R., Gonzalez, A. J., & Abel, T. (2002). A Framework for Validation of Rule-Based Systems. *IEEE Transactions on Systems, Man, and Cybernetics. Part B, Cybernetics, 32*(3), 281–295. doi:10.1109/TSMCB.2002.999805

Koblinsky, C. J., Clarke, R. T., Brenner, A. C., & Frey, H. (1993). Measurement of river level variations with satellite altimetry. *Water Resources Research, 6,* 1839–1848. doi:10.1029/93WR00542

Koch, C. (2004). *The Quest for Consciousness: A Neurobiological Approach.* Englewood, Colorado: Roberts and Company Publishers.

Koen, B. V. (2003). *Discussion of the Method: Conducting the Engineer's Approach to Problem Solving* (p. 260). Oxford, UK: Oxford University Press.

Kolingerova, I. "Probabilistic Methods for Triangulated Models," 8th Int. Conference on Computer Graphics and Artificial Intelligence 3IA 2005, Limoges, France, 93-106, 2005

Kollias, V., Mamalougos, N., Vamvakoussi, X., Lakkala, M., & Vosniadou, S. (2005). Teachers' Attitudes to and Beliefs about Web-Based Collaborative Learning Environments in the Context of An International Implementation. *Computers & Education, 45,* 295–315. doi:10.1016/j.compedu.2005.04.012

Komis, V., Avouris, N., & Fidas, C. (2002). Computer-Supported Collaborative Concept Mapping: Study of Synchronous Peer Interaction. *Education and Information Technologies, 7*(2), 169–188. doi:10.1023/A:1020309927987

Kontonya, G., & Sommerville, I. (1998). *Requirements Engineering: Processes and Techniques.* New York: John Wiley and Sons.

Koschmann, T. (1996). Paradigm Shifts and Instructional Technology: An Introduction. In Koschmann, T. (Ed.), *CSCL: Theory and Practice of An Emerging Paradigm.* Mahwah, NJ, USA: Lawrence Erlbaum Associates.

Kosslyn, S. M. (1973). Scanning visual images: Some structural implications. *Perception & Psychophysics, 14,* 90–94. doi:10.3758/BF03198621

Krasner, Herb; "Accumulating the Body of Evidence for the Payoff of Software Process Improvement – 1997;" Krasner Consulting, Austin, TX.

Kravcik, M. and Gasevic, D. "Knowledge Representation for Adaptive Learning Design," Proceedings of Adaptive Hypermedia. June, Dublin, Ireland, 11 pages, 2006

Kreijns, K., Kirschner, P. A., Jochems, W., & Buuren, H. v. (2005). (in press). Measuring Perceived Sociability of Computer-Supported Collaborative Learning Environments. *Computers & Education.*

Krogh, A., & Vedelsby, J. (1995). Neural Networks Ensembles, Cross validation, and Active Learning. In *Advances in Neural Information Processing Systems* (pp. 231–238). MIT Press Cambridge.

Kruizinga, G. (1997). *Validation and application of satellite radar altimetry.* PhD Dissertation, Univ. of Texas at Austin, Austin, TX, USA.

Kuhl, J. (1994). Motivation and volition. In G. d'ydewalle, P. G. Eelen, & P. Bertelson (Eds.), *International perspectives on psychological science, 2,* 311-340. (England, Drlbaum).

Kurzweil, R. (1990). *The Age of Intelligent Machines* (p. 565). Cambridge, MA: MIT Press.

Kushwaha, D. S., & Misra, A. K. (2006). Robustness Analysis of Cognitive Information Complexity Measure using Weyuker's Properties. *ACM SIGSOFT Software Engineering Notes, 31,* 1–6. doi:10.1145/1108768.1108775

Labrosse, J.J. (1999, December). *MicroC/OS-II, The Real-Time Kernel,* 2nd ed., Gilroy, CA: R&D Books.

Labrosse, J. J. (2000). *Embedded Systems Building Blocks: Complete and Ready-to-Use Modules in C* (2nd ed., p. 611). Lawrence, KS: CMP Books.

Lachman, R., Lachman, J. L., & Butterfield, E. C. (1979, June). *Cognitive Psychology and Information Processing: An Introduction* (1st Edition). Lawrence Erlbaum Associates, Publishers.

Lam, W., Low, K. F., & Ho, C. Y. (1997). Using a Bayesian network induction approach for text categorization. *Proc. 15th International Joint Conference on Artificial Intelligence* (IJCAI-97), (pp. 745-750), Nagoya, Japan.

Lawler, E. E. (1977). Satisfaction and Behaviour. In Hackman, J. R., Lawler, E. E., & Porter, L. W. (Eds.), *Perspectives on Behavior in Organisations.* NY: McGraw-Hill.

Lazebnik, S., Schmid, C., & Ponce, J. (2006). Beyond Bags of Features: Spatial Pyramid Matching for Recognizing Natural Scene Categories. *IEEE Conference on Computer Vision and Pattern Recognition, 2,* 1150-1157.

Lee, Y., & Zhao, W, (2006), An Ontology-based Approach for Domain Requirements Elicitation and Analysis, IEEE Proceedings of the First International Multi-Symposiums on Computer and Computational Sciences.

Lee, J. (2003). *Software Engineering with Computational Intelligence*. Berlin: Springer-Verlag.

Lee, J. (2003). Special Issue on Software Eng with Computational Intelligence. *Information and Software Technology, 45*(7). doi:10.1016/S0950-5849(03)00009-0

Lefton, L. A., Brannon, L., Boyes, M. C., & Ogden, N. A. (2005). *Psychology* (2nd ed.). Toronto: Pearson Education Canada Inc.

Leite, J., Yu, Y., Liu, L., Yu, E., & Mylopoulos, J. (2005, January). Quality-based software reuse. *Lecture Notes in Computer Science, 3520,* 535–550. doi:10.1007/11431855_37

Leonhard, (1995, December). Leonhard Center for the Advancement of Engineering Education, "World-class engineer," *Report*, The Pennsylvania State University. Retrieved June 2007 from http://www.engr.psu.edu/AboutCOE/worldclass.asp

Leonid Kof. (2004), Natural Language Procesing for Requirements Engineering: Applicability to Large Requirements Documents. In Alessandra Russo, Artur Garcez, and Tim Menzies, editors, Automated Software Engineering, Proceedings of the Workshops, Linz, Austria.

Lévy, N., & Losavio, F. (1998, November). Analyzing and comparing architectural styles. In R. Monge & M. Visconti (Eds.), *Proceedings of the 19th international Conference of the Chilean Computer Science Society*. IEEE Computer Society Press. Lewis, C. (1982). *Using the "thinking-aloud" method in cognitive interface design*. Technical Report RC9265, IBM T.J. Watson Research Center.

Lewis, H. R., & Papadimitriou, C. H. (1998). *Elements of the Theory of Computation* (2nd ed.). Englewood Cliffs, NJ: Prentice Hall International.

Lewis, M. (1990). The development of intentionality and the role of consciousness. *Psychological Inquiry, 1,* 231–247. doi:10.1207/s15327965pli0103_13

Li, H., Srihari, R., Niu, C., & Li, W. (2003). Cymfony A hybrid approach to geographical references in information extraction. *Human Language Technology conference: North American chapter of the Association for Computational Linguistics annual meeting*, Edmonton, Canada.

Liang, X. F., & Asano, T. (2004). *A fast denoising method for binary fingerprint image* (pp. 309–313). Spain: IASTED.

Lin, T. Y. (1998). *Granular Computing on Binary Relations (I): Data Mining and Neighborhood Systems, Proc. Rough Sets in Knowledge Discovery* (pp. 107–120). Heidelberg: Physica-Verlag.

Lin, T. Y., Yao, Y. Y., & Zadeh, L. A. (Eds.). (2002). *Data Mining*. Heidelberg: Rough Sets and Granular Computing, Physica-Verlag.

Lipschutz, S., & Lipson, M. (1997). *Schaum's Outline of Theories and Problems of Discrete Mathematics* (2nd ed.). New York, NY: McGraw-Hill Inc.

Li, S., & Jain, A. (2005). *Handbook of Face Recognition*. Springer-Verlag.

Li, S., Liu, X., & Wu, E. (2003). Feature-Based Visibility-Driven CLOD for Terrain. In *Proc. Pacific Graphics 2003* (pp. 313–322). IEEE Press.

Liu, H., & Singh, P. (2004). Commonsense reasoning in and over natural language. *Proceedings of the 8th International Conference on Knowledge-Based Intelligent Information and Engineering Systems (KES-2004)*.

Liu, J. (2000). *Real-Time Systems*. Upper Saddle River, NJ: Prentice Hall.

Liu, K., & Dix, A. (1997). Norm governed agens in CSCW, *The First International Workshop on Computational Semotics*, (Paris, University of De Vince).

Liu, J. (2000). *Real-Time Systems*. Upper Saddle River, NJ: Prentice Hall.

Liu, Y., & Kerre, E. E. (1988). An overview of fuzzy quantifiers. (I) Interpretations. *Fuzzy Sets and Systems, 95,* 1–21. doi:10.1016/S0165-0114(97)00254-6

Locke, E. A., & Latham, G. P. (1990). Work Motivation and Satisfaction: Light at the End of the Tunnel. *Psychological Science*, *4*, 240–246. doi:10.1111/j.1467-9280.1990.tb00207.x

Locke, E. A., & Latham, G. P. (1990). *A theory of goal setting and task performance*. NJ: Prentice-Hall.

Locke, E. A., & Latham, G. P. (1991). Self-regulation through goal setting. *Organizational Behavior and Human Decision Processes*, *50*, 212–247. doi:10.1016/0749-5978(91)90021-K

Locke, E. A., & Latham, G. P. (2004). What should we do about motivation theory? Six recommendations for the twenty-first century. *Academy of Management Review*, *29*, 388–403.

Loop, C. T. Smooth Subdivision Surfaces Based on Triangles. Masters Thesis, University of Utah, Department of Mathematics. 1987

Lopes, H., Oliveira, J. B., & de Figueiredo, L. H. (2002). Robust adaptive polygonal approximation of implicit curves. *Computers & Graphics*, *26*(Issue 6), 841–852. doi:10.1016/S0097-8493(02)00173-5

Lourdusamy, A., Khine, M. S., & Sipusic, M. (2003). Collaborative Learning Tool for Presenting Authentic Case Studies and Its Impact on Student Participation. *Journal of Educational Technology Systems*, *31*(4), 381–392. doi:10.2190/4GBA-UJ45-7WXU-0QVQ

Lowe, D. (1999). Object Recognition From Local Scale-Invariant Features. *Proceedings of the Seventh IEEE Conference on Computer Vision*, *2*, 1150-1157

Lu, H., & Hammersley, R. "Adaptive visualization for interactive geometric modeling in geoscience," the 8th International Conference in Central Europe on Computer Graphics, Visualization and Interactive Digital Media 2000, p.1, Feb. 2000

Luo, Y. and Gavrilova, M.L.. "3D Facial model synthesis using Voronoi Approach," IEEE-CS proceedings, ISVD 2006, pp. 132-137, Banff, AB, Canada, July 2006

Luo, X. F., & Fang, N. (2008). Experimental Study on the Extraction and Distribution of Textual Domain Keywords. *Concurrency and Computation*, *20*(16), 1917–1932. doi:10.1002/cpe.1309

M. R. Genesereth, S. P. Ketchpel, Software agents, *Communications of the ACM*, 37, 7, 1994, 48-53.

Mahalakshmi, G. S., & Geetha, T. V. (2007) Navya-Nyaya Approach to Defect Exploration in Argument Gaming for Knowledge Sharing, In proc.s of International Conference On Logic, Navya-Nyaya & Applications - A Homage To Bimal Krishna Matilal (ICLNNA '07), Jadavpur University, Calcutta, India, pp. 171-182.

Mahalakshmi, G. S., & Saravanan, K. (2007), Design And Implementation Of An Ontology Based Approach To Automate Requirements Generation, International Conf. on Soft Computing techniques in engineering, SOFTECH – 07, Avinashilingam University for Women, Coimbatore, India, pp.301-307.

Mahalakshmi, G. S., & Geetha, T. V. (2008). Reasoning and Evolution of consistent ontologies using NORM, IJAI: Special Issue on theory and applications of soft computing [ISDER]. *Indian Society for Development and Environment Research*, *2*(No.S09), 77–94.

Mallat, S. (1998). *A Wavelet Tour of Signal Processing* (p. 577). San Diego, CA: Academic Press.

Mandrioli, D., & Ghezzi, C. (1987). *Theoretical Foundations of Computer Science*. New York: John Wiley & Sons.

Manlove, S., Lazonder, A. W., & Jong, T. (2006). Regulative Support for Collaborative Scientific Inquiry Learning. *Journal of Computer Assisted Learning*, 87–98. doi:10.1111/j.1365-2729.2006.00162.x

Mann, S. (2001). Humanistic intelligence: WearComp as a new framework and application for intelligent signal processing. In Haykin, S., & Kosko, B. (Eds.), *Intelligent Signal Processing* (pp. 1–39). New York, NY: Wiley-IEEE. doi:10.1109/5.726784

Mann, S. (2002). *Intelligent Image Processing* (p. 342). New York, NY: Wiley/IEEE.

Markie, P. (2004). Rationalism vs. Empiricism. In E. N. Zalta (Ed.), *Stanford Encyclopedia of Philosophy*. Retrieved September 29, 2008, from http://plato.stanford.edu/entries/rationalism-empiricism/

Marr, D. (1982, June). *Vision: A Computational Investigation into the Human Representation and Processing of Visual Information* (1st Edition). Henry Holt & Company.

Marr, D. (1978). Representing visual information. In Hanson, A. R., & Riseman, E. M. (Eds.), *Computer Vision Systems* (pp. 61–80). Academic Press.

Martin, C. (1988). *User-centered Requirements Analysis*. Englewook Cliffs, NJ: Prentice Hall.

Matlin, M. W. (1998). *Cognition* (4th ed.). Orlando, FL: Harcourt Brace College Publishers.

Mayrhauser, A. v. (1995, August). Program comprehension during software maintenance and evolution. *IEEE Computer, 28*(8), 44–55. doi:10.1109/2.402076

MBSE. (accessed 2008). http://www.sei.cmu.edu/mbse/index.html.

McCabe, T. H. (1976). A Complexity Measure. *IEEE Transactions on Software Engineering, SE-2*(6), 308–320. doi:10.1109/TSE.1976.233837

McCallum, A., Freitag, D., & Pereira, F. (2000). Maximum entropy Markov models for information extraction and segmentation. *Proceedings of 17th International Conf. on Machine Learning*, San Francisco, CA.

McCarthy, J. Hayes, P. J. (1987). Some philosophical problems from the standpoint of artificial intelligence. *Readings in nonmonotonic reasoning* 26–45, San Francisco, CA, USA: Morgan Kaufmann Publishers Inc.

McCarthy, J., & Minsky, M. L. M.L., N. Rochester, and C.E. Shannon *(1955)*, Proposal for the 1956 Dartmouth Summer Research Project on Artificial Intelligence, *Dartmouth College, Hanover, NH, USA*, http://www.formal.stanford.edu/jmc/history/dartmouth/dartmouth.html.

McConnell, S. (1996). *Rapid Development: Taming Wild Software Schedules* (p. 680). Bellevue, WA: Microsoft Press.

McConnell, S. (2006). *Software Estimation: Demistifying the Black Art* (p. 308). Bellevue, WA: Microsoft Press.

McCulloch, W. S. (1965). *Embodiments of Mind*. Cambridge, MA: MIT Press.

McDermid, J. A. (1991). *Software Engineer's Reference Book*. Oxford, UK: Butterworth-Heinemann Ltd.

McDermid, J. A. (Ed.). (1991). *Software Engineer's Reference Book*. Oxford, UK: Butterworth-Heinemann Ltd.

McGreal, I. P. (1995). *"Gongsun Long" in Great Thinkers of the Eastern World*. New York: Harper Collins.

McGuinness, D. Harmelen, F. van. (2004). OWL web ontology language overview. W3C Recommendation. Retrieved from the Web 5/8/2008. http://www.w3.org/TR/owl-features/

Mckay, D., & Cunningham, S. (2001, April). Mining dates from historical documents. *The Fourth New Zealand Computer Science Research Students Conference*, New Zealand.

McMinn, P. (2004). Search-based Software Test Data Generation: A Survey. Software: Testing. *Verification and Reliability, 14*(2), 105–156. doi:10.1002/stvr.294

Medin, D. L., & Shoben, E. J. (1988). Context and Structure in Conceptual Combination. *Cognitive Psychology*, (20): 158–190. doi:10.1016/0010-0285(88)90018-7

Medioni, G., & Waupotitsch, R. "Face recognition and modeling in 3D," IEEE Int. Workshop on Analysis and Modeling of Faces and Gestures, pp. 232-233, 2003

Melton, A. (Ed.). (1996). *Software Measurement*. International Thomson Computer Press.

Mendonca, M., & Sunderhaft, N. L. (1999). Mining Software Engineering Data: A Survey. DACS State-of-the-Art Report, http://www.dacs.dtic.mil/techs/datamining/.

Merugu, S., & Ghosh, J. (2005). A privacy-sensitive approach to distributed clustering. *Pattern Recognition Letters, 26*, 399–410. doi:10.1016/j.patrec.2004.08.003

Meystel, A. M., & Albus, J. S. (2002). *Intelligent Systems, Architecture, Design, and Control*. John Wiley & Sons, Inc.

Miao, D. Q., & Hu, G. R. (1999). A heuristic algorithm for reduction of knowledge. *Computer Research & Development, 36*(6), 681–684.

Michaelson, C. (2005). Meaningful motivation for work motivation theory. *Academy of Management Review, 30*, 235–238. doi:10.5465/AMR.2005.16387881

Miclet, L. (1986). *Structural Methods in Pattern Recognition*. London: North Oxford Academic.

Miettinen, M., Kurhiła, J., Nokelainen, P., Floren, P., & Tirri, H. (2003). EDUCOSM - Personalized Writable Web for Learning Communities. in *Proceedings of International Conference on Information Technology Institute of Electrical and Electronics Engineers*, 37-42.

Mill, J. S. (1968). An Examination of Sir William Rowan Hamilton's Philosophy. In A.J. Ayer & R. Winch (Eds.), *British Empirical Philosophers*. New York: Simon and Schuster.

Miller, G. A., Galanter, E., & Pribram, K. H. (1960). *Plans and the structure of behaviour*. New York: Holt, Rinehart, and Winston. doi:10.1037/10039-000

Milner, R. (1980). *A Calculus of Communicating Systems, LNCS 92*. Springer-Verlag.

Mingo, L., Castellanos, J., & Arroyo, F. (2006). Hierarchical Neural Networks to Approximate Functions}. *IEEE International Conference on Cognitive Informatics*. ICCI 2006. (pp. 261-267), Beijing, China.

Mingo, L., Arroyo, F., Diaz, M., & Castellanos, J. (2007). Hierarchical Knowledge Representation: Symbolic Conceptual Trees and Universal Approximation. [IJICS]. *International Journal of Intelligent Control and Systems*, *12*(2), 142–149.

Mingo, L., Aslanyan, L., Castellanos, J., Diaz, M., & Riazanov, V. (2004). Fourier neural networks: An approach with sinusoidal activation functions. *International Journal on Information Theories and Applications*, *11*(1), 52–55.

Minkowski, H. (1908). *Space and Time*. Address, 80th Assembly of German Natural Scientists and Physicians, Cologne.

Minsky, M. (1974). *A framework for representing knowledge. Technical Report Memo 306*. MIT AI Laboratory.

Minsky, M. (1986). *The Society of Mind* (p. 339). New York, NY: Touchstone.

Misra S. and Hurevren Kilic, (2006). Measurement theory and Validation Criteria for Software Complexity measure. *ACM SIGSOFT Software Engineering Notes*. 31,6., pp.1-3.

Misra, S. (2006). Modified Weyuker's Properties, *Proceedings of 5th IEEE International Conference on Cognitive Informatics*, pp.242-247.

Misra, S., & Misra, A. K. (2004). Evaluating Cognitive Complexity Measure with Weyuker Properties. *Proceedings of IEEE (ICCI'04)*, pp.103-108.

Mollestad, T., & Skowron, A. (1996). A rough set framework for data mining of propositional default rules. *Lecture Notes in Computer Science*, *1079*, 448–457.

Moon, M., Yeom, K., & Chae, H. S. (2005). An approach to developing domain requirements as a core asset based on commonality and variability analysis in a product line. *IEEE Transactions on Software Engineering*, *31*(7), 551–569. doi:10.1109/TSE.2005.76

Morasca, S. (2003). Foundations of a Weak Measurement-Theoretic Approach to Software Measurement. *Lecture Notes in Computer Science*, *2621*, 200–215. doi:10.1007/3-540-36578-8_15

Moriguchi, M., & Sugihara, K. (2006). *"A new initialization method for constructing centroidal Voronoi Tessellations on Surface Meshes," ISVD 2006* (pp. 159–165). IEEE-CS Press.

Morrison, J. P. (1971, January). Data Responsive Modular, Interleaved Task Programming System. *IBM Technical Disclosure Bulletin*, *13*(8), 2425–2426.

Moser, P. K., & Trout, J. D. (1995). *Contemporary Materialism: A Reader*. New York, Routledge.

Mostow, J. (1985). Special issue on artificial intelligence and software engineering. *IEEE Trans. SE*, *11*(11), 1253–1408.

Mowday, R., & Colwell, K. (2003). Equity Theory Predictions of Behavior in Organizations. In Bigley, G., Porter, L., & Steers, R. (Eds.), *Motivation and Work Behavior* (7th ed.). New York: Irwin-McGraw Hill.

Murata, T. (1989). Petri Nets: Properties, Analysis and Applications. *Proceedings of the IEEE* (pp. 541-580), Illinois, Chicago, USA, April.

Murphy, G. C., Kersten, M., Robillard, M. P., & Čubraniś, D. (2005, July). The emergent structure of development tasks. In A. P. Black (Ed.), *Proceedings of the 19th European Conference on Object-Oriented Programming* (pp. 33–48). Springer-Verlag.

Murry, R. M., Li, Z., & Sastry, S. S. (1993). *A Mathematical Introduction to Robotic Manipulation*. Boca Raton, FL: CRC Press.

Narayanan, S. McIlraith, S. A. (2002). Simulation, verification and automated composition of web services. WWW '02: Proceedings of the 11th International Conference on World Wide Web (77–88). New York, NY, USA: ACM.

Nattoch, J., Dag, V. G., & Regnell, B". (2004), "Linking Customer Wishes to Product Requirements through Linguistic Engineering", Proceedings of the 12th International Requirements Engineering Conference.

Navabi, Z. (1999). *Verilog Digital System Design* (p. 453). New York, NY: McGraw Hill.

Navarro-Prieto, R. (1998). *The Role of Imagery in Program Comprehension: Visual Programming Languages*. PhD thesis, University of Granada, Newell, A. (1973). You can't play 20 questions with nature and win. In W. G. Chase (Ed.), *Visual Information Processing*. Academic Press.

Nazareth, D. L. (1993). Investigating the Applicability of Petri Nets for Rule-Based Systems Verification. *IEEE Transactions on Knowledge and Data Engineering*, 4(3), 402–415. doi:10.1109/69.224193

Nazareth, D. L., & Kennedy, M. H. (1991). Verification of Rule-Based Knowledge Using Directed Graphs. *Knowledge Acquisition*, 3, 339–360. doi:10.1016/S1042-8143(05)80024-X

Negnevitsky, M. (2005). *Artificial Intelligence. A guide to Intelligent Systems* (2nd ed.). Addison Wesley.

Neisser, U. (1967). *Cognitive Psychology*. Appleton, NY.

Nejdl, W., Wolf, B., Qu, C. S., & Decker, M. Sintek, A. (2002). Naeve, M. Nilsson, M. Palmer, and T. Risch. "EDUTELLA: A P2P Networking Infrastructure Based on RDF. in *Proceedings of the ACM 11th international conference on World Wide Web (WWW)*, Honolulu, Hawaii, USA, 604-615.

Ngolah, C. F., Wang, Y., & Tan, X. (2004). The Real-Time Task Scheduling Algorithm of RTOS+. *IEEE Canadian Journal of Electrical and Computer Engineering*, 29(4), 237-243.

Nguyen, H. S., & Skowron, A. (1995). Quantization of real values attributes: rough set and boolean reasoning approaches. In Wang, P.P. (Ed), *Proceedings of the Second Joint Annual Conference on Information Science* (pp. 34-37), Durham: Duke University Press.

Nielsen, M. A., & Chuang, I. L. (2000). *Quantum Computation and Quantum Information* (p. 676). Cambridge, UK: Cambridge Univ. Press.

Nikolopoulos, C. (1997). *Expert Systems*. Bradley University, Peoria Illinois. Marcel Dekker, Inc.

Okabe, A., Boots, B., & Sugihara, K. (1992). *Spatial tessellation concepts and applications of Voronoi diagrams*. Chichester, England: Wiley & Sons.

OMG. (2002). *MOF 2.0 Query/Views/Transformation RFP*. OMG document ad/2002-04-10, from http://www.omg.org

OMG. (2007). *UML Infrastructure, v2.1.2*. Retrieved November 29, 2007, from http://www.omg.org/cgi-bin/doc?formal/07-11-03

Osgood, C. (1953). *Method and Theory in Experimental Psychology*. UK: Oxford Univ. Press.

Palmer, S. E. (1999, May). *Vision Science: Photons to Phenomenology* (1st Edition). The MIT Press.

Palmer, S. E., & Kimchi, R. (1987, July). The information processing approach to cognition. (pp. 37–77). Lawrence Erlbaum Associates Publishers.

Palnitkar, S. (1996). *Verilog HDL: A Guide to Digital Design and Synthesis* (p. 396). Mountain View, CA: Sun Soft Press / Prentice Hall.

Papa, F., Legre'sy, B., & Re'my, F. (2003). Use of the Topex–Poseidon dual-frequency radar altimeter over land surfaces. *Remote Sensing of Environment*, 87, 136–147. doi:10.1016/S0034-4257(03)00136-6

Papa, F., Legresy, B., Mognard, N. M., Josberger, E. G., & Remy, F. (2002). Estimating Terrestrial Snow Depth with the Topex–Poseidon Altimeter and Radiometer. *IEEE Transactions on Geoscience and Remote Sensing*, 40(10), 2162–2169. doi:10.1109/TGRS.2002.802463

Parker, S. T., & McKinney, M. L. (1999). *Origins of the Intelligence, The Evaluation of Cognitive Development in Monkeys, Apes and Humans*. The John Hopkins University Press.

Park, S., Kim, H., Ko, Y., & Seo, J. (2000). Implementation of an Efficient Requirements-Analysis Supporting System Using Similarity Measure Techniques. *Information and Software Technology, 42*(6), 429–438. doi:10.1016/S0950-5849(99)00102-0

Parnas, D. L., & Clements, P. C. (2001). A rational design process: How and why to fake it. In Hoffman, D. M., & Weiss, D. M. (Eds.), *Collected Papers by David L. Parnas* (pp. 352–368). Upper Saddle River, NJ: Addison-Wesley.

Parsell, M. (2005, March). Review of P.O. Haikonen, The Cognitive Approach to Consious Machines. *Psyche, 11*(2) 1-6. Retrieved May 2006 from http://psyche.cs.monash.edu.au/book_reviews/haikonen/haikone.pdf

Partridge, D. (1998). *Artificial Intelligence and Software Engineering*. Boston: AMACOM.

Patrik Berander, Kashif Ahmed Khan and Laura Lehtola (2006), Towards a research framework on requirements prioritization, SERPS 06.

Pawlak, Z. (1987), Rough Logic, *Bulletin of the Polish Academy of Science, Technical Science*, (5-6), 253-258.

Pawlak, Z. (1998), Granularity of Knowledge, Indiscernibility and Rough Sets, *Proc. 1998 IEEE International Conference on Fuzzy Systems*, 106-110.

Pawlak, Z., Grzymala-Busse, J., Slowinski, R., & Ziarko, W. (1995). Rough sets. *Communications of the ACM, 38*(11), 89–95. doi:10.1145/219717.219791

Payne, D. G., & Wenger, M. J. (1998). *Cognitive Psychology*. Boston: Houghton Mifflin Co.

Pedrycz, W. *Knowledge-Based Fuzzy Clustering*, J. Wiley, N. York, 2005.

Pedrycz, W., & Vukovich, G. Clustering in the framework of collaborative agents, *Proc. 2002 IEEE Int. Conference on Fuzzy Systems*, 1, 2002, 134-138.

Pedrycz, W. (2002). Collaborative fuzzy clustering. *Pattern Recognition Letters, 23*, 675–686. doi:10.1016/S0167-8655(02)00130-7

Pedrycz, W. (Ed.). (2001). *Granular Computing: An Emerging Paradigm*. Heidelberg: Physica-Verlag.

Pedrycz, W., & Gomide, F. (1998). *An Introduction to Fuzzy Sets: Analysis and Design* (p. 465). Cambridge, MA: MIT Press.

Pedrycz, W., & Gomide, F. (2007). *Fuzzy Systems Engineering, J.* Hoboken, NJ: Wiley. doi:10.1002/9780470168967

Pedrycz, W., & Peters, J. F. (1998). *Computational Intelligence in Software Engineering*. Singapore: World Scientific Publisher.

Pedrycz, W., & Rai, P. (to appear). Collaborative clustering with the use of Fuzzy C-Means and Its Quantification. *Fuzzy Sets and Systems*.

Pedrycz, W., & Valente de Oliveira, J. (1996). Optimization of fuzzy models. *IEEE Transaction on Systems, Man, and Cybernetics - Part B, 26*(4), 627–636. doi:10.1109/3477.517038

Peirce, C. S. (1901). Truth and Falsity and Error (in part) (pp. 718–720). In J.M. Baldwin (Ed.), *Dictionary of Philosophy and Psychology* (Vol. 2). Reprinted, CP 5.565–573.

Pennington, N. (1987, July). Stimulus structures and mental representations in expert comprehension of computer programs. *Journal of Cognitive Science, 19*(3), 295–401.

Penrose, R. (1989). *The Emperor's New Mind* (p. 480). Oxford, UK: Oxford Univ. Press.

Penrose, R. (1994). *The Shadows of the Mind: A Search for the Missing Science of Consciousness* (p. 457). Oxford, UK: Oxford Univ. Press.

Pernkopf, F., Van Pham, T., Bilmes, J. A., & Pernkopf, F. (2009). Broad phonetic classification using discriminative Bayesian networks. *Speech Communication, 51*(2), 151–166. doi:10.1016/j.specom.2008.07.003

Perry, S. W., Wong, H. S., & Guan, L. Adaptive Image Processing: A computational Intelligence Perspective, CRC Press, 9 volumes, 272 pages, 2001

Peters, J. F., & Pedrycz, W. (2000). *Software Engineering: An Engineering Approach*. NY: John Wiley & Sons, Inc.

Philip Barry and Kathryn Laskey. (1999), An Application of Uncertain Reasoning to Requirements Engineering, Proceedings of the 15th Annual Conference on Uncertainty in Artificial Intelligence (UAI-99), Morgan Kaufmann, pp. 41-48.

Pinto, D., McCallum, A., Wei, X., & Croft, W. (2003). Table extraction using conditional random fields. *Proceedings of the ACM SIGIR.*

Pistore, M., Traverso, P., & Bertoli, P. Marconi, A. (2005). Automated Synthesis of Composite BPEL4WS Web Services. ICWS '05: Proceedings of the IEEE International Conference on Web Services (293–301). Washington, DC, USA: IEEE Computer Society.

Polkowski, L., & Skowron, A. (1998), Towards Adaptive Calculus of Granules, *Proc. 1998 IEEE International Conference on Fuzzy Systems*, 111-116.

Polkowski, L. (2008). On Foundations and Applications of the Paradigm of Granular Rough Computing, *The International Journal of Cognitive Informatics* (IJCINI). *IGI Publishing, USA, 2*(2), 80–94.

Porter, L. W., & Lawler, E. E. (1968). *Managerial attitudes and performances,* (ILL, Irwin).

Posner, M. (1989) (Ed.). *Foundations of Cognitive Science.* Cambridge, MA: MIT Press, (p. 888).

Powers, W. T. (1992). *Living control systems II.* KY: Control Systems Group.

Prigogine, I., & Nicolis, G. (1972). Thermodynamics of Evolution. *Physics Today,* (25): 23–28. doi:10.1063/1.3071090

Pu, K., & Hristidis, V. Koudas, N. (2006). Syntactic Rule Based Approach to Web Service Composition. ICDE '06: Proceedings of the 22nd International Conference on Data Engineering (31). Washington, DC, USA: IEEE Computer Society.

Qiu, L., Lin, F., & Wan, C. Shi, Z. (2006). Semantic Web Services composition using AI planning of Description Logics. APSCC '06: Proceedings of the 2006 IEEE Asia-Pacific Conference on Services Computing (340–347). Washington, DC, USA: IEEE Computer Society.

Quillian, M. (1968). Semantic memory. In Minsky, E. (Ed.), *Semantic information processing.* Cambridge, Mass., USA: MIT Press.

Quine, W. V. (1976). *The Ways of Paradox and Other Essays.* Cambridge: Harvard University Press.

Quine, W. V. O. (1951). Two Dogmas of Empiricism. *The Philosophical Review, 60*(1), 20–43. doi:10.2307/2181906

Rabiner, L. (1989). A tutorial on hidden Markov models and selected applications in speech recognition. *Proceedings of the IEEE, 77*(2), 257–286. doi:10.1109/5.18626

Raghavan, P. (2002). Social Networks: From the Web to the Enterprise. *IEEE Internet Computing, 6*(1), 91–94. doi:10.1109/4236.989007

Ramaswamy, M., Sarkar, S., & Chen, Y. S. (1997). Using Directed Hypergraphs to Verify Rule-Based Expert Systems. *IEEE Transactions on Knowledge and Data Engineering, 9*(2), 221–237. doi:10.1109/69.591448

Ramirez, J., & De Antonio, A. (2001). Checking Integrity Constraints in Reasoning Systems based on Propositions and Relationships. *Proceedings of the 13th International Conference on Software Engineering and Knowledge Engineering,* SEKE.01 (pp. 188-196), Buenos Aires, Argentina, June.

Ramirez, J., & De Antonio, A. (2007). Checking the Consistency of a Hybrid Knowledge Base System. *Elsevier Science. Knowledge-Based Systems, 20*(3), 225–237. doi:10.1016/j.knosys.2006.05.019

Ramler, R., Biffl, S., & Grunbacher, P. (2006). Value-Based Management of Software Testing. In Biffl, S. (Eds.), *Value-Based Software Engineering* (pp. 225–244). Berlin: Springer. doi:10.1007/3-540-29263-2_11

Rapoport, A., (1962), Mathematical Aspects of General Systems Theory, *General Systems Yearbook,* (11), 3-11.

Rauterberg, M. (1996). How to Measure Cognitive Complexity in Human-Computer Interaction: www.idemployee.id.tue.nl/g.w.m.rauterberg/publications/EMSCR96paper.pdf

Rector, A. L. Horrocks, I. R. (1997). Experience building a large, re-usable medical ontology using a description logic with transitivity and concept inclusions. Proceedings of the Fourteenth National Conference on Artificial Intelligence (AAAI'97).

Reed, S. (1972). Pattern Recognition and Categorization. *Cognitive Psychology, 3*, 383–407. doi:10.1016/0010-0285(72)90014-X

Reid, A., Flatt, M., Stoller, L., & Lepreau, J. Eide, E. (2000, October). Knit: component composition for systems software. Proc. of the 4th Operating Systems Design and Implementation (OSDI) (347–360).

Remy, F., Legresy, B., Bleuzen, S., Vincent, P., & Minster, J. F. (1996). Dual frequency Topex altimeter observations of Greenland. *Journal of Electromagnetic Waves and Applications, 10*, 1507–152. doi:10.1163/156939396X00892

Riabov, A. Liu, Z. (2005, July). Planning for stream processing systems. Proceedings of the Twentieth National Conference on Artificial Intelligence (AAAI'05).

Riabov, A. Liu, Z. (2006). Scalable planning for distributed stream processing systems. Proceedings of the Sixteenth International Conference on Automated Planning and Scheduling (ICAPS 2006).

Rich, C., & Waters, R. C. (1990, January). *The Programmer's Apprentice* (1st Edition). ACM Press Frontier Series and Addison-Wesley.

Richardson, G. P. (1991). *Feedback thought: In social science and systems theory*. Philadelphia: University of Pennsylvania Press.

Rich, C., & Waters, R. (1986). *Readings in Artificial Intelligence and Software Engineering*. San Francisco: Morgan Kaufmann.

Riesenhuber, M., & Poggio, T. (1997). Just One View: Invariances in Inferotemporal Cell Tuning. [MIT Press.]. *Advances in Neural Information Processing Systems*, 215–221.

Riesenhuber, M., & Poggio, T. (1999). Hierarchical Models of Object Recognition in Cortex. *Nature Neuroscience, 2*, 1019–1025. doi:10.1038/14819

Ripley, B. D. (1996). *Pattern Recognition and Neural Networks*. London, UK: Cambridge University Press.

Rock, I., & Gutman, D. (1981). The effect of inattention on form perception. *Journal of Experimental Psychology. Human Perception and Performance, 7*, 275–285. doi:10.1037/0096-1523.7.2.275

Rodriguez, E., & Martin, J. M. (1994). Assessment of the TOPEX Altimeter performance using waveform retracking. *Journal of Geophysical Research, 99*(24), 957–969.

Rosch, E. (1975). Family resemblances: studies in the internal structure of categories. *Cognitive Psychology*, (7): 23–69.

Rosch, E. H. (1973). On the internal structure of perceptual and semantic categories. In Moore, T. E. (Ed.), *Cognitive Development and the Acquisition of Language* (pp. 111–144). Academic Press.

Royce, W. W. (1970). Managing the development of large software systems: Concepts and techniques," *1970 WESCON Technical Papers*, (Western Electronics Show and Convention; Los Angeles; August 1970) pp. A/1-1 to A/1-9. Reprinted in *Proc of the IEEE 11th International Conference on Software Engineering* (Pittsburg, PA; May 1989) (pp. 328-338).

Ruaro, M. E., Bonifazi, P., & Torre, V. (2005, March). Toward the neurocomputer: Image processing and pattern recognition with neuronal cultures. *IEEE Transactions on Bio-Medical Engineering, 52*(3), 371–383. doi:10.1109/TBME.2004.842975

Rubens, W., Emans, B., Leinonen, T., Skarmeta, A. G., & Simons, R.-J. (2005). Design of Web-Based Collaborative Learning Environments. Translating the Pedagogical Learning Principles to Human Computer Interface. *Computers & Education, 45*, 276–294. doi:10.1016/j.compedu.2005.04.008

Rugaber, S. (1995). Program comprehension. *Encyclopedia of Computer Science and Technology, 35*(20), 341–368.

Rumelhart, D. E., & McClelland, J. L. (1986). *Parallel Distributed Processing*. Vols. 1 and 2. Cambridge, MA: MIT Press, (p. 547; 611).

Russell, B. (1970). The Problem of Infinity Considered Historically. In W.C. Salmon (Ed.), *Zeno's Paradoxes*. Indianapolis/Cambridge: Hackett Publishing Co. Inc.

Ryan, R. M., & Deci, E. L. (2000). Self-determination theory and the facilitation of intrinsic motivation, social development, and well-being. *The American Psychologist*, *55*, 68–78. doi:10.1037/0003-066X.55.1.68

Ryan, R. M., Kuhl, J., & Deci, E. l. (1997). Nature and autonomy: Organizational view of social and neurobiological aspects of self-regulation in behaviour and development. *Development and Psychopathology*, *9*, 701–728. doi:10.1017/S0954579497001405

S.C. Stubberud, K.A. Kramer, Data association for multiple sensor types using fuzzy logic, *IEEE Transactions on Instrumentation and Measurement*, 55, 6, 2006, 2292-2303.

Sainsbury, R. M. (1995). *Paradoxes* (2nd ed.). Cambridge: Cambridge University Press.

Salton, G., & Yang, C. S. (1973). On the specification of term values in automatic indexing. *The Journal of Documentation*, *29*(4), 351–372. doi:10.1108/eb026562

Sanchez-Reillo, R., Sanchez-Avila, C., & Gonzalez-Marcos, A. "Multiresolution Analysis and Geometric Measures for Biometric Identification Systems," Secure Networking Proceedings, LNCS, Volume 1740, p. 783, 1999

Santos, F. (1998). *INSS - Un Système Hybride Neuro-Symbolique pour l'Apprentissage Automatique Constructif*, PhD Thesis, LEIBNIZ-IMAG, Grenoble – France.

Saravanan, K., & Mahalakshmi, G. S. (2007), Design And Implementation Of An Ontology Based Approach To Automate Requirements Generation, International Conference on Soft Computing techniques in engineering, SOFTECH – 07, Avinashilingam University for Women, Coimbatore, India.

Schach, S. R. (1999). *Classical and Object-Oriented Software Engineering with UML and Java* (4th ed., p. 616). New York, NY: McGraw Hill.

Schraagen, J. M., Chipman, S. F., & Shalin, V. L. (2000). *Cognitive Task Analysis*. London: Lawrence Erlbaum Associates.

Seamster, T. L., Redding, R. E., & Kaempf, G. L. (1997). *Applied Cognitive Task Analysis in Aviation*. Bodmin, Hartnolls Ltd.

Searle, J. R. (1980). Minds, brains and programs. *The Behavioral and Brain Sciences*, *3*, 417–424. doi:10.1017/S0140525X00005756

Searle, J. R. (1992). *The Rediscovery of the Mind* (p. 288). Cambridge, MA: MIT Press.

Selfridge, O. (1959). Pandemonium: A Paradigm for Learning. In *The Mechanization of Thought Processes*. London: H.M. Stationary Office.

Sendall, S., & Kozacaynski, W. (2003). Model Transformation: the Heart and Soul of Model-Driven Software Development. *IEEE Software*, *20*(5), 42–45. doi:10.1109/MS.2003.1231150

Seo, M., & Barrett, L. R. (2004). The role of affective experience in work motivation. *Academy of Management Review*, *29*, 423–439.

Serrano, M., Romero, R., Trujillo, J. C., & Piattini, M. (2005, July). The advisability of using packages in data warehouse design. In F. B. e Abreu, C. Calero, M. Lanza, G. Poels, & H. A. Sahraoui (Eds.), *Proceedings of the 9th workshop on Quantitative Approaches in Object-Oriented Software Engineering* (pp. 118–128). Montreal: CRIM.

Serre, T., Wold, L., Bileschi, S., & Riesenhuber, M. (2007). Robust Object Recognition with Cortex-Like mechanisms. *IEEE Transactions on Pattern and Machine Intelligence*, *29*(3), 411–426. doi:10.1109/TPAMI.2007.56

Seymore, K., McCallum, A., & Rosenfeld, R. (1999). Learning hidden Markov model structure for information extraction. *AAAI Workshop on Machine Learning for Information Extraction*.

Shannon, C. E. (1948), A Mathematical Theory of Communication, *Bell System Technical Journal*, Vol.27, pp.379-423 and 623-656.

Sharma, N., Joshi, P., & Joshi, R. K. (2006). Applicability of Weyuker's Property 9 to Object Oriented Metrics. *IEEE Transactions on Software Engineering*, *32*(3), 209–211. doi:10.1109/TSE.2006.21

Shen, S., & Davatzikos, C. (2000, August). An Adaptive-Focus Deformable Model Using Statistical and Geometric Information. *IEEE Transactions on Pattern Analysis and Machine Intelligence*, *22*(8), 906–913. doi:10.1109/34.868689

Sheshagiri, M., & desJardins, M. Finin, T. (2003, June). A planner for composing services described in DAML-S. Proceedings of the AAMAS Workshop on Web Services and Agent-based Engineering.

Shevelev, L., Lazareve, N., Sharaev, G., & Novikova, R. (1998). Second-Order Feature Extraction in the Cat Visual Cortex: Selective and Invariant Sensitivity of Neurons to the Shape and Orientation of Crosses and Corners. *Bio Systems*, *48*, 194–204. doi:10.1016/S0303-2647(98)00066-5

Shevelev, L., Lazareve, N., Sharaev, G., & Novikova, R. (1999). Interrelation of Tuning Characteristics to Bar, Cross and Corner in Striate Neurons. *Neuroscience*, *88*, 17–25. doi:10.1016/S0306-4522(98)00168-7

Shi, Z., & Shi, J. (2003). Perspectives on Cognitive Informatics. *Second IEEE International Conference on Cognitive Informatics (ICCI'03)*, August 18-20, (pp. 129-133), London, UK.

Shi, Z., Li, Q., Shi, Z., & Shi, Z. (2006). Semantics-Biased Rapid Retrieval for Video Databases. In Y. Yao, Z. Shi, Y. Wang, & W. Kinsner (Eds.), *Conference on Cognitive Informatics* (pp. 634-639). USA: IEEE Computer Society.

Sienko, T., Adamatzky, A., Rambidi, N. G., & Conrad, M. (2003). *Molecular Computing* (p. 257). Cambridge, MA: MIT Press.

Silerman, S. B., Pogson, C. E., & Cober, A. B. (2005). *When employees at work don't get it: A model for enhancing individual employee change in response to performance feedback. The Academy of Management Executive*, *19*, 135–147. doi:10.5465/AME.2005.16965190

Simon, F., Steinbrückner, F., & Lewerentz, C. (2001, March). Metrics based refactoring. In P. Sousa & J. Ebert (Eds.), *Proceedings of the 5th Conference on Software Maintenance and Reengineering*, (pp. 30–38). IEEE Computer Society Press.

Sirin, E. Parsia, B. (2004). Planning for Semantic Web Services. Semantic Web Services Workshop at the Third International Semantic Web Conference (ISWC 2004). Sivashanmugam, K., Miller, J. A., Sheth, A. P. Verma, K. (04-5). Framework for Semantic Web process composition. International Journal Electronic Commerce, 9(2), 71–106.

Skarda, C. A., & Freeman, W. J. (1987). How Brains Make Chaos into Order. *The Behavioral and Brain Sciences*, 10.

Skogan, D., & Gronmo, R. Solheim, I. (2004). Web Service composition in UML. EDOC '04: Proceedings of the Enterprise Distributed Object Computing Conference, Eighth IEEE International (47–57). Washington, DC, USA: IEEE Computer Society.

Skowron, A., & Stepaniuk, J. (2001). Information Granules: Towards Foundations of Granular Computing. *International Journal of Intelligent Systems*, (16): 57–85. doi:10.1002/1098-111X(200101)16:1<57::AID-INT6>3.0.CO;2-Y

Smith, D. J. (1996). *HDL Chip Design* (p. 448). Madison, AL: Doone Publications.

Soloman, S. (1999). *Sensor Handbook* (p. 1486). New York, NY: McGraw-Hill.

Soloway, E. (1986, September). Learning to program = Learning to construct mechanisms and explanations. *Communications of the ACM*, *29*(9), 850–858. doi:10.1145/6592.6594

Soloway, E., Pinto, J., Letovsky, S., Littman, D., & Lampert, R. (1998, November). Designing documentation to compensate for delocalized plans. *Communications of the ACM*, *31*(11), 1259–1267. doi:10.1145/50087.50088

Sommerville, I. (2006). *Software Engineering* (8th ed., p. 864). Reading, MA: Addison-Wesley.

Sommerville, I., & Sawyer, P. (2004). *Requirements Engineering: A Good Practice Guide* (6th ed.). Pearson Education.

Sperber, D., & Wilson, D. (1995). *Relevance: Communication and Cognition* (2nd ed.). Oxford: Blackwell.

Spinellis, D. (2003, May). *Code Reading: The Open Source Perspective* (1st Edition). Addison Wesley.

Stamper, R. K., & Liu, K. (1994). Organizational dynamics, social norms and information systems. In *proceeding HICSS-27, Los Alamitos (IEEE Computer Society Press)*, VI, 645-654.

Stamper, R. K. (1994). Social Norms in Requirements Analysis – and outline of MEASUR. In Jirotka, M., & Goguen, J. (Eds.), *Requirements Engineering: technical and social aspects*. New York: Academic Press.

Stamper, R. K., Liu, K., Hafkamp, M., & Ades, Y. (2000). Understanding the roles of signs and norms in organizations – a semiotic approach to information systems design. *Behaviour & Information Technology, 19*, 15–27. doi:10.1080/014492900118768

Steece, B. Chulani, S., & Boehm, B. (2002). Determining Software Quality Using COQUALMO. In *Case Studies in Reliability and Maintenance*, W. Blischke and D. Murphy (Ed.), Hoboken, NJ: John Wiley & Sons.

Sternberg, R.J. (2000), Implicit Theory of Intelligence as Exemplar Stories of Success: Why Intelligence Test Validity is in the Eye of the Beholder, *Journal of Psychology, Public Policy, and Law*, (6), 159-167.

Sternberg, R. J. (1997). The Concept of Intelligence and the its Role in Lifelong Learning and Success. *The American Psychologist, 52*(10), 1030–1037. doi:10.1037/0003-066X.52.10.1030

Sternberg, R. J. (2003). *Cognitive Psychology* (3rd ed.). Thomson Wadsworth.

Storer, J. A. (2002). *An Introduction to Data Structures and Algorithms*. Berlin: Springer.

Sugumaran, V., & Storey, V. C. (2003). A semantic-based approach to component retrieval. *SIGMIS Database, 34*(3), 8–24. doi:10.1145/937742.937745

Sutton, R. S., & Barto, A. G. (1998, March). *Reinforcement Learning: An Introduction* (1ˢᵗ Edition). MIT Press.

Tan, X., Wang, Y., & Ngolah, C. F. (2004). A Novel Type Checker for Software System Specifications in RTPA. *Proc. 17th Canadian Conference on Electrical and Computer Engineering* (CCECE'04), IEEE CS Press, Niagara Falls, ON, Canada, May, (pp. 1255-1258).

Tatem, A. J., Lewis, H. G., Atkinson, P. M., & Nixon, M. S. (2002). Super-resolution land cover pattern prediction using a Hopfield neural network. *Remote Sensing of Environment, 79*(1), 1–14. doi:10.1016/S0034-4257(01)00229-2

Taylor, J. G. (2003, June 20-24). The CODAM model of attention and consciousness. In *Proc. Intern. Joint Conf. Neural Networks*, IJCNN03 (Portland. *OR, 1*, 292–297.

Teahan, W., Wen, Y., McNab, R., & Witten, I. (2000, September). A compression-based algorithm for Chinese word segmentation. *Computational Linguistics, 26*(3, 375–393.

Terman, L. M., & Merrill, M. (1961). *Stanford-Binet Intelligence Scale, Manual for the Third Revision*. Houghton Mifflin.

Thomas, D. D., & Moorby, P. R. (1998). *The Verilog Hardware Description Language* (4th ed., p. 354). Boston, MA: Kluwer.

Thomas, L. (1974). *The Lives of a Cell: Notes of a Biology Watcher*. NY: Viking Press.

Thompson, R. A. (2000). *Telephone Switching Systems*. MA, USA: Artech House.

Tikk, D., Biro, G., & Yang, J. (2005). Experiments with a Hierarchical Text Categorization Method on WIPO Patent Collections. In Applied Research in Uncertainty Modeling and Analysis (pp. 283-302). Springer-Verlag.

Triesman, A. (1985, August). Preattentive processing in vision. *Computer Vision Graphics and Image Processing, 31*(2), 156–177. doi:10.1016/S0734-189X(85)80004-9

Tsai, J. J. P., & Weigert, T. (1993). *Knowledge-Based Software Development for Real-Time Distributed Systems*. Singapore: World Scientific Pub.

Tsai, W., & Ghoshal, S. (1998). Social Capital And Value Creation: The Role Of Intrafirm Networks. *Academy of Management Journal, 41*(4), 464–476. doi:10.2307/257085

Tsai, W., Vishnuvajjala, R., & Zhang, D. (1999). Verification and Validation of Knowledge-Based Systems. *IEEE Transactions on Knowledge and Data Engineering, 11*(1), 202–212. doi:10.1109/69.755629

Tsoumakas, G., Angelis, L., & Vlahavas, I. (2004). Clustering classifiers for knowledge discovery from physically distributed databases. *Data & Knowledge Engineering, 49*(3), 223–242. doi:10.1016/j.datak.2003.09.002

Tubbs, M. E., & Ekeberg, S. E. (1991). The role of intentions in work motivation: Implications for goal-setting theory and research. *Academy of Management Review*, *16*, 180–199.

Tulving, E. (1972). Episodic and semantic memory. In Tulving, E., & Donaldson, W. (Eds.), *Organization of memory*. New York, USA: Academic Press.

Turing, A. M. (1950). Computing Machinery and Intelligence. *Mind*, (59): 433–460. doi:10.1093/mind/LIX.236.433

Vahid, F., & Givargis, T. (2002). *Embedded System Design: A Unified Hardware/Software Introduction* (p. 324). New York, NY: Wiley.

Valvano, J. W. (2000). *Embedded Microcomputer Systems: Real-Time Interfacing* (p. 839). Pacific Grove, CA: Brooks/Cole.

Van Eerde, W., & Thierry, H. (1996). Vroom's Expectancy Models and Work-Related Criteria: A Meta-Analysis. *The Journal of Applied Psychology*, *81*, 575–586. doi:10.1037/0021-9010.81.5.575

Vancouver, J. B. (2005). The dept of history and explanation as benefits and bane for psychological control theories. *The Journal of Applied Psychology*, *90*, 38–52. doi:10.1037/0021-9010.90.1.38

Varma, A. K., Gairola, R. M., Kishtawal, C. M., Pandey, P. C., & Singh, K. P. (1999). Rain Rate Estimation From Nadir-Looking TOPEX/POSEIDON Microwave Radiometer (TMR) for Correction of Radar Altimetric Measurements. *IEEE Transactions on Geoscience and Remote Sensing*, *37*(5), 2256–2568. doi:10.1109/36.789650

Vassileva, J. (2004). Harnessing P2P Power in the Classroom. *Intelligent Tutoring Systems (ITS'2004), Lecture Notes in Computer Science 3220*, 305-314.

Veeramachaneni, K., Osadciw, L. A., & Varshney, P. K. "Adaptive Multimodal Biometric Fusion Algorithm Using Particle Swarm," SPIE, vol 5099, pp. 211, Orlando, Florida, April 21- 25, 2003

Vereijken, J. J. (1995, June). A Process Algebra for Hybrid Systems. In A. Bouajjani & O. Maler (Eds.), *Proc. 2nd European Workshop on Real-Time and Hybrid Systems*, Grenoble, France.

Vermesan, A. I. (1998). *Foundation and Application of Expert System Verification and Validation*. The Handbook of Applied Expert Systems. Ed. CRC Press LLC, (pp. 5.1–5.32).

Villanueva, T. J., Cruz, S. V. G., Reyes, S. G., & Benítez, A. (2006). Extracting Refined Rules from Hybrid Neuro-Symbolic Systems. *Proceedings of the International Joint Conference on Neural Networks (IJCNN'06)* (pp. 3021-3025). Vancouver, Canada, July.

Virupakshananda, S. (1994). *Tarka Samgraha*. Madras: Sri Ramakrishna Math.

Viterbi, A. (1967, April). Error bounds for convolutional codes and an asymptotically optimal decoding algorithm. *IEEE Transactions on Information Theory*, *IT-13*(2), 260–269. doi:10.1109/TIT.1967.1054010

von Bertalanffy, L. (1952). *Problems of Life: An Evolution of Modern Biological and Scientific Thought*. London: C.A. Watts.

von Neumann, J. (1946). The Principles of Large-Scale Computing Machines. *Reprinted in Annals of History of Computers*, *3*(3), 263–273. doi:10.1109/MAHC.1981.10025

von Neumann, J. (1958). *The Computer and the Brain*. New Haven: Yale Univ. Press.

von Neumann, J., & Burks, A. W. (1966). *Theory of Self-Reproducing Automata*. Urbana, IL: Univ. of Illinois Press.

Vroom, V. H. (1964). *Work Motivation*. New York: John Wiley and Sons.

Waddinggton, D., & Lardieri, P. (2006). Model-Centric Software Development. *IEEE Computer*, *39*(2), 28–29.

Wallace, J., Silverstein, R., Bluff, K., & Pipingas, A. (1994). Semantic transparency, brain monitoring and evaluation of hybrid cognitive architectures. *Connection Science*, *6*(1). doi:10.1080/09540099408915709

Wang, G.Y. (2001). *Rough set theory and knowledge acquisition*. Xi'an, P.R. China: Press of Xi'an Jiaotong University.

Wang, G.Y. (2001). Uncertainty measurement of decision table information systems. *Computer Science*, *28*(5, Special Issue), 23-26.

Wang, G.Y., & He X. (2002). Knowledge self-learning model based on rough set theory. *Computer Science, 29*(9, Special Issue), pp.24-25.

Wang, X., & Wood, D. (1998). A Conceptual Model for Tables, Principles of Digital Document Processing PODDP '98.In E. Munson, C. Nicholas, & D. Wood (Eds.), *Springer-Verlag Lecture Notes in Computer Science 1481*(1998), 10-23.

Wang, Y. (2002), The Real-Time Process Algebra (RTPA), *Annals of Software Engineering: An International Journal,* 14, USA, Oct., pp. 235-274.

Wang, Y. (2002), Keynote: On Cognitive Informatics, *Proc. 1st IEEE International Conference on Cognitive Informatics* (ICCI'02), Calgary, Canada, IEEE CS Press, August, 34-42.

Wang, Y. (2003). Cognitive informatics models of software agent systems and autonomic computing: Keynote Speech. In *Proc. Intern. Conf. Agent-Based Technologies and Systems (ATS'03)*, U of C Press, Calgary, Canada, August, (p. 25).

Wang, Y. (2003). On cognitive informatics. *Brain and Mind: A Transdisciplinary Journal of Neuroscience and Neuro-philosophy, 4*(2), 151-167.

Wang, Y. (2003). The Measurement Theory for Software Engineering. *Proceedings of Canadian Conference on Electrical and Computer Engineering CCECE 2003*, pp. 1321-1324.

Wang, Y. (2003), Using Process Algebra to Describe Human and Software System Behaviors, *Brain and Mind: A Transdisciplinary Journal of Neuroscience and Neurophilosophy*, 4(2), 199-213.

Wang, Y. (2004), Keynote: On Autonomic Computing and Cognitive Processes, *Proc. 3rd IEEE International Conference on Cognitive Informatics (ICCI'04)*, Victoria, Canada, IEEE CS Press, August, 3-4.

Wang, Y. (2004). On Cognitive Informatics: Foundation of Software Engineering. *Proceeding of the 3rd IEEE International Conference on Cognitive Informatics* (ICCI'04), IEEE CS Press, pp.22-31.

Wang, Y. (2005), Keynote: Psychological Experiments on the Cognitive Complexities of Fundamental Control Structures of Software Systems, *Proc. 4th IEEE International Conference on Cognitive Informatics* (ICCI'05), IEEE CS Press, Irvin, California, USA, August, pp. 4-5.

Wang, Y. (2006), Keynote: Cognitive Informatics - Towards the Future Generation Computers that Think and Feel, *Proc. 5th IEEE International Conference on Cognitive Informatics* (ICCI'06), Beijing, China, IEEE CS Press, July, 3-7.

Wang, Y. (2006). Cognitive Informatics and Contemporary Mathematics for Knowledge Representation and Manipulation, Invited Plenary Talk. *Proc. 1st International Conference on Rough Set and Knowledge Technology (RSKT'06), LNAI 4062*, Springer, Chongqing, China, July, pp. 69-78.

Wang, Y. (2006a, July). Cognitive Complexity of Software and its Measurement. *Proc. 5th IEEE International Conference on Cognitive Informatics* (ICCI'06) (pp. 226-235). Beijing, China: IEEE CS Press.

Wang, Y. (2006b, July). On Concept Algebra and Knowledge Representation. *Proc. 5th IEEE International Conference on Cognitive Informatics* (ICCI'06) (pp. 320-331). Beijing, China: IEEE CS Press.

Wang, Y. (2007, July). *Software Engineering Foundations: A Software Science Perspective*. CRC Series in Software Engineering (Vol. II). Auerbach Publications, USA.

Wang, Y. (2007), *Software Engineering Foundations: A Transdisciplinary and Rigorous Perspective*, CRC Book Series in Software Engineering, Vol. II, Auerbach Publications, NY, USA, July.

Wang, Y. (2007). On Cognitive Informatics Foundations of Knowledge and Formal Knowledge Systems. In D. Zhang, Y. Wang, & W. Kinsner (Eds.), *Conference on Cognitive Informatics* (pp. 263-272). USA: IEEE Computer Society.

Wang, Y. (2007), Wang, Y. (2007), The Theoretical Framework of Cognitive Informatics, *International Journal of Cognitive Informatics and Natural Intelligence*, IGI, Hershey, PA, USA, Jan., 10-22

Wang, Y. (2007). Formal Description of the Cognitive Process of Memorization. *Proc. 6th International Conference on Cognitive Informatics* (ICCI'07), IEEE CS Press, Lake Tahoe, CA., Aug., (pp. 284-293).

Wang, Y. (2007). Formal Linguistics and the Deductive Grammar. In D. Zhang, Y. Wang, & W. Kinsner (Eds.), *Conference on Cognitive Informatics* (pp. 43-51). USA: IEEE Computer Society.

Wang, Y. (2007), Keynote: On Theoretical Foundations of Software Engineering and Denotational Mathematics, *Proc. 5th Asian Workshop on Foundations of Software*, Beihang Univ. Press, Xiamen, China, 99-102.

Wang, Y. (2007), Keynote: Cognitive Informatics Foundations of Nature and Machine Intelligence. *Proc. 6th IEEE International Conference on Cognitive Informatics* (ICCI'07), (pp. 2-12). Lake Tahoe, CA, USA, IEEE CS Press.

Wang, Y. (2007). The Theoretical Framework and Cognitive Process of Learning. *Proc. 6th International Conference on Cognitive Informatics* (ICCI'07), (pp. 470-479). IEEE CS Press.

Wang, Y. (2008). On Visual Semantic Algebra (VSA) and the cognitive process of pattern recognition. *7th IEEE International Conference on Cognitive Informatics* (pp. 384-393), Stanford, CA

Wang, Y. (2008), Keynote: Abstract Intelligence and Its Denotational Mathematics Foundations, *Proc. 7th IEEE International Conference on Cognitive Informatics* (ICCI'08), Stanford University, CA, USA, IEEE CS Press, August, 3-12.

Wang, Y. (2008), *On Contemporary Denotational Mathematics for Computational Intelligence, Transactions of Computational Science, 2*, Springer, August, pp. 6-29.

Wang, Y. (2008), On Cognitive Foundations of Creativity and the Cognitive Process of Creation, *Proc. 7th IEEE International Conference on Cognitive Informatics* (ICCI'08), Stanford University, CA, USA, IEEE CS Press, August, pp. 104-113.

Wang, Y. (2008), Mathematical Laws of Software, *Transactions of Computational Science, 2*, Springer, Aug., pp. 46-83.

Wang, Y. (2008e). The Cognitive Processes of Analysis and Synthesis in Formal Inference. *Proc. 7th IEEE International Conference on Cognitive Informatics* (ICCI'08). Stanford University, CA., USA, IEEE CS Press, August, pp. 223-231.

Wang, Y. (2009), Convergence of Software Science and Computational Intelligence: A New Transdisciplinary research Field, *International Journal of Software Science and Computational Intelligence,* IGI, USA, Jan., 1(1), i-xii.

Wang, Y. (2009), A Cognitive Informatics Reference Model of Autonomous Agent Systems, *International Journal of Cognitive Informatics and Natural Intelligence,* Jan., 3(1), 1-16.

Wang, Y. (2009), On Abstract Intelligence: Toward a Unified Theory of Natural, Artificial, Machinable, and Computational Intelligence, *International Journal of Software Science and Computational Intelligence,* IGI, USA, Jan., 1(1), 1-17.

Wang, Y. (2009d, June). Granular Algebra for Modeling Granular Systems and Granular Computing. *Proc. 8th IEEE International Conference on Cognitive Informatics* (ICCI'09). Hong Kong, IEEE CS Press, to appear.

Wang, Y. "Cognitive informatics: A new transdisciplinary research field." Brain and Mind: A Transdisciplinary Journal of Neuroscience and Neurophilosophy, 4(2), 115-127, 2003

Wang, Y., & Chiew, V. (2009). On the Cognitive Process of Human Problem Solving, *Cognitive Systems Research: An International Journal, 10*(4), Elsevier, to appear.

Wang, Y., & Hu, J. (2002, August). Detecting Tables in HTML Documents. In D. Lopresti, J. Hu, & R. Kashi (Eds.), *Document Image Analysis System V, 5th International Workshop DAS 2002*, Princeton, NJ, USA.

Wang, Y., & King, G. (2000). Software Engineering Processes: Principles and Applications. *CRC Series in Software Engineering* (Vol. I). CRC Press, USA.

Wang, Y., & Noglah, C. F. (2002). Formal Specification of a Real-Time Lift Dispatching System. *Proc. 2002 IEEE Canadian Conference on Electrical and Computer Engineering (CCECE'02),* Winnipeg, Manitoba, Canada, May, (pp. 669-674).

Wang, Y., & Shao, J. (2003), Measurement of the Cognitive Functional Complexity of Software, *Proc. 2nd IEEE International Conference on Cognitive Informatics* (ICCI'03), IEEE CS Press, London, UK, August, pp.67-74.

Wang, Y., & Wang, Y. (2002). Cognitive Models of the Brain. In Proceedings of the 1st IEEE International Conference on Cognitive Informatics (ICCC'02), IEEE CS Press, Calgary, Canada, August 2002, 552.

Wang, Y., & Wang, Y. (2008). The cognitive processes of consciousness and attention. *7th IEEE International Conference on Cognitive Informatics* (pp. 30-39), Stanford, CA.

Wang, Y., & Zhang, Y. (2003), Formal Description of an ATM System by RTPA, *Proc. 16th Canadian Conference on Electrical and Computer Engineering* (CCECE'03), IEEE CS Press, Montreal, Canada, May, 1255-1258.

Wang, Y., Johnston, R., & Smith, M. (Eds.). (2002, August). *Proc. 1st Int. Conf. of Cognitive Informatics* (ICCI'02)., Calgary, Canada: IEEE CS Press.

Wang, Y., L.A. Zadeh, and Y. Yao (2009), On the System Algebra Foundations for Granular Computing, *International Journal of Software Science and Computational Intelligence*, IGI, USA, Jan., 1(1), 64-86.

Wang, G. Y., & He, X. (2003). A self-learning model under uncertain condition. *Journal of Software*, 14(6), 1096-1102.

Wang, H., Gavrilova, M. L., Luo, Y., & Rokne, J. (2006). *"An Efficient Algorithm for Fingerprint Matching"*, *ICPR 2006, Int. C. on Pattern Recognition*. Hong Kong: IEEE-CS.

Wang, Y. (1996). A New Sorting Algorithm: Self-Indexed Sort. *ACM SIGPLAN*, 31(3), 28-36. doi:10.1145/227717.227725

Wang, Y. (2000). *Software Engineering Processes: Principles and Applications, CRC Software Engineering Series* (Vol. 1). USA: CRC Press.

Wang, Y. (2002). The Latest Development on Cognitive Informatics. *Lecture Notes in Computer Science*, 2452, 3-4.

Wang, Y. (2003). On the Latest Development in Cognitive Informatics. [SEN]. *ACM Software Engineering Notes*, 27(2), 28.

Wang, Y. (2003). Using Process Algebra to Describe Human and Software System Behaviors. *Brain and Mind*, 4(2), 199-213. doi:10.1023/A:1025457612549

Wang, Y. (2006). On the Informatics Laws and Deductive Semantics of Software. *IEEE Transactions on Systems, Man and Cybernetics. Part C, Applications and Reviews*, 36(2), 161-171. doi:10.1109/TSMCC.2006.871138

Wang, Y. (2007). *Software Engineering Foundations: A Software Science Perspective. CRC Book Series in Software Engineering* (Vol. 2). NY: Auerbach Publications.

Wang, Y. (2007). The Theoretical Framework of Cognitive Informatics. *International Journal of Cognitive Informatics and Natural Intelligence*, 1(1), 1-27. doi:10.4018/jcini.2007010101

Wang, Y. (2007, July). The OAR Model of Neural Informatics for Internal Knowledge Representation in the Brain. [Hershey, PA, USA: IGI Publishing.]. *International Journal of Cognitive Informatics and Natural Intelligence*, 1(3), 64-75.

Wang, Y. (2007). *Software Engineering Foundations: A Software Science Perspective, CRC Series in Software Engineering* (Vol. II). NY, USA: Auerbach Publications.

Wang, Y. (2007). On The Cognitive Processes of Human Perception with Emotions, Motivations, and Attitudes, *International Journal of Cognitive Informatics and Natural Intelligence. IGI Publishing, USA*, 1(4), 1-13.

Wang, Y. (2008). On Contemporary Denotational Mathematics for Computational Intelligence. *Transactions of Computational Science*, 2, 6-29. doi:10.1007/978-3-540-87563-5_2

Wang, Y. (2008). RTPA: A Denotational Mathematics for Manipulating Intelligent and Computational Behaviors. *International Journal of Cognitive Informatics and Natural Intelligence*, 2(2), 44-62. doi:10.4018/jcini.2008040103

Wang, Y. (2008). Deductive Semantics of RTPA. *International Journal of Cognitive Informatics and Natural Intelligence*, 2(2), 95-121. doi:10.4018/jcini.2008040106

Wang, Y. (2008). On Concept Algebra: A Denotational Mathematical Structure for Knowledge and Software Modeling, *International Journal of Cognitive Informatics and Natural Intelligence. IGI Publishing, USA*, 2(2), 1-19.

Wang, Y. (2008). On the Big-R Notation for Describing Iterative and Recursive Behaviors. *International Journal of Cognitive Informatics and Natural Intelligence*, *2*(1), 17–28. doi:10.4018/jcini.2008010102

Wang, Y. (2008). Mathematical Laws of Software. *Transactions of Computational Science*, *2*, 46–83. doi:10.1007/978-3-540-87563-5_4

Wang, Y. (2008). On System Algebra: A Denotational Mathematical Structure for Abstract Systems, Modeling. *International Journal of Cognitive Informatics and Natural Intelligence*, *2*(2), 20–43. doi:10.4018/jcini.2008040102

Wang, Y. (2008). Deductive Semantics of RTPA. *International Journal of Cognitive Informatics and Natural Intelligence*, *2*(2), 95–121. doi:10.4018/jcini.2008040106

Wang, Y. (2008). On Cognitive Properties of Human Factors and Error Models in Engineering and Socialization. *International Journal of Cognitive Informatics and Natural Intelligence*, *2*(4), 70–84. doi:10.4018/jcini.2008100106

Wang, Y. (2008). RTPA: A Denotational Mathematics for Manipulating Intelligent and Computational Behaviors. *International Journal of Cognitive Informatics and Natural Intelligence*, *2*(2), 44–62. doi:10.4018/jcini.2008040103

Wang, Y. (2009). (to appear). The Formal Design Model of a Telephone Switching System (TSS). *International Journal of Software Science and Computational Intelligence*, *1*(3).

Wang, Y. (2009). On the Cognitive Complexity of Software and its Quantification and Formal Measurement. *International Journal of Software Science and Computational Intelligence*, *1*(2), 31–53. doi:10.4018/jssci.2009040103

Wang, Y. (2009). Formal Description of the Cognitive Process of Memorization. *Transactions of Computational Science*, *5*, 81–98.

Wang, Y. (2009). Formal Descriptions of the Cognitive Processes of Spatiality, Time, and Motion Perceptions. *International Journal of Cognitive Informatics and Natural Intelligence*, *3*(2), 84–98.

Wang, Y. (2009). (to appear). The Cognitive Informatics Theory and Mathematical Models of Visual Information Processing in the Brain. *International Journal of Cognitive Informatics and Natural Intelligence*, *3*(3).

Wang, Y. (2009). A Cognitive Informatics Reference Model of Autonomous Agent Systems (AAS). *International Journal of Cognitive Informatics and Natural Intelligence*, *3*(1), 1–16. doi:10.4018/jcini.2009010101

Wang, Y. (2009). On the Cognitive Complexity of Software and its Quantification and Formal Measurement. *International Journal of Software Science and Computational Intelligence*, *1*(2), 31–53. doi:10.4018/jssci.2009040103

Wang, Y., & King, G. (2000). *Software Engineering Processes: Principles and Applications, CRC Series in Software Engineering* (*Vol. I*). USA: CRC Press.

Wang, Y., King, G., Fayad, M., Patel, D., Court, I., Staples, G., & Ross, M. (2000, March). On Built-in Tests Reuse in Object-Oriented Framework Design. *ACM Journal on Computing Surveys*, *32*(1es), 7–12. doi:10.1145/351936.351943

Wang, Y., & Kinsner, W. (2006). Recent Advances in Cognitive Informatics. *IEEE Transactions on Systems, Man, and Cybernetics*, *36*(2), 121–123. doi:10.1109/TSMCC.2006.871120

Wang, Y., Kinsner, W., Anderson, J. A., Zhang, D., Yao, Y. Y., & Sheu, P. (2009). A Doctrine of Cognitive Informatics. *Fundamenta Informaticae*, *90*(3), 203–228.

Wang, Y., Kinsner, W., & Zhang, D. (2009). Convergence of Cognitive Informatics and Cybernetics—Guest Editorial on Special Issue on Cybernetics and Cognitive Informatics. *IEEE Transactions on Systems, Man, and Cybernetics. Part B, Cybernetics*, *39*(4), 1–5.

Wang, Y., Kinsner, W., & Zhang, D. (2009). Contemporary Cybernetics and its Faces of Cognitive Informatics and Computational Intelligence. *IEEE Trans. on System, Man, and Cybernetics (B)*, *39*(4), 823–833. doi:10.1109/TSMCB.2009.2013721

Wang, Y., & Ruhe, G. (2007). The Cognitive Process of Decision Making. *International Journal of Cognitive Informatics and Natural Intelligence*, *1*(2), 73–85. doi:10.4018/jcini.2007040105

Wang, Y., & Shao, J. (2003). A New Measure of Software Complexity Based on Cognitive Weight. *Canadian Journal of Electrical and Computer Engineering*, 69–74.

Wang, Y., & Sheu, P. (2008). (to appear). Toward Cognitive Computers that Learn and Think. *ACM Transactions on Autonomous and Adaptive Systems*, 2(4).

Wang, Y., Tan, X., & Ngolah, F. C. (2010). (to appear). Design and Implementation of Automatic Code Generators Based on RTPA. *International Journal of Software Science and Computational Intelligence*, 2(3).

Wang, Y., & Wang, Y. (2006). Cognitive Informatics Models of the Brain. *IEEE Transactions on Systems, Man and Cybernetics. Part C, Applications and Reviews*, 36(2), 203–207. doi:10.1109/TSMCC.2006.871151

Wang, Y., & Wang, Y. (2006). On Cognitive Informatics Models of the Brain. *IEEE Transactions on Systems, Man and Cybernetics. Part C, Applications and Reviews*, 36(2), 16–20.

Wang, Y., Wang, Y., Patel, S., & Patel, D. (2006). A Layered Reference Model of the Brain (LRMB). *IEEE Transactions on Systems, Man and Cybernetics. Part C, Applications and Reviews*, 36(2), 124–133. doi:10.1109/TSMCC.2006.871126

Wang, Y., Zadeh, L. A., & Yao, Y. (2009). On the System Algebra Foundations for Granular Computing. *International Journal of Software Science and Computational Intelligence*, 1(1), 64–86. doi:10.4018/jssci.2009010105

Wasko, M. M., & Faraj, S. (2005). Why Should I Share? Examining Social Capital And Knowledge Contribution in Electronic Networks Of Practice. *Management Information Systems Quarterly*, 29(1), 35–57.

Wecker, L., Samavati, F., & Gavrilova, M. L. "Iris Synthesis: A Multi-Resolution Approach," GRAPHITE 2005, ACM Press, in association with SIGGRAPH, pp. 121-125, 2005

Weeks, M. (2007). *Digital Signal Processing Using Matlab and Wavelets* (p. 452). Hingham, MA: Infinity Science press LLC.

Wegener, I. (1987). *The Complexity of Boolean Functions*. Chichester: Wiley.

Weinberger, A., & Fischer, F. (2006). A Framework to Analyze Argumentative Knowledge Construction in Computer-Supported Collaborative Learning. *Computers & Education*, 46, 71–95. doi:10.1016/j.compedu.2005.04.003

Weinberg, G. M. (1971). *The Psychology of Computer Programming*. New York: Van Nostrand Reinhold.

Welty, C. Fikes, R. (2006, November). A reusable ontology for fluents in OWL. Formal Ontology in Information Systems: Proceedings of the 4th Intl Conference (FOIS 2006), Volume 150 Frontiers in Artificial Intelligence and Applications. IOS Press.

Wendorff, P. (2001, March). Assessment of design patterns during software reengineering: Lessons learned from a large commercial project. In P. Sousa & J. Ebert (Eds.), *Proceedings of 5th Conference on Software Maintenance and Reengineering* (pp. 77–84). IEEE Computer Society Press.

Westen, D. (1999). *Psychology: Mind, Brain, and Culture* (2nd ed.). John Wiley & Sons, Inc.

Weyuker, E. J. (1988). Evaluating Software Complexity Measure. *IEEE Transactions on Software Engineering*, 14, 1357–1365. doi:10.1109/32.6178

Whitehead, N. (1925). *Science and the Modern World*. Cambridge: Cambridge Univ. Press.

Whitehouse, K., & Zhao, F. Liu, J. (2006). Semantic streams: A framework for composable semantic interpretation of sensor data. Proceedings of The Third European Workshop on Wireless Sensor Networks (EWSN '06).

Wilson, R. A., & Keil, F. C. (2001). *The MIT Encyclopedia of the Cognitive Sciences*. MIT Press.

Wilson, R. A., & Frank, C. K. (Eds.). (1999). *The MIT Encyclopedia of the Cognitive Sciences*. MA: MIT Press.

Wiswedel, B., & Berthold, M. R. (2007). Fuzzy clustering in parallel universes. *J. of Approximate Reasoning*, 45, 439–454. doi:10.1016/j.ijar.2006.06.020

Witten, I., & Bell, T. (1991). The zero-frequency problem: Estimating the probablities of novel events on adaptive text compression. *IEEE Transactions on Information Theory*, 37(4), 1085–1094. doi:10.1109/18.87000

Wittgenstein, L. (1921). Logisch-Philosophische Abhandlung. In W. Ostwald (Ed.), *Annalen der Naturphilosophie* (vol. 14) (pp. 185-262).

Wolf, W. (2002). *Modern VLSI Design: Systems-on-Chip Design* (3rd ed., p. 640). Upper Saddle River, NJ: Prentice Hall.

Wong, C. C., Chou, M. F., Hwang, C. P., Tsai, C. H., & Shyu, S. R. "A method for obstacle avoidance and shooting action of the robot soccer," Robotics and Automation, proceedings ICRA. IEEE International Conference, pp 3778- 3782 vol.4 2001

Woodward, M. R., & Hennel, M. A. (1979). David. A Measure of Control Flow Complexity in Program Text. *IEEE Transactions on Software Engineering, 1*, 45–50. doi:10.1109/TSE.1979.226497

Wu, Q., Zhou, C., Wu, J., & Wang, C. (2005). Study on Knowledge Base Verification Based on Petri Nets. *International Conference on Control and Automatization (ICCA2005)* (pp. 997–1001), Budapest, Hungry.

Wu, C. H., & Lee, S. J. (1997). Enhanced High Level Petri Nets with Multiple Colors for Knowledge Verification/Validation of Rule-Based Expert Systems. *IEEE Trans. on Systems, Man, and Cybernetics. Part B., 27*(5), 760–773.

Wu, C., & Lee, S. (2000). A Token-Flow Paradigm for Verification of Rule-Based Expert Systems. *IEEE Trans. on Systems, Man, and Cybernetics. Part B., 30*(4), 616–624.

Y. Wang, On Cognitive Informatics, *Brain and Mind, 4*, 2, 2003, 151-167.

Y. Wang, W. Kinsner, Recent advances in Cognitive Informatics, *IEEE Transactions on Systems, Man, and Cybernetics, Part C*, 36, 2, 2006, 121-123.

Yager, R. R. (1995). Linguistic summaries as a tool for database discovery. In *Proceedings of FUZZ-IEEE'95/IFES'95, Workshop on Fuzzy Database Systems and Information Retrieval, (Yokohama, Japan)* (pp. 79 – 82).

Yager, R. R. (1982). A new approach to the summarization of data. *Information Sciences, 28*, 69–86. doi:10.1016/0020-0255(82)90033-0

Yager, R. R. (1988). On ordered weighted avaraging operators in multicriteria decision making. *IEEE Transactions on Systems, Man, and Cybernetics, SMC-18*, 183–190. doi:10.1109/21.87068

Yager, R. R. (1991). On linguistic summaries of data. In Piatetsky-Shapiro, G., & Frawley, B. (Eds.), *Knowledge Discovery in Databases* (pp. 347–363). Cambridge, USA: MIT Press.

Yager, R. R. (1996). Database discovery using fuzzy sets. *International Journal of Intelligent Systems, 11*, 691–712. doi:10.1002/(SICI)1098-111X(199609)11:9<691::AID-INT7>3.0.CO;2-F

Yager, R. R., & Kacprzyk, J. (Eds.). (1997). *The Ordered Weighted Averaging Operators: Theory and Applications*. Boston: Kluwer. doi:10.1007/978-1-4615-6123-1

Yahoo Pipes. (2007) Retrieved from the Web 5/8/2008. http://pipes.yahoo.com/pipes/

Yang, J., Papazoglou, M. P., & Orriëns, B. van Heuvel, W.-J. (2003). A rule based approach to the service composition life-cycle. WISE '03: Proceedings of the Fourth International Conference on Web Information Systems Engineering (295). Washington, DC, USA: IEEE Computer Society.

Yang, S. J. H., Lee, A. S., Chu, W. C., & Yang, H. (1998). Rule Base Verification Using Petri Nets. In *Proccedings 22-nd Annual Int. Computer Software and Applications Conf. (COMPSAC-98)* (pp. 476-481), Vienna, Austria, august.

Yang, S. J. H., Zhang, J., & Chen, I. Y. L. (2007). Web 2.0 Services for Identifying Communities of Practice through Social Networks. in *Proceedings of IEEE International Conference on Services Computing (SCC 2007)*, Salt Lake City, UT, USA, 130-137.

Yanushkevich, S., Wang, P., Srihari, S., & Gavrilova, M. L. (2006). *Image Pattern Recognition: Synthesis and Analysis in Biometrics, Book*. World Scientific.

Yao, Y. Y. (2004). Concept formation and learning: a cognitive informatics perspective. In C. W. Chan, W. Kinsner, Y. Wang, & M. Miller (Eds.), *Proceedings of the 3rd IEEE International Conference on Cognitive Informatics* (pp. 42-51), IEEE CS Press, Victoria, Canada.

Yao, Y. Y. (2004) Granular Computing, *Computer Science, Beijing, China*, (31), 1-5.

Yao, Y. Y. (2005) Perspectives of Granular Computing, *Proc. 2005 IEEE International Conference on Granular Computing*, (1), 85-90.

Yao, Y. Y. (2001). Information Granulation and Rough Set Approximation. *International Journal of Intelligent Systems*, 16(1), 87–104. doi:10.1002/1098-111X(200101)16:1<87::AID-INT7>3.0.CO;2-S

Yao, Y. Y. (2004). A Partition Model of Granular Computing, *Transactions on Rough Sets, 1. Springer, LNCS, 3135*, 232–253.

Yao, Y. Y., & Zhou, B. (2008). A Logic Approach to Granular Computing, *International Journal of Cognitive Informatics and Natural Intelligence. IGI Publishing, USA*, 2(2), 63–79.

Yaremchuk, V., & Dawson, M. R. W. (2008). Artificial Neural Networks That Classify Musical Chords. *International Journal of Cognitive Informatics and Natural Intelligence*, 2(3), 22–30. doi:10.4018/jcini.2008070102

Yourdon, E. (1997). *Death March—The Complete Software Developer's Guide to Surviving "Mission Impossible" Projects*. Upper Saddle River, N.J.: Prentice Hall PTR.

Yuqin Lee and Wenyun Zhao. (2006), "An Ontology-based Approach for Domain Requirements Elicitation and Analysis", In IEEE Proc. of the First International Multi-Symposiums on Computer and Computational Sciences.

Zadeh, L. A. (1965), Fuzzy Sets and Systems, in J. Fox ed., *Systems Theory*, Polytechnic Press, Brooklyn NY, 29-37.

Zadeh, L. A. (1979), Fuzzy Sets and Information Granularity, in M.M. Gupta, R. Ragade, and R. Yager eds., *Advances in Fuzzy Set Theory and Applications*, North-Holland, Amsterdam, 3-18.

Zadeh, L. A., & Kacprzyk, J. (Eds.). (1999). *Computing with Words in Information/Intelligent Systems, 1. Foundations, 2. Applications*. Heidelberg and New York: Physica-Verlag (Springer-Verlag).

Zadeh, L.A. (2003), Some Reflections on Information Granulation and its Centrality in Granular Computing, Computing with Words. The Computational Theory of Perceptions and Precisiated Natural Language. *Proc. Data Mining, Rough Sets and Granular Computing*, Heideberg, 1-19.

Zadeh, L. A. (1965). Fuzzy Sets and Systems. In Fox, J. (Ed.), *Systems Theory* (pp. 29–37). Brooklyn, NY: Polytechnic Press.

Zadeh, L. A. (1983). A computational approach to fuzzy quantifiers in natural languages. *Computers & Mathematics with Applications (Oxford, England)*, 9, 149–184. doi:10.1016/0898-1221(83)90013-5

Zadeh, L. A. (1985). Syllogistic reasoning in fuzzy logic and its application to usuality and reasoning with dispositions. *IEEE Transactions on Systems, Man, and Cybernetics*, SMC-15, 754–763.

Zadeh, L.A. (1997). Towards a Theory of Fuzzy Information Granulation and its Centrality in Human Reasoning and Fuzzy Logic. *Fuzzy Sets and Systems*, (19): 111–127. doi:10.1016/S0165-0114(97)00077-8

Zadeh, L.A. (1998). Some Reflections on Soft Computing, Granular Computing and Their Roles in the Conception, Design and Utilization of Information/Intelligent Systems. *Soft Computing*, (2): 23–25. doi:10.1007/s005000050030

Zadeh, L. A. (1999). From computing with numbers to computing with words-from manipulation of measurements to manipulation of perceptions. *IEEE Transactions on Circuits and Systems*, 45, 105–119.

Zadeh, L.A. (2002). A prototype-centered approach to adding deduction capabilities to search engines – the concept of a protoform. In *BISC Seminar, 2002*. Berkeley: University of California. doi:10.1109/NAFIPS.2002.1018115

Zadeh, L. A. (2005). Toward a generalized theory of uncertainty (GTU)—an outline. *Information Sciences*, 172, 1–40. doi:10.1016/j.ins.2005.01.017

Zadrożny, S., & Kacprzyk, J. (1995) Fuzzy querying using the 'query-by-example' option in a Windows-based DBMS, *Proceedings of Third European Congress on Intelligent Techniques and Soft Computing - EUFIT'95 (Aachen, Germany)*, vol. 2 (pp. 733 – 736).

Zadrożny, S., & Kacprzyk, J. (1999). On database summarization using a fuzzy querying interface. In *Proceedings of IFSA'99 World Congress (Taipei, Taiwan R.O.C.)*, Vol. 1, (pp. 39 – 43).

Zadrożny, S., & Kacprzyk, J. (2007) Summarizing the contents of Web server logs: a fuzzy linguistic approach. *Proceedings of FUZZ-IEEE'2007 – The 2007 IEEE Conference on Fuzzy Systems (London, UK, July 23-26, 2007)*, pp. 1860 – 1865.

Zak, S. H. (2003). *Systems and Control* (p. 704). Oxford, UK: Oxford University Press.

Zanibbi, R., R., Blostein, D., & Cordy, J. (2004, March). A Survey of Table Recognition: Models, Observations, Transformations, and Inferences. *International Journal of Document Analysis and Recognition, 7*(1), 1–16.

Zhang, D. (2000). Applying Machine Learning Algorithms in Software Development. *Proceedings of Monterey Workshop on Modeling Software System Structures*, Santa Margherita Ligure, Italy, pp.275-285.

Zhang, D. (2005). Fixpoint semantics for rule-base anomalies. In W. Kinsner, D. Zhang, Y. Wang & J. Tsai (Eds.), *Computer and Cognitive Informatics* (pp. 10-17). USA: IEEE Computer Society.

Zhang, D. (2006). Machine Learning in Value-Based Software Test Data Generation. Proceedings of the *Eighteenth IEEE International Conference on Tools with AI*, Washington DC, pp.732-736.

Zhang, D. (2008). A Value-Based Framework for Software Evolutionary Testing. Submitted for publication.

Zhang, G. Jin, Q. and Lin, M. (2005). A Framework ff Social Interaction Support for Ubiquitous Learning. in *Proceedings of the 19th International Conference on Advanced Information Networking and Applications (AINA'05).*

Zhang, L., Xie, D.(2002): Comments on 'On the Applicability of Weyuker Property Nine to Object Oriented Structural Inheritance Complexity Metrics. *IEEE Transactions on Software Engineering*, vol. 28, 5, (2002) 526-527.

Zhang, D., & Tsai, J. J. P. (2003). Machine Learning and Software Engineering. *Software Quality Journal, 11*(2), 87–119. doi:10.1023/A:1023760326768

Zhang, D., & Tsai, J. J. P. (2005). *Machine Learning Applications in Software Engineering*. Singapore: World Scientific Publishing Co.

Zhang, D., & Tsai, J. J. P. (2007). *Advances in Machine Learning Applications in Software Engineering*. Hershey, PA: Idea Group Publishing.

Zheng, L., Luo, F., Shan, C., & Yin, W. (2008). A novel cognitive model of reading: Neuropsychology research on internal processing of the brain. *7th IEEE International Conference on Cognitive Informatics* (pp. 122-127), Stanford, CA.

Zhu, L., Rao, A., & Zhang, A. (2002). Theory of Keyblock-based Image Retrieval. *ACM Transactions on Information Systems, 20*, 224–257. doi:10.1145/506309.506313

Ziarko, W. (1993). Variable precision rough set model. *Artificial Intelligence, 46*, 39–59.

Zieger, A. R., Hancock, D. W., Hayne, G. S., & Purdy, C. L. NASA (1991). Radar Altimeter for the TOPEX/POSEIDON Project. *Proceedings of the IEEE, 79*(6), 810-826.

Zowghi, D., Gervasi, V., & McRae, A. (2001), Using default reasoning to discover inconsistencies in natural language requirements, Proceedings of the Eighth Asia-Pacific on Software Engineering Conference, p.133.

Zumbach, J., Hillers, A., & Reimann, P. (2003). Supporting Distributed Problem-Based Learning: the Use of Feedback in Online Learning. In Roberts, T. (Ed.), *Online Collaborative Learning: Theory and Practice* (pp. 86–103). Hershey, PA, USA: Idea. doi:10.4018/978-1-59140-174-2.ch004

Zurada, J. M., Yen, G. G., & Wang, J. (Eds.). (2008). *Computational Intelligence: Research Frontiers, LNCS 5050*. Heidelberg: Springer Verlag. doi:10.1007/978-3-540-68860-0

Zurita, G., & Nussbaum, M. (2004). Computer Supported Collaborative Learning using Wirelessly Interconnected Handheld Computers. *Computers & Education, 42*, 289–314. doi:10.1016/j.compedu.2003.08.005

Zuse, H., (1991). Software Complexity Measures and Methods. de Gruyter.

Zuse, H. (1992). Properties of Software Measures. *Software Quality Journal, 1*, 225–260. doi:10.1007/BF01885772

Zuse, H. (1997). *A Framework of Software Measurement*. Berlin: Walter de Gruyter & Co.

About the Contributors

Yingxu Wang is professor of cognitive informatics, cognitive computing, and software engineering, President of International Institute of Cognitive Informatics and Cognitive Computing (IICICC), and Director of the Cognitive Informatics and Cognitive Computing Lab at the University of Calgary. He is a Fellow of WIF, a P.Eng of Canada, a Senior Member of IEEE and ACM, and a member of ISO/IEC JTC1 and the Canadian Advisory Committee (CAC) for ISO. He received a PhD in Software Engineering from the Nottingham Trent University, UK, and a BSc in Electrical Engineering from Shanghai Tiedao University. He has industrial experience since 1972 and has been a full professor since 1994. He was a visiting professor on sabbatical leaves in the Computing Laboratory at Oxford University in 1995, Dept. of Computer Science at Stanford University in 2008, and the Berkeley Initiative in Soft Computing (BISC) Lab at University of California, Berkeley in 2008, respectively. He is the founder and steering committee chair of the annual IEEE International Conference on Cognitive Informatics and Cognitive Computing (ICCI*CC). He is founding Editor-in-Chief of *International Journal of Cognitive Informatics and Natural Intelligence* (IJCINI), founding Editor-in-Chief of *International Journal of Software Science and Computational Intelligence* (IJSSCI), Associate Editor of *IEEE Trans on System, Man, and Cybernetics* (Part A), associate Editor-in-Chief of *Journal of Advanced Mathematics and Applications*, and Editor-in-Chief of *CRC Book Series in Software Engineering*. Dr. Wang is the initiator of several cutting-edge research fields or subject areas such as cognitive informatics, abstract intelligence, cognitive computing, cognitive computers, denotational mathematics (i.e., concept algebra, inference algebra, real-time process algebra, system algebra, granular algebra, and visual semantic algebra), software science (on unified mathematical models and laws of software, cognitive complexity of software, and automatic code generators, coordinative work organization theory, built-in tests (BITs), and deductive semantics of languages), the layered reference model of the brain (LRMB), the mathematical model of consciousness, and the reference model of cognitive robots. He has published over 120 peer reviewed journal papers, 220+ peer reviewed full conference papers, and 16 books in cognitive informatics, software engineering, and computational intelligence. He is the recipient of dozens international awards on academic leadership, outstanding contributions, research achievement, best papers, and teaching in the last three decades. He can be reached at: yingxu@ucalgary.ca.

* * *

Hadi Ahmadi is a PhD candidate in Department of Computer Science at University of Calgary. He is now working as a research assistant in iCORE information security (iCIS) lab. His main area of research is information and network security. He is also interested in other topics such as coding, complexity theory, and large-scale software development. He has received an MSc degree in electrical engineering, communications, from Sharif University of Technology.

Fernando Arroyo, PhD on artificial intelligence, has a position of full professor at the Universidad Politécnica de Madrid. He has a great number of international publications in leading journals concerning membrane computing and neural networks.

Peter Baranyi received his MSc degrees in electrical engineering and education in engineering sciences in 1994 and 1995, and his PhD degree in 1999 at the Budapest University of Technology and Economics. In 2006, he received the DSc degree of the Hungarian Academy of Sciences. Baranyi's research interests include cognitive informatics and dynamic control theories. He is a member of IEEE.

Nuria Gómez Blas, biologist and IT, obtained her PhD on artficial intelligente in 2008. She has a great number of publications concerning DNA computing and bio informatics. She has been participating in the Natural Computing Group since 2002.

Eric Bouillet is currently at IBM where he has been working on high performance distributed stream processing systems for intelligent data mining and analysis since 2004. Prior to joining IBM, Bouillet has worked at Tellium on the design of optical networks and optimization of lightpath provisioning and fault restoration algorithms, and before that in the Mathematical Sciences Research Center in Bell Labs/Lucent Technologies on routing and optimizations of telecommunication networks. Bouillet holds an MS (1997) and a PhD (1999) in electrical engineering from Columbia University. He also holds a degree from l'Ecole Nationale Supérieure des Télécommunications ENST Paris and EURECOM Sophia Antipolis.

Juan Castellanos, full professor at the Universidad Politécnica de Madrid, with a PhD on artificial intelligence. His research interests lie in the area of bio computing, in particular in the theoretical parts of DNA computing and membrane systems, but also in the area of neural networks. He has more than one hundred papers in these branches of bioinformatics, many of them published in visible journals and in proceedings from notable conferences (7th, 8th International Meeting on DNA Based Computers, etc.)

Ping Chen is an associate professor of computer science and the director of Artificial Intelligence Lab at the University of Houston-Downtown. His research interests include bioinformatics, data mining, and computational semantics. Dr. Chen has received three NSF grants and published over 30 papers in major data mining, artificial intelligence, and bioinformatics conferences and journals. Dr. Chen received his BS degree on information science and technology from Xi'an Jiao Tong University, MS degree on computer science from Chinese Academy of Sciences, and PhD degree on information technology at George Mason University.

Adam Csapo received his MSc degree in computer engineering from the Budapest University of Technology and Economics in 2008. He is currently a PhD student at the Budapest University of Technology and Economics, and visiting research student at the University of Tokyo. He was also previously a research student at the Norwegian University of Science and Technology for 6 months. Csapo is currently working on cognitive models of vision as well as cognitive feedback of control parameters in the remote teleoperation of robots.

Chengmin Ding is a managing consultant at IBM. Ding got his MS degree in computer science in 1998 from American University, and BS degree on computer science in 1994 from Xian Jiaotong

University. Ding's current research interests include leveraging the open source UIMA framework to deliver advanced text mining/analytics solutions and evaluating activity based collaboration paradigm. His long term professional inspiration is to live in the semantic web and have free intelligent agents to handle the daily chores.

Wei Ding received her PhD in computer science from the University of Houston in May 2008, then joined the Department of Computer Science of UMass Boston as an assistant professor in Fall 2008. Wei received her BS degree in computer science and applications from Xi'an Jiao Tong University in 1993 and her MS degree in software engineering from George Mason University in 2000. Wei is currently serving as a program committee member for the 20th IEEE International Conference on Tools with Artificial Intelligence (ICTAI 2008), International Workshop on Spatial and Spatiotemporal Data Mining (SSTDM 2008), the 17th International Conference on Software Engineering and Data Engineering, and she also served as a session chair for the 2007 IEEE International Workshop on Spatial and Spatiotemporal Data Mining in cooperation with IEEE ICDM. She is a member of the ACM and the IEEE.

Yucong Duan is currently a lecturer of Biomedical Engineering Institute, Capital University of Medical Sciences, Beijing, China, since 2008. He received a PhD in software engineering from Institute of Software, Chinese Academy of Sciences, Beijing, China in 2006. He was Post-doc fellow in School of Software, Tsinghua University, Beijing, China from 2006-2007. He was a post-doc fellow in the Software Engineering Laboratory at Pohang University of Science and Technology (POSTECH), Pohang, South Korea, from 2007-2008. He has been a member of IEEE since 2005. His research interests include: Theoretical and empirical software engineering, model driven software development, knowledge representation, cognitive informatics, and biomedical engineering, etc.

Ning Fang is currently a PhD student in the school of computer science and engineering, Shanghai University in China. He got his BEng from Southeast University of China in 1998, and recieved his master's degree from Nanjing University of Post and Telecommunication in China in 2005. His main experience is in modeling, reasoning, integrating and extracting of knowledge. He is participating in the related projects, such as Project of National Science Foundation of China: A Novel Method of Web Knowledge Acquisitions; The Great Research Project of National Science Foundation of China: Web-Based E-science Environment Research. In these project, his tasks involve virtual laboratory building, semantic grid services, ontology inference, knowledge engineering and intelligent personalized searching.

Mark Feblowitz received the Master's of Software Engineering degree at the Wang Institute of Graduate Studies in Tyngsboro, Massachusetts, in 1987, and the Bachelor of Science in computer and communications sciences from the University of Michigan in Ann Arbor, Michigan, in 1980. He was with GTE Laboratories in Waltham, Massachusetts, from 1982 to 2000, performing software engineering research, primarily on requirements modeling and service oriented systems modeling. After a brief stint as XML Architect at Frictionless Commerce, an eProcurement startup, he IBM joined TJ Watson Research Center in 2003, where he is exploring the intersection of high performance stream computing and Semantic Web technologies, with a focus on the application of semantic representations to the description and automated assembly of situational applications. His research interests are in the application of knowledge representation and reasoning techniques to the description and interpretation of semantic models.

Marina L. Gavrilova is an associate professor in the Department of Computer Science, University of Calgary. Dr. Gavrilova's research interests include computational geometry, image processing, optimization, exact computation and computer modeling. Dr. Gavrilova is a founder of two innovative research labs, the SPARCS Laboratory for Spatial Analysis in Computational Sciences and the Biometric Technologies Laboratory. Her publication list includes over 80 research papers, books and book chapters. Prof. Gavrilova is an editor-in-chief of *Transactions on Computational Science*, Springer and serves on the editorial board for *International Journal of Computational Sciences and Engineering and Computer Graphics* and *CAD/CAM Journal*. She is an ACM, IEEE and Computer Society member.

T.V. Geetha obtained her PhD degree in 1992 from Anna University. She is working as professor in the Department of Computer Science and Engineering, Anna University. She is heading a major project titled "Resource Centre For Indian Language Technology Solutions – Tamil" under Ministry of Information Technology, Government of India. In recognition of her significant work in research, the Tamilnadu State Council for Science and Technology has awarded her with the TAMILNADU YOUNG SCIENTIST AWARD for 2000 in the field of Engineering. Her research contributions cover natural language processing, databases, automatic software document generation and distributed artificial intelligence. A Tamil search engine, Tamil spell checker and grammar checker and a Tamil text to speech system have been developed. A Knowledge Representation scheme based on classification and inference techniques available in Indian Logic Systems has been designed.

Yann-Gaël Guéhéneuc is associate professor at the Department of computing and software engineering of Ecole Polytechnique of Montreal where he leads the Ptidej Team on evaluating and enhancing the quality of object-oriented programs by promoting the use of patterns, at the language-, design-, or architectural-levels. He holds a PhD in software engineering from University of Nantes, France (under Professor Pierre Cointe's supervision) since 2003 and an Engineering Diploma from École des Mines of Nantes since 1998. His PhD thesis was funded by Object Technology International, Inc. (now IBM OTI Labs.), where he worked in 1999 and 2000. His research interests are program understanding and program quality during development and maintenance, in particular through the use and the identification of recurring patterns. He was the first to use explanation-based constraint programming in the context of software engineering to identify occurrences of patterns. He is interested also in empirical software engineering; he uses eye-trackers to understand and to develop theories about program comprehension. He has published many papers in international conferences and journals.

Jeff J.S. Huang is a PhD student at the Department of Computer Science and Information Engineering, National Central University, Taiwan. His research interests include Web 2.0, CSCW, and CSCL.

Capers Jones is currently the president of Capers Jones & Associates LLC. He is also the founder and former chairman of Software Productivity Research LLC (SPR). He holds the title of Chief Scientist Emeritus at SPR. Jones founded SPR in 1984. Before founding SPR Capers was assistant director of programming technology for the ITT Corporation at the Programming Technology Center in Stratford, Connecticut. He was also a manager and researcher at IBM in California. Jones is a well-known author and international public speaker. Some of his books have been translated into five languages. Among his book titles are *Patterns of Software Systems Failure and Success* (Prentice Hall 1994), *Applied Software Measurement, 3rd edition*; (McGraw Hill 2008), *Software Quality: Analysis and Guidelines* *for Success* (International Thomson 1997), *Software Cost Estimation, 2nd edition* (McGraw Hill 2007), and *Software Assessments, Benchmarks, and Best Practices* (Addison Wesley Longman 2000). His next book, *Best Practices in Software Engineering*, is in preparation and will be published in the Spring of 2009 by McGraw Hill. Jones and his colleagues from SPR have collected historical data from hundreds of corporations and more than 30 government organizations. This historical data is a key resource for judging the effectiveness of software process improvement methods. This data is also widely cited in software litigation in cases where quality, productivity, and schedules are part of the proceedings. Jones also frequently works as an expert witness in software litigation. Jones is a frequent keynote speaker at international conferences dealing software quality, software measurements, and software project management topics.

Ricardo Rodríguez Jorge is a professor in artificial intelligence and computer science as well as a researcher. He is a member of the Mechatronics Academy at the Technological University of Ciudad Juarez (TUCJ) and also a member of the Computer Science Academy in the Technological Institute of Ciudad Juarez (TICJ). He earned an MS degree in artificial intelligence from the National Center of Research and Technological Development in Mexico (2007), and a BS degree in computer systems engineering from the Technological Institute of Lazaro Cardenas, Mexico (2005). He is a part-time professor in the TICJ in the Computer and Systems Department since 2008 and a full-time professor in the TUCJ in the Mechanical Engineering Department since 2007. His research fields include fuzzy Petri nets for dynamic systems modeling, artificial neural networks training, active rules-based systems, dynamic complex systems, neural-symbolic hybrid systems, and digital image processing. He has published several works in national and international congresses with these areas of research. In addition, he has participated as a speaker in national and international events and in panel discussion boards as a member in such congresses. He has participated as a project consultant in different creativity projects as well.

Morten Lind graduated in the year 1999 with a masters degree in computer science and physics from the University of Southern Denmark. The early parts of the masters education had much emphasis on mathematics, which gradually evolved into computer science. At the final stages of the masters study, as well as in the masters thesis itself, the algorithmic foundation of path planning in industrial robotics was the focus. Following the masters graduation was a period working with implementing laboratory and prototype robotic systems, partially as work at the university, at a company making industrial robotic simulation and planning systems, and as part of post gradual studies. Since 2004, Lind has been working as a researcher at SINTEF Technology and Society at the Department for Production Engineering (now part of SINTEF Raufoss Manufacturing AS), where the focus is on automation and robotisation in merchandise manufacturing. From 2008, Morten Lind has been a PhD student at The Norwegian University of Science and Technology, Department of Production and Quality Engineering, with project in the topic of manufacturing enterprise control. The current work is focused on a bottom up, distributed approach to manufacturing shop floor control.

Zhen Liu received the PhD degree in computer science from the University of Orsay (Paris XI), France. He was with the France Telecom R&D as a research associate from 1986 to 1988. He joined INRIA (the French national research center on information and automation) in 1988, first as a researcher, then became a research director. He joined IBM T. J. Watson Research Center in 2000, and is currently the senior manager of the Next Generation Distributed Systems Department. Zhen Liu is a fellow of IEEE.

He has served NSF Panels and a number of conference program committees. Zhen Liu was the program co-chair of the Joint Conference of ACM Sigmetrics and IFIP Performance 2004, and the general chair of ACM Sigmetrics 2008. Zhen's current research interests are in distributed and networked systems, stream processing systems, sensor networks, performance modeling, distributed optimization and control.

Xiangfeng Luo is an associated professor of the school of computer science and engineering of Shanghai University of China. He received the master degree in Hefei University of Technology in 2000 and the PhD degree in the same school in 2003. He was a post doctor at the China Knowledge Grid Research Group of Institute of Computing Technology (ICT) in Chinese Academy of Sciences (CAS) from Jun, 2003 to Jun, 2005. His major research interest is the semantic grid, knowledge grid and semantics based Web content processing and analysis. He is in charge of several projects, such as National Science Foundation of China (NSFC), the Great Research Project of NSFC, the Innovation Foundation of ICT in CAS and so on. He is also an advanced member of National Basic Research Program of China (973) Semantic Grid Theory, Model and Methodology. He is the program committee member of the First International Conference on Semantics, Knowledge and Grid and the Second International Workshop on Knowledge Grid and Grid Intelligence.

Janusz Kacprzyk, PhD in systems analysis, DSc (habilitation) in computer science, full professor since 1997. He is a member of Polish Academy of Sciences since 2002, and a foreign member of the Spanish Royal Academy of Economic and Financial Sciences (RACEF) since 2007. Currently he is a professor, at the Systems Research Institute, Polish Academy of Sciences, Warsaw, an honorary external professor at the Department of Mathematics, Yli Normal University, Shanxi, China, and a visiting professor, Tijuana Institute of Technology, Mexico. His research interests include: soft computing, fuzzy logic and computing with words, in decisions and optimization, control, database querying, information retrieval. Dr. Kaprzyk is the author of 5 books, (co)editor of 30 volumes, (co)author of 300 papers. He is the president of IFSA (International Fuzzy Systems Association) from June 2007, president of the Polish Society for Operational and Systems Research, a fellow of IEEE (Institute of Electrical and Electronics Engineers), and a fellow of IFSA (International Fuzzy Systems Association).

Witold Kinsner is professor and associate head at the Department of Electrical and Computer Engineering, University of Manitoba, Winnipeg, Canada. He is also affiliate professor at the Institute of Industrial Mathematical Sciences, Winnipeg, and adjunct scientist at the Telecommunications Research Laboratories (TRLabs), Winnipeg. He obtained his PhD in electrical and computer engineering from McMaster University, Hamilton in 1974. He has authored and co-authored over 600 publications in his research areas of computing engines, digital signal processing, and computational intelligence. Dr. Kinsner is a senior member of the Institute of Electrical & Electronics Engineers (IEEE), a member of the Association of Computing Machinery (ACM), a member of Sigma Xi, a Fellow of the Engineering Institute of Canada (EIC), and a life member of the Radio Amateur of Canada (RAC).

Witold Pedrycz is a professor and Canada Research Chair (CRC - Computational Intelligence) in the Department of Electrical and Computer Engineering, University of Alberta, Edmonton, Canada. His main research directions involve computational intelligence, fuzzy modeling, knowledge discovery and data mining, fuzzy control including fuzzy controllers, pattern recognition, knowledge-based neural networks, relational computation, and software engineering. He has published numerous papers in this area. He is also an author of 12 research monographs covering various aspects of computational intelligence and software engineering. Witold Pedrycz has been a member of numerous program committees of IEEE conferences in the area of fuzzy sets and neurocomputing. He currently serves as an associate editor of IEEE Transactions on Fuzzy Systems, and a number of other international journals. He is an editor-in-chief of Information Sciences and editor-in-chief of IEEE Transactions on Systems, Man, and Cybernetics - part A. In 2007 he received a prestigious Norbert Wiener award from the IEEE Systems, Man, and Cybernetics Council. He is a recipient of the IEEE Canada Computer Engineering Medal 2008.

Sugumar Mariappanadar is a senior lecturer in management/HRM at the School of Business and Informatics at Australian Catholic University in Melbourne. His teaching and publications cover sustainable human resource management, human resource measurement, organisational behaviour, and culturally indigenous management practices. His work has been published in IT Professional (IEEE publication), *International Journal of Social Economics, Research and Practice in Human Research Management, the International Journal of Learning, Journal of High Technology Management Research,* and other international journals. He has also contributed to book chapters and conference proceedings. He is currently the associate editor for the *Journal of Spirituality Leadership.* He has had broad management consulting experience in Australia and India. His consultancy includes organisation methods study, employee turnover study for call centres and business process analysis and management systems development. He has been involved along with other IT systems experts in developing business software and HR management software; they are currently used internationally.

Luis F. de Mingo contracted professor at the Universidad Politécnica de Madrid since 1998 obtained a PhD on artificial intelligence in 2000. His research interests lie in the area of learning models, in particular in the theoretical parts of neural networks and pattern recognition, but also in the area of networks of evolutionary processors. He has participated in several EU-INTAS projects and some local projects. He is member of the editorial board of IJITA, and international reviewer of KDS, ITECH conferences and active member of European Molecular Computation Consortium.

Sanjay Misra is assistant professor in Department of Computer Engineering, Atilim University, Ankara, Turkey. He obtained MTech. Degree in software engineering from Motilal Nehru National Institute of Technology, India and PhD from University of Allahabad, India. He has a wide experience (more than 16 years) of research, teaching and academic administration. His areas of interests are software measurement, object oriented technologies, cognitive informatics, SOA, XML technologies and web-services. He published more than 40 research papers in these areas. Presently, he is chief editor of *International Journal of Computer Engineering and Software Technology (IJCSST).*

Cyprian F. Ngolah holds a PhD in software engineering from the University of Calgary, Canada in 2006. He obtained a BSc degree in mathematics and computer science from the University of Essex, England in 1988 and an MSc degree in computer control systems from the University of Bradford, England in 1989. He has taught various computer sciences courses at both the undergraduate and graduate levels. He is currently a lecturer of software engineering at University of Buea, Republic of Cameroon. His main research interests are in real-time process algebra and its applications, tool support for formal specification languages, real-time software systems, formal methods in software engineering, and real-time operating systems.

Shushma Patel is a professor in information systems at London South Bank University. Her background is in medical sciences and she holds a PhD from the Faculty of Medicine, University of London. She heads the Health Informatics research group within the Centre for Information Management & E-Business. She is a Fellow of the British Computer Society and a Chartered IT Professional (CITP). Her research interests are varied, although there is a strong emphasis on cognitive informatics, knowledge management, decision-making, organizational behaviour and related communication issues in both commercial and educational settings. She has published extensively in journals, book chapters and conference proceedings. In addition she has edited special issues of journals and conference proceedings. She has chaired and served on numerous international conferences and programme committees including IEEE ICCI 2003. As a subject specialist reviewer in computing, she has undertaken subject reviews for the UK Quality Assurance Agency in Higher Education. She has worked on a number of research projects funded by the European Union, Department of Trade and Industry (DTI) and industry.

Anand Ranganathan is a research staff member at IBM TJ Watson Research Center. He is currently exploring various aspects of component development and assembly, and the associated knowledge engineering, software engineering and user interaction challenges. He finished his PhD at the Department of Computer Science in the University of Illinois at Urbana-Champaign in 2005. He received his BTech in computer science and engineering from the Indian Institute of Technology in Madras in 2000. His broad research interests include data management, services, Web 2.0, ubiquitous computing, distributed systems, the Semantic Web and artificial intelligence.

Barna Resko received his MSc degree in computer engineering in 2004, and his PhD in 2008 from the Budapest University of Technology and Economics. Currently he is a postdoc researcher at the Computer and Automation Research Institute of the Hungarian Academy of Sciences. Barna Resko was guest researcher for 4 months at the Norwegian University of Science and Technology (2004), and 18 months at the Hashimoto Laboratory of the University of Tokyo (2005-2007). His research interests include cognitive informatics and cognitive infocommunication based robot control.

Anton V. Riabov received the PhD degree in operations research from Columbia University, New York City, in 2004, where he worked on optimization problems arising in multicast routing. Before coming to Columbia, and after graduating with CS degree from Moscow State University, he spent 2 years as a technical lead at a startup developing 3D video games. He joined IBM T. J. Watson Research Center in 2004, and is now the manager of Automated Component Assembly Middleware group within the Next Generation Distributed Systems Department. With his team, he designed and developed MARIO, a prototype of an automatic goal-driven composer, and SPPL, a formalism for describing flow composition tasks. Currently he is working on several projects that aim to simplify the development of flow-based software systems.

Gerardo Reyes Salgado earned a PhD in cognitive sciences from the National Polytechnic Institute of Grenoble, France (2001), an MS in computer sciences from the National Center of Research and Technological Development (CENIDET), México (1995), and a BS degree in civil engineering from Technological Institute of Zacatepec, México (1983). He is a member of the Researchers National System (SNI) of Mexico since 2002. He has also been an undergraduate professor, and currently, he teaches at the doctoral and graduate levels. His research work is registered in more than 60 publications at indexed journals and very prestigious national and international congresses. He has been invited as a lecturer and a speaker in national and international events in more than 20 occasions. At this time, he works as a researcher at the Artificial Intelligence Group at CENIDET, where he is a project consultant of studies in learning process and knowledge automatic extracting. He directs many graduate and doctoral thesis with such projects. Additionally, he is the academic chairperson from CENIDET since February 2006, DVP of Latin American IEEE (2007-2009), and was named honorary collaborator of the Rey Juan Carlos University (RJCU) in Spain, December 2008.

Vianey Guadalupe Cruz Sanchez was born in Cardenas Tabasco, Mexico on September 14th, 1978. She earned her BS degree in computer engineering from the Technological Institute of Cerro Azul, Mexico in 2000, the MS degree in computer science at the "Center of Research and Technological Development (CENIDET)" in 2004. She is a PhD student of computer science at the National Center of Research and Technological Development (CENIDET), Morelos, Mexico. Her research interests include hybrid systems, knowledge representation, neural networks, pattern recognition and digital image processing. She currently serves as a professor at the Autonomous University of Ciudad Juarez (AUCJ), Chihuahua, Mexico. She works for the Electrical and Computer Engineering Department. Prof. Cruz is a member of the IEEE Computer Society.

Frank Schwartz joined The Ohio State University in 1988 as the Ohio Eminent Scholar in hydrogeology, and since 2005, he has served as the director of the newly formed School of Earth Sciences. Schwartz has co-authored several books including *Physical and Chemical Hydrogeology* (1990, 1998), and *Fundamentals of Ground Water* (2003). In recognition of his contributions to hydrogeology, he was named as a co-recipient of the prestigious O.E. Meinzer Award in 1984, a co-recipient of the Excellence in Science and Engineering Award in 1991, and the King Hubbert Science Award in 1997. He was elected as a fellow of the American Geophysical Union in 1992. In addition to teaching and research, Schwartz acts as a consultant to government and industry, and in various advisory capacities. He has served on various NRC Panels and as a member of the Water Science and Technology Board. Dr. Schwartz received his PhD in Geology from the University of Illinois.

Phillip C-Y. Sheu is currently a professor of computer engineering, information and computer science, and biomedical engineering at the University of California, Irvine. He received his PhD and MS degrees from the University of California at Berkeley in electrical engineering and computer science in 1986 and 1982, respectively, and his BS degree from National Taiwan University in electrical engineering in 1978. Between 1982 and 1986, he also worked as a computer scientist at Systems Control Technology, Inc., Palo Alto, CA., where he designed and implemented aircraft expert control systems, and he worked as a product planning engineer at Advanced Micro Devices Inc., Sunnyvale, CA, where he designed and integrated CAD systems. From 1986 to 1988, he was an assistant professor at School of Electrical Engineering, Purdue University. From 1989 to 1993, he was an associate professor of Electrical and Computer Engineering at Rutgers University. He has published two books: (1) Intelligent Robotic Planning Systems and (2) Software Engineering and Environment - An Object-Oriented Perspective, and more than 100 papers in object-relational data and knowledge engineering and their applications, and biomedical computations. He is currently active in research related to complex biological systems, knowledge-based medicine, semantic software engineering, proactive web technologies, and large real-time knowledge systems for defense and homeland security. His current research projects are sponsored by the National Science Foundation, National Institute of Health, and Department of Defense. Dr. Sheu is a Fellow of IEEE.

Mahalakshmi G. Suryanarayanan obtained her Master's of Engineering in Computer Science from Anna University, Chennai, INDIA. She is currently a researcher in the field of Argumentative reasoning pursuing her PhD at Department of Computer Science and Engineering, Anna University, Chennai, INDIA. Her research interests include reasoning, knowledge representation, argumentation, robotics, data mining, information retrieval, requirements engineering, question-answering, cognitive poetics and discourse analysis.

Domonkos Tikk received his BSc and MSc degree in computer science both from Eötvös Loránd Science University in Hungary in the years 1993 and 1995, respectively. He received his PhD in engineering in 2000 from Budapest University of Technology and Economics (BUTE) in Hungary. Since 1998, he has been research assistant at BUTE. From 2003 he works at the same institution as the project leader of an R&D program. He was visiting scholar at Murdoch University, Perth, Australia in 2000; Chonbuk National University, Chonju, Korea in 2001; and Hull University, Hull, UK in 2003. In 2008, he received the Humboldt Foundation scholarship for experienced researchers, and he is now working at Humboldt University in Berlin. His team achieved two 2nd places at the ACM KDD Cup 2005, and won the ACM KDD Cup 2006. He is also the member of Gravity team that is a successful competitor on the Netflix Prize contest. He achieved a first and a second place at the I2B2 2008 Challenge. He is a member of ACM and IFSA. His research interests include text and data mining, automatical categorization methods, computer linguistics, fuzzy systems, and soft computing techniques.

Daoqin Tong is an assistant professor at Department of Geography and Regional Development, University of Arizona. Tong's received MS in civil engineering and PhD in geography from the Ohio State University. Dr. Tong's research interests include spatial analysis, spatial optimization, geocomputation and location analysis.

Jeffrey J.P. Tsai received his PhD degree in computer science from the Northwestern University. He is now a professor of the Department of Computer Science at the University of Illinois, Chicago. He is also a senior research fellow at the University of Texas at Austin. Tsai coauthored 10 books and has published over 230 journal articles and conference papers. Tsai is currently the co-editor-in-chief of the *International Journal on Artificial Intelligence Tools* and an associate editor of the *IEEE Transactions on Services Computing*. He was an associate editor of *IEEE Transactions on Knowledge and Data Engineering*, and sits on many editorial boards of international journals. His current research interests include sensor networks, ubiquitous computing, trustworthy computing, intrusion detection, software reliability and adaptation, knowledge-based software engineering, distributed real-time systems, multimedia systems, and intelligent agents. He is a fellow of the AAAS and the IEEE.

Guoyin Wang, was born in Chongqing, China, in 1970. He received the PhD degree in computer organization and architecture from Xi'an Jiaotong University, Xi'an, China, in 1996. Since then, he has been working at the Chongqing University of Posts and Telecommunications, where he is currently a professor and PhD supervisor, the Chairman of the Institute of Computer Science and Technology (ICST), and the dean of the College of Computer Science and Technology. He also worked at the University of North Texas, USA, and the University of Regina, Canada, as a visiting scholar during 1998-1999. He is the chairman of the Advisory Board of International Rough Set Society (IRSS), chairman of the Rough Set Theory and Soft Computation Society, Chinese Association for Artificial Intelligence. He serves as a program committee member for many international conferences and editorial board member of several international journals. He is the author of 2 books, the editor of many proceedings of international and national conferences, and has over 200 research publications. His research interests include data mining, machine learning, rough set, soft computing, knowledge technology, etc.

Weimin Xu is a professor of the school of computer science and engineering of Shanghai University of China, PhD supervisor. He is senior member of China Computer Society; the sixth open systems professional Committee; the first high-performance computing professional Committee; vice president of the third council of Shanghai Information Society; senior fellow of International Center for Theoretical Physic.

Stephen J.H. Yang received his PhD degree in computer science from the University of Illinois at Chicago in 1995. He is now a professor of the Department of Computer Science and Information Engineering and the Associate Dean of Academic Affairs, National Central University, Taiwan. He is the co-founder and the CEO of T5 Corp, a company providing XML-based Web services. Dr. Yang has published 2 books and over 150 journal articles and conference papers. He is currently the co-editor-in-chief of the *International Journal of Knowledge Management & E-Learning*, and in the advisory board of the *Educational Technology and Society*; and in the editorial boards of the *International Journal of Web Services Research* and the *International Journal of Knowledge and Learning*. He severed as the program co-chair of IEEE MSE 2003, IEEE CAUL 2006, and IEEE W2ME 2007. His research interests include Web services, Web 2.0, software engineering, knowledge engineering, semantic Web, and context aware ubiquitous computing. He is a member of IEEE.

Yiyu Yao received his BEng from Xi'an Jiaotong University, People's Republic of China in 1983, and his MSc and PhD from the University of Regina, Canada in 1988 and 1991, respectively. He was an assistant professor and an associate professor at Lakehead University, Canada from 1992 to 1998. He joined the Department of Computer Science at the University of Regina in 1998, where he is currently a professor of computer science. His research interests include data mining, rough sets, Web intelligence, granular computing, cognitive informatics, machine learning and information retrieval.

Shi Ying is a professor in the State Key Laboratory of Software Engineering at Wuhan University, China. He received the bachelor's degree in computer science in 1986 and the PhD degree in software engineering in 1999 from Wuhan University respectively. His research interests include service-oriented, aspect-oriented and semantic-based software development, software reuse and interoperability. His current research projects include semantic programming language, aspect-oriented software architecture and SOA domain, funded by the National High-Tech Research Development Program, National Natural Science Fund Project, and PhD Degree Foundation Project of the Ministry of Education of China. He has published nearly 90 journal and conference papers.

Lotfi A. Zadeh is professor and director of Berkeley Initiative in Soft Computing (BISC) in Department of Electrical Engineering and Computer science at University of California, Berkeley. He is the founder of fuzzy sets, fuzzy logic, and soft computing. He has initiated a series of fundamental AI and system theories and technologies.

Sławomir Zadrożny is an associate professor (PhD 1994, DSc 2006) at the Systems Research Institute, Polish Academy of Sciences. His current scientific interests include applications of fuzzy logic in group decision making, decision support, database management systems, information retrieval and data analysis. He is the author and co-author of ca. 200 journal/conference papers and chapters in edited volumes. He has been involved in the design and implementation of several prototype software packages. He is also a teacher at the Warsaw School of Information Technology in Warsaw, Poland, where his interests focus on information retrieval and database management systems.

Bo Zhang received his PhD degree in environmental science from The Ohio State University in December 2008. His research interests include data mining, statistical modeling, GIS and remote sensing.

Du Zhang received his PhD degree in computer science from the University of Illinois. He is professor and chair of the computer science department at California State University, Sacramento. His current research interests include: knowledge base inconsistency, machine learning application in software engineering, knowledge-based systems and multi-agent systems. He has authored or coauthored over 130 publications in journals, conference proceedings, and book chapters in these and other areas. He has served as the conference general chair, the program committee chair, a program committee co-chair, or a program area chair for numerous IEEE international conferences. He is an associate editor for International Journal on Artificial Intelligence Tools, a member of editorial board for International Journal of Cognitive Informatics and Natural Intelligence, and a member of editorial board for International Journal of Software Science and Computational Intelligence, and has served as a guest editor for special issues of a number of other journals. He is a senior member of IEEE and a member of ACM.

Jia Zhang received her PhD in computer science from University of Illinois at Chicago in 2000. She is now an assistant professor of Department of Computer Science at Northern Illinois University. Zhang has published 1 book titled "Service Computing" and over 80 technical papers in journals, book chapters, and conference proceedings. She is an associate editor of the *IEEE Transactions on Services Computing (TSC)*, *International Journal of Web Services Research (JWSR)*, and the *Advances in Web Services Research (AWSR)* Book Series, Idea Group. Zhang serves as program vice chair of IEEE International Conference on Web Services (ICWS 2008, 2007 & 2006). Her current research interests center around Services Computing. She is a member of the IEEE.

Jun Zhao, was born in Chongqing, China in 1971. He received the PhD degree on computer software and theory from Chongqing University, Chongqing, China, in 2003. He has been working with Chongqing University of Posts & Telecommunications since 1996, where he currently is a professor and the vice director of Department of Science and Technology. In 2004, under the support of Chinese government, he also worked with London South Bank University, UK. His research interests include data mining, machine learning, soft computing, and information security etc.

Index